Dear Reader:

This book is probably different from any that you have ever seen. It is not meant to be read through and put away as any ordinary book might be. It is meant to be a day-by-day, helpful, cheerful, friendly "Handbook of Life."

We suggest that you keep the book always near you—where you can turn to it easily at any time. Then whenever you face difficult problems—new or old—turn to the chapters and prayers which deal with your own particular and special situation.

"With God
All Things
Are Possible!"

BANTAM BOOKS
TORONTO · NEW YORK · LONDON · SYDNEY

*This low-priced Bantam Book
has been completely reset in a type face
designed for easy reading, and was printed
from new plates. It contains the complete
text of the original hard-cover edition.*
NOT ONE WORD HAS BEEN OMITTED.

🚩

RL 5, IL 8-adult

WITH GOD ALL THINGS ARE POSSIBLE

*A Bantam Book | published by arrangement with
Life-Study Fellowship*

PRINTING HISTORY

*Life-Study Fellowship hardbound edition published June 1944
29 printings to 1972
Life-Study Fellowship paperbound edition published
December 1971
2nd printing .... February 1973*

Bantam edition | January 1974

2nd printing .... April 1974	5th printing .... March 1977
3rd printing .. November 1974	6th printing ...... October 1978
4th printing .... April 1976	7th printing .... February 1980
8th printing .... February 1981	

ISBN 0-553-20084-4

Published simultaneously in the United States and Canada

---

*Bantam Books are published by Bantam Books, Inc. Its trade-
mark, consisting of the words "Bantam Books" and the por-
trayal of a bantam, is Registered in U.S. Patent and Trademark
Office and in other countries. Marca Registrada. Bantam
Books, Inc., 666 Fifth Avenue, New York, New York 10103.*

PRINTED IN THE UNITED STATES OF AMERICA

17 16 15 14 13 12 11

Message
of
Importance to Readers

Dear Reader:

Are you facing any personal problems, worries or troubles at this particular time?

Have the world-wide sin, violence and discontent of our times upset *your* life as they have so many, many others?

For example, are you worried about money troubles, debts or your work? Are you worried about your health in any way?

Are you unhappy or worried about some one dear to you? Are you in love or do you have family troubles of any kind?

Are you worried about the future—afraid of what may lie down the dark, uncertain road ahead?

Do you ever get lonely—and yearn for friends, love and companionship? Do you feel that life should hold more happiness for you in many, many ways?

WONDERFUL NEWS FOR YOU!

If you do have any of these problems, dear reader, or any others, then there is a wonderful message for you in this "Handbook of Life"—for that is what we call this book you now hold in your hands.

In these pages you will find a source of everlasting beauty and strength and happiness. You will find the way to God—to Him Who is all-powerful, all-knowing and all-loving. You will learn His will for you. You will learn to love Him and to live as He wants you to live.

Almost without knowing it, as you read and study, a great peace and calm will enter your life. You will be rising triumphantly above the obstacles and hardships of this drab world. You will be living in a new and better world as your heart and your daily life come under the shelter of God's infinite love and power!

YOUR REWARD SHALL BE GREAT!

Yes, dear reader, before you is great happiness, if you will do your part, as we feel sure you will.

In the first place, please do not try to read all of this book at one time. Read first the page next to this one, marked List of Chapters, then the one after that marked "How to Use This Book." Then read Chapter 1 called: "God Loves You."

Then, after that, turn to whatever chapters and prayers deal with *your own* particular, immediate problems. Read them over carefully and then put the book aside. Live over in your mind and in God's presence, what you have read. Then later on in the same day or the next day, turn again to the chapters and prayers you have read and read them again.

Continue doing this as long as you feel the need still with you. For soon you will begin to *see* and *understand* and *live* the solutions to your problems. You will find yourself living truly "With God"—with all the happiness, joy and abundance of life which that means.

So you see, dear reader, this book is probably different from any that you have ever seen. It is not meant to be read through and put away as any ordinary book might be. It is meant to be a day-by-day, helpful, cheerful, friendly "Handbook of Life."

We suggest that you keep your book always near you— where you can turn to it easily at any time. Then whenever you face difficult problems—new or old—whenever you feel the need of God's love and guidance and power— turn to the chapters and prayers in your book which deal with your own particular and special situation.

May God bless you and be with you every day and hour and minute. May the glorious abundance of life which is His will for you be truly yours. This is our constant prayer.

Noroton, Connecticut. MCMXLIV

A Special Word About the Prayers in This Book

The forty beautiful prayers in this book may be even more helpful and important to you than the chapters themselves.

In fact, if you never read any of the chapters, and if you turned only to the prayers in your times of trouble or of need, of rejoicing or of thankfulness, then you would still find this to be truly a "Handbook of Life." You would find your way to God and to all the joy and happiness and wisdom that true friendship with Him can mean.

We ask you, therefore, to be sure to read all of these forty beautiful prayers and to reread them many times to see for yourself how very, very much they can mean to you.

List of Chapters

How to Use This Book

The way to get the greatest benefit in using this book is like this:

Whenever you face a problem of *any* kind, turn to this page and look through the words and questions listed here until you find the words or questions which deal with your problem.

There you will find the numbers of the chapters you should read, and with those chapters you will find the prayers which will be most helpful to you.

Keep your book always near you, dear friend, so that you can turn to it easily whenever you feel the need of God's help and guidance and love. Try making this book truly your "Handbook of Life," for in that way you will find in it the wonderful joy and happiness that lies waiting here for you!

1

GOD LOVES YOU

Do YOU SOMETIMES WONDER what life is all about?

Do you sometimes wonder where you came from—where you were before you were born?

Do you wonder where you are going after you die—wonder whether there is a life after death?

Do you ever question if God really loves you and is watching over you?

Do you ever wonder whether or not there *is* a God who created you and this world and all that is in it?

Have you ever thought why there is so much sorrow and strife and suffering in the world?

Did you ever ask yourself if there is ever to be any real, true happiness in life for you?

Do you wonder if there is any way that you can call on God to help you overcome your troubles and worries and problems?

If you ever *do* wonder about these things, then there is wonderful news in store for you—right here in this very first chapter.

For here you will read of the most wonderful story in the world—the story of how God created the world, of how He put man in this world, of what God's will for man is!

You will learn that God *does* love you! God *does* care what happens to you! God *does* want you to be well and prosperous and happy!

You will learn that God has laid down some very simple laws of life for man to follow—and that all you have to do to receive God's manifold blessings is to learn what these laws are and abide by them.

"In the Beginning"

So let us not waste any more time. Let's start right here—and tell our story. And, as we should, let us

1

start at the very beginning ... with the very first words of the Bible itself.

For the Bible is the revealed word of God. God put in the Bible what He wanted man to know—and how He wanted man to live. If you want the truth—the secret of real happiness, success and contentment, you have only to look in the Bible and there it is—if you have "eyes to see and ears to hear"!

So opening our Bible to the first page, we find this beautiful passage:

"In the beginning God created the heaven and the earth."

These words and the rest of the first chapter of Genesis form the basic foundation of your life of Faith in God. For that Chapter contains the beautiful story of God's love for you and of the glorious abundance which He created for you!

Could anything be more beautiful than the story of the creation of man? Could God have shown His love for man any more clearly?

You have only to *read* and *understand* the first chapter of the Bible to know that God never, never meant that man should suffer pain and sorrow and lack.

And yet we all know that man *has suffered.* You know it because *you* have suffered and you are seeing mankind throughout the world suffering today.

How does this happen?

Well, the answer is very simple and it, too, is told in the Bible.

The answer is that when God created the world and man to live in the world, He also made some rules by which men should live ... rules such as the Ten Commandments and the Golden Rule and all the beautiful sayings of Jesus.

You know well what happened. You know that throughout all history, men and women have been breaking the commandments of God.

When we stop to realize that, is it hard to understand why there is suffering and sorrow and poverty in the world?

And yet, after mankind had been disobeying God for hundreds of years, God still loved man so very much that He gave him another chance!

This deed of God gives us the second great rock in the foundation of our Faith. It is the clearest, surest proof of God's love for man that there could *be!* And in the words of the Bible itself, this was the act:

> *"For God so loved the world, that He gave His only begotten Son, that whosoever believeth in Him should not perish, but have everlasting life."*

In other words, even after mankind had sinned and disobeyed God's commandments for years and years, God still wanted to save mankind from suffering and sorrow and poverty.

In order to do this, God sent Jesus Christ, His own Son, into the world to show and to teach mankind how to live in such a way as to have health, happiness, prosperity and every other blessing that God, in the greatness of His love, *wants* mankind to have!

Could anything be more clear and positive? Could any story be more thrilling? Is there any doubt that God loves you and all mankind? That He has provided abundance and happiness for you—and that the way you are to receive these blessings is by living your life as nearly as possible as Jesus

Christ has said you are to live it?

The extent to which you can overcome your problems and to which you can have health, happiness and prosperity, really lies in the extent to which you can develop your Faith in these two things:

1. That in the beginning God created a world of abundance and happiness ... that He loves you and wants you to have your share of this happiness and abundance.

2. That Jesus Christ is the Son of God—sent to save you from sin and to show you the way of life eternal—life abundant!

And it is when we turn to the teaching of Jesus Christ that we see the message He brings us from God. For if you read the story of Jesus' life as told in the Bible, you find over and over again that Jesus' answer to any and every problem was FAITH! Jesus' miracles of healing were miracles of FAITH! Jesus' miracle of feeding the multitude was a miracle of FAITH! The walking of Peter upon the waters was a miracle of FAITH!

Yes, FAITH is the answer

to all your problems. If you will only realize this great truth, how different your life will be. You can meet and overcome any problem in life—serene in the confidence that comes with true FAITH in God's love. You can share in all the blessings of health, happiness and prosperity that God has provided out of His great love if you will but keep FAITH *in* Him and *with* Him!

"Yes," you may say, "but how can I have that kind of strong Faith?"

Well, the answer is really very simple. It is given us by Jesus Himself, in the words He spoke to His Disciples when they asked Him the question: "Who is the greatest in the kingdom of heaven?"

For when they asked Him this, Jesus called a little child unto Him and set him in the midst of them and said:

> *"Verily I say unto you, except ye be converted and become as little children, ye shall not enter into the Kingdom of Heaven.*
> *"Whosoever therefore shall humble himself as this little child, the same is greatest in the Kingdom of Heaven."*

Now putting this in the form of two rules for all of us to follow, we have:

1. **Turn your life over to God in childlike trust from this day on.**
2. **Spend at least a few minutes each day with God in humble, sincere prayer and study!**

As you can see, there is nothing at all hard about these two rules. All you need to do is get *started* and then to follow them out every day until they have become a habit. You can't begin to realize what a wonderful change in your life they will bring until you do this.

For no longer will you have to struggle and strain. Because trust in God means that you *know* God loves you, that He will always do what is right for you, that He is always near to you.

And so this leads us to the Second Rule—that you should spend a few minutes each day in humble, sincere prayer.

Sometimes people think that Prayer is a very complicated thing, but really it is very, very simple to understand.

4

Prayer is just talking to God!

Now when a dear friend who loves you is near to you, then you do not try to keep silent. You want to talk to him, to tell him your hopes and plans, to ask for his help.

Well, when you have real, true, abiding Faith in God, you know that He is the best and dearest Friend you ever had. You know that He, too, is always near, always dear, always ready to listen to you. You know you can always tell God, our greatest Friend, all your hopes, your plans, your problems. You know you can always ask Him for help and that He will be ready to give it to you.

That is talking to God. That is Prayer!

And so that is why we have gone even further in trying to help you in this little Handbook of Life. That is why you will find a prayer at the end of each and every Chapter.

Some people think that a church is the only place to pray and indeed it is a lovely place to talk to God. God is happy when we talk to Him there. But that is not the only place God will listen to your prayer.

Jesus often prayed in church. But time and time again, He prayed alone. He prayed at the home of His Disciples and followers. He prayed alone in the garden and in the desert.

And Jesus prayed at all times, too—in the morning and at noon and in the evening. So you, too, whenever you think of God, in times of sorrow, in times of joy, in times of nervousness, in times of worry—in *all* times—can and should speak to God and ask

His help, His abundance, His health, His peace and contentment!

You do not need to think of long, complicated prayers. Such prayers do not always come from the heart. And it is heart-prayers which God loves from His children. God understands even the simple prayer of a child.

The Prayers we give you at the end of each and every chapter are prayers of that kind—just plain, simple talks with God. You will find, as you use them, that they will often give you just the words you may always have wanted to speak to

5

your Father about your sorrows, your joys, your troubles and your problems. Use them, dear Reader, for they are yours out of full and understanding hearts.

And they one and all teach you that God *does* love you—for now you have the proof! Treasure the thought. Come back to it many times. Think of it whatever the problems you face. Think back to this Chapter 1 as you read on in this Handbook of Life.

And now your Prayer called: "That I May Always Know God Loves Me" is at the end of this Chapter. Read it now. Read it many times in the days ahead of you!

Prayer

That

I MAY ALWAYS KNOW GOD LOVES ME

"God is love, and he that dwelleth in love dwelleth in God, and God in him"—1 Jo 4:16

Dear God above, Thou art mighty over all the earth and all the sea and all the heavens and all that in them is. Thou seest all and knowest all.

And yet, Dear God, mighty as Thou art, I know that Thou lookest down upon me with eyes full of love and of friendliness and of understanding. I can see Thy dear, kind face smiling there!

For Thou art my Father. Thou lovest me and Thou watcheth over me. This I know, dear God, and I thank Thee with all my heart!

Please, dear Father above, help me always to have this child-like trust and faith in Thee! Whenever times are dark and troubled, whenever I am afraid or hurt, help me to remember that Thou art there to help me.

Help me, Father, to understand Thy Laws of Life and to live by them always - for I know, dear God, that if I do, then Thou wilt reward me with all the glorious health and happiness, all the joy and abundance of blessings that are Thy will for me and for all Thy children!

In the Name of Thy Love for me, Dear Father, and in the Name of Thy Blessed Son, Jesus Christ, I ask it!

—Amen

7

GOD WANTS YOU TO BE PROSPEROUS

ARE YOU FACING MONEY troubles or debts? Do you often wonder how you are going to keep up with rising prices and changing conditions? Do you worry about property and business affairs?

If these are some of the questions which perplex you, then there is a tremendously important message for you in this chapter. For here you will discover the wonderful truth that God wants you to be prosperous!

It is not God's will that you should lack the things you need in life. God created a world of abundance—enough and to spare for all. He laid down certain laws—laws of life, laws of prosperity. And all He asks is that you *obey* these laws!

Where can you find them? In the Bible, of course. For when you read the Bible, it is as if God were speaking to you. And the place in the Bible where God has shown most clearly His law of prosperity is in the story of the Prophet Elijah and the widow. It is so enlightening that you may want to hear it once more.

A widow was left with two small sons and a heavy burden of debt. In her distress, she went to the Prophet Elijah and begged for help. The Prophet asked her:

"What hast thou in the house?"

"Not any thing save a pot of oil," replied the widow.

Elijah told her to borrow some vessels from her neighbors and pour the oil into them, keeping only a small quantity for her own use. The rest he told her to go and sell and pay her debts. And it is written that the oil continued to flow and that the widow finally freed herself from debt.

God is trying to give you His law of prosperity through this story. It is the law that you should start

with what you have and God will do the rest. It is the law which, translated into popular speech, says that "God helps those who help themselves."

Here is a woman, leaning out of her window wondering how she can get the extra money she needs. Back of her lies a pile of neatly darned clothes—repaired so neatly that you could not see where the cloth ends and the darning begins. Then she remembers that up the street is a lady who has no time to mend her children's clothes. Perhaps she would pay for having them darned neatly. Off goes the lady to see her neighbor. She gets this simple work to do. She has started to help herself!

Here is the need for service and here is the loving service that can supply it. Opportunity lay with what the woman had right where she was and not in some far-off place or happening. She started where she stood!

You should try and remember that right here on this earth, right where you are, your loving Father has provided everything you need for your prosperity and success.

Loving service! When they asked the Psalmist of old who would prosper, he replied: "They shall prosper that love Thee." Isn't that a remarkable thing the Bible says? Why do you think that loving is the most important step in gaining your prosperity?

Because love is the start of all the worthwhile actions of your life. You cannot love God greatly without keeping His commandments and living by the Golden Rule. And you cannot live by the Golden Rule without making friends. You cannot make friends without gaining in prosperity. It is like a magic circle, the centre of which is love!

Love and friendship break down the barriers between people. It makes people *want* to help you. Love greatly and you will forget yourself. You will want to help others. You will give without thought of getting. You will serve without thought of reward.

A young man named George Dunlop loved his invalid mother who was confined to a wheel chair. To save her from being jolted about on the iron rims of the chair's wheels, he used what was then a new substance, looked upon as a curiosity.

It was rubber! He wound strips of it around the steel rims. From this simple service of love grew the famous Dunlop tire which made him many times a rich man.

Jesus knew the secret of such success. He was always trying to get people to give up selfish rewards and pleasures and devote their thoughts to helping others. Do you remember what He said: "For whosoever will save his life shall lose it, but whosoever will lose his life . . . shall save it." How true that is as applied to your prosperity!

The selfish man or woman who "saves" his life is the one who does not give. Such a person is always thinking "What will *I* get out of this?" or "What's in it for *me?*" And how true it is that men and women of this kind, who go through life with the idea of *getting* only, so often neither get nor keep prosperity. You will succeed both spiritually and actually financially! Look for work which will be of real service to others, which will help them in some problem of their own. Sell them goods or services which they really need at a price which is not a grasping one and you will succeed. Be honest to the penny in your dealings—

honest in the way Abraham Lincoln was honest.

Abe Lincoln ran a country store in Salem, Illinois. One day he charged a woman a few pennies more than he felt he ought to have done. Much as he needed the money, "Honest Abe" tramped miles through a blizzard to pay that woman back every cent!

Yes, once in a while people will take advantage of you. But it will bother you no more than it did the honest Quaker who was cheated by a neighbor. Said the Quaker:

"Friend, thou hast taken advantage of me, but that must be because thou needest the money more than do I. Take it and go in peace." The man slunk off with hanging head.

But for every person who *does* take advantage there will be hundreds who will trust you, who will like you, who will be friends of yours, who will want to do things for you. There has never been a man or woman with many friends who was not successful in the truest and deepest sense of the word. Never was there a man with many friends who did not always have a place to sleep and something to eat. Yes,

10

and a great deal more in most cases!

Why, just this attitude of kindly friendship and helpfulness *alone* is often enough to help you in your financial need. For an attitude of friendship makes for a cheerful tolerance of others. It makes for a deep thankfulness for what you have. As our old minister used to say:

"Do not let the empty cup be your first teacher of the blessings you had when it was full."

Thank God and count the prosperity which you have. Thank God and praise everything which comes to you as a symbol of God's love and abundance for you. Count your blessings and they will be magnified and multiplied!

Time after time you will find that if you are thankful to God for the blessings you have, even in small things, your eyes will be opened to the blessings which you would never have noticed if you were not thankful.

Be thankful for the work you have even though it may seem unimportant. There is no work, no position, no talent, no skill, no interest so humble that it can not be

the springboard to the prosperity which God wants you to have!

One winter night a man came to the superintendent of a large apartment house and asked if he could not sleep in the cellar in return for doing some cleaning. The superintendent allowed the man to stay. So cheerfully did the man do his work the next day that he was given a small room in the cellar and a small salary.

His pleasant smile, his happiness in even the humble work he was doing, his thankfulness to have it, endeared him to everyone in the apartment. Always ready to help with baby carriages, to open doors for elderly ladies, to relieve someone of bundles, he soon found himself with all the extra work he could handle for the tenants, such as cleaning, repairing and fixing. In seven months he had taken a little workshop around the corner to handle all the repairing jobs that came his way. And it was not long after that that he was well on the way to modest financial security.

Certainly he had no influence, no outstanding talent. Certainly he started from the bottom. But just those few qualities of thankfulness for what he had, of friendship for others, of willingness to serve, put this man back on the road to well-being.

It is quite probable that you do not *need* to start from the bottom. It is quite probable that you *have* a position or *are* in a better position than this man. So much more the reason for you to be thankful, to be able to start from a higher rung on the ladder.

Perhaps you *have* tried. Perhaps you *have* prayed for prosperity, for more good things in life, for more enjoyable work. And when you see no outward change, you say you have looked at all the ways in which God might have helped you.

But God can see where *you* cannot see. Where *you* may not see an opportunity for prosperity, God may be able to see one. For has He not said: "I will bring the blind by a way that they knew not: I will lead them in paths that they have not known."

You do not know how the watchmaker will fix your watch, how the mechanic will fix your car, how the doctor will heal your body.

Yet you have faith in their power to do their work. Have you just as much faith in God to let Him work in ways you know not of?

Not long ago a woman needed financial help very much. She decided one morning that she would really put her faith in God for her prosperity problems. After morning prayers that day she said to herself:

"I need some money for me and my family. But I am just going to stop struggling. I am going to do whatever God gives me to do. I am going to put all my troubles lovingly into my Father's hands."

And do you know that from that time on her condition steadily improved? True, there were days that were afterwards dark, but time after time she said the same thing to herself. And time after time God responded to her faith.

You, too, will find that with faith in God, good fortune can come to you "in ways you know not." A letter may come from someone you may never have heard from and change your whole life. You may hear a chance word on the street or in a store which may send you off to some place you never thought you would go. An announcement on the radio or an item in the newspaper may give you an idea which may start you off on an entirely different path! All "in ways you knew not." Small things which no one, least of all yourself, would think are turning points in your prosperity!

Believe that God wants you to be prosperous and you will not need to depend only upon your own resources any more. Believe and you will be justified in saying: "With God all things are possible."

And with these words, let us speak to our Father. Let us tell Him our prosperity problems, being brave and not fearing. And let us in His Name ask for our Prosperity!

Let us pray: "For Prosperity and Abundance."

Prayer

For

PROSPERITY AND ABUNDANCE

"The Lord is my shepherd;
I shall not want"—23rd Psalm

Almight God, my heavenly Father, Thine is the
power and glory for ever and ever. Thou art the
Creator of every single thing on earth both large
and small. Thy will is the law of the universe,
the way for us to learn and follow.

Thou hast filled the earth and sea with good
things in infinite abundance. Thou hast created
us, Thy children, to make use of the good things
Thou hast put here. Thou lovest us and it is Thy
will we shall live in plenty if we first seek Thy
kingdom and Thy righteousness.

So I come to Thee, dear Father, to seek Thy help
and guidance in straightening out my prosperity
problems. The way ahead may look troubled and
hard, dear Father, but I know Thou wilt hear
my prayer and help me.

Teach me to be thankful, dear Father, thankful
for the blessings I have now. Teach me to be
faithful in my work, and through it, to serve
my fellow men and women — and that only in so
doing may I prosper.

Even in seeking Thee now, dear Father, my heart
is lightened and I know and feel that things are
going to be better, that Thou knowest my need and
even before I have called Thou wilt answer.
And this gives me new courage to rise and go forth
in hope and peace!

—Amen

14

GOD WANTS YOU TO HAVE A HAPPY MARRIAGE

PERHAPS THE GREATEST source of happiness in life is a contented marriage with the right person, a peaceful home and lovely children to bless it. Is this *your* wish? If you are married already, is *yours* a happy marriage?

It *can* be! And that is why the wonderful news we bring you in this chapter should create such joy for you. Love and a happy marriage is exactly what God wants you to have. They are the glorious ways God has worked out for the passing on of the life He created!

Why, right in the very first chapter of the Bible, God tells you that men and women were made for each other.

"It is not good that the man should be alone," said God. "I will make him a help mate for him." Those are God's own words!

You see? God made men and women for each other's joy and love. Would you like to be in love, to get married? God has planted your yearning for love within your heart and He will satisfy it. And all *you* need to do is to follow just the simple way God has shown, and all those joys shall be added unto you.

God wants you to know there is nothing so beautiful as meeting the one mate meant for you. And God wants love-making to be happy. He does not want you to be old when you are young. He wants happy, wholesome love between men and women in a fine, free, sunny world full of beauty and joy!

In what wondrous way love is awakened, no man can tell. You may meet someone by chance and it can become the beginning of bliss. You will be indeed lucky if love comes to you out of comradeship and friendship. But many and many a time, only one meeting may decide your destiny even though you may not see the other for weeks—or months—or even years!

But how thankful we should be to our Father that love can come to all. Some deep instinct gives a man the power to see the beauty hidden deep in the heart of a plain girl. Some deep feeling gives a woman the insight to see the honesty and sincerity in the heart of a plain man. So do not despair if you are not a beauty or a screen hero.

Love enters in not by doors but by hearts. Love comes to the plain just as often as to the pretty. Love comes as often to the poor as the rich—oftener, for they need it so much more. Love comes to the older as well as the younger—for love has no age and *sees* no age!

For how many times lonely hearts have echoed the question—how can I find love? How can I make myself charming and handsome and ready for love? How can I marry?

Dear reader, the *time* is in God's hands. Many a man has to wait patiently while love stirs in the heart of a woman. Many a woman has to wait and wonder and hope before love is awakened in the heart of a man.

Yes, the time is in God's hands, but the *way* is in yours. To tell you to be clean and pleasant and desirable to *all* in the world would be to tell you something you already know. But the *real* way to charm in love is through the heart.

And the way of the heart is to love! Learn to love all persons—yes, and all things! The more people you love, the more radiant you will become. Love *all* men and women and you will never want for the love of *one;* Others will turn to you as naturally as the flowers turn to the sun.

Attract love by *liking.* The man or the woman who goes around saying: "I don't like this kind of woman" or "I don't like that kind of man"—who can pick flaws in everyone they meet, will rarely find anyone they *do* like. And no one will like *them.*

Liking turns to love. So *like* people. Like them enough to go where they are! Go to church and church affairs. Not by chance may you meet your mate in church and church work. Who will say that the inspiration of love which makes two hearts seek each other does not also bring them to God.

Just the power of loving will transform you. You will be a new person because love *creates!* It is the new person in you which your mate will see! Take this new body, this new soul where it may be seen of men and women. Go to parties, to the homes of friends, abroad in the world. It must be seen to be appreciated—and you cannot be seen if you stay home. *That* is how to meet your mate.

When two people who really love discover each other, a new life begins for both of them—so unlike the old, so radiant, so wonderful, that even the poets have not been able fully to picture it. Deep down in your heart you know this is what God made you for. This is one of His many mansions and He takes you therein with joy and rapture!

So, like the rising chords of a great organ, the course of love runs from companionship and courtship to the sacrament of marriage. And with marriage comes a new life. How close is this tie, you may read in the most beautiful love story ever written—the story of Ruth in your Bible. Just to read it again will give you such a marvelous insight as to how you, too, may go forth with your mate on the wondrous journey of marriage!

If love led only to more love and the satisfaction of desire, then surely it would exhaust itself. Love is crowned with marriage and marriage is made perfect when tiny hands are clutching at the heartstrings. This is but another step in your climb towards God!

There is not a mother or father alive but who will tell you that despite all the cares and troubles which may come, the raising of a family of fine children has brought them something infinitely blessed. Their loves and their lives seem to be lived over again.

Even though father and mother may have to toil with every ounce of their strength to launch their little family, they are rewarded of God in gold which cannot tarnish, in silver which thieves cannot break in and steal. For the miracle of birth, of growth, of unfoldment brings you very close to the root of life which is God!

17

True it is that family cares sometimes overshadow the joys. Children cause trouble and worry. Sometimes they are thoughtless; sometimes they seem mean and unjust. Sometimes husband or wife brings tears.

But if your love has been true all through the years, then there is plenty of love stored up for emergencies such as these. Do you want God's guidance for the wondrous power of love to overcome these stones in your path? Then hearken to the glorious words of St. Paul:

> *"Love suffereth long and*
> *is kind.*
> *Love is not easily*
> *provoked.*
> *Love thinketh no evil.*
> *Love beareth all things,*
> *believeth all things,*
> *hopeth all things,*
> *endureth all things."*

Maybe the husband and father is terribly in need of reform. Maybe the children and others *do* seem like stones in your path. Alone you can do nothing. But with God you can *love* them. Love them right as they are. Just as your heavenly Father loves *you* as you are. Yes, the uplifted heart, the open Bible, the bent knee, the prayer-hearing and prayer-answering God—these alone can bring peace and harmony into your home.

Even though it is true that there comes a time when the plain fact of sin— real or contemplated—must be faced in yourself or in someone on whom you had pinned your hope for marriage seems unfaithful. Someone who has stood before the altar of God with you and promised faithfulness, forgets those vows.

To break into anger, to interfere, to insist on finding out, accomplishes nothing. All too often it gives the erring one an excuse to run to the new love for consolation.

The way to meet this problem is not easy—but the stakes are great. The way is the way of Jesus, who said to the repentant Magdalene:

> *"Neither do I condemn*
> *thee; go and sin no*
> *more."*

Forgive the erring ones and love them in spite of their sin—yes, perhaps because of it. Time wears off the gold on the feet of any idol if its feet be made of clay. To wait is the only thing you will not be sorry for afterwards. And meanwhile be thankful for the love which you *do* have.

For God is not mocked saith the prophet. To those who are tempted to seek further after having vowed faithfulness before God, think and think well before trying to put asunder whom God hath joined together.

Can we say anything to those who love deeply yet who have not found their love; to whom love may bring loss and pain? But there *is* a refuge! It is God! Seek God and He will restore your soul, for so He has promised. With soul restored, the world takes on new meaning. The love which you were ready to give and which seemed for a long time not to be wanted—finds that it *is* needed — many times — in many places—by many people!

For when you trust in God, your love and marriage problems begin to change. When you have faith that God wants you to have a happy marriage, a new peace enters your soul. The way of love and marriage is the way of God. God never closes a door upon any love, but to open it upon another.

One dear old lady, married over fifty years, said that her married life was like a long, sweet song. Before she or her husband fell asleep at night, every fault and grievance of the day was freely confessed. Each new day was like a bright new page.

Never forget the happy hours of early love. Neglect the whole world rather than one another. Here is the work, here is the family given by God to your care! The God-centered life, the life which seeks to give rather than to get, is the life which will give the successful and happy marriage.

The love, the family, the husband or wife which God gave you is the opportunity which He gave you to carry out His plan for you. The invisible strands of helpfulness one to another which bind you to your love or to your family are truly bonds of silk which will lead you to the peace and harmony and happiness in your love and marriage. And you will have guarded the good thing which was committed unto thee.

For it is one of the false witnesses of them who doubt that says married love burns itself out with the graying of the hair and the flying forth of the children. The best is yet to be. All down through the lengthening shadows of life, love sends its golden rays of beauty and romance, transformed into loving service and faith and trust. Until, like the beautiful Greek legend, two souls which have braved sunshine and storm together, stand like two great trees, their branches intertwined, facing the sunrise of God's tomorrow.

Let us, dear reader, make our Prayer "For a Happy Marriage."

𝔓𝔯𝔞𝔶𝔢𝔯

For

A HAPPY MARRIAGE

"Beloved, let us love one another:
for love is of God"—1 John 4:7

Dear heavenly Father, Thou art the only foundation
of my life, for Thy wisdom and power and love
is without end. Thou art the mighty One who hast
created all things and planned all things ever
since the beginning of the world.

And so I know Thou hast planned happiness in .
marriage for me. O how I need such happiness,
dear Father. How my heart aches for love in
marriage, a happy home and good children — all
living together for Thy honor and glory.

Please, please, dear Father, bring happiness
in marriage to me. Teach me that marriage is holy
and sacred. Help me to understand that if
unhappiness and distrust come into marriage it
is because we stray from the example which Thy
dear Son, Jesus, set for us.

O dear Father, help our marriage to be happy.
Help me do my part by being patient and kind and
sympathetic. And in the same way, dear Father,
enter the heart of my mate so that patience and
kindness and love shall be there, too.

With Thy help we will make our marriage a beautiful
thing, dear Father — living together in peace
and happiness! We ask Thy help, Father, and we
know Thou wilt help us, for we ask it in the name
of Thy Son, Jesus!

—Amen

4

GOD WANTS YOU TO BE SUCCESSFUL
IN ALL YOU UNDERTAKE

Do THINGS GO WRONG WITH you lots of times—things you've set your heart on? Goals you've wanted to reach—ambitions? Plans for business or farm, home or personal affairs? Does it often seem you can't make progress—get over obstacles?

If that is the way it is with you, dear reader, then here is wonderful news—God wants you to succeed in your plans!

Yes, sir, He does! God never meant this to be a world of failures. Nothing makes God happier than to see people succeed at what they set out to do—provided, of course, that their ambitions are good and worthy ones.

And you *can* succeed at whatever you try if you will follow God's laws of life— live as He wants you to live, do as He tells you to do. And you have only to turn, as always, to the Bible—that wonderful Book of God's laws—to find the way and the road to realize your ambitions, your plans, to overcome the obstacles which seem to hold you down.

And what is the first thing to do if you want to succeed in any and every undertaking of your life?

"Seek ye first the kingdom of God, and his righteousness; and all these things shall be added unto you."

Because without God's approval, God's help, you are doomed to failure before you start. Be sure that your ambitions, your undertakings, your plans are all in accordance with the best that God wants. And when you are sure—go ahead!

And in this connection we would like to tell you a little story of a man who was afraid to go ahead.

Up in the far north, a man

was floating out to the frozen and deserted sea on an ice-floe. Not a sign of land was near, not a house, not a living soul.

"I am lost," he thought. "No one knows about me. No one can help me." Through his mind ran the words of an old hymn: "My God and Father, while I stray; far from home on life's rough way; O teach me from my heart to say: 'Thy will be done.' "

But, although he did not know it, he was not alone. For hours on a far headland, his friends had been following his floe with strong glasses. And, although the waters were tossing, they were making super-human efforts to reach him. Of all this he knew nothing until they finally came to rescue him.

Perhaps *you* seem to have failed in your undertakings. Perhaps the dreams with which *you* started out in life seem to have been doomed one by one. Perhaps that home, that farm, that business of which you have dreamed is yet beyond your grasp.

You may *think* yourself abandoned and alone. You may think you have no friends who are doing any-thing to help you. But *God* has seen you. He is watching you. He is guiding friends and conditions to your Prosperity, your success and your good fortune.

You need help and need it badly. Please do try and know that God is doing all He can. He will bring you success in your undertakings just as soon as He finds a man or woman or condition through which to work!

God wants you to be successful in all that you undertake which is born of righteousness. It is one of His principal gifts to you. He has placed every good thing in the world for your prosperity and your success. He has placed the power to gain them and the power to *use* them in your heart.

And all that He asks in return is that you obey the few laws He has laid down for His children. A train must run along tracks to get to its destination. God's laws are the tracks along which you must run to get to *your* destination—prosperity, peace and plenty. The reason why so many people fail to realize their ambitions is they are fighting against and breaking God's laws of life.

And it is a marvelous

thing to see that God has so arranged it, that in order for you to be *really* successful and happy, you must first help to make *others* successful and happy. And if every one of us thought in just that way, what a wonderful world this would be!

For this is what Jesus was always trying to get people to do. He was always trying to get people to give up selfish rewards and pleasures and devote their thoughts to helping others. Do you remember what He said?:

"For whosoever will save his life shall lose it, but whosoever will lose his life ... shall save it."

Jesus was talking of the *use* to which you put your life. He meant that the man or woman who tried to live for themselves alone, would *never* be successful in their undertakings. In fact, He made it even *stronger*. He said that such a person would not only not gain their ambition, but would end up with even *less* than what they started with!

And how true that is! Haven't you noticed that nine times out of ten, the person who goes through life saying: "What's in it for

me?" or "What will *I* get out of this?" or "I've got to look out for myself first" not only never *gets* anything permanently, but, in many and many a case, makes enemies and loses that which they got!

"But he that giveth his life shall find it an hundredfold."

How true and how *strong* that is. When you give, you not only get back that which you *give*, says Jesus, but you get it back a *hundred times!*

If you will start out with the idea of *giving* instead of getting, you will succeed not only in a spiritual way, but in a worldy way—in the actual way of more money, more abundance, more prosperity. And this time, real *true* prosperity.

Because, if you will stop to think of it, there is one thing at which you *can* succeed—no matter who you are, what you are, where you are or what you may have done in the past. You *can* succeed at *giving*. People may stop you from making money, from realizing your ambition, but no one can stop you from giving "of your life" just as Jesus commands. No one *wants* to!

But something wonderful happens when you start to give. Now we don't just mean presents or things people ask you. We mean giving of your *self*, your *good will*, your really *best wishes*. We mean you must give of your *own* life, you must *think* of others, want *their* prosperity, help them in their hopes.

Yes, once in a while you will find a suspicious person who cannot understand this. But for everyone like that, you will find a *hundred* who will pour out their pent-up love in return for it.

And from every person to whom you *give*, a wonderful and marvelous thing happens. They cannot *help* giving something to *you*. That is not to say you should ever want or *expect* a return. But it will *come!* Scattered through your life will be many, many friends, all "pulling" for you, all who *want* to see you succeed, who will help you in ways they may not understand *themselves!*

Here will be a person who will show you how to make more money. Here will be another who will open up an entirely new channel in your church work. Here will be a man or woman who will see what your ambition with your farm is. Here will be someone who gives you just the little help you need in your business. You will never, perhaps, be able to tell where this hundredfold return will come from if you only abide by this law, but it will come! Just as surely as day follows night!

Do you want to overcome the obstacles which are holding you back from your future and your plans? Then stop thinking about the past and put the present into God's kind hands. For no matter what you have accomplished in the past, God is ready to start fresh with you today—the minute you stop reading this very Chapter!

You say it is too late? Then hear the words which echo across the centuries right into your room today:

"Him that cometh to me I will in no wise cast out. ...Behold I make all things new."

For where *you* leave off, dear reader, God begins! God's life, God's wisdom, God's help are about your life just as the air surrounds your body. And whenever you call upon God to help you in any undertaking—whether by action or by prayer—then God will come to your rescue, even as the man in the boat was rescued.

Yes, we will grant that there are many hopes and ambitions that may never be realized. Indeed it would take many lifetimes to realize the ambitions of some of us. But deep down inside, dear reader, we all have only one ambition — to live happy, peaceful lives in modest comfort.

And by even the standards of the most unworldly, Jesus was not successful. He lived and died a poor man. The shadow of failure and persecution was always with him. He wanted to bring the whole world His Gospel. But outside of the Holy Land, there were few who heard of Him. Yet was Jesus unhappy because all of his cherished dreams did not come true? Listen to His words: "In the world ye shall have tribulations, but be of good cheer; I have overcome the world."

And to those who might think that Jesus suffered because He did not attain worldly goods, we can still hear His ringing words: "A man's life consisteth not in the abundance of things which he possesses."

Yet with what a triumphant shout He proclaims that He *did* come to bring life and life more abundant:

"Ask, and it shall be given you; seek, and ye shall find; knock, and it shall be opened unto you."

What reserves of ambition will flow into your life, dear reader, once you realize that you are an eternal child of God, the Father. And the wonderful part is that all you need do is to ask, to knock.

God *expects* you to be ambitious. And He who put the desire into your heart surely will see to it that it will be fulfilled to the extent that you are ready for it.

And God will work his wonders in wondrous ways. For one thing you must remember. That is, no matter what God tells you to do, no matter what answer you receive from your Faith in Him or your prayer to Him, what you are told to do will not be too hard even though your sense might tell you that a certain step is impossible. The power and the wisdom and the strength needed to carry God's message through to its completion, is *always* given with the message!

From the place of power will come the supply for every need and the support for every problem and the answer to every ambition.

For you can be O so sure, dear reader, that He who brought you into being will help you and guide you in the way which is best—not always *your* way—but where *your* way is His way, then will He lead you by the hand up the road to fulfillment.

And fulfillment, as we have said, comes only through obeying God's law. *Use* this chapter and if you have ambitions and plans, check them against what is in this chapter and on what about it applies to you.

And pray this Prayer for guidance and strength of God in carrying out your plans:

𝔓rayer

For

SUCCESS IN ALL MY UNDERTAKINGS

*"The Lord will perfect that which
concerneth me"—Psalm 138:8*

Our Father who art in heaven, Thou seest all and
knowest all and plannest all. Thou hast put
me here on earth for the wonderful purpose known
only to Thee. And Thou hast given me my life
that I might make this a better and happier world
for all of Thy children.

O Father, Thou knowest how hard I try to do Thy
will. And sometimes I do wish I could be able to
see into the future and find out whether I will
ever have success and good fortune in my undertakings. But then I know it is enough that
Thou guidest me only one step at a time.

Help me, dear Father, help me to make a wonderful
success of my life. Put my feet on the path
once more to health and happiness and success
in what I undertake.

Guide my steps every day, dear Father, to the
work Thou wantest me to do. Be with me and I
promise to do my best, Father. Make me listen
to what Thou tellest me and help me to be good
and honest and pure in heart. Help me to work
hard that I may overcome all obstacles.

For I shall not grow tired, dear Father, if I know
Thou art leading me on to success. Blessed be
Thy name, dear Father, for I know Thou wilt
never fail me! In Jesus' name I pray.

—Amen

LETTING GOD FILL YOUR LIFE WITH BEAUTY AND HAPPINESS

Is LIFE OFTEN MONOTONOUS to you? Drab, uninteresting, the same, day after day? Do you feel as though you are in a rut? Do you wonder if there is ever going to be any real, true happiness in life for you? Do the days ahead seem to stretch without hope into a dark, gloomy, uncertain future?

Well, if you *do* get discouraged and downhearted like that sometimes, just remember this: *God wants you to be happy!* It is His will that you live a full, useful, beautiful life!

You can prove this to yourself right in the Bible, right in the very words of Jesus himself:

> *"I am come that they might have life — and that they might have it more abundantly."*

Does that really *mean* anything to you, dear reader? Jesus came to give you more than the humdrum life of working and eating and sleeping. He came to give you a life more abundant—a life of beauty and happiness and joy!

Jesus, himself, was a happy man. There was a quiet joy deep down in His heart every hour of His ministry. And many and many a time He spoke of this joy to others.

Do you know why Jesus was happy? It was because He knew that His heavenly Father loved Him. He said it very beautifully and very simply: "The Father hath loved me."

Jesus wants *you* to be happy. God wants you to be happy. Why, then, are you not? Is it because you do not know *how?*

The secret of happiness is so very simple that you can hardly believe it. All you need to do is to live your life by God's laws. "He that keepeth the law, happy is he" you can read in Proverbs 29:18. That simply means that if you do what God wants you to do you will be happy.

And it follows that if you *break* God's laws you will be *unhappy*. This is so easily proved. All of us have done something wrong at one time or another. Were you ever happy after doing something wrong — even though you may have benefitted from it in some material way? Didn't you hear a still, small voice down inside of you saying, "Why did you do that? Didn't you know it was wrong?"

But when you do what you know is right, then you are on the road to contentment and happiness. Yes, if you want to be really happy, you will have to do what God's laws tell you to do.

And there is another way of bringing happiness and joy into your life, dear reader. It is by helping others. Jesus well knew this, for you can read in John 13:17 "If ye know these things, happy are ye if you do them."

There is no question but what you have found this to be true in your own life. Whenever you have done something for another without any thought of return,

hasn't that been one of your happiest moments? Whenever you sent a gift to another, no matter how simple—even a plant cutting—weren't you happy in the thought of the joy it would give them?

Well, there is no greater happiness. For it is one of God's wonderful laws that to help others will always make you happy—and the more you help, the happier you will be!

Why, the Bible is just crammed full with proof that God put you here to be happy. Time after time you can read in the Bible the word "Rejoice." And to rejoice is to be *more* than happy. It is to be so joyful that you want to shout and sing!

> *"Rejoice in the Lord, always; and again I say rejoice." Phil. 4:4*

These are wonderfully happy words. They are just full of joy. You would think they were written by someone who was having a wonderful time, who had all their hearts desired, who did not know what cold and bare surroundings meant; who lived a life of movement and change and happiness.

That passage you have just read was written by St. Paul, one of Jesus' dearest Disciples. And do you know where he was when he wrote them? He was in prison! He was in prison, not because he had committed any crime, but simply because he was a follower of Jesus.

Yet even in the drabness, the monotony, the hopelessness of prison, he was so full of joy at being one with Jesus and the Father, that he wrote the wonderful words you have just read!

Yes, dear reader, it is by living close to God, in tune with His beauty and the world's beauty; thrilling to the challenge of living a God-centered life, helping to build His Kingdom, that you will find the only road to beauty and happiness that there is!

It is so very true that you and I have to do the very same thing, day after day, whether we work out in the world or in household tasks at home. And it does seem to us sometimes that we are in a rut, that life is monotonous.

You are tired and discour-

aged, that may be true. But if you would only understand that God is *within* you—not up there in the sky somewhere—but deep within you—inside as well as out—then a beautiful, happy life can begin for you now—this very minute!

Jesus well knew the power of the presence of God within you. For he says what you, yourself, have probably always really known:

> *"The kingdom of God is within you."*

The answer to your search for beauty and happiness in life is within you. Do you remember the story of the little boy who searched for the Blue Bird of Happiness all over the world, only to find it singing in his back yard all the time?

Happiness and beauty—and we cannot repeat it too often—lie not in your outward circumstances but deep within *yourself!* For no outward circumstances can make you permanently happy unless the spirit is within.

The rich man or woman whose life is just one round of costly possessions rarely sees beauty in them. Those whose life is made up of travel and change will tell you how monotonous they find it. Those whose life is apparently secure are the very ones who tremble most at the future.

We all know the story of the unhappy King who heard that the happiest man in his kingdom lived in a far distant province. The King was told that the secret of the man's happiness lay in the man's shirt. So the King dispatched a messenger to the happy man to buy the shirt of happiness at any price so that the King might be happy once more.

When the messenger arrived at the man's house he found him joking and laughing and full of life. The messenger asked the man to sell him his shirt at any price he should ask the King. And the man roared with laughter. He took off his threadbare cloak and lo—he *had* no shirt!

Of course, that is not to say that all good, believing folks go around grinning and saying: "How good I feel." They see and know that life is serious, that it has its stern hardships. But no matter what happens to them, there is still something within them that makes them see the beauty in the common things of life, that makes them hopeful and happy— the Kingdom of God within!

For there *is* only one beauty. It is the beauty created by God. And it is good that you glory in His handiwork even as was commanded. For God who touches the earth with beauty can make it beautiful for you! God who makes crystal springs of pure water, can purify *your* life, too! And God who makes the waves of the lake dance in the sunshine, can make *you* glad and free if you will only let Him!

All the beauty that is ever worth while is *yours* because it is God's. And you need never say that no beauty is in your life while your eyes can see the jewels in the simplest wild flower, the set of sun in city or hamlet and the innocent beauty of a child. It is a priceless gift because it is *God's* beauty!

Let us thank God we can see this beauty, for to us, the children of God and to us ONLY has this power of seeing beauty been given. Stones have it not, sticks have it not. Only you and I have it. It is given us of God because of His wonderful love for us!

And it is the same with

God's happiness for you. Happiness is just the joy of being alive and well and loved—and it is *nothing else!* When a happy person enters a room it is as if a light were shining from them. Happiness drives away gloom and fear. Even the happiness of others helps us to be good and kind. Yes, even putting on an *appearance* of happiness causes it to grow in your heart.

And the most wonderful thing about God's happiness is that you can lend it to others and yet still keep it. As Emerson said: "Happiness is a perfume; you cannot pour it on others without getting a few drops on yourself."

This feeling of God's beauty and happiness within you gives you the hope, the courage and strength to say to the drabness and monotony and darkness: "Do the worst that you dare! God is within me! You cannot harm me!"

Now—when you come to think about it, haven't you been thinking too much about your own troubles and very little about God?

Maybe that's what's wrong. If you will start thinking about God, you will feel that He is your life and that He can give you the

power to overcome anything in your life which robs it of beauty and happiness—then there is no question but that you will *get* that power!

And how can you start to *let* this presence into your life in the best and quickest way? By bidding it welcome in your heart—through Prayer!

For the Prayer of Faith alone can bring you God's beauty and happiness. Faith and faith alone will lift the burden. Faith alone washes away misery and monotony and unhappiness. Then you become so happy it seems your life has been set to music.

And what wonderful happiness the knowing and the feeling that God loves you, that He wants you to be happy can bring you, dear reader! What a wonderful happiness to know and feel that God, the creator of all beauty and happiness, holds it out to you!

It is this precious thought that we all need to carry us through the everyday cares and troubles which all of us have to face.

For God's beauty and happiness is more than mere loveliness. It cannot be

33

bought with gold for it is greater than gold. God's gift of a healthy body and a calm and contented mind is something which is open to all!

And with them, dear reader, comes the power to *see* God's beauty! Every day, no matter where you live or who you are, you will see at least one beautiful thing created by God. Treasure it! Every day, no matter who you are or where you live, you will see at least one unselfish act performed by one of God's children!

And he who sees these things has laid hold of the truest secret of God's beauty and happiness that there is in the world!

With these thoughts in your soul, can you ever again think your world is drab or monotonous? With your eyes open to God's beauty, with every day a new revelation of it, can you ever again believe you are in a rut? With your heart tuned to God's love, can you ever again doubt His plan for you? Your future stretches on and on—down the endless road of time.

And will you not join us in the Prayer: "That God Will Fill My Life With His Beauty and Happiness."

Prayer

That

GOD WILL FILL MY LIFE WITH HIS BEAUTY AND HAPPINESS

"Light is sown for the righteous, and gladness for the upright in heart" — Psalm 97:11

Almighty God, my heavenly Father, how boundless is Thy power and glory and love. Thou art the One from whom all happiness comes. From Thee alone can help come to me.

For Thou knowest, dear Father, how unhappy I have often been. Thou knowest how many troubles and disappointments have come to me — so many dear ones leaving me, so much poor health. O, Father, it sometimes seems that just everything happens to me — that whatever I do just goes wrong.

Help me to remember, dear Father, that Thou wantest all Thy children to be happy. Thou lookest into my heart, Father. Thou knowest how I long for love and kindness and happiness. So please, dear Father, give me beauty and happiness in my life once more.

Give me the secret of happiness. Teach me that only by making others happy, that only by following Thy Golden Rule can real happiness come. Yes, and I know that my reward for helping others will be Thy kingdom of happiness in my life here and now.

All I ask, dear Father, is that Thou shalt hear my voice and take me in the shelter of Thy love. Yes, even to speak to Thee any time I am unhappy, even as I can now, has made me so happy. Truly I feel the real contentment and happiness and peace of Thy love!

—Amen

6

GOD WANTS YOU TO BE
RADIANT—ATTRACTIVE

ALL OF US KNOW PEOPLE, both men and women, who are glowingly attractive—not only in appearance but also in personality.

They are what we call "charming." They are people we like to *be* with, who make us feel good just to be around them. They are warm, friendly, "human" people. If they are women, men love them and are attracted to them. If they are men, women admire them and seek them.

Would you like to be that kind of person? Would you like to have people admire you and like you and respect you in this way?

You *can* be that kind of a man or woman! No matter what your age, appearance, education, you *can* be radiant and attractive: You *can* develop an inner fire and radiance that will win others to you!

God *wants* you to be like this. Jesus was that kind of

person and His whole life reveals to you the secrets of His charm and influence. Every picture of Jesus shows Him in a haze of radiance, a halo crowning His head. It was because Jesus *was* in contact with a source of life and radiance. It was because Jesus was open to the power of God in His mind and body that even His raiment shone in radiance.

For there are two kinds of people in this old world. You have met people who look like darkened houses with the door barred and the shades all pulled down. But you have also welcomed people who seem like a house set upon a hill—the door wide open and joy and laughter streaming through the open windows.

These are the people who are so radiant, so vital, so filled with the spirit of life. These are the people who, like Jesus, are open to the power of God in their bodies and minds.

You, too, can learn to welcome this spirit of joy and radiance. Your body can lose its dullness, your mind its flatness. The spirit which is God *can* shine through. And it is this spirit and this spirit alone which has the power to make you really attractive and charming and magnetic!

Jesus is the great awakener of your personality. In the company of Jesus you begin to feel better, to see more, to be brave, to love men and women. Jesus was a builder of personalities of men and women in the days of old. He still builds!

That was the deepest reason why people wanted to be with Jesus, the reason they worshipped Him, the reason why He attracted His Disciples. They did it for joy! Losing Himself in love and service to others, Jesus said time after time that He showed them the way "That my joy might remain in you, and that your joy might be full."

What made Jesus joyful? The Bible gives you the secret of that joy in the wonderful words which Jesus uttered: "*I am not alone,* *because the Father is with me.*"

You, too, often may believe you face the problems, the neglect, the stings of life alone. You, too, may think you have no friends to like you, respect you, take your counsel. But you, too, are not alone. The Gospel which Jesus brought can make you, too, sure and confident and unafraid and radiant!

God tells you there is nobody higher or lower than you. Every man and woman you meet will be a child of God. To those whom you thought "higher" you need not be afraid to speak, to ask, to consult. They are *not* higher. And to those whom you thought lower, you need not be afraid to speak, to stoop down, to love. They are *not* lower!

The only way you differ from other people is in the amount of human-ness, the amount of Godliness within you. The amount of *good*-liness within you. That thing which seems to set you apart is the very thing which makes you valuable in God's plan for this world.

Now if you really think you can make yourself attractive by a new way of dressing or doing your hair, then by all means do so.

If you really think that you can make friends and influence people by mechanical "tricks" and studying psychology, then it may be these things will help you.

But actually it is the *hard* way. Because there is no cut-and-dried set of rules on attractiveness and charm and magnetism. What is attractive and charming to one person is just the opposite in another. No, these things are more than a change of clothes, of manners, of appearance. They are a change of heart!

Yes, if your health is not good, by all means use every means in your power to help it. For with health comes the sure step, the firm grasp, the vitality which attracts men and women. If a change of clothes, of "make-up," of manners, of conversation will help you to have more confidence in yourself, by all means acquire them. Both are the "frame" which encloses the picture of your radiant self! But like any frame, they can only add or detract a little from the entire picture.

How many, many times have you, yourself, met a person who made you feel comfortable and warm and good all over? Perhaps they may have violated all the rules of fashion and etiquette and grammar. And when you looked at them perhaps they kept no rules of dress or deportment. All you knew was that while they were talking to you something flowed from them to you. You felt as if you had always known them. *This,* dear reader, is charm, this is attractiveness, this is radiance!

And it flows from old and young, from rich and poor, from learned and humble. It flows from all whose life is not self-centered. As the Bible said of Jesus: *"For power came forth from Him."*

So if you are lonely, if you think your are not attractive, if people do not seem to like you as much as you think they should, won't you face the facts? Nine times out of ten, it is not because of what you do but what you *are!*

And you should *remain* what you are. If you are a man or woman of 35 or 45 or 50 you *can* be more attractive and charming. But only if you have the attraction and charm *of* a man or woman of that age. The older man or woman who tries for the fascination of a boy or girl of 17 is only going to be disappointed and ridiculous.

Some of the most beautiful women, the most charming men in history have been women and men in those ages. Right in your own circle you will have to admit, age has no monopoly on charm or attractiveness or influence. No, the secret is still deeper.

There are only three simple steps to become charming and attractive and compelling. You are all these things to those who *think* you are. So it is easy to see that you must make people *think* differently about you.

That sounds hard, doesn't it? But it is ten times as easy as trying to make yourself over by the beauty parlor, the tailor, or the correspondence course.

This is the first step. Admit frankly that you want to be liked. You don't want to bowl people over by your stunning appearance. You just want people to like you, to like to be with you. It is as simple as that.

The second step is just the opposite. Try to understand that what *you* want, other people want. You want people to respect you? Very well, others want people to

respect *them!* You respect them! You want other people to be friendly to you? Other people want others to be friendly to *them*. *You* be friendly to them. You want people to trust you, you want to influence people for worthy things? Well, if you have gained their respect and their friendship, *whatever* you say or do will influence them!

Is there anything more attractive than a little child, anything more charming? What is the secret of this compelling charm? It is simply that a little child is completely trustful, completely unafraid and completely unconscious of itself. Jesus was giving you the real secret of charm and attractiveness when He said "of such is the Kingdom of Heaven."

For it is not until you become "as a little child" that you can partake of this wonderful thing which has pulled at the hearts of men and women since time began. Be trustful of those about you and you will have the charm of the trustful child. Be unafraid as a child and there will not be a man or woman in the world you will be afraid to meet and to talk to. Be forgetful of yourself and you will plumb the inner secret of *all* attractiveness and charm. In other words, when you meet people in a spirit of friendly interest, knowing they are only flesh and blood with their own problems—sickness, troubles, oppressed, troubled in spirit, you may be sure they will meet you on an entirely different level than you ever thought possible.

We have not forgotten the third step. It is that you pray for inner radiance and for love—but you pray for more! Now Prayer might seem a far cry from getting God's attractiveness to your body and mind. But surely you remember that we are commanded to pray for "all things"!

None of us wants to be attractive, to be magnetic, to influence just people and things in general. Almost all of us have one or at most a few dear friends to whom we want to respond, but find it hard. If you are attractive to just a few people—yes, to even one or two—it is sure you will be attractive to many. So why not concentrate on the one person at a time you want to appeal to?

Pray for that person! The minute you pray for any person your mind and soul are *full* of that person and that is love. And when you think of anyone in a prayerful way, time after time a way to help them comes to you. Pray *further* than "Thy will be done." Add to your prayer: "And here am I, Lord, to do it!"

You may or you may not find a way to help that person. But even if you do not, you are opening to them a wonderful power which, in the end, they must respond to. And they will respond to love as people *always* respond to love—with *more* love! Prayer has more attractive power than any other force in the world!

How much of Jesus' ministry was with the object of drawing people to him, of attracting them, of influencing them! And such was the power that He drew from Prayer that it lit up His entire face and flowed like an electric current out of His body. And, like a magnet, His Disciples watched. The power that they saw moved them so much that they eagerly crowded in upon Him crying: "Lord, teach *us* to pray!" And it was then that Jesus gave unto them the immortal Lord's Prayer.

40

Yes, God, the Father can renew you, too, and give you the same brightness and radiance. Never will you lack attractiveness, never will you lack speech if you smile in loving appreciation of the spirit of love and beauty in another! Never will you lack speech if you express God's love and beauty in your thought and word!

Yes, dear reader, God's laws are there for you to read, the way has been made plain—the way to radiance, to attractiveness, to magnetism—is still the way which Jesus trod and which God created—the way of everlasting love!

Let us pray that Prayer "For Inner Radiance and Attractiveness."

Prayer

INNER RADIANCE AND ATTRACTIVENESS

"He hath made everything beautiful in His time"—Eccl. 3:11

Wonderful, Almighty Father, Thine is the power above all power. Thine is the past, the present and the eternal future. Thine is the glory which lights up the faces of those who love Thee truly.

O, Father, Thou knowest we cannot all be beautiful in body. Thou knowest that sometimes we feel tired and listless and neglected. Sometimes I feel like that, dear Father, and yet I know that is not the way a child of Thine should feel.

For truly I know that Thou hast given us the power to be full of joy and inner radiance and attractiveness. All those things come from Thee, dear Father. They come from a holy spirit and a loving heart.

Please, Father, give me such a heart and such a spirit. Give me the kind of light which comes from being a dear, good child of Thine. O Father, I do want to pass on that light to those I love. I do want the kind of light that others will see what a change Thou hast made in me. I do want to bring others to Thee because they can see what loving Thee has meant for me.

Dear Father, even as I have prayed, I have felt Thy peace entering my spirit, Thy love entering my heart. Thy spirit has lifted me up so that I feel I can go forth once more radiant and joyful and full of Thy light and love!

—Amen

GOD HAS A LIFE WORK FOR YOU

Do you sometimes wonder if the place in life you occupy is really where God wants you to be? Do you wonder if you, perhaps, have hidden talents and abilities that would fit you for bigger things, more satisfaction and happiness than you now have?

Do you feel hindered in your work, not appreciated by others, facing a "dead end"? Well, if you have ever had thoughts of this kind, then right here in this Chapter is light which may shine upon a wonderful new road upon which you may never have traveled.

And that wonderful light is that God *wants* you to have your right work and be happy in it. And He has made the way so sure and plain that you may well marvel that it never struck you in just that way before.

You need look no further than the Bible to know that God created all men and women differently. Some He has fitted for one kind of work and some for another. And in His eyes all kinds of work are equally worthy and useful. He loves us all—both great and small, the "important" among us and the plain people, the famous and the unknown. *All* are children of God.

The only thing that matters to God is how hard we try to do the job we have. If we really *try,* that is all God asks—and He will reward us with just as much happiness—often *more*—than He gives to bigger, more "important" people.

In everyone's life God has lit a candle. And the light of God's candle shines brightest on some one thing which is your *own* life-work. Now there are so many kinds of work and so often you see others apparently happy in theirs, that you may sometimes feel you have made a mistake in the work *you* are doing.

Now you certainly will

agree that in whatever work you *are* doing, you have done your best. Well, if God guides us when we do our best, then He certainly must have guided you to the work you *are* doing. Now maybe you do not think it important work, but it is God's plan for you—of that you may be almost certain.

True you may have often thought of trying something else. But for many reasons—age, family ties, expense, lack of training—you cannot leave the task you are doing. Certainly God would not ask you to start a different work over when He knows how impossible that is for you. So whether it is God's will or not, this is the work you must do for the present at least.

As Barrie, the beloved author says: "Happiness lies not in doing what we think we'd like to do, but in liking what we *have* to do."

But here is a wonderfully illuminating thing. For every ten people who are in the *wrong* kind of life-work and so are discouraged and unhappy, there are a *thousand* people who are in the *right* kind of life-work but are unhappy because they *yearn* for the wrong kind of work. Yes, there may be times when you think the doors of opportunity are closed on you. But time after time when God closes a door upon one kind of work, it is only to open it upon another.

There is only *one* test of whether you are in God's life-work and that is—are you *happy* in it? God *wants* you to "whistle while you work." And in so very many cases the thing which holds you back, the thing which makes your work seem in a rut, the thing which keeps you from your just rewards is your own attitude toward work!

Here is an unhappy, unsuccessful lawyer whom God made to be a plumber—who would be happy and successful at it, yet who plods unhappily along because he thinks being a "professional man" is more worthy.

Here is a store-keeper unhappily making a bare living in a dusty store whom God made to be a farmer, but who feels it beneath his dignity to work in the fields.

Here is a woman unhappily working in a business world who would be gloriously happy as a housewife, but who thinks that cooking meals and making beds are for "servants."

Now here is the wonderful thought God wants you to know, dear reader. There is not a task on this earth which is unimportant or undignified or unrewarding if in doing it you make others happy or comfortable or free!

If your work is to take a towel, as Jesus did, and serve others, then God will give you the same joy and peace and content that He gave Jesus. Yes, if your principal object is to serve others—whether it be as a farmer, a business man, a store-keeper—then and *only* then is your work important!

God has His plan for you, although He does not force His will upon you. Your duty is to find out what He wants you to do.

Are you in business just to make money with no thought of service? Then do not complain if you do not prosper. Are you a farmer who does not love God's earth but looks only for what you can wrest from it? Then do not cry out if you are unhappy and in want. Are you a worker who works only for a few dollars on Saturday, giving as little in service as you possibly can? Then do not complain unhappily as you build your *own* "dead end," dig your own rut.

Do you want success merely for the money and power it gives you and not to make others happy? Well, you may achieve it, but it will be as wormwood when you taste it.

For the marvelous thing about doing your work for the love of God, for the love of service, is not only are you *happy* in it, but you don't have to worry about rewards. God's work improves, it prospers! It prospers because into it goes not only *your* heart and soul and *God's* heart and soul, but the hearts and souls of all who have to do with it!

Believe in God's love and you will believe in yourself. Believe in yourself and you will believe in your work. Believe in your work and you will be happy and prosperous—prosperous in the truest sense of the word!

Yes, if you really *have* talents and believe in God and yourself, then, as surely as day follows night, God will bring them forth. If you really *are* fitted for bigger, better things, and you base your belief in God's plan, then as certain as sunlight God will guide you. For He

45

never puts a craving into a human heart and failed to satisfy it!

But it is always well to remember that all ambitions, all cravings are not *true*. They do not come from God. They are built up out of false pictures of success and truth and what is desirable.

God Himself has told you how and what to think in order to know whether your ambitions and your cravings are true. He tells you in the most noble words of His Bible and here they are:

> *"Whatsoever things are true, whatsoever things are honest, whatsoever things are just, whatsoever things are of good report, if there be any virtue and if there be any praise, think on these things." Phil. 4:8*

Check your ambitions and your cravings against these words. Are they true, honest, just, of good report? Then think on them, dear reader, and think well.

And when you have thought, there are five things to do next and the first is the most important. First ask God to guide you to your life-work. You have asked God in the past for love, for health, for guidance in dark ways. Why not ask His help in finding the best work for you, the best plan?

Tell Him exactly what you think you would like and then wait for His guidance. It will come in ways you may never understand. If you are already in your right work, God will open up new channels for you. If it is not succeeding as it should, He will shine His candle still further into your darkness.

And if you are in the wrong work, then deep, sincere prayer time after time will open a new door for you.

When you have prayed "believe that you have received it." Believe with all your heart that God will do as you ask. Believe it just as much as you believe any promise which God has made. God *will* "look out for something for you" only in a bigger and grander way!

Now thank your Father "in spirit and in truth." Thank Him for the work you already *have*. For many and many a person who looked lightly on their present task, when they lost it, found out what a necessary and comforting and actually happy thing it was! And thank your Father for what He is *going* to give you. Have you never said "thank you" to a friend who promised to do something for you as soon as he got a chance? Well, God has promised, too, and He will *keep* His promise!

And now you are ready for the last step. Go out into the world rejoicing in that promise! Act as if you expected it to come to you quickly—around the next corner. Rejoice and get ready for it. Expect it! And when you get it, resolve you will always use it, not as just a means for reward, but as a means for joy.

One day a stranger was crossing a wide river in the South on an old, dilapidated ferry boat. He noticed the engineer, a white-haired old man sitting in the doorway of the engine room and reading a Bible.

The old man was dressed in worn, old clothes, spotlessly clean. And in his eyes were the wonderful signs of great peace and contentment and happiness. As the stranger talked with the old man, he noticed that, although the rest of the boat was dirty and grimy, the en-gine room was spotlessly clean. He noticed that there was no greasy odor from the engine room, no bilge water under the engine. The engine was so cleaned and polished that it shone like a jewel.

Said the stranger: "Tell me, sir, how do you keep the engine room so clean, and what is the use when the rest of the boat is so dirty? How are you so happy in your work—just going back and forth on this deserted river and keeping your engine room clean without anybody noticing it?"

The old man looked lovingly at his gleaming engine and then at the Bible he was holding in his hand. "It's easy, cap'n. It's like this. I got a glory!"

Just keeping the engine room clean, just making the engine shine and glisten—the cleanest and best engine room on the river—was the old man's God-given work in life—his glory! And with that glory he had everything he needed in life to make him happy. Will you dare say he was not successful?

For success in your work, you will find out sooner or later, is much more than just making money. Yes, it *may* mean making money, but not when you must lose friends to make it!

Success in your work is just doing the best that you can. It is finding what is finest about it and making hard work an adventure and an accomplishment. It means fighting hard and not losing your sense of humor.

Yes, it means taking what life has to offer whether you win or lose, with a smile, for you still can partake of the joy and the happiness of your Father. Because you have taken time from your work to look up at the stars!

Yes, if you want to be truly happy, you must find the *work* which makes you happy, and you must look for happiness in *whatever* work God gives you to do! You must polish the brass whose shining gives you a glory!

Will you not pray now for that glory in our Prayer: "That God Will Lead Me To My Life-Work"?

Prayer

That

GOD WILL LEAD ME TO MY LIFE WORK

*"Blessed is the man whose delight is the law of the Lord . . .
whatsoever he doeth shall prosper"—Interpreted from Psalm 1*

Almighty and Everlasting God, Thou art the
Creator of the whole world. Every blade of grass
is counted and every drop of water is known to
Thee. Every pebble on the beach has its place in
Thy glorious Plan.

And I know and feel that every moment of my life
is provided for and planned by Thee in that way,
dear Father. I know Thou wilt provide for me
and guide me to the place where I can serve
Thee best.

O, Father, I do thank Thee for the work which Thou
hast given me. And before I ask for other work,
truly I shall try to do it well. But sometimes
I feel that I have talents which I have not
used. Sometimes I feel I could do other kinds
of work which would serve Thee more and my dear
ones better.

Help me to find that work if it be part of Thy
Plan, dear Father. Teach me to have faith in
Thee and to know, once I know what my right work is,
to be afraid of no one in going after it.
For knowing that Thou art with me, how can anything
but good come to me?

Give me that faith, dear Father. Help me to know
that no work is so large or so small that I
cannot glorify Thee in it. This thought upholds
me, my Father, and truly I feel that I can face
the world in seeking my right work with
courage and hope and confidence!

—Amen

8

TURNING TO GOD FOR HEALTH AND HEALING

Are you worried about your health? If you are not actually sick, do you feel poorly much of the time—no zest for life—no energy—no pep—just half-sick, half-well?

If that is the way you feel, if you *do* have health problems of any kind, then there is a tremendous message for you right in the Bible itself and right in this chapter of your Handbook of Life.

And that message is that God *wants* you to be healthy. God does not want poor health for anyone on this earth. All of God's powers, all of the powers of nature are on the side of health. You keep well because it is *natural* to be well, because God *wants* you to keep well.

What a joy it is to know that if you will but put yourself under the healing power of God now—today—that

God's power will flow through you, healing every fibre, every muscle, every drop of blood!

Have you felt or seen this power? Of *course* you have. It is the power which keeps you *alive!* It is the power which keeps your heart beating. It is the power which maintains your temperature. It is the power which heals your scars and the power which guides your fever as it turns!

How often have you heard God referred to as the Great Physician? Have you ever really and truly stopped to think what this might mean to your health if you actually *regarded* Him as the Great Physican of your life and health? If you really had such trust and confidence in the love and care of your Father as you *may* have had in a good earthly physician?

Then, imagine for a moment that you are waiting outside the office of a truly great *earthly* physician. The nurse has told you that the doctor will see you in a moment and asked you to sit down in the quiet waiting room. There, on the other side of a large door, is the great doctor whom, perhaps, you have never seen. There he is helping sick people learn to get well. You know he has helped hundreds of others. And there is something about even this waiting room that gives you courage and strength. For you feel that at last you have come to the place where there is the highest earthly knowledge and skill. And you sit quietly in the waiting room, confident that the doctor will help you.

We know you can see the likeness. God is the Great Physician. He is in the "other room" and will soon see you about your health problem. Can you understand in some measure what the Psalmist meant when he said that "they that wait upon the Lord shall renew their strength"?

How may you "wait upon the Lord" as you wait upon your earthly physician?

"In quietness," says the Bible! That is why you should quiet your body and soul before going to God with your health problem. There are many ways of finding quietness. Some people go alone into the deep forest or the upland pasture. Others sit by the limitless sea. There are others who, even though they are surrounded by the streets of the town or the bricks of the city, can go only into their own small room.

In what way *you* can make yourself quiet, you know best. But that is the first thing you must do if you want to turn to God for health and healing. It is not always easy, for so often weariness and worry, pain and trouble remind you of their presence. Yet there are few who cannot give the five minutes needed to bring themselves to God! Just the very thought that a kindly God is ready to listen to you, able and anxious to help you, is often enough to make those few minutes precious jewels set in the ring of the darkest day!

Suppose, for another moment, we go back to the little picture of yourself sitting in the waiting room of a great earthly doctor. As you sit before him a few minutes later, one of the first questions he will ask you is:

"What have you done for this condition?"

Well, before God can help you with your health problem, He, too, wants to know what you have done for your health. He has placed doctors and medicines and hospitals here on earth for the healing of His children and he expects you to use them.

Have you actually faced your health condition or have you been afraid to learn the truth about it? Have you actually sought the best doctor you could get? Have you done what your doctor advised? Have you made the changes in your living that he ordered?

How many times have you witnessed the truth of the fact that "God helps those who help themselves"? Yes, God will help you with your health problem, but He, too, wants to know what *you* have done!

Give thought to all these things as you sit in "God's ante-room" waiting for His help. For it is often where the earthly doctor leaves off that God begins. Every wise doctor will tell you that most

of his work consists in putting the body of his patient into the best condition so that the healing forces of nature may work without obstacle. As one wise doctor said: "I treated the patient, but God cured her!" And Faith and Prayer are two of the strongest forces which can put your mind and body into that condition!

For it is into those parts of your life into which the doctor does not probe that God is most interested. That is why in "waiting upon the Lord" that you prepare yourself to open your heart to Him.

It is not so much a question of making up a list of your trials and tribulations, your pains and your troubles, your symptoms and your sicknesses. It is a question of opening your mind and soul to God. For man knows and *God* knows that so many physical diseases are either caused or prolonged by worry, by fear, by hate, by envy and by uncertainty.

If you are worried, whether about your health or *anything* else, "cast your burden" upon the Lord. If you are afraid of the future, put it into His hands. If there are any you envy or hate, drop your grudge or hate and make yourself forgive.

When you do all these things, you are removing the obstacles which lie in the way of your health. For God does not violate any of His natural laws to bring His health to you. He wants you to have health but you will find that it is *you* who will have to change and not God's laws.

But God *does* make it possible for you to gain glorious health *through* these laws and often in *spite* of conditions which work against them!

You may ask how God's help in health problems does come. By releasing in your own body powers of courage and recovery which you may never have thought existed. We are sure that time after time you have said to yourself, following some great illness or trouble: "God knows how I got through it!"

Yes, God knows! He knows because it was He who gave you the power of getting through it! He and none other! A famous doctor tells the story of a woman who was very sick in a hospital. One day she heard that one of her children had been stricken with pneumonia. Summoning all her strength, she left the hospital to nurse her child. "God knows how she did it," but she nursed that child through the illness and returned to the hospital stronger than when she went in. God had given her this chance to draw upon a limitless power!

God has made it possible for you to take quick and sure advantage of all those things He has placed here on earth for you to get health. He will make it possible for you to use the natural forces for recovery which lie in your body.

Nineteen years ago, a man was told that if he ever expected to live, he would have to give up all work and spend the rest of his life caring for himself. The morning after he received the news, he woke up and saw the sunlight streaming into his room.

As he lay there in bed, he began thinking of how Jesus had healed people so long ago. Now he wasn't ordinarily a praying man and he found it hard to put his thought into words. But just as simply as a child, he closed his eyes and prayed something like this:

"Lord, You know what they told me yesterday. I don't want to quit, Lord, for I have important work to do. I am going to get up and go to work and put myself into Your hands. If You want me to go on, You will let me do it. If You find my work is ended, You will call me home. Whatever You want for me will be all right, Lord."

A great peace entered his heart after praying like that. He got up and did his usual day's work. The next morning before getting up he prayed again:

"Lord, we had a great day together yesterday. Now another day is here. You are with me, Lord, and I will have no fear. If You want me to work this day, too, I shall be glad."

Day after day he prayed. And for long years afterward he lived with Jesus as a companion. He had "waited upon the Lord" and opened his life to God's healing waters!

Suppose, just suppose, that you were to talk like that with God when you are not well—talk very simply about your sickness. Words cannot express what it would mean to you. But you could build glorious health according to God's laws and your own faith.

Does the evil of nervousness and fear walk with you? Do you worry about the future, what may happen to you in the days and years ahead? Then know and feel, dear friend, that in health and sickness God is *still* with you. Feel Him at your side when you are all keyed-up and nervous. Hear Him saying: "Fear not, my child. Hold tightly to My hand. Trust in Me."

Faith in God's power to heal not only drives away fear and nervousness, but it leaves something in their place. It leaves a brave assurance, a deep love for your fellow man and a deep concern for their welfare. This love shines through your eyes and it is that something which men mean when they say: "The glow of health." It is an aliveness which draws people to you, which keeps away the dread of sickness and gives courage to face whatever may come.

So you see that it lies within your own power to be more than conqueror of ill health through Him who loves you. You see that if you will make up your mind to lay hold of those forces, seen and unseen, which are making for your health, they are yours for the taking.

Yes, abide by God's laws of health and healing and when you thirst in fever He will give you the water of His spirit. Abide with Him and He, the Lord of quietness, will take away your pain.

Your Father is closer than ever when you are facing illness and uncertainty. He will not forsake you. He will watch over you even more tenderly. His everlasting care and love will be with you every hour—every minute!

Come then, and let us pray for that health and healing and love in our "Prayer for Health and Healing."

Prayer

HEALTH AND HEALING

"The Lord will take away from thee all sickness"—Deu. 7:15

Dear Father in heaven, to whom all men lift their faces, make me quiet in this time of prayer that Thy loving heart may bring to me all health and all healing.

For I have been so worried about my health, dear Father. Sometimes it just seems that sickness and worry, weariness and pain drain the very strength from my bones.

I know Thou hast pity, loving Father, for Thou didst watch even Thine only Son suffer and cry. So please help me, Thy child, in my weakness and pain.

Truly I thank Thee for Thy servants, the doctors and their medicines, Father, and may they feel they are worthy disciples of the Great Physician. Please guide them so they also can do their part in bringing back health to me.

I want to be well not alone for myself, dear Lord, but for my dear ones who need me and for Thee that I may once again go about Thy business. So please, Father of health, give me this, Thy Blessing.

And now, Father, as I close my prayer, truly I feel the warmth that is the strength of Thy spirit working within my soul and body. Truly I feel so much stronger and full of hope and I do thank Thee, my Father. I do have faith in Thee and I do look forward to Thy help — and even the thought of it gives me hope and peace.

—Amen

LETTING GOD HELP YOU WITH YOUR CHILDREN

Do your children ever cause you trouble and worry? Are they ever mean and unjust to you? Would you like to help them be more successful and happy? If you would, then here is inspiring news—right in this ninth chapter of your Handbook of Living.

And the news is this. God knows all about the problem of the erring, disobedient child. And He *wants* to help you with your children. The patience and the forgiveness of God is simply endless!

> *"How think ye if a man have a hundred sheep and one of them be gone astray, doth he not leave the ninety and nine, and goeth unto the mountains and seeketh that which is gone astray?*
>
> *"Even so, it is not the will of your Father which is in heaven, that one of these little ones should perish."*

Isn't that a wonderful, inspiring passage from God's Word, the Bible? It is not your Father's will that the erring, unruly child should be beyond help!

God *will* help you with your children. He *knows* that you want your child to be successful and happy. Over and over again, Jesus showed his love for children. He was always surrounded by troops of children. His kindest words were spoken concerning them.

> *"Suffer little children and forbid them not, to come unto me, for of such is the Kingdom of heaven."*

What an opportunity *you* have to establish the Kingdom of God on earth through your children! And God *will* help you establish that Kingdom if you obey His laws. For if you obey God's commandments, your children will reflect your life in their own lives as

57

surely as a mirror reflects an image. You must show them by precept and by example that it *pays* to be honest and decent.

Don't wait until your children are grown up before showing them the need for living with God. It may then be too late. As your children grow, the greatest word you can write on the pure white pages of their lives is: "God."

Your children need God today as no generation ever needed Him before. Your children need Faith today as no generation ever needed it before!

And like the three leaves of a clover, you must give your child three Faiths— Faith in himself, Faith in the rest of God's children and Faith in God.

God wants your child to have Faith in himself. Give your child that kind of Faith—Faith that he can do anything which he wants to do if it is done with God's blessing and approval. Give your child the Faith that God has a place for him in the world. Give your child the Faith that he is wanted by you, by the world and by God!

So never laugh at any dream of your child, never scoff at any ambition, no matter how far-fetched it may seem to be.

Some years ago, a little boy told his father: "When I grow up I'm going to build a bridge across the ocean." An unwise father might have mocked at such a childish idea. But this father nodded his approval. He encouraged the boy to learn all he could about bridges and about the ocean. He became one of the greatest bridge builders in the world.

And do you know something? He evolved an idea which is now being seriously considered and which would enable traffic to cross the ocean in a manner very similar to a bridge. He may, with God's help, actually build such a "bridge." And all because his father gave him faith in himself!

You want your children to live honest, decent lives. Some people think this is old fashioned. They think you should want them to become rich and powerful. But the *way* your children live is just as important today as when Jesus walked the earth and gathered little children about him.

You must show your children the way. You must show them that men can live without houses and riches, but that no man can live long without love and respect.

"I pray not that Thou shouldst take them out of the world, but that Thou shouldst keep them from the evil."

Give your children the moral training they need at home. Then they will apply it in the home, the school, the church and in the world. You cannot keep them from going out into the world and even from coming under bad influences. But you *can* make them strong, you can, with God's help, give them Faith in their own power to overcome evil.

That is why it is wrong to "pamper" or "baby" your boy or girl. Help them all you can, but don't try to shield them too much. A vine which is always propped up can only cling to a wall. If your children depend too much on you, they will never develop Faith in themselves.

When the time comes for them to go forth to their life-work, there is only one way to help your child to happiness and success. It is the spirit of St. Paul on the Damascus Road when he said: "Lord, what wilt Thou have me to do?"

Encourage your child to take this noble view of his life-work—whether it be a trade, an art, a profession, or even a life of marriage and motherhood. Assure them that success in the eyes of the world means something, but that success in the eyes of God means *everything!*

Much of the worry you go through about your children is unnecessary. If you have given them faith in themselves, they will right whatever mistakes they have made. It is their *right* to make mistakes. It is the only way they can learn.

But do not magnify the mistakes and troubles of childhood and manhood into something too big. Love and patience with your children will accomplish wonders where scolding and unsought for advice will do little or nothing.

Yes, children often seem mean and selfish to their parents. Often they say and do things which are unjust. But it is the rare child who does not sooner or later feel remorse for unkind words and unjust actions.

Make it possible for your children to seek you out with their troubles and worries by giving them faith in *you*—which is the second great faith the child needs. Give your counsel and advice, but do not force it upon your children. Jesus spent a lifetime giving help and counsel, but He never forced His help on others. Always they had to seek Him out first. He taught through little stories and Parables, and you, too, can teach your children in the same way.

One mother had a young boy who was fond of gossiping about his friends. One day, through idle gossip he got a friend into serious trouble. He came tearfully to his mother and asked her what he should do. The mother knew that the harm had already been done and there was little to do. But she wanted to impress upon him the evil of idle talk.

So she asked him to take a small bag of feathers and scatter them up and down the street. He did so and came back, asking her what to do then.

"Go out and pick them up," she told him. Of course he came back with only a few in his bag. "I couldn't find the rest," he explained, "they had all blown away."

"Of course you couldn't," she pointed out. "And that is what happens when you scatter idle words. You can never recall them."

Don't you think this was a stronger lesson than any beating or scolding?

Yes, the second Faith is faith in you and in all other children of God. The only way you can teach your child Faith in you is by setting him the example you want him to follow. Few things which go on between father and mother are not seen and thought about by your children. Would you have your children bring harmony into your home? Then maintain harmony among yourselves. Would you have your child truthful and honest? Then never allow a falsehood to occur in your home.

An old proverb says: "An apple never falls far from the tree." Your child will reflect in his words and actions most of the things which he sees and hears right in your own home.

And let your child view the world in the same way. Give him *Faith* in that world. Give your child faith in people by having faith in people yourself. The parent who is doubting and suspicious of people will have children who are doubting and suspicious. Teach your child that almost everybody is honest. Teach him that few people are out to harm him or cheat him. Tell him that most folks just want to be liked and comfortable and happy, and that if he will do what he can to bring them those things, they will become his friends.

Faith in himself will give your child faith in others. And faith in others will make friends of them. The man or woman with many friends is almost bound to live a happy, successful life!

Such Faith makes your child proud and happy to be of service to himself, his family, his nation and his God!

And that is the third and most important Faith—faith in God! The child, the boy, the girl, the young man or woman who has faith that God loves him, that God cares for him, that God wants him to be happy—has won half the battle of life!

He has started out in life with a Helper and a Friend who will never leave him. The child who has been taught to bring his problems to God, will rarely be the child who is disobedient and sinful or mean and unjust to

his parents. He will rarely be the child who causes confusion and disharmony in the home. He is rarely the child who causes you worry and nervousness.

A God-fearing, God praying home does not always guarantee a God-fearing, God-praying child. But for every child who fares forth from such a home and becomes a disappointment, there are thousands who go forward to happy, successful lives and homes of their own.

We wish it were possible to impress upon you what high honor and dignity it is to be a parent. God regarded it as a work of supreme dignity. He thought about how mothers and fathers cared for their homes, worked for their families, taught their children. And to the mother who kept these commandments, God wrote:

> *"Her children arise up and call her blessed; her husband also, and he praiseth her."*

Would you like to know what your child will remember about you when he is grown up? He will forget the furniture, the things he wanted and the things he got. He will forget whether his home was shabby or luxurious.

But he *will* remember thoughts of a kindly, honest mother and father and their sheltering care and guidance. He will remember strong bonds woven of love and worship of God in the home.

Yes, the home in which the sense of God's love and care is always present, will make it in his memory the dearest spot on earth, and his parents the dearest people on earth. He will rise up and call you blessed!

Let us pray: "For God's Help in Raising My Family."

Prayer

For

GOD'S HELP IN RAISING MY FAMILY

*"Train up a child in the way he should go: and when
he is old, he will not depart from it"*—Pr. 22:6

Loving, heavenly Father, creator of every living
thing, now is the time I pray to Thee in this home
Thou hast given us and in which Thou hast blessed
me with a dear, good family.

Thou knowest all about us, dear Father, so I
do not need to tell Thee all the trials I often
have in raising my family. Thou knowest how tired
and worn-out I get just trying to look out
for them, and how they sometimes worry me. They
are dear, good children, Father, but sometimes
their words and actions are not what I would
like. Thou understandest, Father.

Help me be a good parent, dear Father, and raise
my family right. Help me always remember what
I know in my heart, that whether small or grown
up, they will always be just my babies. Help me
do this and I know I can understand and help them.
Teach me this and I know I can keep them good
and honest and pure.

O Father, I know Thou hearest my prayer. I know
Thou wilt love and protect and guide me and my
family and help me raise them so we shall all
be one lovely, happy family of Thine.

In the name of Jesus, who took little children
up in His arms and said: "Suffer the little children
to come unto me...for of such is the Kingdom of
Heaven."

—Amen

HELPING OTHERS TO FIND THEIR WAY TO GOD

How many times do you long to set the feet of those you love back on the road to God? How many times have you seen poor, bruised souls right in your own family that you just long to help but do not know how to start?

Here is a father who will not go to church and so find the joy and happiness of the Kingdom of God. Here are other members of your family with bad habits, who need God's guidance and help.

If you *do* have problems like these, then here is a wonderful way of winning souls—the way made plain by the Bible and by our Lord Jesus.

You, too, may feel as Jesus felt when He said: "The spirit of the Lord is upon me, because He hath appointed me to preach the gospel. . . . He hath sent me to heal the broken-hearted, to preach deliverance to the captives, and recovery of sight to the blind, to set at liberty them that are bruised."

Have you ever seen a pilot light upon a gas stove? It is an ever-burning little flame. When you open the burner, the pilot light sets it aflame. You, too, can be God's pilot light. For, like a flame, the love of God cannot be taught . . . it must be caught! You may be only a small flame, but you must be a *true* one. And then, from your flame, a thousand fires may be lit. Isn't that a wonderful thought?

But first the fire must be lit in your own heart. If you want to show others what being "with God" means, you must be a model of what you want that other person to be. You cannot expect someone *else* to stop smoking or drinking or swearing if you, yourself, do these things even occasionally!

Your loved ones will be

more likely to follow you to God if they can see what the influence of God is doing for *you*. You *do* have a wonderful message to bring to your dear ones. You just can't say: "Here is God." You must say: "Here *works* God." You must show in your own words, your bearing, your life, what a wonderful thing it is to be "with God."

In the high mountains of the Andes there are narrow ledges where only one pack animal can walk. When two pack animals meet, one kneels and lets the other walk over him. In that way, both are safe and both go on their ways. They become part of the road.

In the same way, *you* must be part of the road to God. You need not kneel at the feet of the one who travels the road, but at the feet of Jesus.

And that means that you must show your dear ones that not only does God *want* them to be good, but that to live decent, honest lives is good *for* them.

You cannot force anyone along the road to God, whether it be good for them or not. This means that you cannot force your opinions on them no matter how good or true they may be. To force goodness on those you love is like forcing food on them. They will get sick to their stomach from forced food, and sick to their souls from forced counsel.

Jesus never forced goodness upon people. Instead, He told them gentle little stories called Parables. These Parables told of problems which confront people. Then, when Jesus would reach the end of the story, He would ask His Disciple what *he* would do under those circumstances. If you will only read these Parables of Jesus again you will time after time find the exact way to help others find their way to God.

For these Parables never put the person Jesus was speaking to in the wrong. Jesus rarely condemned sinners. Even to the woman who was condemned by law as a great sinner, Jesus gently said: "Neither do I condemn thee; go and sin no more." He didn't excuse the sin, He didn't *condone* it, but neither did He condemn it. He *understood* it.

There is not a person who indulges in a bad habit, who is doing wrong, but who *knows* he is doing wrong and deep down in his heart is sorry for it.

A man who had stolen some money came to a wise old minister because he was troubled. He poured out his heart and expected a stern lecture in return. The minister listened patiently. At the end of his sad confession, the man said to the minister: "Well, should I make restitution or just forget about it and try not to steal any more?"

"What do *you* think?" asked the old minister.

The man stopped and thought a while. Finally after five minutes of silence he said: "You're right."

"But I didn't say a word," replied the minister. "It was your conscience which told you what to do. Go in peace and do it."

No matter how bad the habit, no matter how deep the sin, there is always that still, small voice which cannot be denied. It is the voice of truth, the voice of God in the soul.

Don't you remember in your Bible that time after time when Jesus would finish one of His Parables He would ask: "What think ye?" What do *you* think?

For Jesus knew, as *you* should know, that we are but human. You cannot see all the workings of your loved one's mind and heart. What looks to your eyes as a stain may be in God's sight only a scar. And who knows but what if *you* had to fight the same battle as your dear one, you would not have yielded much more?

That should make you humble. You can accomplish wonders with a loved one if you will begin your talk by confessing that you often *did* or were tempted to do the same thing. And when they see that you, too, have suffered the same temptations, they will surely have more faith in what you say.

Jesus found fault lovingly. He led people to God by praising the good in them. Your loved one *knows* his fault, so you need not tell it. But if he feels that there is *some* good in him despite it, then you will indeed give him the faith he needs to find his way to God.

Yes, even if your family or your loved ones are not ready to understand, you can *still* show that you have faith in them. You can still show them what even one short hour spent with God may mean—how their burdens lighten, how temptations lose their grip; how weak they may be when they kneel, yet how full of power when they rise! You can move the slow of heart by some winning word of love and stay the wayward feet to guide them on the Godward way!

For most bad habits are sicknesses of soul. There is no known medicine which can cure them. There is only God's medicine. And the glorious thing about it is that you—the man or woman, the husband or wife, can give it. It is you who can prepare another for the return of God. It is you who can bring them to the Great Physician for healing!

Show your loved one that church work is *not* dull and uninteresting, but lively and inspiring. That church people are people who are happy and who laugh. Show your loved one that the bad habits of drinking, gambling, swearing do not hurt any one else *half* as much as they hurt the person *himself!* Show them that even *worse* sins can never lead to happiness but only to more sins and more *unhappiness.*

Yes, it is true that your efforts may be feeble at first in leading a loved one to the feet of God. But do you know how even the mightiest of bridges are built?

The builder sends out a tiny kite with a silken cord hanging from it to the other side of the river. Unseen hands draw down the cord. The silken cord is drawn across the river and to its end is attached a cotton cord—then thicker and thicker cords. At last a steel cord is drawn across. And after the steel cord come many more steel cords. Until finally across the river stretches the mighty cable which holds the towering bridge.

The silken cord of love which you send out to your loved one who is troubling you may indeed be a fragile one. But God is on the other side holding it in His willing hands. And as you send out thought after thought, kindness after kindness, forgiveness after forgiveness, you weave a chain of love which nothing can break. You weave a chain so strong that God can draw the erring one to His great heart!

True, there will be times when your dear ones will not seem to care, will not listen to your pleas. And in those dark days there is only one thing to do. You must keep on loving—loving people who do not seem to love.

Beautiful pearls are cultivated by putting a grain of sand under the shell of an oyster. To relieve this intruder, the oyster builds a pearl. You, too, can build a beautiful pearl of love and patience and character about yourself in spite of every one of these irritations. As our dear minister used to say: "When in doubt, do the loving thing."

If you want happiness in your home, if you want to bring husband, wife, son or daughter to God, *practice* your religion. If they will not pray with you, pray yourself. Faith and prayer are so strong that they will not only lift *you* up to God, but they will lift others in whom you have faith and for whom you have prayed!

The story is told of a woman in a far country who prayed she might be able to take her family from the valley where her home stood to the high mountains of God. As she prayed an angel appeared and said: before God is ready to take your home and family, set your house in order. There may be others who might want to stop there after you are gone.

So the woman put her house in order. She became cleanly and kind and forgiving. Then she said to the angel: may I go now that my house is in order? No, said the angel, your garden is full of weeds. Someone may want to watch a while in the garden while you are gone. So the woman weeded her garden and tended it for many years. She uprooted bad habits in herself and pruned poisonous growths of hates and grudges.

Then she said, can I now lead my family to the mountains of God? The angel shook his head: There is a beggar outside your door. Until you have fed him you cannot say all is done. So the woman fed the beggar and served her friends and neighbors and all rejoiced because of her help.

Then she thought she was ready. But the angel asked her to do one thing more: There is someone coming down the road who *also* is seeking God, but they do not have your faith or courage. Give them courage and faith and then ask to see the mountains of God.

So the woman helped the weak and discouraged wherever she found them. And now, she asked the angel, may I take my family to the heights of God? The angel called the family in—the son who was healed of drink through her love—the husband bound to her by the silken cords of love and service, the daughter saved by a mother's prayers—even the grateful neighbors came in.

The angel opened the window of the little house. And, lo, it was on the mountain top of God!

Dear reader, let us pray: "That Others May Find Their Way To God."

𝔓𝔯𝔞𝔶𝔢𝔯

That

OTHERS MAY FIND THEIR WAY TO GOD

"And then shall they see the Son of Man coming in the clouds with great power and glory"—Mark 13:26

Eternal, loving Father in heaven, whose Spirit is all through the universe and the world and whose heart loveth all, draw near to me now in this time of prayer, and strengthen my faith in Thy never-failing love.

I am so happy with Thee, dear Father, that sometimes I just want to shout: "Glory, halleluiah!" And I want to bring Thy message to the whole, wide world.

For there are so many right in my own family and other places who have such a load to carry, who need Thee so much. O, if I could only make them see how happy they could be if they would only live by Thy laws and in Thy love!

With my own words and strength that is not easy, Father dear. But I know Thou hast promised strength to all who ask. So please, Father, help me to show them how to walk closer and closer to Thee. Help me to show them how loving Thee has made such a change in me. Then they will understand what Thy love can do.

Truly, even now I can see the changes which have taken place in some I brought the Glad Tidings to, dear Father. But help me to tell of Thy blessed power to those who still do not listen. Help me to be patient until the spirit works in them even as it does now in me.

Bring me and all suffering souls comfort and rest and peace!

—Amen

70

Chapter 15

the minister. "I have moved. Or as the little brother

11

GOD WANTS YOU TO KNOW THE JOY OF TRUE FRIENDSHIP

ARE YOU SOMETIMES SAD and lonely because you think you have no friends? Do you often wish you could enjoy yourself as do others in the company of dear friends, without that wall which seems to keep people away?

If you *are* lonely for the joys of true friendship, then here is gladsome news. God *wants* you to know the joys of true friendship! His Book shows you the road to friendship if you will only walk it!

Do you not remember the wonderful passage described by the Disciple John? In that passage, Jesus placed the sacrament of friendship as the highest gift He could give to His Disciples. They had undergone trial and tribulation with Jesus. And He turned to them and gave them the highest earthly honor He could bestow:

"I have called you friends."

The way of the Golden Rule had made them the friends of Jesus. And that way, faithfully followed by you, can take you, a sometimes lonely, unhappy, friendless man or woman, and transform you into a happy, joyous child of God with faithful friends on every side!

For loneliness comes only through lack of Faith. If you have real, true, abiding Faith that God *is* your Father, then it follows as the day the night, you will have Faith that all men are your brothers. Friends will come unto you as naturally as brother comes unto brother.

Love for God and Faith in God make men and women humble. You will never see a proud person with many friends. Proud people seem to say to others: "I do not need a friend." And so people do not come to them in friendship. Friendship comes to those

71

who *need* friendship. It goes with those who see the need of others.

Friendship is one of the few things in the world which you can *make*. You *make* friends. You may have to count every penny, yet be rich in friends. You may live in only one room, yet it may be a palace of friendship.

Yet the rules for making friends are so simple that they can be put into four words:

1. Forget yourself.
2. Remember others.

You can forget yourself once you feel this spirit of God in your heart. You will no longer feel shy and sensitive. You will realize that no one is either lower or higher than you—but that all men and women are children of our loving Father.

Every time you forget yourself, you have taken a step on the road to the joys of true friendship. The next time you go out, see how long you can go without talking about yourself. See how much you can put yourself in the place of anyone you talk to.

Do you know how to *start* making friends? You can do it without saying a word. Start smiling! Smile at everybody. Smile at people walking by on the road. Smile at the bus driver as he whizzes by. Smile at the boy behind the counter, the girl across the table. Smile at your fellow church members. And occasionally, smile at yourself!

On a long bus trip, the passengers were glum and fretful and the whole bus was filled with gloom. At a city stop a new driver got on with a broad smile. He smiled as he changed the baggage around. He smiled as he punched the tickets. He chucked a crying baby under the chin. As the bus passed through each village, he turned around with a broad smile and said some funny thing about each village.

In fifteen minutes that smile had spread like a fire. It lit up the people who began to smile at each other. It started them gossiping. A warm, friendly glow—lit by that one smile—came over the lumbering bus as it carried twenty friendly passengers through the night.

A smile is the best friendmaker in the world because it is catching. Try such a smile. Try a smile which says: "I like you," "I'm interested in you," "I'm glad to see you!"

Where do you meet friends? Well, as an old fisherman used to say: "If you want to catch fish you have to go where the fish are." If you want to make friends, you have to go where *people* are — for friends are just people.

Unless you live in a cave, there are people everywhere. Not all of them can or will be your friends. But among them, you will find one — two — three — whom you can call friend. And he who has three true friends has three treasures.

There are people at the place you work, at the place you buy things. There are people at the post office, at the gasoline pump, the roadside stand, the main street, the movies. You can even meet people and have friends if you are a cripple or a "shut-in."

In a Southern village lives a dear old lady who is confined to a wheelchair. Her only contact with the world is by newspaper, magazine or radio. But whenever she hears or reads anything she likes, she writes a note directly to the person concerned. Just a short, kindly, friendly note. You would be astounded at the friendly answers she gets from prominent people whom you never would think had the time to write to an old lady in a little country village.

Every mail brings her letters of friendship and interest. Time after time people have stopped off at this little village just to visit her. Without stirring from her wheel-chair, this fine lady has friends in every corner of the world and never a lonely moment is hers!

If she can accomplish that, don't you think that you, who can probably get around and talk to people, ought to be able to accomplish something, too?

"I *do* go to places," people often say. "I want to make friends. But when I meet people, I can't think of a thing to say. How do I know people will answer when I talk to them?"

Now here is a little secret. EVERYBODY wants to talk if only they can talk about THEMSELVES! The telephone company once took a census of the word used most often in telephone conversations. You probably can guess what the word was. It was "I," "I," "I!" If you can get people just to say "I" they will "fall all over themselves" talking to you.

73

Of course, your interest must be a genuine one or else you will be trapped like the young lady who took a course in conversation. Brightly she asked a well-known chemist to tell her "just everything about his wonderful work." For three minutes she listened and then, smiling all the while, lost herself in her own thoughts, if there were any going on. The chemist noted that and began to speak a string of unintelligible sentences to all of which she smiled and nodded with imitation appreciation. Well, to make a long story short, there was *one* friend which she did not make, even though she played the game according to the "rules."

No, dear reader, you must really believe that every man and woman has something to tell you which you never knew before, as indeed they *have*. As a famous novelist said: "Every man and woman has one novel in him—his own life." God has given every man and woman some one thing to do, to say, to act in this life which is different from what He has given everyone else. Try to find out what this one thing is and you are well on the road to friendship.

Make a game of it. And the more things a person can tell you, the better friends they can become. Many friendships run dry because people run out of inspiration for each other.

Have room for friends, but no room for enemies. Witty old Judge Oliver Wendell Holmes once said: "I had an enemy once and I've been trying to think all day what his name was." Be like the lady who said of someone she didn't like by hearsay: "I wouldn't want to meet Mrs. Winters. I might like her."

Yes, it takes courage to put yourself into the lives of others. Every shy boy and girl, every sensitive man or woman knows that. Most of us who have been buffeted about by the world build a wall about ourselves. One man builds a wall of gruffness to hide a sympathetic heart. One woman builds a wall of rapid, idle chatter to hide an aching soul. One girl builds a wall of silence to hide a heart crying for love. One boy builds a wall of argument to hide a heart aching for comfort.

Once you have the courage to scale these walls, the road to friendship is a straight one. And the way is not through "brilliant" conversation, but the common way, the common things people have talked about for centuries and will continue to talk about.

If talk about the weather, the sorrows and the illnesses of others, the joys of births, marriages and little successes are beneath your notice, you will never make a good friend no matter how "brilliant" your conversation may be.

Why just the faculty of remembering things *about* people will make you more friends, give you more influence, help you get along better with people, make you more successful in your church and other work than all the knowledge in all the books.

Someone said to a great political leader, a "maker" of Presidents: "You must know the names of at least a thousand people." He answered: *"Five* thousand." This man, who counts his friends by the thousands, remembers the face and name of every man or woman he ever met. He remembers where they work, what their wives' names are and dozens of details you or I might consider trivial.

Great as these external things are, the real basis of the joy of true friendship springs from the greater things which are of God. Not for nothing do the greatest friendships arise from your faith and your church.

For in the church there is brotherhood because there is Fatherhood. At the church you bring your heartaches to God's altar. And all about you are others with like faith bringing *their* troubled hearts. This common bond of faith and prayer will draw unto you more friends whose love is deeper than any other friendship in the world.

Do you remember the words of the old hymn: "What a Friend We Have in Jesus"?

Earthly friends, no matter what you do, are bound to disappoint you many, many times. But isn't it glorious to know that you can make a Friend of the greatest Friend a man or a woman can have? Yet how long have you put off making a Friend of Jesus? Yes, how long have you put off making a Friend of your Father?

When your other friends forsake you, your heavenly Friend *never* forsakes you, for so has He promised: "I will never leave thee nor forsake thee." When you walk the road of life by yourself, your heavenly Friend is at your side. When your earthly friends have gone their ways, leaving you to your sorrow or your grief, His arms are about you.

It is not hard to make a Friend of Jesus, for *He* understands *you*. Whether you have succeeded or not, He sees what you have *tried* to do. He is the Friend that "sticketh closer than a brother." Please, dear reader, make a Friend of Jesus just as soon as you can.

And for this heavenly Friendship, will you not take this golden minute and pray: "That God Will Guide Me to the Joys of Friendship."

Prayer

That

GOD WILL GUIDE ME TO THE JOYS OF FRIENDSHIP

"A man that hath friends must show himself friendly; and there is a friend that sticketh closer than a brother"—Prov. 18:24

Almighty God, whose love is beyond understanding and whose wisdom and goodness are without end, the greatest joy of my life is to come to Thee — to know Thee as my truest Friend and Protector.

Yet often, dear Father, I am so lonesome for friends in this world — good men and women. But so many people pass me by with hardly a word or a nod or a smile. And it makes me so unhappy that things should be that way, Father.

For Thou knowest how I want to feel I am wanted and loved in this world. Thou knowest how I long for real friends who will be honest and true.

Please, dear Father, help me have real, true friends. Help me to show myself friendly as Thou hast commanded. When I meet people, no matter where, please help me to remember to be friendly. Please help me to think what I can do for others instead of what they can do for me. And help me, dear Father, to think and say only good things about others, for that way, I know, is the best way to make friends.

O how much better I feel now I have come to Thee in prayer, dear Father. Thou art my heavenly Friend and I know Thou wilt help me. I am at peace, for I know Thou hast listened and that my prayer for friends will be answered. In Jesus' name I say it.

—Amen

DRAWING CLOSE TO GOD FOR COMFORT IN SORROW AND SADNESS

Aʀᴇ ʏᴏᴜ ᴘᴀssɪɴɢ ᴛʜʀᴏᴜɢʜ a time of sorrow and sadness? Have you lost a dear one whose passing has left an aching loneliness? Has someone dear to you with whom you have labored to break a bad habit failed you? Or are you called upon to bear the burdens of others' lives until you hardly know whether you can stand it any longer?

It is at times like these that life sometimes seems unbearable. You ask yourself, will every day be as bad as this one? Will this go on for year after year? Will my life ever again be free of sorrow and sadness?

Yes, it is at these times that you long to draw close to God for comfort in sorrow and sadness, yet do not know how to start on the way. But the way is so very simple, so very easy that it is a wonder you ever stumbled away from it.

It is the way of the Book — the Bible — God's own promise to you. For all through its blessed pages like golden pools of sunshine scattered through a forest, are such promises of God's love that they shine like stars in the blackest night. They are wonderful words and they mean all they say:

"Come unto me all ye that labor and are heavy laden and I will give you rest."

"Whosoever drinketh of the water that I shall give him shall never thirst, but the water that I shall give him shall be in him a well of water springing up into eternal life."

"Peace I leave with you; my peace I give unto you, not as the world giveth, give I unto you. Let not your heart be troubled, neither let it be afraid."

Wonderful, wonderful words. And they are but three of the hundreds and hundreds of jewels scattered in that great, old Book. Oh, if we in this modern age could only take the Bible on our knees and open it whenever sorrow weighed upon us as our grandfathers used to do—just open it almost at random. Why, we could hardly turn one of its golden pages without finding words of God's comfort in pictures of the most marvelous yet simple grandeur.

It may be all too true that you have reached the "end of your rope" with some loved one. They may have promised again and again to reform and do better. But again and again they have failed your trust. Is there any *more* you can do for them?

Yes. It is to lovingly place your own worry and the faults of your dear one in the hands of your Father, for they have been outstretched to you all the time.

Do you remember years ago when you were a little child? You woke in the black of the night and saw what seemed to be terrible shadows on the wall. They were cast by the moon shining through the trees. And your heart filled with fear. You jumped from your bed and ran to your mother's bed crying: "Mother, mother! I'm afraid!"

And she put her tender arms about you and hugged you close to her heart. "Don't be afraid," she crooned. "Here I am, darling. Don't be afraid." And a little later you went peacefully to sleep, all your tears wiped away by tender hands.

Now you are God's grown child. Yet still you wake in the night. Fearsome shapes are cast on your mind— shapes of worry and fear. And you cry: "Father, Father, I am afraid!"

And your Father holds out His everlasting arms to you, saying: "Fear not, my child. I am here. There is nothing to be afraid of!" And you are at peace for "God shall wipe away all tears."

How free of worry and sorrow your life would be if you would but hand them over to God. Your life is weighed down with worry and sorrow because you do not trust your Father with them. Yet there is nothing so small to God if it keeps from you the comfort and the joy He has promised you.

Once you put your troubles into the kind hands of God, you do not need to take them back again. And just think what you get in return for putting them in God's hands! "My *peace* I give unto you!"

One night a minister was wakened by a telephone call. A widower, a stranger, who had merely seen the minister's name on the church tablet, was calling. His only child, a little girl of seven, had been killed by a truck on the highway. The driver never *knew* he had struck the child and had roared on into the distance.

No human help could avail, that the man knew. The minister went to the man's house and found him in terrible grief. Without a word, the minister put his arms about the man's shoulders and said: "Let's go out."

It was storming, but out into the storm they went. They walked mile after mile along the pitch dark road. No word was spoken. What was there to say? But the minister was silently sending his prayer to God, asking that the Father send His healing touch to this stricken man.

So they walked. And, as the man told about it afterwards, every time the lightning flashed he would look into the strong, kind face of the minister. And each time there came over him such a deep feeling of comfort and peace, that at last he was able to humbly say: "Thy will be done" and place his baby girl in God's loving care. And at last he broke into tears—the first tears he had shed—tears of sorrow, yes, but also tears of comfort!

Everywhere there are men and women bowed down with sorrow and sadness. You would think they had enough to take the joy out of *any* life, that such lives would be prison sentences of grief.

But no! They have something within them which is like a roof over their heads when it is raining. They don't talk much about it, but if you could see them while they were praying, you would see a look in their faces which would tell you the whole story.

You would see them as they knelt and you would know that the presence of God as a dear, close Friend was very real to them. This presence, you would see, was not an idle fancy but something they had found for themselves in the hard school of experience!

Sorrow and sadness come to you in many ways. Not always through death, but often through the misspent life of one you love, through the hard blows that life often deals.

But you, too, can lead the kind of life which will bring out the Kingdom of the presence of God which is within you. When you kneel to pray, you are drawing upon a power from the innermost depths of your being—from the Kingdom within you—the only power that can overcome sorrow and sadness.

For, when you come to think about it, aren't many of us thinking too much about our own troubles and not enough about God and our fellow men? We think we are the only ones who suffer. We think that none has suffered before us. We think that none can understand our suffering. Oh, if it were only true!

The story is told of a woman who had suffered great sorrow and sadness. So she went to a Wise Man and asked him for a charm which would insure that never again would they be visited upon her.

For a long time he looked with tender pity in his old eyes and then said: "Yes, I will give you such a charm, but on one condition, and it is this: that you will bring me a handful of earth from before a house into which Sorrow has never entered."

So the woman went forth. At every house she asked: "Has Sorrow never entered this house?" And at every house the people shook their heads. Never did she come to a house where Sorrow had not entered.

But as she went about the country and saw that Sorrow had stopped at every door, her heartache and grief changed. Before the picture of Sorrow everywhere, her heart softened, she stopped being overcome with her own sadness. She became tender towards others. Tears of pity for herself turned into tears of pity for all others. She did not forget her own sorrow, but she lost it in the sorrow of others.

So do not shut yourself up with your sorrow and sadness. Go forth to your work and to the world—even with listless hand and dragging step. For it is in work and in loving service and sympathy for others that God's comfort lies!

You can enter the lives of others so far and no further. When you have done all in your human power to help another break a bad habit like drinking or gambling or swearing or any other—it is *then* that you can call on God.

And do not think that life cannot be bearable even with sorrows that seem at the time *un*bearable. There have been many, many with sorrows much worse than your own. Yet out of their sorrow they have built new lives of peace and comfort— yes and even of happiness— A man past seventy, all alone in the world, was suddenly stricken blind. He lived alone in a small house on the edge of the village. It seemed for a time that nothing was left for him— that he was doomed to a life in the dark, with never a ray of hope or cheer. He could not even read his Bible.

Yet one day as he passed through his front gate and smelled a flower he said: "I shall plant a garden. And even though I cannot see the flowers, I can give them

tender care and feel and smell them and love them."

And he planted such a garden, tending it with loving care. His sensitive hands got to know every little plant. And the flowers seemed to feel the loving care he was giving them. They blossomed as did no flowers in the whole village. Each day he gave a neighbor's boy a handful to bring to the nearest hospital where they just seemed to transport the old man's loving spirit to the sick souls.

Even from the dark, the blind man had drawn peace and contentment through his love for flowers and through his loving service to others.

So can you, too, plant a garden of loving service to those about you.

Yes, you can love even those who have laid a cross upon you. Even as Jesus forgave those who thrust the Cross upon His bent back. You can love people in *spite* of their faults. You can help them and leave their healing to God in His own good time.

You do not have to wait for the blessed comfort and joy of God. Even the Thief upon the Cross heard the promise of Jesus: "*today* thou shalt be with me in paradise!"

You do not have to wait for some future day to walk close to God that your sorrow and your sadness may be taken away. As easy as the turning of a page, as simple as the opening of a window, you can have that comfort today. You can start now—today—to claim the blessed contentment that God has promised you. You can partake now—today—of the living fountain of the Kingdom of God which is within you.

We pray with you: "For God's Comfort in My Sorrow."

Prayer

For

GOD'S COMFORT IN MY SORROW

"As one whom his mother comforteth,
so will I comfort you" — Is. 66:13

Father of infinite mercy and comfort, Thou who hast pity upon all men, make me feel Thy presence even as I pray.

And O how grateful I am to come to the shelter of Thy love in prayer, dear Father. For I do not need to tell Thee how sad and lonely I have been, for I am sure Thou must know all about it.

Yet even in my misery, dear Father, I have known that my comfort and cheer would be to confide in Thee through prayer. I thank Thee for this privilege, dear Father, and I am only sorry that I have so often neglected to take advantage of it.

Please, loving Father, help me to overcome my sorrow and sadness. Help me to realize that only in Thee is true happiness to be found. Strengthen my faith, dear Father, so that I may rejoice in Thy love.

Teach me that sorrow is only for a minute but Thy joy is forever. Teach me to turn to the comfort of my daily tasks that time may heal my troubles. Help me to share the sadness of others that my own sadness may be shared and lightened.

Even this little prayer has made me more cheerful, dear Father. I feel I have come closer to Thee than I have for such a long time — and for the first time I truly begin to see a little of the light of happiness once more.

—Amen

13

GOD'S PROMISE OF ETERNAL LIFE TO YOU

As it must to all men, sorrow and death sooner or later come to every man. There are few who have not drunk the bitter cup of loss. There is none who has not bent over the bed where a loved one tossed in agony. There is none who has not looked down into a grave where it seemed that all of that which we loved was being laid to rest.

And when the minister had spoken the dread words: "Dust to dust," truly the hand of death weighed upon you like a heavy cloak of darkness. And perhaps for the first time in your life you were struck with utter awe and desperation. Oh, how you longed for the touch of a vanished hand, the sound of a voice that was still.

And that age-old question which was wrung from the lips of Job so many, many years ago—that question which neither scientist nor sage can answer—sprang to your own lips:

"If a man die, shall he live again?"

Where, where to turn for the answer? Dear reader, as you have turned to that Blessed Book so many times in the past, so turn now to that Book for the answer to your unspoken question.

Turn to that passage in the great Book of Revelation and hearken to the word of God. For truly, like the benediction of a great organ as it peals out in the darkened church, so come the immortal words to your sorrowing soul.

Do you wonder where your loved ones are, what they have met in the land beyond the sky? Do you ponder what will happen when *you* lie down to rest?

"They shall hunger no more, neither thirst any more, neither shall the

sun light on them, nor any heat . . . he that sitteth on the throne shall dwell among them. For the lamb which is in the midst of them shall feed them and shall lead them unto living fountains of waters; and God shall wipe away all tears from their eyes"

Oh, how beautiful that passage is. And what a wonderful picture it shows of the eternal life which God has promised to those who believe on Him!

Maybe you can remember times in your own life or in those of your loved ones when you were hungry and thirsty. And now you see that God *remembers* those times. And He is waiting with divine food and drink.

Maybe your loved ones left this world with tears in their eyes, as *you* may leave it. It makes you think of a mother coming into a room where her child has been crying. There are still traces of tears on the little face. The mother tucks the blanket about the child to make it warm. She softly wipes away all traces of tears. Then she bends down with a good-night kiss before she tip-toes out.

So, we are told, God, with His great, tender heart "shall wipe away all tears" and even as a mother spreads a warm blanket over her sleeping baby "He shall spread His tabernacle over them."

And when God has wiped away all our tears, when He has warmed and comforted those who have crossed the River, He will lead us to great fountains of sparkling water. Have you ever seen them—tossing great crystals into the sunlit air? And we will drink deep of the water—the water of the spirit—the water of eternal life!

Yes, we leave this earth and go to a strange land. But One has gone on before us. Like a Father meeting His child, Jesus will meet us, holding out his tender hands. For that is what he has told you over and over again:

"In my Father's house are many mansions. If it were not so, I would have told you. I go to prepare a place for you . . . and where I am there ye may be also."

Jesus will *keep* that promise. He knew that in the hour of sadness and death, doubt would creep in. He *prepares* you for that. Oh, how He wants you to believe Him! He wants to impress you so much with the truth of His words:

"If it were not so, I would have told you." What sincerity is there!

For Jesus is the supreme pledge of your Father's love. It is the sweetest note in all the music of life. God so loved the world—God so loved *you*, that He gave His only begotten Son that you might have life eternal!

Do you think for a moment that God would have planted this love for Jesus, this love for your dear ones only to dash it to the earth? Do you think that God would allow the injustices, the sorrows, the lash of the world to bear upon His children only to dash their hopes to pieces?

No, God is a God of law and justice. His universe is a universe of law and justice. Day follows night and there is no variation. Generation follows generation and all go their way to God.

Yes, we *do* want to know if we shall meet our loved ones and be with them. That is what we want perhaps more than anything else.

God's love could never refuse that which His children want most. Nothing is too good or too kind for Him to do for us. He *could* not disappoint us!

Many people ask, why, then, do the dead not return to tell us of these glories? Perhaps a little story will explain the reason.

Some caterpillars in their dull brown coats on the ground were talking about how time after time each caterpillar at the end of his span had wrapped himself up in a silken cocoon and never a caterpillar had come out of his cocoon. So they made a solemn agreement that one of them who was next to go should crawl to the ground and tell his comrades all about what had happened.

The time came for that one to wrap himself in his cocoon and he did so. All the winter he lay there. But while he was there, a wonderful change, a change of a kind he could never *dream* came over him. He found himself a beautiful, shining butterfly, his lacy wings glowing in the sunlight. For a moment he hovered on the edge of the cocoon before flying into the sky. As he looked down into the dark underbrush, he understood how impossible it was to describe the change which had happened to a crawling creature on the ground and turned him into a shining, beautiful creature!

Just so when we lie down to our sleep our lives will be like our lives on earth but our life in heaven will be as different as the caterpillar was from the butterfly.

And the one outstanding fact about the life of Jesus was His freedom from the fear of death and His assurance that God would bless us all with eternal life. Why, just to be with Jesus is enough to give us that assurance!

There are so *many* ways of looking out upon God. You may find God's eternity in the glory of a blossom or a star. The astronomer finds God's eternity in his telescope. The scientist sees God's eternity through his microscope. The thinker finds God's eternity through the great souls who have written and spoken. Some find God through misfortune, while others find Him through loving human service.

But the best windows looking out upon God are the four Gospels. To read and re-read them will give you more promise of God's eternal life for you than you could get if you were to study the stars, the atoms and all the books in all the libraries of the world.

For like jewels set in a ring of eternal joy, so do the words of Jesus ring clear as He pleads with us and promises us that eternal life He was so anxious for us to have. Hearken to them, for you will never read their like anywhere else:

"And this is the will of him that sent me, that everyone which seeth the Son, and believeth on Him, may have everlasting life." John 6:40

"Verily, verily, I say unto you. If a man keep my saying, he shall never see death." John 8:51

"But whosoever drinketh of the water that I shall give him shall never thirst; but the water that I shall give him shall be in him a well of water springing up into everlasting life." John 4:14

"Verily, verily, I say unto you, He that believeth on me hath everlasting life." John 6:47

"He that heareth my word and believeth on Him

*that sent me hath ever-
lasting life." John 5:24
"I am the resurrection and
the life." John 11:25*

How these words tug at
our hearts, for the core of
truth is in them! And how
they take away the terror of
the night of death for us.

Just supposing you were
born but yesterday and had
never seen the coming of
night. What a fearsome
thing it would appear to
you. Is this the end of all
light, you would ask? What
has been the reason for this
beautiful day when all is to
be swallowed up in the
dark? And you would dread
the setting sun with all the
dread that was in you. And
the next day would come
the miracle of dawn. Yes,
the set of sun and the miracle of dawn are known to
you for you have seen them.

"Eye hath not seen nor
ear heard" the miracle of
eternal life. Just so are there
glories which your life cannot reveal and death is but
the veil hiding these glories!

But it is well that you *prepare* for these glories. It is
well that you begin today to
really understand, to be-
lieve!

For what you have just
read *are* God's promises.
That is why this Chapter

was *called* God's promise of
eternal life to you.

And God's promise is that
even as your dear ones who
have crossed the River live,
so shall *you* live. They are
not far away and neither
shall *you* be far away. They
still belong to you and you
belong to them. Forever are
your lives intertwined. Between their world and yours
the distance is not great and
it is probably less than you
imagine.

It is for you to *live* this
joyful gospel. There should
be nothing sad in your
thoughts of your dear ones
nor in thoughts of your own
far journey.

**And the nearer you live to
God, the nearer you hold
communion with Jesus, the
closer will you be to your
departed loved ones and
they to you. They are in
God's keeping and so are
you. They are immortal and
if you are to be one with
them, you must realize your
own immortality more
greatly.**

As the explorer Columbus
was in the darkest hour of
his voyage he received small
signs of the unseen world
not far way. The sea carried
tiny flowers past his ship.
Brilliant birds sang in the

masts and welcomed him to a new world, yet how little did he realize the wonders and the riches and the beauty of the new world.

So God's promises are birds singing their sweet music to your dear ones and calling to us to come to the bright land. The fragrance from God's gardens come to us across the void. And in our dark hours as we cross the darkened sea, we can just see the streaks of days that tell us the story of the new day.

Faith and faith alone will overcome sorrow and death—faith in God's promises. With Faith you can go forth as if your life was set to music. With Faith the peace that passeth all understanding enters your heart and you are at rest.

Let us pray: "For Life Eternal in the Kingdom of Heaven."

Prayer

For

LIFE ETERNAL IN THE KINGDOM OF HEAVEN

"I am the Resurrection, and the life; he that believeth in me, though he were dead, yet shall he live"—John 11:25

Eternal Father, Thou art the rock of my life. Thou art my strength. Thou art my comfort and my consolation. How grateful I am to be able to come to the shelter of Thy love in prayer!

For Thou knowest how sad I often feel at all the sorrow and sadness in the world. Thou knowest how I often think of my dear ones who have passed on and how I wonder where they are and if they are peaceful and happy.

O, dear Father, help me to overcome my sorrow and sadness. Strengthen my faith in Thee more and more. Teach me that life and death, sorrow and joy are all part of Thy great Plan for me. Teach me to look forward, not backward, to look up and not down.

Come to me now with Thy comfort, dear Father. Help me really and truly feel that Jesus is the resurrection and the life. Help me know that he who believeth in Him shall have life eternal in the Kingdom of Heaven. Help me to know that my dear ones are safe and happy with Thee — that Thou hast wiped away all their tears.

What comfort I have felt even to talk to Thee about my sadness, dear Father. Truly I now rest here in quiet peace and know Thou wilt love me and keep me forever, through our Lord and Saviour, Jesus Christ.

—Amen

14

GOD WILL HELP YOU TO GET OUT OF DEBT

ARE YOU WORRIED ABOUT debt or money troubles? Are you in need of greater abundance and prosperity, yet burdened down by debt?

If you *are*, then here is the wonderful news which God has been trying to give you all along if you had eyes to see and ears to hear—the news that God will help you get out of debt!

For God has said that a man in debt is a man caught in a net. Struggle as you may, the net seems to get tighter and tighter about you. Every strange caller brings fear to your heart. You open every letter with trembling. You cross the street to keep out of the way of those to whom you owe money. Verily a net of debt!

And yet from that great lighthouse of divine wisdom, your Bible, you see shining unto you the clear way of God's help in paying your debt.

For you have only to turn to that wonderful Book of Books to find that God has taken thought of you even as you are caught in the net of debt. The Psalmist knew this, for you can still read the wonderfully confident words which he wrote:

"He shall pluck my feet out of the net!"

Yes, God will help you with your debts—no matter how they were incurred. For truly He *knows* that so many debts come to us because of sudden emergencies—times of sickness and lack, times when we must borrow through no fault of our own.

Payment is not always easy and may sometimes mean self-denial but God is there to help.

In your *own* case, self-denial to pay your debts may mean living *beneath* your means for a time. It may mean moving to a cheaper place. It may mean doing

92

without or buying for cash instead of "charging it."

This does take character. It does mean you must save a certain amount each week of what comes in, to pay your debt, "living off the rest." And yet, with God's help, it *can* be done. It *has* been done by thousands who probably owed more than you do right now!

Charles Dickens, the famous writer, toiled for years to pay off his debts. But out of his toil grew some of the loveliest stories the world has ever seen. Abraham Lincoln failed as a country storekeeper and struggled under a mountain of debt. Yet from his struggles grew the great love and understanding he always had for people in debt.

For while debt so often breeds fear, it just as often is the birthplace of courage and sympathy. Only he who has been faced with debt learns sympathy for others who are in debt.

And so the first thing you will need is courage—courage to face your debt and your debtors! It means going to see every single person to whom you are in debt and telling them you are now going to pay them.

The people to whom you talk will *know* that you have courage, for they will know it *takes* courage to do what you are doing. They will feel that you really intend to pay, otherwise you would not have come to them.

But by facing and confessing your debts you will accomplish a wonderful thing. You will at last be free from the demon debt. No longer need you run away.

And another wonderful thing will happen as a result! The people to whom you owe money will become friendly at once! All they have wanted right along was a sign that you sincerely intended to pay them. They will not be hard on you if— and this is a great, big "if"—if they feel you are continuing to be sincere.

Pay your oldest debts first, for they have waited the longest. There will be some people whom you will not be able to pay until you have paid others off. But see these people also and tell them about the older debt. Tell them about when you will start paying *them*.

Then you will find out another thing if you bravely face those you owe. They will take any amount you can give them—a dollar a week—fifty cents a week—even a quarter—anything, as long as they believe you are sincerely trying.

It is better to pay ten people each fifty cents a week than five people a dollar a week. It is better to promise to pay over a longer period than you really think you can. This will take care of emergencies which none of us can foresee—times when you will not be able to pay as you promised. But always keep your promises to pay!

As long as you do *that*, people to whom you are paying back will wish you well. For, come to think of it, no one wants you more to have money, to be successful, than the person to whom you owe money. They will go far out of their way to help you—for they are actually helping themselves!

A man who ran a general store owed a considerable sum to a feed company. Business being poor, he found it impossible to pay them. One day he saw an ad in the paper announcing the company needed a representative in the district.

He knew all about the feed, knew it was good, and knew he could sell it. He went to the manager and found twenty-five applicants for the position. But he explained his debt to the company and added that if he got the job of course he would be able to pay the money he owed them. He got the job, for the company *already* had an "investment" in him. He not only paid back the money but made more than he had done in his general store.

All this shows that where there is a need, God will always give you the supply. God will not wipe out your debts, nor will He give you miracle powers to get around them. His help will come to you in normal, simple ways.

God is bringing you help with your debt problem when you learn from the experience of others. He is helping you when you learn from books like this one you are reading. He is bringing you help when, through *His* Book He brings you new courage to face your debts and pay them.

A lady who was sorely in debt, prayed to God for help. Shortly afterwards she was offered some work. This lasted exactly long enough for her to get out of debt. What clearer assurance that

God had seen her debt and sent the means of making extra money?

For so much depends upon how you regard your debt, whether you regard God's abundance, when you have it, as a gold-seeker or a *God*-seeker. Debts honestly made through love of family or service to loved ones will surely be wiped out with God's help. Seek God's help and you will find it.

In the middle of the last century, two sets of wagons started from Oklahoma toward the West. One was filled with gold-seekers—men who were going to the gold rush in California. The other was filled with God-seekers—men who were seeking a place to worship God in their own way.

Some of the gold-seekers reached California and found the gold. Today a few of these men or their descendants have retained a trace of it. The God-seekers came to a great, salt lake and developed the dry, forbidding country. Today their land, the great State of Utah, is prosperous and thriving. Even their descendants live in plenty and peace and abundance.

Yes, seek God and He will help you pay your debts. He will help you pay them only after you have done everything in your *own* power to pay them with the means at your command. For God will always help those who help themselves. He will be your "partner" in your true efforts to be honest and trustworthy. He will always give you the extra push up the ladder which you need. And with God's help there is "only one step more."

God's way is the way of love. Those to whom you owe money have, in a way, loved you by giving you goods or services or money on your promise to pay them back. Yet how often do people repay this confidence by beginning to dislike those to whom they owe money—sometimes simply because they expect it back!

The one to whom you owe is your brother or your neighbor. He is even *more* deserving of your love, for, while others may have turned away, he has helped you in his own way when you *needed* help. Your concern for him should indeed be greater!

We could tell you the story of a lady whose husband owed money to two

95

neighbors in a small town. Instead of being angry when they expected to be paid, she was grateful and felt sorry that her husband was not able to pay them anything at all.

So she determined to give them a sign of that affection. When she baked a cake one week, she baked two extra cakes, one each for the two families. She took the cake to the wives of the men to whom her husband owed the money and said:

"I am bringing you these cakes for your kindness in giving us time to pay off the money we owe you right now."

The cakes really were delicious and the two families told their neighbors about them. The neighbors said they would like some too, if they could buy them. So the next time the lady brought more cakes, the two women sent them to their neighbors who offered to buy cakes at least once a week.

The fame of the lady's cake spread all over the town and it was not long before her husband had to help her bake all the cakes they could sell. Needless to say, she was able to pay off the two debts. But she was enabled to do even more!

She and her husband made a comfortable living from a growing cake business. And all because this lady loved those she owed money to.

Yes, sincerity in paying debts is the most essential thing. Ask God to give you that sincerity. Did you ever stop to think that if you put an "R" into the word "PAY" you will have the word "PRAY"?

The "R," we feel sure, must stand for Righteousness. "In Righteousness shalt thou be established, thou shalt be far from oppression, for thou shalt not fear." Is. 54:14

To seek God's help in paying your debts, let Him be your "silent partner." Take Him into your confidence. For you can never worry if you will place your debts in God's hands and walk in His way.

Sometimes you hear a story and you try to find out its source before you believe it. So it is with the promised help of God's word, the Bible. It is up to you to search, for there you will find the word you need.

And as you read, you recall these wonderful words of Jesus who said:

"And all things whatsoever ye ask in prayer,

believing, ye shall receive."

You have debts—many of them. You are worried and oppressed by them. Come, dear reader, let us ask that God help you with your debts. Let us believe. And let us receive!

Let us pray: "For God's Help in Getting Out of Debt."

Prayer

For

GOD'S HELP IN GETTING OUT OF DEBT

"Owe to no man anything, but to love one another"
—Ro. 13:8

Almighty, heavenly Father, who has made the earth and all the great universe, how happy I am to come to Thee and open my heart even about the things which trouble me so much.

For Thou knowest how my debts have piled up on me, my Father. Thou knowest the reasons for them, yet how hard I have had to struggle to pay them off. It just seems, dear Father, I never get through.

Father, Thou art the only one I can speak to of these things. And I do know Thou wilt help me if I come to Thee in deep, true, abiding Faith.

Please, please, dear Father, give me Thy help for I really need it. I need to know how to manage so I can pay off my debts. Help me, dear Lord, to put aside a little each week for that purpose. Help me to be brave in facing those I owe and telling them exactly how things are. And I know, dear Father, if I do all these things, then Thou wilt give them Thy blessing.

Yes, Father of mercies, I do want to learn that beautiful lesson of Jesus that Thou knowest of what we are in need. I have told Thee my need and I will seek Thy Kingdom. And I truly know and feel all those things will be added unto me. And O what courage and hope and peace this gives me. I feel right now I can just start getting out of debt in the most wonderful way I have ever tried. Thank you, Father.

—Amen

GOD WILL HELP YOU TO OVERCOME BAD HABITS

Have you got bad habits which are making you unhappy—habits like drinking or smoking or swearing—habits like uncontrolled temper or others equally as distressing?

If you have, then this Chapter brings you the glorious message that God *will* help you overcome bad habits just as willingly and just as lovingly as He can overcome *any* other thing!

For He *knows* how powerless you feel about habits once they have you under their spell. Yet, if you will live as God wants you to live, obey the few simple rules He has laid down for your life, make Him all in all in your life—then as surely as the day follows the night, He will help you.

If you will open your Bible you may read: "Be of good cheer, *for* I have overcome the world." And there is the world of temptation, the world of habit. To overcome means to "come up over." It may be we can explain it more clearly.

Two men saw a flood racing toward them down a long valley. The first was afraid to face the flood and ran down the valley to outstrip it. Of course it caught up with him. The second, who knew what it was to "come up over" faced the flood, started toward it, but *up* the mountain and kept on until he was above the racing waters and was safe.

It will be just like that if you will work with God to "come up over," to overcome your bad habits. God will help you get on the high ground if you will face your habits and do your best to get rid of them.

For it is so easy to get into bad habits, yet so hard to get out of them. How slowly they get a grip on you, how they start from small beginnings, yet how they cling to you!

'At a crossroads in the South where some of the roads are almost impassable in the spring, there was a sign: "Take care which rut you choose—you will be in it for the next twenty-five miles."

Take care which habit rut you start in. You may be in it for the next twenty-five years!

Now there are hundreds of rules and remedies on how to break various habits. Some counsel stopping gradually and some advise stopping all at once. Everyone must find the rule which works best for himself. But habits are like weeds. They spring up in the ground best suited to them. And no matter what habit you may have, there is one ground which nourishes *all* bad habits. That is the ground of tiredness. Off-hand, this might not seem to have much to do with refusing a drink or a cigarette, refraining from losing your temper or doing some other wrong thing, but it *has!*

It is in the hours or minutes of physical and mental tiredness that your self-control weakens. It is when your energy has been worn down by work or worry that you give way to bad habits.

Most bad habits, most sins, are committed at night. Not so much because it is dark, but because at night people are tired. People drink at night to "pep them up" they say. People gamble at night for the "kick" they get, they will tell you. People quarrel easily at night for they get a false sense of stimulation.

But notice how lessened the desire to drink, to smoke, to gamble, to swear—in fact to do *anything* wrong—is in the morning. And all because you are rested and your self-control is stronger!

So when the desire becomes strong, try to get some rest. Don't go out. Stay home and go to bed. Drop your work and also your play and get some sleep. Just this simple thing will do more for you than any "trick" which you might try to break a bad habit!

In the same way you give way to bad habits when you have been through a time of upset—at home, at work or out in the world. These use up a lot of your emotion and this exhausts you. It is then that you lose your self-control, too. It is then that the husband stamps out of the house for a drink, the husband or wife swears, the wife stalks out on a spending or "bingo" spree.

Luckily, every habit has its own danger signals. *You* know what the danger signal of *your* habit is. Your signal may be a very small one, but you can always tell when you are overdrawing your self-control account.

Suddenly you may feel depressed. It is here that the drinker feels he must have a drink, the smoker must have a cigarette. Suddenly you feel all "fed up." It is here that temper and quarrels arise. If you get to recognize these danger signals, you will see yourself *through* these times. And the more you gain control to see yourself through *these* times, the easier it will be to go through the *ordinary* occurrences of life without your bad habits.

Actually, these times often arise, not so much because the body is tired, but because the mind and the spirit are parched for want of rest and for want of something *beyond* themselves!

Rest your spirit as well as your body. In time of stress go to some quiet place of beauty and rest, if you can. Go to a quiet woodland glade or a lovely church if possible. But if you can go to neither, go to your room and shut yourself in. Turn your thoughts inward by shutting the world out.

Even Jesus felt the need of quiet communion with the Father. Much as He enjoyed the comradeship of His Disciples, Jesus time after time went apart to pray.

So you, too, in moments of weakness, can draw added strength from communion with your Father, as you think of the peace, the quietness and the power of God, as you think of his power, His love for you and His promise to help you.

Verily: "They that wait upon the Lord shall renew their strength."

You can be like the traveler to the mountain village. He had come to see the glorious mountain peaks shining in the sun. But a fog covered the whole village for three days. Finally one of the townsfolk said to him: "If you really want to see those peaks, take the trail that leads up yonder mountain. Soon you will come to a bend in the road, where there is a wooden cross. At that point you will be above the fog and you will see the sun shining on the snowbound peaks."

Take the trail to the wooden cross. At that point you will be above the fog of alcohol, of nicotine, of temper, of gambling. And you will see the glory of your Father's love!

Now, as we said, there are many things which people advise others to do to break bad habits. Drinkers have been told to eat candy instead of taking a drink. Smokers have been told to twirl a watch chain instead of reaching for a cigarette. Swearers have been advised to count ten before swearing.

All these little devices are of some use, but behind them, if you look, you will see that their real object is to get you interested in something *else* than your habit. The only trouble with the little "tricks" is that they are too weak, too small!

Bad habits are big! They occupy a big place in your thought and mind. The only way to crowd them out is by crowding something bigger and stronger and *better* in their place!

Get interested in something more stimulating and *powerful* than the stimulation of drinking or smoking

or gambling or swearing. And the biggest thing, which generations of men and women have found to their unspeakable joy, is love and service to others. It is not enough to make good resolutions. We are sure you have seen people who say they have "sworn off" some habit going about boasting how they haven't taken a drink in three days or a cigarette in a week. They rarely go on with the overcoming of their habit.

They are like the captain of the Mississippi steamboat who had a loud and raucous whistle on his boat. He was so fond of scaring the folks at the landings that he used up all his steam blowing the whistle. And the boat always had to wait a half hour longer before she had enough steam to get started again.

No, dear reader. Faith in God's power to help you is dead without works. When you have started with God's help on the road to recovery, it is your duty to help *others* along that road.

A man was sent to meet a minister who was coming from another town. As he started to the station he said to a friend who knew the minister, "I have never seen him. How will I know him?" The friend replied: "Oh, you'll recognize him all right. He'll be helping someone off the train."

Get to be known as the man or the woman who is always "helping someone off the train" and you will be substituting service for habit!

Yes, you will slip back in your bad habits once in a while. The overcoming of bad habits is not an easy road, but it is a road which leads upward. Many times along that road, you will falter as did Peter, and say: "Lord, save me."

For if you are firm in your Faith that God can help you, then you will arise from each set-back stronger than before. There is a power greater than your habit, greater than yourself—and that is the power of God to help you! Turn your will-power over to God and have Faith that He will help you. Expect to be helped and you *will* be helped.

As a country parson once said: "Brothers and sisters, here you are praying for rain. I would like to ask you just one question. Where are your umbrellas?"

Or as the little boy responded to his mother when she said: "Sonny, come into the house while mother prays for rain." And the boy said: "In a minute, mother, I want to bring my wagon in so it won't get wet."

It is that kind of Faith you need to work with God so that He may help you overcome your bad habits. And you cannot imagine how relieved you will feel once you understand that you do not have to fight against your bad habits all the time—and alone. For you know that you *have* fought if you have tried to get rid of a bad habit. No one but yourself *knows* how you have fought. No one, that is, but God!

And you know how many times you have lost. How relieved you will be once you understand that all you have to do is place yourself in the care of your Father, who will make you whole!

For one way, although you may not have thought of it lately, is to get your Father's help through deep, sincere Prayer. Have you ever got down on your knees about your habit and told your Father about it?

At the entrance to a hospital, a famous sculptor carved a figure of Jesus, which he called "Come unto Me." The outstretched arms of our Lord welcomed all who came, but His head was bowed. The sculptor was asked why he modeled the Figure in that way and he answered:

"If you want to see His face, you will see it when you get down on your knees."

Let us pray: **"That God will Help Me To Overcome Bad Habits."**

𝕻𝖗𝖆𝖞𝖊𝖗

That

GOD WILL HELP ME TO OVERCOME
BAD HABITS

"Seek the Lord, and His Strength"—Ps. 105:4

Merciful, loving Father, unto whom all hearts
are open and from whom no secrets are hid, I
lift up my eyes unto the hills from whence cometh
my help — my help in time of temptation.

For I need that help, dear Father — I need it to
give up the habit which is making my life so
unhappy.   Thou knowest how it has tempted me
and how strong it is, dear Father.

Truly, Father, I want to stop, but I just don't
seem to have the power, it has such a hold on me.

O, dear Father, help me get rid of this bad
habit.   Take and remove this thing which is
almost like a sickness.   Help me as if I were
a little child and had no strength at all.

And I will try, Father, truly I will.   I will try
and say "No" each time I am tempted and then
I feel I will get stronger and stronger.

Thank you, dear Father, that even this little
prayer to Thee has made me feel better and
stronger.   Thank you for giving me hope.   Thank
you for taking my hand in Thine — for placing it
in the hands of Thy Son, who was tempted many
times, yet resisted evil unto the very end —
Thy Son, our Lord and Saviour, Jesus Christ.

—Amen

ASKING GOD TO HELP LOVED ONES OVERCOME BAD HABITS

Is SOMEONE YOU LOVE MAKING you unhappy by bad habits—habits of drinking, smoking, swearing? Are you distressed because a loved one is under the spell of some habit which is ruining their own lives and spreading unhappiness among their family and friends?

If you are, then here is the inspiring news which this Chapter wants to give you. You *can* ask God to help a loved one overcome a bad habit and He *will help.* For all through His wonderful Word, the Bible, He has promised divine help—so many promises that it would take almost all of *this* book just to recite them!

Open that blessed Book almost at any page and there in golden words you are almost sure to find a promise of God's help and God's love for you.

And we *do* know you

need that help and that love, for if ever there was a puzzling thing it is this question of the bad habits of a loved one. And sometimes so saddening! How many times have you asked yourself how it was that one you loved could be so cruel as to bring unhappiness and misery to you and others through the curse of some bad habit?

And just when you felt that you just didn't know what to do, the loved one surprised you with some new and good side of their character, some new understanding, some new kindness. For a while, they may have been their old selves—only to slip back into the habit. Yes, they readily agreed that the habit was a bad one and they wanted to break it. But they kept right on. And *still* you knew that deep down in their hearts they *did* want to do right, but didn't have the strength.

Not that habits are weaknesses. They are *sicknesses!* And they must be treated like sickness. A drinking man is not bad. He is sick. A smoking man is not evil when he smokes too much. He is sick because he is drugged.

But habit-sickness is different from other kinds of sickness. There is no human medicine which can cure it. There is only one medicine—and that is God's medicine!

The glorious thing about God's medicine is that you—the wife or husband, the sister or brother, the good friend—can actually help your loved one get it. It is you who can take your loved one to God so that He can pour new life into them. It is you who can take your loved one to the Great Physician for healing!

Have you ever seen an electric heat machine? The doctor gives you two handles and says: "Take hold, it won't hurt you." And if you take hold, a delicious warmth spreads through your body and eases your pain.

So you, too, can hold the handles of Faith and Prayer to your loved one and say: "Take hold; it won't hurt you!" And God's forgiveness and help will flow through their tired, aching bodies and spirits!

But first, dear reader, you must "take hold" yourself. You, too, must have deep, true abiding Faith that God *can* and *will* overcome the bad habits of a loved one.

A country doctor went to the home of a farmer whose wife was very sick. The doctor told the farmer that if the good woman lived until morning she would get well. The following morning the doctor returned and found the farmer still sitting beside the bed, the curtains drawn and the lamp still burning. The farmer tremblingly asked: "How is she?"

Saying no word, the doctor went to the window and threw open the blinds. "The morning has come," he said.

The farmer lingered in the darkness of doubt. He had failed to act on the doctor's promise. Even so, if *you* believe in your Father's promise of help to your loved ones and act on it, you will secure it without fail!

To every man and woman with a bad habit there comes a time when they know the habit is hurting them and they yearn to do something about it. Sooner or later they are going to ask you how *you* think they can stop the habit. And this is the opportunity created by God for you to begin your help.

All you need say is: "God can help you." Yes, maybe they will laugh, but your foundation is on a rock and you don't have to argue about it. All you need do is simply say: "If you are in earnest and you want God to help you, I can show you how we can reach Him!"

Tell your loved one soberly that God *can* stop the habit of drinking or smoking or any other habit just as easily as He can do *any* of His great work. Your loved one may say that they themselves are powerless against drink, against tobacco, against temper. And readily agree that is so for it is so. But you *can* say that there is a power greater than either of you which can do just that. And say: "All I ask is that you turn yourself over to God. All I ask is that you have *faith* that God can help you."

Tell him that neither of you has to apologize for depending upon God, the Father. Tell him that both of you can laugh at those

who say that the way of light is the way of weakness. It is the way of strength. It takes no courage to have no faith, but it takes *great* courage to *have* faith!

Although they may not say so, your loved ones will feel a lightened heart when they realize they do not *have* to fight against alcohol or nicotine or anger. For they *have* fought and they have lost time after time. How lightened they will feel when they understand at last that all they need do is place themselves in the hands of the Father who will make them whole!

An ocean liner hit an iceberg in mid-ocean. Aboard was a man who had accumulated money and had converted it into gold, which he carried in a belt around his waist. He refused to take the belt off when he had to jump overboard. It was only when he loosened the gold and let it sink to the bottom of the sea that he was able to swim and climb into a lifeboat.

God is sending His lifeboat for your loved one, but you must first help him drop his load of fear and doubt before God can rescue him.

Now it may be that your loved one will keep the hurtful habit for a long time. It may be they will cause you many a heartache. Yet it is right here that God is testing your forbearance and your patience. You must learn to live with that person and that habit.

One lady was praying at her bedside for her drinking husband. He came in and saw her on her knees. With an oath he took off his heavy shoes and threw them at her. Both of them struck her but she did not move or turn, but kept on praying. The next morning her husband found the shoes neatly shined beside his bed. He was so ashamed and touched and heartbroken that he never again touched liquor.

For if there was one thing that Jesus taught it was that we are to love one another. He didn't say we were to love good people, righteous people only. He said: "Love one another." And that means everybody—the good and the bad, the strong and the weak, the sinless and the erring!

Jesus loved even publicans and sinners. He could see good even in the Samaritan who was despised by everybody. To the woman who had sinned greatly, He gently said: "Neither do I condemn thee; go and sin no more!"

Jesus found fault, but He found fault lovingly. He praised the good in people. He knew that all men are weak. "Let he who is without sin cast the first stone," He said.

Keep your heart fixed on the good in your loved one even though the distressing habit may go on and on. True, they may drink to much of an excess. But try and remember, perhaps, how generous they are. True, they may swear or smoke to a tremendous degree, but try to remember, perhaps how good they are at heart. And hope! Hope for the turn in the tide which is sure to come.

Have you ever seen glass moulded? Molten glass is poured into moulds—some for dishes, some for glasses, some for pitchers. It is all the same glass, but each mould gives the glass a different form.

So is God's spirit poured into the earthly moulds which we call bodies. There are as many moulds as there are human beings and God needs all kinds to carry His spirit. If some are cracked, they will be mended by God in His own good time.

So you must have patience with your loved one for God's spirit is in them, too. And you will find that when you learn to live with people lovingly and forgivingly, making the best of things as they are, your road will not be as unhappy as you may look forward to right now. You may not reach the desired goal and find every habit blotted out, but surely the road will be more pleasant.

An old minister was asked what he would say if he should not find heaven as he thought. "Well," said the cheerful old man, "I would say 'Hallelujah.' I had a good time getting here, anyway!"

Yes, the storms and the stresses of a bad habit in a loved one may be with you on your road of life for a long time. But if you will live as God wants you to live, then the trials and the tribulations will be to you just a part of God's work in preparing His children for a better life.

One night there was a terrifying storm. The next morning a little girl said to her father, "Daddy, what was God doing last night? Was he making the morning?"

"Yes, dear," said the father. "I guess He *was* making the morning."

So the storms of your own life may be God's way of making the morning for you.

But above all, ask God to help you. Confide in God the fault of your loved one. Ask His help and you may be assured you will not ask in vain. Praise even the least improvement your loved one makes in his habits. Never put him in the wrong and, whenever you can, help him think that the suggestions you made for his good were his own idea. Speak gently and try to really and truly understand the suffering a person with a bad habit is undergoing.

Much can be still gotten by you from your life if you will continue to live with God. With Him you will never be lonely.

A man was driving through a lonely country section and stopped at a far cabin for a drink of water. A sweet-faced old lady gave him a brimming tumbler. As he thanked her, he said: "Mother, do you live here all alone?"

She smiled and answered: "Just me and Jesus."

She had the spirit of God within her and she always felt His presence. Shall we not pray for that presence to help our loved ones overcome their bad habits?

Let us pray: "That God Will Help My Loved Ones to Overcome Bad Habits."

Prayer

That

GOD WILL HELP MY LOVED ONES TO OVERCOME BAD HABITS

"God is faithful, who will not suffer you to be tempted above that ye are able"—I Cor. 10-13

Almighty and everlasting God whom no man has ever seen, yet who are so close that Thy children may always come to Thee! Now I am praying that my loved ones may overcome the bad habits which Thou knowest are making us all so unhappy.

Father, Thou knowest how strong the temptation is for this dear one. Thou knowest how this habit comes and promises so much, yet gives so little. Yes, Thou knowest how much this habit hurts them and hurts all of us who love them, too!

We know they have tried to overcome this habit, dear Father. And I do thank Thee that Thou hast helped them try. But they need more of Thy help, dear Father. They need it that they should not be discouraged when they try and then fail!

Bless the ways we are all trying. Help us encourage them. And put in their heart some good and great ambition that will be stronger than this terrible habit, dear Father.

O Father, bring this dear one closer to Thee in this trouble. Soften their hearts and let me be Thy servant in helping them. That is all I ask, and truly I feel Thou wilt grant it. This makes me so peaceful and so happy. Thank Thee, dear Father, thank Thee from a grateful heart!

—Amen

GOD IS WATCHING OVER YOU

DOES IT SOMETIMES SEEM that you are surrounded by enemies and evil? Are you nervous, worried and afraid of the future much of the time? Are there those who are mean and unjust to you, who try to cross you every chance they get?

If there are, dear reader, then joy can be yours. For over and over again in God's Word you are told that God will protect you from every enemy and evil, that every day and every night He is watching over you!

So often it is just *because* you are good and upright that you have enemies. So often it is just because you cannot be led from the path of righteousness. And so often it is because you simply are surrounded by evil people, evil neighbors and evil conditions.

Yet even with all of this you can be peaceful and happy if the Glad Tidings

of God's love are in you and through you.

It is like the man who said to the minister: "I have been through the Bible forty times and I never found what you are preaching."

"That may be," said the old minister, "but the question is—how much and how many times has the Bible been through *you?*"

For if God's Word is *through* you, then you will know and feel that if you but follow in the footsteps of your Great Teacher, then God's protection from enemies and evil is swift and sure.

"How do you know that God will protect you?" an Arab was once asked.

"How do I know whether it was a man or a camel which passed my tent last night?" answered the Arab, "by his footsteps."

God has left His footsteps in this world and in the Bible. There is One who *walked* in those footsteps and who has left them for

113

you! Follow in those footsteps and you will be out of danger. Your soul will be opened to God's light, and you will hear, as did the poet of old, the voice of Jesus say:

"I am this dark world's light. Look unto me, thy morn shall rise; and all thy days be bright."

For enemies, like evil, are things to be conquered. And the way of conquest *is* the way of Jesus. Jesus understands your problem because it was His own. For He, too, had enemies who reviled Him, who spat upon Him, who dragged him the way of the Cross.

Do you face the hatred of some man or woman? Although Jesus was gentle, good and kind He was hated by many.

How did Jesus triumph over enemies and evil, you may ask. Well, in the first place, Jesus had faith—faith that God was really His Father—faith that God was really watching over Him— faith that God would really protect Him.

Have *you* always had real, true abiding faith that God *was* watching over you when you prayed: "Deliver us from evil?"

For you *must* believe that the God who keeps you in the hollow of His hand neither slumbers nor sleeps. You must believe that the shade of His love hides you by night and the glory of His nearness drives away all the terrors of darkness!

But the real glory of Jesus' ministry unto you came when, hanging upon the Cross at Calvary, He spoke those immortal words which, if the world would but heed them, would drive every trace of enmity out of the hearts of men:

"*Father, forgive them for they know not what they do.*"

Some people try to get around this hard road of forgiveness. Peter, one of Jesus' Disciples, asked Jesus if it wasn't enough to forgive your enemy seven times. Jesus looked at him in reproof "Seventy times seven times," said Jesus. It was almost *unlimited* forgiveness for which Jesus pleaded.

You may say: "Do you mean I should forgive a man who has brought me unhappiness? Do you mean I must forgive a woman who wants to take my husband away? Must I forgive someone who

114

is always plotting to harm me?"

And the answer is still "Yes."

A famous mayor of a great city was almost murdered by a maniac. Yet, all through the time he was getting better at he hospital, he showed no sign of bitterness or hate. When they asked him how he was able to keep so fearless and cheerful, he said:

"Every night I forgive everybody everything."

What a wonderful spirit of forgiveness! Why, just that little sentence said to yourself every night before you go to sleep would work wonders in your life. Try it! Try it tonight! Every night before you go to sleep and start to think of any man or woman who may have wronged you; of any man or woman against whom you feel anger or hate—just say:

"Tonight I forgive them everything."

This is not easy. At first you will not only find it hard to mean it but to *say* it. The first few times you may say it *without* really meaning it. But if you keep at it, a wonderful thing will happen.

You will find that time after time where before you used to toss and turn thinking of the wrongs done to you, planning fanciful revenges upon those who wronged you — you will sleep! You will sleep peacefully and soundly all through the night!

And you will discover something still *more* wonderful. You will wake up morning after morning with a wonderfully peaceful heart. As you go forth you will find that you will be able quietly to face those whom you believe your enemies and waste no emotion in hate or grudge or quarrel! It is the power of forgiveness, the power of faith, the power of resisting not evil in quietness!

It is like the man who was looking at some giant redwood trees in California. "Whatever made those trees grow so tall?" he asked.

"Well, sir," said the guide, "I guess they just stood still and grew tall."

As you love and forgive your enemy, *you* stand still and grow tall.

For here is the great secret. To forgive your enemy may not make any immediate change in them. In many cases they will be just the same as before. But forgiveness will change *you!* It will cause things to happen in your own heart which will truly and actually make your enemy powerless against you!

It takes *two* to make a quarrel. Time after time when people see they cannot disturb you no matter what they do or say, their persecution will stop. Hate and anger are powerless against an open mind, an understanding soul and a forgiving heart!

Only hate and revenge have a way of hanging on. But if you live by the Golden Rule of God's laws, if you can show every man or woman that you do not stand in their way of any good and true thing, if you truly love your neighbor even as was commanded, then time after time, anger and hate melt away like spring snow.

There was a lady whose husband a young widow was trying to take away. The first lady, whom we will call Mrs. Peters, of course regarded the widow as her enemy.

She resolved to try Jesus' way of forgiveness, not an easy thing you will admit. One day she went to the widow's home. She pointed out that she had been married seven years, had two fine children and was very happy.

"Why do you want my husband?" she asked. "Do you love him? Would you be happy if you broke up our home?"

"No," said the widow. "I don't love your husband, but I have to look out for myself. I just think if I can get him, he will be a good provider."

"Come, then," said Mrs. Peters, without showing any hate or anger, "let us see if you cannot be provided for in a better way." And, although it took time, she found a nice position for the widow. On that job, she met a middle-aged man, one of the executives, who fell in love with her. In four months they were married and the widow left her position to keep a prosperous house.

The past was forgotten and both women were happy with their husbands. And all because Mrs. Peters forgave, because she resisted not evil and because she loved enough to do something about her problem.

It is in that spirit of love which you must strive

to meet every man—even though you may think he is your enemy. For if there is one thing which is stronger than hate it is the power of love.

You, yourself, have seen time after time how love can transform people. Here is Mary, a moody, sad-faced, silent girl, who suddenly blossoms into a smiling, happy, lovely sprite. "She's in love!" you say. Here is John, a grouchy, touchy, quarrelsome boy, who one day meets Mary and overnight becomes a fine, happy, loveable fellow. "It's love!" you say.

Not only do Mary and John change in relation to each other, but to their family, their friends, their neighbors and the world. Such *is* the power of love!

It is easy to be silent and to hate. It is hard to forgive. Be not ashamed that you forgive your enemy for you have taken the harder way. You forgive not because you are afraid or weak, but because you are strong.

The minute you are strong enough to forgive your enemy, you have a strength which makes it impossible for him to hurt you. In that moment, your fear departs and you rise gloriously above enemies and evil.

You rise, dear reader, because you rise with God!

Watch a blind man as he taps his way bravely down the street. He walks as if the way was clear before his shuffling feet. He comes to a corner where the traffic eddies about him. But when he hesitates there is always a hand to help him out. So he walks along the street as if he knew there were unknown friends along the road.

You are walking the road of life along paths you cannot see. The future is dark. Pitfalls, enemies and evil may lie ahead. But you are being watched over and led just as surely as is the blind man. And if you will but stop and listen when you come to a crossing in your life, just as surely will a hand find *you* in the dark, a hand guide *you* on the way!

For God *is* watching over you, not like some terrible eye in the heavens, but like a lover watches his beloved, a mother watches her newborn babe. As long as you follow in the path of righteousness, you cannot step out of God's glance. Under his loving eye you may face

117

the day serenely, you may meet the enemies and the evil of the world without fear.

There is an old saying which runs: "Man cannot see God and live." It should be: "Man cannot live unless he sees God." See Him in the sunrise and the sunset; in the brook and the ocean; in the face of a flower and the face of your fellow man. For as you watch these things with love and understanding, so shall God watch over you.

Trust and faith and prayer are the three windows through which your seeking eye may look. Dear reader, shall we not pray: "For God's Protection From Enemies and Evil."

Prayer

For

PROTECTION FROM ENEMIES AND EVIL

"O Lord my God, in Thee do I put my trust; save me from all them that persecute me, and deliver me"—Psalm 7:1

Dear God, lover of my soul, Thou art the greatest Friend and Protector anyone could ever have. That is why I do feel I can open my heart to Thee now — for Thou must know how full of pain and tears it is!

I feel so lonely and misunderstood, dear Father. People are so mean and unjust to me! Thou knowest how quick some of them are to find fault with me and blame me. Yes, Thou knowest who they are and how hard and bare this makes my life!

I don't want to do them any wrong, Father, but so often I see no reason for the way they treat me. O I do try to be kind and helpful to others, but there are some who simply do not want to understand or appreciate.

Please help me understand this, dear Lord. If I do anything which makes them act that way, please help me to be different. But if the fault is not mine, Father, please help me to forgive them, for truly they know not what they do!

And should I be afraid again, dear Father, remind me that if Thou be with me who can be against me? I know Thou art with me and so I should not fear anyone. This makes me stronger, dear Lord — so strong that I really feel I can go forth from here and not be afraid any, any more!

—Amen

DO YOU NEED DEEPER, STRONGER FAITH IN GOD?

Do YOU SOMETIMES FEEL A need for deeper, stronger faith in God? Would you like to know God better as a dear, close Friend? Would you like prayer to be a greater power in your life?

If you would, then turn to that great golden Treasury, your Bible, and there, spread before you in words which have the power to burn into your very soul, you will read the age-old secrets of believing faith, wondrous prayer and everlasting love of God, your Father!

Yes, you can go on for a while and find forgetfulness in your work and your home and your play. But sooner or later there comes a time when they are not enough. There comes a time when the noises of the day press too heavily on your soul.

Once we heard a good man say: "I never understood the consolation of God until I needed him to console me in the loss of my dear wife. Then I learned to know my Father like a sudden revelation."

It is often so. To believe in God's kindness and love in pleasant times is not too hard. But perhaps to you has come the time when you feel the winds of the tempests of life, you hear the crack of the lightning, you feel the anger of life's stormy sea and the fury of life's flood.

Perhaps there has come to you a time when plans go wrong, when love has failed, when the shelf is empty or the stove is cold. There perhaps has come a time when it seems that the joy of the world stops at every door but yours!

And you cry with the cry of Peter: "Lord, help me, or I perish." Your faith weakens, your prayers seem to strike a blank wall and rebound back to your listening ears. And you yearn to cry, even as did Jesus, "My God, my God, why hast Thou forsaken me?"

To many a man and woman, sorrows and trials are the only road they find to God and to deeper, stronger faith. Hard as it may be to understand, it is often only through hard times and struggle that you do, indeed, learn of the love of God!

But even without the sting of misfortune, your soul may cry for an understanding of God and His peace even as the sea shell, when it is placed close to your ear, seems to sigh for its home in the sea.

It is then that you think: there is peace in the blue distances of the sky, there is peace in the still waters of the mountain lake, there is peace in the upland pastures, but where can I find peace for my troubled heart? When will I ever know God as a dear, close friend?

Oh, how well did Jesus know this yearning for faith and love in God. So well that he made of it one of his most tender and glorious promises:

"My peace I give unto you, not as the world giveth, give I unto you."

There was a cobbler once upon a time who lived in a dark basement room and mended the shoes of the village folk. Often he prayed that he might have deeper spiritual understanding, deeper faith in God. Each night as he read his Testament, he wished Jesus would come and visit him in his desolate basement. One night he heard a voice say: "Look out on the street tomorrow, I am coming to visit you."

The next morning he saw a man staggering past his window, weak from cold and hunger. The cobbler took him in and fed him. Later he saw a poor woman braving the snow. He gave her of his few pennies and sent her forth with shoes mended. As day was waning, he made peace between two men who were quarreling outside his window.

That night as he sat down to read his Bible, he felt a wonderful peace as he read: "Inasmuch as ye have done it unto the least of these, my brethren, ye have done it unto me." And at last he knew that Jesus had come to visit him.

That, dear reader, is the way to spiritual understanding, to more faith in God. For how can your eyes be opened to the love and the glory of our Father if they be closed to the need for love that lies within the heart of your fellow man?

Now you may say: "I do have faith, but it is so weak." Dear friend, there is no measuring rod which can measure faith. Even the smallest amount of faith is enough for God. The greatest amount of faith which you might have would not make you more dear to your Father.

For all that He asks is that you *believe*—just believe! Believe greatly or believe less, but believe! The faith of a grain of mustard seed can bring to you the love of God and move the mountain just as greatly as the faith which fills the biggest temple!

And again you may ask yourself: "I wonder if I have the right kind of faith?" All faith, *any* faith is the right kind of faith. There are as many kinds of faith as there are people. You may have the faith that lays down its burdens willingly before the Father. You may have the faith that has not got the courage to lay its burdens down. You may only have the faith which *looks* at God—but that is all the faith that you need.

The only faith you need is the faith that God is in your heart. On St. Valentine's day, a young man sent a heart-shaped carving to the girl he loved. In the center was a mirror with this message: "See what is in my heart." She looked and she saw herself. And she was assured that she had first place in his heart.

Day by day God is looking into your heart. If He sees Himself mirrored there, if He knows that He has a place in your heart, then He *needs* no spoken words of love. Just that reflection is all the spiritual understanding and the faith that He needs to make you very dear to Him!

So how we wish we could make you feel that God is indeed your Friend, that if you are troubled in soul you need not lose courage, for where the *need* is, there God is! How we wish we could make you feel that not only does God guide you, but He takes the journey *with* you!

We know that in most of your moments you know and you feel this. But what a wonderful thing it is to feel that God is here—right where you are. He is beside you. He is beside the fire in the kitchen, in the front room, in the sick room, in the streets of your city, in your place of work. He touches every point in your life.

Isn't it wonderful that looking down upon you, He has said: "I, the Lord, do keep you; I will keep you night and day." What sweet comfort that should bring you. No evil can befall your roof. He has said it. So will it be!

See God everywhere and you will have deeper and deeper faith in Him. See Him in sun-rise and sun-set; in mountain brook and in mighty ocean, in storm cloud and rainbow. See him in the face of the humblest wayside flower and in the face of your fellow man.

Have you ever tried spending a day with God? Shall we tell you how to do it? When you awaken in the morning, before you go forth—whether the day be bright or gloomy, pray to God—tell Him all your plans!

As you go about your daily work, look up once in a while and let God know that you are giving a thought to Him. As daily cares and problems come up one by one, stop for a moment and say: "Is this the right thing to do, Father? Is this what Jesus would do if He were in my place?"

As hour glides by hour you will begin to *feel* God's love and guidance. You will feel your burdens lightened and you will be able to help others with *their* burdens. Yes, you will be able to help the weak ones onward and to raise up those who fall.

As the day nears its close your spirits may droop, you may become tired. It is then that temptation confronts you, it is then that prayer becomes hard. But still, where the need is, there God is, and He is still with you.

And, of course, before you go to your sleep you will feel God as the friend of the twilight hour. It is in the evening when you have laid your daily cares aside, when you have cleansed yourself physically and spiritually that you may touch the hem of God's garment of night. It is the time when you may feel that great robe sweeping over you—bringing rest to your tired eyes and refreshment to your tired soul.

It is then that the God of night reaches down from the dim unknown, keeping watch over you, His own, saying: "Fear not, my child. My hands hold thee fast and thou art wrapped in abiding love." That is the love of God for you—and that, dear Friend, should be your love of God.

That is what a day with God means. And you would find it almost impossible to spend such a day without feeling deeper and deeper spiritual understanding, without *knowing* that God does indeed answer your prayer of faith.

If you deeply desire it, that moment will come to you. And that marvelous revelation will come to you and make that day one of the crowning days of your life.

How shall you know that love? Words cannot describe it, for you must experience it to understand. It is a feeling of wonderful spiritual warmth, a feeling of un-earthly joy.

You may have been weary and heavy laden. You may have been burdened with sin and care and sorrow. You may come feeling how empty your life has been, how full of misery and pain.

Yet, in some strange way, God can make your mind as peaceful as a fireside before which a little child lies sleeping. In some strange way, while remaining in this life, you will enter into the joy of God's eternal life.

That hour will be God's hour. And in that hour, God will change your aching heart into a golden-domed temple of many windows.

Is your heart, then, still hungry for deeper and deeper faith, deeper love?

Someone asked a wise man: "What is the love of God?"

And he answered: "Give me a day to think of the answer." When they came back, he said: "Give me a week to think of the answer." In a week they returned to him and he said: "Give me a month to think of the answer." Again they came and again he said: "Give me a year to think of the love of God." They went away and came back at the end of the year. And when they asked the wise man, "What is the love of God?" he answered, saying:

"I am no nearer. I cannot exhaust the love of God!"

And neither can you, dear reader of this handbook. But it is this picture that you can have before you when you deeply ponder your need for deeper, stronger faith; it is this picture of God which is given to those who hunger and thirst for righteousness.

Let us pray: "For Deeper, Stronger Faith in God."

Prayer

DEEPER, STRONGER FAITH IN GOD

*"Blessed is the man that maketh
the Lord his trust"—Psalms 40:4*

O God and Father, how great and wonderful and
eternal Thou art! And yet how wonderful to know
that with all Thy greatness and power, Thou dost
know my name! Thou dost love me and care for me
just like a dear child!

How true it is, dear Father, that I do not always
understand the reasons for many of the things
that happen to me and my dear ones. No, I do not
always understand the reasons for the pain and
the evil and the hard times which come to us all,
dear Father.

But I do want my faith to be so great that I don't
need to understand — that all I need to do is
trust Thee — and in Thy good time all will be
made clear to me!

Sometimes when I am out in the world, dear Father,
Thou seemest far away. And then I sometimes
forget Thee. But please, loving Father, do not
forget me! For deep down in my heart I do know
how hard it would be to go through life without
Thee!

So please, dear Father, do give me deeper,
stronger faith in Thee. Help me to know Thee as
a dear, good Father, who is always near me and
ready to help and protect me.

That is how I feel now as I say this prayer, my
Father, and that is the way I always want to feel.
I will have faith, dear Father. I do have faith!

—Amen

ASKING GOD TO GUIDE, HELP AND PROTECT YOUR LOVED ONES

ARE YOU WORRIED ABOUT your dear ones for any reason? Do you long to set the feet of those you love back on the path which leads away from trouble and sin and upward to God? Are there poor, bruised souls right in your own family or among your dear ones that you yearn to help?

If there are, then the great good news which we bring to you like a flash of revelation in this chapter, is that you *can* ask God to guide and help and protect your loved ones and He will do so!

Time after time as you turn the pages of your Bible you may read His promises to care for your loved ones. Time after time, God has promised that no harm will come to them. And *you* can help in His work!

Here is a daughter who needs guidance; here is a father who will not attend church; here is a son who is in trouble; here is another who has gone from home to foreign shore. Yes, there are so many things with which you would like to help your loved ones. There are so many things you yearn to do that your own path may be cleared!

It is in moments like that that you just pray to be able to ask God to guide and help and protect them. You feel as Jesus felt, when He said:

"He hath sent me to heal the broken-hearted, to preach deliverance to the captive and recovery of sight to the blind, to set at liberty them that are bruised."

And so you, too, cry: "Oh, if I could only bring God's power to them." You *can,* dear reader! You can help them bring their troubles and problems and pains to their Father, the very minute you, yourself, put on the robes of ministry. You, yourself, must first put yourself under that help and guidance and protection.

Do you remember how Jesus helped, how He healed, how He guided His Disciples? Do you remember how he sought protection for all those who came unto Him with their troubles?

When they were in the wrong did He argue with them? Did He scold? Did He order them to do the things He knew were good for them?

You know that He did not. Jesus helped people by showing them the power of their own faith. He helped them by showing them how strong was His *own* faith! He helped them by showing them how deeply and sincerely He believed in the power of His *own* prayers— how sure He felt that He would receive help and guidance and protection from His Father!

That is the kind of faith *you* must have! It means that *your* life must show that faith. And it means that this faith must be part of your daily life.

Now there are three faiths which every one must have

before God can help and protect them. They must have faith in themselves, faith in their fellow men and faith in God.

So give your loved ones— the ones who give you pain and trouble—faith in themselves. To those who have their own problems, make them feel that they can do anything — *anything* — with God's approval and blessing. Make them feel that God has a place in the world for them. Make them know that all they needed to do is turn sincerely to God with their problems.

Give your loved ones faith in their fellow men. So many earthly problems arise because they *lack* this faith. Faith in men means real friendship. Such faith will make them glad and proud to be of service to you, to their family, to their friends, to their nation and to God!

But, most of all, you must give your dear ones faith in God—faith that God *can* and *will* help them. And it is right here that your own courage and faith must be strongest.

For you, too, must feel with every fibre of your being that you know God will help them. That faith must be part of your daily life—

and your daily life must show it.

How can you *ask* God to help your loved ones in whatever are their problems, in whatever is now causing you unhappiness? How can you help them but by showing them how to help themselves!

There is only one way to work with God in helping them. That is the way of St. Paul on the Damascus Road. Paul has just seen his vision of Jesus, and the first words which sprung to his lips were: "Lord, what wilt Thou have me to do?"

Encourage your dear ones to take this noble view of their troubles. Make it *your* motto in asking God to help and guide them. Assure them that what you or they decide to do means little, but that what God decides for them means much.

If they will but rely on God's word, then both they and you will be ready to face the world and its troubles and problems with bravery. You will face hard times and illness and disappointment with hope and with faith.

For have you ever thought that maybe you have gotten into the habit of looking at your family and dear ones in the wrong way? Surely you do not believe that God put them into your life just by accident. Surely you do not believe they were given to you just by chance!

No, dear reader. God *has* taken thought of you. He *has* taken thought of your dear ones and your family and your friends. He did so before He placed us in this life. We are all placed here by God's will.

Perhaps the husband and father is desperately in need of help and reform. Perhaps the son or daughter is disobedient or unkind. Perhaps there are others who seem like stones in your path.

All alone, there is little that you *can* do. If there is to be any change it must come from two sources— from within your own hearts and from without from God!

And while this wondrous change happens what *can* you do in a real, material way? Well, meanwhile you can *love* them. You can love them as they are and not as you would like them to be. You can love them just as your heavenly Father loves *you*—as *you* are!

Try and see how much there is to love and to cherish in your family and your dear ones. Open up your heart to receive love as well as to give it.

For, with God's help, you *can* bring peace and harmony into your home. You *can* encourage and you can inspire!

Is there someone in your family or among your loved ones who is "trying" you? Is there one who is causing you the most worry and trouble? Then start in to make life a little more comfortable, a little more happy for that person in whatever way you can.

Pray especially for that person. Pray for that one by name, asking God for special help for that erring and troubled one. You will be astounded what a spiritual return you will get from doing just these few simple things.

"Let your requests be made known unto God" and sometimes — perhaps rarely — perhaps often — God will speak to you. He will tell you of something you may have neglected to do. He will open your eyes to some new service you can render to help that person. He will invite you to some new joy or thanksgiving you can share with that loved one.

Commune with God about others. Seek to know God's will for them and work with that will. And prayer will give you the wisdom what to ask and the eagerness and ability to help.

Sometimes you will find that you do not know exactly what to ask for your loved one. But God will understand. He knows of your love and that is all He *needs* to know. If you ask amiss for them God will quietly say: "Nay" And He will rejoice with you when you ask the good and perfect thing so that He may say "Yea."

You may be sure that our Father who gives such great blessings will hold back nothing that is good for your loved one. Just trust Him and do not question the way in which He will work.

You have a friend who is far away. All you know is that his life is one of hardship and danger. In that place much may have happened to disturb his faith. You know that you could help him if you were with him and that you have helped him in the past.

Can you ask God to help him now in your prayers?

Of course you can. There are thousands of times when prayer for others has guided and helped and protected them. What soldier in the thick of battle has not felt his mother's prayers? What soldier does not believe and *know* that those prayers brought him safely through where God decreed it so.

It is not so much what you do or say that will help your dear one to feel God's protection, help and guidance as the atmosphere with which you surround him. You cannot hurry people out of difficult times, nor can you open their eyes all at once.

But if you have confidence that God *will* help them, then something of that confidence will flow in some mysterious way from you to them. Often all you will need to do for them can be done through a glance, a hand-clasp or just a few simple words.

The finest kind of help is that which is given before it is asked. You cannot force God's help. People must be ready for it. All you can do is stand lovingly by until you are convinced that help can come from no other source.

Then it is that you can bring God's help to them.

It is as simple as that. But you will be repaid a thousand times when you see the expression of relief and joy in their eyes when once they realize that at last they have found their Father!

For unquestionably from the man or woman of great faith something *does* flow. You can call it assurance, quiet confidence or the power of God working through them. But that something *does* have the power of comforting and quieting people. It does have the power of making *others* want to be like that.

A man lay very ill in a hospital. To his room came a total stranger. The man knew nothing about him when he came and little more when the stranger left. The stranger said little about himself and asked few questions. He just sat down by the bed-side of the sick man and just talked.

Not great talk. Just small, unhurried talk about plain, simple things—the weather, the lawn outside the room, some flowers in a vase. He asked quietly about the sick man's illness and seemed glad to hear the sick man was improving. Soon he left, saying he had been glad to see the sick man and wished him well.

After he left, the sick man felt a strange peace. Somewhere he felt that he had seen the stranger before, although he knew he had not. It was just something in the stranger's quiet confidence. The sick man knew the stranger had brought him his certainty that God would help him. He just knew that the stranger was living with God and had just placed him before his Friend.

That is the way of asking and giving God's help! Let us pray: "That God Will Guide and Protect Those I Love."

𝔓𝔯𝔞𝔶𝔢𝔯

That

GOD WILL GUIDE AND PROTECT THOSE I LOVE

"Let all those that put their trust in Thee rejoice; let them ever shout for joy, because Thou defendest them"—Ps. 5:11

O heavenly Father, our protector and guide, Thou art the greatest Friend and joy we have! To be able to come to Thee in prayer like this is the most beautiful part of our lives!

It is not for myself that I want to pray today, dear Father, but for those who are near and dear to me and about whom I am worrying. Thou knowest what they are facing, dear Father. And thou knowest the deeper reasons why these things have come upon them!

And Thou knowest how I want to help. Truly I think it would be easier if I could only face what they are facing. But Thou knowest how helpless we are to help another even though we know what is just and right.

Only Thou art left, dear Father. Do be with them in all things at all times. Protect them from enemies and evil, my Father. Forgive them their sins and put love of others in their hearts.

O do make them happy in their lives at home, dear Father, and help them live as Thou wouldst have them live. Above all, put love in their hearts for Thee.

And thank Thee, my Father, for Thy goodness to them and to me. Thank Thee for Thy love and guidance and protection! May we honor Thee all the days of our lives. And be happy and uplifted even as I feel right now!

—Amen

133

GOD IS THE TRUE FRIEND OF THE LONELY

ARE YOU SAD AND LONELY? Do you ever feel so forgotten and neglected that you could sit right down and cry? Do you feel that your life would be happier if you could only have more friends?

If that is the way you feel; if loneliness of heart and spirit is now your burden, then, in the words which follow, there is a message for you—a message which should give you the joy that God is the true friend of the lonely, the beacon of light to the lonely traveler on the road of life!

Do you remember the story of Robinson Crusoe— the tale of a traveler shipwrecked on a desolate island? It is the story of a man faced with the most awful fate which can come to a human being—the doom of being utterly alone! Not for nothing is solitary confinement the most dreaded punishment that man can undergo.

In some ways, all of us— and *you* are among us, dear reader—are all at one time or another cast away on our *own* desert island of loneliness—an island where you long for a friendly voice, a tender hand.

There is the earth-made loneliness of a forest crossroads, a sunless valley, a ruined church. But these are lonelinesses which human occupation can cast forth.

Your island of loneliness may be the physical loneliness of the last farm on the upland road, the last house on the village street, the topmost room in the crowded tenement.

But your greatest loneliness is the loneliness of spirit—the loneliness of the man or woman with no close kin-folks or friends, the man or woman in the small room with but the four walls to answer their unspoken words, the loneliness of the man or woman even in the midst of the swarming city and the surging crowd.

Loneliness of spirit is the waiting for the letter which never comes, the listening for a laugh which never sounds. It is the feeling that on this earth you are still alone—a stranger in a strange world.

It comes to you when you awaken to the fact that you have no close friend. It strikes you when you realize that so many whom you once knew have moved away or passed onward. It follows you when you are facing the sunset of life—when friends are gone, when children have departed, when you are alone in a house which was once full of laughter, but which is now silent and empty.

And it is the final loneliness which deadens you in the loneliness of bereavement—the almost physical ache which is more than you can bear.

Yet even this stone is rolled away. There *is* a one sure touch which can put aside loneliness. There *is* one kind voice which can whisper hope into your ear—the hand and the voice of God—the true friend of the lonely!

God is the true friend of the lonely because He has *always* been the true friend of the lonely. He was a friend to the loneliness of Abraham upon the mountain top, of Isaac and Samuel and David. He was the friend of the loneliness of Jesus when He went apart, the night before He was taken!

And from the loneliness which He, too, had felt, Jesus brings you the message that you, too, can know and feel the friendship and the comradeship and the love of God. Jesus whispers that not to be able to see God is blindness, not to be able to talk to Him and have Him talk to you, is unbearable silence!

Jesus is the doorway through which you may enter the friendship of God, leaving your dark cloak of loneliness behind. He is the door by which God enters into friendship with you, bringing His white garment of love. "No man," says Jesus, "cometh unto the Father but by me."

For loneliness is not something which suddenly comes to you. It creeps upon you slowly and silently. In your younger days, you knew the joy of love and companionship. In former years you had many joys and friendships. Yet somehow—in some way—things changed. Loneliness pressed in upon you.

It is against loneliness you must prepare while friends are still about you. It is against loneliness you must provide when companionship and friendship seem slipping from you.

Little by little you must gain strength of soul and love of God so as to be free from the passing of time. You can keep on loving people if you have always loved them. You can begin to love people if you have not loved them before. But more than anything else, you must make and keep a place in your heart which is a place for God—the true friend of the lonely.

God is eternal. He does not go away nor does He grow old. He does not change, nor does He forsake you. And so, should the time come when none is near, when friends have departed, when kin have gone their ways, you must fill what would be the loneliness of that time with the love and the friendship of God. You must have learned to draw close to God in whom there is no change and to the

spirit which maketh all things new.

But it is right here that a wonderful miracle comes to pass. The minute you draw close to God you can in no wise help but draw close to God's children. Loneliness flees from you if your heart is with God and His children.

If you will just honestly and sincerely try to live in the spirit of Jesus, then you *cannot* be lonely. If you will but believe that God is your loving Father, then you need not study "how to make friends." You will *be* a friend. And if you *are* a friend to other men and women, then you can never be lonely.

You make friends by just being friendly, by just being sympathetic. When you say: "How are you?" it is not just a question to which you do not expect an answer. You really and truly want to *know* how that person is— if they have a burden you can lift or a cross you can help them bear.

You will not always be thinking of yourself and so you will not be "shy." It is so often the people who call themselves "shy" who so often complain of being lonely. Haven't you noticed

136

that whenever you do not think of *yourself*, you are *not* shy? That you can meet people easily at those times?

There has never been a man or woman with a great faith in God who was ever lonely. When you lack faith you lack trust. And if you lack trust in God and in His children, then surely loneliness will be your lot.

You need not be blind to the fact that in the world many people will take advantage of your trust. You may sometimes be misunderstood, sometimes be taken advantage of, sometimes be cheated. But there is more—much more—to be gained by being trustful than there is lost in being untrustful.

For it is an unanswerable fact that most people *want* to be honest and kind and friendly. Most people respond to honesty and kindness and friendliness with the same things. Even the most hardened criminal, given a task in which he is trusted, rarely betrays that trust.

A wise man once said that the happiest man or woman, the least lonely, is the one who thinks the greatest thoughts. So furnish your mind and soul with great and solemn meditation. If you will make the Bible your daily companion you will live in a world of greatness and nobility. You will live in a world with a Father who is above the passing of time and people.

But most of all, you will live in a world in which the closeness of God is very, very real. You will live in a world in which countless people like you have suffered all the pain of loss and separation and still have known and felt that the soul was immortal and that God was their truest friend.

You will live in a world where it will be to God you will turn to solve your problems and to guide your steps. With faith in God, you will feel his wonderful sympathy and His protection so strongly that your own loneliness turns to quiet calm even as His compassion gives you peace.

You are not alone—ever—when God is within your mind and spirit. You *cannot* be alone when you feel that Jesus has come to save you from this loneliness. You cannot be alone when you know that God is your eternal Father and you can go to Him at any time with all your hopes and fears.

"Blessed are the uses of adversity," you may have read. Have you ever thought that out of your own loneliness may spring something much nobler and greater than many of the shallow "friendships" which seem to *you* to make other people's lives so full?

Have you ever thought that when you have passed through the valley of loneliness, it may be so that you can more deeply understand the loneliness of others? "Only the lonely heart can feel my sadness," sang the poet. Only by being lonely yourself can you understand the loneliness of others and count them as friends.

There is the story of the lady who met another one day on the main street.

"I'm so sorry to hear of Aunt Caroline's death, Mrs. Ferris. You must miss her very much—you were such friends."

"Yes, I *do* miss her," said Mrs. Ferris, "but we weren't really friends."

"Why, I always thought you were. I've always seen you laughing and talking together."

"That's so," replied Mrs.

Ferris, "we *did* laugh and talk together, but we were just acquaintances. You see, we never shed any tears together. People have to cry together before they are friends."

How true that is. You have to experience the deeper rather than the surface things of life before friendship can grow.

Don't you, even now, feel that your own loneliness has given you a greater sympathy and understanding for others? If you do, then you have found a truth which the poet so nobly utters:

"Art thou lonely, O my
      brother?
  Then share thy little with
      another.
"Stretch a hand to one
      unfriended,
  And thy loneliness is
      ended."

That is why faith in God, love of His Bible has always been the cornerstone of all friendship—human and divine. The feeling that in your love and faith in God you are bound together with so many, many other men and women is a wondrous one. And time after time, this feeling *alone* is enough to give you that deep sense of comradeship with others which banishes loneliness.

For belief in God, reliance on His Word, the Bible, gives you a real sense of brotherhood with all those many others who likewise believe, a sense of brotherhood because it is based on fatherhood — the Fatherhood of God!

This is the communion of the saints. This is an eternal wall against loneliness.

This knowledge that many of like faith are praying with you, are sharing the same troubles as yours with the same loving Father—this is your eternal shield against spiritual loneliness. For faith and tears and burdens shared lighten the load and light the hope of all who share them.

Shall we not pray? "For God's Comfort and Friendship in Loneliness."

Prayer

For

GOD'S COMFORT AND FRIENDSHIP IN LONELINESS

"I, even I, am he that comforteth you"—Isaiah 51:12

Almighty God, whose love is so much beyond my understanding, the greatest joy of my life is to draw near to Thee — to know Thee as my truest Friend and Comforter!

For Thou knowest, dear Father, that somehow or other I do not seem to make friends easily, nor keep them. It just seems I am left to one side while others have good friends and good times. Sometimes I have been so lonely I could sit right down and cry. O it makes me so unhappy that things should be that way!

Help me, dear Lord, help me to make friends! Help me to forget myself when I am with others. Let me wake up each morning, dear Father, with the feeling that here is another chance to be a good friend of somebody. For that is the way to make friends, truly I know.

Yet also teach me, my Father, that no matter how dark and dreary the day, I am not alone, for Thou art with me, Thy rod and Thy staff they comfort me. O it gives me such comfort to know that although others may forsake me, Thou lovest me always.

Why even as I have prayed I have felt Thy comfort filling my mind and my heart and I am so glad! I am so glad that I am resting now and can always rest in Thy comfort and friendship — and in that of our dear Lord, Jesus, in whose name I pray.

—Amen

GOD ALWAYS ANSWERS PRAYER

Do you ever wonder whether God always answers prayers? When you do not get an immediate answer to your prayers, does your faith sometimes weaken? Would you like to make prayer a greater power in your life?

These questions about prayer sooner or later arise in almost everyone's mind. Yet, if you will but open the glowing pages of your Bible, you will see spread therein like jewels on purple velvet, the many, many assurances that God *does* answer prayer.

For the whole Bible is full of wonderful prayers and the most wonderful is that Prayer of Prayers — the Lord's Prayer.

And even as God has answered His children in ages past, so does He answer today. Our loving Father never fails to answer the soul which sincerely asks—anytime—anywhere. Everyone who seeks will find—something. Everyone who asks will be given something. The value of the gift will depend upon your own faith and the earnestness of your seeking.

God answers your prayer in one of four ways—all of them loving and infinite in wisdom. God says: "Yes," "No," "Wait" or "Here is something better." So when you pray, do not look for just one answer. All the *others* are answers and often *greater* answers than "Yes."

True, when God answers "Yes," you are happy and thankful and stronger in faith. It is the other three answers of God which are sometimes hard to understand and which *really* test your faith.

Has God said "No" to some of your prayers? You will always find there is a very good reason for it. The reason may not be plain to you right away, but sooner or later it *will* be made clear.

For your wishes are limited by so many things. The peasant who has never known of anything more to eat than beans, can pray only for beans. He cannot pray for anything else of God's abundance for he *knows* of nothing else.

Or a small child asks its father for his bright, shining razor to play with as a toy. A razor is a useful thing when you have the capacity and the knowledge to use it. Yet would a loving father not say "No" to such a request? How many times do you think God says "No" to you because He, in His infinite wisdom, knows that to grant your prayer would be disastrous for you?

Even you, yourself, have seen this work out in your own life. Do you remember the many desperate prayers you made when you were sixteen and seventeen and now you see how foolish they often were? Do you shudder to think what would have happened if they had been granted? Do you not think a Wisdom greater than your own was at work when you were told "No"?

How many times may you have said: "Could I have actually prayed to marry that man whom I now see would never have made me happy?" Yet how saddened and disappointed, yes, and how you may have questioned God's wisdom at the time.

A man once said that he had prayed desperately for a certain thing but that if it had been granted, he would have missed the greatest blessing of his life. If your prayer, for instance, to go to South America in your youth had been granted, would you not have missed the one who has made you happy here and now?

Think on these things when God's answer is "No." Try and see God's love behind His kindly refusal. Far better, indeed, you will learn, to pray for what God wants to give you than to trust your own little knowledge as to what to ask for.

For there is never but one reason for God's denial of your prayer. That is His love for you. Time after time you will learn that the thing for which you prayed was denied only that God be able to give you an even greater joy.

When God answers "Wait" to your prayers there is a very good reason for this kindly answer. So many of us are like children who want a stick of candy even though a meal is spread out for us.

God does not want your prayer to be magic. He does not want you to regard prayer as ordering something over a heavenly "telephone."

Suppose you *were* able to sit in your room and order everything you needed over the telephone—food, clothing, amusements. Suppose that because this wish were granted, you never saw or got acquainted with your fellow men—the men and women who made all those things possible. True, you would have abundance of things, but how empty your life would be!

Did you ever stop to think what a weak spineless race of men and women we would be if our every wish were granted, our every problem solved? You have only to look at a pampered child to see the result. If all your wishes were granted, every problem solved, would there be any struggle? Why, there would not even be *love*—for it is *need* which calls forth love. Life would be perfect—but it would be lifeless.

God wants you to regard prayer as talking to a dear Friend who is eager and able to help you, but who, at the same time, is infinitely wise and who is trying to make you see the things you pray for even as He sees them.

God wants you to know Him and to love Him. He wants your life opened to Him. He wants you to realize His power, His wisdom and His infinite love for you, only that He may *give* them to you! To know God and to love Him will be a gift greater than any earthly gift He can grant. That is the supreme purpose and aspiration of prayer!

God asks you in your prayers to love Him in the same manner as you do your earthly friends. The better you know an earthly friend, the more you understand how he feels and thinks, the less he needs to explain why he does things.

How many times, in after years, have you been grateful to an earthly friend for not agreeing with you or for his firm but kind refusal to do a certain thing which he knew was bad for you at the time? You learn after a while to accept the decisions of your earthly friends because you know they are made for your own good out of kind and loving hearts.

Why so hard, then, to accept the decisions of God? Especially when those decisions are so often gifts of so much greater things than those for which you asked?

Columbus set out to find a shorter route to India. No doubt he prayed that he might find that route. God did not answer that prayer. But He *did* answer it with something bigger and better. He put the name Columbus among the immortals, for Columbus discovered America instead of the trade route.

What Pasteur, the great French scientist, started out to find was to help the cattle growers of his district cure a disease among their cattle. What he *did* discover was the cure of that dread dog-madness disease—rabies!

So many, many times, men have prayed for one thing only to be given a far, far greater thing by an all-wise Father. That is why you should not be disappointed that God does not always give you the exact thing you asked for. So often it is because your wishes were for so much smaller and poorer things than God has in store for you.

There is another reason why your prayers are not always answered as you wish. It is because you have not done *your* part! God helps those who help themselves and answers the prayers only of those who have tried to help themselves.

God does not need to give two answers to the same problem. God will not solve a problem when the means of solving it are right at your hand. It is not God's way to miraculously grant health without your first using every means which He has put on earth for the benefit of health. It is useless to ask God to remove an unhappy situation when you, yourself, have made no effort to change yourself so as to stop bringing about the situation.

For, when you come to think of it, how many of your prayers can be answered in no other way than through someone here on earth?

To pray for work means to pray that someone else may give it to you. To pray for health means to find the help of someone else—the right doctor, the right pharmacist, the right advice. To pray for guidance in most cases means to pray to act in a certain way toward someone here on earth.

God has to work through someone else to answer most of your prayers. In like manner, God has to work through *you* to answer someone else's prayer. Remember those words, dear friend—work and pray!

An old fisherman took a young man rowing. On one of the oars the young man saw the word "Pray." On the other he saw the word "Work."

"Why, uncle," said the young man, "what does anyone want with prayer if he works?"

The old man did not answer. But he stopped rowing with the oar marked "Pray," and rowed only with the other. They stopped going forward and only went around in circles.

"Do you see?" pointed out the old man. "If we pray alone without work we accomplish nothing; if we work alone without praying—without God's help we accomplish nothing. But if we work and pray we move ahead because God is helping us!"

So if you want an answer to your prayer you must be willing to be part of a chain. You must be willing to be one of the channels through which the prayers of others may be answered.

To receive, you must be ready to give. To be forgiven you must be ready to forgive. To be healed you must be a healer of others. To be prosperous you must be willing to give your share to someone else's prosperity. To be guided, you must guide where you are able.

Ask God for deeper love and the more you learn of God's ways, the deeper will be your faith and your understanding of His answers. Tell your Father everything. Ask Him for something and then be absolutely certain He will answer—not necessarily with the thing for which you ask—but with a love and a wisdom far beyond anything you could imagine.

For the condition of the answered prayer is still faith. Faith! The faith of a mustard seed. Dead seed has no power. Yet the tiniest seed placed in the ground and allowed to grow can split apart the strongest rock.

There is a mighty power in the seed that grows. So must your faith be a *growing* faith.

True, your faith may grow even from the seed of honest doubt. Still, beginning *with* that doubt, there is faith to be had beyond the valley. The best way to have faith is just to have faith—to believe without seeking for proof or for reason.

Not for nothing did Jesus tell us that we could not enter the kingdom of heaven unless we were as little children.

All you need is the faith that says: "Father, I trust Thee. I believe Thou answerest prayer even though in my belief I doubt." It is faith of this kind that will one day work the miracle.

It is this unquestioning faith that God always answers prayer that will release a power far beyond any you can now imagine—the power of deep-dwelling love and trust in your eternal Father.

Shall we not pray for that trust: "That I May Always Have Faith That God Answers Prayer"?

Prayer

That

I MAY ALWAYS HAVE FAITH THAT GOD ALWAYS ANSWERS PRAYER

*"Let us draw near with a true heart in
full assurance of faith"—Heb. 10:22*

Wonderful God, my heavenly Father, whose boundless love and help will never fail me, I come to
Thee like a tired child who has been a long while
away from home.

And O how I thank Thee for bringing me this quiet
hour away from the work and worries of my life.
I do so want to talk with Thee and walk with Thee
and call Thee my own!

Thou alone knowest, heavenly Father, how many
burdens I am carrying and cannot speak to a human
soul. Thou knowest how often I have prayed,
yet my mind was far from what my lips were saying.
Thou knowest how often I need the Faith that
Thou always dost answer prayer.

Give me that faith, dear Father — deep, true,
abiding Faith. Like a child with a loving Father,
let me place my hand in Thine. Let me walk closer
to Thee and walk in Faith. Give me Faith — faith
that Thou always hearest my prayers and always
dost answer according to Thy wisdom!

Help me, kind Father, to have such Faith that I
will feel it in the sad moments of my life as well
as the happy ones. Fill me with the Faith that
will hold me up on the tossing waters of life —
the faith that knows and feels that my every
prayer is answered one way or another!

Give me the Faith that will make me as happy as I
am now — as uplifted and thankful and rested!

—Amen

GOD WANTS TO BE YOUR OWN DEAR, CLOSE FRIEND

PERHAPS YOU HAVE SUF-FERED some great sorrow or disappointment. Perhaps you have been betrayed by friends in whom you placed your trust. Perhaps you have been hurt by some injustice, some hatred against which you have found it impossible to struggle.

It is at times like these, we are sure, that there comes to you a hunger to know a better and a stronger Friend, a truer and a wiser justice, a finer and fairer life than you have ever lived before.

Do you then yearn to turn over your sorrow and sadness, your loneliness to some Power beyond yourself? Do you then hope to see some life beyond your life, to have some Friend beyond your earthly friends? Do you then yearn to know God as a dear, close Friend?

If you *do*, dear reader, then the Friendship of God is described over and over again in your Bible. Jesus tells you time and time again that God *wants* to be your own, dear, close Friend. Over and over, He tells you what a wonderful Friend our Father is.

"What is the secret of your life? Tell me that I may make mine beautiful, too?" someone asked a happy, radiant woman.

"God is my Friend!" she answered.

To really know and feel God as a dear, close Friend, there is something which you, yourself, must do, something which you, yourself, must believe. For it takes *two* to be a friend of God just as it takes two to make human friends.

You must believe, dear friend, not that God *used* to be a Friend to men nineteen centuries ago, but that God is your Friend *today!* You must believe that not only did men and women know God far off in the Holy Land, but that you and I can know him *today* and can *always* know Him!

Perhaps you have come to think of God as a Being far away, a Being who used to come to this earth centuries ago with thunder and miracle, with lightning and majesty. But if you really want to feel God as a dear, close Friend, you must know and feel that this is not so. You must know and feel that God is in the world about you *now* and in the world *within* you now!

If you want to know God as a dear, close Friend, you must see Him and *feel* Him as a Friend. You must see God's friendship in the very commonest things of nature. You must see His friendship in the ripening of a seed, the springing of the grass, the formation of a feather, the wonders of your own body. All *these* declare the glory of God and show His handiwork!

But most of all you must see God's friendship in the happenings in your *own* life. You may have regarded God as, in some measure, the God of the poet and the singer. He *is* their God, but as well is He the God of the farmer and the laborer. You may have thought of God as the God of the minister and

the speaker. He *is*, but He is no less the God of the housewife and the lonely widow. God is the God and the Friend of the ordinary man and woman. He is *your* Friend!

Sometimes you may have thought that God reveals Himself only at certain consecrated places—the church, the grave, the mountain top, the place of prayer. It is true that He *does* reveal Himself there—for those are the places you would *want* a dear close friend to be.

But God is also your Friend while you are at home, yes, while you are *away* from home; while you are working in field or factory, while you are resting or playing; while you toss in sleepless anxiety!

Sometimes you may have felt that God is present only at the unusual times of your life—at birth, at death, at weddings, at consecrations. Yes, He *is* present then, just as any good friend would be.

But He is no less present at the simple, ordinary happenings of your life—when you walk abroad, when you visit the house of a sick friend, when you sit before the fire, when you go about your errands, when you lie down to sleep.

So do not wait for the unusual times and places and activities to bring you the revelation of God's friendship for you, but rather look for Him not without, but within.

The voice of God, your dear Friend, is speaking when you choose the good deed rather than the bad; when you are sorry for what hurt you may have done. The voice of God, your dear Friend, speaks when you do an unselfish service, when you feel pity for the sorrowing or forgiveness for one who has sinned.

And the wonderful thing about your dear Friend, God, is this: earthly friends become strange, they move away or they die. But God's friendship never changes, it is eternal.

It is like the story of the two hunters who were driven during a great storm to the shelter of a cave in the mountains. It was night when they came out and all the familiar landmarks had been changed or swept away. But one of them

pointed to the evening stars and said: "They're just the same. We can find our way home by them!"

To believe in God as a dear, close Friend is very much different than just believing there *is* a God. Just to believe *that* is of little comfort to you unless out of it comes a longing for Him or a feeling that He is a dear friend whom you can know and tell your troubles to.

Friendship with God is not only the secret of peace and joy, but it is the secret of achievement. With God as a dear, close Friend you will find rest not only *from* your many tasks but *in* whatever you undertake. With God as a dear, close Friend you will know how to carry your burdens without being overcome by them.

A farmer was trying to raise a great stone from the ground with his bare hands. A wise friend said to him: "I will show you how to lift it more easily." The friend made a lever out of another stone and a plank. Soon, with a quarter of the labor, the stone was raised.

In the same way, when you know God as a dear Friend, He says: "Come, I will show you how to raise your sorrow and your loneliness, my child."

God's fellowship, God's friendship was never more clearly understood and pointed out as when Jesus said to His Disciples: "When ye pray, say Father."

Why, just the word "Father" paints a different picture of God. You *can* be a dear friend of your "Father." You can look to your Father as one who supplies your needs, as one who guides you and comforts you, as one to whom you can tell all your little cares and aches and troubles!

A man stopped at a lowly cabin in a remote section of the country and asked for a drink of water. Thanking the sweet-faced old lady who gave it to him, he asked: "Auntie, do you live here all alone?"

With a sweet smile she answered: "Just me and my heavenly Father."

She knew God as a dear, close Friend, just as *you* can know Him.

Yes, your life is full of work and problems and troubles. There are so many problems which seem to demand an immediate answer, there are so many things which take up every minute and seem to leave none for God, your Father and Friend.

But if you really and truly want to know God as a dear, close Friend you *must* put aside time to become acquainted with Him. And surely it *is* possible to put aside ten minutes a day to get better acquainted with God! In these golden minutes you have enough time to relax your body and your mind and your spirit. In these minutes you have enough time to open a little door in your life and let His spirit and His friendship flow gently in!

These few minutes can be an inner temple where you can each day renew your closer friendship with God. As the Psalmist said: "Commune with your own heart upon your bed and be still." Just these few moments of communion will give you such wonderful peace and balance that they will often take you through the most deep-felt sadness and the most difficult day.

Just to be still and commune with your own heart is to *feel* the friendship of God. It is *His* voice which you hear in the silence of your soul.

A Chinese philosopher once said: "Go often to the house of your friend lest weeds spring up in the path and you cannot find the way."

When you have a good earthly friend you get little greater joy than going to visit that friend. To listen to your friend speak or to speak to your friend is in itself a joy. In like manner, if you want God to be your dear, close Friend, you must go often to His house, you must speak to Him and listen to Him.

When you are with a good friend you do not always ask that friend for something. You do not speak all the time. There are moments, even hours, when good friends are together that no words are spoken, yet both experience wonderful peace and joy.

Prayer is the language of God, the language of communion with Him. It is mingling your little life with God's great life. It is listening to God.

Not long ago a man who was bowed down with trou-bles and debts and worries could stand them no longer. Although it was late at night, he went to the house of an old, retired minister. He rang the bell and the old man greeted him quietly and invited him into the front room. For a while the man poured out his many troubles to the old minister who listened sympathetically and quietly.

When the man had ceased speaking, the old man did not give him any advice, but just said: "Let us pray."

The old minister got down on his knees and the man did likewise. As the minister prayed, the man looked at him. His face was a fine, old face, worn by many years of not-too-easy ministry. But it was the face of a fine, old man talking to an old Friend.

The prayer the old minister prayed had no flowery phrases in it. It was the prayer of an old man talking to a Friend to whom he would rather talk than to anyone on earth. He re-told in simple words the problems of the man beside him. He did not ask God immediately to solve all these problems. He just told his dear Friend, God, about them and asked God to give His friendship to this saddened man.

As the man left the house of the old minister, he looked back and saw the little house with the lamp still shining in the window.

At last he felt what dear, close friendship with God meant.

Dear reader, let us pray for that Friendship. "That I May Know God as a Dear, Close Friend."

Prayer

I MAY KNOW GOD AS A DEAR, CLOSE FRIEND

"The mountains shall depart, and the hills be removed; but my kindness shall not depart from thee"—Isaiah 54:10

Dear, loving Father, whose greatness covers the whole, wide universe, yet who comest to me even in a little prayer like this, alone with Thee I am not alone. From out all the great vastness of space Thou comest even to me. Thou makest my darkness light and the light glorious. Thy heart beats with mine. Thy spirit is with me.

O dear Father, be with me when no earthly friend is near. Be with me in times when I can call on no one else. Be with me, Father, from the time I wake up until I go to sleep — and all through the hours of the night. Let me feel Thy friendship which is so different from all the other friendships that I feel.

Help me to feel that friendship so dear and close, loving God. Help me live with Thy friendship so that every day I can look up into Thine eyes without shame or fear.

Help me to feel Thy friendship, dear Father, in every sunset and every star that shines. Help me to feel Thy wonderful love, nearer and dearer than any other!

Yes, dear Father, help me to feel Thee as a dear, close Friend, walking with me today and tomorrow and forever and ever. And so I cannot tell Thee how happy this thought makes me feel, my Father. I can just stay here and be just the happiest person alive.

—Amen

23

THANKING GOD FOR HIS BLESSINGS ON YOU

HAVE YOU EVER THOUGHT of the wondrous power which giving thanks to God has within itself? Would you like to be able to understand how to thank God for His blessings on you so as to bring *forth* that power?

If you would, then the beginning of power is hidden right in the leaves of your own Bible. For if you will open its golden pages, how wonderful are the words which you may read:

"In everything by prayer and supplication, with thanksgiving, let your requests be made unto God."

Notice that the Bible does not say that you are just to thank God for what He has given you, but with thanksgiving let your *requests* be made unto God. There is no doubt that this means you should thank God in *advance* for your needs!

A stranger was passing through a small town in the fruit-growing section of the country. The folks were having a picnic, singing and dancing to the music of an old-fashioned harmonium. Stopping before a white-haired country woman, the stranger said:

"What are you celebrating, Auntie?"

"You must be a stranger," she said. "We're celebrating Apple Blossom Day."

The stranger looked around, but all the trees were bare. "But where are the blossoms?" he asked.

The old lady sighed. "They all froze last week— froze for miles around."

"Then what have you got to be thankful about?" asked the stranger.

She stood up straight and said: "It'd take more than a little frost to stop us folks. We had a mighty good apple harvest last year—and God helpin', there'll be apple blossoms *next* Spring."

Those folks were thank-

155

ing God as commanded—in advance!

For there is no one who has so much trouble but that he has not something to be thankful for. Someone asked: "But should I thank God because I am in debt?"

Yes. There *is* something to be thankful for when you are in debt. You can thank God for having sent such trustful people to help you. You could not *get* into debt unless there were those who trusted you. You can thank God people had confidence in you.

Even if for nothing else, you can still give thanks that you *do* know about God, that the way to His heart is open and that you can call upon Him as a dear, close Friend!

For a wonderful thing happens when you praise or thank someone for something they did for you. We are sure that you, yourself, must have felt what happened.

You must have felt that to praise and thank someone else just seemed to add to their spirit and their powers. People just seem to grow and blossom when they are praised and thanked!

Haven't *you* felt the same

way about someone who thanked or praised you? And when you were sincerely thanked for something you did, weren't you eager to do something *more* for that person that you might again experience that glow?

Don't you think we are justified in believing that God feels something of the same, although in a grander and nobler way, when His children praise and thank Him?

Don't you think that an earthly father, glad as he is to grant the wishes of his child, is joyful and pleased when that child shows appreciation? So, we believe, our heavenly Father must feel when we show Him we appreciate His goodness to us.

You can work no greater miracle than by doing good and praising and thanking!

A wise old man who had lived a blessed life was once offered the power to work miracles. He refused that power. He said he wanted to leave the power of healing to God, the power of leading the wanderer to the angels. He asked only that he be given the power of doing good without knowing it.

He was granted that

power in a wonderful way. It was given to him that wherever his shadow fell, whether to right or left or behind, it would bring good life and health and peace on whomever it fell.

To praise and to thank God is to send forth your shadow. If it is sent forth with thanks and praise, it, too, will bring life and health and peace!

When you praise God and thank Him for His blessings on you, in some mysterious way it raises your own spirit. God brings life and health and peace to *you* in greater abundance!

Praise and thanks freed Silas and Paul from their dungeons. They can free you, too, from your prison of worry, ill-health, fear and lack!

Do you want to have God continue to be bountiful with you? Then thank and praise Him for the things which you now have as *well* as the things which you hope to get.

How little do we really thank God either for His goodness to us or His gifts in the future.

A wise old minister once said: "I am sure that practically all of my flock who ever went to sea never came back safely."

"How is that?" he was asked.

"Well," smiled the minister, "whenever they went to sea, they always asked me to pray for their safe return. But as none of them has ever asked me to thank God for their safe return, I presume none of them returned safely."

Even in the miracles which you read about in the Bible, God always begins with something which is already there. In almost every case, He required that those whom He wanted to help, begin with something they already had.

You will remember that the loaves and fishes were multiplied from loaves and fishes which were already there. The widow who came to Elijah was told to start with the oil which she had in the house; the second widow with the oil and the meal!

In the same way, when you praise God and thank Him for what you have—when you are thankful to Him for what you have, no matter how small, He will *increase* that mite!

A great violinist while playing before a huge audience broke one of the strings on his violin. He kept on playing. Then a second string broke. He did not stop. A third string snapped, and the audience wondered what he would do then.

He stepped to the front of the stage and said: "One string—and God!" And he brought such melting music out of that one string that the audience sat spellbound until the end.

Just God—and the one small string you may have can bring wonderful music into your life—can bring you what your heart yearns for—can bring joy and peace and happiness to others. That one string is trust and thankfulness!

The violinist played with all his heart. And so must you, too, with all your heart give praise and thanks. You must really mean it and feel it from your heart. And those who count their blessings and are thankful for them will always find those blessings increase.

A farmer who always had bountiful crops was asked how he accounted for them. He answered:

"When I plough a field, I bless each furrow. When I plant a seed, I bless each grain that goes into the ground. When I go home at night, I bless my whole farm and put it lovingly into God's hands: I thank Him for the crop to come."

That is the power of praise and thanks and blessing to increase!

But be so thankful to God for what He has given and *will* give that you will be brave enough and strong enough to share.

Two men who had been out of work for a long time were cashing their first pay checks at the bank. The first man, after getting his money, kissed it and said: "I thank God for this pay." The second took two' one-dollar bills and a half-dollar, folded them together and put them into a separate envelope. He said: "I thank God *this* much. How much thankful are *you*?"

How much thankful are *you*? Are you thankful enough so that you want to help others even with the little God starts you off with?

Real, heart-felt thanks is more than just saying a prayer of thanksgiving to our Father. It always leads to action. That is why real, heart-felt thanks makes you a messenger of God

Those whom Jesus cured were more than just thankful for themselves. They went forth into the highways and byways. They not only thanked Jesus, but they spoke aloud of His love and His wonders. They lived better lives because they were thankful. They brought others to Jesus to be healed.

Were you ever healed of a serious illness by a good doctor? That has happened to almost everyone. There is no question but you were thankful to that doctor—that you praised and thanked him.

But didn't you generally do *more*? Whenever you heard of someone suffering from the same trouble, weren't you anxious for them to see the doctor who cured *you*? We are sure you even spoke to utter strangers about that good doctor.

Your thanks led you to help others and you never expected any return from them—only the joy of spreading the good news that others might be healed. And when you heard that someone you recommended had gone to that doctor and had been healed, wasn't your joy a wonderfully glowing thing?

He who really feels and expresses thanks to God finds it almost impossible to keep from speaking of the good which God has given. He finds it almost impossible to live anything but a true and good life. And in living such a life, more blessings are given unto you. So that starting with praise and thanks, you bring more and more blessings to yourself.

It is thanking God for your blessings in this way which will help to establish His kingdom ever more firmly on earth.

Do not leave thankfulness for the time when you are very happy only—when you are happy for something God has already given you. Thankfulness to God should be part of your daily life. Truly, you should try for thankfulness every day, no matter whether you feel that the day calls for thankfulness or not. Every day, if you will but try, you will be able to think of at least three instances of God's goodness.

The real secret of thanking God for His blessings to you is in offering back to Him—sometimes in hope and sometimes in fear—all

159

that He has given you, so that you may act as a messenger of His will!

Yes, thank God for a happy home. But in thanking Him, offer to take your part in the sacrifice of love which it takes to make a happy home. Your thankfulness for God's blessings means that you must be called upon to even deeper resolution that all these gifts be used in His spirit.

As you keep your heart in thankfulness to God, your life will become more full of opportunity time after time—not only to receive His gifts but to use them—and in using them to find your joy increase!

Yes, dear reader, praise God and thank Him and look with love and confidence for your answer to your prayers. When you pray, wait for Him to speak to you for He *will* speak! He will tell you what to do. His answer may be but a thought, a word, a picture in your mind, but if you have praised and thanked Him from your heart, His answer *will* come. With renewed hope you can step forth from your place of prayer, knowing and feeling that you are on the right road because God has placed you there!

Let us pray: "That I May Be Truly Thankful For All My Blessings."

𝔓𝔯𝔞𝔶𝔢𝔯

That

I MAY BE TRULY THANKFUL FOR ALL MY BLESSINGS

"Giving thanks always for all things unto God and the Father in the name of our Lord Jesus Christ"—Ephes. 5:20

Dear, loving Father, whose glory filleth all things, this is the time when I come to Thee, not with a wish or a plea, but with a song — a song of thanksgiving to Thee!

Yes, Thou knowest how many times I have come to Thee with questions and fears. And truly I am thankful that Thou didst calm my fears and answer my questions.

But today, dear Father, I want to come to Thee to learn to be thankful for all my blessings, for such blessings as love and health and happy friendships and home life.

Help me, dear Father, to be thankful for what I have — so that starting with that Thou mayest increase it more and more. May I always be thankful for these good things, dear Father — for my life and my living and for the wonderful joy of family and friends. And for all those who help me understand the wonder of Thy love.

Yes, help me to be doubly thankful for this privilege of praying to Thee, dear Father. But above all, may I be thankful for Thy greatest gift, Thy Son, our Saviour, who, though He was great, humbled himself that we might live more abundantly and be lifted up. In His Name.

—Amen

TURNING TO GOD FOR SUCCESS AND GOOD FORTUNE

WOULD YOU LIKE TO HAVE more success and good fortune at everything you try? Would you like to be more successful and prosperous? Would you like to have less debts and more of the comforts and good things of life?

If you would, then you have a fortune in a place where, perhaps, you never looked for it. Maybe a little story will show you where that fortune is:

In the early days of the far West, a woman who had never seen paper money came to her minister saying she was in dire need. She explained that she had a son who wrote her letters but never sent her anything to get along on.

"All he sends me is letters and pretty pictures," she explained.

"May I see one of the pictures?" asked the minister.

"I have them at home in my Bible," she said. And from between the leaves of the Bible she brought out a handful of bank notes. "These are the pictures," she said.

The minister laughed. "Why you have more money than all of us. You are richer than most of us around here," he pointed out. "You have a fortune in your Bible without knowing it!"

So have *you* a fortune in your Bible. Did you know of it?

You know that God has made a world full of good things. He put you here in the world to use and enjoy them. He laid down certain laws by which you were asked to live in order to get these good things.

These laws are in the Bible. They are the basis of the fortune which is yours. If you will only turn to God and obey these laws, then all the things which you need and want shall be yours.

Jesus had the answer as to how you are to get these things.

"Seek ye first the Kingdom of God and His righteousness and all these things shall be added unto you."

All these things! Yes, when you seek His Kingdom through unswerving faith and heartfelt communion, through loving service, prayer and work—then truly all these things will be added unto you!

The Kingdom of Righteousness is the kingdom of doing *right*—of doing right unto God and your fellow men. That simply means that for success and good fortune you must strive to serve rather than to seek; to give rather than to get.

For you will find that in practically every case where a man or woman achieved success, it was by rendering some service, some work for their fellow men.

As long as you look upon your work as something for which you get paid, just as long will you be dissatisfied and unhappy at your work, no matter how much or how little you may get. It is only when you ask God to give you a new sense of the value of your work, that you are

ready to step up to a pleasanter and better-paying task.

The rewards of better work come to those of us who know what we are doing, who find better ways of doing even the simplest things, who find quicker ways and easier ways of doing whatever task they are assigned to do.

Think on this relation to work. Have you ever studied the work from which you hope to "graduate"? Are you doing it in just the way you were told when you started or have you found out something new about it? Do you know the work of the task just ahead? Those things are your ticket of God's success.

A man carrying a heavy pack came walking along the railroad tracks and stopped at a lonely station on the line. The station agent asked him where he was going and he said he was on his way to Chicago.

The man was a foreigner and the agent had a hard time making him understand. "Don't you know you aren't supposed to walk along the track?" asked the agent.

"But I have a ticket," said the man. And sure enough, he had a ticket to Chicago. But he thought that the ticket gave him only the privilege of walking along the tracks.

The service which you render is God's ticket to your success, good fortune and happiness. You do not need to keep on carrying your burden when you know that your ticket entitles you to give your burdens to Him!

How we would like you to know and feel that the only obstacles to your success and good fortune are your own fears and worries about it!

When you are at peace with yourself, you *know* that you have enough friends, enough ideas, enough faith to do everything you want to do. In those moments you know there is a loving Father who can be trusted to love you and remove all obstacles to your success and good fortune.

Why, knowing all this, do you lose faith and get into a state of not trusting either yourself or your Father? Can it be that you sometimes forget His great truth:

"Thou wilt keep in perfect peace him whose mind is stayed upon Thee."

In perfect peace you will keep your face turned toward your Father and see His face turned toward you!

It is like the little boy who woke up one night, his little heart beating with fright in the dark, with the shadow of waving trees on the wall of his room. He cried:

"Mother, are you there?"

"Yes, darling, mother is here."

"Are you next to me?" asked the boy.

"Yes, dear, mother is next to you."

He was silent for a while and then asked, "But is your face turned toward me?"

"Yes, darling, mother's face is turned toward you."

With a contented sigh the little boy went back to sleep.

When your face is turned toward God and His face is turned to you, then you can go forward in faith and confidence. That is the faith that God *does* love you and *does* care. God will remove every obstacle to your success and give you every good wish of your heart!

Prayer to God for help means more than just asking for something you need. Prayer helps you learn *what to ask for!* Prayer is com-

munion with God in which you try to learn God's will and to work with that will.

From communion with God comes wisdom in asking. For it is not so much what you ask for as the love which you bring to God. How many times have you made short-sighted and foolish prayers? It would be strange indeed if we did not, for our minds are small and our understanding limited.

In an ancient city were two blind men, both of whom roamed the city streets asking help. The first cried: "He is helped whom God helps!" The second cried: "He is helped whom the King helps!"

The King was flattered. He baked a bar of gold in a loaf of bread and sent it to the man who flattered him. Thinking the bread heavy and unfit to eat, the blind man sold it to the man with faith in God for a few pennies. The latter took the bread home, found the treasure and had to beg no more.

The former continued to beg, still crying: "He is helped whom the King helps!" The King sent for him and asked: "What did you do with the bread I sent you?"

The man said: "It seemed heavy and poorly baked, so I sold it to my friend."

"Truly," said the King as he turned the beggar from him, "he is helped whom God helps!"

He is helped who has the *faith* that God will help; he is helped who helps himself!

When it comes to debts and other obligations, God knows you have them. His wonderful Plan includes them, too. When you turn to God prayerfully, He lifts your burdens and lights you on your way. When you follow Him closely, you will find the highway out of most of your questions of success and good fortune.

In the hold of the liner stands the engineer. He never sees the boat move. He does not know in what direction it is going. It is not his duty to know. It is his duty to tend the engines and do as he is directed by the captain.

It is not your part to guide your life through the world. It is just your part to carry out your Father's signals. He is piloting your

165

boat. And, although like the engineer, your work may not be seen by others, it is seen of God and rewarded of Him in success and good fortune.

There is a road to success and good fortune in the days ahead—the road of work and service and thanks to your Father for what you have. Are you ready to turn to God along the way?

God *does* care for your good fortune! He gave you that message through the Prophet Elijah. Do you remember how the widow was told to start with what she *had?*

That is God's message to you in your success problems—that you must start with what you have! There is not a single man or woman who has not some skill, some service, some contribution, something they can do for others which will be the seed of that good fortune.

Perhaps you have wondered whether there is room for those little things, those little extras which make life so much sweeter and happier.

You have but to ask yourself, as was asked so long ago in that Book of Good Things:

"Is not life more than meat and the body more than raiment?"

What a glorious promise that your Father wants you to have these good things! He didn't just promise you life. He promised you more *abundant* life. God truly does want you to have all those good things for which your heart yearns.

The jeweler tests metal with acid to see if it be gold. So must your wants be tested by the acid of righteousness. If they are things of which our Father can approve and find good, then the Source of neverfailing supply will send them to you.

On the table before you is a radio set. It is a wonderful instrument. Through it from the air come all the treasures of mind and music.

How quickly can it bring them to you? In the twinkling of an eye. There is only one small thing which *you* must do. You must turn it on and tune it in. When you do that, your room which was cold and silent becomes warm with sound and music.

In God's world are treasures of good fortune which you want. Right inside of you there is a wonderful instrument. When you turn that instrument on and tune it in, then your life, which may have been drear and in want, can also become filled with God's good fortune and success!

Your Faith is that instrument. Your prayer is the tuning in with the source of the wave of good fortune. As quickly as your faith and prayer can tune in on God's goodness, just as quickly will it bring you success and good fortune.

Let us pray: "For Success and Good Fortune in All Things."

Prayer

For

SUCCESS AND GOOD FORTUNE IN ALL THINGS

"Thou openest thine hand, and satisfiest the desires of every living thing"—Psalm 145:16

God in heaven, Thou art the wonderful Creator of everything there is. Thou art the Shepherd of the sheep on a thousand hills. And because Thou hast made everything there is, Father, lead me to where Thine abundance waits for me.

Thou hast filled the earth and sea with all the good things we need to make us comfortable and happy, dear Father. Thou hast placed them here for our use. And Thou dost offer them to us in return for so little — just that we seek Thy kingdom and its righteousness!

Help me, dear Father, to seek that kingdom. Help me to be thankful for the blessings I have and use them so I may increase them with Thy help. Help me to use whatever talents I have to gain security and prosperity. And help me to use whatever things I own in the right way so as to increase them.

Please, my Father, bless me with success and good fortune. Bless our home with happiness and our work with plenty and our fellowship with others with love.

And as I rise from this prayer to Thee, dear Father, grant that I may carry that wonderful feeling of Thy greatness right into my work and life — that success and good fortune cannot help but be mine.

—Amen

ASKING GOD FOR HIS GUIDANCE, HELP AND PROTECTION

Do you feel the need of God's guidance, help and protection in all that you do? Would you like to feel that God will protect you from all enemies and the evil which they plan? Are there obstacles in your way— standing between you and the things you want?

If you *do* feel like that, then the simple yet sublime message which this chapter brings, should give you new courage, new faith and a new start in life. This message is given to you in that Book of Books, the Bible. So simple is this message that it is almost unbelievable. For generations, men and women have wondered and doubted merely because it *was* so simple.

This message is the message of Jesus, who said that whatever you desire, whatever you want to overcome, whatever you want to do:

"According to your Faith be it unto you."

If you have ever been to sea, you will have noticed the tiny birds far out in the ocean. No matter how high the waves nor how rough the sea, you can see these tiny creatures folding their wings and settling quietly to rest in perfect security on top of the highest wave.

You may be a fearful, storm-tossed traveler on the sea of life. But if your Faith is in the eye which neither slumbers nor sleeps, you, too, can ride the waves of adversity and trouble and pain.

There are three different kinds of Faith which you must have to ask God for His guidance, help and protection. They are: Faith in yourself, Faith in your fellow men and Faith in God. Let us speak of them one after the other until we see how they form a bridge which leads from fear to faith to God!

It will help you to understand the wonderful source of God's help, guidance and protection if you will imagine with us that it is contained in a vast, wonderful, eternal reservoir of pure water high up in the hills. And then imagine all this help and power being held back by three flood-gates which only *you* can open. To bring this eternal water of help, all you have to do is open these flood-gates one after the other.

The first flood-gate is Faith in yourself. Not for nothing has a man or a woman's faith in themselves given them the power to accomplish time after time what has seemed to others impossible. There is hardly a figure in history who did not acquire greatness by having this faith in themselves and their mission.

Fear is nothing but *lack* of faith in yourself. You fear enemies because you lack faith in yourself to overcome them. You fear evil because you lack faith that you can resist temptation. You fear the future because you feel you will not be able to overcome what it may bring.

Faith in yourself banishes fear. Faith in yourself means that you believe your life, your work, your contribution is important both to God and to your fellow men.

Fear is this lack of belief in yourself. If you do not believe you can solve your problems, no matter how, then there is little chance you *will* solve them. If you are afraid of the future, then the future certainly will be black.

Lack of faith in yourself makes it almost impossible to overcome troubles. Perhaps a little story will illustrate the results of lack of faith.

The Golden Gate bridge is the highest and longest single span bridge in the world. There is a mile of it hanging over the bay at San Francisco. When it was being built, the bridge was so high, it looked down from its great height into the black waters so far below that the men who were building it—even though they were experienced bridge builders—felt a terrible fear.

The bridge cost thirty-five million dollars. There is a superstition among builders that for every million dollars spent on a bridge, a human life must be sacrificed. This had already cost the lives of five men on the Golden Gate Bridge, although every safety device was used. Men were ordered to wear steel helmets, rubber shoes, iron girder grippers and every safety device known to science.

Yet still they fell. It was FEAR that was pushing them off that bridge just as certainly as if it stood behind them as they worked. One day it was decided to put a "safety net" under the bridge. This was a net woven of steel strands like a large fish net. It was put under the bridge and swung from one end to the other. If any worker fell off the bridge he fell into the net and could be hauled back to safety.

Now the bridge was as high as before, the girders just as slippery, the water just as black and far below. But a wonderful thing happened.

From that time on not a single man fell off the bridge into the net!

Why? Because they were no longer afraid. And they were no longer afraid because they realized that even if they *did* fall, the safety net was there to catch them. When they lost their fear of falling they did not fall.

Faith is your safety net! Your work may be hard, the way may be slippery, the dark waters of discouragement may swirl beneath your feet. Yet once you realize that between you, and the dark waters of fear and worry is the "safety net" of God's love—you, too, **WILL NOT FALL!**

What happens, you may ask when you *have* that faith. Well, it is an old and true saying that God *does* help those who help themselves. God *does* guide those who try to guide themselves. God *does* protect those who try to protect themselves.

And now let us open the second flood-gate to God's help—faith in your fellow man.

There is hardly a problem which does not find its solution through the action of somebody else. In sickness it might be the finding of the right doctor, in work the meeting of the right employer, in personal affairs the help of the right man or woman.

And it is when you have

171

Faith in your fellow men or women, when you start living at your best, that God is able to help you by working through someone else.

For God's help, in most cases, does not come in the form of miracles. It comes through powers already in your possession. God rarely creates new powers for you, but generally adds to the powers you already have. He just lets those powers work upon others.

You can release God's help and guidance through the love of others, through living the Golden Rule. God will bring you His help just as soon as He finds someone through whom to work.

The third flood-gate is the best and the easiest to open. It is the gate of Faith in God!

How can you get God's help? By the simplest process in the world, the simple process stated by Jesus when He said:

"Everyone that asketh receiveth, Everyone that seeketh findeth, To everyone that knocketh, it shall be opened."

Yes, it is when you have used every ounce of your own strength, your own mind, your own courage; it is when you have brought the power of faith and love to your fellow men and women, that you are ready to draw upon the power and the fullness which is God!

A "rest" in music is the time between two notes. It is really a time of silence. As a great musician said: "There is no music in a rest, but there is the *making* of music in it."

You have hard times, heavy burdens and there seems no music in your life. God sends you pain and disappointment and illness. But may it not be that these "rests" in your life get you ready for the music which always comes?

In order for an astronomer to see the stars, every light in the observatory must be put out. May it not also be that God sometimes sends us burdens to bear that we may see *His* light? The stars are often seen best from the depths of the darkest valley.

Faith in God's help means the sure feeling that God is *with* you, that you can ask Him even when your unhappiness seems the greatest. There is no time, day or night, rain or shine, pain or peace, when God is *not* with you!

True, you may not feel His presence at all times, but neither do we all live on a mountain top. But God is always with every one of His children, everywhere, at all times, always within call!

If your burdens are just too much to bear, if you are in pain or sickness, if you fear greatly, do not try too hard in an earthly way to make sure God is with you.

Just be happy that He is with you in spirit. Feel that He is near in the same way that a dear friend is near. When you are with a dear friend, he does not have to keep assuring you that he is at your side. Even without seeing him, without talking to him you know he is there. Yes, sometimes the mere knowledge that he is in the next room, ready for your instant call is all you need to know.

Surely you know that God has lifted burdens from you before. Do you think that God's power and love was exhausted by the times that He helped you? Not any more than the stream is exhausted by the turning of one mill wheel.

That is why you must feel that you can call on God to help you bear your burdens. There is but one best way you can make yourself feel that God is with you, that you can call upon Him and ask Him to help you. It is the way of Prayer.

It is by praying and then going forth knowing that from morning prayer to evening prayer, from evening prayer to morning prayer, God has drawn ever closer to you.

Beginning with the call of your prayer, know and feel that God is with you. When burdened down, feel He is unravelling your problem. When you go to sleep, feel He is keeping watch over you all through the night so that you can lie down in peace and sleep; so that you need not worry or fret either during the watches of the night or the struggles of the day.

Just be happy that God is with you in spirit—now—that He always *has* been with you in spirit—and always *will* be with you in spirit! And know and feel that there is no pain, no fear, no burden which can long last if you will but remember this.

How best to turn to God for help? Go to some place of peace and quietness—an old church, a quiet wood. And if not these, then even to the quiet of your own room, where you can shut the door and the noises of the world.

And as you look up to God for help, empty your mind of all worry and care; make yourself stop fearing and fretting. Start to think about the greatness and the wonderful peace of God. Think of His power, His love for you—His care for you even up to this hour! And think on the old, old words:

"They that wait on the Lord shall renew their strength."

That is the way to turn to God for help and guidance and protection. The moment you do that, then God, who has been waiting outside your life to help you, will do everything that His wonderful power and love can possibly do!

Let us pray: "For God's Guidance, Help and Protection."

𝔓𝔯𝔞𝔶𝔢𝔯

For

GOD'S GUIDANCE, HELP AND PROTECTION

"The Lord shall guide thee continually and satisfy thy soul in drought"—Isaiah 58:11

My loving Father, Ruler of the World and the Universe to the farthest star, the greatest and the humblest rest their lives in Thy hands. And how glad am I that Thou dost listen even to me!

For my life has had so many trials and troubles, dear Father. I do things I do not want to do. And things I know I should do, dear Father, I do not do. Yes, Thou knowest how much I need Thy guidance with the many, many problems I have to meet.

What I have done, dear Father, I bring to Thee for Thy blessing today, for no work is finished without it. And when tomorrow comes, dear Father, show me again what Thou wantest me to do. Please, loving Father, help me and guide me, for I need it so!

Yes, Father, help me understand that what has happened to me here lately is still Thy will for me. Help me where I am weak and strengthen me where I am strong. Yes, Father, help me always to trust myself to Thee — to let Thee do the guiding and myself the loving.

Speak to me now, dear Father, in the silence and the peace that has come to me from Thee. For I listen humbly and will obey — with trust and faith and hope and courage.

—Amen

GOD WILL HELP YOU BEAR YOUR BURDENS

ARE YOU FACING TROUBLES, worries and burdens which seem almost too great for you to bear? Are you in pain or just recovering from an illness? Do you feel the unhappiness of your life sweeping over you until you are almost ready to "give up"?

If that is the way you feel, then this is one of the most comforting chapters in this, your own handbook of life. For it brings you the glorious assurance right from that Book of Joy, your Bible, that God's hand is true. That the hand that holds your destiny is kind. And that the time of dark is but the tick of a second compared with the eternity of God's light and love.

"I will lift up mine eyes unto the hills,
From whence cometh my help.
My help cometh from the Lord,
Which made heaven and earth.

He will not suffer thy foot to be moved:
He that keepeth thee will not slumber.
Behold, he that keepeth Israel shall neither slumber nor sleep.
The Lord is thy keeper; the Lord is thy shade upon thy right hand.
The sun shall not smite thee by day, nor the moon by night.
The Lord shall preserve thee from evil; he shall preserve thy soul.
The Lord shall preserve thy going out and thy coming in,
From this time forth and even for evermore." (Psalm 121)

Yes, pain and discouragement are indeed hard to bear. It is like climbing a mountain hoping to see the sun shining at the top, only to find the sun shut out by a still *higher* mountain. Just when you had hopes of seeing a little light you were plunged into more darkness!

You may get the feeling that you are living in a world and at a time which is not kind. A great fear may clutch your heart and you may think for a moment that this certainly is not God's world.

But such is not God and such is not the world. God does not stand far off in the sky while you suffer and bear your burdens. He is not stern nor cold. Although you may leave *Him,* God does not leave *you.* The minute you call on Him, He is there at your side, waiting for you—as one who loves you waits for you until you return home.

Two men were walking along a country road. As they neared the home of the first man, they saw in the twilight of his cottage a shining light. The man said:

"Do you know, my friend, I can tell that Jano loves me by the way she places the light in the window. There it is now!"

And there it was! A light of love in a wayside window. So you, too, may know you are loved of God by the way He has placed His Light for you—the Light of His Word and the Light of His Son!

God places a light in every window for those who come home to Him burdened down with sorrow and care. God places a light in every window whether it be the window of a lonely farm, a crowded tenement in the city or on a maple-shaded village street!

It is important that you think of this when trouble and misfortune seem to crush you to the ground. The burden may be too much for you and you, too, like some of the Disciples of old, may doubt. But it is right here that the Faith which we have so often urged you to cultivate will help you when it is most needed!

For Faith in God is never more wonderful than in your hour of trial. It is only then that you realize what a marvelous sure help and refuge that Faith in God is! Faith brings comfort; it brings strength in trouble; it takes the sting from misfortune and brings peace out of worry and confusion.

Faith teaches you that God *knows* of your burdens and that His love helps you carry them. No matter how heavy your burdens are—

even if they seem so heavy you can hardly bear up under them — they cannot crush you, for God's wonderful love will hold you up!

God's love will uphold you, even if you make the feeblest efforts to help yourself in your weakness and discouragement. This may be the very secret of your burdens — that you may make yourself strong to bear.

A boy once found the cocoon of a most beautiful butterfly. He could see the butterfly struggling to get out. But the silk of the cocoon made escape difficult. Thinking to help, the boy tore the silken covering. Instead of flying away, however, the poor butterfly waved its wings a few times and fell to the table.

Years later the boy learned that the cocoon offered just enough resistance to the butterfly so that in struggling to get out it might strengthen its wings. It was only when the butterfly had gained enough strength in its wings to break the silken chains that it would have strength enough to fly!

So may it not be that your burdens and troubles are giving you enough strength to break the cocoon of your earthly life? May it not be that God does not make things too easy for you lest you do not develop enough strength to fly with the wings of your spirit?

Dear reader, when you are faced with problem after problem, do try and remember that, like Indians who fight in single file, you will never have to face more than one problem at a time.

This is something you may have forgotten. You may say to yourself: "How will I ever get through this day? There's this and there's that which I must face—all day long and one thing after another. That is *too* much!"

If you will just try to live just one minute at a time, facing one difficulty at a time in the best way you know how and forgetting all about the others, you will be astonished at how much lighter each one of them will become!

And here is another thought which may help you through many a trouble. It is a practical thought—a little sentence for you to remember. And it had its beginning, so it is said, in this legend:

There was once a king who had a sun-dial in his garden. A sun-dial as you know is a round slab of stone on which the sun casts its shadow thus telling the time of day. As an ornament to the sun-dial, the king commanded his court philosopher to make up an inscription which he could look at during any hour of the day and which furthermore would mean the same whether the king should feel wonderfully happy or unutterably sad, some thing which would help him and comfort him.

As you can imagine, this was not easy to do. For what you might say about happiness, certainly would be hard to say about sadness and trouble. Do you know what the philosopher wrote? Four words:

"This, too, will pass!"

Yes, happiness on earth will pass to days of gray. That is true and while it does not comfort, it helps you prepare for those days. But so, alike, will your pain, your burden, your misfortune—no matter what it is. It always *has* passed and it always *will*. This, too, will pass. And if you will remember this thought, you will find it wonderfully comforting.

You may say right now that disappointment, physical pain are well-nigh too much for you to keep on carrying—that if just one more burden is laid on you, then you can never go on living.

"This, too, will pass."

It will pass because when you go through the valley of pain and sickness and disappointment, truly you need fear no evil; His rod and His staff shall comfort you. When you are sorely tried, truly God's love will take away your fear of the storm. His love and pity will carry you to rest in the harbor of peace.

For with God all things *are* possible. God can lift you from the depths of despair to the heights of hope. He can make you know and feel that your life cannot fail when it is upheld by His everlasting arms.

Whoever you are, wherever you are and whatever happens to you, if you are a child of God you can enter each day with quiet confidence.

This Faith is not always something that you can

secure with one whispered prayer, one day of hope, one night of appeal. It *will*, however, descend upon you just as soon as you know and feel that God *does* love you, God *does* care, God *will* help you to bear your burdens!

Some day — perhaps in the twilight, perhaps when dawn paints the sky, perhaps at work, perhaps at prayer — with a sudden burst, the fact of God's love will come to you!

Your ear will perhaps hear tones which are not of this world and your eyes see things unseen before. And behold you will feel the care and the protection and the love of God!

And with this love, you will find, will come new determination to use your own will power in your struggle for victory over trouble and worry. With this love and from this despair, you will find something deep within you bidding you to take up your load, making you dream of hope and victory even in the day of defeat!

It has often been said that your own burdens grow lighter as you share those of others. They grow lighter even if you *realize* those of others!

One woman said that whenever she felt that her troubles were the worst in the world, she would take a bouquet of flowers to a patient in the nearest hospital. What she would see as she went through the hospital would always prove to her how much less, how less painful, how much smaller her own burdens were.

It reminds one of the story of the village where it was announced the Angel of Worry would be at the village square to look at everybody's burdens. However, as each man and woman reached the square bearing their burdens and saw how much heavier burdens others were bearing, each was glad theirs was lighter. And each silently took his burden home.

To bring your burdens to your Father, you will find is the most wonderfully helpful thing you can do. "Take it to the Lord in prayer" is the title of the old hymn. Generations of men and women have taken their troubles and worries and laid them at the Lord's feet. And in doing so they have found peace and comfort and solace.

High on a hill, so the legend goes, there stands a gray, old monastery. At midnight, the chapel bell rings and all the monks arise to pray.

The prayer is for the sleepless everywhere. They pray for those who cannot sleep from worry. They pray for those who cannot sleep from pain. They pray for those who cannot sleep because of their burden of care.

Some night when you cannot sleep, when your back seems bent with burdens too great for you to bear, think of this legend. See the dim aisles of the monastery, the candles burning low, the whispered prayers of the monks.

But most of all try and feel the spirit of God hovering over this scene—hovering over *you*. All praying—praying, perhaps, for you!

Do you think it would ease your burdened heart to join them?

Let us pray: "That God Will Help Me Bear My Burdens."

𝔓𝔯𝔞𝔶𝔢𝔯

That

GOD WILL HELP ME BEAR MY BURDENS

"Come unto me, all ye that labor and are heavy laden, and I will give you rest"—Matt. 11:28

Dear heavenly Father, Ruler of the Universe, whose spirit reachest out into the endless skies and touchest the loneliest mountain peaks, I turn to Thee. I am heavy laden and I do ask Thy rest!

Thou knowest more than I can tell Thee about my burdens — of home and family, of health and prosperity. Yes, Thou who seest the fall of the lowliest sparrow surely must see the burdens I am carrying.

Dear Father, I come to Thee not in fear and trembling, but in simple faith and love. Just like a child turns to its father. Like a child who knows that help and strength are waiting for his call.

O dear Father, please do help me bear my burdens. Fill me with Thy strength. Teach me to be upright, clean and honest so that no weakness may gain hold of me. Help me draw so close to Thee that I will fear no evil ever.

Yes, dear Father, help me with my burdens just one at a time. And from the time I wake up until I go to sleep, please keep me rested and happy. Keep me always in the secret place of Thy love — where Thou givest to the heart bowed down — rest and strength and hope. In Jesus' name.

—Amen

GOD WANTS YOU TO HAVE A HAPPY HOME

WOULD YOU LIKE MORE peace, harmony and happiness in your home? Does it sometimes seem to you that things at home are just too much to bear? Is your home full of noise and confusion?

If it is, then it should indeed be joyous news for you to know that God wants you to have a happy home. The tenderest passages in His Book, the Bible, are reserved for pictures of the homes where Jesus entered and the families which made Him welcome.

And this, perhaps, is the *secret* of the peaceful and happy home — the home where the spirit of Jesus *is* welcome! For God did not put these precious souls of yours under one roof just by accident. He took thought of you and those in your care.

There is no family without its past and present discords. There is no family where the children are not sometimes noisy and unruly. There is no family in which others do not interfere and become thorns in your side.

It is during times like these, when things seem so full of noise and confusion that you may ask yourself whether all this sacrifice is worth while. But the family is a *place* of sacrifice. Without sacrifice there can *be* no family!

The very *fact* of your family means that you and your mate have chosen to live this way and no other. Yes, father would like to be able to pack up and go to that attractive proposition in California—but there is the house and the children and their schooling! Mother would have it easy if she could go and live with Aunt Eleanor in the city—but there is the house and the children and their schooling!

God has bound your family together with ties of

sacrifice and you cannot draw yourself apart. God wants the burdens of the home to be shared, to make the home a place of unselfishness.

But truly this sacrifice, this labor is *not* wasted. It *does* blossom in ways that you cannot see right now. There is not a mother or a father alive who would exchange the noise and confusion and disharmony of the early years for the *harvest* of those years!

A lady had a very fine rosebush, but one season she found no roses blooming. One day she noticed that there was a crevice in the wall. She went to the other side and found the bush had grown through and there her roses were blooming.

With God's help you can encourage and inspire those in your family and thus bring peace and harmony into your home. But the beginning will have to be made by you. It will have to come from deep within your own heart.

Walking down the street one day, a minister passed a store where the owner was on the street washing a large plate glass window. One soiled spot defied all his attempts to remove it. The minister walked up to him and said: "Sir, the spot is on the inside." That was the only way the window could be cleaned. That is the only way *you* can start to banish noise and confusion from your home.

Do you want to do something right now to start to bring peace and harmony into your home? Then choose today the most trying one in your family, the one who is giving you the most trouble.

Start to make that person a little more happy or a little more comfortable. And do not forget to make that person the object of your own special prayers. Pray for them by name and ask God for special help for them. You may at first meet ungratefulness from them and even unkindness. But the magic of kindness can not be withstood and in one month you almost always will see a change. You can hardly realize how much spiritual comfort you will get from this devotional service.

Just as little droplets of oil can banish the nerve-

184

wracking grinding and squeaking of a rusty hinge, so can little droplets of kindness smooth the noise out of your home life. Shall we give you a few droplets of that harmonizing oil?

Live within your means. So often the struggle to keep up with others brings discontent and worry. And these, in turn, bring tightened nerves, anger and quarrels. It is not until something really important, like desperate sickness or loss, happens in your family, that you sometimes see these things for the harmful things they are—breeders of nerves and disharmony.

Give the soft answer. It still turns away wrath because it still takes two to make a quarrel. If one of you will speak softly even though the other may say things of which they later will be ashamed, the results will astonish you. If noisy and unkind words have no wall against which to bounce back, they are lost in empty air.

Never talk at one another. Surely you know what that means. Father will say to the child in the presence of his mother, "Tell your mother she might mend your dress." Or mother will say before company, perhaps, "Some people in this house don't know what it means to economize."

That is talking *at* one another. It is pure cowardice. To talk at one another only means dragging a third person into your quarrel where you have no right to drag them. If you must say something in criticism, be brave enough to say it directly. No good wife or husband will ever rebuke their mate before others.

Be sure you are right. Never find fault unless you are quite sure you are right. And if you stop to think about it, you will be surprised to find out how often you have been wrong. Don't you know, deep down in your heart, that this is true? You are not the sole carrier of truth. The Bible says that even sinners may have the truth in them. So if there is fault to be found, find fault lovingly!

Be the first to yield. The home is a place of give and take. Stubbornness can cause so much trouble in it. Even if another person is wrong, strive to be the first to yield. Wrongful acts bring their own punishment. You can safely let God take care of the actions of others in His own way.

Never rake over old fires.

We all make mistakes. Once we have admitted them by word or deed, yes, once they have been *made*, they must be forgiven and forgotten. How much family discord is kept alive by continually raking over the ashes of old forgotten fires! How much trouble is caused by opening up old wounds, by bringing up things which happened yesterday, last week or last year. It is worse than useless and leads only to endless argument. "Sufficient unto the days is the evil thereof" it has been said.

Don't grieve over what might have been. Only God knows the future and He, very wisely, keeps it from us. Yet how much family discord is caused by "throwing up" to another what might have been done or should have been done in the past. How much inner discontent results by your being so sure that things would have been better "if."

"If" you *had* married another, things *might* have been better, that is true. But they might also have been wretchedly worse! "If" you had taken that job ten years ago, you *might* be prosperous today, that is true. But you might also be penniless!

It is a most peculiar thing, but human beings, like water, usually find their own level. You are probably in the best work, the best home, with the best man or woman, in the best situation for *you!* God has infinite wisdom in these things.

Love ye one another. How often do people outside your own family get to be more important than those within it! There is *no one*—no matter how much you like them—who must be preferred to your own family. Help and like others, to be sure, but your own family should occupy the central core of your heart.

Walk in the way. A wise man had the following sign engraved over his mantel: "Live righteously—God is present." Strive ever to walk in the way which is righteousness. Strive ever that husband and wife walk in the narrow way. All is not well in the home until God and His beloved Son have a place in your family.

In the Library of Congress at Washington is a series of pictures showing the progress of Civilization—agriculture, science, art, etc. What do you think the first picture is? It is a picture of a man and woman, dressed in skins, kneeling before an altar. The beginning of progress, the beginning of civilization, is the family—the man and the woman—and the altar!

For faith in God gives you the breadth of vision to know and to feel that your years on earth are too few to be darkened by temper and noise and cruel words.

Just as the flag in your home is the symbol of your love of your country, so should the Bible in your home be the symbol of your love of God! The family Bible should *be* the family altar, the core of your home. It should not be placed away on a shelf, but be put on your table where all can see it and open it.

One dear lady said it gave her a deep feeling of peace even in the midst of her household duties and cares, just to place her hand upon it as she passed the table.

For the Bible in the home points to the road of prayer and that is the road of peace. No matter how noisy the day, no matter how everything has been upset with confusion, the home in which the day ends with the Bible and prayer will be a happy and contented one.

The home where the child may hear the old, old stories of the Bible as it sits on mother's lap or father's knee, is the home where peace is already present. The home where the Parables and the sayings of Jesus are explained and thought over is the home where harmony reigns. The home where the Psalms with their majestic poetry and eternal truths are intoned, is a home where the peace which passeth understanding can well enter.

And the home where the Bible is closed and the family kneels in prayer surely is just a small vision of that heaven which is to be.

How many memories of great and happy men center upon such a home. How happy a child's memories may be if they are able to picture in after years their father or mother whenever they open their Bible. Yes, the bended knee, the uplifted heart, the open Bible, the presence of God in the home are the greatest messengers and harbingers of peace and harmony in your home, even when all else is dark and uncertain.

Your family is your portion of heaven right here and now. Sometime, somewhere else, there may be other things you can do, other places you can serve. But right now, God is training you and testing you in the family. It is in the family that the golden cords of helpfulness and unselfishness are being woven which shall bind you to one another and to God.

And it is in the family which abides by the commandments of God, by the love of Jesus, by the words of the Book, that peace and harmony will be found to reign. It was to such a family that the words were spoken:

"That good thing which was committed to thee, guard."

Let us pray: "That God Will Grant Me a Happy Home."

𝕻𝖗𝖆𝖞𝖊𝖗

That

GOD WILL GRANT ME A HAPPY HOME

"My people shall dwell in a peaceful habitation, and in sure dwellings, and in quiet resting places"—Isaiah 32:18

Our God, our help in ages past, our hope for years to come, I turn to Thee like a wanderer in the dark, seeking a way out of the noise and confusion of my life.

For Thou knowest, dear Father, how much noise and confusion enter into our home. Yes, I know that many of the words and deeds are not always badly meant, but they do upset our home so much, Father.

So today, dear Lord, I want to ask Thy blessing on all under this roof. Help us to love one another. Help us to be patient and kind and understanding. Yes, keep us from losing our tempers in arguments and noise and strife. Help us to bear cheerfully together any sickness, any sorrow, any hardship.

Bless those in our home who have tasks in field or factory or right here, dear Father. And bless any small children within our home and any who may have left it for homes of their own. Yes, Father, bless and keep those who have left our dear home for places far away.

Thank Thee, dear Father, that even this little talk with Thee has brought Thy spirit into my heart. I know Thou wilt answer my prayer and I thank Thee — I thank Thee for such comfort and happiness and peace.

—Amen

GOD WILL HELP YOU TO BE A REALLY GOOD AND LOVING WIFE

Do YOU WANT TO BE A really good and loving wife? Do you want to keep your husband's love? Would you like to be the kind of wife who helps her husband to be more successful in every way?

If you would, then here are a few simple suggestions which will help you work with God to make you a happy woman and a successful wife.

For marriage is a sacrament. And if you really want to be a good and loving wife, God will help you. His wonderful Book, the Bible, is just full of the stories of His daughters, whose goodness and faithfulness have come down to us through the ages.

You think immediately of Naomi and Ruth, of Sarah and Mary, the mother of Jesus. And there you can see how they, in their time, became beloved of their husbands.

We know that you, too, started out once upon a time with the wonderful dream of a happy married life. What happened? Can your dream come true?

For we know you did not intend to do anything that would make you anything but a good and loving wife. And time after time, it is not so much what you *do* that makes you anything else, but rather what you *are* or have *become!*

If you really want God to help you become a really good and loving wife, there are seven things you must *be*. God will *help* you become these things if you but ask Him in sincere prayer.

That is why in this illuminating chapter, we want to give you the *seven things you must be* if you want to be a really good and loving wife. They are so important that we are going to devote a great deal of space to them. Now we are going to tell you about them one after the other.

1. You must be your husband's confider. Have you the confidence of your husband? Do you ever discourage him from confiding his questions and worries and troubles to you? Do you ever say: "I don't want to know about that!" or "Don't bother me with those things!"?

Everybody must have *someone* they can confide in, even if it is about something of which they are sorry or ashamed. Welcome that confidence in your husband, even if it is something that hurts you. Be sure he can always tell you anything he wants to. And try to understand it. Above all, never repeat what he has told you in confidence. It is sacred!

Your husband's confidence is not too different from prayer. You feel your Father will listen to you when you confide in Him. So partake in this prayerful thing by helping your husband confide in you.

2. Be your husband's friend. Do you always treat your husband as nicely as

you do your best friend? Do you gossip about your husband when you would hesitate to repeat the same thing about a friend? Do you ever ridicule your husband before others when you would never do that to a good friend?

Try looking at your husband as *others* look at him. Try looking at him as a friend. You will find he is neither all good or all bad— but just a man with some good points and some bad ones. Be proud of his good points and pray for his bad ones.

How many women say, when it is too late: "My husband was the best friend I ever had!" In other words, be a friend, a "pal" to your husband. And ask God to *help* you be such a pal.

3. Be your husband's advisor. Do you ever say: "I'll take care of the house, you take care of the money-making!" Besides your sympathy, your husband wants your advice. Be the first he can bring his problems to.

Often you will not really understand what these problems are. But at least *try*. Make suggestions if you can, but even if he dismisses them, do not be angry. Don't you sometimes laugh when he suggests how the housework should be done?

What your husband wants more than anything else when he asks for advice is to talk about his problems. Did you ever think that this, in a sense, is praying? You tell your Father about your problems and it does your heart good just to *talk* about them. But suppose you felt He did not want to listen. You *love* your Father because you *can* talk to Him about your problems.

Don't you feel you will be a better wife if your husband can come to you with his earthly problems? For be assured, if he cannot get sympathy and counsel from you, he can always get it—good or bad—from someone else!

4. Be your husband's pride. A man wants a wife he can sometimes "show off" or brag about. That doesn't mean he wants a screen beauty. If you are pretty and he is proud of you for that reason, all well and good. But it is more important for you to be the kind of wife of whom he can say something proudly.

It may be only to brag about your cooking or your ways of economizing. But as long as your husband gets compliments from his friends about you, as long as he is proud to have them meet you, as long as he can brag just a little about you, so long will you be the kind of wife you want to be!

5. Be your husband's playmate. Men and women must play. Play softens the hard work and the everyday problems of life. Yes, we know you have children, household cares, meals to prepare, money troubles. But there comes a time when you must forget them and "play" with your husband. Do you "play" with him *now?*

Or do you say: "Oh, I'm too tired to go out. You go out." or "I don't like to go fishing. You go alone." You think you are being kind when you say these things to your husband. But are you? For we always play with people we like.

If you do not join your husband in play he will come to look on you as a housewife, a cook or just a nurse. And be assured, also, that if your husband feels you do not want to play with him, after a while he will not *seek* you when he wants to play. So join your husband in playing as *well* as praying!

6. Be your husband's lover. Now we want to talk to you frankly about a very important thing. Many a wife thinks when she is in her forties or afterward, when she has had several children, that the sex part of marriage is not important any more.

She regards it as something to be "endured" while she believes that attending to her home and her children are more important. Important as they are, we want to say in all earnestness, that while life and love last, the sex part of marriage remains *equally* important!

For the sex life in men remains important even to quite advanced years. And it must be equally shared, equally enjoyed. Not only must life begin at forty, but so must sex life continue after forty—as long as there is love and desire on either side.

And again you may be assured, that the day your husband does not enjoy his sex life with you, he will seek someone he *does* enjoy it with. These are harsh words, but many a wife has

found out how true they are to her sorrow and regret.

7. Be your husband's comforter. You know that your husband wants the world to regard him as a great "he-man" who needs no help or sympathy. Yet you know, too, that at heart your husband is still a grown-up little boy. Deep down inside, you know he is easily hurt and afraid.

Just as a little boy runs to his mother for comfort, so does your husband yearn to run to you when the world has hurt him. You must never make fun of this. You must never say: "That's your business" or "Don't come crying to me" or "You don't deserve any sympathy."

Yes, maybe he *did* bring on his troubles by his own actions. But that does not alter the fact that he is suffering now. If our Lord could forgive those who hurt Him, surely you, too, can forgive. You may have to ask God to *help* you forgive, but God *will* help you!

But be assured that if you deny sympathy and understanding to your husband, he will seek it elsewhere and will get what will pass as a fair imitation of it. So let it always be from *you!*

We have now reached the end of the important seven things we told you about. We know that to carry them out you may have to make many changes in your own life and your ways of living.

But you *must* know that God is willing to help you if you but turn to Him in all faith and sincerity. Ask God to help you do the utmost that you can to make yourself your husband's measure of all he wants a wife to be. And if you fail in your climb and slip back a few steps as we all do, then your Father will surely see that your husband will love and understand.

Ask God to help you not to forget the life you built with your husband, the love that blossomed long ago. Ask Him to recall the promises you both made, the prayers you said when you were first married.

For He has made you the keeper of the hearth and home—but more! He has made you the guiding star of your husband. So very often it is the influence of the wife as to whether her husband is a success or a failure.

You need God's assurance to keep you true to the ideal you have pictured for your husband. Your own soul must be restored constantly that you may have the strength to bear your burden aloft!

You *can* make your husband happy and successful if you will follow the precepts given in this chapter. Yet more important is it that you follow the precepts laid down by God in His *own* Book. And there is no better precept than the one you may read of the height and depths of a woman's love in the golden words therein given:

> *"Love suffereth long and is kind ... love beareth all things, believeth all things, hopeth all things, endureth all things. Love never faileth."*

There is the story of the wife whose married life had almost reached the breaking point. One day it seemed to her as if a voice said: "Pray."

That evening she said: "William, I know you may not understand me, but we don't seem to be getting anywhere with all this arguing and quarreling. I know I haven't been everything I should have, but I want to be different. Will you do just one more thing for me?

Her husband looked at her suspiciously. He asked: "What is that?"

"Will you get down on your knees and pray with me like we used to?"

His face changed and the angry look left it. "You're right," he answered. "I reckon that's the only thing we *haven't* done. We can't seem to talk to each other. Let's talk to God."

They dropped to their knees side by side. They opened their hearts to God as they used to do many years before. All their anger and troubles seemed to melt away. Both saw their mistakes and their weaknesses. Both got new faith and strength for the days to come. Each was united with God and with the other!

Let us pray: "That God Will Make Me A Good Wife."

Prayer

That

GOD WILL MAKE ME A GOOD WIFE

"They two shall be one flesh"—Ephes. 5:31

Wonderful heavenly Father — Father of all wisdom
and power — I come to Thee to whom all men and
women are as little children. I come looking for
Thy great help.

O Father, I do want to be a really good and loving
wife. Yes, for the love which Thou hast given
us, I do thank Thee and ask Thy blessing on it.
Yet sometimes I feel I could be more and do more
for my husband.

I don't want to pray in pride, dear Father, for I
know I am human and have many faults. And maybe
in ways I do not understand, I have not always
been what I would like to be for my husband. If
that is true, my Father, O please show me how I
can change.

Please do help me to be more loving and kind and
patient. Help me to think out what I must do as if it
were happening to somebody else. And I know if
I do my part and really try in the ways I have
now learned — I know that Thy power and love will
help me!

Now that I have told Thee my little secret, dear
Father, I feel so much better. Truly I know Thou
wilt send Thy messenger to my loved one and let
him know in some way how I feel and how I am trying.
And this makes Thy peace and love just enter into
my heart and life at this very minute. And I thank
Thee, dear Father, I thank Thee for that joy.

—Amen

ASKING GOD TO HELP YOU
INFLUENCE OTHER PEOPLE

THERE COMES A TIME IN the life of every one of us when we are faced with the problem of trying to get other people to do something which we feel is best for them.

They may be dear ones whose bad habits are making us unhappy and which we are trying to weed out. They may be mean or unjust to us and we are trying to bring them to their senses of justice and kindness. It may be that we are just trying to make our journey through life a little more pleasant by learning how to get along with others.

When you think about it, what you are really trying to do is to influence people. If that is your problem, dear reader, then if there ever was an example of influence, you have it before you in that Life which is portrayed so wonderfully in your Bible—the life and influence of Jesus!

For you must remember that in His lifetime and, yes, for all the centuries since, Jesus has influenced millions of people, and the end is not yet. Have you ever thought *how* He influenced them? Did He argue with them, scold them, order them to do what He knew was best? You know He did not.

Do you remember the way that Jesus influenced others? By His own life and His words. And by His deep abiding faith that His Father was sharing His responsibility and His work.

Do you recall the Parables? When Jesus wanted to illustrate a point, to influence one of His Disciples to do a certain thing, He sat down and told a little story which is called a Parable.

He did not even mention the fault which may have existed. He did not upbraid or scold the person to whom He was speaking. When He finished the little story, you will remember, He would mildly ask which was the better choice of action. And the Disciple to whom it was told understood what Jesus was so gently suggesting. Time after time the Disciples were set back in that way on the road to salvation and peace.

The Parables picture Jesus as a humble man. He did not tell the little stories as His own adventures, His own opinions. Do *you* want to influence others? Then be humble in the way Jesus was humble. Confess your own faults and understand them well before you try to influence the life of another.

Show the person to whom you are speaking that you are not standing on a high pedestal, but are human— with the same longings and weaknesses—but that through the wondrous power which God has given you, you have been able to *overcome* these weaknesses.

Love ye one another. The moral of all of the Parables of Jesus was the power of love. Jesus could see good in the Samaritan who was despised by all, in the publican who was repentant. Don't try to change people because changing them would just make *you* more

comfortable. Desire to change people, to influence them because you *love* them and wish them well.

"Speak not the fault in man." Jesus did not speak the fault in man. He knew that deep down in their hearts, most people realize well enough what their habits and faults are. If you show you know and understand, yet condemn not, people will try with all their might to live up to that faith in them.

"Neither do I condemn thee." Even to a great sinner, Jesus said that. "Go and sin no more." Because Jesus well knew the soothing power of considering other people's feelings. How often do *you* consider the feelings of those whom you are trying to change or influence?

There are some things which make you unhappy— things like personal failure and pain and sickness. But the habits and the words and the actions of others have no power to make you unhappy if you will but remember that in most cases they are not directed at you at all.

It may be true that some people have been mean and unjust to you. And can you question that for some of those things you, too, have been in part responsible? Can you question that you, yourself, have said things that were not always fine and just, that you did things that were not always well considered?

Even with all that being true, however, you are in no way responsible for many, if not most of the mean and unjust things said and done to you. Why was it that someone took an instant dislike to you when you had hardly spoken a word to them? Why was it that someone deliberately insulted you and you racked your brains trying to figure out the reason?

You were looking for the fault in yourself. But the fault is not *always* in yourself. The same injustice, the same meanness, would have struck *anyone* who had appeared before the person who was mean. Nothing you could have said or done would have stopped it.

If you *were* responsible for the meanness, then no one would have to tell you what to do. But if you are not responsible, then a great deal of your unhappiness over other people's meanness and bad habits would be banished if you will but remember that *you are not always responsible!*

Certainly many people were mean and unjust to Jesus. But do you recall what He did? He did not bear all the load Himself. Certainly He pitied people who were so blind they could not see. But He also took it for granted, as you must, that He would *meet* undeserved injustice and meanness.

But He did *more.* He expected His Father to share the load. He said: "Father, forgive them for they know not what they do." He gave God a part in His life.

While it is true that God wants you to do your best to care for people, to help people to break bad and destructive habits such as drinking or gambling or swearing or smoking, you may be sure that God did not delegate you as the only one to cure the evils of the world.

One day a group of old timers were sitting in front of the general store when a high-hatted, silk-frocked reformer was rushing around the village square, mopping his brow, arguing and in general competing with the busy beaver for activity. Grandpa Ferris pointed him out, saying:

"There goes Ed Emerson

attendin' single-handed to the salvation of the country."

Do not think of yourself as the only one responsible for the life and habits of another—even someone dear to you. Often they may be the nearest and dearest in your family, but they, too, have their own lives to live for good or evil.

You can remind yourself—and it will take a great deal of your unhappiness away—that God, too, has plans for that erring one. You can remind yourself that while you are doing your best to influence them for good, God, also, is doing *His* share.

Let God help you influence others by leaving your dear ones *to* Him. Such faith that God will bring them to the light, will enable you to overcome so many of your fears about them and live hopefully with them.

Such faith in God's power to help you will mean much to you. If you can draw upon this great, unseen Power through your sincere prayer, then you will indeed receive your answer. Prayer brings you this answer not so much by changing the dear one about whom you pray, but rather by delivering you, yourself, from their power to hurt you or make you unhappy.

If you have a dear one with a bad habit, much of your worry and unhappiness usually comes from worrying and wondering what "people will think." You get the feeling that everybody is talking about things at your house—how this one drinks, how that one gambles, and so on.

It will ease your unhappiness to remember that this is not true. Most people have "troubles of their own" ... too many to give so much thought to yours. You would be surprised how little people think about the bad habits of those you love, but how little they think about *yours* and *you!*

So don't worry too much or feel too badly about what people are saying when someone dear to you has a bad habit. People are so busy about their own affairs that they can spare only a very small part of their lives to thinking about others. From many standpoints, this is unfortunate, but from this standpoint in the habits of others, it is fortunate for you and helpful to remember.

Once a newspaper published some very insulting

things about a man who was trying to start a movement which he believed would benefit his fellow citizens. He went to a wise old man who often had things of this nature printed about him.

"What shall I do?" he asked, shaking with rage and thrusting the paper before the older man. "Shall I sue the paper? Shall I offer to fight the writer? Shall I put an advertisement in the same paper denying it?"

The older man answered quietly: "Don't do anything."

"Don't do *anything*? But think of all the people who will be talking about me when they read that!"

"I *am* thinking of them," said the older man. "Do you see that article? Well, half the readers of that paper never saw it. Half of those who saw it read the headline only. Half of those who read the article never heard of you and don't care one way or the other. Half of those who care one way or the other didn't believe it. And half of those who *did* believe it will forget all about it and you tomorrow. How many people do you think are left to do all that talking?"

Well, dear reader, that ought to convince you that other people are not "talking about things at your house" as much as you think.

Do you really want to influence a dear one, to get them to break habits which are making you unhappy, to live a life which will make all of you happy?

Then give God a greater part in your life, as Jesus did. There are those who think the minister is the only one who has been given the power to receive help and power from God. The minister would be the first to tell you that this is not so. Time and time again plain, ordinary individuals like you and me have been able to partake of the powers to move others given by God.

For faith in God's help does many important things for you. It helps you overcome your fear of the results of bad habits. It helps you live hopefully, knowing that in His own good time, God will work in His own way to bring light. It makes it impossible for those with bad habits to make you too unhappy and it makes it possible for you to look confidently to God for the changes which are sure to come.

Faith in God brings a new

power to you—a power upon which you can draw through deep, sincere prayer. This faith will support you if you but remember that there is One who is ready to help you when all else fails. This is the realest of strength from within.

You can talk to God in deep, sincere prayer. You can go to Him as a child goes to its parents for advice. You can listen to His answers as you meditate. And time after time, all will become clear to you as the morning sun rising over the mountains.

Let us pray: "That God Will Grant Me the Power to Influence Others."

𝕻𝖗𝖆𝖞𝖊𝖗

That

GOD WILL GRANT ME POWER TO INFLUENCE OTHERS

"Be thou an example of the believers, in word, in conversation, in charity, in spirit, in faith, in purity"—1 Tim. 4:12

Dear Father of us all, Maker of the night and day, how I thank Thee that I can come to Thee in prayer like this—and make so many things which were dark become clear to me!

I do not need to tell Thee, dear Father, that there are those among us who are not walking in Thy path. There are some who need to be changed. And it seems that I am the only one who sees this clearly and must try to influence them.

I do not judge, lest I be judged, dear Father, but truly I need Thy help in influencing these others. Not for myself, Father, but that they may be shown how to do what is right. Show me what is Thy will for them, dear Father, that I may get them to carry it out.

And guide and influence me, my Father, that I may be an example of the right way. Help me to understand that people must trust me if I want to show them the way. Help me to be patient with them for I know this is so important.

Yes, dear Father, I know it is hard to break old habits and change other people. But Thou knowest this must be done if things are to be different. And that is why I do so need Thy loving help.

And this I ask in the name of Thy Son who led the multitude to salvation and joy and glory.

—Amen

GOD WILL HELP YOU FIND WORK

Do YOU SOMETIMES THINK you are in the wrong work? Or do you often feel that you ought to have more pay for the work you are doing? Would you like to feel that you are in the right work for *you?*

If you *would,* then this may perhaps be one of the most helpful chapters in this, your Handbook of Life. For it shows you how wonderfully God moves to help you find the right work for you and to reward you for it!

In the first place, there is no such thing as the wrong place for anybody. All work, well and faithfully performed is right and good. The work you do—whatever it may be—is good even though it may not be the right work for *you.*

You will not make such a great mistake by doing the wrong work as by not finding *out* that it is the wrong work for you. It is when you

do find out that your problems arise.

Yet we know what so often happens. You have put so much thought and time and strength into what you have done. And then you are faced with the question as to whether you should give it up and try some other kind of work.

Yes, it is better to try some other kind of work if you can. Providing, of course, that you make sure that your new work will not give you the same problems which your old work gave. We shall talk about that later.

But suppose—as most always happens — that you *cannot* change your work. Suppose you are tied to it by experience, by age, by family responsibility? What can you do *then* to ease your problems?

Well, in the first place, you can convince yourself that no matter what other work you might get, most of the things you dislike about your present work will also probably be present.

The same day-after-day tasks will be part of your new job, too. It is this routine, this daily "grind" which so often makes us dissatisfied with our work and makes us think it is the wrong work for us.

If you visit the Empire State Building in New York City, they will give you statistics about that enormous building. There are 6,500 windows in the building and it takes a large number of window cleaners to clean them. They spend all their time on that job. They start from the upper floors and when the first floor windows are cleaned one hundred and two floors below, they must start all over again.

That is a routine job if there ever was one. It seems just an endless routine of pails and mops and water.

But it is not the only routine job. Most of us have routine jobs. The machine worker turns out the same pieces day after day. The grocery clerk sells the same things to the same people day after day. The housekeeper cleans the same rooms, washes the same dishes, makes the same beds day after day.

Even the professional worker is not free of routine. The teacher starts out in the fall back where she started the year before, with a new class. The doctor sees the same colds and sore throats and stomach aches year after year.

No matter what you believe, there is hardly a job which does not require that you do the same thing over and over again each day, year in and year out. So if you are dissatisfied because you are doing routine work, you have plenty of company. For almost everybody in this world has the same kind of a job. There are few others.

Changing your work to get rid of routine is not the answer to your problem of right work.

But there *is* one thing you can prove to yourself—no matter what your job or what you do. You can look upon it as carrying out God's plan for your life. That is an old expression, isn't it and you have heard it before. God's plan for your life!

Sometimes you may have got the impression that after

everybody's name God wrote something like: "Robert Jones—to be a carpenter" "Helen Howard—to be a housewife" "William Smith—to be a clerk" "Jane Robinson—to be a teacher."

We do not believe that is what God intended. God did not definitely assign some one job to everyone. He did not lay down rules which said: "This man or this woman is to do this work and no other."

Do you know what God did write after each name? "This man to be a man" and "This woman to be a woman!"

God has decreed that all should work. Right in the first Chapter of the Bible you have read that. But we believe that God wants us to work for only two reasons. First that you may use all the powers which he has given you. And second that through work you may help others.

Sometimes you can develop more of your powers by changing your work. When that is the case, God will see that you change it. Sometimes you can help others more by changing your work. And when you *can* help others, God will

help you change it. But for *those two reasons only!* If you want to change for any *other* reason, you will find that you have *made* no change.

That is where the question of more money for your work comes in. If you believe you should have more money for your work, God will help you get it *for those two reasons only!* He will help you get more money *when* you develop more of the powers He gave you *or* when your work helps *others* more.

You can get more money, as a rule, by doing that right in the work in which you are now engaged. If you develop more powers, it will be worth more to your employer. If your work helps others more—and this includes your employer and those you must serve—then God will see to it that you are justly rewarded.

For God is interested only in what you *are* and not in what you *do.* You may search the Scriptures from cover to cover and never find that Jesus asked any man or woman what they did as a condition for His prayers or His help. But often and often He asked what a man or a woman *was!*

206

And what you *are* comes from what you made of the work you have done. God would rather see you faithful in your work than successful in the worldly meaning of the term. "Be thou faithful unto death, and I will give thee a crown of life." Rev. 2:10

God wants to know where you are traveling rather than how fast you get there or how far it may be. Small, daily duties faithfully performed mean more in God's sight than sudden spurts of things done once in a while. And the results of any work—whether it be the ordinary tasks of life or the exceptional achievements—come as the total of small things done every day—faithfully and cheerfully.

A great bar of steel was hung from the roof by a cable. Next to it a cork was suspended by a silk thread. A scientist struck the steel bar by swinging the cork against it once every second. At first nothing happened. But after a few hours the great bar began to quiver. After a few days it began to move ever so slightly. In a month it began to sway. And in several months it was swaying under the almost imperceptible strokes of the tiny cork.

The flowering of your work may come just as unnoticeably and slowly. In the process you may very often feel that you have worn yourself out—that you are a failure. It is a feeling that comes to every one of us.

An old wood carver stood looking at what was once a fine, sharp knife. Its edge was dull and worn and it could no longer cut. Yet he placed it lovingly in a velvet box in a cabinet and said:

"It means much to me because it has worn itself out making the beautiful carvings for which people have praised me. It has worn itself out making beauty for others."

Was the tool a failure? You know it was not. *You* can mean much — very much—to God when you are worn out making beauty for others!

You have read of soldiers who have fought a rearguard action in order that their comrades might retire to stronger positions, while they delayed the enemy. They do not even *expect* victory. They expect *defeat!* Yet are they failures? They triumph because they fight and fall that others might live!

So you, too, have worked and struggled and worn yourself out in what may have seemed to you to have been hard and drudging work. Yet if you have used yourself to make beauty for others and to serve others, then you may be sure that God will say: "Well done, thou good and faithful servant."

Even in these days of changing war and reconstruction work, the same yard-stick applies. The question arises as to where you can be of best service. And the answer is: in those things which serve others best. And this means whether we have fought on distant fields or whether we are working on tasks of rebuilding and reconstruction.

Sometimes you *can* develop your powers and help others by changing your work. But just as often you can do exactly the same thing right in your own work, right where you are, right in your own community.

That is why when you need a job, God does not say: "There is a job at such and such a place." But He *does* answer your sincere prayer for your right work by pointing out to you in ways which you do not always notice, where such openings lie.

For years a man may have been contented and happy to work in his spare time with seeds and plants although his work may be as store clerk. He may have prayed to God to give him more interesting and better work. One day he may get talking to a greenhouse man and is told: "I wish I knew of a man who would take an interest in my business. That last man is leaving." If the man who prayed was alert, he would there see God putting his powers forward and giving him an opportunity for his right work.

Yes, God works in mysterious ways His wonders to perform. He works through others to find the right work for you.

There was a young lad who wanted to be off "on his own" to the city. After a while his father gave him permission to go to the city alone. He started out bravely enough, but soon became afraid and discouraged.

But the conductor seemed

to know where he was going and told him how to get around the city. A stranger sat down beside him and pointed out the towns they were passing. When the boy reached the city, a kindly man spoke to him and said he would walk with him to a good place for him to stay.

It was not until long afterwards that the boy learned that his father had traveled in the same train, seated unseen in a car behind and had sent all those helpful people to help his boy.

That is in some measure how God will work through others to help you to your right work—if you will but have deep, true, abiding faith in His love and His care.

Let us pray: "That God Will Help Me To Find My Right Work."

𝕻𝖗𝖆𝖞𝖊𝖗

That

GOD WILL HELP ME TO FIND MY RIGHT WORK

"Neglect not the gift that is in thee"—1 Tim. 4:14

O Lord, our Light on the path of life, who knowest our days from the time we are born, help me to be still and listen to Thy voice that I may know what to do and which way to go.

For Thou hast commanded that no one be idle, dear Father, and I have tried to obey that commandment. Yet sometimes truly I feel I am not using all the gifts that are in me — that I am not in my right work.

Dear Father, please do help me to find that right work, if I do not have it now. I know Thou wilt guide me to the work Thou wantest me to do. And when I <u>have</u> found my right work, dear Father, help me to do it well. Help me to work with others, to work hard and save, to be neat and clean and, most of all, to have real true faith in Thy plan for me.

Whatever my hands find to do, dear Father, in home or field or factory, help me to do it with all my might. Truly I feel if I work in that way Thou wilt promote me to better work and greater rewards!

Dear Father, I truly have faith in Thee. I have got Thy guidance in my work before and I know I will get it again if I only listen closely and try to understand. And truly I thank Thee and I feel I am being guided and upheld — and able to face the world once more with hope and confidence. In Jesus' name I pray.

—Amen

GOD WILL PROVIDE

Suppose someone asked you why you are careworn and worried. Well, at first you would be very surprised at the question, for you might immediately answer:

"Well, I'm up against it. I've simply exhausted every means at my disposal and I'm simply overwhelmed with money troubles and debts. My loved ones and I have even known hunger. Can you blame us for wanting greater prosperity, for wanting to be successful and prosperous?"

No one would *think* of blaming you, dear reader. One would only say: "But did you know that you could call on your Father who is rich?"

We could tell you the story of a dear lady who needed fifty dollars for an operation at the same time that her husband was worried about the sale of his only crop. But the season was bad and the crop just brought barely enough money to live on, with no money for the operation.

Now this lady had prayed for the success of the crop, but her faith had begun to waiver — even as yours might. But one day she remembered more strongly God's promise to provide the life more abundant. And she said to herself:

"If I lose my faith, I am not true to my Father. If I lose my faith it shows I do not believe in His Word, the Bible, and in His wonderful promises." And this brought an entirely new thought to her.

"How often my husband and I have sung the old hymn: 'My Father is rich in houses and lands.' I wonder if we really understood it. My Father is rich! Why, if I had an earthly father and he was rich, I would just laugh at these trials. I would send him a wire and back would come what we need. God is my Father and He is richer than the richest millionaire.

What is fifty dollars and the other things we need to Him! He is my Father and I know He will provide. I need it and it is right I should have it. I'm going to send him a 'wire.' I don't know from what 'office' it is coming, but my Father has ways I know not of. I will send him a 'prayer-wire'."

Her hope and faith were made stronger by this thought. She kept on working with a song on her lips and a light heart. She told her husband:

"I know we are going to get what we need. I sent a wire."

"Where?" he asked. "I don't see a single way. How can you be so sure?"

"Because I sent Him a 'prayer-wire' and because He is rich," she answered smilingly. She really trusted God.

A week later her husband came to her happily. "Well," he said "we've heard from your Father. And He sent a government official to buy a strip of our land which we never use, for a transcontinental oil line. We're getting five hundred dollars for it."

"Didn't I tell you," cried the wife, "that my Father was rich?" For this blessed lady, faith had triumphed. For Faith is not just believing that God *can*, but that He *will!*

If there be any good thing you need or want that is good for you to have, you can ask God and He will grant it. How often do you realize that everything — everything in the world belongs to God. "All the gold and silver and cattle on a thousand hills." Men hold things for a while, but they pass. They pass to other men and those material things which go to make wealth always—always—go back to the earth which is God's and which waits only God's next move to pass it on!

What God has is yours! How do you make connections with that vast supply? Here is how God will provide. The path is so light and the way so plain that it becomes like walking along a broad highway.

If you do that which is right in His sight, if you listen to His voice and His commandments, if you will but have faith, then all the Lord's treasure house is open to you.

And your call to God is in Prayer. A life of Prayer is a life of power. God talks to you in His Word, the Bible, and you talk to God in your Prayer. Just have faith in the power of God to answer your prayer and you will be using the greatest power in the universe!

When you have talked to God in prayer, when you have trusted in Him and asked His guidance, what should you do *then?* Wait! Wait upon God for guidance. Wait, saying, "Lord, what would Thou have me to do?"

If God wants you to make some move which will help you get rid of your problem, He will put the thought into your mind, so there will not be the slightest shadow of a doubt He is talking to you. God works in mysterious ways His wonders to perform. He can make things happen for your good. He can bring certain people to help you. He can direct your steps to others whom you may not even know, but who are there to help you. He can cause things to happen hundreds of miles away which will be to your good!

It is the middle of winter. The square of a small town is covered with ice and snow. On a certain corner the hungry birds are flying about waiting, although there is not a sign of food.

At twelve o'clock a man comes out of a building nearby and spreads handfuls of crumbs on the snow. With happy chirps, the birds sweep all about him. All are fed. The birds have come to know that there is a human kindness, that there is a man who knows their need and their hunger.

The birds do not reason. Yet they have the faith which God has given them. They know that at the appointed time, a wise and kindly friend who knows what the tiny creatures face in winter will take care they are fed.

So you, too, may be in a cold and wintry world. You may have financial and other desperate needs. You may be worrying and anxious about the future. But hearken. You, too, have a wise and kindly Friend. The power which notes the fall of a sparrow also has noted *your* distress!

Do you think that the Father who cares for His little creatures the birds, is likely to forget his dear creatures, men and women?

God *does* care about you and your loved ones. He wants you to be healthy and happy and prosperous. God cares about the world and about all the people in it. He is watching over all. God will show each and every man and woman that He *does* care!

"*Who* shall prosper?" they asked the Psalmist of old, when this very same problem came up which is troubling you. And he made them a very strange answer.

"They shall prosper who love God."

When you think of it, that is a very remarkable thing to say. It doesn't say they shall prosper who *believe* in God. The Psalmist didn't say they shall prosper who *serve* God. He *did* say they shall prosper who *love* God!

Why do you think that loving is the most important thing in gaining your prosperity? Because love is the heart from whence comes all the worth-while actions of your life. The father who does not love his wife and children will not work very hard to care for them. The mother who does not love her husband and little ones almost always spends her time in idleness and gossip.

The young folks who do not love one thing greatly—whether it be one another or their future work, will just drift along with the tide.

Truly prosperity comes from love! Isn't that a wonderful thought?

For unless you love something very much it doesn't mean much to you. If you do not care for flowers they mean little or nothing to you. If you do not care for a person, that person means little or nothing to you. And if you do not love God, then He actually means little or nothing to you in your life!

But to those who love God, the whole color of life changes. God means everything. He means love and faith and obedience and trust and hope. And you cannot love God without keeping His commandments. And you cannot keep His great commandment — the Golden Rule—without loving your fellow men. And when you love your fellow men a wonderful thing happens.

The minute you begin to love your fellow men, a really powerful thing happens. Such love breaks down the barriers between people. It changes those

214

whom you meet. It turns strangers into friends and even turns enemies into friends. It opens up opportunities which you never thought existed before. By the application of this kind of love, daily problems—money problems—financial problems—debt problems—are solved miraculously and quickly!

Love greatly and you will gain more friends. Love greatly and you will forget yourself in the service of others. Love greatly and you will be tolerant and helpful and sympathetic. Love greatly and you will give even of your little. Love greatly and you are casting miracle bread upon the waters. In your hours of need, these come back to you with interest added—to cheer and bless and sustain!

For we have yet to see a man or woman with friends made through love who did not always have enough to see them through life. True, they may not be millionaires, they may not even be prosperous in the common sense of the word. But the abundance gained through love—the abundance of the needs of the body and the needs of the spirit is the true abundance no matter in what degree it comes to you.

Yes, you have prayed for prosperity, for the better things of life. And perhaps you have risen full of hope with head held high. But as the hours passed into days and perhaps the days into months, you began to waver. You could see no outward change in your circumstance and you began to wonder how God was going to bring your prosperity about.

You cannot see! That is where God makes His answer to your question. You cannot see that your prosperity can come from any place other than the place and the people you know right now!

> *"I will bring the blind by a way they know not, in paths they know not, I will lead them."*

"They know not." These are the magic words! You do not know how the watchmaker is going to fix your watch, the mechanic is going to fix the machine you have taken to him, nor how the doctor is going to heal you! Yet time after time it happened. A letter comes from someone you hadn't heard from in years which will change the whole picture. A chance word heard on the street sends you off to some place you never went before. An item in the paper or on the radio gives you an idea which sends you on an entirely different path. All placed in paths "you knew not."

No, dear reader, just the simple statement "With God all things are possible" is all the answer you need to your prosperity prayer.

Try and remember, only that when you say "our Father" you are really and truly talking to a loving Father able, willing and anxious to give you all your heart's desires — in ways which only a loving Father can devise.

Let us pray: "For Faith that God Will Provide."

𝔓𝔯𝔞𝔶𝔢𝔯

For

FAITH THAT GOD WILL PROVIDE

"Therefore I say unto you, what things soever ye desire, when ye pray, believe that ye receive them and ye shall have them"—Mark 11:24

O Lord our heavenly Father, who dost feed the birds and clothe the flowers, with what peace I come to Thee in this hour to tell Thee of the many things facing me.

That times are hard, I do not need to tell Thee, dear Father. For I am sure that Thou dost see us struggling down here on Thine earth. Thou knowest how we are trying to keep home and family together, to get out of debt and to get just a little ahead.

O Father, I do thank Thee that Thou hast been so good to us so many times in the past. And I thank Thee for Thy Bible which tells us that whatsoever things we desire, if we believe that we will receive them when we pray, we shall have them.

What a wonder thought, dear Father. And how I shall try to believe, how I _shall_ try to have deep, true, abiding Faith! Truly Father, I will not worry, seeing that Thou art at my side.

I shall believe now — right in this prayer, dear Father! Just to think about that wonderful promise just takes such a load off my shoulders. And into my heart comes a great peace like one who has heard his Father say, Peace, be still and it shall be done!

—Amen

GOD WILL GRANT PEACE UNTO YOU

ARE YOU NERVOUS AND worried a good deal of the time? Are you unhappy, bored with life and feel you are in a rut? Would you like to have more real, true happiness in life—to know deeper peace and understanding in your own heart and soul?

Then your greatest need is God. Without Him you truly are in a rut and can easily find life flat, stale and unprofitable. Without God you can easily convince yourself that there is no end to the life of noise and nervousness and confusion which may surround you.

True it may be that you are passing through a time of deep care and trouble and worry. One thing happens after another, arguments arise, problems perplex. The love which you trusted may have failed. Footsteps which once you welcomed may echo no more. You may have to leave the paths of peace and go into strange places and strange tasks.

Or you may suddenly be called upon to take up a new burden of failing health or money. Yes, there may seem no end to the things that come to drive peace from your life.

And you ask yourself, will every day be as long as this day? Will the slow-moving months ever pass so that things may be as before? Will my life ever be quiet again or has God forgotten me?

Some people—and you may be one of them—begin to think that their troubles and lack of peace is some "punishment" for something they have done, some mistake they may have made in the past. How untrue this is! True it may be that sin is punished, but the punishment is immediate and is not withheld for years. Even if the sinner is not punished outwardly, he is punished in the depths of his heart. This

218

is the dread knowledge which every sinner learns.

But God does not punish you in later times for your sins. God *forgives* them and forgets them. The peace which may have left you is not because you are near to God, but because you are *far* from God! For God offers you that peace— now—no matter what you have done in the past, no matter what your mistakes, no matter what road you have taken.

God does not ask you what mistakes you may have made. He knows them. He does not ask you for a list of your sins. He knows them, too. The only thing God asks is what you have done with your body, your mind, your spirit in the service of His Children!

A minister was called to see a very sick girl who had worn herself out nursing her sister who had been very ill. "If I should die, will I go to heaven?" asked the girl. "I am sure you will," replied the minister.

"But God does not know my name; how will He know me?"

"My dear," said the minister, "He does not need to know your name. Show Him your hands."

Yes, show God your hands. If they are hands which have comforted and helped others then He will grant His peace unto you.

An old man was going along a lonely highway and came at evening to a deep, wide chasm through which flowed a raging torrent. When he was safe on the other side, he turned and built a bridge.

A fellow traveler said to him, "Old man, you are wasting your time building here. You will never pass this way again. Why are you building this bridge?"

The old man lifted his fine, old head and looked with eyes of peace into the eyes of the traveler. "My son," he said, "along the road we have walked today is a young couple. Their feet also must pass this way. That river which was deep and dangerous for me will be twice as dangerous for them. Yet they too, must cross. Good friend, I am building a bridge for *them!*"

Jesus himself walked a road which was dangerous and stony all the way. Although peace was in Him and through Him, it was far from peace which surrounded Him. Yet he has turned and built a bridge for you!

As you look backward you can see that so many of those who trod the road before you have crossed by that bridge, are now resting in peace on the other side, what a comfort to know that Jesus built a bridge for you!

For surely you know men and women whose lives are steady, happy and content even though they have had fully as much noise and trouble and confusion as *you* have had. But almost always you will find that they have been people with Faith, people who turned that Faith into Prayer. They have consecrated some part of every day to thoughts of God. They have opened some parts of their bodies and souls each day to the divine peace of God that it flow into them!

A blind woman whose face was radiant with inner joy and peace once said: "It is easy to believe in God and His peace when you live alone with Him in the dark."

Alone with God! Happily for you, not in the dark, but in the light! You can live there! You can pray for God's peace. Oh, if you only

knew how easy it was there for you to take!

There was a woman who bought a steamship ticket from Boston to New Orleans. The cost of her ticket was so high that she brought along a case of crackers and packages of cheese, feeling she could not afford the meals on the boat. All through the voyage she lived on the crackers and cheese. On the last day of the trip, she decided to have one good, warm dinner. When she offered to pay for the dinner, she was told that the meals had been included in the price of the ticket!

Are *you* living on a meagre diet of the crackers and cheese of life, when you could dine from God's abundance? Are you traveling on the ticket to the port of peace which God so freely gives?

The price? The price is free! It is the secret of peace. If you want peace, hand all your fears and nervousness and worry over to God! Do not let them accumulate in your mind.

Do not wait until they accumulate, until the night or the Sunday. Do not wait until the day or the week is done to turn your cares over to God. But in the midst of the day's cares, in the rush of the streets, the noise and confusion of the tasks of home and shop and farm—stand still for a moment, ask the cause of your lack of peace and, lifting up your heart, give your cares and worries to your loving Father!

How different your life would be if you only would! You are weighed down with care and confusion, with worry and nervousness because, actually, you do not trust Jesus with all your life's worries! Do you think sometimes that what disturbs your peace is a small thing and that He would not want to be troubled with it?

There is nothing small to Jesus if it disturbs your quietness and peace. "In Me ye shall have peace." Could anything be simpler and plainer than that? In Jesus you shall have peace! Live in Jesus and with Jesus. Walk with Him and talk with Him. Make Him the ever-lighted and secret altar, the quiet place where you can go—any hour, any minute, any second!

If you live with Jesus in that way, then nothing can disturb you, nothing can touch you. The peace that fills the heart of Jesus will flow into your heart. The peace of God, like the fluttering wings of a bird, will settle down into your own body and mind and spirit and there make its home!

And this means rest. Relax in the peace of God! Relax your body by going to a quiet place. But more than that, relax your mind and spirit to let God in. Let go of your cares. Say: "At least I shall not worry during these moments when I meditate and relax." Look upon your life not as a life of a moment or of a year. Look upon your life as something eternal—which it is. Look upon your cares and worries as only a small part of the eternal life which stretches out before you. Beyond your life if you really and truly have faith in God and in His Word, His promise of eternal life makes our few cares but the tick of a second in the unending hours which God's grace gives us!

If you can only gain this eternal view of your life, much of the pain and unhappiness of your daily life will vanish. What difference the little annoyances of the day or the month or the year when beyond them lies the unending vista of life with God!

You may drift for years without God, but you cannot be happy or at ease. There comes a time in *everyone's* life when they need God. And today you need him more than ever to answer the hundreds of problems which are brought on by the sin and violence in the world today.

God's greatest gift is peace—peace of mind, peace of heart, peace of spirit. To the man or woman with faith in God and love for his fellow men, work is a pleasant thing, troubles are light as feathers, and evil cannot come near!

"In Me ye shall have peace," said Jesus. Let yourself live in Him and abide in Him and you shall have peace. As you are joined with Jesus, so will peace fill your heart like the waters of the ocean fill the bays at high tide, covering every rock of worry, every reef of care. You will be filled with the very fullness of God!

For the peace of God is perfect. "Thou wilt keep him in *perfect* peace whose mind is stayed on Thee because he trusteth in Thee." His peace cannot be touched by any wordly care, it can-

not be reached by the highest wave of sorrow.

Look upon the peace of God as upon a river which follows you along your road of life. As you arise in the morning it is there in the early dawn. It is flowing nearby as you do your daily tasks. You have only to look out of the window of your soul to see it. It is there when evening comes and the stars come out—the peace which hushes you to sleep.

When you were a child you wandered in the peace of God, picking flowers on its banks. In the ages of growth, youths and maidens walked hand in hand in love along its banks. In age there are shady seats by quiet pools. And when feet which now tread the source of the river of peace, walk no more on the river of earth, then the children of children shall come to wander by its banks!

Yes, dear reader, God hears the unspoken thought of your soul for peace. You will hear His footsteps bring you that peace through the stirring of the evening wind. You will feel His presence as you pray.

It is the peace which passeth understanding.

You will feel a new calm that truly shall pass understanding. A new fountain of peace shall bring life to your drooping spirits. With God you will sleep in peace and awake rejoicing with the morning light—happy and eager to do His will. Your soul will be restored to joy and your spirit lay hold anew of the peace which passeth the understanding as you go forth!

Let us pray: "For the Knowledge of the Peace of God."

Prayer

For

THE KNOWLEDGE OF THE PEACE OF GOD

"Thou wilt keep him in perfect peace whose mind is stayed upon Thee"—Is. 26:3

Almighty Father, who dost fix the tides and the rising of the sun and moon, I turn to Thee with a heart filled with trouble and hurt and weariness. It is with a sad and humble heart that I pray. Give me peace and the rest I need so much!

I believe in Thy goodness with all my heart, dear Father. And I thank Thee so very much for the never-ending love which Thou givest. And in return, I give Thee <u>my</u> love, knowing that in Thine eyes it is the most precious gift in the world!

O dear Father, take away from my heart the fears of today and tomorrow. Teach me that I have no reason to fear anything at all in my life. Teach me that if only I make Thee a part of my very life nothing can hurt me. And help me to know, dear Father, that for every sincere effort I make to help myself, Thou wilt give me twice again as much help!

These are the things I need and ask, my Father. Dear Lord, give me the knowledge of Thy peace I need so much. Let me always feel the kind of peace I feel when I pray like this, a deep, deep peace. A peace which knows that no matter what may happen, Thou lovest me, Thy child. The peace which knows Thou wilt guide and protect and calm my soul for all the days of my life.

—Amen

ASKING GOD FOR STRENGTH TO OVERCOME ALL OBSTACLES

ARE THERE OBSTACLES IN your way — standing between you and the things you want? Do you feel that other people are putting these obstacles in your path, defeating some particular ambition you have in life?

If you *do*, then you will find that this chapter in your Handbook of Living will open a window which God has furnished you—the window of His Word—the window of victory and eternal life.

For if there is one thing you *must* believe, it is that God *does* care, that God *is* interested in you, that He has created the world and your own mind and body so that all will work together with you in overcoming all obstacles.

To even the hard life— your life which has many obstacles standing between you and the things you want, God has a message. It is the message that He will give you the strength to overcome every obstacle!

God will give you the strength because He gives it to *all* of His children. For if there is one thing you must admit, it is that everyone on this earth has had obstacles to overcome. You must admit that your life, as full of heart-aches and set-backs and disappointments as it has been, is no harder than the lives of thousands of others all about you.

"Yes," you will say, "other people have troubles and problems but that doesn't help *me*. I'm interested in mine."

It is like the little girl who said to the dentist: "I have the worst toothache in the world."

"Why?" asked the dentist.

"Because it's *my* tooth-ache," she answered.

Readily we must admit that some people have more obstacles than others. Why this should be there is no way of telling. But, although everyone in the world is faced with problems and obstacles, there are hundreds, yes thousands, of people who have learned to overcome them.

You will find in learning the life-stories of practically every great man or woman, that their lives were one series of obstacles successfully overcome. Some even had obstacles still remaining in their lives at the highest moments of their fame and success.

Jesus, Himself, reached with His Gospel only a limited number of people in the small world of His time. He died a comparatively young man on that symbol of defeat—the Cross. Yet who can say His victory was not finally achieved?

And who can say that what you accomplish in the *face* of obstacles would have amounted to more had they not been present? For you, too, will find that in many and many a case, the obstacles placed in your path were for your good rather than for your harm. You will find out, later in life, as so many people have, that there is One, far wiser than you who had said: "Not this way"—only to open a better way!

Sometimes people say: "I can stand trouble and obstacles and defeat, if these things didn't come all at once. But obstacles all seem to come at the same time."

There is an old Eastern saying which goes: "Only one camel can pass through a gate at a time."

Only one obstacle can confront you at a time. You *cannot* take care of two and there is no use trying. And God *does* give you the strength to overcome one obstacle at a time. Of that you may be sure. It is only when you get confused and try to take care of *all* of them at the same time that you waste God's power and help.

Obstacles, whether they be in the form of the actions of people or in conditions you meet, are peculiar things. The same obstacle varies in size depending upon how you look at it.

There are three windows, three glasses through which you can look at obstacles. They are the windows of space and time and God!

Do you remember how large certain obstacles loomed when you were

226

seventeen? Would you ever finish school? Would you ever get work? Would you ever get married? Would your appearance ever improve? Do they seem as large to you now? Were they not *small*, compared with what you thought have been *bigger* ones? You are looking at them through the window of time!

Do you remember the obstacles which faced you when you lived at home or when you lived in some other street or city? Yet now that you have moved somewhere else, isn't it true that many of those which seemed so large at the old place, now have shrunken in size? You are looking at them through the window of space.

There is the story of the man who was worrying what would happen if a certain man would make a certain decision on the next day. His whole future seemed to hang on that decision.

Walking through the woods, he met an astronomer and a geologist. The astronomer spoke of the awesome depths of space, the millions of light years the nearest stars were from the earth, the smallness of our earth as compared with some of the giant stars. The geologist spoke of the uncounted millions of years which were the age of our earth, the centuries which had passed while life slowly climbed from the prehistoric mud.

After a while the man said with a relieved sort of sigh: "Well, I don't suppose it makes such a difference whether or not I hear from Mr. Jones." He was beginning to look at his obstacles through the windows of space and time.

And this is the window which God opens for you in His Bible. It is the window of creation and of eternal life. God has promised eternal life for those who believe in Him. And this promise means that life—*your* life—stretches far into the future—that it goes eternally forward. With God's immensity, with such eternity before you, cannot you see that the plans of the people who seem to put obstacles in your way, that the obstacles *themselves* are indeed small and short-lived as compared with the glorious promises of God?

But there is another way of looking through windows at your obstacles. It is through a magnifying and diminishing window! That is to say the size and importance of the obstacles confronting you is often determined by *yourself*. They can vary from day to day, even from hour to hour!

When you are upset and physically tired, when you toss sleeplessly in bed, verily your problems and obstacles grow like giants. Your power to meet even the slightest obstacle grows weaker and the obstacle grows larger.

But when you have gotten a good night's sleep and feel rested, your own *powers* to meet obstacles grow. When you get up in the morning after a good night's sleep, no obstacle seems too great for you and your courage is high. As the day wears on you get tired, your powers wane and your obstacles seem to grow.

Isn't there a lesson in overcoming obstacles to be learned here? Do not *expect* to be able to meet obstacles equally well at all times. Expect to feel worse about the actions of people and of events at certain times. Say to yourself when an obstacle looms like a giant:

"This happens to be one of the times when my powers are low. They will be greater another time. I will make no decisions now and I will not even *think* about this problem. Now is not the time!"

Some folks can surmount many obstacles if they are only the obstacles of events. But when they meet the obstacles of people who do not seem to like them, who criticize them, who seem to stand between them and something they want—well, they simply go to pieces!

This happens to every one of us. Whatever you want to do, someone is always there to say you haven't got the ability or the talent. Whatever you do, someone is always there to discourage you. Whatever you want, someone is always there to refuse it. Some folks, it seems, even go out of their way to hurt you.

There is little you can do about the actions or the criticisms of others. Agree to yourself that to a certain number of others, you will never be able to please them. Do not let yourself be disheartened by the actions or the criticism of people like that. Just pay no attention to them. Let it be as if they did not exist for you. Forget them completely and do what seems to you best.

For you will find that the people who criticize, who

put obstacles in your way, are a very small number compared with the folks who are ready to help you the minute they are convinced that you are sincerely trying.

And it will help you greatly in meeting the actions and the opinions of others, if you will remember one thing. Other people are not as different from yourself as you think they are! Most other people have about the same ambitions and desires as *you* have. They are not paying half as much attention to your plans as you *think* they are. They are twice as much interested in carrying out their *own* plans as they ever could be in putting obstacles in *your* way.

And another thing. The people whose actions you fear, whose decisions you tremble to meet, are neither so much more great nor so much more smart nor so much more wise than yourself! They, too, in most cases, are just as uncertain and groping as *you* are. You are just as able and alert and smart as the next ninety-six people you will be likely to meet.

Obstacles truly are evil

things. And you can do little better than learn to the best of your ability that you can overcome them by "resisting not evil." The less you think about the obstacles in your way and the more about the positive things you can do to attain your end, the easier it will be to overcome them.

God is your Friend and He will be trusted. He will keep His promises better than any earthly friend. And how full of God's promise of victory over obstacles is your Bible! What a heartening thing to have this promise of God right there in your home — every hour, every minute—for your use when you worry and your ambition is thwarted!

For when you have done all in your own power to overcome your obstacles, *then* place your trust in our Father. And as you do, deep down in your heart will come the feeling that there is not an obstacle, not an enemy over whom you cannot triumph. Again you will hear the voice of Jesus say: "Come unto me ... and I will give you rest."

The moment you start to worry over an obstacle, put

that obstacle in God's care. Hand it over to Him to deal with. You may be sure *He* can look ahead where *you* cannot and manage things. You can ask Him to take whatever is troubling you and work it out according to His own way of wisdom.

Work, yes work greatly. Work, filled with the blessed trust in God expressed by Jesus. Throw your cares to the winds, bid your worries depart and accept what comes with peace and thankfulness.

They who trust in God, they who seek His Kingdom, cannot worry over obstacles. While Peter kept his eyes fixed in faith on Jesus, he walked upon the waters unafraid. It was only when he looked upon the tossing waves about him that he faltered and sank.

The man or woman, fixed in faith, can overcome the world. Let us pray: "That God will Grant Me The Strength to Overcome All Obstacles."

Prayer

That

GOD WILL GRANT ME THE STRENGTH TO OVERCOME ALL OBSTACLES

"If ye shall say unto this mountain, Be thou removed, and be thou cast into the sea, it shall be done"—Matt. 21:21

Dear Father, wonderful maker of life and joy and peace, the very thought of Thee is so comforting that my heart is made strong even by the thought of Thy power.

And O that is the power I need, dear Father, for Thou knowest the many obstacles that stand in my way. Thou knowest those people and those things which are against me, my Father. Thou knowest where I am weak and what strength I need.

I do remember in my childhood, dear Father, Thou didst remove obstacles one by one which I thought would never end. And truly I see as I look back on my life that there are so many obstacles Thou helped me over that I could not count them.

Please, dear Father, teach me that all the obstacles of the future are no greater and that Thou wilt even so help me overcome them, too! O Father, make Thy hand my hand. For truly I know Thou canst remove every stone, every cord which binds my hopes. Thou canst change dark clouds into sunshine if only I have faith, dear Father.

Let me always look up to Thee in love and trust as I do now, Father. Keep me steadfast in my faith even as I am in this hour.

—Amen

GOD WANTS TO SEE LASTING PEACE ON EARTH

ARE YOU WORRIED AND unhappy about war? Would you like to see a lasting peace on earth?

If these and other fears and hopes crowd into your mind, then perhaps this little chapter in your Handbook of Life is given to you that many things which are far from clear to you about the terrors of war may be made more plain, viewed in the light of God's Word and God's love.

For it is so natural to ask why, when everyone knows how terrible war is, do nations go to war? And few have answered that question. No one answered it in the time of Alexander, in the time of Caesar, in the time of Napoleon, in the time of the last World War. And no one answers it today.

There *is* no answer save that men and women will not learn that God has laid down certain laws and that they are to be obeyed. And that violation of these laws brings certain punishment, yea, even unto the third and fourth generation—for that is one of the most terrible punishments of war — its burden on children of men still unborn.

There is only one law between men and women which God has given us to bring lasting peace on earth. And this is the law:

"Thou shalt not kill."

Given to Moses, engraved on tablets of stone, this law stands like the granite which it is. Oh, yes, men great and small have tried to justify killing under this circumstance and that. They have said it was all right to kill under this circumstance and at that time. They have said that certain crimes of killing such as murder, could be expiated only by more killing. They have said that you could kill at certain times. They have said that it was all right to kill certain men and women of certain races and colors and creeds.

But wherever there has been any other statement of this law, there has come trouble and disaster and war.

"Thou shalt not kill" means just exactly what God wrote. It means thou shalt not kill!

It is *because* God wants to see lasting peace on earth that He made that law—with no amendments. He made no changes and no exceptions to it. It is engraved on granite and it will outlast the centuries.

Yet the peace of God comes slowly. True it is that God could abolish war tomorrow if He wanted to. Yet the peace which would follow would be so easily earned that it would be a hollow, soft and flabby people that would live under it.

A father sends his son out into the world. The father knows the son will encounter temptation, danger, hardship, violence, sin, yes, even war. Yet it is the only thing the father can do. To keep the son sheltered and at home would result only in a weak, spineless man.

The son has to learn by his own experience that wrongdoing brings its own punishment quickly and inexorably.

In like manner, it is probable that God could have instantly made a race of perfect men and women. There are animals which are perfect for the environment they inhabit. Shellfish, for instance, are protected by a thick shell, their food is washed to them by the waves, they need not move from the spot where they are born. Yet the shellfish is one of the few animals which has never developed in its whole history of evolution. It is the same as it was ten billion years ago. It did not suffer, it did not need to learn. And it stood still!

Yet not for nothing do you read in your Bible that the years of men are but a second in God's sight. The children of God have come up out of great depths and through long ages of darkness. Behind us lie ages of the dusty relics of cruel superstitions, frightening fears. The dark shadows of the past still flicker over the paths we walk. Old jungle ways and old hatreds still cling to us. And there are mockers along the way who say we cannot walk forward. And true it is that there are dangers ahead which, like the waves of the sea, beat us back from the rising tide of peace.

But the race of man *does* go forward. Persecutions and cruelties, barbarous punishmment, "scientific" cruelty, all are practiced, here and now. But where once they were practiced with no thought of their cruelty, today even the most ferocious of their practitioners try to justify them on some ground or other, no matter how full of quicksand that ground may be.

The warm light of the presence of God and the courage and the cheer which His Word and His Book and His Son have been to us, keeps us on the march. We have not reached the top of the hill where we can see the city not built by hands, the city of peace. There is a long climb ahead and there is little use for us to be blind to that fact. Most of us will never reach the top, will never even catch a glimpse of the dawn. But where our feet may never tread, the feet of our children and our children's children may stand and see the dawn over the far-off hills.

No, for us, the living, it is our place to struggle upward in the valley. And it is so hard for us to learn. The leaders of men and women are but the reflections of their people. When people are greedy their leaders are greedy. When people refuse to sacrifice material possessions that others might live, their leaders refuse to sacrifice them. When people refuse to lay up treasures of kindness, of goodness, of helpfulness on earth, then their leaders are neither kind nor good nor helpful.

Wherever in the world there are men and women who in their own individual lives are greedy, are trying to get the most they can for themselves without any thought of others, there will always be leaders to lead them into war. For war is only the final expression of what a country and its people have all along been living and thinking.

God wants lasting peace, but God's power is there for those who use it for war. The power which is in the crashing shell is the same power which turns the mill-wheel. The voice of the cannon is the voice of God, condemning waste and greed and jealousy.

And it is one of God's laws

that although you are innocent, you must suffer with those who are guilty. That is because all human lives on earth are like one body. If one part of the body is hurt, the rest of the body suffers. If one member of a family is hurt, the whole family suffers.

So true it may be that among the millions who march to war, there are few who have not tried to be good and fair and kind. Most of them truly have tried to live sincere, upright lives and most of them *did* live such lives.

It is only sad that they are victims—victims not only of their own passions, but also the tools of men in high places who desire power and wealth more than truth and goodness. They are the victims of misunderstanding and ignorance.

The news of the battle of Waterloo was brought to England by means of signal flags waved in France across the English Channel. A dense fog was over the channel and all that the people could see were the words "WELLINGTON DEFEATED." All England was bowed in grief. Yet when the fog lifted in the morning, they read the rest of the message "THE ENEMY." Tears of sorrow turned to joy at the completed message "WELLINGTON DEFEATED THE ENEMY."

Sin and hate and greed and violence are signalling "GOD DEFEATED." But when the fog of ignorance and selfishness is lifted, we shall be able to read the rest of the message "GOD DEFEATED THE ENEMY!"

When one speaks of Jesus, the man of peace, people sometimes say that He could not understand the passion for war that sweeps through men's souls. Yet Jesus *did* face war. He did face persecution by a conquering dictator. Judea was under the heel of the Roman dictator. Herod was ruler over Galilee just the same as Adolf Hitler placed rulers over the territories his hordes overran.

Into this atmosphere of seething underground revolt Jesus came and lived. The people were looking for a leader to lead them against their Roman conquerors. With His incomparable qualities of leadership, Jesus could easily have led it.

Do you not think that Jesus was forced to study the use of force and war?

Was He not tempted in the Wilderness to use the great power at His command to restore His country?

Yet Jesus knew God's law of peace. "Thou shalt not kill"! Jesus knew that the road to war is always over the bodies of thousands of men and women, of innocent men and women. To wage a war Jesus would have had to lead an army, an army which like every other army would have to kill and inspire terror in the hearts of men and women, soldiers and civilians alike. If Jesus had decided to lead an army His gentle Disciples would have become soldiers instead of saints. Would they then have been fitted to write the chronicle of Jesus' life as they did in the New Testament?

No, Jesus took the road of peace—the harder path. He took the path that made the dictators of the time pass Him by, ignore Him as a power. But His path lead to the place where the names of killers and conquerors have gathered but infamy and dust, and the name of Jesus is remembered and revered!

For there is only one answer to gain lasting peace. You cannot confuse man's cruelty with the purposes of God for peace. You must first see peace in the smiles of children, peace in the love in the hearts of mothers, peace in kindness among the poor.

Be at peace with yourself and the God who is in heaven, the God who has been your help in ages past will surely answer your cry for help today. He will give you the strength and the courage that cannot falter in these days which try men's souls.

In a warring world, where else but to God can you turn for security and peace? In days when your heart fails you, when your life is turned away from its well-worn paths, when new hardships and new responsibilities crowd in upon you, God will be your one source of strength and peace.

The trust you have in God will give you confidence that even through the noise and smoke of battle, the purpose of God for lasting peace among His children cannot be turned aside.

To your dear ones who may be far from home, who may be in the air or under the sea or on foreign shores, God will give a vision of

Himself. He will give a vision to those who are marching along in the darkness. God will give a vision of Himself to those in prison, in concentration camp, in exile and in hospital cot—men who have chosen the way which was hard and lonely rather than to prove false to their own conscience and to Him.

God will give a vision of Himself to those who have marched off in youth to fields of battle, to those who are afraid, to those who are missing and to those who are wounded. Yes, He will give a vision of Himself even to those who offer their lives in a cause which denies Him! Let us pray: "For Lasting Peace On Earth."

Prayer

For

LASTING PEACE ON EARTH

"They shall beat their swords into plowshares and their spears into pruning hooks"—Is. 2:4

Almighty God, from whose heart all thoughts of truth and peace come forth, light in this world the eternal light of lasting peace. And bring to all nations Thy kingdom in peace!

O dear Father, so many people are suffering, hungering and persecuted. And I can just see the thousands of hearts and homes that are sad and sorrowful because there is no peace. And so often I wonder where it is going to end!

Right now I am in my own peaceful home, dear Father. And O how I pray that peace may stay within these walls, yes, and spread forth unto all the world. O I do pray that the clouds of darkness which hang over the world may be driven away by the sunshine of Thy smile.

Begin Thy peace with me, dear Father, with me, Thy child. Cleanse my heart of all envy and greed and strife. Bless me that I may be humble in the face of suffering, that I may learn the lesson of Thy peace.

Yes, Father, in the midst of noise, even as I go out and face the world, give me a quiet and holy place within my heart where peace may dwell even as it dwells this minute — where my tired spirit may be made peaceful by Thee.

—Amen

35

GOD WANTS YOU TO REALLY ENJOY LIFE

WOULD YOU LIKE TO HAVE more real, true happiness in life? Would you like to have more fun out of life, more "pep," more zest for living?

If you *would*, then deep in that wonderful treasure chest of happiness — your Bible — there is such an array of joyful jewels that they have been treasured by the world all down through the years. In words that still echo in men's hearts, God brings you His tidings of great joy.

For God *wants* you to be really happy. He has strewn with the generosity of a loving Father all the good things of earth for you to enjoy and to be happy with. And to add wonder to wonders, God sent His own Son into this world to bring you such happiness and joy. Even now those wonderful words may ring in your heart:

"These things have I spoken unto you, that my joy might remain in you and that your joy might be full."

"Ye shall go out with joy, and be led forth with peace."

Joy! Joy! Over and over again that word echoes in the Word of God. If there is anything that can truly be called God-given, it is the happiness which God wants you to have, the enjoyment of life which God wants to bring to you!

For centuries men and women have been searching for true happiness. They have asked themselves over and over again in what it consisted. And no doubt you, too, have often questioned what you would really need to enjoy life.

Men have sought to enjoy life through money but it has turned their lives to dust. They have found if they look at the world through a glass coated with silver they see only their own reflections. Men have sought to enjoy life through fame and power, but have met only envy and resistance. And they have sought happiness through food and sex and drink, but at the last have kept only a bitter taste.

No, God does not give you happiness through any of these things, although, rightly used, all of them can help you enjoy life. You need not search afar for happiness. You will find it as the two children found it in the legend.

The two children started out to seek the Blue Bird of Happiness. Over all the world they looked and it was nowhere to be found. Tired and discouraged they came home. And there it was—singing joyfully in their own back yard.

And the things God wants to give you to make you enjoy life are the things you can find right in your own life—things which are freely open to you whether you are rich or poor—no matter what your age or race or creed or color! What *are* these things?

If you will look at the Cross you will see that it has four wings. Evenly balanced, they make the Cross a thing of beauty and holiness and inspiration.

There are four things which God offers you to make you happy—evenly balanced in your life they can make your life a thing of beauty and holiness and inspiration to yourself and others.

God gives you four things which are yours to be used to really enjoy life. They are: work, play, love and faith.

God wants you to enjoy life through your work. No one can enjoy life without it and truly God is wise in knowing this to be true. That is not to say that your work should be toil or drudgery. True work—the kind that God wants you to have to be happy—is the accomplishment of something by hand or brain which shall help others.

For no matter how well paid the work, how fine the surroundings, how "easy" it may be, if you do not get a sense of accomplishment in it, you will be unhappy in it. And then you will not enjoy your life. One-fourth of your happiness in life will be missing.

That is why God has made the most enjoyable work, the work which will be the most service to others. That is why often you are the happiest in some work for which you are not paid, but which you know is making others happy.

So look at your work anew. If you do not get this feeling of happy service from it, then you are in the wrong work and should look for something else. Very often, however, if you will look at the work you *have* with new eyes you will see which part of it means service to others. If you will devise *new* ways of adding to this service of others through your work, then in that degree will you be happy in your work.

Your work, looked at from the viewpoint of loving service to others can turn what was once a dull chore into a challenging and stimulating occupation which can set your heart singing.

The second wing of your cross of happiness is play. It is perfectly true that "all work and no play makes Jack a dull boy." All work and no play makes life a dull

life. **God wants you to be happy through your play.**

Play, of course, like other good things which God gives, can be made a means and an end in life, which it is not. The housewife who lives to do her housework only that she may spend four hours in the movies every day is playing—but playing too much. The man who works only to earn enough to spend in play is also making it an end in life. If you do not think this is so, watch the rich man who has nothing else to do but play and see how little real enjoyment he gets from it.

Play is good. It is good even when there is no apparent purpose in it. Many people do not want to play because they say it does not accomplish anything. But play *does* accomplish something. It accomplishes what it is intended to accomplish—what God wants it to accomplish for you. It preserves the rhythm of life. Play is—or should be—release from concentration of body and mind. Play, the doing of something different, the relaxing with a hobby, the spending of time in the open air, in the woods, in the garden, in friendly games and in pleasant talk is one of the necessary things.

God wants you to really enjoy life through your play. And play, like work, is there for every man and woman who knows its God-sent purpose.

The third wing of your happiness cross is the wing of love. And by love, we are not speaking in the narrow meaning of sex, although that, too, is an important part of it.

God has so created you that to be truly happy, to really enjoy life, you must love and be loved. To love and be loved—and the greatest of these is to love!

Every man and woman is born with this capacity for love, although so very many stifle it. Love in its broader sense is the desire to help, to protect, to guide, to share and to console. You can accomplish all of these things without the element of sex entering into it.

Some of the noblest men and women have been gloriously happy in this kind of love without the faintest part of sex entering. Jesus, Himself, knew neither the love of wife nor family, yet His love flowed out to the whole world and it flows today—bringing peace and joy and comfort to aching hearts.

True, Nature has planted the sex instinct within men and women and its natural exercise in God's sacrament of marriage brings happiness to men and women. But where this relationship is not to be, even where the springtime of love has passed, there are still deeper happinesses and rewards of love.

The tender story is told of the stranger who stopped at the door of a distant little house in the hills. He looked about the beautiful front yard, the tidy painted home and the lovely flowers blooming all about. An older man answered the door.

"How is it that your place is the nicest looking in these parts?" asked the stranger. "You and your wife must work hard here."

"Do you see that graveyard over there?" asked the man. "My wife is there. She died a year after we moved out here. But *she* made this place. It's not hard work that made it. She was my heart and my heart is in this place. I treasure her love even though she is not here. And I learned from my Bible that where my treasure is, there will my heart be also."

That is the ennobling power of love.

It is important that you be *loved* as well as loving—that what you do will give you the esteem of others. It is this feeling of being loved that makes a happy child and it is the same feeling of being loved that makes a happy man or woman.

God wants you to enjoy life through the esteem and love of others and through learning to love others yourself. Again, this gift of God is open to every man and woman no matter of what age or where you happen to be. Love and you will be loved. Be loved and you will enjoy life and be happy.

The fourth wing of your cross of happiness is the most enduring and the noblest. To really enjoy life you must have faith—faith in yourself, faith in your fellow men and women and faith in God. And from faith in God will spring the other two faiths.

Truly it has been said that man does not live by bread alone. To be truly happy, you must feel that life has a purpose, that it is surging toward some great event to which the whole creation moves. You must feel that you, yourself, have some part, no matter how small, in this march of the universe.

Faith means that you must believe in a God who loves you, who bears your troubles in His heart and so makes it possible for *you* to bear them. You must feel that God is a God of infinite love and will hold you up and not suffer you to be dismayed.

For even with your work, even with your play, even with your love, there will come a time when you need much more. Hard situations, difficult problems will arise. You will be sorely tried. It is then that faith in God will give you the capacity to see life and to see it whole. It will be the great anchor of your happiness. It is this faith which will give meaning to your work, sacrament to your love and direction to your life.

Faith in God will do even more for your happiness. It will give you a great "measuring rod" by which to measure all those things which are for your enjoyment of life. Faith in God will indicate to you the worthiness of your work, the beauty of your play, the

243

sacredness of your love and the eternal road which your happy life must take.

You can have energy and "pep" and bring enjoyment into your life if you once understand that your strength and your happiness is of God—that He wants you to be happy and is just waiting for you to give you all the help that a loving Father *can* give!

If strength is your need, if love is your need, if happiness is your need, to enable you to really enjoy life— then you may be sure that it is there for you to take—

Let us pray: "For Real Zest and Joy in Living."

Prayer

REAL ZEST AND JOY IN LIVING

"Rejoice in the Lord always; and again I say, Rejoice"—Phil. 4:4

Almighty God, my heavenly Father, whose boundless love and help will never fail me, I come
to Thee tired and worn out and without any
enjoyment in life.

And I ask Thy help to make me truly happy
again, dear Father, to give me real zest and
joy in living like I used to have.

Help me to remember, my Father, that happiness
and joy are my birthright and it is Thy will
that I be happy. Help me to be grateful for
the joys of living, the joys of friendship, the
joys of being alive in a world where I may
meet so many brave and kindly people if I wish.

Yes, Father, help me find joy and happiness in
the simple love and companionship of Thy children. Help me to find happiness and joy and
zest for living in the contentment of good
health and in my daily tasks.

But help me to be happiest, dear Father, in
loving service to Thee and to my fellow men.
And teach me that my reward shall be the kingdom
of happiness in my life here and now.

Truly, Father, nothing can make me happier than
to speak to Thee like this. Please help me
carry that feeling of joy out of this room and
into the days to come. That will be the finest
joy and happiness I could feel!

—Amen

GOD DOES NOT LIKE PRIDE, VANITY AND HAUGHTINESS

ARE YOU OFTEN TEMPTED to look down on other people? Do you sometimes feel "stuck up" and haughty and pretty pleased with yourself? If that is the way you feel, then you are disobeying one of God's most often-repeated injunctions—that you be not proud.

For it is surprising to see how many times God's word, the Bible, mentions pride and vanity. Someone figured out that there are more than a hundred places in the Bible where pride and vanity are condemned.

Now why do you think that God does not like pride, vanity and haughtiness? Because it is something that not only makes you unhappy, makes *others* unhappy and miserable, but also makes you forget God. In fact, God not only does not like pride and vanity, but you may read "God resisteth the proud, but giveth

grace unto the humble." James 4:6

Yes, pride is bound to make you unhappy. It is pride that leads you to think that no one is as good as you are. It is pride that makes it hard for you to see the good in other people. It is pride that even blinds you to the goodness of God. It is pride that makes you envious and haughty and scornful and leads to heartbreaks, quarrels and even wars.

How many times have you heard the expression "foolish pride"? It is a wise expression, for there are few things as foolish as pride. For pride in the insignificant things that most proud people cherish is indeed foolish.

Nine times out of ten, whenever you see a proud person, it is rarely anything great or noble or worth while of which they are proud. It is more likely to be because they have a bigger barn than anyone else in the township, a fine house or automobile, a little more education or a little more money. And you can see at once that all these things do not add an inch to your stature as a man or a woman or as a child of God.

For pride makes you forget that unusual possessions and talents are all gifts of God, intended not to set you apart but to make you more of a servant to your fellow man. Instead of being proud of your possessions or talents, realize that you have a double obligation because you have been doubly endowed.

There is the tale told of the master organ builder who built such an organ for the church that God gave it the gift of playing all by itself whenever any who was true and good and humble entered the church. On his wedding day, the master organ builder was puffed up with pride as he thought of his wonderful genius and how the people would marvel. His bride entered the church first and the organ burst out with joyful music. But when the organ builder came through the portals, it was silent!

The organ builder was astonished and could not understand it. But the old minister who was to perform the ceremony pointed out to him that his pride at a gift of God's was what kept the organ silent. The builder was truly repentant and as he and his bride went back up the aisle and through the doors, the organ pealed for both of them. As a general rule, however, you will find that the least talented, the people who do the least useful or important work are the very ones who are the most vain. You have only to look at the strut of a headwaiter, the self-important pose of a butler, the pomposity of a doorman in front of an expensive hotel, the swagger of a gambler, to see examples before you.

Really important and useful men and women—the people who do the necessary work of the world, as a general rule are humble, whether they be the greatest or the least. The carpenter who does a workmanlike job is usually essentially a humble man in the finest sense of the word. The worker at the lathe or bench who turns out valuable and useful things is usually a humble man in that sense. The mother goes about her daily tasks humbly. The scientist and the doctor, aware of their responsibility, the vast knowledge of the universe which still lies beyond their grasp, are humble in the face of God's wonder and miracles. It is upon people like these that the world depends. These are the people whom God exalteth.

During the Revolutionary War, a group of soldiers were piling up lumber. The work was heavy and the squad was short-handed. Superintending the work, but not moving, was a sergeant. A plainly dressed officer came up and asked the sergeant why he did not help the men. "Why, I'm the sergeant," answered the surprised man proudly.

Without a word the officer took off his coat and helped the men with the lumber, while the sergeant looked on. When the lumber was piled he put on his coat and started away. The sergeant stopped him and asked: "Who are you? What's your name?" The officer stiffened to a salute and said: "General George Washington."

The sergeant looked ridiculous and he *was* ridiculous. Proud and vain people are *always* ridiculous. There is something about the puffed-up man or woman that seems to make others want to "take them down a peg." It is that something which makes small boys want to throw snowballs at gentlemen in high hats. It is that something which makes a theatre audience laugh when the self-important man in the frock coat falls down.

Yes, people can stand many things in your character without caring to do anything about it, but there is something about foolish pride that seems to make people want to take you down.

It reminds one of the story of the young man all puffed up with pride who came to a very learned man and said: "I am going to graduate with the highest honors in my school." The old man asked: "What then?" Said the young fellow, "Why then I am going to become one of the country's most famous lawyers." The old man nodded, "What then?" he said. "Why then I ought to become one of the richest men in the country

248

with everything money can buy."

The old man continued, "What then?" And the answer was: "Why then I suppose I'll receive all kinds of honors and live to a good old age." "Yes, and what then?" prodded the old man. "Why then, why then, I guess I'll die," stammered the young man by now considerably deflated. "What then?" finally asked the wise old man. The young man couldn't answer. His pride did not take him that far— it did not take him to God. Then he knew how vain and silly were his thoughts— thinking nothing of eternity and of God.

Yes, it is a good thing whenever you feel too self-important, too pleased with yourself to measure yourself by the yardstick of immensity and the clock of eternity. Ages and ages rolled past, millions of men and women were born, died and were dust before *you* were born. Your life on this earth is but a tick of a second on the clock of the universe which goes on eternally. Before you is eternity. And measured by the yardstick of immensity—with all the vastness of space on every side of you — up and down — east and west — in every direction—stretching on without beginning or end—how big do you think you are? It is thoughts like these which keep sensible people from being too important and proud and vain.

It is a good thing to sit down and think of yourself in that way once in a while. Yes, whenever you feel like getting too puffed up with your own importance, you need not even *measure* yourself by those immense measuring rods. There are millions and millions of people who are living their lives all over this earth who do not even know you are alive— who will never in all likelihood hear about you. This is always a sobering thought.

It is like the explorer in Africa who went into the hut of a native chief. The chief had rings in his ears and nose. He was chief over a small tribe and was simply bursting with importance. The explorer paid him a few simple compliments on his well-stocked village. The chief brushed them impatiently aside and said through an interpreter: "Yes, yes, but what do they think of me in America?"

Chiefs and kings and generals are not always the ones who deem themselves to be greater than they are. Ordinary folks give way to it also. It was pride that drove Adam out of the Garden of Eden, that drove Saul from his kingdom, that has driven man and wife, sister and brother apart. Foolish pride which was too proud to say: "I was wrong, forgive me."

But he that humbleth himself shall be exalted."

Humility does not mean that you must always go about with lowered head and eyes, looking and feeling like a "poor worm." You can practice humility and still have confidence in yourself and your ability.

It simply means that you do not push yourself forward. The test will come when you can take either the place of honor at the table of life or the least important place with the same grace. The test will come when you can do the most important work you can imagine or even the smallest task with the same ability and good spirit. If you can do these things, then your humility is the kind that God exalts and Jesus typifies.

It is the kind of humility that is not ashamed of honest work or which feels that certain jobs are beneath you. God has put you into this world to work and he does not rate one occupation over another. All have their place.

There is the story of the big clock in the steeple of the town hall in the village square and the little gold watch. The watch said to the clock: "I do not like you. You are big and course and vulgar and made of brass. Now *I* am covered with gold. I have jewels within me and a beautiful crystal face. I am ever so delicately balanced and I certainly am a finer timepiece than you!"

The big clock in the tower smiled gently. "That is true," he rumbled. "You have much to be proud of. But there is a man down there in the square who wants to know what time it is. My great hands will shine in his eyes and my bronze bell will ring the time in his ears. But supposing you come up here and tell him what time it is."

In other words, we are all put here to serve our fellow men and God in the way we are best fitted. If we are best fitted to lead, then that is our work and not a source of vain pride. If we are fitted

250

to follow, then that is our work and it is nothing of which we need be ashamed.

Be proud and you will build a wall which will shut you out from your fellow men. Be humble and frank and honest and you will find your fellow men making a pleasant path to your door. Be proud and you will al-ways have to remember how superior you are. Be humble, yes, be childlike, and you will not have to strain or strut or pose. Your body and your mind will be relaxed and you will be happy in the truest sense of the word.

Let us pray: "For True Humbleness and Respect Before God."

Prayer

For

TRUE HUMBLENESS AND RESPECT BEFORE GOD

"God giveth grace unto the humble"—Ja. 4:6

Dear heavenly Father, Lord of the ages, whose presence is in the farthest reaches of the universe, yet Who art forever near, today I come to Thee with a humble heart.

O Father I do confess that sometimes I have been tempted to be proud and vain and satisfied with myself. And I have been tempted to be haughty to and look down on some of Thy children. I have said and done things in pride for which I truly am sorry now.

But, dear Father, Thou hast promised that if we confess our sins, Thou wilt forgive us and make us new again. Please, dear Father, give me that forgiveness now. And from this time on keep me from all pride which might lead me to think of myself more highly than I should.

Teach me that pride goeth before a fall, Father, and so keep me from the foolishness of pride. Teach me not to boast about my possessions or my talents, but humbly to remember that they are all gifts of Thine, just loaned to me so that I might serve Thy children. Help me to know that whatever I do, I do it not with my strength alone, but with Thine.

Dear heavenly Father, truly I shall try to do better. Truly I have felt Thy wonderful promise of help and forgiveness so much. And now I feel that I can go forth with thoughts of Thee — with thoughts of reverence and thankfulness and love.

—Amen

ASKING GOD FOR GUIDANCE IN HANDLING YOUR PROPERTY

ARE YOU WORRIED FOR ANY reason about property that you own? For instance, have you debts or mortgages on your property, or rents which you have to meet? Do you feel the need of God's guidance and blessing in your property matters? These and many other questions like them are pressing problems which many people have to meet.

Sometimes the question of property and mortgages and debts seems a far cry from the ministry of the spirit. Many people wonder how they can ask God for guidance in solving these problems which are often the most insistent and distressing they have to face.

You, too, may have hesitated to ask God's help and guidance in handling your property and business matters because you may have felt that houses and farms, lots and business ventures are something with which God does not concern Himself—that somehow He has left "business matters" entirely to us.

Yet you do know that nothing — absolutely nothing is outside God's interest for you. You know that the goods and the property and the business which God created and put into your hands is of as much interest to Him as it is to you. You should know that He wants you to be happy in the possession and handling of it.

When you study the life of God's dear Son, Jesus, closely, you see at once that Jesus spent as much of His time caring for the bodies of men and women as He did their spirits. Jesus knew what poverty was. He hated it and never praised it. He commanded the rich to share with the poor, but regarded poverty as merely another opportunity to mould character, not as a good thing in itself. Time after time he recognized that houses and farms brought property problems and He tried to help people with them.

Yet Jesus always taught that all property and land and earthly possessions belonged first to God. He taught that we were but caretakers or stewards of the property and that whatever we did with it should be devoted to using it for God's purposes.

The minute you take this attitude toward your property and its problems, you will find that the solution of many of these problems becomes immediately clear.

There is only one rule you need in your property and business matters. That is the Golden Rule. Yes, we know that this Rule has been twisted around so as to mean little in business dealings. But a better one has never been given!

And it is also true that in many cases where you try to put the Golden Rule into your property and business transactions you are, as Jesus said, like a sheep in the midst of wolves. But remember this, said Jesus, and be "as wise as serpents" as well as "harmless as doves."

Some people think that if you want to put the Golden Rule into your business and property, that you must lose all your senses entirely—that the lender must loan to anyone who asks, that the seller of property would have to sell the property at less than he could afford to.

But somehow, when you carry on your property matters in the service of God, He *does* give you the wisdom which Jesus said you should have. Everyone knows that the mission workers in the poorer sections of the cities are wholeheartedly devoted to the service of God and their fellow men. But they are far less likely to be taken in by the people who unworthily ask for help than the supposedly "hard-headed" rich people who come down to help them!

Honesty and open-heartedness in property and business dealings somehow brings you the real help of God. It somehow gives you a deeper wisdom in their handling—in buying, in selling, in renting and in financial matters in general. Because you have nothing to hide, you do not have to keep thinking about yourself all the time.

You are able to think clearly about the person who wants to buy or sell or rent or loan. If they are not acting honestly, you are so often able to detect it more quickly than if you had your mind solely on *yourself*. God *does* give you this wisdom!

You will find that if you start out in God's way with an honest and open heart, people will respond in the same way. Most people, when they start out to buy or rent or sell property or to do business, are on their guard. They *expect* deceit and lying and double-dealing.

But when they see you are honest, that you do not have to hide anything, that what you say they can see is true, then they drop all their own pretenses and are *glad* to do so. It is so much easier to do business with a decent, honest man. The whole transaction takes place on an entirely different footing.

People respond to trustfulness *with* trustfulness. On the corner in many a great city you will find a little pile of newspapers with a tin cup, placed there while the small merchant has gone to dinner. It will be only one person in a thousand who will take a paper without dropping a coin into the little cup.

One of the largest restaurant chains in New York City allows its customers to take whatever they want of the food freely displayed and open on their counters. The customer eats what he feels he can afford and on the way out tells the cashier the amount of his "check" and pays that amount. The customer is entirely trusted. That company has prospered all through the years and its losses are practically nothing.

It is so much more easy to tell the truth that it is a wonder people often take a life-time to find this little fact out. When you tell the truth in a business matter, then indeed God is on your side, for it is even a commandment: "Thou shalt not bear false witness." Thou shalt not lie.

When you tell the truth you need not fumble for words. You need not blush nor stammer. You do not need to tell one person one story and another person another story and hope they do not "get together."

If you tell the truth and truly act as a steward of God's property, then you will want to be of service to the buyer of your property as well as yourself. You will want to help the seller that he, too, prosper.

Desire prosperity for the person who wants to buy your house or farm. Desire prosperity for the person who wants to rent it. Desire prosperity for the one of whom you wish to buy. Desire peace and comfort for the one who wants to rent your room or your store. Pray and work for their good as well as your own, for your good cannot be separated from theirs.

Suppose you have some property to sell. Now instead of looking at a customer and thinking: "How much can I squeeze out of this man or woman for what I have to sell?" suppose instead of that you looked at them and thought: "How, in justice to what I need, can I render this man or woman the greatest possible service?" You would find it gives a new and wonderful lift to

your everyday life. It would influence that man or woman in a like manner, so that time after time you would be able to come to a good, friendly understanding. And all because of taking God's way.

Sometimes you may ask the question: "But what should I do in the face of debts—of taxes and mortgages and loans due? What should I do at the prospect of losing my home or my business if my debts are not paid? Should I have these same loving thoughts?"

And the answer is "Yes." God does not always believe it wise that you hold property and, although the way is hard, it is *still* God's plan that you do something else. But in most cases when you think that people are "hard" on you, it is often your own thought. Do you remember how glad you were when you got the mortgage, the loan, the extension of taxes, the property? You thought at the time that the persons responsible for it were pretty good, didn't you?

Well, they have not changed. Money must be repaid, often at great sacrifice. The prophet Elijah counseled the widow who was deep in debt to sacrifice the oil which she had in the house. He advised her to start with what she *had*.

That is the way God will help you to pay your obligations—by helping you to start where you stand and work from there! It is here that your real honesty will stand you in good stead.

When you come to think of it, few people desire your prosperity more than the people to whom you owe money. For if you prosper, you will pay them the money you owe them. Time after time they will go further out of their way to help you than many of your "friends."

There is the story of the storekeeper who owed a large amount of money to a stove company whose stoves he sold, but could not pay them. They were pressing him for the money. He knew the stoves were good and saleable. Hearing that the territory where his store was located was vacant he asked the company for the job. He promised to pay them from his commissions. Of course, they were glad to give him the territory, for it assured them of their money. So suc-

cessful was he that he soon paid their bill and was working full time, making more than he had made in the store.

Few people to whom you owe money are deliberately hard. If they see you are sincerely trying to pay them and are absolutely honest, they will give you every opportunity in the world.

So, dear reader, do not be afraid to talk over your property problems with God for truly He will listen. Tell Him about the property that you want to rent or sell. Confide in him your plans for a business of your own or your ambition to improve a business you may have. Ask his blessings and guidance in your affairs. And if things are going wrong, if you are in danger of losing any property, *still* be not afraid to tell your Father.

And God will answer, make no mistake about it. God will bring a buyer for your property just as soon as He finds one who will be best served by it. God will send those to prosper your business just as soon as He knows you are truly going forth to serve them. God will bless your farm the minute you ask him for that blessing!

And the way to ask God's help and guidance is through honest, sincere prayer—the kind of prayer that knoweth it receiveth even before it is asked—the kind of prayer that fears not to ask of the Father even those every-day helps with every-day problems which are so often shut out from your confidence with God.

Let us pray: "For God's Guidance in Handling Property."

Prayer

For

GOD'S GUIDANCE IN HANDLING PROPERTY

"The upright shall have good things in possession"—Prov. 28:10

Dear heavenly Father, Thou who art the greatest Teacher in all the world, it is I, Thy child, who comes to Thee that I may gain Thy wisdom and Thy understanding which I need so much.

For Thou hast promised that no trouble is too great and none too small for Thy help, dear Father. And that is why I come to Thee with my problem which has been troubling me so long — just how to handle the property entrusted to me.

Thou knowest, dear Father, how we have toiled to secure it and keep it up. And it is now that I need Thy help in the problem which has come up. O Father, cleanse my heart from all selfishness in handling it. Not for what it may do or bring do I ask Thy help, my Father, but that I may continue faithful to Thee in handling it.

If, in Thine infinite wisdom it is best to dispose of it, please Father, guide the steps of those who may find more and better use for it. And if it be best for us to keep it, please show us the way that Thy will be done.

But always, dear Father, teach me it is better to give than to receive, better to forget than step forward, better to minister than be ministered unto.

And grant, dear Father, that through this property, I may be at peace with all men and all women and with Thee. That is what gives me hope and strength.

—Amen

259

GOD IS ALWAYS READY TO FORGIVE YOUR SINS

Are you worried because some time in the past you may have yielded to the temptation of sin? Are you often tempted beyond your strength to commit some sin? And would you like God's forgiveness, yet hesitate lest it be asking too much?

If you are, then the wonderful tidings which are engraved in words which will never die in God's glorious Word, the Bible, should set your heart at peace. For there is one sure and simple way you can seek God's forgiveness of sin and sinful thinking. It is the way which St. Paul pointed out:

"If any man be in Christ, he is a new creature, old things are passed away, behold all things are become new." Old things are passed away! Yes, Jesus has the power to change you from a worried, unhappy man or woman to a contented, happy child of God. For he has changed and will *still* change millions of men and women from lives of sin and unhappiness to lives of welldoing and joy!

Yes, the world is full of people who have taken the key and locked in their hearts and memories unhappy thoughts which they will not reveal to anyone— even to their nearest and dearest. Here is a man who appears happy and carefree. How surprised others would be if they could look into his heart. They would see a boiling cauldron of unhappy thoughts—regrets— guilt and moral failure!

Here is a woman apparently gay and happy. How surprised her friends would be to see the load and the heartache which she carries about with her every day— dreams that never came true, temptations that will not down, sins that she herself will not admit!

The great, big enormous sins which blaze their sign

to all who pass by are not the ones which bring the most unhappiness and sorrow. It is the small, hidden sins which are your own secret, which eat at the heart of your happiness. It is the sins which often you, alone, know you committed, sins which are not always *called* sins but which you know have brought tears and heartache to others—things you have done, words you have said which can never be recalled.

And yet, so often they were things which you regretted almost the instant you said them or did them. Well, whatever you did in the past—whether the sin was great or small, whether outward or hidden, it is now beyond anything you can recall!

And you ask yourself— "Can I let the past go? Will God forgive me? *Has* he forgiven me?"

Yes, dear friend, God has forgiven you if you have truly repented. He does not bear grudges. True it is that many people picture God as an angry God always looking for sins and then punishing sinners grievously. Unfortunately this has been the picture which many people have built up in their own minds of God, our Father.

It is precisely this picture that Jesus came to paint over for you. Jesus has given us a picture of God as a loving, forgiving Father—forgiving us even when we dare not forgive ourselves!

Jesus has made for you the forgiveness of the Father as simple as the little story of the boy who asked his mother: "How do you know that God forgives sin, mother?"

"Do you remember when you were naughty the other day and how you came to me and said you were sorry for what you had done?"

"Yes," said the boy.

"And do you remember how I said I was sure you would never do it again and forgave you? Do you remember how happy you were? You believed me, didn't you?"

"Oh, yes," answered the boy.

"Well, that is the way our Father forgives us," explained the mother. "Tell Him you are sorry and that you will never do it again and just as quickly as I forgave you or father would forgive you, so God will forgive you. Believe *Him* as you believe me!"

The forgiveness of God for your sins is so very simple and yet how complicated we often make it. For Jesus has told us that if we will face our temptations and our sins honestly then there is glorious hope for us. But Jesus has said that we must really and truly face them without trying to make excuses for ourselves. That is not always so easy.

There is the story of the lady who came to her minister to tell him about her struggle with a certain temptation. "I have prayed and prayed," she told the minister, "and have asked God to tell me what to do."

"What did you tell Him to tell you?" dryly asked the wise old minister.

"Why I asked Him to tell me what I knew was right—that would be the right thing to do, wouldn't it?"

"Did you ever think of asking Him what *He* knew was right?" questioned the shrewd old parson.

Yes, so many times we are willing to give up our sins and temptations if we can keep all the pleasant things which they seem to promise.

But Jesus said we must not make excuses for ourselves. He has told us we must confess our sins and temptations to ourselves first and then to God—and then *do* something—start to do what we know is right!

It is this last step which so often holds us back from actually seeking God's help in overcoming our sins and receiving His forgiveness. Deep within our hearts we feel we may have to change our entire way of thinking and living.

How can you begin to seek God's forgiveness? Well, one way is to start forgiving others. You will remember that in one version of our Lord's Prayer, Jesus taught us to say: "Forgive us our trespasses as we forgive those who trespass against us." In other words, Jesus is telling us that we should ask God's forgiveness exactly to the extent we are willing to forgive others.

Jesus made it still more clear. You will remember that a man once asked Jesus whether, if he made public prayers and sacrifices, his sins would be forgiven. Jesus turned to him with scorn. He told the man that if he came to worship with hate in his heart, then no amount of prayer or sacrifices would do him any good. "First be reconciled with thy brother, then come and offer thy gift," He said.

It was this stress upon forgiveness *yourself* which Jesus made again and again. For He well knew that there are few sins which do not harm *others*. And unless you are willing to renounce the attitude which allows you to harm others, then Jesus knew you were not ready to receive forgiveness, for you have not learned the lesson which God has been trying to teach — the Golden Rule — the lesson that true happiness lies only in doing unto others as you would have them do unto you!

So many times, many of the things which have caused you such suffering were questions of bad judgment more than anything else. It is true that there are many grievous sins, but so few people commit them. So few people actually *try* to harm others for the sake of doing harm. In so many instances, what you did was what you thought best at the time. It was not until later that the real seriousness of your action dawned upon you. And when it *did* dawn, then it was that it took its place in the background of your thought and mind as a sin.

Let us by all means admit that some of the things you did were real sins. Well, nothing that you can do now will bring back the vanished moment of wrongdoing. Under those circumstances, the only thing you can do is let the past go, "forgetting the things that are behind."

God wants you to do only one thing in order that He may forgive you. All he asks is that you begin at once — today — to start living at the best you know how — and then reach out and take His forgiveness!

God will forgive you no matter who you are or what you are, if you will respond to Him in this way. God's help and forgiveness is promised to everyone. There are no strings attached.

> *"Everyone that asketh receiveth,*
> *Everyone that seeketh findeth,*
> *To everyone that knocketh it shall be opened."*

Right now — this very day — God is ready to do everything for you that His love can do. He is waiting for only one thing on your part—for you to start living a new life.

For God is a Father of love. And He can be trusted to take care of whatever has happened in the past. If you sinned and truly repented, your sins were forgiven long ago. If you stumbled off the right path, God can be trusted to lead you faithfully back.

How often have you read in the Bible that God's mercies are new each morning? Each dawning of day gives you the chance to build a new life no matter what your past life has been.

A drunkard was helped by a minister to reform. For a time he came regularly to church and then came no more. Many years passed and one day the minister was called to preach a funeral service in the slums. The man who asked him said that his "friend" had requested it. As the minister came into the little room where the body of the man he had helped lay, he said: "Poor Tom, where did you find him?"

"*Find* him?" asked the astonished man. "It was he who found *us!* For years he has been going through these streets night and day bringing Jesus home to *us!*"

You, too, can start today building a life that will please God. At the end of each day when you have lived your best, when you may have tried to make up for what you did in the past, you have the privilege of going up to your Father and saying: "Are you pleased with me, Father?"

And from your Father will come the answer. You will know at once which of your thoughts and deeds should have been turned away. And your Father is ready to forgive you, not once, but seventy times seven!

For when you stop to think of it, to forgive is made up of two words— "for" and "give." Forgiving really means "to give for." Give for the joy of making others happy. Give for the happiness of others. Give for others without thought of personal reward, and, as day follows night, God will give for *you*.

When you give for others, when you help them realize the power of God's love, when you "for-give" them, you are almost giving them the keys of heaven. And as there is no limit to the blessing which you can open to them from God, so is there no limit to the forgiveness which God can open for you.

A mind and soul attuned like that is really beginning to live at its best. It is a

264

mind which has returned to the Father.

Yes, even though your sins were as scarlet, if you truly repent and begin to live as best you know, you will be forgiven every day as you return to your Father.

For in Him you will find forgiveness and peace and joy. And He shall say: "This my son was dead and is alive again, he was lost and was found."

Let us pray: "For God's Forgiveness of My Sins."

Prayer

For

GOD'S FORGIVENESS OF MY SINS

"For thou, Lord, art good, and ready to forgive; and plenteous in mercy unto all them that call upon thee"—Psalms 86:5

Eternal God, who sitteth in judgment, yet whose mercy endureth forever, it is not easy for me to come into Thy presence this day. But alone with Thee, with none to hear or condemn, I know Thou wilt listen and understand.

Father, I humbly confess that in many ways I have not kept Thy commands. It is with sorrow that I look back on those things I have done and some of which I am still doing.

All I can say, dear Father, is what was said so many years ago: "Be merciful unto me, a sinner." O Father, please help me mend my ways. Be patient with me — for without Thee I am lost. Strengthen me that sin have no power over me. Help me, help me drive all evil from my heart.

In Thy love for me, dear Father, Thou hast given me the love of family and friends. In Thy mercy, Father, help me to be worthy of that love. O how I need faith and prayer right now, dear Father, for I know so well that the prayers of the righteous avail so much!

Dear Father, somehow I do feel that having confessed to Thee, having cast my burden upon Thee, I truly will receive Thy forgiveness. Yes, somehow I feel Thy kindly hand, hear Thy kindly voice saying: "Peace, be still...Thy sins are forgiven...in His Name."

—Amen

TURNING TO GOD FOR HELP IN OVERCOMING TEMPTATION

WOULD YOU LIKE TO BREAK yourself of some bad habit which is making you and your loved ones unhappy— the habit, for instance, of drink, of gambling, of profanity, of temper or any of the many, many other habits which make life so hard and miserable?

Would you like God's help in overcoming these and other temptations—to resist the temptations which call to every man and woman—temptations to sin or to do what you know is wrong?

If you would, then here in this short space of this chapter in your Handbook of Life, is given to you the Word and the Way—the word of God in His Bible and the Way of Jesus in His wonderful life so often, too, beset by the tempter's whisper.

For, make no mistake about it, there are two differ-ent battles going on in your body and mind as they go on in *everyone's* body and mind. You can call this battle the struggle between right and wrong, between good and evil, between the devil and the angels, between the spirit and the flesh—but whatever you *call* it, it is there and it is very real!

But happily, as in *all* struggles, it is in the very struggle that there is hope. For when you cease to struggle then, indeed, you are dead, physically and spiritually. As long as you *ask* yourself the question as to whether you can overcome temptation, so is the spark of God alive in you and so will God help you to fan that spark into living flame.

And just as flame purifies, so does Faith in God and His wondrous power purify your thought even as your struggle goes on. So you can arise from the ashes and the

flame of the fire of temptation a new man or woman.

"If any man be in Christ,
he is a new creature, old
things are passed away."
Yes, God has the power to
transform you from a weak,
tempted man or woman to a
strong, upright child of our
Father!

For God is not so much
interested in keeping men
and women free from the
thought and knowledge of
temptation, as He is in building *strong* men and women
with *full* knowledge of the
world's sin and the world's
temptation.

A stranger was spending
the summer in the back-
woods where he met an old
man toiling with his three
strong sons on a rocky farm.
The stranger stopped to
talk to the old man.

"Tell me," he said, "whatever can you raise in a
rocky, mountain place like
this?"

The old man slowly
straightened up, wiped his
perspiring brow with a
gnarled hand and proudly
gave him his answer:

"Men!"

God wants men and
women, not to be free from
all contact with the world
and its sin, but to be able to
meet the world and over-
come that temptation, to
make their virtues and their
personalities grow in soil
which to unseeing eyes only
might be stony and rocky
and full of thorns.

God will not do away
with drink or gambling or
tobacco or the lusts of the
body. They are part of the
world and they are still *in*
the world. And God will not
instantly wipe away all the
bad habits which you have
so carefully grown all these
years. You will be disap-
pointed if you expect as a
result of a day or two of
determination — even of
prayer — to secure un-
earned strength to resist
temptation.

God *will* help you to overcome temptations and sin,
but He will do it in natural,
normal ways—ways which
you sometimes may not be
able to see, so natural and
simple they may be. God
will help you overcome your
temptations just as soon as
He can find the way which
is natural and normal to
you!

Some people worry about
what they call "bad
thoughts." At times, no matter how they try to keep
them away, they have

thoughts of hate or passion or immorality or temptation. Visions of what they would like to do pass through their minds. And sometimes the visions are not good ones nor holy ones. And then they are troubled because they think that the thought which passed through their minds has made them guilty of the sin about which they thought.

But look upon it this way, dear reader, and you will find that God is helping you to resist temptation in ways you know not.

Your mind and your heart are two different things. Your heart is deep within you and beats with the heart of God. Your mind is like a waiting room where all thoughts may come—invited or uninvited. And like a waiting room, your mind is open to thoughts which are not always welcome—sinful, mean, yes and impure thoughts!

True, you may have a thought of hate or passion, of temptation or of lust. But as that thought enters the waiting room of your mind it can go no further than the portals of your heart. It must stand before that guardian which you call your conscience.

If your heart and your conscience see the thought for the evil thing it is, if your heart and your conscience bid it leave, if your heart and your conscience give no room for that thought to act, then you have committed no sin, you have resisted a temptation which might come to anyone.

Instead of being made weaker by that thought, you have been made strong by God and have been given the strength to resist it. You have gone far on the road to making yourself a worthy member of the Kingdom of God.

There is the story of the famous man who was visiting a schoolroom and wished to test a little girl. Holding up an apple, he asked to what kingdom it belonged. "The vegetable," she answered.

Then he held up an iron bar and asked to what kingdom *that* belonged. "The mineral," she said.

He pointed to himself and asked to what kingdom *he* belonged. The little girl hesitated, for she did not want to say that the famous man belonged to the animal kingdom. Suddenly her face brightened and she replied: "To God's kingdom."

The man was deeply stirred and a tear came to his eye. "God help me be worthy of that kingdom," he softly said.

To enter that kingdom is not easy. The powers of temptation have ways that are attractive and cunning. Perhaps you, too, have noticed their way of working. Perhaps, you, too, have seen how they seem to be able to flash pictures on your mind, how they make sin and wrongdoing seem easy and pleasant.

The drinker sees a picture of the inviting glass of liquor. The gambler sees a picture of the money he will have when and if he wins. The lustful man or woman sees a picture of the unholy attraction which beckons them. But there is one thing you can do about any temptation which casts such pictures. If you can banish them the moment they appear, you will be able to withstand them all the *other* moments.

You cannot make your mind a blank. If you are to keep these pictures of temptation out of your mind, you must put something in their place. And it is here that God is most ready to help you overcome your temptation. For in His Book

He has given you still *greater* pictures to fill your mind—purer, finer pictures than any which the temptation can furnish.

Well did the Psalmist know how God would help the tempted, when he said: "Thou wilt keep him in perfect peace whose mind is stayed upon Thee." Whose mind is stayed upon Thee! If your mind gives pictures of temptation no abiding place, but keeps its gaze fixed upon God, then God will keep you in perfect peace. And surely peace can only come where there is freedom from temptation and sin!

Keep your mind upon God by thinking of those many wonderful words in the Bible which bring to you His promises of help and deliverance:

"Ye shall not fear them, for the Lord your God, he shall fight for you."

"The Lord is my rock and my fortress and my deliverer."

"Giving thanks unto the Father—who hath delivered us from the power of darkness, and hath translated us in the kingdom of His dear Son."

"Thou hast delivered my

soul from death, wilt not Thou deliver my feet from falling."

"When thou passeth through the waters, I will be with thee. I will never leave thee nor forsake thee."

And from these moments of peace will come God's help in overcoming your temptations. They will come to you as you learn from others how they solved the same problems which are facing you. You will learn from others through your eyes, through your ears and through the knowledge which is the heritage of the race.

God will help you overcome temptation and sin when you feel a new determination to use all your willpower and strength to overcome them. God will help you overcome your temptation as you feel an old memory tugging at your heartstrings—a memory of times when you did not have that temptation or that habit.

Yes, and God will help you whenever in your moments of despair as to whether you will ever overcome the temptation you feel something deep down in your heart telling you to keep up the good fight.

Self-control is not easy. Resistance to temptation is not easy. Breaking an unhappy habit is not easy. There is hardly a man or woman—even the best and finest—who is not almost daily faced with temptations of one kind or another, who does not hear the siren song of some bad habit whispering to them to try this or that bad action because it is so easy and pleasant.

Some one asked the famous evangelist, Dwight L. Moody, what person in his lifetime gave him the most trouble. He immediately answered, "Myself."

And so it is wise to remember that temptations are more strong at some times than at others. They vary with your physical strength. In other words you are able to resist temptation better at some times rather than others. When you are physically or mentally tired, then it is easier to listen to the call of temptation. It is then that your heart opens your mind to the thoughts which your mind has allowed to enter and which have stayed awaiting judgment.

So the answer would seem natural. Keep yourself as rested physically and mentally as you can and you will find it easier to resist whatever habit or temptation against which you are struggling.

Yes, dear friend, God will let you walk with Him free of temptation. He will help you bear the sting of spite, the hate of men who fear Him. If you will do *your* best to overcome your bad habits, then God can indeed be trusted to do *His* best. And the courage to resist temptation will not only be a part of your own achievement, but also God's great gift.

Let us pray: "That God Will Help Me To Overcome Temptation."

Prayer

That

GOD WILL HELP ME TO OVERCOME TEMPTATION

"God is faithful, who will not suffer you to be tempted above that ye are able; but will with the temptation also make a way to escape"
—I Cor. 10:13

Almighty and everlasting God, whom no man has ever seen, Who art spirit and Father of spirits, unto Thee do I come in my fear and weakness.

For Thou knowest, dear Father, what temptations I face now. Thou knowest how tempting is the way of evil, how narrow is the way of good!

I am trembling and tired, dear Father, like one who has run a long way. Temptations that wait in the darkness call to me. I am weak, my Father, and afraid lest I listen to them.

Help me, dear Father, help me when I am tempted. Help me to remember the temptations which have overcome me in the past and which can overcome me again unless I receive Thy help!

O Father, help me to choose the better way to overcome these temptations. Truly I know Thou wilt help, for I seem to see Thee nodding Thy head. I seem to feel Thee taking my hand in Thine!

While Thou leadest, I do not fear, dear Father, for Thou art with me — Thy rod and Thy staff keep temptation from me. Yes, Father, with Thee I have strength to overcome — overcome all the temptations which call to me. With Thee I am strong — ready to go forth — not afraid — able to say "No" — true and brave!

With Thee I shall overcome!

—Amen

ASKING GOD'S HELP IN CONTROLLING YOUR TEMPER AND EMOTIONS

Do YOU EVER LOOSE YOUR temper and allow your emotions to get control of you? Would you like to break yourself of the habit of losing your temper and "going to pieces" at every little obstacle which confronts you?

If you would, then take heart, dear reader, for the lesson of the world and the lesson which God has given here for you, teaches you that you *can* control your emotions in a greater and finer way than you ever thought possible.

Loss of control takes many forms. You cannot stand noise; you fly into anger at being interrupted at whatever you are doing, you get enraged if your desires or your opinions are crossed in the slightest. Perhaps up to now you have been "easy" with yourself when it comes to temper and loss of control. You probably have said: "Oh, I am so high-strung" or "Who wouldn't get angry?"

Yet deep in your heart, if you are honest with yourself, how many times has your life been made unhappy, yes even saddened by the thoughtless word of anger, the unplanned action which your emotions drove you into.

Even though you knew you were doing wrong at the moment, you said the word which could not be recalled—you lost control of yourself. Even though you knew at the moment you were doing wrong, you did the deed which could not be undone. Think of the unhappiness which you may have brought to your dear ones and friends, the friendships of years spoiled or even wrecked, the hearts torn by your outbursts of temper and anger.

And yet, although you may not always believe it, temper and emotion *can* be controlled. Thousands of people with natures every bit as sensitive as yours, with just as much cause, yes, even *more*, for outbursts as you, have learned to control their temper and emotions.

God says that you *can* control your temper. By the example of His dear Son, He has shown you that it can be done. Jesus faced evil. You yourself know how people went out of their way to misunderstand Him. You know how some of His followers took advantage of His friendship and His love. You know how suspicion and abuse followed Jesus whereever He went.

Yet you also know that His calm and self-control were indeed marvelous. For Jesus was drawing upon a power which is just as open to you today for control if you will only use it!

When you begin to accept evils which you cannot change, without anger, something actually happens with *you*, too. Somehow or other there comes into your heart a peace—the peace which Jesus knew — the peace which cannot give nor take away!

Remember that temper is not one of those things which happens without reason and warning, even though you may like to *believe* it does. For to believe that gives you your excuse that you are not to blame. It gives you your chance to excuse yourself by saying "I don't know what happened. I just lost my temper."

No, dear reader, temper and emotional outbursts come to you as the result of very definite things and at very definite times. If you will study these things and these times, you will be far on the way to understanding *yourself* and controlling them.

It is important to know the *times* when you are most likely to give way to temper. If you know *that*, then things will not matter—for you will know that at certain times almost *any* little thing—even things which pass unnoticed at other times—bring on your temper.

First, it is always at times when you are tired and weary that it is easiest to give way to temper and emotional outbursts. Everyone knows that things look different at night than they do in the morning or the daytime. In the morning you seem to be able to answer any questions, overcome any obstacles, handle any situation. But as the day goes on, your ability to do these things seems to lessen. Problems and obstacles loom larger and larger. Small wonder, then, that as they loom large they overcome you.

Almost always after a sleepless night or perhaps two or three, you will find your temper mounting. Nine-tenths of the arguments and quarrels of people take place at night.

Other times when you give way to temper and loss of control is when you have had your self-control sapped by pain, suffering, disappointment, worry or uncertainty about something. Remember those five things— for they are the roots of temper. They are the real causes of your temper and anger— not your sensitive nature.

And still further. Temper does not come on without warning. If you knew what the warning signals are you would be able to recognize them. Just as a thunder storm gives warning of its approach by lowering clouds on the horizon, by oppressive heat, by a sudden stillness in the air, so do storms of temper and anger give warning of their coming to those who know how to heed them.

If you will learn to recognize the warning signals that come to you before your storm of temper, time after time you will be able to keep the storm from coming. It will go "around you" as sudden storms sometimes do!

One of the most frequent signs of coming temper is the feeling that you will never be able to accomplish what you have to do. A man will feel he will never finish his work, and may as well give up. A woman will feel that no matter how she works in the house, more and more work stretches on endlessly. A mother will feel that her children will *never* stop being disobedient and noisy. This feeling of "endlessness" is one of the largest warning signals. Look for it in yourself.

Another warning signal is when you find it impossible to make up your mind. You seem tugged one way or the other. Should you go here or there? What should you say or do? Should you do this or that? You can't make up your mind. This is a warning signal of temper ahead.

A third warning signal is a general feeling of anger. You aren't angry at anyone in particular just yet—but just angry in general. You say "I got out of bed with the wrong foot this morning." You feel angry about something in the news. You feel angry about something a total stranger said or did. You feel angry about some condition you notice in the house or on the street. It is only a step from feeling angry in general to feeling angry about someone in particular.

All these things are storm-warnings. They are signs of approaching battle. And when you find a battle coming, the wise thing is to "post a guard."

If you really want God to help you control your temper and emotions, here is the way to start. When you notice any of these danger signals, when you start to feel nervous and irritable or angry over trifles—do this simple thing:

Drop whatever you are doing, if you can, and give yourself a rest. If you *can*, lie down and deliberately drive all thought from your mind. At first you may toss and turn, but gradually peace will come. But whether in your room or anywhere else, turn your thought to God!

For in many cases, your mind and your spirit need as much rest as your body. Go to a church or some quiet place if you can and there turn to God. Sit in quiet before Him. Empty your mind of all thought except the wonder and the greatness and peace of God!

"Wait on the Lord." For those who wait on the Lord shall renew their strength—and control their temper and emotions! And the time you have been nervous and irritable and out of control, God has been waiting to help you, to give you His peace. He has been waiting for you to open your heart and mind to Him that He might pour out His comfort and His peace into it!

That was the secret of Jesus. Whenever He was worried or perplexed He went apart, quieted Himself and prayed to His Father for help and strength and guidance. He would come back from even a few moments spent in prayer with such a wonderfully relaxed and peaceful expression, that His Disciples were amazed and begged Him to give them the secret of His peace. And it was then that He gave them the prayer which they were to say to their Father—the Lord's Prayer!

And the secret was the resisting not of evil. How often have you read those words of Jesus and yet how little you may have understood them. Yet in their understanding lies one of the greatest secrets of controlling your temper and emotions. And within them lies one of the greatest forces for your happiness that the world has to offer—strange as these words are.

For they are strange indeed. You may well ask yourself if you are not to "fight back" when things go against you, if you must let anyone do anything they want to you without your raising your voice.

Yes, this is the secret of Jesus. It lies not in acting quickly and unthinkingly, but in remaining calm when things are going on, in seeing evil as the small and temporary thing it is. It is in having faith that God will overcome it—overcome it in His own marvelous and unchanging way.

Do you want a simple little "exercise" in beginning to learn to control your temper? Here it is.

Suppose you are standing in line at a store, a ticket window, the post office and the line moves like a snail. And you are in the habit of fuming and fretting. Is anything to be gained by grumbling and peering at those ahead, by demanding quicker attention? You know there is not.

Begin your practice of resisting not evil by not chafing at the line ahead. Look at the line behind! Relax and look at the person in front of you or behind you. Strike up a pleasant conversation with the person on either side of you. You have the common task of waiting to "break the ice." Don't grumble, but make some pleasant comment. Make up your mind to use the time getting acquainted with that person. Look about you for something interesting or humorous. Point it out to the person near you. The line will seem to move like magic and you will reach the window fresh and reposed. You will have controlled your temper and emotions. This is only a small practice test, but used in conjunction with the rest of the counsel given in this chapter, you should be well on the way to control!

These are little "tricks" to be sure. Yet you need no trick if you will just place your worries and cares in the kind hands of God just as fast as they come to you. That is so simple, so easy that you can do it—begin this very day—by turning to God "with whom all things are possible!"

Let us pray: "For God's Help in Controlling My Temper and Emotions."

𝔓𝔯𝔞𝔶𝔢𝔯

For

GOD'S HELP IN CONTROLLING MY TEMPER AND EMOTIONS

"He that is slow to anger is better than the mighty; and he that ruleth his spirit than he that taketh a city"—Prov. 16:32

Eternal Father, who makest the heavens Thy home, yet who livest in humble hearts, I come to Thee with a heart which is ashamed of my temper and my emotions of anger.

O dear Father, I do not know what is the matter with me when I get those spells. I just don't seem able to control them. Truly, almost as soon as I say mean things, I am ashamed. But in my pride and vanity it is so hard to admit I was wrong.

Help me, dear Father, help me, for I know I am not only hurting others, but hurting myself. Yes, I know they lose me friends and make me miserable. Please, Father in heaven, do help me to control myself better. I want to change with all my heart!

Yes, Father, forbid that I should willingly hurt anyone by word or deed. My heart loves Thee and I want to do what is right. Thou knowest how sorry I am and how I have made up my mind to do better.

I have opened my heart to Thee, dear Father, And I do feel Thou wilt cleanse it and make it more pure. I do feel that Thou wilt give me Thy blessing and help me to control myself. And this makes my mind and my heart so much stronger, dear Father — strong to go forth calm and controlled for many a long day!

—Amen

Heartwarming Books
of
Faith and Inspiration

☐	23363	**MAN OF STEEL AND VELVET** Dr. Aubrey Andelin	$3.50
☐	22706	**FASCINATING WOMANHOOD** Dr. Aubrey Andelin	$3.95
☐	23196	**STEPS ON THE STAIRWAY** R. Ransom	$2.95
☐	22739	**CONFESSIONS OF A HAPPY CHRISTIAN** Zig Ziglar	$2.75
☐	23748	**THE SCREWTAPE LETTERS** C. S. Lewis	$2.25
☐	23069	**A SEVERE MERCY** Sheldon Vanauken	$3.50
☐	20831	**THE GUIDEPOSTS TREASURY OF LOVE**	$2.95
☐	23255	**GUIDEPOST'S TREASURY OF FAITH**	$3.50
☐	20168	**THREE STEPS FORWARD TWO STEPS BACK** Charles S. Swindoll	$2.95
☐	23977	**MEETING GOD AT EVERY TURN** Catherine Marshall	$3.50
☐	23277	**POSITIVE PRAYERS FOR POWER-FILLED LIVING** Robert H. Schuller	$2.95
☐	22623	**TWO FROM GALILEE** Marjorie Holmes	$2.95
☐	23614	**THE GREATEST SECRET IN THE WORLD** Og Mandino	$2.95
☐	23479	**THE GREATEST MIRACLE IN THE WORLD** Og Mandino	$2.95
☐	24139	**CHRIST COMMISSION** Og Mandino	$3.50
☐	20102	**THE 1980'S COUNTDOWN TO ARMAGEDDON** Hal Lindsey	$2.95
☐	23268	**I'VE GOT TO TALK TO SOMEBODY, GOD** Marjorie Holmes	$2.95
☐	23539	**A GRIEF OBSERVED** C. S. Lewis	$2.95
☐	23166	**WITH GOD ALL THINGS ARE POSSIBLE—** Life Fellowship Study	$3.50

Prices and availability subject to change without notice.

Buy them at your local bookstore or use this handy coupon for ordering:

Bantam Books, Inc., Dept. HF, 414 East Golf Road, Des Plaines, Ill. 60016

Please send me the books I have checked above. I am enclosing $_____
(please add $1.25 to cover postage and handling). Send check or money order
—no cash or C.O.D.'s please.

Mr/Mrs/Miss _____

Address _____

City_____State/Zip_____

HF—12/83

Please allow four to six weeks for delivery. This offer expires 6/84.

MS READ-a-thon—
a simple way
to start youngsters reading.

Boys and girls between 6 and 14 can join the MS READ-a-thon and by reading books, raise money for Multiple Sclerosis research. They get two rewards—the enjoyment of reading, and the great feeling that comes from helping others.

Parents and educators: For complete information call your local MS chapter. Or mail the coupon below.

Kids can help, too!

Books by One of the Great
Inspirational Writers
of Our Time

OG MANDINO

"For many years I have eagerly read everything Og Mandino has written, always to my profit, and I personally owe him a great debt of gratitude. This sentiment, I am sure, will be echoed by his wide circle of readers."—Norman Vincent Peale

SPECIAL MONEY SAVING OFFER

Now you can have an up-to-date listing of Bantam's hundreds of titles plus take advantage of our unique and exciting bonus book offer. A special offer which gives you the opportunity to purchase a Bantam book for only 50¢. Here's how!

By ordering any five books at the regular price per order, you can also choose any other single book in the catalog (up to a $4.95 value) for just 50¢. Some restrictions do apply, but for further details why not send for Bantam's illustrated Shop-At-Home Catalog today!

Just send us your name and address plus 50¢ to defray the postage and handling costs.

Les Misérables

VICTOR HUGO

Ouvrage publié sous la direction de
ANNETTE FLOBERT

Édition présentée par
FLORENCE NAUGRETTE
Ancienne élève de l'ENS
Agrégée de lettres modernes
Professeur à l'université de Rouen

www.universdeslettres.com

Voir « LE TEXTE ET SES IMAGES » p. 276
pour l'exploitation de l'iconographie de ce dossier.

1. Eugène Delacroix, *La Liberté guidant le peuple*, 1830.
(Musée du Louvre, Paris.)

LE PEUPLE AU XIXᵉ SIÈCLE :
MISÈRE ET RÉVOLUTION

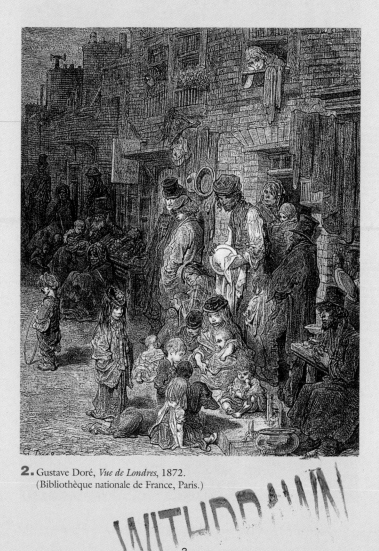

2. Gustave Doré, *Vue de Londres*, 1872.
(Bibliothèque nationale de France, Paris.)

3. Jean Gabin (Jean Valjean) et Fernand Ledoux (Mgr Myriel) dans *Les Misérables* de Jean-Paul Le Chanois, 1957.

4. Jean Gabin (Jean Valjean), Elfreide Florin (La Thénardier) et Bourvil (Thénardier) dans le film de Jean-Paul Le Chanois, 1957.

5. Robert Marien (JEAN VALJEAN) et Marie Zamora (COSETTE) dans la comédie musicale d'Alain Boublil et Claude Michel Schönberg, théâtre Mogador, 1991.

6. Bernard Blier (JAVERT), Lucien Baroux (M. GILLENORMAND), Giani Esposito (MARIUS), Jean Gabin (JEAN VALJEAN) dans le film de J.-P. Le Chanois, 1957.

7. Émile Genevoix (GAVROCHE)
dans *Les Misérables* de Raymond Bernard, 1933.

8. François Pompon, *Cosette*, 1888. (Maison de Victor Hugo, Paris.)

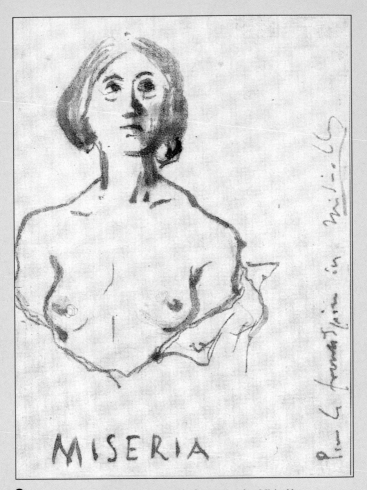

9. Victor Hugo, *Miseria*, dessin pour le frontispice des *Misérables*.
(Maison de Victor Hugo, Paris.)

REGARDS
SUR L'ŒUVRE

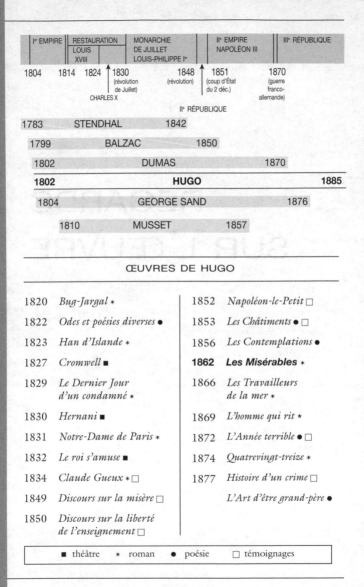

| Ier EMPIRE | RESTAURATION | | MONARCHIE DE JUILLET | IIe EMPIRE | IIIe RÉPUBLIQUE |
| | LOUIS XVIII | | LOUIS-PHILIPPE Ier | NAPOLÉON III | |

| 1804 | 1814 | 1824 | 1830 (révolution de Juillet) | 1848 (révolution) | 1851 (coup d'État du 2 déc.) | 1870 (guerre franco-allemande) |

CHARLES X

IIe RÉPUBLIQUE

1783	STENDHAL	1842
1799	BALZAC	1850
1802	DUMAS	1870
1802	**HUGO**	**1885**
1804	GEORGE SAND	1876
1810	MUSSET	1857

ŒUVRES DE HUGO

1820	*Bug-Jargal* ∗
1822	*Odes et poésies diverses* ●
1823	*Han d'Islande* ∗
1827	*Cromwell* ■
1829	*Le Dernier Jour d'un condamné* ∗
1830	*Hernani* ■
1831	*Notre-Dame de Paris* ∗
1832	*Le roi s'amuse* ■
1834	*Claude Gueux* ∗ □
1849	*Discours sur la misère* □
1850	*Discours sur la liberté de l'enseignement* □

1852	*Napoléon-le-Petit* □
1853	*Les Châtiments* ● □
1856	*Les Contemplations* ●
1862	***Les Misérables*** ∗
1866	*Les Travailleurs de la mer* ∗
1869	*L'homme qui rit* ∗
1872	*L'Année terrible* ● □
1874	*Quatrevingt-treize* ∗
1877	*Histoire d'un crime* □
	L'Art d'être grand-père ●

| ■ théâtre | ∗ roman | ● poésie | □ témoignages |

LIRE AUJOURD'HUI
LES MISÉRABLES

Opposant au régime de Napoléon III, Victor Hugo vit en exil. En 1862, il publie *Les Misérables*, roman commencé dix-sept ans plus tôt. Dès sa sortie, le succès est immense. Aujourd'hui, ses traductions et ses adaptations cinématographiques et théâtrales ont fait le tour du monde.

Tout à la fois roman d'aventures, roman psychologique et roman social, c'est un livre original et puissant. On se passionne pour le destin mouvementé du forçat Jean Valjean, qui cherche toute sa vie à racheter son passé, pour les malheurs de Fantine, la femme déchue, pour la métamorphose de sa petite Cosette, enfant martyre, pour les élans patriotiques et sentimentaux du jeune Marius, pour l'impertinence de Gavroche, le gamin de Paris. On frémit à l'approche du vil Thénardier, rusé et prêt à tout, et devant Javert, l'inspecteur de police impitoyable qui traque Jean Valjean. Les évasions du bagnard, les peurs de la fillette, les filatures dans les rues sombres, le soulèvement révolutionnaire, la fuite infernale du vieillard et du jeune homme, le premier portant l'autre sur ses épaules dans les égouts de Paris, frappent vivement l'imagination.

Cette peinture vivante de la société du XIXe siècle, qui a profondément ému et même parfois choqué les contemporains de Hugo, soulève des questions qui concernent directement le lecteur d'aujourd'hui : les préjugés sociaux, la misère humaine, l'exploitation de l'enfant et de la femme, les abus de la justice. Pourtant, il s'agit d'un roman optimiste : Hugo rêve de la venue de jours meilleurs.

En attendant, les personnages, qu'ils soient courageux, dévoués, amoureux, ou encore sordides, cruels et injustes, se transforment au fil du récit palpitant de leurs aventures en figures de légende.

REPÈRES

L'AUTEUR : Victor Hugo.

PREMIÈRE PUBLICATION : 1862.

LE GENRE : roman populaire, philosophique, d'aventures, social, romantique et réaliste : dépassant les catégories traditionnelles ? Illustré par les meilleurs dessinateurs de son temps, puis inlassablement adapté au théâtre et au cinéma, et plus récemment en bande dessinée.

LE CONTEXTE : le second Empire, l'exil, la révolution industrielle, la paupérisation du prolétariat.

LE ROMAN

• **Structure** : cinq parties, divisées en livres, puis en chapitres.

• **Lieu et temps** : en France (avec une incursion à Waterloo, en Belgique) au début du XIXe siècle. L'essentiel de l'intrigue se déroule sous la Restauration et le début de la monarchie de Juillet.

• **Personnages** : le héros Jean Valjean, ancien bagnard ; Mgr Myriel, évêque de Digne ; Petit-Gervais, ramoneur ; Fantine, mère célibataire réduite à la misère ; Cosette, sa fille, laissée en pension chez des aubergistes : Thénardier, le « mauvais pauvre », et sa femme ; leurs enfants Éponine, Azelma, Gavroche et ses frères ; Javert, le policier zélé ; Marius, étudiant amoureux de Cosette ; M. Gillenormand, son grand-père ; le baron Pontmercy, son père ; Enjolras, Courfeyrac, Grantaire, ses amis ; Fauchelevent, charretier à Montreuil-sur-Mer, puis jardinier à Paris ; le père Mabeuf, vieil homme ami de Marius ; religieuses, révolutionnaires, fonctionnaires de justice et de police, enfants des rues, gardes nationaux, forçats, etc.

• **Intrigue** : plusieurs intrigues enlacées qui se rejoignent pour n'en former qu'une seule. Jean Valjean parviendra-t-il à

Victor Hugo, *Gavroche à onze ans.*
(Maison de Victor Hugo, Paris).

échapper à Javert, qui le poursuit et le reconnaît malgré ses changements d'identité ?

LES ENJEUX

• Roman-fleuve, ouvert à divers niveaux de lecture.

• Le premier roman qui prend le peuple comme héros collectif, et lui donne la parole : que signifie le titre ?

• Une réflexion révolutionnaire sur les causes de la misère, sur la responsabilité collective, sur les implications sociales du respect des valeurs chrétiennes, sur les droits de l'enfant, sur la condition féminine, sur le fonctionnement de la justice.

HUGO
ET *LES MISÉRABLES*

UN JEUNE HOMME PASSIONNÉ

Né à Besançon le 26 février 1802, Victor Hugo est le fils d'un père bonapartiste et d'une mère royaliste. La mésentente du couple partagera les trois jeunes frères entre l'admiration pour leur père Léopold, capitaine, colonel, puis général de l'Empire, qu'ils suivront dans ses garnisons en France, en Italie, en Espagne, et l'amour de leur mère Sophie, qui leur donne une éducation libre et studieuse à Paris.

Victor débute très jeune dans la carrière littéraire. Il fonde avec ses frères un journal monarchiste et publie des *Odes* qui lui valent une pension royale. Après la mort de sa mère, il épouse son amie d'enfance, Adèle Foucher, dont il aura quatre enfants (un cinquième meurt en bas âge), et se rapproche peu à peu de son père. Il tient un salon où se réunit la nouvelle génération romantique.

Son succès trouve sa consécration au théâtre, avec l'entrée fracassante du drame romantique à la Comédie-Française : lors de la bataille d'*Hernani*, en 1830, ses jeunes amis soutiennent sa pièce dans une lutte acharnée contre les partisans du classicisme. Son bonheur conjugal est fragile ; son ami Sainte-Beuve lui fait part de son amour pour Adèle. Victor rencontre en 1833 la belle Juliette Drouet, qui devient sa maîtresse et se consacre à lui jusqu'à son dernier jour, le suivant, le soutenant, le protégeant dans toutes les circonstances de sa vie, même les plus périlleuses.

UN HOMME ENGAGÉ

Après *Le Dernier Jour d'un condamné* (1829) et *Claude Gueux* (1834), qui dénoncent la peine de mort, Hugo se tourne de plus en plus vers les thèmes politiques et la question sociale. Sa carrière d'écrivain se double d'une activité politique importante. D'abord royaliste, puis libéral, Victor Hugo se rapproche du pouvoir sous la monarchie de Juillet ; il devient académicien, puis pair de France (1845). Mais deux ans plus tôt, il a perdu sa fille aînée, Léopoldine, noyée dans la Seine avec son jeune époux. À la suite de ce deuil, Hugo cesse un temps de publier. En 1845, il s'enferme et commence la rédaction du roman qui deviendra *Les Misérables*, interrompu en 1848 « pour cause de révolution ».

Il soutient la candidature de Louis-Napoléon Bonaparte à la présidence de la seconde République, mais il est vite déçu par les orientations conservatrices de son gouvernement. Élu député, il prononce à la Chambre un *Discours sur la misère* (1849) qui est mal reçu. En 1851, il visite les affreuses caves de Lille, où habitent et travaillent des ouvriers misérables (voir p. 284). Ses prises de position à l'Assemblée l'éloignent peu à peu de la droite. Il milite pour l'assistance publique, pour la liberté de la presse et du théâtre, pour le suffrage universel, pour le développement d'un enseignement laïc, gratuit et obligatoire (1850, *Discours sur la liberté de l'enseignement*). Se méfiant des dangers du pouvoir personnel, il s'oppose à la révision de la constitution qui permettrait à Louis-Napoléon Bonaparte de briguer un second mandat présidentiel.

L'EXILÉ

Après le coup d'État du 2 décembre 1851, Hugo participe à la résistance, mais, protégé par Juliette, il doit quitter Paris sous un faux nom. Banni sous le second Empire, il fustige Napoléon III dans *Napoléon-le-Petit* et *Les Châtiments*. Suivi par les siens, il se retire en Belgique, puis dans les îles anglo-normandes. L'exil est pour Hugo une période de grande fécondité littéraire qui ne l'empêche pas de poursuivre son activité politique et sociale. Il soutient les mouvements républicains européens, combat la peine de mort, vient en aide aux autres proscrits et aux enfants pauvres de Guernesey à qui il offre des repas, des jouets et des vêtements. Même après la loi d'amnistie de 1859, qui autorise les proscrits à rentrer en France, Hugo refuse de revenir en métropole tant que

Napoléon III est au pouvoir, préférant rester à Guernesey. C'est là, dans sa maison de Hauteville-House, qu'il reprend en 1860 la rédaction des *Misérables*. Le roman paraît en 1862.

LA LÉGENDE DE SON SIÈCLE

Le 4 septembre 1870, l'empire est déchu et la république proclamée. Victor Hugo rentre le lendemain même dans la capitale assiégée par les Prussiens. Il est élu député dans les rangs républicains. Le 18 mars 1871, la Commune de Paris se révolte. Hugo ne soutient pas l'insurrection, mais il réclamera inlassablement l'amnistie des communards, et se fera l'écho de cette période troublée de guerre civile dans *L'Année terrible* (1871).

Sur la fin de sa vie, Hugo perd de nombreux proches. Mais il reste très entouré. Sa femme meurt en 1868. Après le décès de son fils Charles, en 1871, il obtient la tutelle de ses petits enfants, Georges et Jeanne. Des hommes politiques, des écrivains viennent lui rendre visite. Sénateur en 1876, il siège à l'extrême gauche. Le jour de son entrée dans sa quatre-vingtième année, des centaines de milliers de personnes défilent sous ses fenêtres et l'acclament. Il meurt le 22 mai 1885. Il avait souhaité le corbillard des pauvres et refusé « l'oraison de toutes les églises ». Ses désirs seront exaucés, mais le 1er juin, jour de ses obsèques, une foule immense, après avoir veillé le corps du grand homme exposé sous l'arc de triomphe, l'accompagnera jusqu'au Panthéon.

L'INSPIRATION DES *MISÉRABLES*

Plusieurs éléments biographiques sont à l'origine de l'inspiration des *Misérables*.

Parmi eux, le souvenir de la désunion des parents de Hugo. Désunion matrimoniale, mais aussi politique : le général Léopold Hugo était un soldat de Napoléon, un héros de l'Empire, alors que Sophie Trébuchet était voltairienne et royaliste. Le petit Victor, élevé principalement par sa mère, redécouvre les mérites de son père à l'âge adulte. On retrouve ce schéma dans le roman, *via* le personnage de Marius, influencé par son grand-père royaliste Gillenormand, avant de découvrir la stature de son père à la mort de ce dernier.

Une anecdote, racontée par Hugo dans *Choses vues*, est directement transposée dans le roman : en 1841, Hugo assiste à une altercation entre une prostituée et un bourgeois qui l'a humiliée. La fille est conduite au commissariat et Hugo lui évite la prison en témoignant en sa faveur auprès du policier.

La mort de Léopoldine en septembre 1843 a sans doute été aussi un événement déterminant. On peut lire *Les Misérables* comme une tentative de redonner vie, par la fiction, à l'enfant disparue. Jean Valjean donne en effet une seconde naissance à Cosette.

L'année qui suit la mort de Léopoldine, Hugo noue une liaison avec une jeune femme mariée, Léonie Biard. Le mari de cette dernière n'appréciant pas du tout la situation, il dépêche la police, qui constate le flagrant délit d'adultère. Léonie est envoyée à la prison des femmes (Saint-Lazare) qui accueille aussi les prostituées, où elle reste deux mois avant d'être transférée au couvent des Augustines. Hugo, pair de France depuis 1845, est « inviolable » ; il n'est donc pas poursuivi. Mais le scandale est tel qu'il est contraint de s'isoler quelque temps. La culpabilité qu'il ressent à l'égard de Léonie est peut-être un autre élément qui contribue à la naissance du personnage de Fantine.

La vie de Hugo, à cette époque, lui apparaît « misérable ». Il est certes académicien et pair de France, au sommet des honneurs, donc, mais sa vie privée est tissée de douleurs. Depuis longtemps, son mariage est malheureux, sa fille est morte à la fleur de l'âge, il a fait le malheur de la femme qu'il aimait (sans compter le tort et le chagrin infligés à Juliette Drouet).

Cette « misère » personnelle s'articule, dans l'inspiration du roman, autour de la misère collective et de la « question sociale » (voir p.290) : le développement du prolétariat urbain, entraîné par la révolution industrielle, fait apparaître une nouvelle forme de misère, et de délinquance, laquelle engendre une grande peur sociale. Dans son *Discours sur la misère* (1849), Hugo avait prédit l'abolition possible de la misère : parole impossible à entendre pour ceux qui croient qu'elle est inévitable, dans l'ordre des choses, voulue par Dieu.

LA GENÈSE DES *MISÉRABLES*

La rédaction débute en 1845. Le roman s'intitule d'abord *Jean Tréjean*, puis *Les Misères*.

La révolution de 1848 contraint Hugo à s'interrompre : il se consacre alors directement à l'action politique, en tant que député. Le manuscrit est mis dans une malle, et Hugo ne s'y replongera que douze ans plus tard.

Lorsqu'il reprend son projet en 1860, il passe d'abord de longs mois à relire et à méditer son premier manuscrit. Contrairement à son habitude, il revient sur son texte à plusieurs reprises, le grossissant à partir d'une mince trame initiale. Les corrections et les additions (digressions, apparition de personnages secondaires, esquisse d'une foule de silhouettes, addition de nombreux détails réalistes) vont doubler le volume du texte originel. Entre le début et la fin de la rédaction, dix-sept ans se seront écoulés.

LA PARUTION

Le livre, fébrilement attendu par le public, paraît en 1862 chez un jeune éditeur bruxellois, Albert Lacroix, et connaît immédiatement un immense succès. La publication, qui s'échelonne d'avril à juin, est un grand événement populaire. Des ouvriers se cotisent, « chacun pour vingt sous », afin d'acheter les dix volumes de cette collection assez coûteuse, et tirent au sort le nom de celui d'entre eux qui la gardera. Les contrefaçons du livre sont nombreuses : l'éditeur de Hugo lui écrit à maintes reprises pour obtenir son aide dans la lutte contre les faussaires. Malgré ce manque à gagner, les recettes sont excellentes. Hugo avait obtenu par contrat 300 000 francs de droits d'auteur (un peu moins d'un million d'euros). Lacroix fait un bénéfice trois fois supérieur.

La critique est partagée, l'Église est embarrassée. Certains se scandalisent, tandis que le journaliste Louis Veuillot récupère habilement le propos du livre en y lisant une apologie* de la religion catholique. Le roman est mis à l'Index, vainement. Les partisans de Hugo saluent dans *Les Misérables* un chef-d'œuvre. Cependant quelques écrivains, et non des moindres – Lamartine notamment –, y voient un livre dangereux ou de mauvais goût, qui menace l'ordre social en donnant au peuple des espoirs chimériques et en lui inculquant « la passion de l'impossible ». Baudelaire publie un article élogieux, mais écrit à sa mère que « ce livre est immonde et inepte ». Rimbaud, quant à lui, verra dans *Les Misérables* « un véritable poème » (voir « Lectures des *Misérables* », p. 326).

Depuis cette époque, le succès du roman, maintes fois adapté et traduit, ne s'est jamais démenti : au cinéma, au théâtre, en comédie musicale ou en bande dessinée. *Les Misérables* est le livre français le plus connu dans le monde.

---

* Les mots suivis d'un astérisque sont définis p. 339.

Auguste Rodin (1840-1917),
Buste de Victor Hugo, bronze, 1908.
(Maison de Victor Hugo, Paris.)

Les
Misérables

VICTOR HUGO

roman

Tant qu'il existera, par le fait des lois et des mœurs, une damnation sociale créant artificiellement, en pleine civilisation, des enfers, et compliquant d'une fatalité[1] humaine la destinée qui est divine ; tant que les trois problèmes du siècle, la dégradation[2] de l'homme par le prolétariat[3], la déchéance[4] de la femme par la faim, l'atrophie[5] de l'enfant par la nuit, ne seront pas résolus ; tant que, dans de certaines régions, l'asphyxie[6] sociale sera possible ; en d'autres termes, et à un point de vue plus étendu encore, tant qu'il y aura sur la terre ignorance et misère, des livres de la nature de celui-ci pourront ne pas être inutiles.

Hauteville-House, 1862.

---

1. **Fatalité :** destin inévitable
2. **Dégradation :** abaissement.
3. **Prolétariat :** condition ouvrière.
4. **Déchéance :** chute morale.
5. **Atrophie :** arrêt maladif de la croissance.
6. **Asphyxie :** étouffement.

PREMIÈRE PARTIE
FANTINE

LIVRE PREMIER : UN JUSTE

1. Mgr Myriel

En 1815, M. Charles-François-Bienvenu Myriel était évêque de Digne. C'était un vieillard d'environ soixante-quinze ans ; il occupait le siège de Digne depuis 1806.

Quoique ce détail ne touche en aucune manière au fond même de ce que nous avons à raconter, il n'est peut-être pas inutile, ne fût-ce que pour être exact en tout, d'indiquer ici les bruits et les propos qui avaient couru sur son compte au moment où il était arrivé dans le diocèse[1]. Vrai ou faux, ce qu'on dit des hommes tient souvent autant de place dans leur vie et surtout dans leur destinée que ce qu'ils font. M. Myriel était fils d'un conseiller au parlement d'Aix ; noblesse de robe[2]. On contait que son père, le réservant pour hériter de sa charge, l'avait marié de fort bonne heure, à dix-huit ou vingt ans, suivant un usage assez répandu dans les familles parlementaires. Charles Myriel, nonobstant[3] ce mariage, avait, disait-on, beaucoup fait parler de lui. Il était bien fait de sa personne, quoique d'assez petite taille, élégant, gracieux, spirituel ; toute la première partie de sa vie avait été donnée au monde et aux galanteries.

---

1. **Diocèse :** territoire placé sous l'autorité d'un évêque.
2. **Noblesse de robe :** noblesse des membres de la haute magistrature.
3. **Nonobstant :** malgré.

La révolution survint, les événements se précipitèrent, les familles parlementaires décimées[1], chassées, traquées, se dispersèrent. M. Charles Myriel, dès les premiers jours de la révolution, émigra en Italie. Sa femme y mourut d'une maladie de poitrine dont elle était atteinte depuis longtemps. Ils n'avaient point d'enfants. Que se passa-t-il ensuite dans la destinée de M. Myriel ? L'écroulement de l'ancienne société française, la chute de sa propre famille, les tragiques spectacles de 93, plus effrayants encore peut-être pour les émigrés qui les voyaient de loin avec le grossissement de l'épouvante, firent-ils germer en lui des idées de renoncement et de solitude ? Fut-il, au milieu d'une de ces distractions et de ces affections qui occupaient sa vie, subitement atteint d'un de ces coups mystérieux et terribles qui viennent quelquefois renverser, en le frappant au cœur, l'homme que les catastrophes publiques n'ébranleraient pas en le frappant dans son existence et dans sa fortune ? Nul n'aurait pu le dire ; tout ce qu'on savait, c'est que, lorsqu'il revint d'Italie, il était prêtre.

En 1804, M. Myriel était curé de B. (Brignolles[2]). Il était déjà vieux, et vivait dans une retraite profonde.

Vers l'époque du couronnement, une petite affaire de sa cure, on ne sait plus trop quoi, l'amena à Paris. Entre autres personnes puissantes, il alla solliciter[3] pour ses paroissiens M. le cardinal Fesch. Un jour que l'empereur était venu faire sa visite à son oncle, le digne curé, qui attendait dans l'antichambre, se trouva sur le passage de sa majesté. Napoléon, se voyant

---

1. **Décimées** : détruites.
2. **Brignolles** : ville du Var.
3. **Solliciter** : adresser une demande à.

regarder avec une certaine curiosité par ce vieillard, se
retourna, et dit brusquement :

55 – Quel est ce bonhomme qui me regarde ?

– Sire, dit M. Myriel, vous regardez un bonhomme,
et moi je regarde un grand homme. Chacun de nous
peut profiter.

L'empereur, le soir même, demanda au cardinal le
60 nom de ce curé, et quelque temps après M. Myriel fut
tout surpris d'apprendre qu'il était nommé évêque de
Digne.

*[Mgr Myriel, simple et charitable, est apprécié de tous.
Il consacre l'essentiel de son revenu aux pauvres, et laisse
sa porte ouverte à tous. « Les pauvres gens du pays [...]
avec une sorte d'instinct affectueux [...] ne l'appelaient
que monseigneur Bienvenu. » Il accompagne un jour un
condamné sur la guillotine ; cette expérience l'horrifie.
Bravant les préjugés de la population, il se rend au
chevet d'un vieux conventionnel[1] agonisant ; les deux
hommes évoquent longuement la Révolution ;
Mgr Myriel ne peut pardonner le sang versé et le régi-
cide, mais le conventionnel lui fait entrevoir la grandeur des idéaux révolutionnaires : lutter pour la fin du
véritable tyran, c'est-à-dire « la fin de la prostitution
pour la femme, la fin de l'esclavage pour l'homme, la fin
de la nuit pour l'enfant ». (I, I, 2 à 14)[2]]*

---

1. **Conventionnel :** député à la Convention (1792-1795).
2. **I, I, 2 à 14 :** signifie Ire partie, livre I, chapitres 2 à 14.

Gustave Brion, *Jean Valjean*,
gravure pour l'édition Hetzel des *Misérables* de 1865.
(Bibliothèque nationale de France, Paris.)

LIVRE DEUXIÈME : LA CHUTE

1. Le soir d'un jour de marche

Dans les premiers jours du mois d'octobre 1815, une heure environ avant le coucher du soleil, un homme qui voyageait à pied entrait dans la petite ville de Digne. Les rares habitants qui se trouvaient en ce
5 moment à leurs fenêtres ou sur le seuil de leurs maisons regardaient ce voyageur avec une sorte d'inquiétude. Il était difficile de rencontrer un passant d'un aspect plus misérable. C'était un homme de moyenne taille, trapu et robuste, dans la force de l'âge.
10 Il pouvait avoir quarante-six ou quarante-huit ans. Une casquette à visière de cuir rabattue cachait en partie son visage brûlé par le soleil et le hâle et ruisse-lant de sueur. Sa chemise de grosse toile jaune, ratta-chée au col par une petite ancre d'argent, laissait voir
15 sa poitrine velue ; il avait une cravate tordue en corde, un pantalon de coutil[1] bleu usé et râpé, blanc à un genou, troué à l'autre, une vieille blouse grise en haillons, rapiécée à l'un des coudes d'un morceau de drap vert cousu avec de la ficelle, sur le dos un sac de
20 soldat fort plein, bien bouclé et tout neuf, à la main un énorme bâton noueux, les pieds sans bas dans des souliers ferrés, la tête tondue et la barbe longue.

La sueur, la chaleur, le voyage à pied, la poussière, ajoutaient je ne sais quoi de sordide[2] à cet ensemble
25 délabré.

---

1. **Coutil** : tissu épais, en fil ou en coton.
2. **Sordide** : sale, dégoûtant.

Les cheveux étaient ras, et pourtant hérissés ; car ils commençaient à pousser un peu, et semblaient n'avoir pas été coupés depuis quelque temps.

Personne ne le connaissait. Ce n'était évidemment qu'un passant. D'où venait-il ? Du midi. Des bords de la mer peut-être. Car il faisait son entrée dans Digne par la même rue qui sept mois auparavant avait vu passer l'empereur Napoléon allant de Cannes à Paris[1]. Cet homme avait dû marcher tout le jour. Il paraissait très fatigué. Des femmes de l'ancien bourg qui est au bas de la ville l'avaient vu s'arrêter sous les arbres du boulevard Gassendi et boire à la fontaine qui est à l'extrémité de la promenade. Il fallait qu'il eût bien soif, car des enfants qui le suivaient le virent encore s'arrêter et boire, deux cents pas plus loin, à la fontaine de la place du marché.

Arrivé au coin de la rue Poichevert, il tourna à gauche et se dirigea vers la mairie. Il y entra ; puis sortit un quart d'heure après. Un gendarme était assis près de la porte sur le banc de pierre où le général Drouot monta le 4 mars pour lire à la foule effarée des habitants de Digne la proclamation du golfe Juan[2]. L'homme ôta sa casquette et salua humblement le gendarme.

Le gendarme, sans répondre à son salut, le regarda avec attention, le suivit quelque temps des yeux, puis entra dans la maison de ville[3].

---

1. Après son abdication en avril 1814, Napoléon a dû se retirer à l'île d'Elbe. Le 1er mars 1815, il débarque sur la plage du golfe Juan, près de Cannes, et entre à Paris le 20 mars. Les populations acclament le long des routes ce « vol de l'aigle ».
2. Le général Drouot, resté fidèle à Napoléon, l'avait accompagné à l'île d'Elbe.
3. **Maison de ville** : mairie.

■ SITUER

À Digne, petite ville tranquille où l'évêque, Mgr Myriel, jouit d'une très bonne réputation, arrive un soir un mystérieux personnage qui éveille la méfiance des habitants.

■ RÉFLÉCHIR

STRUCTURE : décrire, raconter

1. Étudiez la construction grammaticale de la première phrase. Quels indices nous renseignent sur les circonstances de la scène ? Quelle périphrase* désigne le sujet de l'action ? Que suggère-t-elle ?

2. Quel est le rôle du premier paragraphe ? Comment le personnage est-il présenté dans les paragraphes suivants ? Commentez la composition de ce passage.

3. Quels indices (dans son aspect physique, son habillement et ses accessoires) donnent à l'inconnu un aspect inquiétant ? Peut-on les interpréter à coup sûr ?

4. Pourquoi l'homme salue-t-il le gendarme ? Pourquoi celui-ci entre-t-il dans la maison de ville ? Quelles questions le lecteur se pose-t-il ?

QUI PARLE ? QUI VOIT ? Le point de vue du narrateur

5. Relevez les verbes qui introduisent une observation, ceux qui introduisent une déduction. Sait-on ce que ressent l'inconnu ? Quel est le point de vue* adopté par le narrateur* ? Quelle est l'attitude des habitants envers l'inconnu ?

6. Ce texte est le début du livre II de la Ire partie. Quels renseignements, traditionnellement attendus à l'entrée en scène d'un nouveau personnage, nous manquent encore ? Quel effet cette attente produit-elle ?

7. Si vous deviez filmer la scène, quels plans tourneriez-vous successivement ? Quel serait le mouvement général de votre caméra ?

THÈMES : La société et l'individu

8. Le visage de l'homme est en partie masqué par sa casquette. Quelle est la signification symbolique de ce détail, premier élément du portrait ?

9. L'homme est étranger à la ville. Quels éléments du texte indiquent qu'il est déjà « traqué » par le regard des habitants ?

■ ÉCRIRE

10. Un monologue intérieur : Racontez la scène du point de vue de Jean Valjean, en imaginant ses sentiments et ses propres observations sur la ville de Digne et l'accueil de ses habitants.

Il y avait alors à Digne une belle auberge à l'enseigne de la *Croix-de-Colbas*. [...]

55 L'homme se dirigea vers cette auberge, qui était la meilleure du pays. Il entra dans la cuisine, laquelle s'ouvrait de plain-pied[1] sur la rue. Tous les fourneaux étaient allumés ; un grand feu flambait gaîment dans la cheminée. L'hôte, qui était en même temps le chef,

60 allait de l'âtre aux casseroles, fort occupé et surveillant un excellent dîner destiné à des rouliers[2] qu'on entendait rire et parler à grand bruit dans une salle voisine. Quiconque a voyagé sait que personne ne fait meilleure chère que les rouliers. Une marmotte grasse,

65 flanquée de perdrix blanches et de coqs de bruyère, tournait sur une longue broche devant le feu ; sur les fourneaux cuisaient deux grosses carpes du lac de Lauzet et une truite du lac d'Alloz.

L'hôte, entendant la porte s'ouvrir et entrer un

70 nouveau venu, dit sans lever les yeux de ses fourneaux :

– Que veut monsieur ?

– Manger et coucher, dit l'homme.

– Rien de plus facile, reprit l'hôte. En ce moment il tourna la tête, embrassa d'un coup d'œil tout l'ensemble

75 du voyageur, et ajouta : En payant.

L'homme tira une grosse bourse de cuir de la poche de sa blouse et répondit :

– J'ai de l'argent.

– En ce cas on est à vous, dit l'hôte.

80 L'homme remit sa bourse en poche, se déchargea de son sac, le posa à terre près de la porte, garda son bâton à la main, et alla s'asseoir sur une escabelle[3] basse

---

1. **De plain-pied :** au même niveau que la rue, au rez-de-chaussée.
2. **Rouliers :** transporteurs de marchandises.
3. **Escabelle :** escabeau.

près du feu. Digne est dans la montagne. Les soirées d'octobre y sont froides.

85 Cependant, tout en allant et venant, l'hôte considérait le voyageur.

– Dîne-t-on bientôt ? dit l'homme.

– Tout à l'heure[1], dit l'hôte.

Pendant que le nouveau venu se chauffait, le dos 90 tourné, le digne aubergiste Jacquin Labarre tira un crayon de sa poche, puis il déchira le coin d'un vieux journal qui traînait sur une petite table près de la fenê- tre. Sur la marge blanche il écrivit une ligne ou deux, plia sans cacheter et remit ce chiffon de papier à un 95 enfant qui paraissait lui servir tout à la fois de marmiton et de laquais. L'aubergiste dit un mot à l'oreille du marmiton, et l'enfant partit en courant dans la direction de la mairie.

Le voyageur n'avait rien vu de tout cela.

100 Il demanda encore une fois : – Dîne-t-on bientôt ?

– Tout à l'heure, dit l'hôte.

L'enfant revint. Il rapportait le papier. L'hôte le déplia avec empressement, comme quelqu'un qui attend une réponse. Il parut lire attentivement, puis 105 hocha la tête, et resta un moment pensif. Enfin, il fit un pas vers le voyageur qui semblait plongé dans des réflexions peu sereines.

– Monsieur, dit-il, je ne puis vous recevoir.

L'homme se dressa à demi sur son séant.

110 – Comment ! avez-vous peur que je ne paye pas ? voulez-vous que je paye d'avance ? J'ai de l'argent, vous dis-je.

– Ce n'est pas cela.

– Quoi donc ?

---

1. **Tout à l'heure :** tout de suite.

115 – Vous avez de l'argent…

– Oui, dit l'homme.

– Et moi, dit l'hôte, je n'ai pas de chambre.

L'homme reprit tranquillement : – Mettez-moi à l'écurie.

120 – Je ne puis.

– Pourquoi ?

– Les chevaux prennent toute la place.

– Eh bien, repartit l'homme, un coin dans le grenier. Une botte de paille. Nous verrons cela après 125 dîner.

– Je ne puis vous donner à dîner.

Cette déclaration, faite d'un ton mesuré, mais ferme, parut grave à l'étranger. Il se leva.

– Ah bah ! mais je meurs de faim, moi. J'ai marché 130 dès le soleil levé. J'ai fait douze lieues[1]. Je paye. Je veux manger.

– Je n'ai rien, dit l'hôte.

L'homme éclata de rire et se tourna vers la cheminée et les fourneaux.

135 – Rien ! et tout cela ?

– Tout cela m'est retenu.

– Par qui ?

– Par ces messieurs les rouliers.

– Combien sont-ils ?

140 – Douze.

– Il y a là à manger pour vingt.

– Ils ont tout retenu et tout payé d'avance.

L'homme se rassit et dit sans hausser la voix :

– Je suis à l'auberge, j'ai faim, et je reste.

145 L'hôte alors se pencha à son oreille, et lui dit d'un accent qui le fit tressaillir : – Allez-vous-en.

---

1. **Lieue :** mesure de distance qui équivaut à environ quatre kilomètres.

Le voyageur était courbé en cet instant et poussait quelques braises dans le feu avec le bout ferré de son bâton, il se retourna vivement, et, comme il ouvrait la
150 bouche pour répliquer, l'hôte le regarda fixement et ajouta toujours à voix basse : – Tenez, assez de paroles comme cela. Voulez-vous que je vous dise votre nom ? Vous vous appelez Jean Valjean. Maintenant voulez-vous que je vous dise qui vous êtes ? En vous voyant
155 entrer, je me suis douté de quelque chose, j'ai envoyé à la mairie, et voici ce qu'on m'a répondu. Savez-vous lire ?

En parlant ainsi il tendait à l'étranger, tout déplié, le papier qui venait de voyager de l'auberge à la mairie et
160 de la mairie à l'auberge. L'homme y jeta un regard. L'aubergiste reprit après un silence :

– J'ai l'habitude d'être poli avec tout le monde. Allez-vous-en.

L'homme baissa la tête, ramassa le sac qu'il avait
165 déposé à terre, et s'en alla.

[La nouvelle de l'arrivée en ville de l'ancien forçat s'est répandue comme une traînée de poudre. Après avoir été chassé par l'aubergiste, Jean Valjean est rejeté par un cabaretier. Même la prison ne veut pas l'accueillir. Attiré par le spectacle d'un ménage heureux, il demande l'hospitalité. Le mari, comprenant qu'il s'agit de « l'homme » dont tout le monde parle, ferme sa porte à double tour.]

La nuit continuait de tomber. Le vent froid des Alpes soufflait. À la lueur du jour expirant, l'étranger aperçut dans un des jardins qui bordent la rue une sorte de hutte qui lui parut maçonnée en mottes de
170 gazon. Il franchit résolument une barrière de bois et se trouva dans le jardin. Il s'approcha de la hutte ; elle

avait pour porte une étroite ouverture très basse et elle
ressemblait à ces constructions que les cantonniers se
bâtissent au bord des routes. Il pensa sans doute que
175 c'était en effet le logis d'un cantonnier ; il souffrait du
froid et de la faim ; il s'était résigné à la faim, mais
c'était du moins là un abri contre le froid. Ces sortes
de logis ne sont habituellement pas occupés la nuit. Il
se coucha à plat ventre et se glissa dans la hutte. Il y
180 faisait chaud, et il y trouva un assez bon lit de paille. Il
resta un moment étendu sur ce lit, sans pouvoir faire
un mouvement tant il était fatigué. Puis, comme son
sac sur son dos le gênait et que c'était d'ailleurs un
oreiller tout trouvé, il se mit à déboucler une des cour-
185 roies. En ce moment, un grondement farouche se fit
entendre. Il leva les yeux. La tête d'un dogue énorme
se dessinait dans l'ombre à l'ouverture de la hutte.

C'était la niche d'un chien.

Il était lui-même vigoureux et redoutable ; il s'arma
190 de son bâton, il se fit de son sac un bouclier, et sortit
de la niche comme il put, non sans élargir les déchiru-
res de ses haillons.

Il sortit également du jardin, mais à reculons,
obligé, pour tenir le dogue en respect, d'avoir recours
195 à cette manœuvre de bâton que les maîtres en ce genre
d'escrime appellent *la rose couverte*.

Quand il eut, non sans peine, repassé la barrière et
qu'il se retrouva dans la rue, seul, sans gîte, sans toit,
sans abri, chassé même de ce lit de paille et de cette
200 niche misérable, il se laissa tomber plutôt qu'il ne
s'assit sur une pierre, et il paraît qu'un passant qui
traversait l'entendit s'écrier : – Je ne suis pas même un
chien !

Bientôt il se releva et se remit à marcher. Il sortit de
205 la ville, espérant trouver quelque arbre ou quelque
meule dans les champs, et s'y abriter.

Il chemina ainsi quelque temps, la tête toujours baissée. Quand il se sentit loin de toute habitation humaine, il leva les yeux et chercha autour de lui. Il
210 était dans un champ, il avait devant lui une de ces collines basses couvertes de chaume coupé ras, qui après la moisson ressemblent à des têtes tondues.

L'horizon était tout noir ; ce n'était pas seulement le sombre de la nuit ; c'étaient des nuages très bas qui
215 semblaient s'appuyer sur la colline même et qui montaient, emplissant tout le ciel. Cependant, comme la lune allait se lever et qu'il flottait encore au zénith[1] un reste de clarté crépusculaire, ces nuages formaient au haut du ciel une sorte de voûte blanchâtre d'où
220 tombait sur la terre une lueur.

La terre était donc plus éclairée que le ciel, ce qui est un effet particulièrement sinistre, et la colline, d'un pauvre et chétif contour, se dessinait vague et blafarde[2] sur l'horizon ténébreux. Tout cet ensemble était
225 hideux, petit, lugubre et borné. Rien dans le champ ni sur la colline qu'un arbre difforme qui se tordait en frissonnant à quelques pas du voyageur.

Cet homme était évidemment très loin d'avoir de ces délicates habitudes d'intelligence et d'esprit qui font
230 qu'on est sensible aux aspects mystérieux des choses ; cependant il y avait dans le ciel, dans cette colline, dans cette plaine et dans cet arbre, quelque chose de si profondément désolé qu'après un moment d'immobilité et de rêverie, il rebroussa chemin brusquement. Il
235 y a des instants où la nature semble hostile.

Il revint sur ses pas. Les portes de Digne étaient fermées. Digne, qui a soutenu des sièges dans les

---

1. **Au zénith :** au plus haut du ciel.
2. **Blafarde :** blême, pâle.

guerres de religion, était encore entourée en 1815 de
vieilles murailles flanquées de tours carrées qu'on a
240 démolies depuis. Il passa par une brèche et rentra dans
la ville.

Il pouvait être huit heures du soir. Comme il ne
connaissait pas les rues, il recommença sa promenade à
l'aventure.

245 Il parvint ainsi à la préfecture, puis au séminaire[1]. En
passant sur la place de la cathédrale, il montra le poing
à l'église.

Il y a au coin de cette place une imprimerie. C'est là
que furent imprimées pour la première fois les procla-
250 mations de l'empereur et de la garde impériale à
l'armée, apportées de l'île d'Elbe et dictées par
Napoléon lui-même.

Épuisé de fatigue et n'espérant plus rien, il se
coucha sur le banc de pierre qui est à la porte de cette
255 imprimerie.

Une vieille femme sortait de l'église en ce moment.
Elle vit cet homme étendu dans l'ombre. – Que faites-
vous là, mon ami ? dit-elle.

Il répondit durement et avec colère : – Vous le
260 voyez, bonne femme, je me couche.

La bonne femme, bien digne de ce nom en effet,
était madame la marquise de R.

– Sur ce banc ? reprit-elle.

– J'ai eu pendant dix-neuf ans un matelas de bois,
265 dit l'homme ; j'ai aujourd'hui un matelas de pierre.

– Vous avez été soldat ?

– Oui, bonne femme. Soldat.

– Pourquoi n'allez-vous pas à l'auberge ?

– Parce que je n'ai pas d'argent.

---

1. **Séminaire :** école où l'on prepare les jeunes prêtres.

270 – Hélas ! dit madame de R., je n'ai dans ma bourse que quatre sous.

– Donnez toujours.

L'homme prit les quatre sous. Madame de R. continua : – Vous ne pouvez vous loger avec si peu dans une
275 auberge. Avez-vous essayé pourtant ? Il est impossible que vous passiez ainsi la nuit. Vous avez sans doute froid et faim. On aurait pu vous loger par charité.

– J'ai frappé à toutes les portes.

– Eh bien ?

280 – Partout on m'a chassé.

La « bonne femme » toucha le bras de l'homme et lui montra de l'autre côté de la place une petite maison basse à côté de l'évêché.

– Vous avez, reprit-elle, frappé à toutes les portes ?

285 – Oui.

– Avez-vous frappé à celle-là ?

– Non.

– Frappez-y.

[Chez Mgr Myriel, on s'apprête à dîner. Sa sœur, Mlle Baptistine, écoute la servante, Mme Magloire, qui s'inquiète de la proximité du rôdeur. Mais Mgr Myriel n'a pas l'intention de changer ses habitudes, et il laisse sa porte ouverte. Soudain, on frappe. (I, II, 2)]

3. Héroïsme de l'obéissance passive

La porte s'ouvrit.

Elle s'ouvrit vivement, toute grande, comme si quelqu'un la poussait avec énergie et résolution.

Un homme entra.

5 Cet homme, nous le connaissons déjà. C'est le voyageur que nous avons vu tout à l'heure errer cherchant un gîte.

Il entra, fit un pas et s'arrêta, laissant la porte ouverte derrière lui. Il avait son sac sur l'épaule, son bâton à la main, une expression rude, hardie, fatiguée et violente dans les yeux. Le feu de la cheminée l'éclairait. Il était hideux. C'était une sinistre apparition.

Madame Magloire n'eut pas même la force de jeter un cri. Elle tressaillit, et resta béante[1].

Mademoiselle Baptistine se retourna, aperçut l'homme qui entrait et se dressa à demi d'effarement[2], puis, ramenant peu à peu sa tête vers la cheminée, elle se mit à regarder son frère, et son visage redevint profondément calme et serein.

L'évêque fixait sur l'homme un œil tranquille.

Comme il ouvrait la bouche, sans doute pour demander au nouveau venu ce qu'il désirait, l'homme appuya ses deux mains à la fois sur son bâton, promena ses yeux tour à tour sur le vieillard et les femmes, et, sans attendre que l'évêque parlât, dit d'une voix haute :

– Voici. Je m'appelle Jean Valjean. Je suis un galérien. J'ai passé dix-neuf ans au bagne. Je suis libéré depuis quatre jours et en route pour Pontarlier[3] qui est ma destination. Quatre jours que je marche depuis Toulon. Aujourd'hui, j'ai fait douze lieues à pied. Ce soir, en arrivant dans ce pays, j'ai été dans une auberge, on m'a renvoyé à cause de mon passeport jaune[4] que j'avais montré à la mairie. Il avait fallu. J'ai été à une auberge. On m'a dit : Va-t'en ! Chez l'un, chez l'autre.

---

1. **Béante :** qui regarde avec étonnement.
2. **Effarement :** stupeur, effroi.
3. **Pontarlier :** ville du Doubs.
4. Les prisonniers du bagne, à leur libération, devaient montrer leur passeport jaune dans les mairies des villes qu'ils traversaient. La police pouvait ainsi vérifier leur itinéraire.

Personne n'a voulu de moi. J'ai été à la prison, le guichetier ne m'a pas ouvert. J'ai été dans la niche d'un chien. Ce chien m'a mordu et m'a chassé, comme s'il avait été un homme. On aurait dit qu'il savait qui

40 j'étais. Je m'en suis allé dans les champs pour coucher à la belle étoile. Il n'y avait pas d'étoile. J'ai pensé qu'il pleuvrait, et qu'il n'y avait pas de bon Dieu pour empêcher de pleuvoir, et je suis rentré dans la ville pour y trouver le renfoncement d'une porte. Là, dans

45 la place, j'allais me coucher sur une pierre, une bonne femme m'a montré votre maison et m'a dit : Frappe là. J'ai frappé. Qu'est-ce que c'est ici ? êtes-vous une auberge ? J'ai de l'argent. Ma masse[1]. Cent neuf francs quinze sous que j'ai gagnés au bagne par mon travail

50 en dix-neuf ans. Je payerai. Qu'est-ce que cela me fait ? j'ai de l'argent. Je suis très fatigué, douze lieues à pied, j'ai bien faim. Voulez-vous que je reste ?

– Madame Magloire, dit l'évêque, vous mettrez un couvert de plus.

55 L'homme fit trois pas et s'approcha de la lampe qui était sur la table. – Tenez, reprit-il, comme s'il n'avait pas bien compris, ce n'est pas ça. Avez-vous entendu ? Je suis un galérien. Un forçat. Je viens des galères. – Il tira de sa poche une grande feuille de papier jaune qu'il

60 déplia. – Voilà mon passeport. Jaune, comme vous voyez. Cela sert à me faire chasser de partout où je vais. Voulez-vous lire ? Je sais lire, moi. J'ai appris au bagne. Il y a une école pour ceux qui veulent. Tenez, voilà ce qu'on a mis sur le passeport : « Jean Valjean,

65 forçat libéré, natif de… – cela vous est égal… – Est resté dix-neuf ans au bagne. Cinq ans pour vol avec

---

1. **Masse :** sommes prélevées sur le salaire d'un prisonnier, qu'on lui remet à sa libération.

effraction[1]. Quatorze ans pour avoir tenté de s'évader quatre fois. Cet homme est très dangereux » – Voilà ! Tout le monde m'a jeté dehors. Voulez-vous me rece-
70 voir, vous ? Est-ce une auberge ? Voulez-vous me donner à manger et à coucher ? avez-vous une écurie ?

– Madame Magloire, dit l'évêque, vous mettrez des draps blancs au lit de l'alcôve.

Nous avons déjà expliqué de quelle nature était
75 l'obéissance des deux femmes.

Madame Magloire sortit pour exécuter ces ordres.

L'évêque se tourna vers l'homme.

– Monsieur, asseyez-vous et chauffez-vous. Nous allons souper dans un instant, et l'on fera votre lit
80 pendant que vous souperez.

Ici l'homme comprit tout à fait. L'expression de son visage, jusqu'alors sombre et dure, s'empreignit[2] de stupéfaction, de doute, de joie, et devint extraordi-naire. Il se mit à balbutier comme un homme fou :
85 – Vrai ? quoi ! vous me gardez ? vous ne me chassez pas ? un forçat ! Vous m'appelez *monsieur* ! vous ne me tutoyez pas ? Va-t'en, chien ! qu'on me dit toujours. Je croyais bien que vous me chasseriez. Aussi j'avais dit tout de suite qui je suis. Oh ! la brave
90 femme qui m'a enseigné ici ! Je vais souper ! Un lit avec des matelas et des draps ! comme tout le monde ! Un lit ! il y a dix-neuf ans que je n'ai couché dans un lit ! Vous voulez bien que je ne m'en aille pas ! Vous êtes de dignes gens ! D'ailleurs j'ai de l'argent. Je
95 payerai bien. Pardon, monsieur l'aubergiste, comment vous appelez-vous ? Je payerai tout ce qu'on voudra.

---

1. **Vol avec effraction :** vol avec dégâts matériels, tels que bris de portes, de vitrines, de serrures.
2. **S'empreignit :** prit la marque.

Vous êtes un brave homme. Vous êtes aubergiste, n'est-ce pas ?

– Je suis, dit l'évêque, un prêtre qui demeure ici.

100 – Un prêtre ! reprit l'homme. Oh ! un brave homme de prêtre ! Alors vous ne me demandez pas d'argent ? Le curé, n'est-ce pas ? le curé de cette grande église ? Tiens ! c'est vrai, que je suis bête ! je n'avais pas vu votre calotte.

105 Tout en parlant il avait déposé son sac et son bâton dans un coin, avait remis son passeport dans sa poche, et s'était assis. Mademoiselle Baptistine le considérait avec douceur. Il continua :

– Vous êtes humain, monsieur le curé, vous n'avez
110 pas de mépris. C'est bien bon un bon prêtre. Alors vous n'avez pas besoin que je paye ?

– Non, dit l'évêque, gardez votre argent. Combien avez-vous ? ne m'avez-vous pas dit cent neuf francs ?

– Quinze sous, ajouta l'homme.

115 – Cent neuf francs quinze sous. Et combien de temps avez-vous mis à gagner cela ?

– Dix-neuf ans.

[Mgr Myriel offre l'hospitalité à Jean Valjean ; voulant faire honneur à son invité, l'évêque demande à Mme Magloire de sortir les six couverts en argent. Après dîner, s'éclairant des chandeliers d'argent, il mène son hôte à sa chambre. Jean Valjean, épuisé, s'endort profondément tout habillé. Mais il se réveille en pleine nuit.

Le narrateur raconte alors le passé du personnage. Orphelin très tôt, l'émondeur[1] Jean Valjean a dû s'occuper de sa sœur et de ses sept neveux. Réduit à la misère

---

1. Émondeur : personne qui entretient les arbres en les débarrassant de leurs branches inutiles ou nuisibles et de leurs plantes parasites.

par le manque de travail, il a volé un pain pour les
nourrir. Condamné au bagne, il fait plusieurs tentatives
d'évasion, qui allongent sa peine. Ses dix-neuf ans de
détention l'ont endurci. « Que s'était-il passé dans cette
âme ? » (I, II, 4 à 6.)]

7. Le dedans du désespoir

Essayons de le dire.

Il faut bien que la société regarde ces choses puisque c'est elle qui les fait.

C'était, nous l'avons dit, un ignorant ; mais ce
5 n'était pas un imbécile. La lumière naturelle était allumée en lui. Le malheur, qui a aussi sa clarté, augmenta le peu de jour qu'il y avait dans cet esprit. Sous le bâton, sous la chaîne, au cachot, à la fatigue, sous l'ardent soleil du bagne, sur le lit de planches des forçats, il se
10 replia en sa conscience et réfléchit.

Il se constitua tribunal.

Il commença par se juger lui-même.

Il reconnut qu'il n'était pas un innocent injustement puni. Il s'avoua qu'il avait commis une action extrême
15 et blâmable ; qu'on ne lui eût peut-être pas refusé ce pain s'il l'avait demandé ; que dans tous les cas il eût mieux valu l'attendre, soit de la pitié, soit du travail ; que ce n'est pas tout à fait une raison sans réplique de dire : peut-on attendre quand on a faim ? que d'abord
20 il est très rare qu'on meure littéralement de faim ; ensuite que, malheureusement ou heureusement, l'homme est ainsi fait qu'il peut souffrir longtemps et beaucoup, moralement et physiquement, sans mourir ; qu'il fallait donc de la patience ; que cela eût mieux
25 valu même pour ces pauvres petits enfants ; que c'était un acte de folie, à lui, malheureux homme chétif, de prendre violemment au collet la société tout entière et

de se figurer qu'on sort de la misère par le vol ; que c'était, dans tous les cas, une mauvaise porte pour
30 sortir de la misère que celle par où l'on entre dans l'infamie[1] ; enfin qu'il avait eu tort.

Puis il se demanda :

S'il était le seul qui avait eu tort dans sa fatale histoire ? Si d'abord ce n'était pas une chose grave
35 qu'il eût, lui travailleur, manqué de travail, lui laborieux, manqué de pain. Si, ensuite, la faute commise et avouée, le châtiment n'avait pas été féroce et outré[2]. S'il n'y avait pas plus d'abus de la part de la loi dans la peine qu'il n'y avait eu d'abus de la part du coupable
40 dans la faute. S'il n'y avait pas excès de poids dans un des plateaux de la balance, celui où est l'expiation[3]. Si la surcharge de la peine n'était point l'effacement du délit, et n'arrivait pas à ce résultat de retourner la situation, de remplacer la faute du délinquant par la faute
45 de la répression, de faire du coupable la victime et du débiteur le créancier[4], et de mettre définitivement le droit du côté de celui-là même qui l'avait violé. Si cette peine, compliquée des aggravations successives pour les tentatives d'évasion, ne finissait pas par être une
50 sorte d'attentat du plus fort sur le plus faible, un crime de la société sur l'individu, un crime qui recommençait tous les jours, un crime qui durait dix-neuf ans.

Il se demanda si la société humaine pouvait avoir le droit de faire également subir à ses membres, dans un
55 cas son imprévoyance déraisonnable, et dans l'autre cas sa prévoyance impitoyable, et de saisir à jamais un

---

1. **Infamie :** déshonneur, honte.
2. **Outré :** exagéré.
3. **Expiation :** punition d'une faute commise.
4. Le **débiteur** est celui qui doit quelque chose à une personne ; cette dernière devient son **créancier**.

pauvre homme entre un défaut et un excès, défaut de travail, excès de châtiment.

S'il n'était pas exorbitant[1] que la société traitât ainsi précisément ses membres les plus mal dotés dans la répartition de biens que fait le hasard, et par conséquent les plus dignes de ménagements.

Ces questions faites et résolues, il jugea la société et la condamna.

Il la condamna à sa haine.

[...]

Il y avait à Toulon une école pour la chiourme[2] tenue par des frères ignorantins[3] où l'on enseignait le plus nécessaire à ceux de ces malheureux qui avaient de la bonne volonté. Il fut du nombre des hommes de bonne volonté. Il alla à l'école à quarante ans, et apprit à lire, à écrire, à compter. Il sentit que fortifier son intelligence, c'était fortifier sa haine. Dans de certains cas, l'instruction et la lumière peuvent servir de rallonge au mal.

Cela est triste à dire, après avoir jugé la société qui avait fait son malheur, il jugea la providence[4] qui avait fait la société, et il la condamna aussi.

Ainsi, pendant ces dix-neuf ans de torture et d'esclavage, cette âme monta et tomba en même temps. Il y entra de la lumière d'un côté et des ténèbres de l'autre.

Jean Valjean n'était pas, on l'a vu, d'une nature mauvaise. Il était encore bon lorsqu'il arriva au bagne. Il y condamna la société et sentit qu'il devenait

---

1. **Exorbitant :** excessif, exagéré, monstrueux.
2. **Chiourme :** ensemble des forçats.
3. Les **frères ignorantins** (ainsi nommés par modestie) étaient des religieux qui se consacraient à l'éducation.
4. **Providence :** Dieu gouvernant la création.

SITUER

Jean Valjean se réveille en pleine nuit. Le narrateur revient sur le passé de cet émondeur qui, ayant volé un pain pour nourrir sa famille, a passé dix-neuf ans de sa vie au bagne. Comment l'homme juge-t-il la société qui l'a condamné ? Voyage dans une conscience.

RÉFLÉCHIR

GENRES : la délibération

1. Quelles sont les deux phrases-paragraphes qui introduisent les étapes du raisonnement ? L'ordre de ces deux parties est-il indifférent ?

2. Dans les lignes 13 à 31, quel mot suit systématiquement les points virgules ? Quel type de propositions cette conjonction de subordination introduit-elle ? Quel est l'effet de cette accumulation ?

3. Dans les lignes 33 à 62, toutes les phrases commencent par « si ». Quel verbe complètent-elles ? De quel type de propositions s'agit-il ? Montrez que ces questions rhétoriques* n'autorisent qu'une seule réponse.

4. Le narrateur rapporte indirectement les questions que Jean Valjean s'est posées. En fin de compte, à qui s'adressent-elles ?

CARACTÈRES : Jean Valjean juge et partie

5. Quelles qualités de Jean Valjean apparaissent dans ce passage ?

6. Quel est l'intérêt de ce retour en arrière ?

SOCIÉTÉ : la société face à ses responsabilités

7. Peut-on dire que l'auteur fasse l'apologie* du vol ? Sur quels points la critique des institutions porte-t-elle dans ce chapitre ?

8. Quels sont, d'après ce texte, les droits fondamentaux du travailleur et du citoyen que la société doit garantir ?

ÉCRIRE

9. Un plaidoyer : avocat de Jean Valjean, vous essayez d'obtenir sa libération lors de la révision de son procès. Rédigez un plaidoyer en sa faveur en montrant au jury l'injustice de la peine qui lui a été infligée.

85 méchant ; il y condamna la providence et sentit qu'il devenait impie[1] [...].

Un détail que nous ne devons pas omettre, c'est qu'il était d'une force physique dont n'approchait pas un des habitants du bagne. À la fatigue, pour filer un câble, 90 pour virer un cabestan[2], Jean Valjean valait quatre hommes. Il soulevait et soutenait parfois d'énormes poids sur son dos, et remplaçait dans l'occasion cet instrument qu'on appelle cric et qu'on appelait jadis orgueil, d'où a pris nom, soit dit en passant, la rue 95 Montorgueil près des halles de Paris. Ses camarades l'avaient surnommé Jean-le-Cric. Une fois, comme on réparait le balcon de l'hôtel de ville de Toulon, une des admirables cariatides de Puget[3] qui soutiennent ce balcon se descella[4] et faillit tomber. Jean Valjean, qui se 100 trouvait là, soutint de l'épaule la cariatide et donna le temps aux ouvriers d'arriver.

Sa souplesse dépassait encore sa vigueur. Certains forçats, rêveurs perpétuels d'évasions, finissent par faire de la force et de l'adresse combinées une véritable 110 science. C'est la science des muscles. Toute une statique mystérieuse est quotidiennement pratiquée par les prisonniers, ces éternels envieux des mouches et des oiseaux. Gravir une verticale, et trouver des points d'appui là où l'on voit à peine une saillie[5], était un jeu 115 pour Jean Valjean. Étant donné un angle de mur, avec la tension de son dos et de ses jarrets, avec ses coudes

---

1. **Impie :** qui offense la religion, incroyant.
2. **Cabestan :** treuil servant à manipuler de gros fardeaux.
3. **Puget** est un sculpteur français du XVIIᵉ siècle. Les **cariatides** sont des statues de femmes soutenant une corniche sur leur tête.
4. **Se descella :** se détacha de son socle.
5. **Saillie :** relief sur une paroi, qui permet à celui qui l'escalade de prendre appui.

et ses talons emboîtés dans les aspérités de la pierre, il se hissait comme magiquement à un troisième étage. Quelquefois il montait ainsi jusqu'au toit du bagne.

120   Il parlait peu. Il ne riait pas. Il fallait quelque émotion extrême pour lui arracher, une ou deux fois l'an, ce lugubre rire du forçat qui est comme un écho du rire du démon. À le voir, il semblait occupé à regarder continuellement quelque chose de terrible.

125   [...]

    Pour résumer, en terminant, ce qui peut être résumé et traduit en résultats positifs dans tout ce que nous venons d'indiquer, nous nous bornerons à constater qu'en dix-neuf ans, Jean Valjean, l'inoffensif émondeur de
130 Faverolles[1], le redoutable galérien de Toulon, était devenu capable, grâce à la manière dont le bagne l'avait façonné, de deux espèces de mauvaises actions : premièrement, d'une mauvaise action rapide, irréfléchie, pleine d'étourdissement, toute d'instinct, sorte de représailles
135 pour le mal souffert ; deuxièmement, d'une mauvaise action grave, sérieuse, débattue en conscience et méditée avec les idées fausses que peut donner un pareil malheur. Ses préméditations passaient par les trois phases successives que les natures d'une certaine trempe peuvent seules
140 parcourir, raisonnement, volonté, obstination. Il avait pour mobiles l'indignation habituelle, l'amertume de l'âme, le profond sentiment des iniquités[2] subies, la réaction, même contre les bons, les innocents et les justes, s'il y en a. Le point de départ comme le point d'arrivée de
145 toutes ses pensées était la haine de la loi humaine ; cette haine qui, si elle n'est arrêtée dans son développement par quelque incident providentiel, devient, dans un temps

---

1. **Faverolles** : village d'où est originaire Jean Valjean.
2. **Iniquités** : injustices.

donné, la haine de la société, puis la haine du genre humain, puis la haine de la création, et se traduit par un
150 vague et incessant et brutal désir de nuire, n'importe à qui, à un être vivant quelconque. – Comme on voit, ce n'était pas sans raison que le passeport qualifiait Jean Valjean d'homme très dangereux.

D'année en année, cette âme s'était desséchée de
155 plus en plus, lentement, mais fatalement. À cœur sec, œil sec. À sa sortie du bagne, il y avait dix-neuf ans qu'il n'avait versé une larme.

[...]

10. L'homme réveillé

Donc comme deux heures du matin sonnaient à l'horloge de la cathédrale, Jean Valjean se réveilla.

Ce qui le réveilla, c'est que le lit était trop bon. Il y avait vingt ans bientôt qu'il n'avait couché dans un lit,
5 et, quoiqu'il ne se fût pas déshabillé, la sensation était trop nouvelle pour ne pas troubler son sommeil.

Il avait dormi plus de quatre heures. Sa fatigue était passée. Il était accoutumé à ne pas donner beaucoup d'heures au repos.

10 Il ouvrit les yeux, et regarda un moment dans l'obscurité autour de lui, puis il les referma pour se rendormir.

Quand beaucoup de sensations diverses ont agité la journée, quand des choses préoccupent l'esprit, on s'endort, mais on ne se rendort pas. Le sommeil vient
15 plus aisément qu'il ne revient. C'est ce qui arriva à Jean Valjean. Il ne put se rendormir, et il se mit à penser.

Il était dans un de ces moments où les idées qu'on a dans l'esprit sont troubles. Il avait une sorte de va-et-vient obscur dans le cerveau. Ses souvenirs anciens et ses
20 souvenirs immédiats y flottaient pêle-mêle et s'y croisaient confusément, perdant leurs formes, se grossis-

sant démesurément, puis disparaissant tout à coup comme dans une eau fangeuse[1] et agitée. Beaucoup de pensées lui venaient, mais il y en avait une qui se repré-
25 sentait continuellement et qui chassait toutes les autres. Cette pensée, nous allons la dire tout de suite : – il avait remarqué les six couverts d'argent et la grande cuiller que madame Magloire avait posés sur la table.

Ces six couverts d'argent l'obsédaient. – Ils étaient là.
30 – À quelques pas. – À l'instant où il avait traversé la chambre d'à côté pour venir dans celle où il était, la vieille servante les mettait dans un petit placard à la tête du lit.– Il avait bien remarqué ce placard. – À droite, en entrant par la salle à manger.– Ils étaient massifs. – Et de
35 vieille argenterie. – Avec la grande cuiller, on en tirerait au moins deux cents francs. – Le double de ce qu'il avait gagné en dix-neuf ans.– Il est vrai qu'il eût gagné davantage si l'*administration* ne l'avait pas *volé*.

Son esprit oscilla toute une grande heure dans des
40 fluctuations[2] auxquelles se mêlait bien quelque lutte. Trois heures sonnèrent. Il rouvrit les yeux, se dressa brusquement sur son séant, étendit le bras et tâta son havresac[3] qu'il avait jeté dans le coin de l'alcôve, puis il laissa pendre ses jambes et poser ses pieds à terre, et se
45 trouva, presque sans savoir comment, assis sur son lit.

Il resta un certain temps rêveur dans cette attitude qui eût eu quelque chose de sinistre pour quelqu'un qui l'eût aperçu ainsi dans cette ombre, seul éveillé dans la maison endormie. Tout à coup il se baissa, ôta ses souliers et les
50 posa doucement sur la natte près du lit, puis il reprit sa posture de rêverie et redevint immobile.

---

1. **Fangeuse** : sale, bourbeuse.
2. **Fluctuations** : hésitations.
3. **Havresac** : sac à dos.

Au milieu de cette méditation hideuse[1], les idées que nous venons d'indiquer remuaient sans relâche son cerveau, entraient, sortaient, rentraient, faisaient sur lui une sorte de pesée ; et puis il songeait aussi, sans savoir pourquoi, et avec cette obstination machinale de la rêverie, à un forçat nommé Brevet qu'il avait connu au bagne, et dont le pantalon n'était retenu que par une seule bretelle de coton tricoté. Le dessin en damier de cette bretelle lui revenait sans cesse à l'esprit.

Il demeurait dans cette situation, et y fût peut-être resté indéfiniment jusqu'au lever du jour, si l'horloge n'eût sonné un coup, – le quart ou la demie. Il sembla que ce coup lui eût dit : allons !

Il se leva debout, hésita encore un moment, et écouta ; tout se taisait dans la maison ; alors il marcha droit et à petits pas vers la fenêtre qu'il entrevoyait. La nuit n'était pas très obscure ; c'était une pleine lune sur laquelle couraient de larges nuées chassées par le vent. Cela faisait au dehors des alternatives d'ombre et de clarté, des éclipses, puis des éclaircies, et au dedans une sorte de crépuscule. Ce crépuscule, suffisant pour qu'on pût se guider, intermittent à cause des nuages, ressemblait à l'espèce de lividité[2] qui tombe d'un soupirail de cave devant lequel vont et viennent des passants. Arrivé à la fenêtre, Jean Valjean l'examina. Elle était sans barreaux, donnait sur le jardin et n'était fermée, selon la mode du pays, que d'une petite clavette[3]. Il l'ouvrit, mais, comme un air froid et vif entra brusquement dans la chambre, il la referma tout de suite. Il regarda le jardin de ce regard attentif qui étudie plus qu'il ne regarde. Le jardin était enclos d'un

---

1. **Hideuse** : affreuse.
2. **Lividité** : lumière blanche.
3. **Clavette** : petite cheville amovible.

mur blanc assez bas, facile à escalader. Au fond, au delà, il distingua des têtes d'arbres également espacées, ce qui indiquait que ce mur séparait le jardin d'une avenue ou d'une ruelle plantée.

Ce coup d'œil jeté, il fit le mouvement d'un homme déterminé, marcha à son alcôve, prit son havresac, le fouilla, en tira quelque chose qu'il posa sur le lit, mit ses souliers dans une de ses poches, referma le tout, chargea le sac sur ses épaules, se couvrit de sa casquette dont il baissa la visière sur ses yeux, chercha son bâton en tâtonnant, et l'alla poser dans l'angle de la fenêtre, puis revint au lit et saisit résolument l'objet qu'il y avait déposé. Cela ressemblait à une barre de fer courte, aiguisée comme un épieu à l'une de ses extrémités.

Il eût été difficile de distinguer dans les ténèbres pour quel emploi avait pu être façonné ce morceau de fer. C'était peut-être un levier ? C'était peut-être une massue ?

Au jour on eût pu reconnaître que ce n'était autre chose qu'un chandelier de mineur. On employait alors quelquefois les forçats à extraire de la roche des hautes collines qui environnent Toulon, et il n'était pas rare qu'ils eussent à leur disposition des outils de mineur. Les chandeliers des mineurs sont en fer massif, terminés à leur extrémité inférieure par une pointe au moyen de laquelle on les enfonce dans le rocher.

Il prit le chandelier dans sa main droite, et retenant son haleine, assourdissant son pas, il se dirigea vers la porte de la chambre voisine, celle de l'évêque, comme on sait. Arrivé à cette porte, il la trouva entrebâillée. L'évêque ne l'avait point fermée.

[Jean Valjean vole les couverts d'argent et s'enfuit. Mais, le lendemain, il est repris par la police qui le ramène chez l'évêque. Celui-ci, au lieu de l'accuser de vol, dit aux gendarmes qu'il s'agit d'un don, auquel il ajoute sa dernière richesse, les chandeliers. Il demande à Jean Valjean d'utiliser cet argent pour devenir honnête homme : « C'est votre âme que je vous achète ; je la retire aux pensées noires et à l'esprit de perdition, et je la donne à Dieu. » (I, II, 11 et 12)]

13. Petit-Gervais

Jean Valjean sortit de la ville comme s'il s'échappait. Il se mit à marcher en toute hâte dans les champs, prenant les chemins et les sentiers qui se présentaient sans s'apercevoir qu'il revenait à chaque instant sur ses
5 pas. Il erra ainsi toute la matinée, n'ayant pas mangé et n'ayant pas faim. Il était en proie à une foule de sensations nouvelles. Il se sentait une sorte de colère ; il ne savait contre qui. Il n'eût pu dire s'il était touché ou humilié. Il lui venait par moments un attendrissement
10 étrange qu'il combattait et auquel il opposait l'endurcissement de ses vingt dernières années. Cet état le fatiguait. Il voyait avec inquiétude s'ébranler au dedans de lui l'espèce de calme affreux que l'injustice de son malheur lui avait donné. Il se demandait qu'est-ce qui
15 remplacerait cela. Parfois il eût vraiment mieux aimé être en prison avec les gendarmes, et que les choses ne se fussent point passées ainsi ; cela l'eût moins agité. Bien que la saison fût assez avancée, il y avait encore çà et là dans les haies quelques fleurs tardives dont
20 l'odeur, qu'il traversait en marchant, lui rappelait des souvenirs d'enfance. Ces souvenirs lui étaient presque insupportables, tant il y avait longtemps qu'ils ne lui étaient apparus.

Des pensées inexprimables s'amoncelèrent ainsi en
25 lui toute la journée.

Comme le soleil déclinait au couchant, allongeant sur
le sol l'ombre du moindre caillou, Jean Valjean était
assis derrière un buisson dans une grande plaine rousse
absolument déserte. Il n'y avait à l'horizon que les
30 Alpes. Pas même le clocher d'un village lointain. Jean
Valjean pouvait être à trois lieues de Digne. Un sentier
qui coupait la plaine passait à quelques pas du buisson.

Au milieu de cette méditation qui n'eût pas peu
contribué à rendre ses haillons effrayants pour quelqu'un
35 qui l'eût rencontré, il entendit un bruit joyeux.

Il tourna la tête, et vit venir par le sentier un petit
Savoyard[1] d'une dizaine d'années qui chantait, sa vielle[2]
au flanc et sa boîte à marmotte[3] sur le dos ; un de ces
doux et gais enfants qui vont de pays en pays, laissant
40 voir leurs genoux par les trous de leur pantalon.

Tout en chantant l'enfant interrompait de temps en
temps sa marche et jouait aux osselets avec quelques
pièces de monnaie qu'il avait dans sa main, toute sa
fortune probablement. Parmi cette monnaie il y avait
45 une pièce de quarante sous.

L'enfant s'arrêta à côté du buisson sans voir Jean
Valjean et fit sauter sa poignée de sous que jusque-là il
avait reçue avec assez d'adresse tout entière sur le dos
de sa main.

50 Cette fois la pièce de quarante sous lui échappa, et
vint rouler vers la broussaille jusqu'à Jean Valjean.

---

1. Petit Savoyard : jeune ramoneur. La Savoie fournissait beaucoup d'hommes
   et d'enfants exerçant ce métier itinérant.
2. Vielle : instrument de musique dont les cordes sont frottées par une roue
   actionnée par une manivelle, accessoire traditionnel des petits Savoyards.
3. Les petits Savoyards transportaient avec eux une marmotte qu'ils
   montraient.

Jean Valjean posa le pied dessus.

Cependant l'enfant avait suivi sa pièce du regard, et l'avait vu.

55 Il ne s'étonna point et marcha droit à l'homme.

C'était un lieu absolument solitaire. Aussi loin que le regard pouvait s'étendre, il n'y avait personne dans la plaine ni dans le sentier. On n'entendait que les petits cris faibles d'une nuée d'oiseaux de passage qui 60 traversaient le ciel à une hauteur immense. L'enfant tournait le dos au soleil qui lui mettait des fils d'or dans les cheveux et qui empourprait[1] d'une lueur sanglante la face sauvage de Jean Valjean.

– Monsieur, dit le petit Savoyard, avec cette 65 confiance de l'enfance qui se compose d'ignorance et d'innocence, – ma pièce ?

– Comment t'appelles-tu ? dit Jean Valjean.

-- Petit-Gervais, monsieur.

– Va-t'en, dit Jean Valjean.

70 – Monsieur, reprit l'enfant, rendez-moi ma pièce.

Jean Valjean baissa la tête et ne répondit pas.

L'enfant recommença :

– Ma pièce, monsieur !

L'œil de Jean Valjean resta fixé à terre.

75 – Ma pièce ! cria l'enfant, ma pièce blanche ! mon argent !

Il semblait que Jean Valjean n'entendît point. L'enfant le prit au collet de sa blouse et le secoua. Et en même temps il faisait effort pour déranger le gros 80 soulier ferré posé sur son trésor.

– Je veux ma pièce ! ma pièce de quarante sous !

L'enfant pleurait. La tête de Jean Valjean se releva. Il était toujours assis. Ses yeux étaient troubles. Il

---

1. **Empourprait :** couvrait d'une lumière rouge.

considéra l'enfant avec une sorte d'étonnement, puis
85 il étendit la main vers son bâton et cria d'une voix
terrible : – Qui est là ?

– Moi, monsieur, répondit l'enfant. Petit-Gervais !
moi ! moi ! Rendez-moi mes quarante sous, s'il vous
plaît ! Ôtez votre pied, monsieur, s'il vous plaît !

90 Puis irrité, quoique tout petit, et devenant presque
menaçant :

– Ah çà, ôterez-vous votre pied ? Ôtez donc votre
pied, voyons.

– Ah ! c'est encore toi ! dit Jean Valjean, et se dres-
95 sant brusquement tout debout, le pied toujours sur la
pièce d'argent, il ajouta : – Veux-tu bien te sauver !

L'enfant effaré[1] le regarda, puis commença à trembler de la tête aux pieds, et, après quelques secondes de
stupeur, se mit à s'enfuir en courant de toutes ses
100 forces sans oser tourner le cou ni jeter un cri.

Cependant à une certaine distance l'essoufflement le
força de s'arrêter, et Jean Valjean, à travers sa rêverie,
l'entendit qui sanglotait.

Au bout de quelques instants l'enfant avait disparu.

105 Le soleil s'était couché.

L'ombre se faisait autour de Jean Valjean. Il n'avait pas
mangé de la journée ; il est probable qu'il avait la fièvre.

Il était resté debout, et n'avait pas changé d'attitude
depuis que l'enfant s'était enfui. Son souffle soulevait sa
110 poitrine à des intervalles longs et inégaux. Son regard,
arrêté à dix ou douze pas devant lui, semblait étudier
avec une attention profonde la forme d'un vieux tesson[2]
de faïence bleue tombé dans l'herbe. Tout à coup il tressaillit ; il venait de sentir le froid du soir.

---

1. **Effaré :** effrayé.
2. **Tesson :** débris de vaisselle.

115 Il raffermit sa casquette sur son front, chercha machinalement à croiser et à boutonner sa blouse, fit un pas, et se baissa pour reprendre à terre son bâton.

En ce moment il aperçut la pièce de quarante sous que son pied avait à demi enfoncée dans la terre et qui
120 brillait parmi les cailloux.

Ce fut comme une commotion galvanique[1]. – Qu'est-ce que c'est que ça ? dit-il entre ses dents. Il recula de trois pas, puis s'arrêta, sans pouvoir détacher son regard de ce point que son pied avait foulé
125 l'instant d'auparavant, comme si cette chose qui luisait là dans l'obscurité eût été un œil ouvert fixé sur lui.

Au bout de quelques minutes, il s'élança convulsivement vers la pièce d'argent, la saisit, et, se redressant, se mit à regarder au loin dans la plaine, jetant à la fois
130 ses yeux vers tous les points de l'horizon, debout et frissonnant comme une bête fauve effarée qui cherche un asile.

Il ne vit rien. La nuit tombait, la plaine était froide et vague, de grandes brumes violettes montaient dans
135 la clarté crépusculaire.

Il dit : Ah ! et se mit à marcher rapidement dans une certaine direction, du côté où l'enfant avait disparu. Après une trentaine de pas, il s'arrêta, regarda, et ne vit rien.

140 Alors il cria de toute sa force : – Petit-Gervais ! Petit-Gervais !

Il se tut, et attendit.

Rien ne répondit.

La campagne était déserte et morne. Il était envi-
145 ronné de l'étendue. Il n'y avait rien autour de lui

---

1. **Commotion galvanique :** choc électrique.

SITUER

Ayant quitté la ville, le forçat libéré, troublé par la bonté de l'évêque, rencontre un petit ramoneur à qui il vole sa pièce. Mais il prend conscience de son forfait, et subit alors une conversion décisive.

RÉFLÉCHIR

STRATÉGIES : un dialogue de sourds

1. Sous forme de tableau, notez les éléments qui opposent les deux personnages de la scène.

2. Quels sont les réactions successives de Petit-Gervais devant la dureté de Jean Valjean ?

3. Caractérisez les répliques et les attitudes physiques de Jean Valjean dans le dialogue. Que révèlent-elles sur son état d'esprit ?

PERSONNAGES : innocence et culpabilité

4. D'après son attitude et ses réactions, quelle image de l'enfance le petit Savoyard offre-t-il ?

5. Pourquoi Jean Valjean vole-t-il la pièce à l'enfant ? À quelle motivation obéit-il ?

THÈMES : l'expérience de la conversion

6. Relevez les notations temporelles qui décrivent la tombée progressive de la nuit. À quelles étapes de l'évolution psychologique de Jean Valjean correspondent-elles ?

7. Comment peut-on interpréter symboliquement les caractéristiques du paysage dans lequel se déroule la scène ?

8. Quelles sont les manifestations physiques et psychologiques de la conversion morale de Jean Valjean ?

9. Comment comprenez-vous la comparaison* de la pièce avec un « œil ouvert fixé sur lui » ?

ÉCRIRE

10. Un récit : Petit-Gervais raconte l'épisode aux gendarmes, en décrivant Jean Valjean et en leur rapportant les sentiments qu'il a lui-même éprouvés.

qu'une ombre où se perdait son regard et un silence où sa voix se perdait.

Une bise glaciale soufflait, et donnait aux choses autour de lui une sorte de vie lugubre. Des arbrisseaux
150 secouaient leurs petits bras maigres avec une furie incroyable. On eût dit qu'ils menaçaient et poursuivaient quelqu'un.

[Jean Valjean croise un homme à qui il demande s'il a vu Petit-Gervais. Il s'agit d'un prêtre, qui ne peut le renseigner. Jean Valjean lui donne de l'argent pour ses pauvres.]

Il fit de la sorte un assez long chemin, regardant, appelant et criant, mais il ne rencontra plus personne.
155 Deux ou trois fois il courut dans la plaine vers quelque chose qui lui faisait l'effet d'un être couché ou accroupi ; ce n'était que des broussailles ou des roches à fleur de terre.

Enfin, à un endroit où trois sentiers se croisaient, il
160 s'arrêta.

La lune s'était levée. Il promena sa vue au loin et appela une dernière fois : Petit-Gervais ! Petit-Gervais ! Petit-Gervais ! Son cri s'éteignit dans la brume, sans même éveiller un écho. Il murmura encore Petit-
165 Gervais ! mais d'une voix faible et presque inarticulée. Ce fut là son dernier effort ; ses jarrets fléchirent brusquement sous lui comme si une puissance invisible l'accablait tout à coup du poids de sa mauvaise conscience ; il tomba épuisé sur une grosse pierre, les
170 poings dans ses cheveux et le visage dans ses genoux, et il cria : Je suis un misérable !

Alors son cœur creva et il se mit à pleurer. C'était la première fois qu'il pleurait depuis dix-neuf ans.

Jean Valjean pleura longtemps. Il pleura à chaudes
175 larmes, il pleura à sanglots, avec plus de faiblesse
qu'une femme, avec plus d'effroi qu'un enfant. [...]

Pendant qu'il pleurait, le jour se faisait de plus en plus
dans son cerveau, un jour extraordinaire, un jour ravissant et terrible à la fois. Sa vie passée, sa première faute, sa
180 longue expiation[1], son abrutissement extérieur, son
endurcissement intérieur, sa mise en liberté réjouie par
tant de plans de vengeance, ce qui lui était arrivé chez
l'évêque, la dernière chose qu'il avait faite, ce vol de
quarante sous à un enfant, crime d'autant plus lâche et
185 d'autant plus monstrueux qu'il venait après le pardon de
l'évêque, tout cela lui revint et lui apparut, clairement,
mais dans une clarté qu'il n'avait jamais vue jusque-là. Il
regarda sa vie, et elle lui parut horrible ; son âme, et elle
lui parut affreuse. Cependant un jour doux était sur cette
190 vie et sur cette âme. Il lui semblait qu'il voyait Satan à la
lumière du paradis.

Combien d'heures pleura-t-il ainsi ? que fit-il après
avoir pleuré ? où alla-t-il ? on ne l'a jamais su. Il paraît
seulement avéré[2] que, dans cette même nuit, le voiturier
195 qui faisait à cette époque le service de Grenoble et qui
arrivait à Digne vers trois heures du matin, vit en traver-
sant la rue de l'évêché un homme dans l'attitude de la
prière, à genoux sur le pavé, dans l'ombre, devant la
porte de monseigneur Bienvenu.

*[En 1817, dans la joyeuse société des étudiants pari-
siens, quatre jeunes gens font « une bonne farce » à
leurs maîtresses en les quittant lâchement après une
partie de campagne. La jeune et jolie Fantine est ainsi
abandonnée par son amant, Tholomyès, père de sa petite
Cosette (I, III)].*

---

1. **Expiation :** punition d'une faute commise.
2. **Avéré :** établi, démontré, prouvé.

CONFIER, C'EST PARFOIS LIVRER

[Fantine décide de retourner au pays, à Montreuil-sur-Mer, dans le Pas-de-Calais, pour y gagner sa vie. Mais elle craint d'avoir des difficultés à trouver un emploi avec une enfant illégitime. Sur la route, elle confie Cosette à un couple d'aubergistes, les Thénardier, qu'elle croit dignes de confiance, et à qui elle paie régulièrement une pension pour l'éducation et l'entretien de son enfant. (I, IV, 1 et 2)]

3. L'alouette

Il ne suffit pas d'être méchant pour prospérer[1]. La gargote[2] allait mal.

Grâce aux cinquante-sept francs de la voyageuse, Thénardier avait pu éviter un protêt[3] et faire honneur à
5 sa signature[4]. Le mois suivant ils eurent encore besoin d'argent ; la femme porta à Paris et engagea au Mont-de-piété[5] le trousseau[6] de Cosette pour une somme de soixante francs. Dès que cette somme fut dépensée, les Thénardier s'accoutumèrent à ne plus voir dans la
10 petite fille qu'un enfant qu'ils avaient chez eux par

---

1. Prospérer : s'enrichir.

2. Gargote : petite auberge bon marché et peu soignée.

3. Protêt : un commerçant peut payer ses fournitures en plusieurs fois. Il signe des traites qui devront être payées à intervalles précis. Si le commerçant ne paye pas le jour dit, son fournisseur peut faire dresser par la justice un protêt, acte qui rend le mauvais payeur responsable de tous les frais.

4. Faire honneur à sa signature : respecter l'engagement qu'on a signé. Thénardier avait réussi à payer à temps.

5. Mont-de-piété : organisme public qui prête de l'argent contre le dépôt d'objets personnels (bijoux, vêtements, meubles, etc.).

6. Trousseau : ensemble des vêtements de l'enfant.

charité, et la traitèrent en conséquence. Comme elle n'avait plus de trousseau, on l'habilla des vieilles jupes et des vieilles chemises des petites Thénardier, c'est-à-dire de haillons. On la nourrit des restes de tout le monde, un peu mieux que le chien, et un peu plus mal que le chat. Le chat et le chien étaient du reste ses commensaux[1] habituels ; Cosette mangeait avec eux sous la table dans une écuelle de bois pareille à la leur.

La mère qui s'était fixée, comme on le verra plus tard, à Montreuil-sur-Mer, écrivait, ou, pour mieux dire, faisait écrire tous les mois afin d'avoir des nouvelles de son enfant. Les Thénardier répondaient invariablement : Cosette est à merveille.

Les six premiers mois révolus, la mère envoya sept francs pour le septième mois, et continua assez exactement ses envois de mois en mois. L'année n'était pas finie que le Thénardier dit : – Une belle grâce qu'elle nous fait là ! que veut-elle que nous fassions avec ses sept francs ? Et il écrivit pour exiger douze francs. La mère, à laquelle ils persuadaient que son enfant était heureuse et « venait bien »[2], se soumit et envoya les douze francs.

Certaines natures ne peuvent aimer d'un côté sans haïr de l'autre. La mère Thénardier aimait passionnément ses deux filles à elle, ce qui fit qu'elle détesta l'étrangère. Il est triste de songer que l'amour d'une mère peut avoir de vilains aspects. Si peu de place que Cosette tînt chez elle, il lui semblait que cela était pris aux siens, et que cette petite diminuait l'air que ses filles respiraient. Cette femme, comme beaucoup de femmes de sa sorte, avait une somme de caresses et une somme

---

1. **Commensaux** : compagnons de table.
2. **Venait bien :** grandissait bien.

de coups et d'injures à dépenser chaque jour. Si elle
n'avait pas eu Cosette, il est certain que ses filles, tout
idolâtrées qu'elles étaient, auraient tout reçu ; mais
45 l'étrangère leur rendit le service de détourner les coups
sur elle. Ses filles n'eurent que les caresses. Cosette ne
faisait pas un mouvement qui ne fît pleuvoir sur sa tête
une grêle de châtiments violents et immérités. Doux
être faible qui ne devait rien comprendre à ce monde ni
50 à Dieu, sans cesse punie, grondée, rudoyée, battue et
voyant à côté d'elle deux petites créatures comme elle,
qui vivaient dans un rayon d'aurore !

La Thénardier étant méchante pour Cosette,
Éponine et Azelma furent méchantes. Les enfants, à
55 cet âge, ne sont que des exemplaires de la mère. Le
format est plus petit, voilà tout.

Une année s'écoula, puis une autre.

On disait dans le village :

– Ces Thénardier sont de braves gens. Ils ne sont
60 pas riches, et ils élèvent un pauvre enfant qu'on leur a
abandonné chez eux !

On croyait Cosette oubliée par sa mère.

Cependant le Thénardier, ayant appris par on ne sait
quelles voies obscures que l'enfant était probablement
65 bâtard et que la mère ne pouvait l'avouer, exigea quinze
francs par mois, disant que « la créature » grandissait et
mangeait, et menaçant de la renvoyer. « Qu'elle ne
m'embête pas ! s'écriait-il, je lui bombarde[1] son mioche
tout au milieu de ses cachotteries. Il me faut de
70 l'augmentation. » La mère paya les quinze francs.

D'année en année, l'enfant grandit, et sa misère aussi.

Tant que Cosette fut toute petite, elle fut le souffre-
douleur des deux autres enfants ; dès qu'elle se mit à se

---

1. **Bombarde :** renvoie (familier).

développer un peu, c'est-à-dire avant même qu'elle eût
75 cinq ans, elle devint la servante de la maison.

Cinq ans, dira-t-on, c'est invraisemblable. Hélas,
c'est vrai. La souffrance sociale commence à tout âge.
N'avons-nous pas vu, récemment, le procès d'un
nommé Dumolard, orphelin devenu bandit, qui, dès
80 l'âge de cinq ans, disent les documents officiels, étant
seul au monde « travaillait pour vivre, et volait ».

On fit faire à Cosette les commissions, balayer les
chambres, la cour, la rue, laver la vaisselle, porter
même des fardeaux. Les Thénardier se crurent
85 d'autant plus autorisés à agir ainsi que la mère qui était
toujours à Montreuil-sur-Mer commença à mal payer.
Quelques mois restèrent en souffrance[1].

Si cette mère fût revenue à Montfermeil au bout de
ces trois années, elle n'eût point reconnu son enfant.
90 Cosette, si jolie et si fraîche à son arrivée dans cette
maison, était maintenant maigre et blême[2]. Elle avait je
ne sais quelle allure inquiète. Sournoise ! disaient les
Thénardier.

L'injustice l'avait faite hargneuse et la misère l'avait
95 rendue laide. Il ne lui restait plus que ses beaux yeux
qui faisaient peine, parce que, grands comme
ils étaient, il semblait qu'on y vît une plus grande
quantité de tristesse.

C'était une chose navrante[3] de voir, l'hiver, ce
100 pauvre enfant, qui n'avait pas encore six ans, grelottant
sous de vieilles loques de toile trouées, balayer la rue
avant le jour avec un énorme balai dans ses petites
mains rouges et une larme dans ses grands yeux.

---

1. **En souffrance :** impayés.
2. **Blême :** d'une blancheur maladive.
3. **Navrante :** désolante.

SITUER

Fantine a mis sa petite Cosette en pension chez les Thénardier. Sachant la mère vulnérable, l'homme abuse de la situation en exigeant toujours davantage d'argent et la femme fait de Cosette son souffre-douleur. Portrait d'une enfant martyre.

RÉFLÉCHIR

PERSONNAGES : le bourreau et sa victime

1. Relevez dans un tableau les antithèses* qui opposent l'attitude de la Thénardier à l'égard de ses filles et son attitude à l'égard de Cosette.

2. Dans le portrait de Cosette, quelle est la fonction des énumérations ? Montrez comment le malheur et la misère ont dégradé l'apparence physique et morale de Cosette.

3. Quelle est la signification du surnom donné à Cosette ? Outre les explications données par le narrateur, que suggère la métaphore * ?

4. Dans quelle mesure la Thénardier est-elle monstrueuse ? Dans quelle mesure est-elle humaine ?

QUI PARLE ? QUI VOIT ? La lâcheté collective

5. Le pronom « on » est employé à plusieurs reprises dans ce passage. Qui désigne-t-il tour à tour ?

6. Le narrateur rapporte l'opinion de la population de Montfermeil sur Cosette. Selon vous, les habitants sont-ils dupes ou hypocrites ?

REGISTRES ET TONALITÉS : une dénonciation indignée

7. Dans quelles phrases la voix du narrateur se fait-elle entendre directement ? Quel est l'effet de ces interventions ?

8. Quelles réflexions, quels sentiments l'auteur cherche-t-il à provoquer chez le lecteur ?

SOCIÉTÉ : le déterminisme social

9. Pourquoi Éponine et Azelma sont-elles méchantes ? Pourquoi Cosette est-elle « hargneuse » et « laide » ?

10. À quoi sert l'exemple du procès de Dumolard ? Quelle réalité de son époque Hugo cherche-t-il à dénoncer ici ?

Dans le pays on l'appelait l'Alouette. Le peuple, qui
105 aime les figures, s'était plu à nommer de ce nom ce
petit être pas plus gros qu'un oiseau, tremblant, effa-
rouché et frissonnant, éveillé le premier chaque matin
dans la maison et dans le village, toujours dans la rue
ou dans les champs avant l'aube.

110 Seulement la pauvre alouette ne chantait jamais.

LIVRE CINQUIÈME : LA DESCENTE

*[En revenant à Montreuil-sur-Mer, Fantine découvre
que sa ville natale a prospéré depuis l'arrivée, en 1815,
d'un inconnu qui y a repris une usine de verroterie
noire. Grâce à son esprit inventif, il a mis au point de
nouvelles méthodes de fabrication qui réduisent les coûts
et enrichissent les ouvriers en même temps que le proprié-
taire de l'usine. Cet homme avait, le jour de son arrivée
dans la ville, sauvé deux enfants d'un incendie. On
n'avait alors pas songé à lui demander son passeport. « Il
s'appelait le père Madeleine. » (I, V, 1)]*

2. Madeleine

C'était un homme d'environ cinquante ans, qui
avait l'air préoccupé et qui était bon. Voilà tout ce
qu'on en pouvait dire.

Grâce aux progrès rapides de cette industrie qu'il avait
5 si admirablement remaniée, Montreuil-sur-Mer était
devenu un centre d'affaires considérable. L'Espagne, qui
consomme beaucoup de jais[1] noir, y commandait chaque
année des achats immenses. Montreuil-sur-Mer, pour ce
commerce, faisait presque concurrence à Londres et à

---

1. **Jais :** pierre dure et très noire.

10 Berlin. Les bénéfices du père Madeleine étaient tels que,
dès la deuxième année, il avait pu bâtir une grande fabrique dans laquelle il y avait deux vastes ateliers, l'un pour
les hommes, l'autre pour les femmes. Quiconque avait
faim pouvait s'y présenter, et était sûr de trouver là de
15 l'emploi et du pain. Le père Madeleine demandait aux
hommes de la bonne volonté, aux femmes des mœurs
pures, à tous de la probité[1]. Il avait divisé les ateliers, afin
de séparer les sexes et que les filles et les femmes pussent
rester sages. Sur ce point, il était inflexible. C'était le seul
20 où il fût en quelque sorte intolérant. Il était d'autant
plus fondé à cette sévérité que, Montreuil-sur-Mer étant
une ville de garnison[2], les occasions de corruption abon-
daient. Du reste sa venue avait été un bienfait, et sa
présence était une providence[3]. Avant l'arrivée du père
25 Madeleine, tout languissait dans le pays ; maintenant
tout y vivait de la vie saine du travail. Une forte circulation échauffait tout et pénétrait partout. Le chômage et
la misère étaient inconnus. Il n'y avait pas de poche si
obscure où il n'y eût un peu d'argent, pas de logis si
30 pauvre où il n'y eût un peu de joie.

Le père Madeleine employait tout le monde. Il
n'exigeait qu'une chose : soyez honnête homme !
soyez honnête fille !

Comme nous l'avons dit, au milieu de cette activité
35 dont il était la cause et le pivot[4], le père Madeleine
faisait sa fortune, mais, chose assez singulière dans un
simple homme de commerce, il ne paraissait point que
ce fût là son principal souci. Il semblait qu'il songeât
beaucoup aux autres et peu à lui. En 1820, on lui

---

1. **Probité :** honnêteté.
2. **Ville de garnison :** ville où séjournent des troupes de soldats.
3. **Providence :** chance inespérée.
4. **Pivot :** centre, base.

40 connaissait une somme de six cent trente mille francs
placée à son nom chez Laffitte[1] ; mais avant de se réser-
ver ces six cent trente mille francs, il avait dépensé plus
d'un million pour la ville et pour les pauvres.

L'hôpital était mal doté ; il y avait fondé dix lits.
45 Montreuil-sur-Mer est divisé en ville haute et ville
basse. La ville basse qu'il habitait n'avait qu'une école,
méchante masure qui tombait en ruine ; il en avait
construit deux, une pour les filles, l'autre pour les
garçons. Il allouait de ses deniers[2] aux deux instituteurs
50 une indemnité double de leur maigre traitement officiel, et un jour, à quelqu'un qui s'en étonnait, il dit :
« Les deux premiers fonctionnaires de l'État, c'est la
nourrice et le maître d'école. » Il avait créé à ses frais
une salle d'asile, chose alors presque inconnue en
55 France, et une caisse de secours pour les ouvriers vieux
et infirmes. Sa manufacture étant un centre, un
nouveau quartier où il y avait bon nombre de familles
indigentes avait rapidement surgi autour de lui ; il y
avait établi une pharmacie gratuite.

60 Dans les premiers temps, quand on le vit commencer,
les bonnes âmes dirent : C'est un gaillard qui veut
s'enrichir. Quand on le vit enrichir le pays avant de
s'enrichir lui-même, les mêmes bonnes âmes dirent :
C'est un ambitieux. Cela semblait d'autant plus probable
65 que cet homme était religieux, et même pratiquait
dans une certaine mesure, chose fort bien vue à cette
époque. Il allait régulièrement entendre une basse
messe tous les dimanches. Le député local, qui flairait
partout des concurrences, ne tarda pas à s'inquiéter de
70 cette religion. Ce député, qui avait été membre du

---

1. **Laffitte :** banquier et homme politique français (1767-1844).
2. **De ses deniers :** de son argent.

corps législatif de l'empire, partageait les idées religieuses d'un père de l'Oratoire connu sous le nom de
Fouché, duc d'Otrante, dont il avait été la créature et
l'ami. À huis clos il riait de Dieu doucement. Mais
75 quand il vit le riche manufacturier Madeleine aller à la
basse messe de sept heures, il entrevit un candidat
possible, et résolut de le dépasser ; il prit un confesseur
jésuite et alla à la grand-messe et à vêpres. L'ambition
en ce temps-là était, dans l'acception[1] directe du mot,
80 une course au clocher. Les pauvres profitèrent de cette
terreur comme le bon Dieu, car l'honorable député
fonda aussi deux lits à l'hôpital ; ce qui fit douze.

Cependant en 1819 le bruit se répandit un matin
dans la ville que, sur la présentation de M. le préfet et
85 en considération des services rendus au pays, le père
Madeleine allait être nommé par le roi maire de
Montreuil-sur-Mer. Ceux qui avaient déclaré ce
nouveau venu « un ambitieux », saisirent avec transport cette occasion que tous les hommes souhaitent de
90 s'écrier : Là ! qu'est-ce que nous avions dit ? Tout
Montreuil-sur-Mer fut en rumeur. Le bruit était
fondé. Quelques jours après, la nomination parut dans
Le Moniteur[2]. Le lendemain, le père Madeleine refusa.

Dans cette même année 1819, les produits du
95 nouveau procédé inventé par Madeleine figurèrent à
l'exposition de l'industrie ; sur le rapport du jury, le roi
nomma l'inventeur chevalier de la Légion d'honneur.
Nouvelle rumeur dans la petite ville. Eh bien ! c'est la
croix[3] qu'il voulait ! Le père Madeleine refusa la croix.

---

1. **Acception :** signification.
2. *Le Moniteur* **:** journal officiel.
3. **La croix :** la Légion d'honneur.

100 Décidément cet homme était une énigme. Les bonnes âmes se tirèrent d'affaire en disant : Après tout, c'est une espèce d'aventurier.

On l'a vu, le pays lui devait beaucoup, les pauvres lui devaient tout ; il était si utile qu'il avait bien fallu qu'on 105 finît par l'honorer, et il était si doux qu'il avait bien fallu qu'on finît par l'aimer ; ses ouvriers en particulier l'adoraient, et il portait cette adoration avec une sorte de gravité mélancolique. Quand il fut constaté riche, « les personnes de la société » le saluèrent, et on l'appela dans 110 la ville monsieur Madeleine ; ses ouvriers et les enfants continuèrent de l'appeler *le père Madeleine*, et c'était la chose qui le faisait le mieux sourire. À mesure qu'il montait, les invitations pleuvaient sur lui. « La société » le réclamait. Les petits salons guindés de Montreuil-sur-Mer 115 qui, bien entendu, se fussent dans les premiers temps fermés à l'artisan, s'ouvrirent à deux battants au million-naire. On lui fit mille avances. Il refusa.

Cette fois encore les bonnes âmes ne furent point empêchées. – C'est un homme ignorant et de basse 120 éducation. On ne sait d'où cela sort. Il ne saurait pas se tenir dans le monde. Il n'est pas du tout prouvé qu'il sache lire.

Quand on l'avait vu gagner de l'argent, on avait dit : c'est un marchand. Quand on l'avait vu semer son 125 argent, on avait dit : c'est un ambitieux. Quand on l'avait vu repousser les honneurs, on avait dit : c'est un aventurier. Quand on le vit repousser le monde, on dit : c'est une brute.

En 1820, cinq ans après son arrivée à Montreuil-sur-130 Mer, les services qu'il avait rendus au pays étaient si éclatants, le vœu de la contrée fut tellement unanime[1], que le roi le nomma de nouveau maire de la ville. Il refusa

---

1. **Unanime :** général.

encore, mais le préfet résista à son refus, tous les notables
vinrent le prier, le peuple en pleine rue le suppliait, l'insis-
135 tance fut si vive qu'il finit par accepter. On remarqua que
ce qui parut surtout le déterminer, ce fut l'apostrophe
presque irritée d'une vieille femme du peuple qui lui cria
du seuil de sa porte avec humeur : *Un bon maire, c'est
utile. Est-ce qu'on recule devant du bien qu'on peut faire ?*
140   Ce fut là la troisième phase de son ascension. Le
père Madeleine était devenu monsieur Madeleine,
monsieur Madeleine devint monsieur le maire.

    *[M. Madeleine conquiert peu à peu l'estime de la
population. Il est charitable et de bon conseil. Mais son
passé reste mystérieux. Un jour de 1821, apprenant par
les journaux la mort de Mgr Myriel, il porte le deuil. Il
donne de l'argent à tous les petits Savoyards qui passent
dans la ville. (I, V, 3 et 4)]*

5. Vagues éclairs à l'horizon

    *[Une seule personne résiste à l'engouement général
pour M. Madeleine, le policier Javert, persuadé qu'il a
déjà vu cet homme quelque part.]*

    Javert était né dans une prison d'une tireuse de cartes
dont le mari était aux galères. En grandissant, il pensa
qu'il était en dehors de la société et désespéra d'y rentrer
jamais. Il remarqua que la société maintient
5 irrémissiblement[1] en dehors d'elle deux classes d'hommes,
ceux qui l'attaquent et ceux qui la gardent ; il n'avait le
choix qu'entre ces deux classes ; en même temps il se
sentait je ne sais quel fond de rigidité, de régularité et de

---

1. **Irrémissiblement :** sans indulgence, sans espoir de pardon.

probité[1], compliqué d'une inexprimable haine pour cette
10 race de bohèmes[2] dont il était. Il entra dans la police. Il y
réussit. À quarante ans il était inspecteur.

[...]

Cet homme était composé de deux sentiments très
simples et relativement très bons, mais qu'il faisait pres-
15 que mauvais à force de les exagérer, le respect de l'autorité, la haine de la rébellion[3] ; et à ses yeux le vol, le
meurtre, tous les crimes, n'étaient que des formes de la
rébellion. Il enveloppait dans une sorte de foi aveugle et
profonde tout ce qui a une fonction dans l'État, depuis
20 le premier ministre jusqu'au garde-champêtre. Il
couvrait de mépris, d'aversion et de dégoût tout ce qui
avait franchi une fois le seuil légal du mal. Il était absolu
et n'admettait pas d'exceptions. D'une part il disait :
– Le fonctionnaire ne peut se tromper ; le magistrat n'a
25 jamais tort. – D'autre part il disait : – Ceux-ci sont
irrémédiablement[4] perdus. Rien de bon n'en peut sortir.
– Il partageait pleinement l'opinion de ces esprits extrê-
mes qui attribuent à la loi humaine je ne sais quel
pouvoir de faire ou, si l'on veut, de constater des
30 démons, et qui mettent un Styx[5] au bas de la société. Il
était stoïque[6], sérieux, austère ; rêveur triste ; humble et
hautain comme les fanatiques. Son regard était une
vrille[7], cela était froid et cela perçait. Toute sa vie tenait

---

1. **Probité :** honnêteté.
2. La mère de Javert étant tireuse de cartes, profession de bohémienne
   (= gitane), Javert désire s'intégrer dans la société : il déteste les marginaux
   qui lui rappellent des origines dont il a honte.
3. **Rébellion :** révolte.
4. **Irrémédiablement :** pour toujours, sans espoir de salut.
5. **Styx :** fleuve des Enfers dans la mythologie grecque.
6. **Stoïque :** ferme, rigoureux, insensible à la souffrance.
7. **Vrille :** outil utilisé pour faire des trous. La métaphore* signifie ici que
   son regard était impitoyablement perçant.

dans ces deux mots : veiller et surveiller. Il avait intro-
duit la ligne droite dans ce qu'il y a de plus tortueux au
monde ; il avait la conscience de son utilité, la religion
de ses fonctions, et il était espion comme on est prêtre.
Malheur à qui tombait sous sa main ! Il eût arrêté son
père s'évadant du bagne et dénoncé sa mère en rupture
de ban[1]. Et il l'eût fait avec cette sorte de satisfaction
intérieure que donne la vertu. Avec cela une vie de
privations, l'isolement, l'abnégation[2], la chasteté, jamais
une distraction.

[...]

Javert était comme un œil toujours fixé sur M. Madeleine. Œil plein de soupçon et de conjectures[3].
M. Madeleine avait fini par s'en apercevoir, mais il
sembla que cela fût insignifiant pour lui. Il ne fit pas
même une question à Javert, il ne le cherchait ni ne
l'évitait, il portait, sans paraître y faire attention, ce
regard gênant et presque pesant. Il traitait Javert
comme tout le monde, avec aisance et bonté.

À quelques paroles échappées à Javert, on devinait
qu'il avait recherché secrètement, avec cette curiosité
qui tient à la race et où il entre autant d'instinct que de
volonté, toutes les traces antérieures que le père Madeleine avait pu laisser ailleurs. Il paraissait savoir, et il
disait parfois à mots couverts, que quelqu'un avait pris
certaines informations dans certain pays sur une
certaine famille disparue. Une fois il lui arriva de dire,
se parlant à lui-même : – Je crois que je le tiens ! – Puis
il resta trois jours pensif sans prononcer une parole. Il
paraît que le fil qu'il croyait tenir s'était rompu.

---

1. **En rupture de ban :** recherchée par la police.
2. **Abnégation :** détachement, dévouement total, oubli de soi.
3. **Conjectures :** hypothèses, suppositions.

Du reste, et ceci est le correctif[1] nécessaire à ce que
65 le sens de certains mots pourrait présenter de trop
absolu, il ne peut y avoir rien de vraiment infaillible[2]
dans une créature humaine, et le propre de l'instinct
est précisément de pouvoir être troublé, dépisté et
dérouté. Sans quoi il serait supérieur à l'intelligence, et
70 la bête se trouverait avoir une meilleure lumière que
l'homme.

Javert était évidemment quelque peu déconcerté[3] par
le complet naturel et la tranquillité de M. Madeleine.

Un jour pourtant son étrange manière d'être parut faire
75 impression sur M. Madeleine. Voici à quelle occasion.

6. Le père Fauchelevent

*[Un des rares ennemis irréductibles de M. Madeleine,
le paysan Fauchelevent, se retrouve un jour renversé sous
sa charrette qui, s'enfonçant de plus en plus, menace de
l'écraser. En attendant les secours, la population assiste
impuissante à la détresse du vieil homme. M. Madeleine
propose dix louis à qui soulèvera la charrette.]*

Les assistants baissaient les yeux. Un d'eux
murmura : – Il faudrait être diablement fort. Et puis,
on risque de se faire écraser !

– Allons ! recommença Madeleine, vingt louis[4] !
5 Même silence.

– Ce n'est pas la bonne volonté qui leur manque, dit
une voix.

---

1. **Correctif :** rectification.
2. **Infaillible :** qui ne se trompe jamais.
3. **Déconcerté :** désorienté.
4. **Louis :** pièce d'or d'une valeur approximative de 60 euros.

M. Madeleine se retourna, et reconnut Javert. Il ne l'avait pas aperçu en arrivant.

10   Javert continua :

– C'est la force. Il faudrait être un terrible homme pour faire la chose de lever une voiture comme cela sur son dos.

Puis, regardant fixement M. Madeleine, il poursuivit 15 en appuyant sur chacun des mots qu'il prononçait :

– Monsieur Madeleine, je n'ai jamais connu qu'un seul homme capable de faire ce que vous demandez là.

Madeleine tressaillit.

Javert ajouta avec un air d'indifférence, mais sans 20 quitter des yeux Madeleine :

– C'était un forçat.

– Ah ! dit Madeleine.

– Du bagne de Toulon.

Madeleine devint pâle.

25   Cependant la charrette continuait à s'enfoncer lentement. Le père Fauchelevent râlait et hurlait :

– J'étouffe ! Ça me brise les côtes ! Un cric ! quelque chose ! Ah !

Madeleine regarda autour de lui :

30   – Il n'y a donc personne qui veuille gagner vingt louis et sauver la vie à ce pauvre vieux ?

Aucun des assistants ne remua. Javert reprit :

– Je n'ai jamais connu qu'un homme qui pût remplacer un cric, c'était ce forçat.

35   – Ah ! voilà que ça m'écrase ! cria le vieillard.

Madeleine leva la tête, rencontra l'œil de faucon de Javert toujours attaché sur lui, regarda les paysans immobiles, et sourit tristement. Puis, sans dire une parole, il tomba à genoux, et avant même 40 que la foule eût eu le temps de jeter un cri, il était sous la voiture.

Il y eut un affreux moment d'attente et de silence.

Gustave Brion, *Javert*, 1862.

On vit Madeleine presque à plat ventre sous ce poids effrayant essayer deux fois en vain de rapprocher ses 45 coudes de ses genoux. On lui cria : – Père Madeleine ! retirez-vous de là ! – Le vieux Fauchelevent lui-même lui dit : – Monsieur Madeleine ! allez-vous-en ! C'est qu'il faut que je meure, voyez-vous ! Laissez-moi ! Vous allez vous faire écraser aussi ! – Madeleine ne 50 répondit pas.

Les assistants haletaient. Les roues avaient continué de s'enfoncer, et il était déjà devenu presque impossible que Madeleine sortît de dessous la voiture.

Tout à coup on vit l'énorme masse s'ébranler, la 55 charrette se soulevait lentement, les roues sortaient à demi de l'ornière. On entendit une voix étouffée qui criait : Dépêchez-vous ! aidez ! C'était Madeleine qui venait de faire un dernier effort.

Ils se précipitèrent. Le dévouement d'un seul avait 60 donné de la force et du courage à tous. La charrette fut enlevée par vingt bras. Le vieux Fauchelevent était sauvé.

Madeleine se releva. Il était blême, quoique ruisselant de sueur. Ses habits étaient déchirés et couverts de boue. Tous pleuraient. Le vieillard lui baisait les 65 genoux et l'appelait le bon Dieu. Lui, il avait sur le visage je ne sais quelle expression de souffrance heureuse et céleste, et il fixait son œil tranquille sur Javert qui le regardait toujours.

[Le père Fauchelevent garde après l'accident un handicap au genou. M. Madeleine lui trouve un emploi de jardinier dans un couvent parisien. La nomination de M. Madeleine à la mairie indispose Javert.

Fantine est embauchée dans la fabrique de M. Madeleine. Elle est heureuse de pouvoir gagner sa vie. Mais ses collègues, jalouses et cancanières, la suspectent et découvrent qu'elle correspond avec un certain M. Thénardier. Une commère,

I, V, 6, lignes 1 à 68

SITUER

M. Madeleine est aimé de la population, mais a éveillé les soupçons de l'inspecteur de police Javert. Un matin, le vieux Fauchelevent tombe sous sa charrette, qui menace de l'écraser. Qui aura le courage et la force de le sauver ?

RÉFLÉCHIR

STRUCTURE : une décision urgente

1. Quelles sont les étapes de cet épisode ? Commentez la longueur des paragraphes et des phrases.

2. Quels personnages prennent successivement la parole ? Comment les dialogues entretiennent-ils le suspense ?

STRATÉGIES : un redoutable défi

3. Est-il vraisemblable que M. Madeleine n'ait pas aperçu Javert en arrivant ? Comment le policier intervient-il dans le dialogue ? Montrez l'impact dramatique* de cette présence inattendue.

4. Pourquoi Javert évoque-t-il le souvenir du forçat de Toulon ?

5. Commentez les réactions de M. Madeleine aux remarques de Javert.

6. Pourquoi M. Madeleine hésite-t-il avant de porter lui-même secours à Fauchelevent ? Quels sont les enjeux de son combat inté-rieur ? Pourquoi finit-il par intervenir ?

7. Quel sens donnez-vous à l'expression « l'œil de faucon » (l. 36) Quelle indication cette métaphore* fournit-elle sur le personnage ?

8. Que signifient les regards échangés entre Javert et M. Madeleine ?

THÈMES : le sauveur

9. Quelles sont les réactions successives de la foule au cours de cet épisode ? Expliquez la phrase : « Le dévouement d'un seul avait donné de la force et du courage à tous. »

10. « Sans dire une parole », M. Madeleine « tombe à genoux ». Si l'on compare cette attitude à celle de Jean Valjean, devant la porte de l'évêque, après le vol de la pièce à Petit-Gervais (I, II, 13, p. 62), quelle interprétation symbolique peut-on lui donner ?

11. Comment M. Madeleine peut-il ressentir une « souffrance heureuse et céleste » après avoir accompli son exploit ? Expliquez cet oxymore*.

12. À qui M. Madeleine est-il comparé dans le dernier paragraphe ? Justifiez cette image.

Mme Victurnien, mène l'enquête et révèle à l'atelier l'exis-
tence de l'enfant. La jeune femme est aussitôt renvoyée par la
surveillante. Fantine, qui s'était meublée à crédit, ne peut
plus faire face à ses dettes. Après avoir essayé en vain de se
placer comme servante, elle coud des chemises et renonce à son
maigre confort. La misère la guette. (I, V, 7 à 9)]

10. Suite du succès

[...]

Fantine gagnait trop peu. Ses dettes avaient grossi.
Les Thénardier, mal payés, lui écrivaient à chaque
instant des lettres dont le contenu la désolait et dont le
port[1] la ruinait. Un jour ils lui écrivirent que sa petite
5 Cosette était toute nue par le froid qu'il faisait, qu'elle
avait besoin d'une jupe de laine, et qu'il fallait au
moins que la mère envoyât dix francs pour cela. Elle
reçut la lettre, et la froissa dans ses mains tout le jour.
Le soir elle entra chez un barbier[2] qui habitait le coin
10 de la rue, et défit son peigne. Ses admirables cheveux
blonds lui tombèrent jusqu'aux reins.

– Les beaux cheveux ! s'écria le barbier.

– Combien m'en donneriez-vous ? dit-elle.

– Dix francs.

15 – Coupez-les.

Elle acheta une jupe de tricot et l'envoya aux Thénardier.

Cette jupe fit les Thénardier furieux. C'était de
l'argent qu'ils voulaient. Ils donnèrent la jupe à
Éponine. La pauvre Alouette continua de frissonner.

20 Fantine pensa : – Mon enfant n'a plus froid. Je l'ai
habillée de mes cheveux. – Elle mettait de petits

---

1. **Port :** prix du timbre, payé par la destinataire de la lettre.
2. **Barbier :** coiffeur.

bonnets ronds qui cachaient sa tête tondue et avec lesquels elle était encore jolie.

Un travail ténébreux se faisait dans le cœur de Fantine. Quand elle vit qu'elle ne pouvait plus se coiffer, elle commença à tout prendre en haine autour d'elle. Elle avait longtemps partagé la vénération[1] de tous pour le père Madeleine ; cependant, à force de se répéter que c'était lui qui l'avait chassée, et qu'il était la cause de son malheur, elle en vint à le haïr lui aussi, lui surtout. Quand elle passait devant la fabrique aux heures où les ouvriers sont sur la porte, elle affectait de rire et de chanter.

Une vieille ouvrière qui la vit une fois chanter et rire de cette façon dit : – Voilà une fille qui finira mal.

Elle prit un amant, le premier venu, un homme qu'elle n'aimait pas, par bravade, avec la rage dans le cœur. C'était un misérable, une espèce de musicien mendiant, un oisif gueux[2], qui la battait, et qui la quitta comme elle l'avait pris, avec dégoût.

Elle adorait son enfant.

Plus elle descendait, plus tout devenait sombre autour d'elle, plus ce doux petit ange rayonnait dans le fond de son âme. Elle disait : Quand je serai riche, j'aurai ma Cosette avec moi ; et elle riait. La toux ne la quittait pas, et elle avait des sueurs dans le dos.

Un jour elle reçut des Thénardier une lettre ainsi conçue : « Cosette est malade d'une maladie qui est dans le pays. Une fièvre miliaire[3], qu'ils appellent. Il faut des drogues[4] chères. Cela nous ruine et nous ne

---

1. **Vénération :** adoration respectueuse.
2. **Gueux :** misérable.
3. **Fièvre miliaire :** grave maladie, souvent mortelle, caractérisée par une transpiration abondante et une éruption de boutons, qui avait provoqué une épidémie en 1821.
4. **Drogues :** médicaments.

⁵⁰ pouvons plus payer. Si vous ne nous envoyez pas quarante francs avant huit jours, la petite est morte. »

Elle se mit à rire aux éclats, et elle dit à sa vieille voisine : – Ah ! ils sont bons ! quarante francs ! que ça ! ça fait deux napoléons[1] ! Où veulent-ils que je les ⁵⁵ prenne ? Sont-ils bêtes, ces paysans !

Cependant elle alla dans l'escalier près d'une lucarne et relut la lettre.

Puis elle descendit l'escalier et sortit en courant et en sautant, riant toujours.

⁶⁰ Quelqu'un qui la rencontra lui dit : – Qu'est-ce que vous avez donc à être si gaie ?

Elle répondit : – C'est une bonne bêtise que viennent de m'écrire des gens de la campagne. Ils me demandent quarante francs. Paysans, va !

⁶⁵ Comme elle passait sur la place, elle vit beaucoup de monde qui entourait une voiture de forme bizarre, sur l'impériale[2] de laquelle pérorait[3] tout debout un homme vêtu de rouge. C'était un bateleur dentiste en tournée, qui offrait au public des râteliers[4] complets, ⁷⁰ des opiats[5], des poudres et des élixirs.

Fantine se mêla au groupe et se mit à rire comme les autres de cette harangue[6] où il y avait de l'argot pour la canaille et du jargon[7] pour les gens comme il faut. L'arracheur de dents vit cette belle fille qui riait, et ⁷⁵ s'écria tout à coup : – Vous avez de jolies dents, la fille

---

1. **Napoléons** : pièces d'or d'environ trois euros à l'effigie de Napoléon.
2. **Impériale** : étage supérieur d'un véhicule.
3. **Pérorait** : discourait longuement et avec prétention.
4. **Râteliers** : dentiers.
5. **Opiats** : pâtes dentifrices ; **élixirs** : préparations médicamenteuses liquides.
6. **Harangue** : discours destiné à persuader la foule, boniment.
7. **Jargon** : vocabulaire technique incompréhensible au profane.

qui riez là. Si vous voulez me vendre vos deux palettes, je vous donne de chaque un napoléon d'or.

– Qu'est-ce que c'est que ça, mes palettes ? demanda Fantine.

80 – Les palettes, reprit le professeur dentiste, c'est les dents de devant, les deux d'en haut.

– Quelle horreur ! s'écria Fantine.

– Deux napoléons ! grommela une vieille édentée qui était là. Qu'en voilà une qui est heureuse !

85 Fantine s'enfuit et se boucha les oreilles pour ne pas entendre la voix enrouée de l'homme qui lui criait : – Réfléchissez, la belle ! deux napoléons, ça peut servir. Si le cœur vous en dit, venez ce soir à l'auberge du *Tillac d'argent*, vous m'y trouverez.

90 Fantine rentra, elle était furieuse et conta la chose à sa bonne voisine Marguerite : – Comprenez-vous cela ? ne voilà-t-il pas un abominable homme ? comment laisse-t-on des gens comme cela aller dans le pays ! M'arracher mes deux dents de devant ! mais je 95 serais horrible ! Les cheveux repoussent, mais les dents ! Ah ! le monstre d'homme ! j'aimerais mieux me jeter d'un cinquième la tête la première sur le pavé ! Il m'a dit qu'il serait ce soir au *Tillac d'argent*.

– Et qu'est-ce qu'il offrait ? demanda Marguerite.

100 – Deux napoléons.

– Cela fait quarante francs.

– Oui, dit Fantine, cela fait quarante francs.

Elle resta pensive, et se mit à son ouvrage. Au bout d'un quart d'heure, elle quitta sa couture et alla relire 105 la lettre des Thénardier sur l'escalier.

En rentrant, elle dit à Marguerite qui travaillait près d'elle :

– Qu'est-ce que c'est donc que cela, une fièvre miliaire ? Savez-vous ?

110 – Oui, répondit la vieille fille, c'est une maladie.

– Ça a donc besoin de beaucoup de drogues ?

– Oh ! des drogues terribles.

– Où ça vous prend-il ?

– C'est une maladie qu'on a comme ça.

115 – Cela attaque donc les enfants ?

– Surtout les enfants.

– Est-ce qu'on en meurt ?

– Très bien, dit Marguerite.

Fantine sortit et alla encore une fois relire la lettre
120 sur l'escalier.

Le soir elle descendit, et on la vit qui se dirigeait du
côté de la rue de Paris où sont les auberges.

Le lendemain matin, comme Marguerite entrait
dans la chambre de Fantine avant le jour, car elles
125 travaillaient toujours ensemble et de cette façon n'allu-
maient qu'une chandelle pour deux, elle trouva
Fantine assise sur son lit, pâle, glacée. Elle ne s'était
pas couchée. Son bonnet était tombé sur ses genoux.
La chandelle avait brûlé toute la nuit et était presque
130 entièrement consumée[1].

Marguerite s'arrêta sur le seuil, pétrifiée[2] de cet
énorme désordre, et s'écria :

– Seigneur ! la chandelle qui est toute brûlée ! il
s'est passé des événements !

135 Puis elle regarda Fantine qui tournait vers elle sa
tête sans cheveux.

Fantine depuis la veille avait vieilli de dix ans.

– Jésus ! fit Marguerite, qu'est-ce que vous avez,
Fantine ?

---

1. **Consumée :** brûlée.
2. **Pétrifiée :** stupéfaite, saisie.

140 – Je n'ai rien, répondit Fantine. Au contraire. Mon enfant ne mourra pas de cette affreuse maladie, faute de secours. Je suis contente.

En parlant ainsi, elle montrait à la vieille fille deux napoléons qui brillaient sur la table.

145 – Ah ! Jésus Dieu ! dit Marguerite. Mais c'est une fortune ! Où avez-vous eu ces louis d'or ?

– Je les ai eus, répondit Fantine.

En même temps elle sourit. La chandelle éclairait son visage. C'était un sourire sanglant. Une salive 150 rougeâtre lui souillait le coin des lèvres, et elle avait un trou noir dans la bouche.

Les deux dents étaient arrachées.

Elle envoya les quarante francs à Montfermeil.

Du reste c'était une ruse des Thénardier pour avoir 155 de l'argent. Cosette n'était pas malade.

[Fantine sombre dans la misère. Elle renonce à sa coquetterie, n'arrive plus à rembourser ses dettes, tombe malade. Après avoir vendu ses cheveux et ses dents, elle vend « le reste », et devient « fille publique ».]

12. Le désœuvrement de M. Bamatabois

Il y a dans toutes les petites villes, et il y avait à Montreuil-sur-Mer en particulier, une classe de jeunes gens qui grignotent quinze cents livres de rente[1] en province du même air dont[2] leurs pareils dévorent à 5 Paris deux cent mille francs par an. Ce sont des êtres de la grande espèce neutre, hongres[3], parasites, nuls,

---

1. Il s'agit d'un revenu annuel.
2. **Du même air dont :** de la même manière que.
3. **Hongres :** châtrés (habituellement en parlant du cheval).

qui ont un peu de terre, un peu de sottise et un peu
d'esprit, qui seraient des rustres[1] dans un salon et se
croient des gentilshommes au cabaret, qui disent : mes
prés, mes bois, mes paysans, sifflent les actrices du
théâtre pour prouver qu'ils sont gens de goût, querellent
les officiers de la garnison pour montrer qu'ils sont
gens de guerre, chassent, fument, bâillent, boivent,
sentent le tabac, jouent au billard, regardent les voyageurs descendre de diligence, vivent au café, dînent à
l'auberge, ont un chien qui mange les os sous la table
et une maîtresse qui pose les plats dessus, tiennent à un
sou, exagèrent les modes, admirent la tragédie, mépri-
sent les femmes, usent leurs vieilles bottes, copient
Londres à travers Paris et Paris à travers Pont-à-
Mousson[2], vieillissent hébétés[3], ne travaillent pas, ne
servent à rien et ne nuisent pas à grand'chose.

M. Félix Tholomyès[4], resté dans sa province et
n'ayant jamais vu Paris, serait un de ces hommes-là.

S'ils étaient plus riches, on dirait : ce sont des
élégants ; s'ils étaient plus pauvres, on dirait : ce sont
des fainéants. Ce sont tout simplement des
désœuvrés[5]. Parmi ces désœuvrés, il y a des ennuyeux,
des ennuyés, des rêvasseurs, et quelques drôles.

[...]

Huit ou dix mois donc après ce qui a été raconté dans
les pages précédentes, vers les premiers jours de janvier
1823, un soir qu'il avait neigé, un de ces élégants, un de
ces désœuvrés, un « bien pensant », car il avait un

---

1. **Rustres** : paysans grossiers.
2. **Pont-à-Mousson** : ville de Meurthe-et-Moselle.
3. **Hébétés** : abrutis.
4. **Tholomyès** est le jeune homme qui a abandonné Fantine et Cosette. Voir
p. 62.
5. **Désœuvrés** : oisifs, inactifs.

35 morillo[1], de plus chaudement enveloppé d'un de ces
grands manteaux qui complétaient dans les temps froids
le costume à la mode, se divertissait à harceler[2] une créature qui rôdait en robe de bal et toute décolletée avec des
fleurs sur la tête devant la vitre du café des officiers. Cet
40 élégant fumait, car c'était décidément la mode.

Chaque fois que cette femme passait devant lui, il lui
jetait, avec une bouffée de la fumée de son cigare,
quelque apostrophe qu'il croyait spirituelle et gaie,
comme : – Que tu es laide ! – Veux-tu te cacher ! – Tu
45 n'as pas de dents ! etc., etc. – Ce monsieur s'appelait
monsieur Bamatabois. La femme, triste spectre paré
qui allait et venait sur la neige, ne lui répondait pas, ne
le regardait même pas, et n'en accomplissait pas moins
en silence et avec une régularité sombre sa promenade
50 qui la ramenait de cinq minutes en cinq minutes sous
le sarcasme[3], comme le soldat condamné qui revient
sous les verges[4]. Ce peu d'effet piqua sans doute l'oisif
qui, profitant d'un moment où elle se retournait,
s'avança derrière elle à pas de loup et en étouffant son
55 rire, se baissa, prit sur le pavé une poignée de neige et
la lui plongea brusquement dans le dos entre ses deux
épaules nues. La fille poussa un rugissement, se tourna,
bondit comme une panthère, et se rua sur l'homme,
lui enfonçant ses ongles dans le visage, avec les plus
60 effroyables paroles qui puissent tomber du corps de
garde[5] dans le ruisseau. Ces injures, vomies d'une voix

---

1. **Morillo** : sorte de chapeau à petits bords porté par les royalistes.
2. **Harceler** : tourmenter, persécuter.
3. **Sarcasme** : moquerie cruelle.
4. **Verges** : baguettes avec lesquelles on frappe et on châtie.
5. **Corps de garde** : troupe qui monte la garde ; ses membres étaient
réputés pour la grossièreté de leur langage. **Tomber dans le ruisseau :**
tomber dans la misère.

SITUER

Fantine, chassée de son travail, endettée, a sombré dans la misère. Elle finit par se prostituer. Un soir d'hiver, elle doit subir les moqueries d'un jeune bourgeois désœuvré, qui lui glisse de la neige dans le dos. La jeune femme réagit violemment. Mais la dispute tourne mal.

RÉFLÉCHIR

**PERSONNAGES : la femme bafouée
et l'« honorable bourgeois »**

1. La femme en robe de bal accomplit-elle véritablement une « promenade » devant le café des officiers ? Quel est l'effet produit par le contraste entre son apparence et la réalité de sa condition ?

2. Expliquez la métaphore « triste spectre paré » (l. 46). Relevez les autres images employées pour décrire Fantine. Est-elle encore une femme ?

3. Pourquoi Fantine est-elle d'abord indifférente aux provocations de M. Bamatabois ?

4. Comment expliquez-vous la brusquerie de sa colère, et son indifférence au scandale ?

5. Comment expliquez-vous, dans le contexte, la différence entre « livide » (l. 77) et « pâle » (l. 78) ? Pourquoi Fantine craint-elle la police ?

6. Commentez les attitudes successives de M. Bamatabois à l'égard de Fantine tout au long du passage. Quelles sont ses motivations ? Comment jugez-vous son comportement ?

QUI PARLE ? QUI VOIT ? Démasquer les faux-semblants

7. Quelles sont les caractéristiques du vêtement de M. Bamatabois ? Que suggère le nom de ce personnage ?

8. Relevez les expressions et les signes de ponctuation qui traduisent le jugement du narrateur sur M. Bamatabois.

9. Pourquoi Javert arrête-t-il la femme et non pas le bourgeois ?

SOCIÉTÉ : « la déchéance de la femme par la faim »

10. À quelle expression de l'avant-propos (voir p. 23) ce passage renvoie-t-il ? De quelle réalité sociale la déchéance physique et morale de Fantine est-elle le symbole ?

11. Dans cet épisode, quel personnage exerce un métier réprouvé ? Quels personnages se comportent de manière effectivement immorale ?

12. Que pensez-vous de l'attitude des spectateurs pendant le combat ? Quels sont les préjugés dénoncés par l'auteur dans ce passage ?

enrouée par l'eau-de-vie, sortaient hideusement d'une bouche à laquelle manquaient en effet les deux dents de devant. C'était la Fantine.

65 Au bruit que cela fit, les officiers sortirent en foule du café, les passants s'amassèrent, et il se forma un grand cercle riant, huant et applaudissant, autour de ce tourbillon composé de deux êtres où l'on avait peine à reconnaître un homme et une femme, l'homme se
70 débattant, son chapeau à terre, la femme frappant des pieds et des poings, décoiffée, hurlant, sans dents et sans cheveux, livide de colère, horrible.

Tout à coup un homme de haute taille sortit vive-ment de la foule, saisit la femme à son corsage de satin
75 couvert de boue, et lui dit : Suis-moi !

La femme leva la tête ; sa voix furieuse s'éteignit subitement. Ses yeux étaient vitreux, de livide elle était devenue pâle, et elle tremblait d'un tremblement de terreur. Elle avait reconnu Javert.
80 L'élégant avait profité de l'incident pour s'esquiver[1].

[Javert arrête la jeune femme qui, d'après lui, menace l'ordre public. M. Madeleine, entendant Fantine se défen-dre et raconter par quel enchaînement de circonstances malheureuses elle a sombré dans la misère, la fait libérer, contre l'avis de Javert, scandalisé. Fantine, qui croyait M. Madeleine responsable de son licenciement, est éperdue de reconnaissance pour son bienfaiteur (I, V, 13).

M. Madeleine, décidé à s'occuper de Fantine, la confie aux sœurs de son infirmerie. Il envoie de l'argent aux Thénardier. Mais Fantine s'affaiblit. Le médecin juge bon de faire revenir l'enfant. Fantine écrit donc aux Thénar-dier, leur demandant de confier Cosette au porteur du

---

1. **S'esquiver :** disparaître discrètement.

message. M. Madeleine est prêt à s'y rendre lui-même, mais un événement imprévu va perturber ses plans.

Javert, qui avait cru démasquer M. Madeleine, l'a dénoncé auprès des autorités comme étant Jean Valjean, le forçat en rupture de ban. Mais un matin de juillet 1823, le policier vient demander sa destitution au maire : il l'a accusé à tort, car on vient de découvrir le véritable Jean Valjean, un voleur de pommes, qui se fait appeler Champmathieu. Le procès, auquel Javert est appelé à témoigner, a lieu le lendemain à Arras. (I, VI)]

LIVRE SEPTIÈME : L'AFFAIRE CHAMPMATHIEU

[Dans l'après-midi qui suit la visite de Javert, M. Madeleine se rend auprès de Fantine ; il lui promet l'arrivée prochaine de Cosette, et reste longtemps avec elle. Puis il retient une voiture et des chevaux pour le milieu de la nuit. (I, VII, 1 et 2)]

3. Une tempête sous un crâne

[« Le lecteur a sans doute deviné que M. Madeleine n'est autre que Jean Valjean. » *Après le vol de Petit-Gervais, il a disparu, vendu les couverts en argent, gardé les chandeliers, et a traversé la France jusqu'à Montreuil-sur-Mer, pour y devenir le brave homme que l'on sait,* « n'ayant plus que deux pensées : cacher son nom et sanctifier sa vie ; échapper aux hommes et revenir à Dieu ». *La révélation de Javert le plonge dans un trouble inexprimable : que faire ? Laisser la justice condamner Champmathieu, et être ainsi débarrassé pour toujours de son lourd passé, ou se dénoncer pour sauver un innocent ?]*

Il examina la situation et la trouva inouïe ; tellement inouïe qu'au milieu de sa rêverie, par je ne sais quelle impulsion d'anxiété presque inexplicable, il se leva de sa chaise et ferma sa porte au verrou. Il craignait qu'il n'entrât encore quelque chose. Il se barricadait contre le possible.

Un moment après il souffla sa lumière. Elle le gênait.

Il lui semblait qu'on pouvait le voir.

Qui, on ?

Hélas ! ce qu'il voulait mettre à la porte était entré ; ce qu'il voulait aveugler, le regardait. Sa conscience.

Sa conscience, c'est-à-dire Dieu.

Pourtant, dans le premier moment, il se fit illusion ; il eut un sentiment de sûreté et de solitude ; le verrou tiré, il se crut imprenable ; la chandelle éteinte, il se sentit invisible. Alors il prit possession de lui-même ; il posa ses coudes sur la table, appuya la tête sur sa main, et se mit à songer dans les ténèbres.

– Où en suis-je ? – Est-ce que je ne rêve pas ? – Que m'a-t-on dit ? – Est-il bien vrai que j'aie vu ce Javert et qu'il m'ait parlé ainsi ? – Que peut être ce Champ-mathieu ? – Il me ressemble donc ? – Est-ce possible ? – Quand je pense qu'hier j'étais si tranquille et si loin de me douter de rien ! – Qu'est-ce que je faisais donc hier à pareille heure ? – Qu'y a-t-il dans cet incident ? – Comment se dénouera t-il ? – Que faire ?

Voilà dans quelle tourmente il était. Son cerveau avait perdu la force de retenir ses idées, elles passaient comme des ondes, et il prenait son front dans ses deux mains pour les arrêter.

De ce tumulte qui bouleversait sa volonté et sa raison, et dont il cherchait à tirer une évidence et une résolution, rien ne se dégageait que l'angoisse.

Sa tête était brûlante. Il alla à la fenêtre et l'ouvrit
35 toute grande. Il n'y avait pas d'étoiles au ciel. Il revint
s'asseoir près de la table.

La première heure s'écoula ainsi.

Peu à peu cependant des linéaments[1] vagues commencèrent à se former et à se fixer dans sa méditation[2], et il
40 put entrevoir avec la précision de la réalité, non l'ensemble de la situation, mais quelques détails.

Il commença par reconnaître que, si extraordinaire
et si critique que fût cette situation, il en était tout à
fait le maître.

45 Sa stupeur ne fit que s'en accroître.

Indépendamment du but sévère et religieux que se
proposaient ses actions, tout ce qu'il avait fait jusqu'à ce
jour n'était autre chose qu'un trou qu'il creusait pour y
enfouir son nom. Ce qu'il avait toujours le plus redouté,
50 dans ses heures de repli sur lui-même, dans ses nuits
d'insomnie, c'était d'entendre jamais prononcer ce nom ;
il se disait que ce serait là pour lui la fin de tout ; que le
jour où ce nom reparaîtrait, il ferait évanouir autour de lui
sa vie nouvelle, et, qui sait même peut-être ? au dedans de
55 lui sa nouvelle âme. Il frémissait de la seule pensée que
c'était possible. Certes, si quelqu'un lui eût dit en ces
moments-là qu'une heure viendrait où ce nom retentirait
à son oreille, où ce hideux mot, Jean Valjean, sortirait
tout à coup de la nuit et se dresserait devant lui, où cette
60 lumière formidable faite pour dissiper le mystère dont il
s'enveloppait, resplendirait subitement sur sa tête, et que
ce nom ne le menacerait pas, que cette lumière ne
produirait qu'une obscurité plus épaisse, que ce voile
déchiré accroîtrait le mystère, que ce tremblement de
65 terre consoliderait son édifice, que ce prodigieux incident

---

1. **Linéaments** : traits, fils (ici conducteurs de la pensée).
2. **Méditation** : profonde réflexion.

n'aurait d'autre résultat, si bon lui semblait, à lui, que de rendre son existence à la fois plus claire et plus impénétrable, et que, de sa confrontation avec le fantôme de Jean Valjean, le bon et digne bourgeois monsieur Madeleine
70 sortirait plus honoré, plus paisible et plus respecté que jamais, – si quelqu'un lui eût dit cela, il eût hoché la tête et regardé ces paroles comme insensées. Eh bien ! tout cela venait précisément d'arriver, tout cet entassement de l'impossible était un fait, et Dieu avait permis que ces
75 choses folles devinssent des choses réelles !
    […]
    La clarté devint complète, et il s'avoua ceci : – Que sa place était vide aux galères, qu'il avait beau faire, qu'elle l'y attendait toujours, que le vol de Petit-
80 Gervais l'y ramenait, que cette place vide l'attendrait et l'attirerait jusqu'à ce qu'il y fût, que cela était inévitable et fatal. – Et puis il se dit : – Qu'en ce moment il avait un remplaçant, qu'il paraissait qu'un nommé Champmathieu avait cette mauvaise chance, et que,
85 quant à lui, présent désormais au bagne dans la personne de ce Champmathieu, présent dans la société sous le nom de M. Madeleine, il n'avait plus rien à redouter, pourvu qu'il n'empêchât pas les hommes de sceller sur la tête de ce Champmathieu cette pierre de
90 l'infamie[1] qui, comme la pierre du sépulcre[2], tombe une fois et ne se relève jamais.

    [La rêverie de Jean Valjean se prolonge dans la nuit. Son cas de conscience lui semble insoluble.]

    Sa rêverie n'avait point dévié. Il continuait de voir clairement son devoir écrit en lettres lumineuses qui

---

1. **Infamie** : déshonneur, honte.
2. **Sépulcre** : tombeau.

flamboyaient devant ses yeux et se déplaçaient avec son
95 regard : – *Va ! nomme-toi ! dénonce-toi !*

Il voyait de même, et comme si elles se fussent mues
devant lui avec des formes sensibles, les deux idées qui
avaient été jusque-là la double règle de sa vie : cacher son
nom, sanctifier[1] son âme. Pour la première fois, elles lui
100 apparaissaient absolument distinctes, et il voyait la différence qui les séparait. Il reconnaissait que l'une de ces
idées était nécessairement bonne, tandis que l'autre
pouvait devenir mauvaise ; que celle-là était le dévouement
et que celle-ci était la personnalité ; que l'une disait : *le*
105 *prochain*, et que l'autre disait : *moi* ; que l'une venait de la
lumière et que l'autre venait de la nuit.

[...]

Il était plein d'épouvante, mais il lui semblait que la
bonne pensée l'emportait.

[Jean Valjean part pour Arras dans la nuit. Voyage
plein de péripéties. Plusieurs fois, le destin semble vouloir
l'empêcher de se rendre au procès, mais il trouve toujours
une solution. Au tribunal, après une dernière hésitation,
il révèle son identité devant une assistance interloquée.
Champmathieu est acquitté. (I , VII, 5 à 11)

De retour à Montreuil-sur-Mer, il se rend au chevet de
Fantine ; celle-ci croit qu'il lui ramène Cosette. Survient
Javert, triomphant, qui arrête M. Madeleine sous les yeux de
la pauvre malade. Saisie de terreur, Fantine meurt. Dans la
nuit, Jean Valjean s'échappe de la prison de la ville, retourne
chez lui régler quelques affaires, échappe encore à Javert
grâce au mensonge complice de la religieuse qui a soigné
Fantine, et part à pied dans la direction de Paris. Le corps de
Fantine est jeté à la fosse commune. (I, VIII, 1 à 5)]

---

1. **Sanctifier :** élever jusqu'à la sainteté.

THÈMES : la conversion de Jean Valjean

1. Dans une version antérieure, le roman commençait par l'entrée de Jean Valjean dans Digne. Pourquoi l'auteur a-t-il modifié le début ? Quel rôle Mgr Myriel joue-t-il dans le destin de Jean Valjean ?

2. La seule ébauche de plan connue des *Misérables* est :

> Histoire d'un saint ;
>
> Histoire d'un homme ;
>
> Histoire d'une femme ;
>
> Histoire d'une poupée.

Quel lien peut-on faire entre « histoire d'un saint » et « histoire d'un homme » ?

SOCIÉTÉ : le déterminisme social

3. Selon Hugo, le fonctionnement de la justice de son époque engendre la criminalité. Montrez par quel enchaînement fatal Jean Valjean s'est laissé prendre dans la spirale de la délinquance, depuis le vol du pain jusqu'à celui de la pièce de Petit-Gervais.

4. Dans son *Discours sur la misère*, Hugo proclame que la misère n'est pas une fatalité. Quelle est la responsabilité de la société dans le destin de Fantine ?

5. Jean Valjean et Fantine sont les victimes des préjugés de la société. Par quels personnages sont-ils traqués ou martyrisés ? Quelle mentalité l'auteur cherche-t-il à dénoncer ?

6. Les sens de « misérables » sont nombreux : il peut s'agir aussi bien du pauvre que de l'homme mauvais. Ils peuvent être victimes, ou bourreaux, ou les deux à la fois. Qui sont les « misérables » dans cette première partie ? Quels sont leurs points communs ?

7. M. Madeleine se comporte en patron philanthrope (voir p.69), en s'intéressant à l'éducation, à l'hygiène et à la protection sociale de ses ouvriers. Quels sont les principes de son action ?

8. Hugo a milité pour le développement de l'école gratuite, laïque et obligatoire. Expliquez la phrase de M. Madeleine : « Les deux premiers fonctionnaires de l'État, c'est la nourrice et le maître d'école » (p. 70, l. 52-53).

L'ART DU RÉCIT : l'identité perdue de Jean Valjean

9. En ne révélant pas tout de suite la véritable identité de M. Madeleine, le narrateur crée-t-il un véritable effet de suspense ? Pourquoi, dès lors, maintenir si longtemps le nom d'emprunt ? Justifiez le choix de ce nom.

10. À quels moments décisifs de l'intrigue Javert est-il présent ? De quelle manière intervient-il dans le récit ?

11. Quelles sont les convictions de Javert ? Que suggère la comparaison de ce personnage avec « un œil toujours fixé sur M. Madeleine » (p. 75, l. 46) ? Rapprochez cette image du poème de *la Légende des siècles* intitulé « La Conscience ». (Voir p. 319 et p. 59, l. 126.)

12. « Tempête sous un crâne » est devenue, depuis son invention par Hugo, une expression toute faite. Expliquez son sens, dans le roman, et dans la langue courante.

DEUXIÈME PARTIE
COSETTE

LIVRE PREMIER : WATERLOO

*[L'auteur prend la parole pour raconter sa visite, en
1861, du champ de bataille de Waterloo, occasion d'une
méditation sur la grande défaite de Napoléon en 1815.
L'armée française fut décimée par les troupes de Wellington et Blücher, alors qu'elle attendait en vain les renforts
de Grouchy. Les cavaliers français, mal dirigés, périrent
en grand nombre, écrasés pêle-mêle dans un ravin, le
chemin d'Ohain. (II, I, 1 à 18)]*

19. Le champ de bataille la nuit

*[Sur le champ de bataille dévasté, d'étranges créatures
rôdent la nuit autour des cadavres, bravant l'interdiction de dépouiller les morts.]*

La lune était sinistre sur cette plaine.

Vers minuit, un homme rôdait, ou plutôt rampait
du côté du chemin creux d'Ohain. C'était, selon toute
apparence, un de ceux que nous venons de caractériser,
5 ni Anglais, ni Français, ni paysan, ni soldat, moins
homme que goule[1], attiré par le flair[2] des morts, ayant
pour victoire le vol, venant dévaliser Waterloo. Il était
vêtu d'une blouse qui était un peu une capote[3], il était
inquiet et audacieux, il allait devant lui et regardait
10 derrière lui. Qu'était-ce que cet homme ? La nuit

---

1. **Goule :** démon femelle des légendes orientales, qui dévore les cadavres
dans les cimetières.
2. **Flair :** odeur.
3. **Capote :** manteau militaire.

probablement en savait plus sur son compte que le jour. Il n'avait point de sac, mais évidemment de larges poches sous sa capote. De temps en temps, il s'arrêtait, examinait la plaine autour de lui comme pour voir s'il
15 n'était pas observé, se penchait brusquement, dérangeait à terre quelque chose de silencieux et d'immobile, puis se redressait et s'esquivait. Son glissement, ses attitudes, son geste rapide et mystérieux le faisaient ressembler à ces larves[1] crépusculaires qui
20 hantent les ruines et que les anciennes légendes normandes appellent les Alleurs.

De certains échassiers nocturnes font de ces silhouettes dans les marécages.

[...]

25 Nous avons dit la catastrophe du chemin d'Ohain. Ce qu'avait été cette mort pour tant de braves, le cœur s'épouvante d'y songer.

Si quelque chose est effroyable, s'il existe une réalité qui dépasse le rêve, c'est ceci : vivre, voir le soleil, être
30 en pleine possession de la force virile, avoir la santé et la joie, rire vaillamment, courir vers une gloire qu'on a devant soi, éblouissante, se sentir dans la poitrine un poumon qui respire, un cœur qui bat, une volonté qui raisonne, parler, penser, espérer, aimer, avoir une mère,
35 avoir une femme, avoir des enfants, avoir la lumière, et tout à coup, le temps d'un cri, en moins d'une minute, s'effondrer dans un abîme, tomber, rouler, écraser, être écrasé, voir des épis de blé, des fleurs, des feuilles, des branches, ne pouvoir se retenir à rien, sentir son
40 sabre inutile, des hommes sous soi, des chevaux sur soi, se débattre en vain, les os brisés par quelque ruade dans les ténèbres, sentir un talon qui vous fait jaillir les

---

1. Larves : génies malfaisants, errant sous des formes hideuses.

yeux, mordre avec rage des fers de chevaux, étouffer, hurler, se tordre, être là-dessous, et se dire : tout à l'heure j'étais un vivant !

45

Là où avait râlé[1] ce lamentable désastre, tout faisait silence maintenant. L'encaissement du chemin creux était comblé de chevaux et de cavaliers inextrica-blement[2] amoncelés. Enchevêtrement terrible. Il n'y avait plus de talus, les cadavres nivelaient[3] la route avec la plaine et venaient au ras du bord comme un bois-seau d'orge bien mesuré. Un tas de morts dans la partie haute, une rivière de sang dans la partie basse ; telle était cette route, le soir du 18 juin 1815. Le sang coulait jusque sur la chaussée de Nivelles et s'y extravasait[4] en une large mare devant l'abatis[5] d'arbres qui barrait la chaussée, à un endroit qu'on montre encore. C'est, on s'en souvient, au point opposé, vers la chaussée de Genappe, qu'avait eu lieu l'effondrement des cuirassiers[6]. L'épaisseur des cadavres se proportionnait à la profondeur du chemin creux. Vers le milieu, à l'endroit où il devenait plane, là où avait passé la division Delord, la couche des morts s'amincissait.

50

55

60

Le rôdeur nocturne que nous venons de faire entrevoir au lecteur allait de ce côté. Il furetait[7] cette immense tombe. Il regardait. Il passait on ne sait

65

---

1. **Avait râlé** : avait gémi en agonisant.
2. **Inextricablement** : les cadavres sont empilés de telle sorte qu'on ne peut les séparer, les démêler les uns des autres.
3. **Nivelaient la route** : mettaient la route au niveau de la plaine, supprimant fossés et talus.
4. **S'y extravasait** : s'y élargissait.
5. **L'abatis d'arbres** : les arbres coupés.
6. **Cuirassiers** : soldats de cavalerie, porteurs d'une cuirasse.
7. **Furetait** : fouillait.

quelle hideuse revue[1] des morts. Il marchait les pieds dans le sang.

Tout à coup il s'arrêta.

70 À quelques pas devant lui, dans le chemin creux, au point où finissait le monceau des morts, de dessous cet amas d'hommes et de chevaux, sortait une main ouverte, éclairée par la lune.

Cette main avait au doigt quelque chose qui brillait, 75 et qui était un anneau d'or.

L'homme se courba, demeura un moment accroupi, et quand il se releva, il n'y avait plus d'anneau à cette main.

Il ne se releva pas précisément ; il resta dans une attitude fausse et effarouchée, tournant le dos au tas de 80 morts, scrutant l'horizon, à genoux, tout l'avant du corps portant sur les deux index appuyés à terre, la tête guettant par-dessus le bord du chemin creux. Les quatre pattes du chacal conviennent à de certaines actions.

Puis, prenant son parti, il se dressa.

85 En ce moment il eut un soubresaut. Il sentit que par derrière on le tenait.

Il se retourna ; c'était la main ouverte qui s'était refermée et qui avait saisi le pan de sa capote.

Un honnête homme eût eu peur. Celui-ci se mit à 90 rire.

– Tiens, dit-il, ce n'est que le mort. J'aime mieux un revenant qu'un gendarme.

Cependant la main défaillit et le lâcha. L'effort s'épuise vite dans la tombe.

95 – Ah ça ! reprit le rôdeur, est-il vivant, ce mort ? Voyons donc.

Il se pencha de nouveau, fouilla le tas, écarta ce qui faisait obstacle, saisit la main, empoigna le bras, dégagea

---

1. **Passait la revue** : vérifiait la tenue des soldats.

la tête, tira le corps, et quelques instants après il traînait
100 dans l'ombre du chemin creux un homme inanimé, au
moins évanoui. C'était un cuirassier, un officier, un
officier même d'un certain rang ; une grosse épaulette
d'or sortait de dessous la cuirasse ; cet officier n'avait
plus de casque. Un furieux coup de sabre balafrait son
105 visage où l'on ne voyait que du sang. Du reste, il ne
semblait pas qu'il eût de membre cassé, et par quelque
hasard heureux, si ce mot est possible ici, les morts
s'étaient arc-boutés au dessus de lui de façon à le
garantir de l'écrasement. Ses yeux étaient fermés.

110   Il avait sur sa cuirasse la croix d'argent de la Légion
d'honneur.

Le rôdeur arracha cette croix qui disparut dans un
des gouffres qu'il avait sous sa capote.

Après quoi, il tâta le gousset[1] de l'officier, y sentit
115 une montre et la prit. Puis, il fouilla le gilet, y trouva
une bourse et l'empocha.

Comme il en était à cette phase des secours qu'il
portait à ce mourant, l'officier ouvrit les yeux.

– Merci, dit-il faiblement.

120   La brusquerie des mouvements de l'homme qui le
maniait, la fraîcheur de la nuit, l'air respiré librement,
l'avaient tiré de sa léthargie[2].

Le rôdeur ne répondit point. Il leva la tête. On
entendait un bruit de pas dans la plaine ; proba-
125 blement quelque patrouille qui approchait.

L'officier murmura, car il y avait encore de l'agonie[3]
dans sa voix :

– Qui a gagné la bataille ?

---

1. **Gousset :** petite poche pour la montre.
2. **Léthargie :** torpeur, sommeil profond.
3. **Agonie :** combat final contre la mort.

– Les Anglais, répondit le rôdeur.

130 L'officier reprit :

– Cherchez dans mes poches. Vous y trouverez une bourse et une montre. Prenez-les.

C'était déjà fait.

Le rôdeur exécuta le semblant demandé[1], et dit :

135 – Il n'y a rien.

– On m'a volé, reprit l'officier, j'en suis fâché. C'eût été pour vous.

Les pas de la patrouille devenaient de plus en plus distincts.

140 – Voici qu'on vient, dit le rôdeur, faisant le mouvement d'un homme qui s'en va.

L'officier, soulevant péniblement le bras, le retint :

– Vous m'avez sauvé la vie. Qui êtes-vous ?

Le rôdeur répondit vite et bas :

145 – J'étais comme vous de l'armée française. Il faut que je vous quitte. Si l'on me prenait, on me fusillerait. Je vous ai sauvé la vie. Tirez-vous d'affaire maintenant.

– Quel est votre grade ?

– Sergent.

150 – Comment vous appelez-vous ?

– Thénardier.

– Je n'oublierai pas ce nom, dit l'officier. Et vous, retenez le mien. Je me nomme Pontmercy.

[Jean Valjean a été repris peu après son évasion de la prison de Montreuil-sur-Mer. Il a eu le temps de retirer une grosse somme d'argent chez le banquier Laffitte, qu'il a enterrée dans un lieu connu de lui seul. Il renonce à se défendre et reconnaît le vol de la pièce à Petit-Gervais. Le roi ramène sa condamnation à mort à

---

1. **Exécuta le semblant demandé :** fit semblant d'exécuter le geste demandé.

SITUER

Après la bataille de Waterloo, l'armée française est défaite. La nuit venue, des rôdeurs, au risque d'être fusillés s'ils sont pris en flagrant délit, dépouillent les morts. L'un d'eux va, malgré lui, sauver sa victime.

RÉFLÉCHIR

STRUCTURE : de surprise en surprise

1. Relevez les notations de temps qui marquent le progrès de la narration. Trouvez un titre pour chaque étape ainsi délimitée.

2. Relevez, dans leur ordre d'apparition, les termes désignant le voleur. Quel effet la révélation de son nom produit-elle sur le lecteur ?

PERSONNAGES : le bandit et le soldat

3. À quel animal le rôdeur est-il comparé ? Qu'évoque cette comparaison* ?

4. Étudiez les divers comportements de Thénardier. Choisissez cinq adjectifs pour définir son attitude et son caractère.

5. Que suggère la métaphore du « gouffre » (l. 113) où le rôdeur empoche les objets volés ?

6. Thénardier réussit à se donner le beau rôle dans le dialogue. Appréciez sa présence d'esprit.

7. Quel aspect de la personnalité de l'officier sa première question révèle-t-elle ? Quels autres traits de son caractère apparaissent dans le dialogue ?

REGISTRES ET TONALITÉS : le mélange des genres

8. Dans la première moitié du texte, combien de fois le mot « main » est-il sujet de l'action ? Quelle impression est créée par la personnification* de cette partie du corps ?

9. « L'homme se courba, demeura un moment accroupi, et quand il se releva, il n'y avait plus d'anneau à cette main. » Quelle action est passée sous silence ? Soulignez l'intérêt de cette ellipse*.

10. En quoi cet épisode est-il grave et émouvant ? Comment le lecteur réagit-il devant le sort de l'officier et l'attitude de Thénardier ?

11. Quels passages font pourtant sourire ? Quel effet crée cette intrusion du comique dans le tragique ?

ÉCRIRE

12. Un récit : Thénardier raconte l'épisode à sa manière devant les hôtes de son auberge. Il s'adresse directement à son auditoire, prend sa femme à témoin, et se fait passer pour un héros, maquillant son geste en acte de bravoure.

une peine de travaux forcés à perpétuité. Il est envoyé au
bagne de Toulon.

Quatre mois plus tard, un forçat de corvée à bord du
*vaisseau l'*Orion, *mouillé dans le port de Toulon, sauve*
un matelot en grimpant à son secours dans la mâture.
Après son geste héroïque, il tombe à la mer devant l'assis-
tance horrifiée. Le journal annonce qu'il s'est noyé, et
donne son nom : Jean Valjean. (II, II)]

LIVRE TROISIÈME : ACCOMPLISSEMENT DE LA PROMESSE FAITE À LA MORTE

[Le soir de Noël de la même année 1823, plusieurs
clients sont attablés dans l'auberge de Montfermeil.
Cosette, en haillons, tricote des bas de laine pour les
petites Thénardier. Le dernier-né du couple, un petit
garçon mal-aimé de sa mère, crie. (II, III, 1)]

2. Deux portraits complétés

[...]

Thénardier venait de dépasser ses cinquante ans ;
madame Thénardier touchait à la quarantaine, qui est
la cinquantaine de la femme ; de façon qu'il y avait
équilibre d'âge entre la femme et le mari. Les lecteurs
5 ont peut-être, dès sa première apparition, conservé
quelque souvenir de cette Thénardier grande,
blonde, rouge, grasse, charnue, carrée, énorme et
agile ; elle tenait, nous l'avons dit, de la race de ses
sauvagesses colosses[1] qui se cambrent dans les foires
10 avec des pavés pendus à leur chevelure. Elle faisait
tout dans le logis, les lits, les chambres, la lessive, la
cuisine, la pluie, le beau temps, le diable. Elle avait

---

1. **Colosses :** énormes.

Marguerite Moreno et Charles Dullin (les Thénardier)
dans *Les Misérables* de Raymond Bernard, 1933.

pour tout domestique Cosette ; une souris au service
d'un éléphant. Tout tremblait au son de sa voix, les
15 vitres, les meubles et les gens. Son large visage, criblé
de taches de rousseur, avait l'aspect d'une écumoire[1].
Elle avait de la barbe. C'était l'idéal d'un fort de la
halle[2] habillé en fille. Elle jurait splendidement ; elle
se vantait de casser une noix d'un coup de poing.
20 Sans les romans qu'elle avait lus, et qui, par moments,
faisaient bizarrement reparaître la mijaurée sous
l'ogresse, jamais l'idée ne fût venue à personne de
dire d'elle : c'est une femme. Cette Thénardier était

---

1. Écumoire : ustensile de cuisine (large cuillère à trous).
2. Fort de la halle : transporteur faisant le service du marché qui
approvisionnait Paris, doué d'une grande force musculaire.

comme le produit de la greffe d'une donzelle[1] sur une
25 poissarde. Quand on l'entendait parler, on disait :
C'est un gendarme ; quand on la regardait boire, on
disait : C'est un charretier[2] ; quand on la voyait
manier Cosette, on disait : C'est le bourreau. Au
repos, il lui sortait de la bouche une dent.

30 Le Thénardier était un homme petit, maigre, blême,
anguleux, osseux, chétif[3], qui avait l'air malade et qui
se portait à merveille, sa fourberie commençait là. Il
souriait habituellement par précaution, et était poli à
peu près avec tout le monde, même avec le mendiant
35 auquel il refusait un liard[4]. Il avait le regard d'une
fouine[5] et la mine d'un homme de lettres. Il ressemblait
beaucoup aux portraits de l'abbé Delille[6]. Sa coquetterie consistait à boire avec les rouliers[7]. Personne n'avait
jamais pu le griser[8]. Il fumait dans une grosse pipe. Il
40 portait une blouse et sous sa blouse un vieil habit noir.
Il avait des prétentions à la littérature et au matérialisme[9].
Il y avait des noms qu'il prononçait souvent, pour
appuyer les choses quelconques qu'il disait, Voltaire[10],

---

1. **Donzelle :** jeune fille. **Poissarde :** femme de la halle (au sens figuré :
femme qui a des manières hardies, un langage grossier).
2. **Charretier :** conducteur de charrette.
3. **Chétif :** petit, faible, misérable.
4. **Liard :** petite monnaie de cuivre qui valait trois deniers, le quart d'un sou.
5. **Fouine :** petit mammifère. Le terme est utilisé par métaphore* pour
évoquer la ruse et la sournoiserie.
6. L'abbé **Delille** (1738-1813) était un poète de la nature dont les œuvres
connurent un grand succès.
7. **Rouliers :** transporteurs de marchandises.
8. **Griser :** enivrer.
9. **Matérialisme :** système philosophique de ceux qui pensent que rien
n'existe en dehors de la matière.
10. **Voltaire, Raynal :** philosophes éclairés et anticléricaux du XVIIIᵉ siècle.
Parny : écrivain du XVIIIᵉ siècle, auteur de *Poésies érotiques* annonçant
le romantisme. **Saint Augustin** (354-430) : évêque africain, philosophe et
théologien.

Raynal, Parny, et, chose bizarre, saint Augustin. Il affir-
45 mait avoir « un système ». Du reste fort escroc. Un filou-
sophe. Cette nuance existe. On se souvient qu'il
prétendait avoir servi ; il contait avec quelque luxe qu'à
Waterloo, étant sergent dans un 6ᵉ ou 9ᵉ léger[1]
quelconque, il avait, seul contre un escadron de hussards[2]
50 de la mort, couvert de son corps et sauvé à travers la
mitraille « un général dangereusement blessé ». De là,
venait, pour son mur, sa flamboyante enseigne, et, pour
son auberge, dans le pays, le nom de « cabaret du sergent
de Waterloo ». Il était libéral, classique, et bonapartiste. Il
55 avait souscrit pour le champ d'Asile[3]. On disait dans le
village qu'il avait étudié pour être prêtre.

Nous croyons qu'il avait simplement étudié en
Hollande pour être aubergiste. Ce gredin de l'ordre
composite[4] était, selon les probabilités, quelque
60 Flamand de Lille en Flandre, Français à Paris, Belge à
Bruxelles, commodément à cheval sur deux frontières.
Sa prouesse à Waterloo, on la connaît[5]. Comme on
voit, il l'exagérait un peu. Le flux et le reflux, le méandre,
l'aventure, était l'élément de son existence ; conscience
65 déchirée entraîne vie décousue ; et vraisemblablement,
à l'orageuse époque du 18 juin 1815, Thénardier
appartenait à cette variété de cantiniers maraudeurs[6]
dont nous avons parlé, battant l'estrade[7], vendant à
ceux-ci, volant ceux-là, et roulant en famille, homme,

---

1. **Léger :** régiment, unité de l'armée qui se déplace facilement.
2. **Hussards :** soldats de la cavalerie légère.
3. **Champ d'Asile :** colonie française fondée au Texas en 1818 par des proscrits
   bonapartistes et libéraux, et pour laquelle une souscription avait été lancée.
4. **Composite :** mélangé.
5. Voir II, I, 19, p. 99.
6. **Cantiniers :** personnes qui tiennent une cantine militaire ; **maraudeurs :**
   voleurs.
7. **Battant l'estrade :** courant la campagne.

70 femme et enfants, dans quelque carriole boiteuse, à la
suite des troupes en marche, avec l'instinct de se
rattacher toujours à l'armée victorieuse. Cette
campagne faite, ayant, comme il disait, « du quibus »[1],
il était venu ouvrir gargote à Montfermeil.

75 Ce quibus, composé des bourses et des montres, des
bagues d'or et des croix d'argent, récoltées au temps
de la moisson dans les sillons ensemencés de cadavres,
ne faisait pas un gros total et n'avait pas mené bien loin
ce vivandier[2] passé gargotier[3].

80 [...]
Cet homme et cette femme, c'était ruse et rage
mariées ensemble, attelage hideux et terrible.

Pendant que le mari ruminait et combinait, la
Thénardier, elle, ne pensait pas aux créanciers[4] absents,
85 n'avait souci d'hier ni de demain, et vivait avec emportement, toute dans la minute.

Tels étaient ces deux êtres. Cosette était entre eux,
subissant leur double pression, comme une créature
qui serait à la fois broyée par une meule et déchiquetée
90 par une tenaille[5]. L'homme et la femme avaient chacun
une manière différente ; Cosette était rouée de coups,
cela venait de la femme ; elle allait pieds nus l'hiver,
cela venait du mari.

Cosette montait, descendait, lavait, brossait, frottait,
95 balayait, courait, trimait[6], haletait, remuait des choses

---

1. **Avoir du quibus :** avoir de l'argent ; exactement avoir « de quoi » (sens
de *quibus* en latin), expression familière.
2. **Vivandier :** celui qui suit un corps de troupe et qui vend des vivres (voir
« cantinier »).
3. **Gargotier :** tenancier d'une gargote, petite auberge bon marché et peu
soignée.
4. **Créanciers :** personnes à qui on doit de l'argent.
5. **Tenaille :** grosse pince aux mâchoires acérées.
6. **Trimait :** allait et venait en pure perte (familier).

Cosette, gravure d'après un dessin de Gustave Brion
pour l'édition Hetzel des *Misérables* de 1865.
(Maison de Victor Hugo, Paris).

lourdes, et, toute chétive, faisait les grosses besognes. Nulle pitié ; une maîtresse farouche, un maître venimeux. La gargote Thénardier était comme une toile où Cosette était prise et tremblait. L'idéal de l'oppres-
100 sion était réalisé par cette domesticité[1] sinistre. C'était quelque chose comme la mouche servante des araignées.

La pauvre enfant, passive, se taisait.

Quand elles se trouvent ainsi, dès l'aube, toutes petites, toutes nues, parmi les hommes, que se passe-
105 t-il dans ces âmes qui viennent de quitter Dieu ?

[Un voyageur demande qu'on donne à boire à son cheval. Il n'y a plus d'eau. La Thénardier envoie Cosette en chercher à la source, dans la forêt, en pleine nuit. Elle lui donne une pièce de quinze sous pour acheter du pain en chemin. Dans la rue, la petite passe devant une vitrine illuminée, où elle contemple une magnifique poupée. (II, III, 3 et 4)]

5. La petite toute seule

Comme l'auberge Thénardier était dans cette partie du village qui est près de l'église, c'était à la source du bois du côté de Chelles que Cosette devait allait puiser de l'eau.
5 Elle ne regarda plus un seul étalage de marchand. Tant qu'elle fut dans la ruelle du Boulanger et dans les environs de l'église, les boutiques illuminées éclairaient le chemin, mais bientôt la dernière lueur de la dernière baraque disparut. La pauvre enfant se trouva dans
10 l'obscurité. Elle s'y enfonça. Seulement, comme une certaine émotion la gagnait, tout en marchant elle

---

1. **Domesticité** : asservissement, esclavage.

agitait le plus qu'elle pouvait l'anse du seau. Cela faisait un bruit qui lui tenait compagnie.

Plus elle cheminait, plus les ténèbres devenaient épaisses. Il n'y avait plus personne dans les rues. Pourtant, elle rencontra une femme qui se retourna en la voyant passer, et qui resta immobile, marmottant entre ses lèvres : Mais où peut donc aller cet enfant ? Est-ce que c'est un enfant-garou[1] ? Puis la femme reconnut Cosette. – Tiens, dit-elle, c'est l'Alouette !

Cosette traversa ainsi le labyrinthe de rues tortueuses et désertes qui termine du côté de Chelles le village de Montfermeil. Tant qu'elle eut des maisons et même seulement des murs des deux côtés de son chemin, elle alla assez hardiment. De temps en temps, elle voyait le rayonnement d'une chandelle à travers la fente d'un volet, c'était de la lumière et de la vie, il y avait là des gens, cela la rassurait. Cependant, à mesure qu'elle avançait, sa marche se ralentissait comme machinalement. Quand elle eut passé l'angle de la dernière maison, Cosette s'arrêta. Aller au-delà de la dernière boutique avait été difficile ; aller plus loin que la dernière maison, cela devenait impossible. Elle posa le seau à terre, plongea sa main dans ses cheveux et se mit à se gratter lentement la tête, geste propre aux enfants terrifiés et indécis. Ce n'était plus Montfermeil, c'étaient les champs. L'espace noir et désert était devant elle. Elle regarda avec désespoir cette obscurité où il n'y avait plus personne, où il y avait des bêtes, où il y avait peut-être des revenants. Elle regarda bien, et elle entendit les bêtes qui marchaient dans l'herbe, et elle vit distinctement les revenants qui remuaient dans les arbres.

---

1. **Garou :** personnage maléfique légendaire, mi-homme, mi-loup, errant la nuit.

Alors elle ressaisit le seau, la peur lui donnait de l'audace :
– Bah ! dit-elle, je lui dirai qu'il n'y avait plus d'eau ! – Et
45 elle rentra résolument dans Montfermeil.

À peine eut-elle fait cent pas qu'elle s'arrêta encore, et se
remit à se gratter la tête. Maintenant, c'était la Thénardier
qui lui apparaissait ; la Thénardier hideuse avec sa bouche
d'hyène et la colère flamboyante dans les yeux. L'enfant
50 jeta un regard lamentable en avant et en arrière. Que faire ?
que devenir ? où aller ? Devant elle le spectre de la Thénardier ; derrière elle tous les fantômes de la nuit et des bois.
Ce fut devant la Thénardier qu'elle recula. Elle reprit le
chemin de la source et se mit à courir. Elle sortit du village
55 en courant, elle entra dans le bois en courant, ne regardant
plus rien, n'écoutant plus rien. Elle n'arrêta sa course que
lorsque la respiration lui manqua, mais elle n'interrompit
point sa marche. Elle allait devant elle, éperdue.

Tout en courant elle avait envie de pleurer.

60 Le frémissement nocturne de la forêt l'enveloppait tout
entière. Elle ne pensait plus, elle ne voyait plus. L'immense
nuit faisait face à ce petit être. D'un côté, toute l'ombre ;
de l'autre, un atome.

Il n'y avait que sept ou huit minutes de la lisière du bois
65 à la source. Cosette connaissait le chemin pour l'avoir fait
plusieurs fois le jour. Chose étrange, elle ne se perdit pas.
Un reste d'instinct la conduisait vaguement. Elle ne jetait
cependant les yeux ni à droite ni à gauche, de crainte de
voir des choses dans les branches et dans les broussailles.
70 Elle arriva ainsi à la source.

C'était une étroite cuve naturelle creusée par l'eau dans
un sol glaiseux, profonde d'environ deux pieds, entourée
de mousse et de ces grandes herbes gaufrées[1] qu'on appelle

---

1. **Gaufrées :** aux feuilles plissées (comme la fraise ou collerette portée aux
   XVIe et XVIIe siècles).

collerettes de Henri IV, et pavée de quelques grosses
75 pierres. Un ruisseau s'en échappait avec un petit bruit
tranquille.

Cosette ne prit pas le temps de respirer. Il faisait très
noir, mais elle avait l'habitude de venir à cette fontaine.
80 Elle chercha de la main gauche dans l'obscurité un
jeune chêne incliné sur la source qui lui servait ordinai-
rement de point d'appui, rencontra une branche, s'y
suspendit, se pencha et plongea le seau dans l'eau. Elle
était dans un moment si violent que ses forces étaient
85 triplées. Pendant qu'elle était ainsi penchée, elle ne fit
pas attention que la poche de son tablier se vidait dans
la source. La pièce de quinze sous tomba dans l'eau.
Cosette ne la vit ni ne l'entendit tomber. Elle retira le
seau presque plein et le posa sur l'herbe.
90 Cela fait, elle s'aperçut qu'elle était épuisée de lassi-
tude. Elle eût bien voulu repartir tout de suite ; mais
l'effort de remplir le seau avait été tel qu'il lui fut
impossible de faire un pas. Elle fut bien forcée de
s'asseoir. Elle se laissa tomber sur l'herbe et y demeura
95 accroupie.

Elle ferma les yeux, puis elle les rouvrit, sans savoir
pourquoi, mais ne pouvant faire autrement.

À côté d'elle, l'eau agitée dans le seau faisait des
cercles qui ressemblaient à des serpents de feu blanc.
100 Au-dessus de sa têtc, le ciel était couvert de vastes
nuages noirs qui étaient comme des pans de fumée. Le
tragique masque de l'ombre semblait se pencher
vaguement sur cet enfant.

Jupiter se couchait dans les profondeurs. L'enfant
105 regardait d'un œil égaré cette grosse étoile qu'elle ne
connaissait pas et qui lui faisait peur. La planète, en
effet, était en ce moment très près de l'horizon et
traversait une épaisse couche de brume qui lui donnait
une rougeur horrible. La brume, lugubrement

110 empourprée[1], élargissait l'astre. On eût dit une plaie lumineuse.

Un vent froid soufflait de la plaine. Le bois était ténébreux, sans aucun froissement de feuilles, sans aucune de ces vagues et fraîches lueurs de l'été. De 115 grands branchages s'y dressaient affreusement. Des buissons chétifs et difformes sifflaient dans les clairières. Les hautes herbes fourmillaient sous la bise comme des anguilles. Les ronces se tordaient comme de longs bras armés de griffes cherchant à prendre des 120 proies. Quelques bruyères sèches, chassées par le vent, passaient rapidement et avaient l'air de s'enfuir avec épouvante devant quelque chose qui arrivait. De tous les côtés il y avait des étendues lugubres.

[...]

125 Sans se rendre compte de ce qu'elle éprouvait, Cosette se sentait saisir par cette énormité noire de la nature. Ce n'était plus seulement de la terreur qui la gagnait, c'était quelque chose de plus terrible même que la terreur. Elle frissonnait. Les expressions manquent pour dire ce 130 qu'avait d'étrange ce frisson qui la glaçait jusqu'au fond du cœur. Son œil était devenu farouche. Elle croyait sentir qu'elle ne pourrait peut-être pas s'empêcher de revenir là à la même heure le lendemain.

Alors, par une sorte d'instinct, pour sortir de cet état 135 singulier qu'elle ne comprenait pas, mais qui l'effrayait, elle se mit à compter à haute voix un, deux, trois, quatre, jusqu'à dix, et, quand elle eut fini, elle recommença. Cela lui rendit la perception vraie des choses qui l'entouraient. Elle sentit le froid à ses mains qu'elle avait 140 mouillées en puisant de l'eau. Elle se leva. La peur lui était revenue, une peur naturelle et insurmontable. Elle

---

1. **Empourprée** : rougeoyante.

La Thénardier a envoyé Cosette chercher de l'eau en pleine nuit dans la forêt. L'enfant, terrifiée, arrive à la source où elle remplit son seau. La nature qui l'entoure prend des formes fantastiques…

■ **RÉFLÉCHIR**

THÈMES : terreurs enfantines

1. Dans les deux derniers paragraphes, relevez le champ lexical* de la peur. Précisez les connotations* propres à chaque mot retenu.

2. Les peurs de l'enfant sont-elles rationnelles ? Quels sont les dangers effectivement encourus par Cosette dans cet épisode ?

3. Relevez les expressions qui montrent que Cosette obéit à une force qui la dépasse.

QUI PARLE ? QUI VOIT ? Émotion partagée

4. Cosette ne voit ni n'entend tomber la pièce de quinze sous. Quelles conséquences de cette perte le lecteur peut-il prévoir ?

5. Quels sont les points de vue* adoptés tour à tour par le narrateur ? Dans quelles positions le lecteur est-il successivement placé ?

GENRES : une description fantastique

6. Quelles formes se dessinent dans ce tableau ? Quelle impression leur mouvement produit-il ?

7. Quelles sont les teintes dominantes dans ce paysage nocturne ? Qu'évoque, dans le contexte, chacune d'entre elles ? Quel effet leur association produit-elle ?

8. Analysez les comparaisons et les métaphores* utilisées pour décrire le paysage.

9. Dans le dernier paragraphe, repérez les allitérations et les assonances*, et précisez, dans chaque cas, ce qu'elles évoquent.

10. Les quatre éléments (eau, terre, air, feu) sont présents dans le paysage. À quels endroits sont-ils personnifiés* ? Quelle impression se dégage de ces descriptions ?

11. En quoi l'atmosphère de ce passage est-elle fantastique* ?

n'eut plus qu'une pensée, s'enfuir ; s'enfuir à toutes
jambes, à travers bois, à travers champs, jusqu'aux
maisons, jusqu'aux fenêtres, jusqu'aux chandelles
145 allumées. Son regard tomba sur le seau qui était devant
elle. Tel était l'effroi que lui inspirait la Thénardier qu'elle
n'osa pas s'enfuir sans le seau d'eau. Elle saisit l'anse à
deux mains. Elle eut de la peine à soulever le seau.

Elle fit ainsi une douzaine de pas, mais le seau était
150 plein, il était lourd, elle fut forcée de le reposer à terre.
Elle respira un instant, puis elle enleva l'anse de
nouveau, et se remit à marcher, cette fois un peu plus
longtemps. Mais il fallut s'arrêter encore. Après
quelques secondes de repos, elle repartit. Elle marchait
155 penchée en avant, la tête baissée, comme une vieille ; le
poids du seau tendait et roidissait[1] ses bras maigres ;
l'anse de fer achevait d'engourdir et de geler ses petites
mains mouillées ; de temps en temps elle était forcée
de s'arrêter, et chaque fois qu'elle s'arrêtait l'eau froide
160 qui débordait du seau tombait sur ses jambes nues.
Cela se passait au fond d'un bois, la nuit, en hiver, loin
de tout regard humain ; c'était un enfant de huit ans.
Il n'y avait que Dieu en ce moment qui voyait cette
chose triste.

165 Et sans doute sa mère, hélas !

Car il est des choses qui font ouvrir les yeux aux
mortes dans leur tombeau.

Elle soufflait avec une sorte de râlement douloureux ; des sanglots lui serraient la gorge, mais elle
170 n'osait pas pleurer, tant elle avait peur de la Thénardier, même loin. C'était son habitude de se figurer
toujours que la Thénardier était là.

---

1. **Roidissait** : raidissait.

Cependant elle ne pouvait pas faire beaucoup de
175 chemin de la sorte, et elle allait bien lentement. Elle
avait beau diminuer la durée des stations et marcher
entre chaque le plus longtemps possible. Elle pensait
avec angoisse qu'il lui faudrait plus d'une heure
pour retourner ainsi à Montfermeil et que la
180 Thénardier la battrait. Cette angoisse se mêlait à son
épouvante d'être seule dans le bois la nuit. Elle était
harassée de fatigue et n'était pas encore sortie de la
forêt. Parvenue près d'un vieux châtaignier qu'elle
connaissait, elle fit une dernière halte plus longue
185 que les autres pour se bien reposer, puis elle rassem-
bla toutes ses forces, reprit le seau et se remit à
marcher courageusement. Cependant le pauvre petit
être désespéré ne put s'empêcher de s'écrier : Ô
mon Dieu ! mon Dieu !
190 En ce moment, elle sentit tout à coup que le seau
ne pesait plus rien. Une main, qui lui parut énorme,
venait de saisir l'anse et la soulevait vigoureusement.
Elle leva la tête. Une grande forme noire, droite et
debout, marchait auprès d'elle dans l'obscurité.
195 C'était un homme qui était arrivé derrière elle et
qu'elle n'avait pas entendu venir. Cet homme, sans
dire un mot, avait empoigné l'anse du seau qu'elle
portait.

Il y a des instincts pour toutes les rencontres de la
vie. L'enfant n'eut pas peur.

*[Dans l'après-midi, cet homme, vêtu misérablement,
mais d'une allure digne, marchait sur le boulevard de
l'Hôpital, à Paris. Après avoir vu passer la voiture du
roi et avoir échappé à un agent, il a pris le coche, est
descendu à Chelles, et s'est enfoncé dans le bois, où il a vu
l'enfant. (II, III, 6)]*

7. Cosette côte à côte dans l'ombre avec l'inconnu

Cosette, nous l'avons dit, n'avait pas eu peur.

L'homme lui adressa la parole. Il parlait d'une voix grave et presque basse.

– Mon enfant, c'est bien lourd pour vous ce que vous portez là.

Cosette leva la tête et répondit :

– Oui, monsieur.

– Donnez, reprit l'homme, je vais vous le porter.

Cosette lâcha le seau. L'homme se mit à cheminer près d'elle.

– C'est très lourd, en effet, dit-il entre ses dents. Puis il ajouta :

– Petite, quel âge as-tu ?

– Huit ans, monsieur.

– Et viens-tu de loin comme cela ?

– De la source qui est dans le bois.

– Et est-ce loin où tu vas ?

– À un bon quart d'heure d'ici.

L'homme resta un moment sans parler, puis il dit brusquement :

– Tu n'as donc pas de mère ?

– Je ne sais pas, répondit l'enfant.

Avant que l'homme eût eu le temps de reprendre la parole, elle ajouta :

– Je ne crois pas. Les autres en ont. Moi, je n'en ai pas.

Et après un silence, elle reprit :

– Je crois que je n'en ai jamais eu.

L'homme s'arrêta, il posa le seau à terre, se pencha et mit ses deux mains sur les deux épaules de l'enfant, faisant effort pour la regarder et voir son visage dans l'obscurité.

La figure maigre et chétive de Cosette se dessinait vaguement à la lueur livide du ciel.

35 – Comment t'appelles-tu ? dit l'homme.

– Cosette.

L'homme eut comme une secousse électrique. Il la regarda encore, puis il ôta ses mains de dessus les épaules de Cosette, saisit le seau, et se remit à marcher.

40 Au bout d'un instant, il demanda :

– Petite, où demeures-tu ?

– À Montfermeil, si vous connaissez.

– C'est là que nous allons ?

– Oui, monsieur.

45 Il fit encore une pause, puis il recommença :

– Qui est-ce donc qui t'a envoyée à cette heure chercher de l'eau dans le bois ?

– C'est madame Thénardier.

L'homme repartit d'un son de voix qu'il voulait 50 s'efforcer de rendre indifférent, mais où il y avait pourtant un tremblement singulier :

– Qu'est-ce qu'elle fait, ta madame Thénardier ?

– C'est ma bourgeoise[1], dit l'enfant. Elle tient l'auberge.

55 – L'auberge ? dit l'homme. Eh bien, je vais aller y loger cette nuit. Conduis-moi.

– Nous y allons, dit l'enfant.

L'homme marchait assez vite. Cosette le suivait sans peine. Elle ne sentait plus la fatigue. De temps en 60 temps, elle levait les yeux vers cet homme avec une sorte de tranquillité et d'abandon inexprimable. Jamais on ne lui avait appris à se tourner vers la providence[2] et à prier. Cependant elle sentait en elle quelque chose

---

1. **Ma bourgeoise :** signifie ici « ma patronne ».
2. **Providence :** un Dieu secourable.

qui ressemblait à de l'espérance et à de la joie et qui
85 s'en allait vers le ciel.

Quelques minutes s'écoulèrent. L'homme reprit :

– Est-ce qu'il n'y a pas de servante chez madame
Thénardier ?

– Non, monsieur.

90 – Est-ce que tu es seule ?

– Oui, monsieur.

Il y eut encore une interruption. Cosette éleva la
voix :

– C'est-à-dire il y a deux petites filles.

95 – Quelles petites filles ?

– Ponine et Zelma.

L'enfant simplifiait de la sorte les noms romanesques chers à la Thénardier.

– Qu'est-ce que c'est que Ponine et Zelma ?

100 – Ce sont les demoiselles de madame Thénardier.
Comme qui dirait ses filles.

– Et que font-elles, celles-là ?

– Oh ! dit l'enfant, elles ont de belles poupées, des
choses où il y a de l'or, tout plein d'affaires. Elles
105 jouent, elles s'amusent.

– Toute la journée ?

– Oui, monsieur.

– Et toi ?

– Moi, je travaille.

110 – Toute la journée ?

L'enfant leva ses grands yeux où il y avait une larme
qu'on ne voyait pas à cause de la nuit, et répondit
doucement :

– Oui, monsieur.

115 Elle poursuivit après un intervalle de silence :

– Des fois, quand j'ai fini l'ouvrage et qu'on veut
bien, je m'amuse aussi.

– Comment t'amuses-tu ?

– Comme je peux. On me laisse. Mais je n'ai pas
120 beaucoup de joujoux. Ponine et Zelma ne veulent pas
que je joue avec leurs poupées. Je n'ai qu'un petit
sabre en plomb, pas plus long que ça.

L'enfant montra son petit doigt.

– Et qui ne coupe pas ?

125 – Si, monsieur, dit l'enfant, ça coupe la salade et les
têtes de mouches.

Ils atteignirent le village ; Cosette guida l'étranger
dans les rues. Ils passèrent devant la boulangerie, mais
Cosette ne songea pas au pain qu'elle devait rapporter.
130 L'homme avait cessé de lui faire des questions et
gardait maintenant un silence morne. Quand ils eurent
laissé l'église derrière eux, l'homme, voyant toutes ces
boutiques en plein vent, demanda à Cosette :

– C'est donc la foire ici ?

135 – Non, monsieur, c'est Noël.

Comme ils approchaient de l'auberge, Cosette lui
toucha le bras timidement.

– Monsieur ?

– Quoi, mon enfant ?

140 – Nous voilà tout près de la maison.

– Eh bien ?

– Voulez-vous me laisser reprendre le seau à
présent ?

– Pourquoi ?

145 – C'est que, si madame voit qu'on me l'a porté, elle
me battra.

L'homme lui remit le seau. Un instant après, ils
étaient à la porte de la gargote.

8. Désagrément de recevoir chez soi un pauvre qui est peut-être un riche

[L'homme s'installe pour dîner et dormir chez les Thénardier, qui le regardent d'un mauvais œil car il a l'air d'un pauvre.]

Cosette était laide. Heureuse, elle eût peut-être été jolie. Nous avons déjà esquissé cette petite figure sombre. Cosette était maigre et blême ; elle avait près de huit ans, on lui en eût donné à peine six. Ses grands
5 yeux enfoncés dans une sorte d'ombre étaient presque éteints à force d'avoir pleuré. Les coins de sa bouche avaient cette courbe de l'angoisse habituelle, qu'on observe chez les condamnés et chez les malades désespérés. Ses mains étaient, comme sa mère l'avait
10 deviné, « perdues d'engelures[1] ». Le feu qui l'éclairait en ce moment faisait saillir[2] les angles de ses os et rendait sa maigreur affreusement visible. Comme elle grelottait toujours, elle avait pris l'habitude de serrer ses deux genoux l'un contre l'autre. Tout son vêtement
15 n'était qu'un haillon qui eût fait pitié l'été et qui faisait horreur l'hiver. Elle n'avait sur elle que de la toile trouée ; pas un chiffon de laine. On voyait sa peau çà et là, et l'on y distinguait partout des taches bleues ou noires qui indiquaient les endroits où la Thénardier
20 l'avait touchée. Ses jambes nues étaient rouges et grêles[3]. Le creux de ses clavicules était à faire pleurer. Toute la personne de cette enfant, son allure, son attitude, le son de sa voix, ses intervalles entre un mot et

---

1. **Perdues d'engelures :** abîmées par les crevasses dues au froid.
2. **Saillir :** apparaître distinctement, ressortir.
3. **Grêles :** maigres.

l'autre, son regard, son silence, son moindre geste,
25 exprimaient et traduisaient une seule idée, la crainte.

La crainte était répandue sur elle ; elle en était pour
ainsi dire couverte ; la crainte ramenait ses coudes
contre ses hanches, retirait ses talons sous ses jupes, lui
faisait tenir le moins de place possible, ne lui laissait de
30 souffle que le nécessaire, et était devenue ce qu'on
pourrait appeler son habitude de corps, sans variation
possible que d'augmenter. Il y avait au fond de sa
prunelle un coin étonné où était la terreur.

*[La Thénardier menace de fouetter Cosette qui a
oublié d'acheter le pain et ne retrouve pas la pièce de
quinze sous. L'homme fait semblant de l'avoir trouvée
par terre, et donne à la Thénardier une pièce de vingt
sous. L'enfant échappe ainsi au martinet. Arrivent les
petites Thénardier, qui jouent à la poupée tandis que
Cosette leur tricote des bas. L'homme achète le travail
de l'enfant, pour qu'elle puisse s'amuser. Les petites
Thénardier, délaissant un instant leur poupée, jouent
avec le chat.]*

Comme les oiseaux font un nid avec tout, les
35 enfants font une poupée avec n'importe quoi. Pendant
qu'Éponine et Azelma emmaillotaient le chat, Cosette
de son côté avait emmailloté le sabre. Cela fait, elle
l'avait couché sur ses bras, et elle chantait doucement
pour l'endormir.

40 La poupée est un des plus impérieux besoins et en
même temps un des plus charmants instincts de
l'enfance féminine. Soigner, vêtir, parer, habiller,
déshabiller, rhabiller, enseigner, un peu gronder,
bercer, dorloter, endormir, se figurer que quelque
45 chose est quelqu'un, tout l'avenir de la femme est là.
Tout en rêvant et tout en jasant, tout en faisant de
petits trousseaux et de petites layettes, tout en cousant

de petites robes, de petits corsages et de petites bras-
sières, l'enfant devient jeune fille, la jeune fille devient
50 grande fille, la grande fille devient femme. Le premier
enfant continue la dernière poupée.

Une petite fille sans poupée est à peu près aussi
malheureuse et tout à fait aussi impossible qu'une
femme sans enfants.

55 Cosette s'était donc fait une poupée avec le sabre.

La Thénardier, elle, s'était rapprochée de l'*homme
jaune*[1]. – Mon mari a raison, pensait-elle, c'est peut-
être monsieur Laffitte[2]. Il y a des riches si farces !

Elle vint s'accouder à sa table.

60 – Monsieur… dit-elle.

À ce mot *monsieur*, l'homme se retourna. La
Thénardier ne l'avait encore appelé que *brave homme*
ou *bonhomme*.

– Voyez-vous, monsieur, poursuivit-elle en prenant
65 son air douceâtre qui était encore plus fâcheux à voir
que son air féroce, je veux bien que l'enfant joue, je ne
m'y oppose pas, mais c'est bon pour une fois, parce
que vous êtes généreux. Voyez-vous, cela n'a rien. Il
faut que cela travaille.

70 – Elle n'est donc pas à vous, cette enfant ? demanda
l'homme.

– Oh, mon Dieu, non, monsieur ! c'est une petite
pauvre que nous avons recueillie comme cela, par
charité. Une espèce d'enfant imbécile. Elle doit avoir
75 de l'eau dans la tête. Elle a la tête grosse, comme vous
voyez. Nous faisons pour elle ce que nous pouvons,
car nous ne sommes pas riches. Nous avons beau écrire

---

1. L'homme porte un grand manteau jaune.
2. **Laffitte** : riche banquier de l'époque (voir note 1, p. 70).

à son pays, voilà six mois qu'on ne nous répond plus. Il faut croire que sa mère est morte.

80   – Ah ! dit l'homme, et il retomba dans sa rêverie.

– C'était une pas grand'chose que cette mère, ajouta la Thénardier. Elle abandonnait son enfant.

Pendant toute cette conversation, Cosette, comme si un instinct l'eût avertie qu'on parlait d'elle, n'avait
85 pas quitté des yeux la Thénardier. Elle écoutait vaguement. Elle entendait çà et là quelques mots.

Cependant les buveurs, tous ivres aux trois quarts, répétaient leur refrain immonde avec un redoublement de gaîté. C'était une gaillardise de haut goût[1] où
90 étaient mêlés la Vierge et l'enfant Jésus. La Thénardier était allée prendre sa part des éclats de rire. Cosette, sous la table, regardait le feu qui se réverbérait dans son œil fixe ; elle s'était remise à bercer l'espèce de maillot qu'elle avait fait, et, tout en le berçant, elle
95 chantait à voix basse : Ma mère est morte ! ma mère est morte ! ma mère est morte !

Sur de nouvelles instances[2] de l'hôtesse, l'homme jaune, « le millionnaire », consentit enfin à souper.

– Que veut monsieur ?

100   – Du pain et du fromage, dit l'homme.

– Décidément, c'est un gueux[3], pensa la Thénardier.

Les ivrognes chantaient toujours leur chanson, et l'enfant, sous la table, chantait aussi la sienne.

Tout à coup Cosette s'interrompit. Elle venait de se
105 retourner et d'apercevoir la poupée des petites Thénardier qu'elles avaient quittée pour le chat et laissée à terre à quelques pas de la table de cuisine.

---

1. La chanson est **gaillarde**, c'est-à-dire leste. L'expression « de haut goût » est donc ironique.
2. **Instances** : sollicitations.
3. **Gueux** : misérable.

Alors elle laissa tomber le sabre emmailloté qui ne
lui suffisait qu'à demi, puis elle promena lentement ses
110 yeux autour de la salle. La Thénardier parlait bas à son
mari, et comptait de la monnaie, Ponine et Zelma
jouaient avec le chat, les voyageurs mangeaient, ou
buvaient, ou chantaient, aucun regard n'était fixé sur
elle. Elle n'avait pas un moment à perdre. Elle sortit de
115 dessous la table en rampant sur les genoux et sur les
mains, s'assura encore une fois qu'on ne la guettait
pas, puis se glissa vivement jusqu'à la poupée, et la
saisit. Un instant après elle était à sa place, assise,
immobile, tournée seulement de manière à faire de
120 l'ombre sur la poupée qu'elle tenait dans ses bras. Ce
bonheur de jouer avec une poupée était tellement rare
pour elle qu'il avait toute la violence d'une volupté[1].

Personne ne l'avait vue, excepté le voyageur, qui
mangeait lentement son maigre souper.

125 Cette joie dura près d'un quart d'heure.

Mais quelque précaution que prît Cosette, elle ne
s'apercevait pas qu'un des pieds de la poupée *passait*,
et que le feu de la cheminée l'éclairait très vivement.
Ce pied rose et lumineux qui sortait de l'ombre frappa
130 subitement le regard d'Azelma qui dit à
Éponine : – Tiens ! ma sœur !

Les deux petites filles s'arrêtèrent, stupéfaites.
Cosette avait osé prendre la poupée !

Éponine se leva, et, sans lâcher le chat, alla vers sa
135 mère et se mit à la tirer par sa jupe.

– Mais laisse-moi donc ! dit la mère. Qu'est-ce que
tu me veux ?

– Mère, dit l'enfant, regarde donc !

Et elle désignait du doigt Cosette.

---

1. **Volupté** : plaisir intense.

140 Cosette, elle, tout entière aux extases[1] de la possession, ne voyait et n'entendait plus rien.

Le visage de la Thénardier prit cette expression particulière qui se compose du terrible mêlé aux riens de la vie et qui a fait nommer ces sortes de femmes : 145 mégères[2].

Cette fois, l'orgueil blessé exaspérait encore sa colère. Cosette avait franchi tous les intervalles, Cosette avait attenté à la poupée de « ces demoiselles ».

Une czarine[3] qui verrait un moujik essayer le grand 150 cordon bleu[4] de son impérial fils n'aurait pas une autre figure.

Elle cria d'une voix que l'indignation enrouait :

– Cosette !

Cosette tressaillit comme si la terre eût tremblé sous elle. Elle se retourna.

155 – Cosette ! répéta la Thénardier.

Cosette prit la poupée et la posa doucement à terre avec une sorte de vénération[5] mêlée de désespoir. Alors, sans la quitter des yeux, elle joignit les mains, et, ce qui est effrayant à dire dans un enfant de cet âge, elle se les tordit ; puis, ce que n'avait pu lui arracher 160 aucune des émotions de la journée, ni la course dans le bois, ni la pesanteur du seau d'eau, ni la perte de l'argent, ni la vue du martinet, ni même la sombre parole qu'elle avait entendu dire à la Thénardier, – elle pleura. Elle éclata en sanglots.

165 Cependant le voyageur s'était levé.

– Qu'est-ce donc ? dit-il à la Thénardier.

---

1. **Extases :** ravissements.
2. **Mégères :** femmes méchantes et emportées.
3. **Czarine :** impératrice de Russie ; **moujik :** paysan russe.
4. **Grand cordon bleu :** distinction honorifique.
5. **Vénération :** adoration respectueuse.

— Vous ne voyez pas ? dit la Thénardier en montrant du doigt le corps du délit qui gisait aux pieds de Cosette.

170 — Eh bien, quoi ? reprit l'homme.

— Cette gueuse, répondit la Thénardier, s'est permis de toucher à la poupée des enfants !

— Tout ce bruit pour cela ! dit l'homme. Eh bien, quand elle jouerait avec cette poupée ?

175 — Elle y a touché avec ses mains sales ! poursuivit la Thénardier, avec ses affreuses mains !

Ici Cosette redoubla ses sanglots.

— Te tairas-tu ! cria la Thénardier.

L'homme alla droit à la porte de la rue, l'ouvrit et 180 sortit.

Dès qu'il fut sorti, la Thénardier profita de son absence pour allonger sous la table à Cosette un grand coup de pied qui fit jeter à l'enfant les hauts cris.

La porte se rouvrit, l'homme reparut, il portait dans 185 ses deux mains la poupée fabuleuse dont nous avons parlé et que tous les marmots du village contemplaient depuis le matin, et il la posa debout devant Cosette en disant :

— Tiens, c'est pour toi.

190 Il faut croire que, depuis plus d'une heure qu'il était là, au milieu de sa rêverie, il avait confusément remarqué cette boutique de bimbeloterie[1] éclairée de lampions et de chandelles si splendidement qu'on l'apercevait à travers la vitre du cabaret comme une illumination.

195 Cosette leva les yeux, elle avait vu venir l'homme à elle avec cette poupée comme elle eût vu venir le soleil, elle entendit ces paroles inouïes : *c'est pour toi*, elle le regarda, elle regarda la poupée, puis elle recula lente-

---

1. **Boutique de bimbeloterie :** bazar.

ment, et s'alla cacher tout au fond sous la table dans le
200 coin du mur.

Elle ne pleurait plus, elle ne criait plus, elle avait l'air
de ne plus oser respirer.

La Thénardier, Éponine, Azelma étaient autant de
statues. Les buveurs eux-mêmes s'étaient arrêtés. Il
205 s'était fait un silence solennel dans tout le cabaret.

La Thénardier, pétrifiée et muette, recommençait
ses conjectures[1] : – Qu'est-ce que c'est que ce vieux ?
est-ce un pauvre ? est-ce un millionnaire ? C'est peut-
être les deux, c'est-à-dire un voleur.

210 La face du mari Thénardier offrit cette ride expressive qui accentue la figure humaine chaque fois que
l'instinct dominant y apparaît avec toute sa puissance
bestiale. Le gargotier considérait tour à tour la poupée
215 et le voyageur ; il semblait flairer cet homme comme il
eût flairé un sac d'argent. Cela ne dura que le temps
d'un éclair. Il s'approcha de sa femme et lui dit bas :

– Cette machine coûte au moins trente francs. Pas
220 de bêtises. À plat ventre devant l'homme !

Les natures grossières ont cela de commun avec les
natures naïves qu'elles n'ont pas de transitions.

– Eh bien, Cosette, dit la Thénardier d'une voix qui
voulait être douce et qui était toute composée de ce
225 miel aigre des méchantes femmes, est-ce que tu ne
prends pas ta poupée ?

Cosette se hasarda à sortir de son trou.

– Ma petite Cosette, reprit le Thénardier d'un air
caressant, monsieur te donne une poupée. Prends-la.
230 Elle est à toi.

Cosette considérait la poupée merveilleuse avec une
sorte de terreur. Son visage était encore inondé de

---

1. **Conjectures :** hypothèses, suppositions.

■ **SITUER**

L'homme qui a aidé Cosette à porter son seau s'est installé à l'auberge pour dîner et dormir. Il a remplacé la pièce perdue et a payé pour que la petite puisse jouer. Celle-ci emprunte subrepticement la poupée des filles Thénardier, qui finissent par s'en apercevoir. La mère, alertée, s'apprête à sévir.

■ **RÉFLÉCHIR**

QUI PARLE ? QUI VOIT ? Le jeu du narrateur avec son lecteur

1. Observez le rythme* de la phrase : « puis, ce que n'avait pu lui arracher […] elle pleura » (l. 159 à 164). Quel effet l'énumération produit-elle ? Justifiez la rupture finale de la construction syntaxique.

2. Que se passe-t-il à l'extérieur de l'auberge pendant que la Thénardier donne un grand coup de pied à Cosette ? Quel effet cette ellipse* produit-elle ?

3. Comment le narrateur réussit-il à entretenir le suspense* dans cet épisode ?

4. Les Thénardier ignorent l'identité du voyageur, que le narrateur prend soin de ne pas dévoiler. De quels éléments le lecteur dispose-t-il malgré tout pour deviner qui se cache derrière cet étranger ?

GENRES : un dialogue théâtral

5. Relevez les paroles et gestes qui expriment la colère de la Thénardier.

6. L'homme lui répond-il avec violence ? Peut-on deviner ses pensées pendant le dialogue avec la Thénardier ?

7. Observez les gestes de l'homme : comment engage-t-il la conversation ? comment clôt-il le débat ?

8. Le retour de l'homme pétrifie les autres personnages, soudain réduits au silence et au rôle de figurants. Quel est l'effet de ce coup de théâtre ?

THÈMES : la nuit de Noël

9. La boutique de bimbeloterie est éclairée, Jean Valjean est comparé au soleil. En cette nuit de Noël, quel est le symbolisme de la lumière ?

10. Que représente la poupée pour Cosette ? Quel rôle Jean Valjean joue-t-il auprès de la fillette ?

11. Par quels signes la révolte de Cosette se manifeste-t-elle dans ce passage ? Dans quelle mesure la présence de l'étranger et l'approche de Noël peuvent-elles l'encourager ?

larmes, mais ses yeux commençaient à s'emplir, comme le ciel au crépuscule du matin, des rayonne-
235 ments étranges de la joie. Ce qu'elle éprouvait en ce moment-là était un peu pareil à ce qu'elle eût ressenti si on lui eût dit brusquement : Petite, vous êtes la reine de France.

Il lui semblait que si elle touchait à cette poupée, le
240 tonnerre en sortirait.

Ce qui était vrai jusqu'à un certain point, car elle se disait que la Thénardier gronderait, et la battrait.

Pourtant, l'attraction l'emporta. Elle finit par s'approcher, et murmura timidement en se tournant
245 vers la Thénardier :

– Est-ce que je peux, madame ?

Aucune expression ne saurait rendre cet air à la fois désespéré, épouvanté et ravi.

– Pardi ! fit la Thénardier, c'est à toi. Puisque monsieur te la donne.

– Vrai, monsieur ? reprit Cosette, est-ce que c'est
250 vrai ? c'est à moi, la dame ?

L'étranger paraissait avoir les yeux pleins de larmes. Il semblait être à ce point d'émotion où l'on ne parle pas pour ne pas pleurer. Il fit un signe de tête à Cosette, et mit la main de « la dame » dans sa petite
255 main.

Cosette retira vivement sa main, comme si celle de *la dame* la brûlait, et se mit à regarder le pavé. Nous sommes forcé d'ajouter qu'en cet instant-là elle tirait la langue d'une façon démesurée. Tout à coup, elle se
260 retourna et saisit la poupée avec emportement.

– Je l'appellerai Catherine, dit-elle.

Ce fut un moment bizarre que celui où les haillons de Cosette rencontrèrent et étreignirent les rubans et les fraîches mousselines roses de la poupée.

265 – Madame, reprit-elle, est-ce que je peux la mettre sur une chaise ?

– Oui, mon enfant, répondit la Thénardier.

Maintenant c'était Éponine et Azelma qui regardaient Cosette avec envie.

270 Cosette posa Catherine sur une chaise, puis s'assit à terre devant elle, et demeura immobile, sans dire un mot, dans l'attitude de la contemplation.

– Joue donc, Cosette, dit l'étranger.

– Oh ! je joue, répondit l'enfant.

[Thénardier, comprenant que l'homme a de l'argent, s'adoucit. Le lendemain, l'étranger emmène Cosette avec lui, après avoir dédommager Thénardier d'une forte somme d'argent. Pour obtenir davantage, l'aubergiste poursuit l'homme et l'enfant dans la campagne ; l'homme refuse de céder au chantage, produit la lettre de Fantine, et remet Thénardier à sa place. L'homme n'est autre que Jean Valjean, qui ne s'était pas noyé, mais avait plongé sous le bateau pour s'évader du bagne. (II, III, 9 à 11)

Il ramène Cosette à Paris et s'installe avec elle dans la masure Gorbeau. Mais il se sent surveillé ; Javert est à ses trousses. Il doit fuir, en pleine nuit, pour lui échapper. (II, IV)

Après une folle poursuite, Jean Valjean et Cosette se retrouvent dans le quartier de Picpus, encerclés par la police. Jean Valjean, portant la fillette, escalade un mur, et se retrouve dans un couvent. Il tombe alors nez à nez avec le vieux Fauchelevent, qui réussit à le faire passer pour son frère auprès des religieuses. Ultime Fauchelevent (c'est le nouveau nom de Jean Valjean) devient lui aussi jardinier, et Cosette est élevée par les religieuses. (II, V et VIII)]

PERSONNAGES : **les Thénardier**

1. Au cours de cette partie, nous voyons Thénardier dans deux épisodes différents, à huit ans d'intervalle. Quels aspects de la personnalité de l'aubergiste trouvait-on déjà chez le rôdeur de Waterloo ?

2. Chez Hugo, aucun personnage n'est jamais totalement noir. Sa vision n'est pas manichéenne. Comment se comporte la Thénardier avec ses filles ? avec Cosette ? avec son dernier-né ? Comment expliquez-vous la diversité de ses attitudes envers les enfants ?

THÈMES : **l'enfance malheureuse**

3. Jean Valjean vient chercher Cosette le soir de Noël. Quelle est la signification symbolique de cette date pour l'intrigue ?

4. Dans ses romans, Hugo invente souvent des noms et des prénoms originaux. « Cosette » signifie « petite chose ». Qu'évoque pour vous le prénom de ce personnage ?

5. Les contes pour enfants mettent souvent en scène des enfants martyrisés, qui réussissent à vaincre leur condition. Quels exemples vous viennent à l'esprit ?

6. Hugo a été le premier à employer l'expression « droit de l'enfant », dans son *Discours sur la liberté de l'enseignement*. Quels droits de l'enfant revendique-t-il dans cette partie ?

L'ART DU RÉCIT : **comment ménager ses effets**

7. Le tressement des intrigues permet au narrateur de ne pas révéler l'identité de l'homme qui vient chercher Cosette. À quels indices peut-on le reconnaître ? Pourquoi maintenir son anonymat ?

8. Quels sont les chapitres qui se terminent par une révélation ou une surprise ? Mettez en évidence la structure du feuilleton* dans cette partie.

9. Dans ces extraits, le narrateur considère l'étranger d'un point de vue* extérieur. Pourquoi ? Nous ne le connaissons que par ses paroles et par ses actes. Que nous révèlent-ils de sa personnalité ?

10. À la fin de la seconde partie, Jean Valjean trouve refuge dans un couvent. Protégé par cette enceinte, il est à l'abri de la police. Mais ce lieu a aussi une importance symbolique : les sœurs donnent l'exemple de la vertu. Le premier livre montrait la conversion de Jean Valjean, la fin du deuxième livre oriente son parcours vers la sainteté. Montrez que la narration renoue ici avec le début de la première partie.

REGISTRES ET TONALITÉS : le mélange des genres

11. Le mélange des genres et des tonalités est propre à l'écriture de Hugo. Quel effet le mélange de réalisme et de fantastique crée-t-il dans cette partie ?

Gustave Brion, *Marius*, 1862.

TROISIÈME PARTIE
MARIUS

[Quelques années plus tard, la masure Gorbeau a de nouveaux locataires : une famille misérable, les Jondrette, dont le fils, Gavroche, est un gamin de Paris, effronté et gouailleur. Leur voisin est un jeune étudiant très pauvre, nommé M. Marius.

Orphelin de mère, fils d'un colonel d'Empire, Marius Pontmercy a été élevé par son grand-père, M. Gillenormand, grand bourgeois royaliste, qui l'a arraché à son père. À la mort de ce dernier, Marius découvre que le baron Pontmercy, anobli par l'empereur sur le champ de bataille de Waterloo, aimait son fils, et était un héros. Le jeune homme se plonge dans la légende napoléonienne, et se brouille à cette occasion avec son grand-père. Il s'installe dans la masure Gorbeau, où il vit difficilement.

Il rencontre un groupe de jeunes gens préoccupés de questions sociales et politiques, les Amis de l'A.B.C., qui se réunissent au café : Enjolras, un jeune homme farouche, chaste, pur, intransigeant ; Combeferre, plus humain, le théoricien du groupe ; Jean Prouvaire, Feuilly, Courfeyrac, Bahorel, Bossuet, Joly, sont leurs amis. Quant à Grantaire, sceptique et bon vivant, il admire, aime et vénère Enjolras, malgré leurs tempéraments opposés. (III, I à V)]

LIVRE SIXIÈME : LA CONJONCTION DE DEUX ÉTOILES

1. Le sobriquet[1] : mode de formation des noms de famille

Marius à cette époque était un beau jeune homme de moyenne taille, avec d'épais cheveux très noirs, un front haut et intelligent, les narines ouvertes et passionnées, l'air sincère et calme, et sur tout son visage je ne
5 sais quoi qui était hautain, pensif et innocent. Son profil, dont toutes les lignes étaient arrondies sans cesser d'être fermes, avait cette douceur germanique qui a pénétré dans la physionomie française par l'Alsace et la Lorraine, et cette absence complète d'angles qui
10 rendait les Sicambres[2] si reconnaissables parmi les Romains et qui distingue la race léonine[3] de la race aquiline. Il était à cette saison de la vie où l'esprit des hommes qui pensent se compose, presque à proportions égales, de profondeur et de naïveté. Une situation
15 grave étant donnée, il avait tout ce qu'il fallait pour être stupide ; un tour de clef de plus, il pouvait être sublime. Ses façons étaient réservées, froides, polies, peu ouvertes. Comme sa bouche était charmante, ses lèvres les plus vermeilles et ses dents les plus blanches du monde,
20 son sourire corrigeait ce que toute sa physionomie avait de sévère. À de certains moments, c'était un singulier contraste que ce front chaste et ce sourire voluptueux. Il avait l'œil petit et le regard grand[4].

---

1. **Sobriquet** : surnom.
2. **Sicambres** : peuplade germanique établie sur la rive droite du Rhin. Les Sicambres furent battus par les Romains au début de notre ère.
3. **Race léonine** : race du lion ; **race aquiline** : race de l'aigle.
4. Hugo fait ici son autoportrait. Marius ressemble étrangement à l'auteur quand il avait vingt ans, à cette différence près que Hugo avait les cheveux châtains.

[Lors de ses promenades au jardin du Luxembourg, Marius remarque la présence régulière d'un couple constitué d'un vieil homme aux cheveux blancs et d'une fillette sage et « presque laide », qui occupent toujours le même banc. Courfeyrac, un des amis de Marius, surnomme le couple « mademoiselle Lanoire » et « monsieur Leblanc ».]

2. *Lux facta est* [1]

[L'année suivante, la fillette s'est métamorphosée en une jolie jeune fille.]

La personne qu'il voyait maintenant était une grande et belle créature ayant toutes les formes les plus charmantes de la femme à ce moment précis où elles se combinent encore avec toutes les grâces les plus naïves
5 de l'enfant ; moment fugitif et pur que peuvent seuls traduire ces deux mots : quinze ans. C'étaient d'admirables cheveux châtains nuancés de veines dorées, un front qui semblait fait de marbre, des joues qui semblaient faites d'une feuille de rose, un incarnat[2] pâle, une blan-
10 cheur émue, une bouche exquise d'où le sourire sortait comme une clarté et la parole comme une musique, une tête que Raphaël[3] eût donnée à Marie posée sur un cou que Jean Goujon[4] eût donné à Vénus. Et, afin que rien ne manquât à cette ravissante figure, le nez n'était pas
15 beau, il était joli ; ni droit ni courbé, ni italien ni grec ;

---

1. *Lux facta est* (citation en latin de la Genèse) : « La lumière fut ».
2. **Incarnat :** teint.
3. **Raphaël :** célèbre peintre de la Renaissance italienne (1483-1520), qui donna une expression parfaite à la beauté féminine.
4. **Jean Goujon :** sculpteur français (1510-1566), dont les œuvres sont caractérisées par la grâce et la pureté.

c'était le nez parisien ; c'est-à-dire quelque chose de spirituel, de fin, d'irrégulier et de pur, qui désespère les peintres et qui charme les poètes.

20 Quand Marius passa près d'elle, il ne put voir ses yeux qui étaient constamment baissés. Il ne vit que ses longs cils châtains pénétrés d'ombre et de pudeur.

Cela n'empêchait pas la belle enfant de sourire tout en écoutant l'homme à cheveux blancs qui lui parlait, et rien n'était ravissant comme ce frais sourire avec des 25 yeux baissés.

Dans le premier moment, Marius pensa que c'était une autre fille du même homme, une sœur sans doute de la première. Mais, quand l'invariable habitude de la promenade le ramena pour la seconde fois près du 30 banc, et qu'il l'eut examinée avec attention, il reconnut que c'était la même. En six mois, la petite fille était devenue jeune fille ; voilà tout. Rien n'est plus fréquent que ce phénomène. Il y a un instant où les filles s'épanouissent en un clin d'œil et deviennent 35 des roses tout à coup. Hier on les a laissées enfants, aujourd'hui on les retrouve inquiétantes.

Celle-ci n'avait pas seulement grandi, elle s'était idéa-lisée. Comme trois jours en avril suffisent à certains arbres pour se couvrir de fleurs, six mois lui avaient suffi 40 pour se vêtir de beauté. Son avril à elle était venu.

[…]

Et puis ce n'était plus la pensionnaire avec son chapeau de peluche[1], sa robe de mérinos[2], ses souliers d'écolier et ses mains rouges ; le goût lui était venu 45 avec la beauté ; c'était une personne bien mise avec une sorte d'élégance simple et riche et sans manière.

---

1. **Peluche** : étoffe dont les fils sont très longs sur l'endroit.
2. **Mérinos** : étoffe de laine fine.

Elle avait une robe de damas[1] noir, un camail[2] de même étoffe et un chapeau de crêpe[3] blanc. Ses gants blancs montraient la finesse de sa main qui jouait avec
50 le manche d'une ombrelle en ivoire chinois, et son brodequin[4] de soie dessinait la petitesse de son pied. Quand on passait près d'elle, toute sa toilette exhalait un parfum jeune et pénétrant.

Quant à l'homme, il était toujours le même.
55 La seconde fois que Marius arriva près d'elle, la jeune fille leva les paupières. Ses yeux étaient d'un bleu céleste et profond, mais dans cet azur voilé il n'y avait encore que le regard d'un enfant. Elle regarda Marius avec indifférence, comme elle eût regardé le marmot
60 qui courait sous les sycomores, ou le vase de marbre qui faisait de l'ombre sur le banc ; et Marius de son côté continua sa promenade en pensant à autre chose.

[...]

3. Effet de printemps

Un jour, l'air était tiède, le Luxembourg était inondé d'ombre et de soleil, le ciel était pur comme si les anges l'eussent lavé le matin, les passereaux[5] poussaient de petits cris dans les profondeurs des marronniers. Marius
5 avait ouvert toute son âme à la nature, il ne pensait à rien, il vivait et il respirait, il passa près de ce banc, la jeune fille leva les yeux sur lui, leurs deux regards se rencontrèrent.

---

1. **Damas :** tissu de laine ou de soie de couleur unie, dont le tissage forme un dessin.
2. **Camail :** pèlerine à capuchon.
3. **Crêpe :** étoffe légère.
4. **Brodequin :** bottine.
5. **Passereaux :** moineaux.

Qu'y avait-il cette fois dans le regard de la jeune fille ?
10 Marius n'eût pu le dire. Il n'y avait rien et il y avait tout.
Ce fut un étrange éclair.

Elle baissa les yeux, et il continua son chemin.

Ce qu'il venait de voir, ce n'était pas l'œil ingénu et
simple d'un enfant, c'était un gouffre mystérieux qui
15 s'était entr'ouvert, puis brusquement refermé.

Il y a un jour où toute jeune fille regarde ainsi.
Malheur à qui se trouve là !

Ce premier regard d'une âme qui ne se connaît pas
encore est comme l'aube dans le ciel. C'est l'éveil de
20 quelque chose de rayonnant et d'inconnu. Rien ne
saurait rendre le charme dangereux de cette lueur inattendue qui éclaire vaguement tout à coup d'adorables
ténèbres et qui se compose de toute l'innocence du
présent et de toute la passion de l'avenir. C'est une
25 sorte de tendresse indécise qui se révèle au hasard et
qui attend. C'est un piège que l'innocence tend à son
insu et où elle prend des cœurs sans le vouloir et sans
le savoir. C'est une vierge qui regarde comme une
femme.

30 Il est rare qu'une rêverie profonde ne naisse pas de
ce regard là où il tombe. Toutes les puretés et toutes
les candeurs se rencontrent dans ce rayon céleste et
fatal qui, plus que les œillades les mieux travaillées des
coquettes, a le pouvoir magique de faire subitement
35 éclore au fond d'une âme cette fleur sombre, pleine de
parfums et de poisons, qu'on appelle l'amour.

Le soir, en rentrant dans son galetas[1], Marius jeta les
yeux sur son vêtement, et s'aperçut pour la première
fois qu'il avait la malpropreté, l'inconvenance et la
40 stupidité inouïe d'aller se promener au Luxembourg

---

1. **Galetas :** logement misérable.

avec ses habits « de tous les jours », c'est-à-dire avec un chapeau cassé près de la ganse[1], de grosses bottes de roulier[2], un pantalon noir blanc aux genoux et un habit noir pâle aux coudes.

[Marius, amoureux, devient coquet. Il cherche à découvrir l'adresse et l'identité de la jeune fille. Mais les deux promeneurs disparaissent brutalement, ce qui afflige le jeune homme. (III, VI, 4 à 9)

La société parisienne a, comme les théâtres, un troisième dessous[3] : dans les bas-fonds, les bandits font la loi. Babet, Gueulemer, Claquesous et Montparnasse forment une bande redoutable nommée Patron-Minette. *(III, VII)]*

LIVRE HUITIÈME : LE MAUVAIS PAUVRE

[Un jour, Marius est bousculé par deux jeunes filles en haillons qui viennent d'échapper à la police ; elles laissent tomber dans leur fuite un paquet qu'il ramasse. Celui-ci contient des lettres, toutes de la même écriture mais signées de noms différents, adressées à des personnes aisées pour leur demander un secours financier ; il ignore qui peut en être l'auteur. Le lendemain matin, on frappe à sa porte. (III, VIII, 1 à 3)]

4. Une rose dans la misère

Une toute jeune fille était debout dans la porte entrebâillée. La lucarne du galetas où le jour paraissait était précisément en face de la porte et éclairait cette figure

---

1. **Ganse :** bande de tissu qui borde un chapeau.
2. **Roulier :** transporteur de marchandises.
3. **Dessous :** étages à planchers mobiles situés sous les scènes des théâtres.

d'une lumière blafarde[1]. C'était une créature hâve[2], chétive,
5 décharnée ; rien qu'une chemise et une jupe sur une
nudité frissonnante et glacée. Pour ceinture une ficelle,
pour coiffure une ficelle, des épaules pointues sortant de
la chemise, une pâleur blonde et lymphatique[3], des clavicules terreuses, des mains rouges, la bouche entrouverte
10 et dégradée, des dents de moins, l'œil terne, hardi et bas,
les formes d'une jeune fille avortée et le regard d'une
vieille femme corrompue ; cinquante ans mêlés à quinze
ans ; un de ces êtres qui sont tout ensemble faibles et
horribles et qui font frémir ceux qu'ils ne font pas pleurer.
15 Marius s'était levé et considérait avec une sorte de
stupeur cet être, presque pareil aux formes de l'ombre
qui traversent les rêves.

Ce qui était poignant surtout, c'est que cette jeune
fille n'était pas venue au monde pour être laide. Dans
20 sa première enfance, elle avait dû même être jolie. La
grâce de l'âge luttait encore contre la hideuse vieillesse
anticipée de la débauche et de la pauvreté. Un reste de
beauté se mourait sur ce visage de seize ans, comme ce
pâle soleil qui s'éteint sous d'affreuses nuées à l'aube
25 d'une journée d'hiver.

Ce visage n'était pas absolument inconnu à Marius.
Il croyait se rappeler l'avoir vu quelque part.

– Que voulez-vous, mademoiselle ? demanda-t-il.

La jeune fille répondit avec sa voix de galérien ivre :
30 – C'est une lettre pour vous, monsieur Marius.

Elle appelait Marius par son nom ; il ne pouvait douter
que ce ne fût à lui qu'elle eût affaire ; mais qu'était-ce que
cette fille ? comment savait-elle son nom ?

---

1. **Blafarde :** blanche et pâle.
2. **Hâve :** pâle et amaigrie ; **chétive :** petite, faible, misérable.
3. **Lymphatique :** anémiée, maladive.

Sans attendre qu'il lui dît d'avancer, elle entra. Elle
35 entra résolument, regardant avec une sorte d'assurance
qui serrait le cœur toute la chambre et le lit défait. Elle
avait les pieds nus. De larges trous à son jupon lais-
saient voir ses longues jambes et ses genoux maigres.
Elle grelottait.
40 Elle tenait en effet une lettre à la main qu'elle
présenta à Marius.

Marius en ouvrant cette lettre remarqua que le pain
à cacheter large et énorme était encore mouillé. Le
message ne pouvait venir de bien loin. Il lut :

45 « Mon aimable voisin, jeune homme !

« J'ai apris[1] vos bontés pour moi, que vous avez payé
mon terme il y a six mois. Je vous bénis, jeune homme. Ma
fille aînée vous dira que nous sommes sans un morceau de
pain depuis deux jours, quatre personnes, et mon épouse
50 malade. Si je ne suis point déssu dans ma pensée, je crois
dcvoir espérer que votre cœur généreux s'humanisera à cet
exposé et vous subjuguera le désir de m'être propice en
daignant me prodiguer un léger bienfait.
Je suis avec la considération distinguée qu'on doit
55 aux bienfaiteurs de l'humanité,

JONDRETTE

« P.S. – Ma fille attendra vos ordres, cher monsieur
Marius. »

Cette lettre, au milieu de l'aventure obscure qui occupait Marius depuis la veille au soir, c'était une chandelle
60 dans une cave. Tout fut brusquement éclairé.

---

1. Les fautes d'orthographe et de langue sont de Jondrette.

Cette lettre venait d'où venaient les quatre autres. C'était la même écriture, le même style, la même orthographe, le même papier, la même odeur de tabac. [...]

65 Cependant, tandis que Marius attachait sur elle un regard étonné et douloureux, la jeune fille allait et venait dans la mansarde avec une audace de spectre. Elle se démenait sans se préoccuper de sa nudité. Par instants, sa chemise défaite et déchirée lui tombait 70 presque à la ceinture. Elle remuait les chaises, elle dérangeait les objets de toilette posés sur la commode, elle touchait aux vêtements de Marius, elle furetait ce qu'il y avait dans les coins.

– Tiens, dit-elle, vous avez un miroir !

75 Et elle fredonnait, comme si elle eût été seule, des bribes[1] de vaudeville, des refrains folâtres[2] que sa voix gutturale[3] et rauque faisait lugubres. Sous cette hardiesse perçait je ne sais quoi de contraint, d'inquiet et d'humilié. L'effronterie est une honte.

80 Rien n'était plus morne que de la voir s'ébattre et pour ainsi dire voleter dans la chambre avec des mouvements d'oiseau que le jour effare, ou qui a l'aile cassée. On sentait qu'avec d'autres conditions d'éducation et de destinée, l'allure gaie et libre de 85 cette jeune fille eût pu être quelque chose de doux et de charmant. Jamais parmi les animaux la créature née pour être une colombe ne se change en une orfraie[4]. Cela ne se voit que parmi les hommes.

Marius songeait, et la laissait faire.

---

1. **Bribes :** morceaux ; **vaudeville :** pièce légère entremêlée de chansons faciles.
2. **Folâtres :** légers.
3. **Voix gutturale :** voix rauque, de gorge.
4. **Orfraie :** variété de chouette.

90   Elle s'approcha de la table.

– Ah ! dit-elle, des livres !

Une lueur traversa son œil vitreux. Elle reprit, et son accent exprimait le bonheur de se vanter de quelque chose, auquel nulle créature humaine n'est insensible :

95   – Je sais lire, moi.

Elle saisit vivement le livre ouvert sur la table, et lut assez couramment :

« … Le général Bauduin reçut l'ordre d'enlever avec les cinq bataillons de sa brigade le château de Hougo-
100 mont qui est au milieu de la plaine de Waterloo… »

Elle s'interrompit :

– Ah ! Waterloo ! Je connais ça. C'est une bataille dans les temps. Mon père y était. Mon père a servi dans les armées. Nous sommes joliment bonapartistes
105 chez nous, allez ! C'est contre les Anglais Waterloo.

Elle posa le livre, prit une plume, et s'écria :

– Et je sais écrire aussi !

Elle trempa la plume dans l'encre, et se tournant vers Marius :

110 – Voulez-vous voir ? Tenez, je vais écrire un mot pour voir.

Et avant qu'il eût eu le temps de répondre, elle écrivit sur une feuille de papier blanc qui était au milieu de la table : *Les cognes*[1] *sont là*.

115 Puis jetant la plume :

– Il n'y a pas de fautes d'orthographe. Vous pouvez regarder. Nous avons reçu de l'éducation, ma sœur et moi. Nous n'avons pas toujours été comme nous sommes. Nous n'étions pas faites…

120 Ici elle s'arrêta, fixa sa prunelle éteinte sur Marius, et éclata de rire en disant avec une intonation qui

---

1. **Cognes :** gendarmes (argot).

contenait toutes les angoisses étouffées par tous les cynismes[1] :

– Bah !

125 Et elle se mit à fredonner ces paroles sur un air gai :

> J'ai faim, mon père,
> Pas de fricot[2].
> J'ai froid, ma mère,
> Pas de tricot.
> 130 Grelotte,
> Lolotte !
> Sanglote,
> Jacquot !

À peine eut-elle achevé ce couplet qu'elle s'écria :

135 – Allez-vous quelquefois au spectacle, monsieur Marius ? Moi, j'y vais. J'ai un petit frère qui est ami avec des artistes et qui me donne des fois des billets. Par exemple, je n'aime pas les banquettes de galeries. On y est gêné, on y est mal. Il y a quelquefois du gros 140 monde ; il y a aussi du monde qui sent mauvais.

Puis elle considéra Marius, prit un air étrange, et lui dit :

– Savez-vous, monsieur Marius, que vous êtes très joli garçon ?

145 Et en même temps il leur vint à tous les deux la même pensée, qui la fit sourire et qui le fit rougir.

Elle s'approcha de lui, et lui posa une main sur l'épaule.

– Vous ne faites pas attention à moi, mais je vous 150 connais, monsieur Marius. Je vous rencontre ici dans

---

1. **Cynismes :** attitudes provocantes causées par la désillusion.
2. **Fricot :** ragoût.

SITUER

Marius, l'esprit absorbé par le souvenir de sa charmante prome-
neuse du Luxembourg, ne prête guère attention à ses étranges
voisins de la masure Gorbeau. Jondrette envoie sa fille chez le jeune
homme, pour lui demander l'aumône. La jeune fille, dénaturée par la
misère, offre à Marius le spectacle sordide de sa déchéance.

RÉFLÉCHIR

SOCIÉTÉ : une rose dans la misère

1. Comment la coquetterie de la jeune fille se manifeste-t-elle ?

2. Expliquez la métaphore* contenue dans l'expression « avec une
audace de spectre » (l. 67). Dans quel contexte avons-nous déjà
rencontré cette image ?

3. À quel animal la jeune fille est-elle comparée ? Où avons-nous
déjà rencontré la même image ? Que suggère cette comparaison ?

4. Sur quel ton la jeune fille chante-t-elle ? Quel est le sens des
paroles de sa chanson ? Quel effet ce contraste produit-il ?

5. Relevez les antithèses* qui décrivent le comportement de la
jeune fille. Que cache son apparente gaieté ?

6. Avec quels personnages féminins du roman cette jeune fille a-
t-elle des points communs ? Lesquels ?

7. Pourquoi la jeune fille est-elle fière de savoir lire et écrire ? Quelle
importance l'auteur accorde-t-il à l'éducation ?

PERSONNAGES : une jeune fille effrontée

8. Comment la jeune fille se conduit-elle avec Marius ? Expliquez la
dernière phrase.

9. Comparez l'attitude des deux jeunes gens. Comment expliquez-
vous le silence de Marius ?

QUI PARLE ? QUI VOIT ? Une fausse inconnue

10. Le narrateur n'a pas encore dévoilé le prénom de la jeune fille.
Quelle réplique permet malgré tout au lecteur de deviner son identité ?

11. Que signifient les mots qu'elle écrit instinctivement ? Quel indice
cette phrase peut-elle donner à Marius et au lecteur ?

12. Quelles peuvent être les conséquences de la rencontre de ces
deux personnages pour la suite du récit ? Quelles questions le
lecteur se pose-t-il ?

ÉCRIRE

13. Une confidence : de retour chez elle, la jeune fille confie à sa sœur les sentiments variés qu'elle a éprouvés pendant cette visite chez Marius.

l'escalier, et puis je vous vois entrer chez un appelé le Père Mabeuf[1] qui demeure du côté d'Austerlitz, des fois, quand je me promène par là. Cela vous va très bien, vos cheveux ébouriffés.

155 Sa voix cherchait à être très douce et ne parvenait qu'à être très basse.

Une partie des mots se perdait dans le trajet du larynx aux lèvres comme sur un clavier où il manque des notes.

Marius s'était reculé doucement.

160 – Mademoiselle, dit-il avec sa gravité froide, j'ai là un paquet qui est, je crois, à vous. Permettez-moi de vous le remettre.

Et il lui tendit l'enveloppe qui renfermait les quatre lettres.

165 [...]

– Tiens ! dit-elle, c'est celle pour ce vieux qui va à la messe. Au fait, c'est l'heure. Je vais lui porter. Il nous donnera peut-être de quoi déjeuner.

Puis elle se remit à rire, et ajouta :

170 – Savez-vous ce que cela fera si nous déjeunons aujourd'hui ? Cela fera que nous aurons eu notre déjeuner d'avant hier, notre dîner d'avant-hier, notre déjeuner d'hier, notre dîner d'hier, tout ça en une fois, ce matin. Tiens ! parbleu ! si vous n'êtes pas contents,
175 crevez, chiens.

Ceci fit souvenir Marius de ce que la malheureuse venait chercher chez lui.

Il fouilla dans son gilet, il n'y trouva rien.

La jeune fille continuait, et semblait parler comme si
180 elle n'avait plus conscience que Marius fût là.

---

1. **Le Père Mabeuf :** vieil homme, ami de Marius, passionné par les plantes et les « bouquins ».

– Des fois je m'en vais le soir. Des fois je ne rentre pas. Avant d'être ici, l'autre hiver, nous demeurions sous les arches des ponts. On se serrait pour ne pas geler. Ma petite sœur pleurait. L'eau, comme c'est triste ! Quand je
185 pensais à me noyer, je disais : Non, c'est trop froid. Je vais toute seule quand je veux, je dors des fois dans les fossés. Savez-vous, la nuit, quand je marche sur le boulevard, je vois les arbres comme des fourches, je vois des maisons toutes noires grosses comme les tours de Notre-Dame, je
190 me figure que les murs blancs sont la rivière, je me dis : Tiens, il y a de l'eau là ! Les étoiles sont comme des lampions d'illuminations, on dirait qu'elles fument et que le vent les éteint, je suis ahurie, comme si j'avais des chevaux qui me soufflent dans l'oreille ; quoique ce soit
195 la nuit, j'entends des orgues de Barbarie[1] et les mécaniques des filatures[2], est-ce que je sais, moi ? Je crois qu'on me jette des pierres, je me sauve sans savoir, tout tourne, tout tourne. Quand on n'a pas mangé, c'est très drôle.

Et elle le regarda d'un air égaré.

200 À force de creuser et d'approfondir ses poches, Marius avait fini par réunir cinq francs seize sous. C'était en ce moment tout ce qu'il possédait au monde. – Voilà toujours mon dîner d'aujourd'hui, pensa-t-il, demain nous verrons. – Il prit les seize sous et donna les cinq
205 francs à la fille.

[...]

[Marius s'aperçoit que ses voisins sont encore plus pauvres que lui ; en regardant par un trou dans la cloi-

---

1. **Orgue de Barbarie :** instrument de musique portatif reproduisant des mélodies à partir de cartes perforées tournant sur un cylindre.
2. **Filatures :** usines où l'on fabrique du fil pour étoffe, et dont les machines sont bruyantes.

son, il découvre l'intérieur du réduit où habitent Jondrette et sa famille. (III, VIII, 5.)]

6. L'homme fauve au gîte

Les villes, comme les forêts, ont leurs antres où se cachent tout ce qu'elles ont de plus méchant et de plus redoutable. Seulement, dans les villes, ce qui se cache ainsi est féroce, immonde et petit, c'est-à-dire laid ;
5 dans les forêts, ce qui se cache est féroce, sauvage et grand, c'est-à-dire beau. Repaires pour repaires, ceux des bêtes sont préférables à ceux des hommes. Les cavernes valent mieux que les bouges[1].

Ce que Marius voyait était un bouge.
10 Marius était pauvre et sa chambre était indigente ; mais, de même que sa pauvreté était noble, son grenier était propre. Le taudis où son regard plongeait en ce moment était abject[2], sale, fétide, infect, ténébreux, sordide. Pour tous meubles, une chaise de paille, une table infirme,
15 quelques vieux tessons[3], et dans deux coins deux grabats[4] indescriptibles ; pour toute clarté, une fenêtre-mansarde à quatre carrcaux, drapée de toiles d'araignée. Il venait par cette lucarne juste assez de jour pour qu'une face d'homme parût une face de fantôme. Les murs avaient un
20 aspect lépreux[5], et étaient couverts de coutures et de cicatrices comme un visage défiguré par quelque horrible maladie. Une humidité chassieuse[6] y suintait. On y distinguait des dessins obscènes grossièrement charbonnés.

---

1. **Bouges :** logements malpropres, taudis.
2. **Abject :** dégoûtant, repoussant ; **fétide :** puant.
3. **Tessons :** débris de verre ou de vaisselle.
4. **Grabats :** mauvais lits, lits de pauvres.
5. **Aspect lépreux :** décrépit, en ruine.
6. **Chassieuse :** visqueuse.

La chambre que Marius occupait avait un pavage de
25 briques délabré ; celle-ci n'était ni carrelée, ni plan-
chéiée ; on y marchait à cru[1] sur l'antique plâtre de la
masure devenu noir sous les pieds. Sur ce sol inégal, où
la poussière était comme incrustée et qui n'avait qu'une
virginité, celle du balai, se groupaient capricieusement
30 des constellations de vieux chaussons, de savates et de
chiffons affreux ; du reste cette chambre avait une
cheminée ; aussi la louait-on quarante francs par an. Il y
avait de tout dans cette cheminée, un réchaud, une
marmite, des planches cassées, des loques pendues à des
35 clous, une cage d'oiseau, de la cendre, et même un peu
de feu. Deux tisons y fumaient tristement.

Une chose qui ajoutait encore à l'horreur de ce
galetas[2], c'est que c'était grand. Cela avait des saillies[3],
des angles, des trous noirs, des dessous de toits, des
40 baies et des promontoires. De là d'affreux coins inson-
dables où il semblait que devaient se blottir des araignées grosses comme le poing, des cloportes larges
comme le pied, et peut-être même on ne sait quels
êtres humains monstrueux.

45 L'un des grabats était près de la porte, l'autre près
de la fenêtre. Tous deux touchaient par une extrémité
à la cheminée et faisaient face à Marius.

[...]

Près de la table, sur laquelle Marius apercevait une
50 plume, de l'encre et du papier, était assis un homme
d'environ soixante ans, petit, maigre, livide, hagard[4],
l'air fin, cruel et inquiet ; un gredin hideux.

---

1. **À cru :** sur le sol même, sans plancher.
2. **Galetas :** logement misérable.
3. **Saillies :** avancées, reliefs.
4. **Hagard :** qui a une expression égarée et sauvage.

Lavater[1], s'il eût considéré ce visage, y eût trouvé le vautour mêlé au procureur ; l'oiseau de proie et
55 l'homme de chicane[2] s'enlaidissant et se complétant l'un par l'autre, l'homme de chicane faisant l'oiseau de proie ignoble, l'oiseau de proie faisant l'homme de chicane horrible.

Cet homme avait une longue barbe grise. Il était
60 vêtu d'une chemise de femme qui laissait voir sa poitrine velue et ses bras nus hérissés de poils gris. Sous cette chemise, on voyait passer un pantalon boueux et des bottes dont sortaient les doigts de ses pieds.

65 Il avait une pipe à la bouche et il fumait. Il n'y avait plus de pain dans le taudis, mais il y avait encore du tabac.

Il écrivait, probablement quelque lettre comme celles que Marius avait lues.

[*Un riche bienfaiteur vient rendre visite à Jondrette. Par le trou dans le mur, Marius observe la scène, et s'aperçoit avec stupeur qu'il s'agit de « monsieur Leblanc », accompagné de la jeune fille ! Jondrette cherche à apitoyer son visiteur, et lui fixe un second rendez-vous, pour l'attirer dans un piège et le dépouiller.*

Jondrette croit avoir reconnu son visiteur. Tandis qu'il prépare son méfait et engage des hommes de main, Marius s'active : il va prévenir la police du coup que prépare son voisin. L'inspecteur Javert lui confie deux pistolets : Marius tirera en l'air au moment critique, afin que la police, postée dans la rue, puisse prendre les

---

1. **Lavater** : écrivain, penseur et théologien suisse du XVIIIᵉ siècle, resté célèbre pour sa théorie de la physiognomonie, méthode par laquelle on interprète les caractères par les traits du visage, à partir des ressemblances animales.
2. **Homme de chicane** : homme de loi qui vit des procès.

bandits sur le fait. Le soir venu, M. Leblanc revient chez Jondrette ; il lui donne de l'argent pour régler son loyer. Marius se tient prêt à intervenir. (III, VIII, 7 à 18.)]

19. Se préoccuper des fonds obscurs

[M. Leblanc observe un étrange remue-ménage : au fil de la conversation, la pièce se remplit peu à peu d'hommes patibulaires au visage noirci. Jondrette tente de vendre à son bienfaiteur un tableau qui ne vaut rien. M. Leblanc proteste : « C'est quelque enseigne de cabaret, cela vaut bien trois francs. »]

Jondrette répondit avec douceur :

– Avez-vous votre portefeuille là ? je me contenterais de mille écus.

M. Leblanc se leva debout, s'adossa à la muraille et
5 promena rapidement son regard dans la chambre. Il avait Jondrette à sa gauche du côté de la fenêtre et la Jondrette et les quatre hommes à sa droite du côté de la porte. Les quatre hommes ne bougeaient pas et n'avaient pas même l'air de le voir ; Jondrette s'était
10 remis à parler d'un accent plaintif, avec la prunelle si vague et l'intonation si lamentable que M. Leblanc pouvait croire que c'était tout simplement un homme devenu fou de misère qu'il avait devant les yeux.

– Si vous ne m'achetez pas mon tableau, cher bienfai-
15 teur, disait Jondrette, je suis sans ressource, je n'ai plus qu'à me jeter à même la rivière. Quand je pense que j'ai voulu faire apprendre à mes deux filles le cartonnage demi-fin, le cartonnage des boîtes d'étrennes. Eh bien ! il faut une table avec une planche au fond pour que les
20 verres ne tombent pas par terre, il faut un fourneau fait exprès, un pot à trois compartiments pour les différents degrés de force que doit avoir la colle selon qu'on

l'emploie pour le bois, pour le papier, ou pour les étoffes,
un tranchet pour couper le carton, un moule pour l'ajus-
25 ter, un marteau pour clouer les aciers, des pinceaux, le
diable, est-ce que je sais, moi ? et tout cela pour gagner
quatre sous par jour ! et on travaille quatorze heures ! et
chaque boîte passe treize fois dans les mains de
l'ouvrière ! et mouiller le papier ! et ne rien tacher ! et
30 tenir la colle chaude ! le diable ! je vous dis ! quatre sous
par jour ! comment voulez-vous qu'on vive ?

Tout en parlant, Jondrette ne regardait pas
M. Leblanc qui l'observait. L'œil de M. Leblanc était
fixé sur Jondrette et l'œil de Jondrette sur la porte.
35 L'attention haletante de Marius allait de l'un à l'autre.
M. Leblanc paraissait se demander : Est-ce un idiot ?
Jondrette répéta deux ou trois fois avec toutes sortes
d'inflexions variées dans le genre traînant et suppliant :
Je n'ai plus qu'à me jeter à la rivière ! j'ai descendu
40 l'autre jour trois marches pour cela du côté du pont
d'Austerlitz !

Tout à coup sa prunelle éteinte s'illumina d'un flam-
boiement hideux, ce petit homme se dressa et devint
effrayant, il fit un pas vers M. Leblanc, et lui cria d'une
45 voix tonnante :

– Il ne s'agit pas de tout cela ! me reconnaissez-vous ?

20. Le guet-apens

*[D'autres complices continuent à arriver. Marius voit
le piège se refermer autour de M. Leblanc qui s'apprête
maintenant à se défendre.]*

Marius pensa qu'avant quelques secondes le
moment d'intervenir serait arrivé, et il éleva sa main
droite vers le plafond, dans la direction du corridor,
prêt à lâcher son coup de pistolet.

5 Jondrette, son colloque[1] avec l'homme à la trique[2] terminé, se tourna de nouveau vers M. Leblanc et répéta sa question en l'accompagnant de ce rire bas, contenu et terrible qu'il avait :

– Vous ne me reconnaissez donc pas ?

10 M. Leblanc le regarda en face et répondit :

– Non.

Alors Jondrette vint jusqu'à la table. Il se pencha par-dessus la chandelle, croisant les bras, approchant sa mâchoire anguleuse et féroce du visage calme de 15 M. Leblanc, et avançant le plus qu'il pouvait sans que M. Leblanc reculât, et, dans cette posture de bête fauve qui va mordre, il cria :

– Je ne m'appelle pas Fabantou[3], je ne m'appelle pas Jondrette, je me nomme Thénardier ! je suis l'aubergiste 20 de Montfermeil ! entendez-vous bien ? Thénardier ! Maintenant me reconnaissez-vous ?

Une imperceptible rougeur passa sur le front de M. Leblanc, et il répondit sans que sa voix tremblât, ni s'élevât, avec sa placidité[4] ordinaire :

25 – Pas davantage.

Marius n'entendit pas cette réponse. Qui l'eût vu en ce moment dans cette obscurité l'eût vu hagard[5], stupide et foudroyé. Au moment où Jondrette avait dit : *Je me nomme Thénardier*, Marius avait tremblé de tous ses 30 membres et s'était appuyé au mur comme s'il eût senti le froid d'une lame d'épée à travers son cœur. Puis son bras droit, prêt à lâcher le coup de signal, s'était abaissé

---

1. **Colloque :** conversation.
2. **L'homme à la trique :** il s'agit de l'un des bandits.
3. **Fabantou :** faux nom dont Thénardier avait signé sa lettre à M. Leblanc pour lui demander de l'argent.
4. **Placidité :** calme.
5. **Hagard :** qui a une expression égarée et sauvage.

lentement, et au moment où Jondrette avait répété :
Entendez-vous bien, Thénardier ? les doigts défaillants de
35 Marius avaient manqué laisser tomber le pistolet.
Jondrette, en dévoilant qui il était, n'avait pas ému
M. Leblanc, mais bouleversé Marius. Ce nom de Thénardier, que M. Leblanc ne semblait pas connaître, Marius le
connaissait. Qu'on se rappelle ce que ce nom était pour
40 lui ! Ce nom, il l'avait porté sur son cœur, écrit dans le
testament de son père ! il le portait au fond de sa pensée,
au fond de sa mémoire, dans cette recommandation
sacrée : « Un nommé Thénardier m'a sauvé la vie. Si mon
fils le rencontre, il lui fera tout le bien qu'il pourra. » Ce
45 nom, on s'en souvient, était une des piétés[1] de son âme ;
il le mêlait au nom de son père dans son culte. Quoi !
c'était là ce Thénardier, c'était là cet aubergiste de Montfermeil qu'il avait vainement et si longtemps cherché ! Il
le trouvait enfin, et comment ! ce sauveur de son père
50 était un bandit ! cet homme, auquel lui Marius brûlait de
se dévouer, était un monstre ! ce libérateur du colonel
Pontmercy était en train de commettre un attentat dont
Marius ne voyait pas encore bien distinctement la forme,
mais qui ressemblait à un assassinat ! et sur qui, grand
55 Dieu ! Quelle fatalité ! quelle amère moquerie du sort !

*[Marius ne sait que faire : s'il tire, il fait arrêter
Thénardier, le sauveur de son père ; s'il ne tire pas, c'en
est fait de M. Leblanc, le père de sa bien-aimée.]*

Il lui semblait d'un côté entendre « son Ursule[2] » le
supplier pour son père, et de l'autre le colonel lui

---

1. **Piété :** attachement fait de tendresse et de respect.
2. Marius, ayant ramassé sur un banc du jardin du Luxembourg un
   mouchoir brodé aux initiales *U. F.* (Ultime Fauchelevent), croit que sa
   bien-aimée s'appelle Ursule.

▬▬ **SITUER**

Marius, voyant que les choses tournent mal pour le père de sa bien-aimée, attiré dans un guet-apens par Jondrette, s'apprête à tirer en l'air pour avertir la police. Coup de théâtre : en entendant le bandit révéler son nom, il comprend qu'il s'agit du sauveur de son père. Le moment est dramatique : quel parti Marius va-t-il prendre ?

▬▬ **RÉFLÉCHIR**

THÈMES : l'homme et la bête

1. Sur le champ de bataille de Waterloo, Thénardier était comparé à un chacal (voir p. 102, l. 83). À quel animal est-il identifié ici ? Relevez dans le même paragraphe les termes qui nourrissent cette comparaison. Quel aspect de son caractère ce texte révèle-t-il ?

2. À partir de « Ce nom, il l'avait porté sur son cœur... » (l. 40), observez la ponctuation, la personne et le temps des verbes. Qui ressent les sentiments exprimés ici ? Dans quel style le discours est-il rapporté* ? Quelle est l'impression produite ?

REGISTRES ET TONALITÉS : l'ironie du sort

3. Expliquez l'exclamation : « Quelle amère moquerie du sort ! » (l. 55). Cette rencontre inattendue est-elle vraisemblable ? En quoi est-elle hautement romanesque ?

4. Étudiez les anaphores*, les exclamations, et les autres effets stylistiques qui expriment l'émotion de Marius.

PERSONNAGES : être et paraître

5. Comment comprenez-vous les réactions physiques et les réponses de M. Leblanc ?

6. Quel problème nouveau Marius doit-il résoudre ? À quelles lois contradictoires doit-il obéir ? En quoi peut-on dire qu'il s'agit d'un choix cornélien ?

STRATÉGIES : coup de théâtre

7. Quelle est l'importance dramatique de la révélation du nom de Thénardier : a. sur M. Leblanc ; b. sur Marius ; c. sur le lecteur ? De ces trois destinataires, lequel est le plus surpris ? Lequel est le moins surpris ? Quelle relation s'installe entre le narrateur et le lecteur ?

8. Pourquoi Thénardier a-t-il pris des pseudonymes ? et Jean Valjean ? Dites, pour chacun des deux personnages, quelles conséquences peut entraîner le dévoilement de son identité.

recommander Thénardier. Il se sentait fou. Ses genoux
se dérobaient sous lui. Et il n'avait pas même le temps
60 de délibérer, tant la scène qu'il avait sous les yeux se
précipitait avec furie. C'était comme un tourbillon
dont il s'était cru maître et qui l'emportait. Il fut au
moment de s'évanouir.

Cependant Thénardier, nous ne le nommerons plus
65 autrement désormais, se promenait de long en large
devant la table dans une sorte d'égarement et de
triomphe frénétique.

Il prit à plein poing la chandelle et la posa sur la
cheminée avec un frappement si violent que la mèche
70 faillit s'éteindre et que le suif[1] éclaboussa le mur.

Puis il se tourna vers M. Leblanc, effroyable, et
cracha ceci :

– Flambé ! fumé ! fricassé ! à la crapaudine[2] !

Et il se remit à marcher en pleine explosion.

75 – Ah ! criait-il, je vous retrouve enfin, monsieur le
philanthrope[3] ! monsieur le millionnaire râpé ! monsieur le
donneur de poupées ! vieux Jocrisse[4] ! Ah ! vous ne me
reconnaissez pas ! Non, ce n'est pas vous qui êtes venu à
Montfermeil, à mon auberge, il y a huit ans, la nuit de
80 Noël 1823 ! ce n'est pas vous qui avez emmené de chez
moi l'enfant de la Fantine, l'Alouette ! ce n'est pas vous
qui aviez un carrick[5] jaune ! non ! et un paquet plein de
nippes à la main comme ce matin chez moi ! Dis donc, ma
femme ! c'est sa manie, à ce qu'il paraît, de porter dans les
85 maisons des paquets pleins de bas de laine ! vieux charitable, va ! Est-ce que vous êtes bonnetier, monsieur le

---

1. **Suif :** graisse animale, utilisée entre autres pour fabriquer des chandelles.
2. **À la crapaudine** (terme de cuisine) : manière de faire rôtir une volaille.
3. **Philanthrope :** personne généreuse qui cherche à améliorer le sort des autres hommes.
4. **Jocrisse :** personnage traditionnel de la farce, niais et crédule.
5. **Carrick :** grand manteau.

Gustave Brion, *Jean Valjean*,
dessin pour l'édition Hetzel, 1866.

millionnaire ? vous donnez aux pauvres votre fonds de boutique[1], saint homme ! quel funambule ! Ah ! vous ne me reconnaissez pas ? Eh bien, je vous reconnais, moi ! je
90 vous ai reconnu tout de suite dès que vous avez fourré votre mufle ici. Ah ! on va voir enfin que ce n'est pas tout rose d'aller comme cela dans les maisons des gens, sous prétexte que ce sont des auberges, avec des habits minables, avec l'air d'un pauvre, qu'on lui aurait donné
95 un sou[2], tromper les personnes, faire le généreux, leur prendre leur gagne-pain, et menacer dans les bois, et qu'on n'en est pas quitte pour rapporter après, quand les gens sont ruinés, une redingote trop large et deux méchantes couvertures d'hôpital, vieux gueux, voleur
100 d'enfants !

[Jondrette, de plus en plus menaçant, tente vainement d'intimider M. Leblanc. Ce dernier, ligoté, réussit à couper ses liens avec une pièce de monnaie aiguisée ; il s'applique lui-même le fer rouge sur le bras pour montrer son courage. Jondrette n'a plus qu'une chose à faire : il sort son couteau.]

Marius égaré promenait ses yeux autour de lui, dernière ressource machinale du désespoir.

Tout à coup il tressaillit.

À ses pieds, sur la table, un vif rayon de pleine lune
105 éclairait et semblait lui montrer une feuille de papier. Sur cette feuille il lut cette ligne écrite en grosses lettres le matin même par l'aînée des filles Thénardier.

– LES COGNES SONT LÀ.

---

1. **Fonds de boutique :** ensemble des biens d'un commerçant.
2. Voir II, III, 8, p. 125-135.

Une idée, une clarté traversa l'esprit de Marius ;
c'était le moyen qu'il cherchait, la solution de cet
affreux problème qui le torturait, épargner l'assassin et
sauver la victime. Il s'agenouilla sur sa commode, étendit
le bras, saisit la feuille de papier, détacha doucement
un morceau de plâtre de la cloison, l'enveloppa dans le
papier, et jeta le tout par la crevasse au milieu du
bouge.

Il était temps. Thénardier avait vaincu ses dernières
craintes ou ses derniers scrupules et se dirigeait vers le
prisonnier.

– Quelque chose qui tombe ! cria la Thénardier.

– Qu'est-ce ? dit le mari.

La femme s'était élancée et avait ramassé le plâtras
enveloppé du papier. Elle le remit à son mari.

– Par où cela est-il venu ? demanda Thénardier.

– Pardié ! dit la femme, par où veux-tu que cela soit
entré ?

C'est venu par la fenêtre.

– Je l'ai vu passer, dit Bigrenaille[1].

Thénardier déplia rapidement le papier et l'approcha
de la chandelle.

– C'est de l'écriture d'Éponine. Diable !

Il fit signe à sa femme, qui s'approcha vivement, et il
lui montra la ligne écrite sur la feuille de papier, puis il
ajouta d'une voix sourde :

– Vite ! l'échelle ! laissons le lard dans la souricière
et fichons le camp !

– Sans couper le cou à l'homme ? demanda la
Thénardier.

– Nous n'avons pas le temps.

– Par où ? reprit Bigrenaille.

_____

1. **Bigrenaille :** l'un des bandits.

– Par la fenêtre, répondit Thénardier. Puisque Ponine a jeté la pierre par la fenêtre, c'est que la maison n'est pas cernée de ce côté-là.

Le masque à voix de ventriloque[1] posa à terre sa 145 grosse clef, éleva ses deux bras en l'air et ferma trois fois rapidement ses mains sans dire un mot. Ce fut comme le signal du branle-bas[2] dans un équipage. Les brigands qui tenaient le prisonnier le lâchèrent ; en un clin d'œil l'échelle de corde fut déroulée hors de la 150 fenêtre et attachée solidement au rebord par les deux crampons de fer.

Le prisonnier ne faisait pas attention à ce qui se passait autour de lui. Il semblait rêver ou prier.

Sitôt l'échelle fixée, Thénardier cria :

155 – Viens ! la bourgeoise !

Et il se précipita vers la croisée.

Mais comme il allait enjamber, Bigrenaille le saisit rudement au collet.

– Non pas, dis donc, vieux farceur ! après nous !

160 – Après nous ! hurlèrent les bandits.

– Vous êtes des enfants, dit Thénardier, nous perdons le temps. Les railles[3] sont sur nos talons.

– Eh bien, dit un des bandits, tirons au sort à qui passera le premier.

165 Thénardier s'exclama :

– Êtes-vous fou ! êtes-vous toqués ! en voilà-t-il un tas de jobards[4]! perdre le temps, n'est-ce pas ? tirer au sort, n'est-ce pas ? au doigt mouillé ! à la courte paille ! écrire nos noms ! les mettre dans un bonnet !…

---

1. **Le masque à voix de ventriloque :** l'un des bandits.
2. **Branle-bas :** préparatifs d'un équipage en vue du combat.
3. **Railles :** gendarmes (argot).
4. **Jobards :** crédules, niais (familier).

170 – Voulez-vous mon chapeau ? cria une voix du seuil de la porte.

Tous se retournèrent. C'était Javert.

Il tenait son chapeau à la main, et le tendait en souriant.

[Javert arrête les bandits. Quant au vieux monsieur, il s'est échappé discrètement, à l'insu de la police, en sautant par la fenêtre. (III, VIII, 21.)]

PERSONNAGES : Marius, le jeune premier

1. Hugo a découvert à l'âge adulte les mérites de son père, général de Napoléon. Quels sont les enjeux de la querelle politique opposant M. Gillenormand, royaliste, à son petit-fils, qui découvre les mérites de l'Empire ?

2. Justifiez le titre de cette partie : montrez que Marius en est le personnage principal, et que le narrateur adopte le plus souvent son point de vue dans le récit des événements.

3. Marius est le jeune premier* de ce roman. Or il n'apparaît qu'à la troisième partie. Cette construction romanesque est inhabituelle. Comment se justifie-t-elle ? Pensez-vous que Marius soit réellement le héros du roman ?

GENRES : roman réaliste et roman sentimental

4. Dans la troisième partie, la rencontre de Marius et de Cosette oriente la narration vers le roman sentimental. Quelles étapes habituelles du roman d'amour retrouve-t-on ici ?

5. *Les Misérables* est un roman qui mélange les catégories et les genres. Quel effet l'entrelacement des intrigues et des styles (sentimental, réaliste, dramatique) produit-il ?

SOCIÉTÉ : les bas-fonds

6. Le roman est construit de telle sorte que les destins d'Éponine et de Cosette s'inversent entre la seconde et la troisième partie. Quels rôles leurs « pères » respectifs ont-ils joués dans cette évolution ? Selon vous, est-ce le destin, la providence, la valeur personnelle des êtres, ou une justice supérieure à celle des hommes qui est responsable de ce retournement ?

7. Après Fantine et Cosette, c'est au tour d'Éponine d'incarner « la déchéance de la femme par la faim ». Comment se comporte-t-elle avec Marius ? Quels sentiments inspire-t-elle ?

8. Dans l'esprit des contemporains de Hugo, le prolétariat est considéré comme une classe dangereuse, constituée de « barbares ». Expliquez la comparaison entre la ville et la forêt (p. 155, l. 1). Quels sont les personnages du roman qui incarnent la misère et la délinquance dans la jungle des villes ?

THÈMES : le nom

9. Thénardier, alias Jondrette, collectionne les noms d'emprunt. Pourquoi ? Quelle est la signification symbolique de cette attitude ?

10. Courfeyrac a surnommé l'inconnu du Luxembourg « Monsieur Leblanc ». Quelles sont les connotations* de ce nom de famille ? Dans quelle mesure est-il représentatif de la condition de Jean Valjean ?

L'ART DU RÉCIT : les ficelles de l'intrigue

11. Dans l'épisode qui l'oppose à Jondrette, à quels détails reconnaît-on l'ancien forçat derrière M. Leblanc ?

12. Les retrouvailles, les révélations, les hasards, l'ironie du sort sont des ressorts habituels du mélodrame et du roman-feuilleton. Après avoir dressé la liste des coïncidences dramatiques dans cette partie, montrez qu'elles se jouent du vraisemblable.

QUATRIÈME PARTIE

L'IDYLLE RUE PLUMET ET L'ÉPOPÉE RUE SAINT-DENIS

[Sous la monarchie de Juillet, malgré certaines quali-tés de Louis-Philippe, l'agitation gronde. Des sociétés secrètes se forment, qui réfléchissent sur les questions poli-tiques et sociales. À Paris, certains quartiers sont particulièrement effervescents. Enjolras réunit ses amis de l'A.B.C. au café Musain.

Écœuré par la scène dont il a été témoin dans la masure Gorbeau, et afin de ne pas avoir à témoigner contre Thénardier, Marius déménage. Il se languit toujours de la belle jeune fille dont il ignore le nom. Un jour, il rencontre Éponine, la fille des Thénardier, qui a retrouvé pour lui l'adresse de la jeune fille. (IV, I et II)]

LIVRE TROISIÈME

LA MAISON DE LA RUE PLUMET

[« Le lecteur a sans doute moins tardé encore que Thénardier à reconnaître Jean Valjean » et Cosette derrière le couple du jardin du Luxembourg. Pourquoi ont-ils quitté le couvent du Petit-Picpus ? Une fois Cosette élevée, Jean Valjean a estimé qu'elle devait mener une vie normale, qu'il n'avait pas le droit d'en faire une religieuse privée de liberté. Il a saisi l'occasion de la mort de son « frère » pour quitter le couvent, et s'installer avec Cosette dans une maison de la rue Plumet, sous le nom de M. Fauchelevent. Il loue en même temps deux autres appartements dans Paris, pour échap-per plus facilement à la police en cas de besoin. Cosette est la maîtresse de la maison de la rue Plumet ; elle y vit dans la plus grande harmonie avec Jean Valjean, qui sort peu, et Toussaint, la servante. Une grande tendresse unit Cosette et son « père ». (IV, III, 1 à 4)]

5. La rose s'aperçoit
qu'elle est une machine de guerre

Un jour Cosette se regarda par hasard dans son miroir et se dit : tiens ! Il lui semblait presque qu'elle était jolie. Ceci la jeta dans un trouble singulier. Jusqu'à ce moment elle n'avait point songé à sa figure. Elle se
5 voyait dans son miroir, mais elle ne s'y regardait pas. Et puis, on lui avait souvent dit qu'elle était laide ; Jean Valjean seul disait doucement : Mais non ! mais non ! Quoi qu'il en fût, Cosette s'était toujours crue laide, et avait grandi dans cette idée avec la résignation facile de
10 l'enfance. Voici que tout d'un coup son miroir lui disait comme Jean Valjean : Mais non ! Elle ne dormit pas de la nuit. – Si j'étais jolie ? pensait-elle, comme cela serait drôle que je fusse jolie ! – Et elle se rappelait celles de ses compagnes dont la beauté faisait effet dans le
15 couvent, et elle se disait : Comment ! je serais comme mademoiselle une telle !

Le lendemain elle se regarda, mais non par hasard, et elle douta : – Où avais-je l'esprit ? dit-elle, non, je suis laide. – Elle avait tout simplement mal dormi, elle
20 avait les yeux battus[1] et elle était pâle. Elle ne s'était pas sentie très joyeuse la veille de croire à sa beauté, mais elle fut triste de n'y plus croire. Elle ne se regarda plus, et pendant plus de quinze jours elle tâcha de se coiffer tournant le dos au miroir.

25 Le soir, après le dîner, elle faisait assez habituellement de la tapisserie dans le salon ou quelque ouvrage de couvent, et Jean Valjean lisait à côté d'elle. Une fois elle leva les yeux de son ouvrage et elle fut toute surprise de la façon inquiète dont son père la regardait.

---

1. **Les yeux battus** : les yeux cernés.

30   Une autre fois, elle passait dans la rue, et il lui
sembla que quelqu'un qu'elle ne vit pas disait derrière
elle : Jolie femme ! mais mal mise[1]. – Bah ! pensa-
t-elle, ce n'est pas moi. Je suis bien mise et laide. – Elle
avait alors son chapeau de peluche[2] et sa robe de
35 mérinos[3].

    Un jour enfin, elle était dans le jardin, et elle enten-
dit la pauvre vieille Toussaint qui disait : Monsieur,
remarquez-vous comme mademoiselle devient jolie ?
Cosette n'entendit pas ce que son père répondit, les
40 paroles de Toussaint furent pour elle une sorte de
commotion[4]. Elle s'échappa du jardin, monta à sa
chambre, courut à la glace, il y avait trois mois qu'elle
ne s'était regardée, et poussa un cri. Elle venait de
s'éblouir elle-même.

45   Elle était belle et jolie ; elle ne pouvait s'empêcher
d'être de l'avis de Toussaint et de son miroir. Sa taille
s'était faite, sa peau avait blanchi, ses cheveux s'étaient
lustrés, une splendeur inconnue s'était allumée dans
ses prunelles bleues. La conscience de sa beauté lui vint
50 tout entière, en une minute, comme un grand jour qui
se fait, les autres la remarquaient d'ailleurs, Toussaint
le disait, c'était d'elle évidemment que le passant avait
parlé, il n'y avait plus à douter ; elle redescendit au
jardin, se croyant reine, entendant les oiseaux chanter,
55 c'était en hiver, voyant le ciel doré, le soleil dans les
arbres, des fleurs dans les buissons, éperdue, folle, dans
un ravissement inexprimable.

    De son côté, Jean Valjean éprouvait un profond et
indéfinissable serrement de cœur.

---

1. **Mise :** habillée.
2. **Peluche :** étoffe dont les fils sont très longs sur l'endroit.
3. **Mérinos :** étoffe de laine fine.
4. **Commotion :** choc, émotion violente.

60 C'est qu'en effet, depuis quelque temps, il contemplait avec terreur cette beauté qui apparaissait chaque jour plus rayonnante sur le doux visage de Cosette. Aube riante pour tous, lugubre pour lui.

Cosette avait été belle assez longtemps avant de s'en 65 apercevoir. Mais, du premier jour, cette lumière inattendue qui se levait lentement et enveloppait par degrés toute la personne de la jeune fille blessa la paupière sombre de Jean Valjean. Il sentit que c'était un changement dans une vie heureuse, si heureuse 70 qu'il n'osait y remuer dans la crainte d'y déranger quelque chose. Cet homme qui avait passé par toutes les détresses, qui était encore tout saignant des meurtrissures[1] de sa destinée, qui avait été presque méchant et qui était devenu presque saint, qui, après 75 avoir traîné la chaîne du bagne, traînait maintenant la chaîne invisible, mais pesante, de l'infamie[2] indéfinie, cet homme que la loi n'avait pas lâché et qui pouvait être à chaque instant ressaisi et ramené de l'obscurité de sa vertu au grand jour de l'opprobre[3] public, cet 80 homme acceptait tout, excusait tout, pardonnait tout, bénissait tout, voulait bien tout, et ne demandait à la providence, aux hommes, aux lois, à la société, à la nature, au monde, qu'une chose, que Cosette l'aimât !
[...]
85 Cette beauté qui s'épanouissait de plus en plus triomphante et superbe à côté de lui, sous ses yeux, sur le front ingénu et redoutable de l'enfant, du fond de sa laideur, de sa vieillesse, de sa misère, de sa réprobation, de son accablement, il la regardait effaré.

---

1. **Meurtrissures :** blessures.
2. **Infamie :** déshonneur, indignité.
3. **Opprobre :** honte, humiliation.

■ SITUER

Rue Plumet, Cosette et son « père » mènent une existence apparemment tranquille, ponctuée par les promenades au jardin du Luxembourg. Un jour, Cosette découvre qu'elle est devenue une jolie jeune fille. Jean Valjean s'inquiète.

■ RÉFLÉCHIR

STRUCTURE : Cosette au miroir

1. Notez les articulations temporelles qui marquent les observations de Cosette. Quelles sont les étapes de sa prise de conscience ?

2. Relevez les exclamations et les interrogations de Cosette. Pour chacune d'entre elles, précisez la nature du sentiment exprimé.

3. Analysez l'enchaînement des propositions dans la phrase « La conscience de sa beauté […] ravissement inexprimable. » (l. 49-57). La syntaxe est-elle régulière ? Quelle impression le rythme de cette phrase produit-il ?

4. Relevez les verbes et les signes de ponctuation qui introduisent les paroles ou les pensées de Cosette, ainsi que les réflexions du narrateur que l'on pourrait aussi attribuer à la jeune fille elle-même. Repérez les paroles et les pensées exprimées : a. au style direct ; b. au style indirect ; c. au style indirect libre. Quelle impression ce mélange de discours rapportés* produit-il ?

THÈMES : la chrysalide et le papillon

5. Dans la seconde moitié du texte, relevez et expliquez les comparaisons et les métaphores* illustrant la transformation de Cosette et la prise de conscience qu'entraîne cette transformation.

6. De qui proviennent les différents regards qui signalent à Cosette sa métamorphose ?

**PERSONNAGES : le bonheur de l'une
fait le malheur de l'autre**

7. Quels nouveaux traits de caractère apparaissent chez Cosette ?

8. « Aube riante pour tous, lugubre pour lui » (l. 63). Analysez le rythme et la structure de cette phrase. Expliquez l'antithèse*.

9. Que cache la « paupière sombre » (l. 68) de Jean Valjean ? Commentez la longueur et le rythme de la dernière phrase. Quels sentiments sont exprimés par ce flux de la pensée ?

10. L'antithèse entre la lumière et l'obscurité parcourt tout le passage. Comment l'interprétez-vous ?

90 Il se disait : Comme elle est belle ! Qu'est-ce que je vais devenir, moi ?

Là du reste était la différence entre sa tendresse et la tendresse d'une mère. Ce qu'il voyait avec angoisse, une mère l'eût vu avec joie.

95 Les premiers symptômes ne tardèrent pas à se manifester.

[…]

Avec la foi en sa beauté, toute l'âme féminine s'épanouit en elle. Elle eut horreur du mérinos et honte
100 de la peluche. Son père ne lui avait jamais rien refusé. Elle sut tout de suite toute la science du chapeau, de la robe, du mantelet, du brodequin[1], de la manchette, de l'étoffe qui va, de la couleur qui sied[2], cette science qui fait de la femme parisienne quelque chose de si char-
105 mant, de si profond et de si dangereux. Le mot *femme capiteuse*[3] a été inventé pour la Parisienne. […]

Jean Valjean considérait ces ravages avec anxiété. Lui qui sentait qu'il ne pourrait jamais que ramper, marcher tout au plus, il voyait des ailes venir à Cosette.
110 […]

Le premier jour que Cosette sortit avec sa robe et son camail[4] de damas noir et son chapeau de crêpe blanc, elle vint prendre le bras de Jean Valjean, gaie, radieuse, rose, fière, éclatante. – Père, dit-elle,
115 comment me trouvez-vous ainsi ? Jean Valjean répondit d'une voix qui ressemblait à la voix amère d'un envieux : – Charmante ! Il fut dans la promenade

---

1. **Brodequin** : bottine.
2. **Qui sied** : qui convient.
3. **Capiteuse** : enivrante.
4. **Camail** : pèlerine à capuchon ; **damas** : étoffe de laine ou de soie de couleur unie, dont le tissage forme un dessin.

comme à l'ordinaire. En rentrant il demanda à Cosette :

120 – Est-ce que tu ne remettras plus ta robe et ton chapeau, tu sais ?

Ceci se passait dans la chambre de Cosette. Cosette se tourna vers le porte-manteau de la garde-robe où sa défroque de pensionnaire était accrochée.

125 – Ce déguisement ! dit-elle. Père, que voulez-vous que j'en fasse ? Oh ! par exemple, non, je ne remettrai jamais ces horreurs. Avec ce machin-là sur la tête, j'ai l'air de madame Chien-fou.

Jean Valjean soupira profondément.

130 À partir de ce moment, il remarqua que Cosette qui autrefois demandait toujours à rester, disant : Père, je m'amuse mieux ici avec vous, demandait maintenant toujours à sortir. En effet, à quoi bon avoir une jolie figure et une délicieuse toilette, si 135 on ne les montre pas ?

Il remarqua aussi que Cosette n'avait plus le même goût pour l'arrière-cour. À présent, elle se tenait plus volontiers au jardin, se promenant sans déplaisir devant la grille. Jean Valjean, farouche, ne mettait pas les pieds 140 dans le jardin. Il restait dans son arrière-cour, comme le chien.

Cosette, à se savoir belle, perdit la grâce de l'ignorer ; grâce exquise, car la beauté rehaussée[1] de naïveté est ineffable, et rien n'est adorable comme une innocente 145 éblouissante qui marche tenant en main, sans le savoir, la clef d'un paradis. Mais ce qu'elle perdit en grâce ingénue[2], elle le regagna en charme pensif et sérieux. Toute sa personne, pénétrée des joies de la jeunesse, de

---

1. **Rehaussée** : soulignée, relevée.
2. **Ingénue** : naïve.

l'innocence et de la beauté, respirait une mélancolie
150 splendide.

Ce fut à cette époque que Marius, après six mois
écoulés, la revit au Luxembourg.

*[Un échange de regard a suffi pour que s'enflamment
les cœurs de Cosette et Marius. Jean Valjean, jaloux, a
brusquement interrompu les promenades. Cosette est triste,
mais ne veut pas contrarier son « père ». (IV, III, 6 et 7)]*

8. La cadène[1]

*[Jean Valjean aime sortir aux premières lueurs du
jour avec Cosette. Un matin d'automne, tandis qu'ils se
promènent aux portes de Paris, leur sérénité est troublée
par l'arrivée d'un effrayant convoi.]*

Sept voitures marchaient à la file sur la route. Les six
premières avaient une structure singulière. Elles
ressemblaient à des haquets[2] de tonneliers ; c'étaient
des espèces de longues échelles posées sur deux roues
5 et formant brancard à leur extrémité antérieure.
Chaque haquet, disons mieux, chaque échelle était
attelée de quatre chevaux bout à bout. Sur ces échelles
étaient traînées d'étranges grappes d'hommes. Dans le
peu de jour qu'il faisait, on ne voyait pas ces hommes,
10 on les devinait. Vingt-quatre sur chaque voiture,
douze de chaque côté, adossés les uns aux autres,
faisant face aux passants, les jambes dans le vide, ces
hommes cheminaient ainsi ; et ils avaient derrière le
dos quelque chose qui sonnait et qui était une chaîne

---

1. **Cadène :** chaîne de fer à laquelle on attachait les forçats.
2. **Haquets :** charrettes longues, servant à transporter du vin ou des ballots ;
   tonneliers : fabricants de tonneaux.

15 et au cou quelque chose qui brillait et qui était un
carcan[1]. Chacun avait son carcan, mais la chaîne était
pour tous ; de façon que ces vingt-quatre hommes, s'il
leur arrivait de descendre du haquet et de marcher,
étaient saisis par une sorte d'unité inexorable[2] et devaient
20 serpenter sur le sol avec la chaîne pour vertèbre à peu
près comme le mille-pieds. À l'avant et à l'arrière de
chaque voiture, deux hommes, armés de fusils, se
tenaient debout, ayant chacun une des extrémités de la
chaîne sous son pied. Les carcans étaient carrés. La
25 septième voiture, vaste fourgon à ridelles[3], mais sans
capote[4], avait quatre roues et six chevaux, et portait un
tas sonore de chaudières de fer, de marmites de fonte,
de réchauds et de chaînes, où étaient mêlés quelques
hommes garrottés et couchés tout de leur long, qui
30 paraissaient malades. Ce fourgon, tout à claire-voie[5],
était garni de claies[6] délabrées qui semblaient avoir
servi aux vieux supplices.

Ces voitures tenaient le milieu du pavé[7]. Des deux
côtés marchaient en double haie des gardes d'un aspect
35 infâme, coiffés de tricornes claques[8] comme les soldats
du Directoire[9], tachés, troués, sordides, affublés
d'uniformes d'invalides et de pantalons de croque-
morts, mi-partis[10] gris et bleus, presque en lambeaux,

---

1. **Carcan** : collier de fer servant à attacher les condamnés.
2. **Unité inexorable** : solidarité inévitable. Les forçats sont condamnés à
   rester attachés les uns aux autres, ils n'ont aucune autonomie de
   déplacement.
3. **Ridelles** : côtés d'une charrette, faits en forme de râtelier.
4. **Capote** : couverture amovible d'une voiture.
5. **À claire-voie** : fermé par un grillage de bois ou de fer.
6. **Claies** : treillages, grilles.
7. Les voitures roulaient au milieu de la chaussée.
8. **Tricornes claques** : chapeaux à trois cornes, que l'on peut aplatir.
9. **Directoire** : un des régimes de la Révolution française (1795-1799).
10. **Mi-partis** : à moitié.

avec des épaulettes rouges, des bandoulières jaunes, des
40 coupe-choux[1], des fusils et des bâtons ; espèces de
soldats goujats[2]. Ces sbires[3] semblaient composés de
l'abjection[4] du mendiant et de l'autorité du bourreau.
Celui qui paraissait leur chef tenait à la main un fouet de
poste. Tous ces détails, estompés par le crépuscule, se
45 dessinaient de plus en plus dans le jour grandissant. En
tête et en queue du convoi, marchaient des gendarmes à
cheval, graves, le sabre au poing.

Ce cortège était si long qu'au moment où la
première voiture atteignait la barrière, la dernière
50 débouchait à peine du boulevard.

Une foule, sortie on ne sait d'où et formée en un clin
d'œil, comme cela est fréquent à Paris, se pressait des
deux côtés de la chaussée et regardait. On entendait
dans les ruelles voisines des cris de gens qui s'appelaient
55 et les sabots des maraîchers[5] qui accouraient pour voir.

[Les prisonniers entassés ont un air farouche, malsain,
horrible et pitoyable. Livrés aux coups et aux intempéries,
ils sont emportés vers une terrible destination.]

Les coups de bâton n'épargnaient pas même les
malades, qui gisaient noués de cordes et sans mouvement sur la septième voiture et qu'on semblait avoir
jetés là comme des sacs pleins de misère.
60 Brusquement, le soleil parut ; l'immense rayon de
l'orient jaillit, et l'on eût dit qu'il mettait le feu à
toutes ces têtes farouches. Les langues se délièrent ; un

---

1. Coupe-choux : sabres très courts (ironique).
2. Goujats : hommes sales et grossiers.
3. Sbires : hommes de main au service du pouvoir (péjoratif).
4. Abjection : avilissement, honte.
5. Maraîchers : jardiniers spécialisés dans la culture des légumes.

incendie de ricanements, de jurements et de chansons
fit explosion. La large lumière horizontale coupa en
65 deux toute la file, illuminant les têtes et les torses, laissant les pieds et les roues dans l'obscurité. Les pensées
apparurent sur les visages ; ce moment fut épouvantable ; des démons visibles à masques tombés, des
âmes féroces toutes nues. Éclairée, cette cohue resta
70 ténébreuse. Quelques-uns, gais, avaient à la bouche
des tuyaux de plume d'où ils soufflaient de la vermine
sur la foule, choisissant les femmes ; l'aurore accentuait
par la noirceur des ombres ces profils lamentables ; pas
un de ces êtres qui ne fût difforme à force de misère ;
75 et c'était si monstrueux qu'on eût dit que cela changeait la clarté du soleil en lueur d'éclair. La voiturée
qui ouvrait le cortège avait entonné et psalmodiait[1] à
tue-tête avec une jovialité hagarde[2] un pot-pourri[3] de
Désaugiers, alors fameux, *la Vestale* ; les arbres frémis-
80 saient lugubrement ; dans les contre-allées, des faces
de bourgeois écoutaient avec une béatitude[4] idiote ces
gaudrioles[5] chantées par des spectres.

Toutes les détresses étaient dans ce cortège comme
un chaos ; il y avait là l'angle facial de toutes les bêtes,
85 des vieillards, des adolescents, des crânes nus, des
barbes grises, des monstruosités cyniques[6], des résigna-
tions hargneuses, des rictus sauvages, des attitudes
insensées, des groins coiffés de casquettes, des espèces
de têtes de jeunes filles avec des tire-bouchons sur les

---

1. **Psalmodier :** manière de chanter les psaumes, chants religieux.
2. **Hagarde :** qui a une expression égarée et sauvage.
3. **Pot-pourri :** mélange de chansons ; Désaugiers est un compositeur français du XVIIIe siècle.
4. **Béatitude :** bonheur parfait.
5. **Gaudrioles :** propos gais, plaisanteries.
6. **Cyniques :** d'une laideur provocante.

90 tempes, des visages enfantins et, à cause de cela, horribles, de maigres faces de squelettes auxquelles il ne manquait que la mort. [...]

Marche des damnations vers les supplices, faite sinistrement, non sur le formidable char fulgurant[1] de
95 l'Apocalypse[2], mais, chose plus sombre, sur la charrette des gémonies[3].

Un des gardes, qui avait un crochet au bout de son bâton, faisait de temps en temps mine de remuer ces tas d'ordure humains. Une vieille femme dans la foule
100 les montrait du doigt à un petit garçon de cinq ans, et lui disait : *Gredin, cela t'apprendra !*

Comme les chants et les blasphèmes grossissaient, celui qui semblait le capitaine de l'escorte fit claquer son fouet, et, à ce signal, une effroyable bastonnade sourde
105 et aveugle qui faisait le bruit de la grêle tomba sur les sept voiturées ; beaucoup rugirent et écumèrent ; ce qui redoubla la joie des gamins accourus, nuée de mouches sur ces plaies.

L'œil de Jean Valjean était devenu effrayant. Ce
110 n'était plus une prunelle ; c'était cette vitre profonde qui remplace le regard chez certains infortunés, qui semble inconsciente de la réalité, et où flamboie la réverbération des épouvantes et des catastrophes. Il ne regardait pas un spectacle ; il subissait une vision. Il
115 voulut se lever, fuir, échapper ; il ne put remuer un pied. Quelquefois les choses qu'on voit vous saisissent, et vous tiennent. Il demeura cloué, pétrifié, stupide, se

---

1. **Fulgurant :** accompagné d'éclairs.
2. **Apocalypse :** vision de la fin du monde par saint Jean, rapportée dans le dernier livre du Nouveau Testament.
3. **Gémonies :** dans l'ancienne Rome, escalier sur lequel on exposait les corps des condamnés qui avaient été étranglés dans la prison ; de là on traînait ces corps avec des crocs dans le Tibre.

demandant, à travers une confuse angoisse inexprimable,
ce que signifiait cette persécution sépulcrale, et d'où
120 sortait ce pandémonium[1] qui le poursuivait. Tout à
coup il porta la main à son front, geste habituel de
ceux auxquels la mémoire revient subitement ; il se
souvint que c'était là l'itinéraire en effet, que ce détour
était d'usage pour éviter les rencontres royales
125 toujours possibles sur la route de Fontainebleau, et
que, trente-cinq ans auparavant, il avait passé par cette
barrière-là.

Cosette, autrement épouvantée, ne l'était pas moins.
Elle ne comprenait pas ; le souffle lui manquait ; ce
130 qu'elle voyait ne lui semblait pas possible ; enfin elle
s'écria :

– Père ! qu'est-ce qu'il y a donc dans ces voitures-là ?

Jean Valjean répondit :

– Des forçats.

135 – Où donc est-ce qu'ils vont ?

– Aux galères.

En ce moment la bastonnade, multipliée par cent
mains, fit du zèle, les coups de plat de sabre s'en
mêlèrent, ce fut comme une rage de fouets et de
140 bâtons ; les galériens se courbèrent, une obéissance
hideuse se dégagea du supplice, et tous se turent
avec des regards de loups enchaînés. Cosette
tremblait de tous ses membres ; elle reprit :

– Père, est-ce que ce sont encore des hommes ?

145 – Quelquefois, dit le misérable.

C'était la Chaîne en effet qui, partie avant le
jour de Bicêtre, prenait la route du Mans pour
éviter Fontainebleau où était alors le roi. Ce
détour faisait durer l'épouvantable voyage trois ou

---

1. **Pandémonium :** assemblée de démons, d'esprits infernaux.

SITUER

Cosette et son « père » mènent enfin une existence paisible. Un matin, pendant qu'ils se promènent aux barrières de Paris, leur tranquillité est troublée par l'irruption d'un convoi effrayant : des forçats enchaînés en route pour le bagne. Cette vision terrifiante stupéfie Cosette, et rappelle à Jean Valjean le passé qu'il cherche à effacer.

RÉFLÉCHIR

THÈMES : « Est-ce que ce sont encore des hommes ? »

1. Étudiez le vocabulaire de l'horreur et de l'épouvante.

2. Commentez l'expression « ces tas d'ordure humains » (l. 99).

3. Que signifie la dernière question de Cosette ?

4. Pourquoi Jean Valjean est-il ici qualifié de « misérable » (l. 145) ?

5. La remarque de la vieille femme vous paraît-elle appropriée à la situation ?

6. La « joie des gamins » est-elle compréhensible ? Que révèle-t-elle ? Que cache-t-elle ? Expliquez la métaphore* : « nuée de mouches sur ces plaies » (l. 107-108).

7. Dans les phrases qui décrivent la bastonnade, les gardes sont-ils directement nommés comme sujets de l'action ? Que suggèrent les expressions « sourde et aveugle » (l. 104-105) et « multipliée par cent mains » (l. 137-138) ?

PERSONNAGES : le douloureux combat de Jean Valjean

8. Quels sont les effets physiques de cette vision sur Jean Valjean ? Quel est l'impact psychologique de cette scène à ce stade du récit ?

9. Expliquez l'expression « persécution sépulcrale » (l. 119). Quel combat intérieur agite Jean Valjean ?

10. Pourquoi Jean Valjean répond-il à Cosette de façon aussi évasive ?

SOCIÉTÉ : le scandale du bagne

11. En quoi cette scène est-elle insoutenable pour le bagnard, pour la jeune fille, pour le lecteur ?

12. À quelles réflexions cet épisode livre-t-il le lecteur ?

ÉCRIRE

13. UN RÉQUISITOIRE : Victor Hugo prononce un discours dénonçant l'institution du bagne.

150 quatre jours de plus ; mais, pour épargner à la
personne royale la vue d'un supplice, on peut bien le
prolonger.

Jean Valjean rentra accablé. De telles rencontres
sont des chocs et le souvenir qu'elles laissent ressemble
155 à un ébranlement.

Pourtant Jean Valjean, en regagnant avec Cosette la
rue de Babylone, ne remarqua point qu'elle lui fit
d'autres questions au sujet de ce qu'ils venaient de
voir ; peut-être était-il trop absorbé lui-même dans son
160 accablement pour percevoir ses paroles et pour lui
répondre. Seulement le soir, comme Cosette le quittait
pour s'aller coucher, il l'entendit qui disait à demi-voix
et comme se parlant à elle-même : – Il me semble que
si je trouvais sur mon chemin un de ces hommes-là, ô
165 mon Dieu, je mourrais rien que de le voir de près !

*[Un voyou attaque Jean Valjean pour lui dérober son
porte-monnaie. Mais le vieil homme terrasse le garçon, et
finit par lui laisser sa bourse après un long et puissant
sermon.*

*Cosette s'inquiète : elle a cru repérer la présence d'un
rôdeur dans le jardin. Le mystère s'éclaircit quand elle
découvre une lettre que lui adresse son admirateur, et
dont la lecture la transporte dans une délicieuse rêverie,
jusqu'au soir de leur premier tête-à-tête dans le jardin
de la rue Plumet. L'inconnu se révèle être Marius. Ils
échangent leur premier baiser. (IV, IV et V.)]*

LIVRE SIXIÈME : LE PETIT GAVROCHE

[Les Thénardier ont vendu leurs deux derniers-nés à la Magnon, qui vient d'être arrêtée par la police. Abandonnés à eux-mêmes, les deux enfants errent dans les rues à la recherche d'un logis. (IV, VI, 1)]

2. Où le petit Gavroche
tire parti de Napoléon le Grand

[Les deux garçons tombent sur Gavroche, le fils aîné des Thénardier, « celui qui criait au tome II » (II, III, 1 voir p. 107) ; il les prend sous sa protection, sans savoir qu'il s'agit de ses frères.]

Comme ils passaient devant un de ces épais treillis grillés qui indiquent la boutique d'un boulanger, car on met le pain comme l'or derrière des grillages de fer, Gavroche se tourna :

5 – Ah ça, mômes, avons-nous dîné ?

– Monsieur, répondit l'aîné, nous n'avons pas mangé depuis tantôt ce matin.

– Vous êtes donc sans père ni mère ? reprit majestueusement Gavroche.

10 – Faites excuse, monsieur, nous avons papa et maman, mais nous ne savons pas où ils sont.

– Des fois, cela vaut mieux que de le savoir, dit Gavroche qui était un penseur.

– Voilà, continua l'aîné, deux heures que nous

15 marchons, nous avons cherché des choses au coin des bornes, mais nous ne trouvons rien.

– Je sais, fit Gavroche. C'est les chiens qui mangent tout.

Il reprit après un silence :

20   – Ah ! nous avons perdu nos auteurs[1]. Nous ne savons plus ce que nous en avons fait. Ça ne se doit pas, gamins. C'est bête d'égarer comme ça des gens d'âge. Ah ça ! il faut licher[2] pourtant.

Du reste il ne leur fit pas de questions. Être sans
25 domicile, quoi de plus simple ?

L'aîné des deux mômes, presque entièrement revenu à la prompte insouciance de l'enfance, fit cette exclamation :

– C'est drôle tout de même. Maman qui avait dit qu'elle nous mènerait chercher du buis bénit le
30 dimanche des rameaux.

– Neurs, répondit Gavroche.

– Maman, reprit l'aîné, est une dame qui demeure avec mamselle Miss.

– Tanflûte, repartit Gavroche.

35 Cependant il s'était arrêté, et depuis quelques minutes il tâtait et fouillait toutes sortes de recoins qu'il avait dans ses haillons.

Enfin il releva la tête d'un air qui ne voulait qu'être satisfait, mais qui était en réalité triomphant.

40   – Calmons-nous, les momignards. Voici de quoi souper pour trois.

Et il tira d'une de ses poches un sou.

Sans laisser aux deux petits le temps de s'ébahir, il les poussa tous deux devant lui dans la boutique du
45 boulanger, et mit son sou sur le comptoir en criant :

– Garçon ! cinq centimes de pain.

Le boulanger, qui était le maître en personne, prit un pain et un couteau.

– En trois morceaux, garçon ! reprit Gavroche, et il
50 ajouta avec dignité :

---

1. **Nos auteurs :** nos parents.
2. **Licher :** manger (populaire).

– Nous sommes trois.

Et voyant que le boulanger, après avoir examiné les trois soupeurs, avait pris un pain bis, il plongea profondément son doigt dans son nez avec une aspiration aussi impérieuse que s'il eût au bout du pouce la prise de tabac du grand Frédéric[1], et jeta au boulanger en plein visage cette apostrophe indignée :

– Keksekça ?

Ceux de nos lecteurs qui seraient tentés de voir, dans cette interpellation de Gavroche au boulanger un mot russe ou polonais, ou l'un de ces cris sauvages que les Yoways et les Botocudos se lancent du bord d'un fleuve à l'autre à travers les solitudes, sont prévenus que c'est un mot qu'ils disent tous les jours (eux nos lecteurs) et qui tient lieu de cette phrase : qu'est-ce que c'est que cela ? Le boulanger comprit parfaitement et répondit :

– Eh mais ! c'est du pain, du très bon pain de deuxième qualité.

– Vous voulez dire du larton brutal[2], reprit Gavroche, calme et froidement dédaigneux. Du pain blanc, garçon ! du larton savonné ! je régale.

Le boulanger ne put s'empêcher de sourire, et tout en coupant le pain blanc, il les considérait d'une façon compatissante qui choqua Gavroche.

– Ah ça, mitron[3] ! dit il, qu'est-ce que vous avez donc à nous toiser[4] comme ça ?

---

1. **Le grand Frédéric** : Frédéric II, roi de Prusse au XVIIIᵉ siècle, admirateur de Voltaire.
2. **Larton brutal** : pain noir (note de Hugo).
3. **Mitron** : garçon boulanger.
4. **Toiser** : mesurer du regard avec distance. La toise est une ancienne unité de mesure (1,949 m).

Mis tous trois bout à bout, ils auraient à peine fait une toise.

80 Quand le pain fut coupé, le boulanger encaissa le sou, et Gavroche dit aux deux enfants :

– Morfilez.

Les petits garçons le regardèrent interdits.

Gavroche se mit à rire :

85 – Ah ! tiens, c'est vrai, ça ne sait pas encore, c'est si petit.

Et il reprit :

– Mangez.

En même temps, il leur tendait à chacun un morceau de pain.

90 Et, pensant que l'aîné, qui lui paraissait plus digne de sa conversation, méritait quelque encouragement spécial et devait être débarrassé de toute hésitation à satisfaire son appétit, il ajouta en lui donnant la plus grosse part :

– Colle-toi ça dans le fusil.

95 Il y avait un morceau plus petit que les deux autres ; il le prit pour lui.

Les pauvres enfants étaient affamés, y compris Gavroche. Tout en arrachant leur pain à belles dents, ils encombraient la boutique du boulanger qui, main-
100 tenant qu'il était payé, les regardait avec humeur.

– Rentrons dans la rue, dit Gavroche.

Ils reprirent la direction de la Bastille.

[...]

Il y a vingt ans, on voyait encore dans l'angle sud-est
105 de la place de la Bastille près de la gare du canal creusée dans l'ancien fossé de la prison-citadelle, un monument bizarre qui s'est effacé déjà de la mémoire des Parisiens, et qui méritait d'y laisser quelque trace, car c'était une pensée du « membre de l'Institut, général
110 en chef de l'armée d'Égypte[1] ».

---

1. Périphrase* pour désigner Bonaparte.

Nous disons monument, quoique ce ne fût qu'une maquette. Mais cette maquette elle-même, ébauche prodigieuse, cadavre grandiose d'une idée de Napoléon que deux ou trois coups de vent successifs avaient
115 emportée et jetée à chaque fois plus loin de nous, était devenue historique, et avait pris je ne sais quoi de définitif qui contrastait avec son aspect provisoire. C'était un éléphant de quarante pieds[1] de haut, construit en charpente et en maçonnerie, portant sur son dos sa tour
120 qui ressemblait à une maison, jadis peint en vert par un badigeonneur quelconque, maintenant peint en noir par le ciel, la pluie et le temps. Dans cet angle désert et découvert de la place, le large front du colosse, sa trompe, ses défenses, sa tour, sa croupe énorme, ses
125 quatre pieds pareils à des colonnes faisaient, la nuit, sur le ciel étoilé, une silhouette surprenante et terrible. On ne savait ce que cela voulait dire. C'était une sorte de symbole de la force populaire. C'était sombre, énigmatique et immense. C'était on ne sait quel fantôme puis-
130 sant, visible et debout à côté du spectre invisible de la Bastille.

Peu d'étrangers visitaient cet édifice, aucun passant ne le regardait. Il tombait en ruine ; à chaque saison, des plâtras qui se détachaient de ses flancs lui faisaient
135 des plaies hideuses. Les « édiles[2] », comme on dit en patois élégant, l'avaient oublié depuis 1814. Il était là dans son coin, morne, malade, croulant, entouré d'une palissade pourrie, souillée à chaque instant par des cochers ivres ; des crevasses lui lézardaient le ventre,
140 une latte lui sortait de la queue, les hautes herbes lui

---

1. **Pied :** ancienne mesure de longueur (0,324 m) ; l'éléphant a donc environ 13 mètres de haut.
2. **Édiles :** magistrats chargés de la voirie à Rome ; emploi ironique ici.

poussaient entre les jambes ; et comme le niveau de la
place s'élevait depuis trente ans tout autour par ce
mouvement lent et continu qui exhausse[1] insensiblement
le sol des grandes villes, il était dans un creux et il
145 semblait que la terre s'enfonçât sous lui. Il était
immonde, méprisé, repoussant et superbe, laid aux
yeux du bourgeois, mélancolique aux yeux du penseur.
Il avait quelque chose d'une ordure qu'on va balayer et
quelque chose d'une majesté qu'on va décapiter.
150 Comme nous l'avons dit, la nuit, l'aspect changeait.
La nuit est le véritable milieu de tout ce qui est ombre.
Dès que tombait le crépuscule, le vieil éléphant se
transfigurait ; il prenait une figure tranquille et redoutable dans la formidable sérénité des ténèbres. Étant
155 du passé, il était de la nuit ; et cette obscurité allait à sa
grandeur.
[…]
Qu'on nous permette de nous interrompre ici et de
rappeler que nous sommes dans la simple réalité, et qu'il
160 y a vingt ans les tribunaux correctionnels eurent à juger,
sous prévention[2] de vagabondage et de bris d'un monument public, un enfant qui avait été surpris couché dans
l'intérieur même de l'éléphant de la Bastille.
Ce fait constaté, nous continuons.
165 En arrivant près du colosse, Gavroche comprit
l'effet que l'infiniment grand peut produire sur
l'infiniment petit, et dit :
– Moutards ! n'ayez pas peur.
Puis il entra par une lacune[3] de la palissade dans
170 l'enceinte de l'éléphant et aida les mômes à enjamber

---

1. **Exhausse** : relève.
2. **Prévention** : accusation.
3. **Lacune** : trou, brèche.

la brèche. Les deux enfants, un peu effrayés, suivaient sans dire mot Gavroche et se confiaient à cette petite providence[1] en guenilles qui leur avait donné du pain et leur avait promis un gîte.

175 Il y avait là, couchée le long de la palissade, une échelle qui servait le jour aux ouvriers du chantier voisin. Gavroche la souleva avec une singulière vigueur, et l'appliqua contre une des jambes de devant de l'éléphant. Vers le point où l'échelle allait aboutir,
180 on distinguait une espèce de trou noir dans le ventre du colosse.

Gavroche montra l'échelle et le trou à ses hôtes et leur dit :

– Montez et entrez.

185 Les deux petits garçons se regardèrent terrifiés.

– Vous avez peur, mômes ! s'écria Gavroche.

Et il ajouta :

– Vous allez voir.

Il étreignit le pied rugueux de l'éléphant, et en un
190 clin d'œil, sans daigner se servir de l'échelle, il arriva à la crevasse. Il y entra comme une couleuvre qui se glisse dans une fente, et s'y enfonça, et un moment après les deux enfants virent vaguement apparaître comme une forme blanchâtre et blafarde, sa tête pâle
195 au bord du trou plein de ténèbres.

– Eh bien, cria-t-il, montez donc, les momignards ! vous allez voir comme on est bien ! – Monte, toi ! dit-il à l'aîné, je te tends la main.

Les petits se poussèrent de l'épaule, le gamin leur
200 faisait peur et les rassurait à la fois, et puis il pleuvait bien fort. L'aîné se risqua. Le plus jeune, en voyant monter son frère et lui resté tout seul entre les pattes

---

1. **Providence :** aide inespérée.

de cette grosse bête, avait bien envie de pleurer, mais il n'osait.

205 L'aîné gravissait, tout en chancelant, les barreaux de l'échelle ; Gavroche, chemin faisant, l'encourageait par des exclamations de maître d'armes à ses écoliers ou de muletier à ses mules :

– Aye pas peur !

210 – C'est ça !

– Va toujours !

– Mets ton pied là !

– Ta main ici.

– Hardi !

215 Et quand il fut à sa portée, il l'empoigna brusquement et vigoureusement par le bras et le tira à lui.

– Gobé, dit-il.

Le môme avait franchi la crevasse.

– Maintenant, fit Gavroche, attends-moi. Monsieur, 220 prenez la peine de vous asseoir.

Et, sortant de la crevasse comme il y était entré, il se laissa glisser avec l'agilité d'un ouistiti le long de la jambe de l'éléphant, il tomba debout sur ses pieds dans l'herbe, saisit le petit de cinq ans à bras-le-corps et le 225 planta au beau milieu de l'échelle, puis il se mit à monter derrière lui en criant à l'aîné :

– Je vas le pousser, tu vas le tirer.

En un instant le petit fut monté, poussé, traîné, tiré, bourré, fourré dans le trou sans avoir eu le temps de se 230 reconnaître, et Gavroche, entrant après lui, repoussant d'un coup de talon l'échelle qui tomba sur le gazon, se mit à battre des mains et cria :

– Nous y v'là ! Vive le général Lafayette[1] !

---

1. **Lafayette :** général français (1757-1834), héros de la guerre d'Indépendance américaine.

Cette explosion passée, il ajouta :

235 – Les mioches, vous êtes chez moi.

Gavroche était en effet chez lui.

Ô utilité inattendue de l'inutile ! charité des grandes choses ! bonté des géants ! Ce monument démesuré qui avait contenu une pensée de l'empereur était devenu la
240 boîte d'un gamin. Le môme avait été accepté et abrité par le colosse. Les bourgeois endimanchés qui passaient devant l'éléphant de la Bastille disaient volontiers en le toisant d'un air de mépris avec leurs yeux à fleur de tête : – À quoi cela sert-il ? – Cela servait à sauver du froid, du
245 givre, de la grêle, de la pluie, à garantir du vent d'hiver, à préserver du sommeil dans la boue qui donne la fièvre et du sommeil dans la neige qui donne la mort, un petit être sans père ni mère, sans pain, sans vêtements, sans asile. Cela servait à recueillir l'innocent que la société
250 repoussait.

[…]

Le trou par où Gavroche était entré était une brèche à peine visible du dehors, cachée qu'elle était, nous l'avons dit, sous le ventre de l'éléphant, et si étroite
255 qu'il n'y avait guère que des chats et des mômes qui pussent y passer.

– Commençons, dit Gavroche, par dire au portier que nous n'y sommes pas.

Et plongeant dans l'obscurité avec certitude comme
260 quelqu'un qui connaît son appartement, il prit une planche et en boucha le trou.

Gavroche replongea dans l'obscurité. Les enfants entendirent le reniflement de l'allumette enfoncée dans la bouteille phosphorique[1]. L'allumette chimique n'existait

---

1. **Bouteille phosphorique :** bouteille contenant du phosphore dans lequel on plongeait l'allumette (dite « phosphorique »).

270 pas encore ; le briquet Fumade[1] représentait à cette
époque le progrès.

Une clarté subite leur fit cligner les yeux ; Gavroche
venait d'allumer un de ces bouts de ficelle trempés
dans la résine qu'on appelle rats de cave. Le rat de
275 cave, qui fumait plus qu'il n'éclairait, rendait confusément visible le dedans de l'éléphant.

Les deux hôtes de Gavroche regardèrent autour
d'eux et éprouvèrent quelque chose de pareil à ce
qu'éprouverait quelqu'un qui serait enfermé dans la
280 grosse tonne de Heidelberg[2], ou mieux encore, à ce
que dut éprouver Jonas[3] dans le ventre biblique de la
baleine. Tout un squelette gigantesque leur apparaissait et les enveloppait. En haut, une longue poutre
brune d'où partaient de distance en distance de massives
285 membrures cintrées figurait la colonne vertébrale avec
les côtes, des stalactites de plâtre y pendaient comme
des viscères, et d'une côte à l'autre de vastes toiles
d'araignée faisaient des diaphragmes poudreux. On
voyait çà et là dans les coins de grosses taches noirâtres
290 qui avaient l'air de vivre et qui se déplaçaient rapidement avec un mouvement brusque et effaré.

Les débris tombés du dos de l'éléphant sur son
ventre en avaient comblé la concavité, de sorte qu'on
pouvait y marcher comme sur un plancher.

295 Le plus petit se rencogna contre son frère et dit à
demi-voix :

---

1. Le **briquet Fumade** : bouteille contenant de l'acide sulfurique dans
lequel on trempait l'allumette chimique.
2. **Heidelberg** : ville allemande ; son tonneau (« tonne ») est célèbre par ses
dimensions énormes.
3. **Jonas** : personnage de la Bible. Fuyant l'ordre divin, il est avalé par un
gros poisson (une baleine ?) dans le ventre duquel il passe trois jours et
trois nuits.

Le Petit Gavroche, gravure d'après un dessin de Gustave Brion
pour l'édition de 1865 des *Misérables* (Hetzel et A. Lacroix).
(Bibliothèque nationale de France, Paris.)

– C'est noir.

Ce mot fit exclamer Gavroche. L'air pétrifié des deux mômes rendait une secousse nécessaire.

300 – Qu'est-ce que vous me fichez ? s'écria-t-il. Blaguons-nous ? faisons-nous les dégoûtés ? vous faut-il pas les Tuileries[1] ? Seriez-vous des brutes ? Dites-le. Je vous préviens que je ne suis pas du régiment des godiches. Ah çà, est-ce que vous êtes les moutards du
305 moutardier du pape ?

Un peu de rudoiement est bon dans l'épouvante. Cela rassure. Les deux enfants se rapprochèrent de Gavroche.

Gavroche, paternellement attendri de cette
310 confiance, passa « du grave au doux[2] » et s'adressant au plus petit :

– Bêta, lui dit-il en accentuant l'injure d'une nuance caressante, c'est dehors que c'est noir. Dehors il pleut,
315 ici il ne pleut pas ; dehors il fait froid, ici il n'y a pas une miette de vent ; dehors il y a des tas de monde, ici il n'y a personne ; dehors il n'y a pas même la lune, ici il y a ma chandelle, nom d'unch !

Les deux enfants commençaient à regarder l'appar-
320 tement avec moins d'effroi ; mais Gavroche ne leur laissa pas plus longtemps le loisir de la contemplation.

– Vite, dit-il.

Et il les poussa vers ce que nous sommes très heureux de pouvoir appeler le fond de la chambre.
325 Là était son lit.

Le lit de Gavroche était complet. C'est-à-dire qu'il y avait un matelas, une couverture et une alcôve avec rideaux.

---

1. **Les Tuileries :** palais parisien, résidence royale.
2. Citation de Boileau, écrivain du XVIIᵉ siècle.

SITUER

Gavroche est fier d'accueillir les deux enfants abandonnés dans son logis secret : la statue délabrée de l'éléphant de la Bastille, intérieur effrayant et accueillant tout à la fois.

RÉFLÉCHIR

PERSONNAGES : Gavroche et ses frères

1. Relevez et expliquez les tournures populaires ou imagées du langage de Gavroche.

2. Gavroche est fier de faire visiter son logis. À quoi le voit-on ?

3. Étudiez la variété des tons employés par Gavroche avec les petits. Montrez comment il réussit à les rassurer en faisant mine de les rudoyer.

4. Quel rôle Gavroche joue-t-il auprès des deux petits ? Que pense le lecteur, qui, lui, connaît le lien de parenté entre les trois enfants ?

REGISTRES ET TONALITÉ : un univers fantastique

5. Quelle impression se dégage du contraste entre l'ombre et la clarté dans ce tableau ?

6. En quoi cet endroit est-il effrayant ? En quoi est-il rassurant ?

7. Quels traits sont particulièrement accentués dans le dessin de Hugo (p. 13) ? Quels aspects de la personnalité de Gavroche expriment-ils ?

THÈMES : l'imaginaire enfantin

8. Relevez les champs lexicaux* de la couleur et de la lumière dans ce texte. Comment les enfants perçoivent-ils progressivement l'espace dans lequel ils pénètrent ?

9. Quelle est l'image utilisée pour désigner la charpente de l'édifice ? Dressez le tableau des correspondances entre l'architecture du monument et les parties du corps de l'animal représenté.

10. Deux comparaisons, celle de la tonne d'Heidelberg, et celle de la baleine de Jonas, sont employées pour décrire l'intérieur de l'éléphant. Quelles sont leurs connotations* respectives ?

11. Que représente symboliquement cet espace creux pour les trois enfants abandonnés ?

Le matelas était une natte de paille, la couverture un
330 assez vaste pagne de grosse laine grise fort chaude et
presque neuve. Voici ce que c'était que l'alcôve :

Trois échalas[1] assez longs, enfoncés et consolidés
dans les gravois[2] du sol, c'est-à-dire du ventre de
l'éléphant, deux en avant, un en arrière, et réunis par
335 une corde à leur sommet, de manière à former un faisceau pyramidal. Ce faisceau supportait un treillage de
fil de laiton qui était simplement posé dessus, mais
artistement appliqué et maintenu par des attaches de fil
de fer de sorte qu'il enveloppait entièrement les trois
340 échalas.

Un cordon de grosses pierres fixait tout autour ce
treillage sur le sol de manière à ne rien laisser passer.
Ce treillage n'était autre chose qu'un morceau de ces
grillages de cuivre dont on revêt les volières dans les
345 ménageries. Le lit de Gavroche était sous ce grillage
comme dans une cage. L'ensemble ressemblait à une
tente d'esquimau.

*[Gavroche installe un lit de fortune pour ses hôtes. Il
leur raconte les joies de sa vie parisienne : les baignades, les
farces aux blanchisseuses, les combines pour entrer gratui-
tement au théâtre et à l'Opéra, les exécutions capitales...
Les petits ont peur des bruits. Gavroche les rassure : ce n'est
qu'une cavalcade de rats ! Les trois enfants, blottis l'un
contre l'autre, finissent par s'endormir.]*

Les heures de la nuit s'écoulèrent. L'ombre couvrait
l'immense place de la Bastille, un vent d'hiver qui se
350 mêlait à la pluie soufflait par bouffées, les patrouilles

---

1. **Échalas :** pieu en bois.
2. **Gravois :** gravats, débris, décombres.

furetaient[1] les portes, les allées, les enclos, les coins obscurs, et, cherchant les vagabonds nocturnes, passaient silencieusement devant l'éléphant ; le monstre, debout, immobile, les yeux ouverts dans les ténèbres, avait l'air de rêver comme satisfait de sa bonne action, et abritait du ciel et des hommes les trois pauvres enfants endormis.

370

[*Aidé par Gavroche, Thénardier s'évade de prison (IV, VI, 3).*

Avec sa bande, il médite un mauvais coup contre le bourgeois de la rue Plumet. Pour protéger les amours de Marius, Éponine s'interpose, tient tête à son père, et empêche les bandits d'exécuter leur plan.

Jean Valjean, depuis quelque temps, a vu Thénardier rôder. Il décide brusquement de partir en Angleterre. Marius ne peut envisager de perdre Cosette. Il décide de l'épouser ; le lendemain, il renoue donc avec son grand-père, qui ne veut pas entendre parler de ce mariage, et lui conseille de prendre Cosette pour maîtresse. Marius, scandalisé, rompt une nouvelle fois avec son grand-père.

Ce même jour, un message anonyme conseille à Jean Valjean de déménager. Quand Marius revient le lendemain rue Plumet, Cosette est partie sans laisser d'adresse. Une voix qui ressemble à celle d'Éponine l'avertit que ses amis l'attendent à la barricade du quartier des Halles. (IV, VIII et IX.)]

---

1. **Furetaient :** fouillaient.

LIVRE DIXIÈME : LE 5 JUIN 1832

[Le 5 juin 1832, le peuple de Paris suit les funérailles du général Lamarque, ancien soldat de Napoléon. La révolte gronde, la tension monte entre la foule et les forces de l'ordre, des barricades se forment. C'est l'insurrection. (IV, X, 1 à 3)]

4. Les bouillonnements d'autrefois

Rien n'est plus extraordinaire que le premier fourmillement d'une émeute. Tout éclate partout à la fois. Était-ce prévu ? oui. Était-ce préparé ? non. D'où cela sort-il ? des pavés. D'où cela tombe-t-il ? des nues. Ici l'insurrection a
5 le caractère d'un complot ; là d'une improvisation. Le premier venu s'empare d'un courant de la foule et le mène où il veut. Début plein d'épouvante où se mêle une sorte de gaîté formidable. Ce sont d'abord des clameurs, les magasins se ferment, les étalages des marchands
10 disparaissent ; puis des coups de feu isolés ; des gens s'enfuient ; des coups de crosse heurtent les portes cochères ; on entend les servantes rire dans les cours des maisons et dire : *Il va y avoir du train !*
    […]

LIVRE DOUZIÈME : CORINTHE

[Rue de la Chanvrerie, les insurgés, rejoints par Gavroche, ont leur quartier général dans le café Corinthe, tenu par la veuve Hucheloup. Grantaire (voir p. 139) boit. Les insurgés renversent un omnibus, arrachent des pavés pour dresser une barricade. (IV, XII, 1 à 3)]

A. Bellenger, *La Barricade*.
(Maison de Victor Hugo, Paris.)

4. Essai de consolation sur la veuve Hucheloup

[…]

La pluie avait cessé. Des recrues étaient arrivées. Des ouvriers avaient apporté sous leurs blouses un baril de poudre, un panier contenant des bouteilles de vitriol, deux ou trois torches de carnaval et une bourriche[1] pleine
5 de lampions « restés de la fête du roi ». Laquelle fête était toute récente, ayant eu lieu le 1er mai. On disait que ces munitions venaient de la part d'un épicier du faubourg Saint-Antoine nommé Pépin. On brisait l'unique réverbère de la rue de la Chanvrerie, la lanterne corres-
10 pondante de la rue Saint-Denis, et toutes les lanternes des rues circonvoisines, de Mondétour, du Cygne, des Prêcheurs, et de la Grande et de la Petite-Truanderie[2].

Enjolras, Combeferre et Courfeyrac[3] dirigeaient tout. Maintenant deux barricades se construisaient en même
15 temps, toutes deux appuyées à la maison de Corinthe et faisant équerre ; la plus grande fermait la rue de la Chanvrerie, l'autre fermait la rue Mondétour du côté de la rue du Cygne. Cette dernière barricade, très étroite, n'était construite que de tonneaux et de pavés. Ils
20 étaient là environ cinquante travailleurs ; une trentaine armés de fusils ; car, chemin faisant, ils avaient fait un emprunt en bloc à une boutique d'armurier.

Rien de plus bizarre et de plus bigarré[4] que cette troupe. L'un avait un habit veste, un sabre de cavalerie et
25 deux pistolets d'arçon[5], un autre était en manches de chemises avec un chapeau rond et une poire à poudre

---

1. **Bourriche :** sorte de grand panier.
2. Rues du quartier des Halles.
3. Amis de Marius, jeunes révolutionnaires.
4. **Bigarré :** coloré, varié.
5. **Pistolets d'arçon :** pistolets que l'on met dans les fourreaux de cuir accrochés à la selle.

pendue au côté, un troisième était plastronné[1] de neuf feuilles de papier gris et armé d'une alêne de sellier[2]. Il y en avait un qui criait : *Exterminons jusqu'au dernier et*
30 *mourons au bout de notre baïonnette*[3] ! Celui-là n'avait pas de baïonnette. Un autre étalait par-dessus sa redingote[4] une buffleterie[5] et une giberne de garde national avec le couvre-giberne orné de cette inscription en laine rouge : Ordre public. Force fusils portant des numéros de
35 légions, peu de chapeaux, point de cravates, beaucoup de bras nus, quelques piques. Ajoutez à cela tous les âges, tous les visages, de petits jeunes gens pâles, des ouvriers du port bronzés. Tous se hâtaient, et, tout en s'entr'aidant, on causait des chances possibles, – qu'on
40 aurait des secours vers trois heures du matin,– qu'on était sûr d'un régiment, – que Paris se soulèverait. Propos terribles auxquels se mêlait une sorte de jovialité cordiale. On eût dit des frères ; ils ne savaient pas les noms les uns des autres. Les grands périls ont cela de beau qu'ils
45 mettent en lumière la fraternité des inconnus.

Un feu avait été allumé dans la cuisine et l'on y fondait dans un moule à balles brocs, cuillers, fourchettes, toute l'argenterie d'étain du cabaret. On buvait à travers tout cela. Les capsules et les chevrotines[6] traînaient pêle-
50 mêle sur les tables avec les verres de vin. Dans la salle de

---

1. **Plastronné** : vêtu d'un plastron, pièce d'habillement ou de cuirasse qui protège la poitrine.
2. **Alêne de sellier** : poinçon de fer servant à percer et coudre le cuir, utilisé par le fabricant de selles.
3. **Baïonnette** : arme pointue qui s'adapte au bout du fusil.
4. **Redingote** : manteau long (de bourgeois).
5. **Buffleterie** : ensemble des peaux de buffle qui font partie de l'équipement d'un soldat ; **giberne** : boîte à cartouches ; **garde national** : membre de la garde nationale, milice bourgeoise anti-émeute présente dans les grandes villes.
6. **Capsules :** dispositifs de mise à feu contenus dans les cartouches ; **chevrotines :** gros plomb.

billard, mame Hucheloup[1], Matelote et Gibelotte, diversement modifiées par la terreur, dont l'une était abrutie, l'autre essoufflée, l'autre éveillée, déchiraient de vieux torchons et faisaient de la charpie[2] ; trois insurgés les assistaient, trois gaillards chevelus, barbus et moustachus, qui épluchaient la toile avec des doigts de lingère et qui les faisaient trembler.

[...]

Gavroche, complètement envolé et radieux, s'était chargé de la mise en train. Il allait, venait, montait, descendait, remontait, bruissait, étincelait. Il semblait être là pour l'encouragement de tous. Avait-il un aiguillon ? oui certes, sa misère ; avait-il des ailes ? oui certes, sa joie. Gavroche était un tourbillonnement. On le voyait sans cesse, on l'entendait toujours. Il remplissait l'air, étant partout à la fois. C'était une espèce d'ubiquité[3] presque irritante ; pas d'arrêt possible avec lui. L'énorme barricade le sentait sur sa croupe. Il gênait les flâneurs, il excitait les paresseux, il ranimait les fatigués, il impatientait les pensifs, mettait les uns en gaieté, les autres en haleine, les autres en colère, tous en mouvement, piquait un étudiant, mordait un ouvrier ; se posait, s'arrêtait, repartait, volait au-dessus du tumulte et de l'effort, sautait de ceux-ci à ceux-là, murmurait, bourdonnait, et harcelait tout l'attelage ; mouche de l'immense Coche[4] révolutionnaire.

---

1. La veuve Hucheloup tient le café Corinthe, quartier général des amis de Marius. *Matelotte* et *Gibelotte* sont les serveuses.
2. **Charpie :** lambeaux de toile, préparés pour servir de pansements.
3. **Ubiquité :** faculté d'être en plusieurs lieux à la fois.
4. Allusion à la fable de La Fontaine *Le Coche et la Mouche* ; l'expression désigne celui qui s'agite beaucoup sans rendre de réels services.

[Javert, qui s'est infiltré parmi les révolutionnaires, est reconnu par Gavroche, et fait prisonnier (IV, XII, 5 à 8).

Ayant perdu Cosette, Marius veut mourir. Dans un élan suicidaire, il se dirige vers le quartier des Halles pour rejoindre ses amis. (IV, XIII.]

LIVRE QUATORZIÈME
LES GRANDEURS DU DÉSESPOIR

[Marius arrive à l'instant critique où les forces de l'ordre renversent la barricade. Il abat les deux gardes qui s'apprêtaient à tuer Courfeyrac et Gavroche. (IV, XIV, 1 à 3.)]

4. Le baril de poudre

[...]

Marius n'avait plus d'armes, il avait jeté ses pistolets déchargés, mais il avait aperçu le baril de poudre dans la salle basse près de la porte.

Comme il se tournait à demi, regardant de ce côté,
5 un soldat le coucha en joue. Au moment où le soldat ajustait Marius, une main se posa sur le bout du canon du fusil, et le boucha. C'était quelqu'un qui s'était élancé, le jeune ouvrier au pantalon de velours. Le coup partit, traversa la main, et peut-être aussi l'ouvrier, car il
10 tomba, mais la balle n'atteignit pas Marius. Tout cela dans la fumée, plutôt entrevu que vu. Marius, qui entrait dans la salle basse, s'en aperçut à peine. Cependant il avait confusément vu ce canon de fusil dirigé sur lui et cette main qui l'avait bouché, et il avait entendu le
15 coup. Mais dans des minutes comme celle-là, les choses qu'on voit vacillent et se précipitent, et l'on ne s'arrête à rien. On se sent obscurément poussé vers plus d'ombre encore, et tout est nuage.

Les insurgés, surpris, mais non effrayés, s'étaient
20 ralliés. Enjolras avait crié : Attendez ! ne tirez pas au
hasard ! Dans la première confusion en effet ils
pouvaient se blesser les uns les autres. La plupart étaient
montés à la fenêtre du premier étage et aux mansardes
d'où ils dominaient les assaillants. Les plus déterminés,
25 avec Enjolras, Courfeyrac, Jean Prouvaire et Combeferre, s'étaient fièrement adossés aux maisons du fond, à
découvert[1] et faisant face aux rangées de soldats et de
gardes qui couronnaient la barricade.

Tout cela s'accomplit sans précipitation, avec cette
30 gravité étrange et menaçante qui précède les mêlées.
Des deux parts on se couchait en joue, à bout portant,
on était si près qu'on pouvait se parler à portée de
voix. Quand on fut à ce point où l'étincelle va jaillir,
un officier en hausse-col[2] et à grosses épaulettes éten-
35 dit son épée et dit :

– Bas les armes !

– Feu ! dit Enjolras.

Les deux détonations partirent en même temps, et
tout disparut dans la fumée.

40 Fumée âcre et étouffante où se traînaient, avec des
gémissements faibles et sourds, des mourants et des
blessés.

Quand la fumée se dissipa, on vit des deux côtés les
combattants, éclaircis, mais toujours aux mêmes
45 places, qui rechargeaient les armes en silence.

Tout à coup, on entendit une voix tonnante qui
criait :

– Allez-vous-en, ou je fais sauter la barricade !

---

1. **À découvert :** exposés aux balles ennemies.
2. **Hausse-col :** petite plaque dorée, en forme de croissant, portée au-
dessous du cou par les officiers en service.

Tous se retournèrent du côté d'où venait la voix.

50 Marius était entré dans la salle basse, et y avait pris le baril de poudre, puis il avait profité de la fumée et de l'espèce de brouillard obscur qui emplissait l'enceinte retranchée, pour se glisser le long de la barricade jusqu'à cette cage de pavés où 55 était fixée la torche. En arracher la torche, y mettre le baril de poudre, pousser la pile de pavés sous le baril, qui s'était sur-le-champ défoncé, avec une sorte d'obéissance terrible, tout cela avait été pour Marius le temps de se baisser et de se relever ; 60 et maintenant tous, gardes nationaux, gardes municipaux, officiers, soldats, pelotonnés à l'autre extrémité de la barricade, le regardaient avec stupeur le pied sur les pavés, la torche à la main, son fier visage éclairé par une résolution fatale, 65 penchant la flamme de la torche vers ce monceau redoutable où l'on distinguait le baril de poudre brisé, et poussant ce cri terrifiant :

– Allez-vous-en, ou je fais sauter la barricade !

Marius sur cette barricade après l'octogénaire[1], 70 c'était la vision de la jeune révolution après l'apparition de la vieille.

– Sauter la barricade ! dit un sergent, et toi aussi !

Marius répondit :

– Et moi aussi.

75 Et il approcha la torche du baril de poudre.

Mais il n'y avait déjà plus personne sur le barrage. Les assaillants, laissant leurs morts et leurs blessés, refluaient pêle-mêle et en désordre vers l'extrémité de

---

1. Allusion au père Mabeuf, ami de Marius, mort sur la barricade en allant rechercher le drapeau rouge (IV, XIV, 2).

la rue et s'y perdaient de nouveau dans la nuit. Ce fut
80 un sauve-qui-peut.

La barricade était dégagée.

*[Marius est fêté par ses camarades. On soigne les blessés.
La situation des insurgés est très critique. (IV, XIV, 5.)]*

6. L'agonie de la mort après l'agonie de la vie

[Marius va inspecter la petite barricade de derrière.]

Marius [...] entendit son nom prononcé faiblement
dans l'obscurité :

– Monsieur Marius !

Il tressaillit, car il reconnut la voix qui l'avait appelé
5 deux heures auparavant à travers la grille de la rue
Plumet[1].

Seulement cette voix maintenant semblait n'être
plus qu'un souffle.

Il regarda autour de lui et ne vit personne.

10 Marius crut s'être trompé, et que c'était une illusion
ajoutée par son esprit aux réalités extraordinaires qui se
heurtaient autour de lui. Il fit un pas pour sortir de
l'enfoncement reculé où était la barricade.

– Monsieur Marius ! répéta la voix.

15 Cette fois il ne pouvait douter, il avait distinctement
entendu ; il regarda, et ne vit rien.

– À vos pieds, dit la voix.

---

1. Voir IV, IX, 2, p. 201. Rue Plumet, une voix ressemblant à celle
d'Éponine a averti Marius, désespéré par le déménagement de
Cosette, que ses amis l'attendent à la barricade de la rue de la
Chanvrerie.

Il se courba et vit dans l'ombre une forme qui se traînait vers lui. Cela rampait sur le pavé. C'était cela qui lui parlait.

20 Le lampion permettait de distinguer une blouse, un pantalon de gros velours déchiré, des pieds nus, et quelque chose qui ressemblait à une mare de sang. Marius entrevit une tête pâle qui se dressait vers lui et qui lui dit :

– Vous ne me reconnaissez pas ?

25 – Non.

– Éponine.

Marius se baissa vivement. C'était en effet cette malheureuse enfant. Elle était habillée en homme.

– Comment êtes-vous ici ? que faites-vous là ?

30 – Je meurs, lui dit-elle.

Il y a des mots et des incidents qui réveillent les êtres accablés. Marius s'écria comme en sursaut :

– Vous êtes blessée ! Attendez, je vais vous porter dans la salle. On va vous panser. Est-ce grave ?

35 comment faut-il vous prendre pour ne pas vous faire de mal ? où souffrez-vous ? Du secours ! mon Dieu ! Mais qu'êtes-vous venue faire ici ?

Et il essaya de passer son bras sous elle pour la soulever. En la soulevant il rencontra sa main.

40 Elle poussa un cri faible.

– Vous ai-je fait mal ? demanda Marius.

– Un peu.

– Mais je n'ai touché que votre main.

Elle leva sa main vers le regard de Marius, et Marius

45 au milieu de cette main vit un trou noir.

– Qu'avez-vous donc à la main ? dit-il.

– Elle est percée.

– Percée !

– Oui.

50 – De quoi ?

– D'une balle.

– Comment ?

– Avez-vous vu un fusil qui vous couchait en joue ?

– Oui, et une main qui l'a bouché.

55 – C'était la mienne.

Marius eut un frémissement.

– Quelle folie ! Pauvre enfant ! Mais tant mieux, si c'est cela, ce n'est rien. Laissez-moi vous porter sur un lit. On va vous panser, on ne meurt pas d'une main percée.

60 Elle murmura :

– La balle a traversé la main, mais elle est sortie par le dos. C'est inutile de m'ôter d'ici. Je vais vous dire comment vous pouvez me panser, mieux qu'un chirurgien. Asseyez-vous près de moi sur cette pierre.

65 Il obéit ; elle posa sa tête sur les genoux de Marius, et, sans le regarder, elle dit :

– Oh ! que c'est bon ! Comme on est bien ! Voilà ! Je ne souffre plus.

Elle demeura un moment en silence, puis elle 70 tourna son visage avec effort et regarda Marius.

– Savez-vous cela, monsieur Marius ? Cela me taquinait que vous entriez dans ce jardin, c'était bête, puisque c'était moi qui vous avais montré la maison, et puis enfin je devais bien me dire qu'un 75 jeune homme comme vous…

Elle s'interrompit et, franchissant les sombres transitions qui étaient sans doute dans son esprit, elle reprit avec un déchirant sourire :

– Vous me trouviez laide, n'est-ce pas ?

80 Elle continua :

– Voyez-vous, vous êtes perdu ! Maintenant personne ne sortira de la barricade. C'est moi qui vous ai amené ici, tiens ! Vous allez mourir, j'y compte bien. Et pourtant, quand j'ai vu qu'on vous visait, j'ai mis la main sur la 85 bouche du canon du fusil. Comme c'est drôle ! Mais c'est que je voulais mourir avant vous. Quand j'ai reçu cette balle, je me suis traînée ici, on ne m'a pas vue, on ne m'a

pas ramassée. Je vous attendais, je disais : Il ne viendra
donc pas ? Oh ! si vous saviez, je mordais ma blouse, je
90 souffrais tant ! Maintenant je suis bien. Vous rappelez-
vous le jour où je suis entrée dans votre chambre et où je
me suis mirée dans votre miroir[1], et le jour où je vous ai
rencontré sur le boulevard près des femmes en journée[2] ?
Comme les oiseaux chantaient ! Il n'y a pas bien long-
95 temps. Vous m'avez donné cent sous, et je vous ai dit : Je
ne veux pas de votre argent. Avez-vous ramassé votre
pièce au moins ? Vous n'êtes pas riche. Je n'ai pas pensé à
vous dire de la ramasser. Il faisait beau soleil, on n'avait
pas froid. Vous souvenez-vous, monsieur Marius ? Oh ! je
100 suis heureuse ! Tout le monde va mourir.

Elle avait un air insensé, grave et navrant[3]. Sa blouse
déchirée montrait sa gorge nue. Elle appuyait en
parlant sa main percée sur sa poitrine où il y avait un
autre trou, et d'où il sortait par instant un flot de sang
105 comme le jet de vin d'une bonde ouverte.

Marius considérait cette créature infortunée avec
une profonde compassion.

– Oh ! reprit-elle tout à coup, cela revient.
J'étouffe !

110 Elle prit sa blouse et la mordit, et ses jambes se
raidissaient sur le pavé.

En ce moment la voix de jeune coq du petit
Gavroche retentit dans la barricade. L'enfant était
monté sur une table pour charger son fusil et chantait
115 gaîment la chanson alors si populaire :

En voyant Lafayette,

1. Voir III, VIII, 4, p. 148.
2. **Femmes en journée :** femmes employées à des travaux domestiques,
payées à la journée.
3. **Navrant :** désolant, pitoyable.

Le gendarme répète :

Sauvons-nous ! sauvons-nous ! sauvons-nous !

Éponine se souleva, et écouta, puis elle murmura :

120 — C'est lui.

Et se tournant vers Marius :

— Mon frère est là. Il ne faut pas qu'il me voie. Il me gronderait.

— Votre frère ! demanda Marius qui songeait dans le
125 plus amer et le plus douloureux de son cœur aux devoirs que son père lui avait légués envers les Thénardier, qui est votre frère ?

— Ce petit.

— Celui qui chante ?

130 — Oui.

Marius fit un mouvement.

— Oh ! ne vous en allez pas ! dit-elle, cela ne sera pas long à présent !

Elle était presque sur son séant, mais sa voix était
135 très basse et coupée de hoquets. Par intervalles le râle l'interrompait. Elle approchait le plus qu'elle pouvait son visage du visage de Marius. Elle ajouta avec une expression étrange :

— Écoutez, je ne veux pas vous faire une farce. J'ai
140 dans ma poche une lettre pour vous. Depuis hier. On m'avait dit de la mettre à la poste. Je l'ai gardée. Je ne voulais pas qu'elle vous parvînt. Mais vous m'en voudriez peut-être quand nous allons nous revoir tout à l'heure. On se revoit, n'est-ce pas ? Prenez votre lettre.

145 Elle saisit convulsivement la main de Marius avec sa main trouée, mais elle semblait ne plus percevoir la souffrance. Elle mit la main de Marius dans la poche de sa blouse. Marius y sentit en effet un papier.

— Prenez, dit-elle.

150 Marius prit la lettre.

Elle fit un signe de satisfaction et de consentement.

– Maintenant, pour ma peine, promettez-moi…
Et elle s'arrêta.

– Quoi ? demanda Marius.

155 – Promettez-moi !

– Je vous promets.

– Promettez-moi de me donner un baiser sur le front quand je serai morte. – Je le sentirai.

Elle laissa retomber sa tête sur les genoux de Marius 160 et ses paupières se fermèrent. Il crut cette pauvre âme partie. Éponine restait immobile ; tout à coup, à l'instant où Marius la croyait à jamais endormie, elle ouvrit lentement ses yeux où apparaissait la sombre profondeur de la mort, et lui dit avec un accent dont la 165 douceur semblait déjà venir d'un autre monde :

– Et puis, tenez, monsieur Marius, je crois que j'étais un peu amoureuse de vous.

Elle essaya encore de sourire et expira.

[La lettre vient de Cosette, qui indique à Marius son adresse, rue de l'Homme-Armé, et l'avertit que le départ pour l'Angleterre (voir p. 201) est prévu dans huit jours. Éponine avait tout manigancé : elle avait écrit le message anonyme (« Déménagez », voir p. 201) à Jean Valjean, intercepté la lettre de Cosette et envoyé Marius sur la barricade, pour y mourir avec lui. Marius charge Gavroche de porter sa réponse à Cosette : étant sans fortune, il ne peut l'épouser, et va mourir sur la barricade (IV, XIV, 7).

Par hasard, Jean Valjean a déchiffré sur le buvard de Cosette sa lettre à Marius ; l'amoureux de Cosette lui inspire une haine violente. Dans la rue de l'Homme-Armé, Gavroche, pressé de revenir sur la barricade, confie la lettre de Marius au vieil homme.

Rentré chez lui, Valjean lit la lettre : il sait maintenant que Marius est perdu, « pris dans l'engrenage ». Il suffit de laisser s'accomplir les choses. Mais soudain, il revêt son habit de garde national, et se dirige vers la barricade. (IV, XV.)]

CARACTÈRES : Éponine et Gavroche, enfants de la rue

1. Gavroche est l'archétype du gamin de Paris, au point d'être devenu un nom commun. Quels traits de ce personnage retrouve-t-on dans son caractère et son mode de vie ?

2. Quel est le rôle d'Éponine dans le destin de Marius et de Cosette ? Dans quelle mesure son action est-elle décisive dans l'intrigue de la quatrième partie ?

3. Quels sont les éléments qui font de la mort d'Éponine un épisode particulièrement émouvant ? À quels indices le lecteur avait-il déjà pu deviner ses sentiments pour Marius ?

4. Gavroche confie à Jean Valjean la lettre destinée à Cosette. Quelles peuvent être les conséquences de ce geste ? En quoi son rôle de messager fait-il de lui le double de sa sœur ?

SOCIÉTÉ : monstruosités sociales

5. Hugo connaît les bagnes de Brest et de Toulon. Dans l'épisode de la cadène, montrez comment la captivité a déshumanisé les malheureux.

6. Sur quels points la critique de la société porte-t-elle dans cette partie ? Quels scandales l'auteur cherche-t-il à dénoncer ?

THÈMES : amour et jalousie, l'innocence perdue

7. Quelles sont les conséquences diverses de la métamorphose physique et psychologique de Cosette, sur elle-même, sur Marius, et sur Jean Valjean ?

8. Dans quelle mesure le passage de Cosette à l'âge adulte marque-t-il un tournant déterminant dans ses relations avec Jean Valjean ?

9. *Les Misérables* racontent aussi la force aliénante du passé sur les destins individuels. Ultime Fauchelevent, comme jadis M. Madeleine, est un bourgeois honorable. Pourtant, la réalité finit toujours par lui rappeler son passé de bagnard. Que représente pour lui le spectacle de la cadène ? Montrez que Jean Valjean, sous son nom d'emprunt, reste un homme traqué.

REGISTRES ET TONALITÉS : l'écriture romanesque de l'histoire

10. L'éléphant de la Bastille, maquette en plâtre d'un monument de bronze que souhaitait ériger Napoléon, a été démoli en 1846. Hugo en a alors emporté un morceau. De quel glorieux passé l'éléphant de la Bastille est-il le souvenir ? Quelle interprétation peut-on donner de son délabrement ?

11. Pourquoi Marius se jette-t-il dans le combat ? Ses motivations sont-elles purement politiques ? Que pensez-vous de l'alliance des faits historiques et de l'intrigue sentimentale ?

LIVRE PREMIER

LA GUERRE ENTRE QUATRE MURS

[Le 6 juin, la situation s'est dégradée. Les insurgés ne sont plus soutenus par les Parisiens. Leur défaite est inévitable. Enjolras décide que cinq hommes chargés de famille revêtiront les habits des gardes nationaux tués pour s'enfuir. Il manque un habit. Survient Jean Valjean, qui donne le sien. Le combat redouble de violence. On tire au canon sur les insurgés. Gavroche profite d'une accalmie pour aller faire provision de cartouches sur les soldats morts. (V, I, 1 à 14)]

15. Gavroche dehors

Courfeyrac[1] tout à coup aperçut quelqu'un au bas de la barricade, dehors dans la rue, sous les balles.

Gavroche avait pris un panier à bouteilles dans le cabaret, était sorti par la coupure[2], et était paisiblement
5 occupé à vider dans son panier les gibernes[3] pleines de cartouches des gardes nationaux[4] tués sur le talus de la redoute[5].

– Qu'est-ce que tu fais là ? dit Courfeyrac.

Gavroche leva le nez.

---

1. **Courfeyrac** est l'un des jeunes amis de Marius.
2. **Coupure** : voir IV, XII, 5 : « Une coupure suffisante pour qu'un homme y pût passer avait été ménagée entre le mur des maisons et l'extrémité de la barricade la plus éloignée du cabaret, de façon qu'une sortie était possible. »
3. **Gibernes** : boîtes à cartouches.
4. **Gardes nationaux** : membres de la garde nationale, milice bourgeoise anti-émeute présente dans les grandes villes.
5. **Redoute** : petite fortification isolée.

10 – Citoyen, j'emplis mon panier.
– Tu ne vois donc pas la mitraille ?
Gavroche répondit :
– Eh bien, il pleut. Après ?
Courfeyrac cria.
15 – Rentre !
– Tout à l'heure, fit Gavroche.
Et, d'un bond, il s'enfonça dans la rue.

On se souvient que la compagnie Fannicot, en se retirant, avait laissé derrière elle une traînée de cadavres.
20 Une vingtaine de morts gisaient çà et là dans toute la longueur de la rue sur le pavé. Une vingtaine de gibernes pour Gavroche, une provision de cartouches pour la barricade.

La fumée était dans la rue comme un brouillard.
25 Quiconque a vu un nuage tombé dans une gorge de montagnes, entre deux escarpements à pic, peut se figurer cette fumée resserrée et comme épaissie par deux sombres lignes de hautes maisons. Elle montait lentement et se renouvelait sans cesse ; de là un obs-
30 curcissement graduel qui blêmissait même le plein jour. C'est à peine si d'un bout à l'autre de la rue, pourtant fort courte, les combattants s'apercevaient.

Cet obscurcissement, probablement voulu et calculé par les chefs qui devaient diriger l'assaut de la barri-
35 cade, fut utile à Gavroche.

Sous les plis de ce voile de fumée et grâce à sa peti-tesse, il put s'avancer assez loin dans la rue sans être vu. Il dévalisa les sept ou huit premières gibernes sans grand danger.

40 Il rampait à plat ventre, galopait à quatre pattes, prenait son panier aux dents, se tordait, glissait, ondu-lait, serpentait d'un mort à l'autre, et vidait la giberne ou la cartouchière comme un singe ouvre une noix.

De la barricade, dont il était encore assez près, on
45 n'osait lui crier de revenir, de peur d'appeler l'attention sur lui.

Sur un cadavre, qui était un caporal, il trouva une
poire à poudre.

– Pour la soif, dit-il, en la mettant dans sa poche.

50 À force d'aller en avant, il parvint au point où le
brouillard de la fusillade devenait transparent.

Si bien que les tirailleurs de la ligne rangés et à
l'affût derrière leur levée de pavés, et les tirailleurs de la
banlieue massés à l'angle de la rue, se montrèrent sou-
55 dainement quelque chose qui remuait dans la fumée.

Au moment où Gavroche débarrassait de ses cartouches un sergent gisant près d'une borne, une balle
frappa le cadavre.

– Fichtre ! fit Gavroche. Voilà qu'on me tue mes
60 morts.

Une deuxième balle fit étinceler le pavé à côté de
lui. Une troisième renversa son panier.

Gavroche regarda, et vit que cela venait de la
banlieue.

65 Il se dressa tout droit, debout, les cheveux au vent, les
mains sur les hanches, l'œil fixé sur les gardes nationaux
qui tiraient, et il chanta :

> On est laid à Nantcrre,
> C'est la faute à Voltaire,
70 > Et bête à Palaiseau,
> C'est la faute à Rousseau[1].

---

1. Hugo a expliqué en III, I, 5 le mépris des gamins de Paris pour la
banlieue. Il invente ici de nouvelles paroles, sur un air et un refrain de
l'époque, écrits pour se moquer des réactionnaires attribuant tous les
maux à la Révolution et aux philosophes du XVIIIᵉ siècle, qui l'avaient
influencée.

Puis il ramassa son panier, y remit, sans en perdre une seule, les cartouches qui en étaient tombées, et, avançant vers la fusillade, alla dépouiller une autre giberne. Là une quatrième balle le manque encore. Gavroche chanta :

> Je ne suis pas notaire,
> C'est la faute à Voltaire ;
> Je suis petit oiseau,
> C'est la faute à Rousseau.

Une cinquième balle ne réussit qu'à tirer de lui un troisième couplet :

> Joie est mon caractère,
> C'est la faute à Voltaire ;
> Misère est mon trousseau,
> C'est la faute à Rousseau.

Cela continua ainsi quelque temps.

Le spectacle était épouvantable et charmant. Gavroche, fusillé, taquinait la fusillade. Il avait l'air de s'amuser beaucoup. C'était le moineau becquetant les chasseurs. Il répondait à chaque décharge par un couplet. On le visait sans cesse, on le manquait toujours. Les gardes nationaux et les soldats riaient en l'ajustant. Il se couchait, puis se redressait, s'effaçait dans un coin de porte, puis bondissait, disparaissait, reparaissait, se sauvait, revenait, ripostait à la mitraille par des pieds de nez, et cependant pillait les cartouches, vidait les gibernes et remplissait son panier. Les insurgés, haletants d'anxiété, le suivaient des yeux. La barricade tremblait ; lui, il chantait. Ce n'était pas un enfant, ce n'était pas un homme ; c'était un étrange gamin fée. On eût dit le nain invulnérable de la mêlée. Les balles couraient après lui, il était plus leste qu'elles. Il jouait on ne sait quel effrayant jeu de cache-cache avec la

105 mort ; chaque fois que la face camarde[1] du spectre
s'approchait, le gamin lui donnait une pichenette.

Une balle pourtant, mieux ajustée ou plus traître
que les autres, finit par atteindre l'enfant feu follet. On
vit Gavroche chanceler, puis il s'affaissa. Toute la barri-
110 cade poussa un cri ; mais il y avait de l'Antée[2] dans ce
pygmée ; pour le gamin toucher le pavé, c'est comme
pour le géant toucher la terre ; Gavroche n'était tombé
que pour se redresser ; il resta assis sur son séant, un
long filet de sang rayait son visage, il éleva ses deux
115 bras en l'air, regarda du côté d'où était venu le coup,
et se mit à chanter :

> Je suis tombé par terre,
> C'est la faute à Voltaire,
> Le nez dans le ruisseau,
120 > C'est la faute à…

Il n'acheva point. Une seconde balle du même
tireur l'arrêta court. Cette fois il s'abattit la face contre
le pavé, et ne remua plus. Cette petite grande âme
venait de s'envoler.

*[En allant chercher le corps de Gavroche, Marius est
blessé au front. La barricade va bientôt céder. Enjolras
ordonne qu'on exécute Javert. Jean Valjean se porte
volontaire. Il emmène l'inspecteur de police à l'écart, tire
en l'air et libère le prisonnier interloqué.*

*Un suprême assaut renverse la barricade ; les insurgés
se réfugient dans le cabaret. Marius, blessé à la clavicule,
reste dehors ; il sent qu'il s'évanouit. Une main vigoureuse*

---

1. **Camarde :** qui a le nez plat et écrasé. En langage populaire, la *camarde* signifie la « mort ».
2. **Antée :** géant de la mythologie grecque qui reprend force chaque fois qu'il s'étend sur la terre.

■ **SITUER**

Légère accalmie. Enjolras prévient ses camarades : il ne reste presque plus de munitions. Entendant cela, Gavroche descend imprudemment dans la rue pour faire provision de cartouches sur les soldats morts.

■ **RÉFLÉCHIR**

MISE EN SCÈNE : mouvement, arrêt sur image

1. Notez la fréquence des verbes. Justifiez l'effet de leur accumulation.

2. « Il se dressa […] il chanta » (l. 65-67) : analysez la syntaxe et le rythme de cette phrase. Commentez la posture du personnage.

3. Analysez l'effet produit par la longueur et le rythme des phrases du dernier paragraphe.

4. Relevez les groupements binaires, les antithèses, les paradoxes*, et commentez chacun de ces procédés.

REGISTRES ET TONALITÉS : pudeur d'une mort annoncée

5. Qu'est-ce ce qu'une « poire à poudre » ? Expliquez l'humour de la réplique : « Pour la soif » (l. 49). Quelle autre réplique de Gavroche fait également sourire ? Expliquez pourquoi.

6. Observez les vers de la chanson. Justifiez l'emploi des rimes. Quelle est la tonalité de la chanson ?

7. Quelles sont les réactions successives des spectateurs de la scène ? des lecteurs de cet épisode ?

8. Dans les deux derniers paragraphes, quel ton le narrateur emploie-t-il pour raconter la mort de Gavroche ?

PERSONNAGES : l'étrange gamin fée

9. Relevez et expliquez les comparaisons et les métaphores* appliquées à Gavroche. Laquelle était déjà présente dans la chanson ?

10. Quels traits du caractère de Gavroche connaissions-nous déjà ? Quels nouveaux traits découvrons-nous ici ?

11. Quelle est la dernière image que le lecteur retiendra de Gavroche ?

THÈMES : les idéaux révolutionnaires

12. Gavroche adapte à la situation une chanson en vogue, dont il reprend le refrain. Quel sens donnez-vous aux paroles qu'il compose ? Justifiez l'allusion à Voltaire et à Rousseau dans ce contexte.

le saisit alors. Avant de perdre connaissance, Marius a
une dernière « pensée mêlée au suprême souvenir de
Cosette : – Je suis fait prisonnier. Je serai fusillé. » *Le*
cabaret est assailli à son tour ; le combat est sanglant ;
les rares survivants se réfugient au premier étage. (V, I,
17 à 22)]

23. Oreste à jeun et Pylade ivre[1]

Enfin, se faisant la courte échelle, s'aidant du squelette
de l'escalier, grimpant aux murs, s'accrochant au plafond,
écharpant[2], au bord de la trappe même, les derniers qui
résistaient, une vingtaine d'assiégeants, soldats, gardes
5 nationaux, gardes municipaux, pêle-mêle, la plupart
défigurés par des blessures au visage dans cette ascension
redoutable, aveuglés par le sang, furieux, devenus sauvages, firent irruption dans la salle du premier étage. Il n'y
avait plus là qu'un seul homme qui fût debout, Enjolras.
10 Sans cartouches, sans épée, il n'avait plus à la main que le
canon de sa carabine dont il avait brisé la crosse sur la tête
de ceux qui entraient. Il avait mis le billard entre les
assaillants et lui ; il avait reculé à l'angle de la salle, et là,
l'œil fier, la tête haute, ce tronçon d'arme au poing, il
15 était encore assez inquiétant pour que le vide se fût fait
autour de lui. Un cri s'éleva :
— C'est le chef. C'est lui qui a tué l'artilleur.
Puisqu'il s'est mis là, il y est bien. Qu'il y reste.
Fusillons-le sur place.
20 — Fusillez-moi, dit Enjolras.

---

1. **Oreste et Pylade :** deux héros de l'Antiquité grecque dont l'amitié est
devenue légendaire.
2. **Écharper :** faire une grande blessure avec un instrument tranchant.

Et, jetant le tronçon de sa carabine, et croisant les bras, il présenta sa poitrine.

L'audace de bien mourir émeut toujours les hommes. Dès qu'Enjolras eut croisé les bras, acceptant la fin, l'assourdissement de la lutte cessa dans la salle, et ce chaos s'apaisa subitement dans une sorte de solennité sépulcrale. Il semblait que la majesté menaçante d'Enjolras désarmé et immobile pesât sur ce tumulte, et que, rien que par l'autorité de son regard tranquille, ce jeune homme, qui seul n'avait pas une blessure, superbe, sanglant, charmant, indifférent comme un invulnérable, contraignît cette cohue sinistre à le tuer avec respect. Sa beauté, en ce moment-là augmentée de sa fierté, était un resplendissement, et, comme s'il ne pouvait pas plus être fatigué que blessé, après les effrayantes vingt-quatre heures qui venaient de s'écouler, il était vermeil et rose. C'était de lui peut-être que parlait le témoin qui disait plus tard devant le conseil de guerre : « Il y avait un insurgé que j'ai entendu nommer Apollon. » Un garde national qui visait Enjolras abaissa son arme en disant : « Il me semble que je vais fusiller une fleur. »

[Enjolras est prêt à mourir. Les soldats le couchent en joue. Soudain, Grantaire, son ami, ivre-mort depuis la veille, se réveille.]

L'ivresse qui finit ressemble à un rideau qui se déchire. On voit, en bloc et d'un seul coup d'œil, tout ce qu'elle cachait. Tout s'offre subitement à la mémoire ; et l'ivrogne, qui ne sait rien de ce qui s'est passé depuis vingt-quatre heures, n'a pas achevé d'ouvrir les paupières qu'il est au fait. Les idées lui reviennent avec une lucidité brusque ; l'effacement de l'ivresse, sorte de buée qui aveuglait le cerveau, se dissipe, et fait place à la claire et nette obsession des réalités.

Relégué qu'il était dans un coin et comme abrité derrière le billard, les soldats, l'œil fixé sur Enjolras, n'avaient pas même aperçu Grantaire, et le sergent se préparait à répéter l'ordre : En joue ! quand tout à coup ils entendirent une voix forte crier à côté d'eux :

– Vive la république ! J'en suis.

Grantaire s'était levé.

L'immense lueur de tout le combat qu'il avait manqué, et dont il n'avait pas été, apparut dans le regard éclatant de l'ivrogne transfiguré.

Il répéta : Vive la république ! traversa la salle d'un pas ferme, et alla se placer devant les fusils debout près d'Enjolras.

– Faites-en deux d'un coup, dit-il.

Et, se tournant vers Enjolras avec douceur, il lui dit :

– Permets-tu ?

Enjolras lui serra la main en souriant.

Ce sourire n'était pas achevé que la détonation éclata.

Enjolras, traversé de huit coups de feu, resta adossé au mur comme si les balles l'y eussent cloué. Seulement il pencha la tête.

Grantaire, foudroyé, s'abattit à ses pieds.

Quelques instants après, les soldats délogeaient les derniers insurgés réfugiés au haut de la maison. Ils tiraillaient à travers un treillis de bois dans le grenier. On se battait dans les combles[1]. On jetait des corps par les fenêtres, quelques-uns vivants. Deux voltigeurs[2], qui essayaient de relever l'omnibus fracassé, étaient tués de deux coups de carabine tirés des mansardes. Un homme en blouse en était précipité, un coup de

---

1. **Combles :** espaces compris entre le dernier étage et le toit d'un édifice.
2. **Voltigeurs :** fantassins d'élite, très mobiles.

baïonnette dans le ventre, et râlait à terre. Un soldat et un insurgé glissaient ensemble sur le talus de tuiles du toit, et ne voulaient pas se lâcher, et tombaient, se tenant embrassés d'un embrassement féroce. Lutte pareille dans la cave. Cris, coups de feu, piétinement farouche. Puis le silence. La barricade était prise.

Les soldats commencèrent la fouille des maisons d'alentour et la poursuite des fuyards.

24. Prisonnier

Marius était prisonnier en effet. Prisonnier de Jean Valjean.

La main qui l'avait étreint par derrière au moment où il tombait, et dont, en perdant connaissance, il avait senti le saisissement, était celle de Jean Valjean.

Jean Valjean n'avait pas pris au combat d'autre part que de s'y exposer. Sans lui, à cette phase suprême de l'agonie[1], personne n'eût songé aux blessés. Grâce à lui, partout présent dans le carnage comme une providence[2], ceux qui tombaient étaient relevés, transportés dans la salle basse, et pansés. Dans les intervalles, il réparait la barricade. Mais rien qui pût ressembler à un coup, à une attaque, ou même à une défense personnelle, ne sortit de ses mains. Il se taisait et secourait. Du reste, il avait à peine quelques égratignures. Les balles n'avaient pas voulu de lui. Si le suicide faisait partie de ce qu'il avait rêvé en venant dans ce sépulcre, de ce côté-là il n'avait point réussi. Mais nous doutons qu'il eût songé au suicide, acte irréligieux.

---

1. **Agonie :** combat ultime contre la mort.
2. **Providence :** aide inespérée.

20 Jean Valjean, dans la nuée épaisse du combat, n'avait pas l'air de voir Marius ; le fait est qu'il ne le quittait pas des yeux. Quand un coup de feu renversa Marius, Jean Valjean bondit avec une agilité de tigre, s'abattit sur lui comme sur une proie, et l'emporta.

25 Le tourbillon de l'attaque était en cet instant-là si violemment concentré sur Enjolras et sur la porte du cabaret que personne ne vit Jean Valjean, soutenant dans ses bras Marius évanoui, traverser le champ dépavé de la barricade et disparaître derrière l'angle de
30 la maison de Corinthe[1].

On se rappelle cet angle qui faisait une sorte de cap dans la rue ; il garantissait des balles et de la mitraille, et des regards aussi, quelques pieds[2] carrés de terrain. Il y a ainsi parfois dans les incendies une chambre qui
35 ne brûle point, et dans les mers les plus furieuses, en deçà d'un promontoire ou au fond d'un cul-de-sac d'écueils, un petit coin tranquille. C'était dans cette espèce de repli du trapèze intérieur de la barricade qu'Éponine avait agonisé.

40 Là Jean Valjean s'arrêta, il laissa glisser à terre Marius, s'adossa au mur, et jeta les yeux autour de lui.

La situation était épouvantable.

Pour l'instant, pour deux ou trois minutes peut-être, ce pan de muraille était un abri, mais comment sortir
45 de ce massacre ? Il se rappelait l'angoisse où il s'était trouvé rue Polonceau, huit ans auparavant, et de quelle façon il était parvenu à s'échapper[3] ; c'était difficile alors, aujourd'hui c'était impossible. Il avait devant lui

---

1. Le quartier général des insurgés est le *café Corinthe*.
2. Le **pied** est une ancienne unité de mesure (0,324 m).
3. Valjean, traqué par Javert dans un labyrinthe de rues, s'était sauvé en escaladant le mur du couvent du Petit-Picpus, où il avait trouvé refuge (voir II, V, p. 135).

cette implacable et sourde maison à six étages qui ne
semblait habitée que par l'homme mort penché à sa
fenêtre ; il avait à sa droite la barricade assez basse qui
fermait la Petite-Truanderie ; enjamber cet obstacle
paraissait facile, mais on voyait au-dessus de la crête du
barrage une rangée de pointes de baïonnettes. C'était la
troupe de ligne, postée au delà de cette barricade, et
aux aguets. Il était évident que franchir la barricade
c'était aller chercher un feu de peloton[1], et que toute
tête qui se risquerait à dépasser le haut de la muraille de
pavés servirait de cible à soixante coups de fusil. Il avait
à sa gauche le champ de combat. La mort était derrière
l'angle du mur.

Que faire ?

Un oiseau seul eût pu se tirer de là.

Et il fallait se décider sur-le-champ, trouver un expé-
dient, prendre un parti. On se battait à quelques pas de
lui ; par bonheur tous s'acharnaient sur un point unique, sur la porte du cabaret ; mais qu'un soldat, un
seul, eût l'idée de tourner la maison, ou de l'attaquer
en flanc, tout était fini.

Jean Valjean regarda la maison en face de lui, il
regarda la barricade à côté de lui, puis il regarda la
terre, avec la violence de l'extrémité suprême, éperdu,
et comme s'il eût voulu y faire un trou avec ses yeux.

À force de regarder, on ne sait quoi de vaguement
saisissable dans une telle agonie se dessina et prit forme
à ses pieds, comme si c'était une puissance du regard
de faire éclore la chose demandée. Il aperçut à quelques pas de lui, au bas du petit barrage si impitoyablement gardé et guetté au dehors, sous un écroulement
de pavés qui la cachait en partie, une grille de fer posée

---

1. **Feu de peloton** : tir de soldats.

à plat et de niveau avec le sol. Cette grille, faite de forts barreaux transversaux, avait environ deux pieds carrés. L'encadrement de pavés qui la maintenait avait été arraché, et elle était comme descellée. À travers les bar-
85 reaux on entrevoyait une ouverture obscure, quelque chose de pareil au conduit d'une cheminée ou au cylindre d'une citerne. Jean Valjean s'élança. Sa vieille science des évasions lui monta au cerveau comme une clarté. Écarter les pavés, soulever la grille, charger sur
90 ses épaules Marius inerte comme un corps mort, des- cendre, avec ce fardeau sur les reins, en s'aidant des coudes et des genoux, dans cette espèce de puits heu- reusement peu profond, laisser retomber au-dessus de sa tête la lourde trappe de fer sur laquelle les pavés
95 ébranlés croulèrent de nouveau, prendre pied sur une surface dallée à trois mètres au-dessous du sol, cela fut exécuté comme ce qu'on fait dans le délire, avec une force de géant et une rapidité d'aigle ; cela dura quel- ques minutes à peine.

100 Jean Valjean se trouva avec Marius toujours évanoui, dans une sorte de long corridor souterrain.

Là, paix profonde, silence absolu, nuit.

L'impression qu'il avait autrefois éprouvée en tom- bant de la rue dans le couvent, lui revint. Seulement,
105 ce qu'il emportait aujourd'hui, ce n'était plus Cosette, c'était Marius.

C'est à peine maintenant s'il entendait au-dessus de lui comme un vague murmure, le formidable tumulte du cabaret pris d'assaut.

[...]

LIVRE TROISIÈME : LA BOUE, MAIS L'ÂME

1. Le cloaque et ses surprises

C'est dans l'égout de Paris que se trouvait Jean Valjean.

Ressemblance de plus de Paris avec la mer. Comme dans l'océan, le plongeur peut y disparaître.

La transition était inouïe. Au milieu même de la ville, Jean Valjean était sorti de la ville, et, en un clin d'œil, le temps de lever un couvercle et de le refermer, il avait passé du plein jour à l'obscurité complète, de midi à minuit, du fracas au silence, du tourbillon des tonnerres à la stagnation[1] de la tombe, et, par une péripétie bien plus prodigieuse encore que celle de la rue Polonceau, du plus extrême péril à la sécurité la plus absolue.

Chute brusque dans une cave ; disparition dans l'oubliette de Paris ; quitter cette rue où la mort était partout pour cette espèce de sépulcre où il y avait la vie, ce fut un instant étrange. Il resta quelques secondes comme étourdi ; écoutant, stupéfait. La chausse-trape[2] du salut s'était subitement ouverte sous lui. La bonté céleste l'avait en quelque sorte pris par trahison. Adorables embuscades de la providence[3] !

Seulement, le blessé ne remuait point, et Jean Valjean ne savait pas si ce qu'il emportait dans cette fosse était un vivant ou un mort.

Sa première sensation fut l'aveuglement. Brusquement, il ne vit plus rien. Il lui sembla aussi qu'en une minute

---

1. **Stagnation** : immobilité.
2. **Chausse-trape** : piège.
3. **Providence** : suprême sagesse par laquelle Dieu conduit tout.

il était devenu sourd. Il n'entendait plus rien. Le frénétique orage de meurtre qui se déchaînait à quelques
pieds au-dessus de lui n'arrivait jusqu'à lui, nous
l'avons dit, grâce à l'épaisseur de terre qui l'en séparait,
qu'éteint et indistinct, et comme une rumeur dans une
profondeur. Il sentait que c'était solide sous ses pieds ;
voilà tout ; mais cela suffisait. Il étendit un bras, puis
l'autre, et toucha le mur des deux côtés, et reconnut
que le couloir était étroit ; il glissa, et reconnut que la
dalle était mouillée. Il avança un pied avec précaution,
craignant un trou, un puisard[1], quelque gouffre ; il
constata que le dallage se prolongeait. Une bouffée de
fétidité[2] l'avertit du lieu où il était.

Au bout de quelques instants, il n'était plus aveugle.
Un peu de lumière tombait du soupirail où il s'était
glissé, et son regard s'était fait à cette cave. Il commença à distinguer quelque chose. Le couloir où il
s'était terré, nul autre mot n'exprime mieux la situation, était muré derrière lui. C'était un de ces culs-de-
sac que la langue spéciale appelle branchements.
Devant lui, il y avait un autre mur, un mur de nuit. La
clarté du soupirail expirait à dix ou douze pas du point
où était Jean Valjean, et faisait à peine une blancheur
blafarde[3] sur quelques mètres de la paroi humide de
l'égout. Au-delà, l'opacité était massive ; y pénétrer
paraissait horrible, et l'entrée y semblait un engloutis-
sement. On pouvait s'enfoncer pourtant dans cette
muraille de brume, et il le fallait. Il fallait même se
hâter. Jean Valjean songea que cette grille, aperçue par
lui sous les pavés, pouvait l'être par les soldats, et que

---

1. Puisard : espèce de puits destiné à recevoir et à écouler les eaux inutiles.
2. Fétidité : puanteur.
3. Blafarde : pâle.

tout tenait à ce hasard. Ils pouvaient descendre eux aussi dans le puits et le fouiller. Il n'y avait pas une minute à perdre. Il avait déposé Marius sur le sol, il le
60 ramassa, ceci est encore le mot vrai, le reprit sur ses épaules et se mit en marche. Il entra résolument dans cette obscurité.

La réalité est qu'ils étaient moins sauvés que Jean Valjean ne le croyait. Des périls d'un autre genre et non
65 moins grands les attendaient peut-être. Après le tourbillon fulgurant du combat, la caverne des miasmes[1] et des pièges ; après le chaos, le cloaque[2]. Jean Valjean était tombé d'un cercle de l'enfer dans l'autre.

Quand il eut fait cinquante pas, il fallut s'arrêter.
70 Une question se présenta. Le couloir aboutissait à un autre boyau qu'il rencontrait transversalement. Là s'offraient deux voies.

Laquelle prendre ? fallait-il tourner à gauche ou à droite ? Comment s'orienter dans ce labyrinthe noir ?
75 Ce labyrinthe, nous l'avons fait remarquer, a un fil ; c'est sa pente. Suivre la pente, c'est aller à la rivière.

Jean Valjean le comprit sur-le-champ.

Il se dit qu'il était probablement dans l'égout des Halles ; que, s'il choisissait la gauche et suivait la
80 pente, il arriverait avant un quart d'heure à quelque embouchure sur la Seine entre le pont au Change et le Pont-Neuf, c'est-à-dire à une apparition en plein jour sur le point le plus peuplé de Paris. Peut-être aboutirait-il à quelque cagnard[3] de carrefour. Stupeur des
85 passants de voir deux hommes sanglants sortir de terre sous leurs pieds. Survenue[4] des sergents de ville, prise

---

1. **Miasmes :** émanations transportant des maladies.
2. **Cloaque :** lieu destiné à recevoir les immondices, égout.
3. **Cagnard :** sortie d'égout.
4. **Survenue :** arrivée.

d'armes du corps de garde[1] voisin. On serait saisi avant
d'être sorti. Il valait mieux s'enfoncer dans le dédale[2],
se fier à cette noirceur, et s'en remettre à la providence
90 quant à l'issue.

Il remonta la pente et prit à droite.

*[Jean Valjean continue sa marche dans le noir, et
s'inquiète. Sortira-t-il vivant de ce labyrinthe ?]*

Tout à coup il vit son ombre devant lui. Elle se
découpait sur une faible rougeur presque indistincte
qui empourprait[3] vaguement le radier[4] à ses pieds et la
95 voûte sur sa tête, et qui glissait à sa droite et à sa gauche sur les deux murailles visqueuses du corridor. Stupéfait, il se retourna.

Derrière lui, dans la partie du couloir qu'il venait de
dépasser, à une distance qui lui parut immense, flam-
100 boyait, rayant l'épaisseur obscure, une sorte d'astre
horrible qui avait l'air de le regarder.

C'était la sombre étoile de la police qui se levait
dans l'égout.

Derrière cette étoile remuaient confusément huit ou
105 dix formes noires, droites, indistinctes, terribles.

*[Les policiers cherchent les fuyards dans les égouts.
Jean Valjean parvient à leur échapper, et poursuit sa
longue marche épuisante. Soudain, « tâtonnant dans
l'ombre », il sent son pied s'enfoncer dans la vase. (V,
III, 2 à 5.)]*

---

1. **Corps de garde :** petite troupe qui monte la garde.
2. **Dédale :** labyrinthe.
3. **Empourprait :** éclairait d'une lumière rouge.
4. **Radier :** plancher artificiel de l'égout.

6. Le fontis

Jean Valjean se trouvait en présence d'un fontis.

Ce genre d'écroulement était alors fréquent dans le sous-sol des Champs-Élysées, difficilement maniable aux travaux hydrauliques et peu conservateur des constructions
5 souterraines à cause de son excessive fluidité. Cette fluidité dépasse l'inconsistance des sables même du quartier Saint-Georges, qui n'ont pu être vaincus que par un enrochement sur béton, et des couches glaiseuses infectées de gaz du quartier des Martyrs, si liquides que le passage n'a pu
10 être pratiqué sous la galerie des Martyrs qu'au moyen d'un tuyau en fonte. Lorsqu'en 1836 on a démoli sous le faubourg Saint-Honoré, pour le reconstruire, le vieil égout en pierre où nous voyons en ce moment Jean Valjean engagé, le sable mouvant, qui est le sous-sol des Champs-Élysées
15 jusqu'à la Seine, fit obstacle, au point que l'opération dura près de six mois, au grand récri[1] des riverains, surtout des riverains à hôtels et à carrosses. Les travaux furent plus que malaisés ; ils furent dangereux. Il est vrai qu'il y eut quatre mois et demi de pluies et trois crues de la Seine.
20 Le fontis que Jean Valjean rencontrait avait pour cause l'averse de la veille. Un fléchissement du pavé mal soutenu par le sable sous-jacent avait produit un engorgement d'eau pluviale. L'infiltration s'étant faite, l'effondrement avait suivi. Le radier, disloqué, s'était affaissé dans la vase.
25 Sur quelle longueur ? Impossible de le dire. L'obscurité était là plus épaisse que partout ailleurs. C'était un trou de boue dans une caverne de nuit.

Jean Valjean sentit le pavé se dérober sous lui. Il entra dans cette fange. C'était de l'eau à la surface, de
30 la vase au fond. Il fallait bien passer. Revenir sur ses pas

---

1. **Récri :** protestation.

était impossible. Marius était expirant et Jean Valjean
exténué. Où aller d'ailleurs ? Jean Valjean avança. Du
reste la fondrière[1] parut peu profonde aux premiers
pas. Mais à mesure qu'il avançait, ses pieds
35 plongeaient. Il eut bientôt de la vase jusqu'à mi-jambe
et de l'eau plus haut que les genoux. Il marchait,
exhaussant[2] de ses deux bras Marius le plus qu'il pouvait au-dessus de l'eau. La vase lui venait maintenant
aux jarrets et l'eau à la ceinture. Il ne pouvait déjà plus
40 reculer. Il enfonçait de plus en plus. Cette vase, assez
dense pour le poids d'un homme, ne pouvait évidemment en porter deux. Marius et Jean Valjean eussent
eu chance de s'en tirer isolément. Jean Valjean continua d'avancer, soutenant ce mourant qui était un cada-
45 vre peut-être.

L'eau lui venait aux aisselles ; il se sentait sombrer ;
c'est à peine s'il pouvait se mouvoir dans la profondeur
de bourbe où il était. La densité, qui était le soutien,
était aussi l'obstacle. Il soulevait toujours Marius, et,
50 avec une dépense de force inouïe, il avançait ; mais il
enfonçait. Il n'avait plus que la tête hors de l'eau, et ses
deux bras élevant Marius. Il y a, dans les vieilles pein-
tures du déluge[3], une mère qui fait ainsi de son enfant.

Il enfonça encore, il renversa sa face en arrière pour
55 échapper à l'eau et pouvoir respirer ; qui l'eût vu dans
cette obscurité eût cru voir un masque flottant sur de
l'ombre ; il apercevait vaguement au-dessus de lui la
tête pendante et le visage livide[4] de Marius ; il fit un

---

1. **Fondrière** : trou produit par un affaissement où les eaux bourbeuses
s'amassent.
2. **Exhaussant** : soulevant.
3. **Déluge** : épisode de la Bible où Dieu envoie sur la Terre des pluies
torrentielles pendant quarante jours et quarante nuits.
4. **Livide** : blanc, très pâle.

effort désespéré, et lança son pied en avant ; son pied
60 heurta on ne sait quoi de solide, un point d'appui. Il
était temps.

Il se dressa et se tordit et s'enracina avec une sorte
de furie sur ce point d'appui. Cela lui fit l'effet de la
première marche d'un escalier remontant à la vie.

65 Ce point d'appui, rencontré dans la vase au moment
suprême, était le commencement de l'autre versant du
radier, qui avait plié sans se briser et s'était courbé sous
l'eau comme une planche et d'un seul morceau. Les
pavages bien construits font voûte et ont de ces ferme-
70 tés-là. Ce fragment du radier, submergé en partie, mais
solide, était une véritable rampe, et, une fois sur cette
rampe, on était sauvé. Jean Valjean remonta ce plan
incliné et arriva de l'autre côté de la fondrière.

En sortant de l'eau, il se heurta à une pierre et
75 tomba sur les genoux. Il trouva que c'était juste, et y
resta quelque temps, l'âme abîmée[1] dans on ne sait
quelle parole à Dieu.

Il se redressa, frissonnant, glacé, infect[2], courbé sous
ce mourant qu'il traînait, tout ruisselant de fange[3],
80 l'âme pleine d'une étrange clarté.

[Jean Valjean poursuit son chemin, et finit par arri-
ver à une sortie. Il reprend espoir, mais la grille est fer-
mée. Soudain, dans l'ombre, il se retrouve face à face
avec Thénardier, qui ne le reconnaît pas, tant son visage
est sale. Croyant qu'il a affaire à un meurtrier qui
s'apprête à dépouiller sa victime, Thénardier propose de
lui ouvrir la grille contre une part du butin : « – Tu as

---

1. **Abîmée :** absorbée, plongée, perdue.
2. **Infect :** sale, immonde, souillé.
3. **Fange :** boue.

▄ SITUER

Après la chute de la barricade, Jean Valjean a sauvé Marius d'une mort certaine. Pour échapper aux soldats, l'ancien forçat, portant Marius inconscient sur ses épaules, s'est engouffré dans les égouts. Jean Valjean s'épuise dans le labyrinthe humide. Soudain, le sol se dérobe sous ses pieds : les deux hommes vont-ils être engloutis ?

▄ RÉFLÉCHIR

STRUCTURE : la force de la volonté

1. Dégagez la structure du passage en observant les indices temporels et l'alternance des temps du récit.

2. À quels champs lexicaux* appartiennent les verbes ayant pour sujet le personnage de Jean Valjean ? Que traduisent-ils ?

3. Analysez l'impression produite par la ponctuation et la longueur des phrases dans le premier paragraphe.

4. Commentez le rythme et la construction syntaxique de la dernière phrase.

THÈMES : la passion de Jean Valjean

5. Relevez les champs lexicaux de l'horizontalité et de la verticalité. Sur un schéma retraçant l'avancée de Valjean, figurez ses postures successives. Lesquelles vous semblent les plus significatives ?

6. Quels sont les éléments qui rapprochent cet épisode d'une descente au tombeau ?

7. Montrez comment l'instinct de survie de Jean Valjean l'emporte sur la tentation d'abandonner la lutte.

8. Dans quels épisodes Jean Valjean était-il déjà tombé à genoux ? Quelle est la signification de cette attitude ?

9. Quelle est la signification symbolique de la boue dans ce passage ? D'où vient l'« étrange clarté » (l. 80) qui remplit l'âme de Jean Valjean ? Interprétez l'opposition entre la descente dans la boue et la remontée vers la clarté.

▄ ÉCRIRE

Imaginez le monologue intérieur de Jean Valjean portant sur son dos le corps de Marius. Vous mettrez en valeur la complexité de ses sentiments.

tué l'homme ; c'est bien. Moi, j'ai la clef. » *Jean Valjean le paye avec le peu d'argent qu'il a sur lui et sort de l'égout. (V, III, 7 et 8)]*

9. Marius fait l'effet d'être mort à quelqu'un qui s'y connaît

[Jean Valjean profite enfin de l'air libre. Il asperge le visage de Marius, qui respire encore.]

Jean Valjean allait plonger de nouveau sa main dans la rivière, quand tout à coup il sentit je ne sais quelle gêne, comme lorsqu'on a, sans le voir, quelqu'un derrière soi.

5 Nous avons déjà indiqué ailleurs cette impression, que tout le monde connaît.

Il se retourna.

Comme tout à l'heure, quelqu'un en effet était derrière lui.

Un homme de haute stature, enveloppé d'une longue redingote, les bras croisés, et portant dans son 10 poing droit un casse-tête[1] dont on voyait la pomme de plomb, se tenait debout à quelques pas en arrière de Jean Valjean accroupi sur Marius.

C'était, l'ombre aidant, une sorte d'apparition. Un homme simple en eût eu peur à cause du crépuscule, et 15 un homme réfléchi à cause du casse-tête.

Jean Valjean reconnut Javert.

[C'est Thénardier, poursuivi par Javert, qui a livré le fuyard en pâture au policier. Celui-ci empoigne Jean Valjean.]

---

1. **Casse-tête :** petit bâton très court, plombé à l'une de ses extrémités.

Jean Valjean demeura inerte sous l'étreinte de Javert comme un lion qui consentirait à la griffe d'un lynx.

20 – Inspecteur Javert, dit-il, vous me tenez. D'ailleurs, depuis ce matin je me considère comme votre prisonnier. Je ne vous ai point donné mon adresse pour chercher à vous échapper. Prenez-moi. Seulement, accordez-moi une chose.

25 – Que faites-vous là ? et qu'est-ce que c'est que cet homme ?

Il continuait de ne plus tutoyer Jean Valjean.

Jean Valjean répondit, et le son de sa voix parut réveiller Javert :

30 – C'est de lui précisément que je voulais vous parler. Disposez de moi comme il vous plaira ; mais aidez-moi à le rapporter chez lui. Je ne vous demande que cela.

[Jean Valjean trouve dans le portefeuille de Marius l'adresse de son grand-père. Accompagné de Javert, il dépose le corps de Marius évanoui chez M. Gillenormand. Il obtient du policier l'autorisation de passer chez lui avant d'être emmené. Javert laisse l'ancien forçat monter seul. Il l'attendra dehors, en bas de l'immeuble. Tandis qu'il monte l'escalier, Jean Valjean jette un coup d'œil par la fenêtre. Javert a disparu. (V, III, 10 et 11)]

LIVRE QUATRIÈME : JAVERT DÉRAILLÉ

Javert déraillé

*[Javert a volontairement laissé s'échapper son prison-
nier. Il se dirige vers la Seine, l'esprit troublé.]*

Sa situation était inexprimable.

Devoir la vie à un malfaiteur, accepter cette dette et
la rembourser, être, en dépit de soi-même, de plain-
pied[1] avec un repris de justice, et lui payer un service
5 avec un autre service, se laisser dire : Va-t'en, et lui dire
à son tour : Sois libre ; sacrifier à des motifs personnels
le devoir, cette obligation générale, et sentir dans ces
motifs personnels quelque chose de général aussi, et de
supérieur peut-être ; trahir la société pour rester fidèle
10 à sa conscience ; que toutes ces absurdités se réalisas-
sent et qu'elles vinssent s'accumuler sur lui-même,
c'est ce dont il était atterré[2].

Une chose l'avait étonné, c'était que Jean Valjean lui
eût fait grâce, et une chose l'avait pétrifié, c'était que,
15 lui Javert, il eût fait grâce à Jean Valjean.

Où en était-il ? Il se cherchait et ne se trouvait plus.

Que faire maintenant ? Livrer Jean Valjean, c'était
mal ; laisser Jean Valjean libre, c'était mal. Dans le premier cas, l'homme de l'autorité tombait plus bas que
20 l'homme du bagne ; dans le second, un forçat montait
plus haut que la loi et mettait le pied dessus. Dans les
deux cas, déshonneur pour lui Javert. Dans tous les
partis qu'on pouvait prendre, il y avait de la chute. La
destinée a de certaines extrémités à pic sur l'impossible

---

1. **De plain-pied :** au même niveau.
2. **Atterré :** étonné, abattu, stupéfait.

25 et au delà desquelles la vie n'est plus qu'un précipice. Javert était à une de ces extrémités-là.

Une de ses anxiétés, c'était d'être contraint de penser. La violence même de toutes ces émotions contradictoires l'y obligeait. La pensée, chose inusitée pour lui, 30 et singulièrement douloureuse.

Ce qu'il venait de faire lui donnait le frisson. Il avait, lui Javert, trouvé bon de décider, contre tous les règlements de police, contre toute l'organisation sociale et judiciaire, contre le code[1] tout entier, une mise en 35 liberté ; cela lui avait convenu ; il avait substitué ses propres affaires aux affaires publiques ; n'était-ce pas inqualifiable ? Chaque fois qu'il se mettait en face de cette action sans nom qu'il avait commise, il tremblait de la tête aux pieds. À quoi se résoudre ? Une seule 40 ressource lui restait : retourner en hâte rue de l'Homme-Armé[2], et faire écrouer[3] Jean Valjean. Il était clair que c'était cela qu'il fallait faire. Il ne pouvait.

Quelque chose lui barrait le chemin de ce côté-là.

Quelque chose ? Quoi ? Est-ce qu'il y a au monde 45 autre chose que les tribunaux, les sentences exécutoires[4], la police et l'autorité ? Javert était bouleversé.

Un galérien sacré ! un forçat imprenable à la justice ! et cela par le fait de Javert !

Que Javert et Jean Valjean, l'homme fait pour sévir, 50 l'homme fait pour subir, que ces deux hommes, qui étaient l'un et l'autre la chose de la loi, en fussent venus à ce point de se mettre tous les deux au-dessus de la loi, est-ce que ce n'était pas effrayant ?

---

1. **Le code :** ensemble des lois.
2. Jean Valjean habite rue de l'Homme-Armé.
3. **Écrouer :** emprisonner.
4. **Sentences exécutoires :** jugements qui doivent être mis à exécution.

Quoi donc ! de telles énormités arriveraient et per-
55 sonne ne serait puni ! Jean Valjean, plus fort que
l'ordre social tout entier, serait libre, et lui Javert con-
tinuerait de manger le pain du gouvernement !

Sa rêverie devenait peu à peu terrible.

Il eût pu à travers cette rêverie se faire encore
60 quelque reproche au sujet de l'insurgé rapporté rue
des Filles-du-Calvaire[1] ; mais il n'y songeait pas. La faute
moindre se perdait dans la plus grande. D'ailleurs cet
insurgé était évidemment un homme mort, et, légalement, la mort éteint la poursuite.

65 Jean Valjean, c'était là le poids qu'il avait sur l'esprit.

Jean Valjean le déconcertait. Tous les axiomes[2] qui
avaient été les points d'appui de toute sa vie s'écrou-
laient devant cet homme. La générosité de Jean Valjean
envers lui Javert l'accablait. D'autres faits, qu'il se rap-
70 pelait et qu'il avait autrefois traités de mensonges et de
folies, lui revenaient maintenant comme des réalités.
M. Madeleine reparaissait derrière Jean Valjean, et les
deux figures se superposaient de façon à n'en plus faire
qu'une, qui était vénérable. Javert sentait que quelque
75 chose d'horrible pénétrait dans son âme, l'admiration
pour un forçat. Le respect d'un galérien, est-ce que
c'est possible ? Il en frémissait, et ne pouvait s'y soustraire. Il avait beau se débattre, il était réduit à confesser
dans son for intérieur la sublimité[3] de ce misérable.
80 Cela était odieux.

Un malfaiteur bienfaisant, un forçat compatissant[4],
doux, secourable, clément[5], rendant le bien pour le

---

1. **Rue des Filles-du-Calvaire :** adresse du grand-père de Marius, chez qui Javert et Jean Valjean ont ramené le jeune homme.
2. **Axiome :** vérité évidente et non démontrable.
3. **Sublimité :** caractère de ce qui mérite l'admiration et le respect.
4. **Compatissant :** sensible, charitable.
5. **Clément :** indulgent.

Javert, après avoir arrêté le forçat qu'il poursuivait depuis tant d'années, vient de le laisser échapper volontairement. Bouleversé, il cherche à comprendre son geste. Y aurait-il des valeurs supérieures à la loi ? Toutes ses certitudes s'effondrent.

STRUCTURE : l'idée fixe

1. Repérez les signes de ponctuation qui expriment le désarroi de Javert. Quelles émotions variées traduisent-ils ?

2. Certaines phrases sont particulièrement courtes. Lesquelles ? Certains paragraphes sont constitués d'une seule phrase. Lesquels ? Quelle impression ce morcellement produit-il ?

3. Expliquez les antithèses et les oxymores* des deux derniers paragraphes. En quoi Jean Valjean, pour Javert, est-il un « monstre » (l. 88) ?

4. Quelles expressions traduisent l'impossibilité où se trouve Javert de formuler une réponse à ses interrogations ?

CARACTÈRES : drame de conscience

5. À quelles lois contraires Javert est-il contraint d'obéir ?

6. Étudiez le portrait de Valjean par Javert : est-ce celui d'un ennemi ?

7. Analysez les raisons profondes du bouleversement que ressent Javert. Ne poursuivait-il pas Jean Valjean pour les mêmes raisons ?

8. Comment le lecteur percevait-il Javert jusqu'à présent ? Quelle dimension nouvelle le personnage prend-il dans ce chapitre ?

THÈMES : le hors-la-loi sublime

9. Dans quelle mesure peut-on dire que Jean Valjean et Javert se sont mis « tous les deux au-dessus de la loi » (l. 52-53) ?

10. Quel rapprochement peut-on faire entre le cas de conscience de Javert et le procès que Valjean fait de lui-même et de la société (I, II, 7, p. 45). Quels sont les enjeux idéologiques de l'alternative entre sauver et punir ?

11. Une lettre testament : avant de mettre fin à ses jours. Javert écrit à Jean Valjean une lettre expliquant pourquoi il lui a rendu sa liberté.

mal, rendant le pardon pour la haine, préférant la pitié
à la vengeance, aimant mieux se perdre que de perdre
85 son ennemi, sauvant celui qui l'a frappé, agenouillé sur
le haut de la vertu, plus voisin de l'ange que de
l'homme ! Javert était contraint de s'avouer que ce
monstre existait.

Cela ne pouvait durer ainsi.

90 Sa suprême angoisse, c'était la disparition de la certitude. Il se sentait déraciné. Le code n'était plus qu'un
tronçon dans sa main. Il avait affaire à des scrupules
d'une espèce inconnue. Il se faisait en lui une révélation
sentimentale entièrement distincte de l'affirmation
95 légale, son unique mesure jusqu'alors. Rester dans
l'ancienne honnêteté, cela ne suffisait plus. Tout un
ordre de faits inattendus surgissait et le subjuguait[1].
Tout un monde nouveau apparaissait à son âme, le bienfait accepté et rendu, le dévouement, la miséricorde[2],
100 l'indulgence, les violences faites par la pitié à l'austérité[3],
l'acception de personnes[4], plus de condamnation définitive, plus de damnation, la possibilité d'une larme
dans l'œil de la loi, on ne sait quelle justice selon Dieu
allant en sens inverse de la justice selon les hommes. Il
105 apercevait dans les ténèbres l'effrayant lever d'un soleil
moral inconnu ; il en avait l'horreur et l'éblouissement.
Hibou forcé à des regards d'aigle.

Il se disait que c'était donc vrai, qu'il y avait des
exceptions, que l'autorité pouvait être décontenancée,
110 que la règle pouvait rester court devant un fait, que tout
ne s'encadrait pas dans le texte du code, que l'imprévu
se faisait obéir, que la vertu d'un forçat pouvait tendre

---

1. **Subjuguait** : dominait.
2. **Miséricorde** : clémence, pardon, pitié.
3. **Austérité** : rigueur, dureté.
4. **Acception de personnes** : fait de prendre en compte les individus.

un piège à la vertu d'un fonctionnaire, que le monstrueux pouvait être divin, que la destinée avait de ces
115 embuscades-là, et il songeait avec désespoir que lui-
même n'avait pas été à l'abri d'une surprise.

Il était forcé de reconnaître que la bonté existait. Ce
forçat avait été bon. Et lui-même, chose inouïe, il
venait d'être bon. Donc il se dépravait[1].
120 Il se trouvait lâche. Il se faisait horreur.

L'idéal pour Javert, ce n'était pas d'être humain, d'être
grand, d'être sublime ; c'était d'être irréprochable.

Or il venait de faillir.

Comment en était-il arrivé là ? comment tout cela
125 s'était-il passé ? Il n'aurait pu se le dire à lui-même. Il
prenait sa tête dans ses deux mains, mais il avait beau
faire, il ne parvenait pas à se l'expliquer.

Il avait certainement toujours eu l'intention de
remettre Jean Valjean à la loi dont Jean Valjean était le
130 captif, et dont lui, Javert, était l'esclave. Il ne s'était pas
avoué un seul instant pendant qu'il le tenait qu'il eût la
pensée de le laisser aller. C'était en quelque sorte à son
insu que sa main s'était ouverte et l'avait lâché.

*[Le doute envahit Javert. Ses valeurs, sa vision du
monde, tout s'écroule.]*

Ainsi, – et dans le grossissement de l'angoisse, et
135 dans l'illusion d'optique de la consternation, tout ce
qui eût pu restreindre et corriger son impression
s'effaçait, et la société, et le genre humain, et l'univers
se résumaient désormais à ses yeux dans un linéament[2]
simple et terrible, – ainsi la pénalité, la chose jugée, la

---

1. **Se dépravait :** se dégradait moralement.
2. **Linéament :** ligne.

140 force due à la législation, les arrêts des cours sou-
veraines, la magistrature, le gouvernement, la prévention et la répression, la sagesse officielle, l'infaillibilité
légale[1], le principe d'autorité[2], tous les dogmes[3] sur
lesquels repose la sécurité politique et civile, la sou-
145 veraineté[4], la justice, la logique découlant du code,
l'absolu social, la vérité publique, tout cela, décombre,
monceau, chaos ; lui-même Javert, le guetteur de
l'ordre, l'incorruptibilité au service de la police, la
providence-dogue de la société, vaincu et terrassé ; et
150 sur toute cette ruine un homme debout, le bonnet
vert[5] sur la tête et l'auréole au front ; voilà à quel bouleversement il en était venu ; voilà la vision effroyable
qu'il avait dans l'âme.

Que cela fût supportable. Non.

155 État violent, s'il en fut. Il n'y avait que deux manières d'en sortir. L'une d'aller résolument à Jean Valjean,
et de rendre au cachot l'homme du bagne. L'autre...
[...]

L'obscurité était complète. C'était le moment sépul-
160 cral qui suit minuit. Un plafond de nuages cachait les
étoiles. Le ciel n'était qu'une épaisseur sinistre. Les maisons de la Cité n'avaient plus une seule lumière ; personne ne passait ; tout ce qu'on apercevait des rues et des
quais était désert ; Notre-Dame et les tours du Palais de
165 justice semblaient des linéaments de la nuit. Un réverbère
rougissait la margelle du quai. Les silhouettes des ponts
se déformaient dans la brume les unes derrière les autres.
Les pluies avaient grossi la rivière.

---

1. **Infaillibilité légale :** impossibilité pour la loi de se tromper.
2. **Principe d'autorité :** obligation d'obéir à une autorité supérieure.
3. **Dogmes :** doctrines considérées comme des vérités incontestables.
4. **Souveraineté :** autorité suprême.
5. Les forçats condamnés « à temps » portaient une casaque et un bonnet verts.

L'endroit où Javert s'était accoudé était, on s'en
170 souvient, précisément situé au-dessus du rapide de la
Seine, à pic sur cette redoutable spirale de tourbillons
qui se dénoue et se renoue comme une vis sans fin.

Javert pencha la tête et regarda. Tout était noir. On
ne distinguait rien. On entendait un bruit d'écume ;
175 mais on ne voyait pas la rivière. Par instants, dans cette
profondeur vertigineuse, une lueur apparaissait et serpentait vaguement, l'eau ayant cette puissance, dans la
nuit la plus complète, de prendre la lumière on ne sait
où et de la changer en couleuvre. La lueur s'évanouissait,
180 et tout redevenait indistinct. L'immensité semblait
ouverte là. Ce qu'on avait au-dessous de soi, ce n'était
pas de l'eau, c'était du gouffre. Le mur du quai,
abrupt, confus, mêlé à la vapeur, tout de suite dérobé,
faisait l'effet d'un escarpement de l'infini.

185 On ne voyait rien, mais on sentait la froideur hostile
de l'eau et l'odeur fade des pierres mouillées. Un souffle farouche montait de cet abîme. Le grossissement du
fleuve plutôt deviné qu'aperçu, le tragique chucho-
tement du flot, l'énormité lugubre des arches du pont,
190 la chute imaginable dans ce vide sombre, toute cette
ombre était pleine d'horreur.

Javert demeura quelques minutes immobile, regardant cette ouverture de ténèbres ; il considérait l'invisible
avec une fixité qui ressemblait à de l'attention. L'eau
195 bruissait. Tout à coup, il ôta son chapeau et le posa sur
le rebord du quai. Un moment après, une figure haute
et noire, que de loin quelque passant attardé eût pu
prendre pour un fantôme, apparut debout sur le parapet,
se courba vers la Seine, puis se redressa, et tomba droite
200 dans les ténèbres ; il y eut un clapotement sourd ; et
l'ombre seule fut dans le secret des convulsions de cette
forme obscure disparue sous l'eau.

[Marius, gravement blessé, reste longtemps entre la vie et la mort, veillé affectueusement par son grand-père. Un monsieur aux cheveux blancs vient régulièrement demander de ses nouvelles et apporter des pansements préparés par Cosette.

M. Gillenormand accepte le mariage de son petit-fils avec Mlle Fauchelevent. Jean Valjean est allé chercher sa fortune enterrée dans le bois de Montfermeil. Il garde cinq cents francs pour lui, et remet à Cosette une dot considérable de près de six cent mille francs.

Marius donnerait tout pour retrouver son sauveur. Mais Jean Valjean observe la plus grande discrétion à ce sujet et ne se fait pas connaître (V, V).]

LIVRE SIXIÈME : LA NUIT BLANCHE

[Dans la maison Gillenormand, où habiteront les mariés, une chambre a été préparée pour M. Fauchelevent. Cosette le supplie de venir habiter avec eux. Le mariage a lieu le jour de Mardi gras. Le cortège croise le carnaval. M. Fauchelevent, blessé quelques jours plus tôt, a le bras en écharpe, et ne peut signer. M. Gillenormand signe pour lui. (V, VI, 1)]

2. Jean Valjean a toujours son bras en écharpe

[Cosette et Marius sont radieux. Au retour de l'église, le repas de noces est prêt chez M. Gillenormand.]

Cosette n'avait jamais été plus tendre avec Jean Valjean. Elle était à l'unisson[1] du père Gillenormand ; pendant qu'il érigeait la joie en aphorismes[2] et en

---

1. **Unisson :** ici, entente des âmes, communauté de sentiments.
2. **Aphorismes :** sentences.

maximes, elle exhalait l'amour et la bonté comme un
5 parfum. Le bonheur veut tout le monde heureux.

Elle retrouvait, pour parler à Jean Valjean, des
inflexions de voix du temps qu'elle était petite fille.
Elle le caressait du sourire.

Un banquet avait été dressé dans la salle à manger.

10 Un éclairage *a giorno*[1] est l'assaisonnement nécessaire
d'une grande joie. La brume et l'obscurité ne sont point
acceptées par les heureux. Ils ne consentent pas à être
noirs. La nuit, oui ; les ténèbres, non. Si l'on n'a pas de
soleil, il faut en faire un.

15 La salle à manger était une fournaise de choses gaies.
Au centre, au-dessus de la table blanche et éclatante, un
lustre de Venise à lames plates, avec toutes sortes
d'oiseaux de couleur, bleus, violets, rouges, verts, per
chés au milieu des bougies ; autour du lustre des giran-
20 doles[2], sur le mur des miroirs-appliques à triples et
quintuples branches ; glaces, cristaux, verreries,
vaisselles, porcelaines, faïences, poteries, orfèvreries,
argenteries, tout étincelait et se réjouissait. Les vides
entre les candélabres[3] étaient comblés par les bouquets,
25 en sorte que, là où il n'y avait pas une lumière, il y avait
une fleur.

Dans l'antichambre trois violons et une flûte
jouaient en sourdine des quatuors de Haydn[4].

Jean Valjean s'était assis sur une chaise dans le salon,
30 derrière la porte, dont le battant se repliait sur lui de
façon à le cacher presque. Quelques instants avant
qu'on se mît à table, Cosette vint, comme par coup de

---

1. **Éclairage a giorno** (de l'italien) : éclairage très brillant, comme « en
plein jour ».
2. **Girandoles :** guirlandes.
3. **Candélabres :** grands chandeliers.
4. **Haydn :** compositeur autrichien du XVIIIe siècle.

tête, lui faire une grande révérence en étalant de ses deux mains sa toilette de mariée, et, avec un regard
35 tendrement espiègle, elle lui demanda :

– Père, êtes-vous content ?

– Oui, dit Jean Valjean, je suis content.

– Eh bien, riez alors.

Jean Valjean se mit à rire.

40 Quelques instants après, Basque[1] annonça que le dîner était servi.

Les convives, précédés de M. Gillenormand donnant le bras à Cosette, entrèrent dans la salle à manger, et se répandirent, selon l'ordre voulu, autour de la
45 table.

Deux grands fauteuils y figuraient, à droite et à gauche de la mariée, le premier pour M. Gillenormand, le second pour Jean Valjean. M. Gillenormand s'assit. L'autre fauteuil resta vide.

50 On chercha des yeux « monsieur Fauchelevent ».

Il n'était plus là.

M. Gillenormand interpella Basque.

– Sais-tu où est monsieur Fauchelevent ?

– Monsieur, répondit Basque, précisément. Mon-
55 sieur Fauchelevent m'a dit de dire à monsieur qu'il souffrait un peu de sa main malade, et qu'il ne pourrait dîner avec monsieur le baron et madame la baronne[2]. Qu'il priait qu'on l'excusât, qu'il viendrait demain matin. Il vient de sortir.

60 Ce fauteuil vide refroidit un moment l'effusion du repas de noces. Mais, M. Fauchelevent absent, M. Gillenormand était là, et le grand-père rayonnait pour deux. Il affirma que M. Fauchelevent faisait bien de se

---

1. **Basque** est le serviteur de M. Gillenormand.
2. Marius a repris le titre de son père, anobli sur le champ de bataille.

SITUER

Repas de noces chez M. Gillenormand. La gaieté est de mise. Cosette rayonne de bonheur. Au moment de passer à table, on remarque l'absence de M. Fauchelevent. Mais la fête continue.

RÉFLÉCHIR

THÈMES : L'envers du décor

1. Que cachent les excès de tendresse de Cosette envers son « père » ? Comment comprenez-vous la réponse et le rire de Jean Valjean ?

2. Quelles sont les caractéristiques du décor ? Est-il gai ou surchargé ? Quel effet les énumérations produisent-elles ?

3. Marius vient occuper le fauteuil laissé vide par Jean Valjean. Quelle est la signification symbolique de ce geste ?

4. Jean Valjean fait-il partie de la nouvelle famille formée par l'union de Marius et Cosette ? Pourquoi s'efface-t-il volontairement ?

QUI PARLE ? QUI VOIT ? Le père présent-absent.

5. Sur quel mode les paroles de Jean Valjean sont-elles rapportées* par Basque ? Quelle est l'impression produite ?

6. Pourquoi le narrateur fait-il alterner les noms de Jean Valjean et de M. Fauchelevent ?

PERSONNAGES : la solitude de Jean Valjean

7. Lors de sa première apparition dans le roman, Jean Valjean était caché par sa casquette. Au début de cette scène, il est installé derrière le battant de la porte. Que suggère cette position ?

8. Montrez que la souffrance de Jean Valjean est à la fois celle du père et celle de l'exclu.

9. Comment jugez-vous l'attitude de Cosette et de Marius après le départ de Jean Valjean ?

10. Hugo a perdu deux fois sa fille Léopoldine : le jour de son mariage, et le jour de sa mort (par noyade) survenue peu après. Dans quelle mesure ce passage est-il autobiographique ?

coucher de bonne heure, s'il souffrait, mais que ce
65 n'était qu'un « bobo ». Cette déclaration suffit.
D'ailleurs, qu'est-ce qu'un coin obscur dans une telle
submersion de joie ? Cosette et Marius étaient dans un
de ces moments égoïstes et bénis où l'on n'a pas d'autre
faculté que de percevoir le bonheur. Et puis, M. Gille-
70 normand eut une idée. – Pardieu, ce fauteuil est vide.
Viens-y, Marius. Ta tante, quoiqu'elle ait droit à toi, te
le permettra. Ce fauteuil est pour toi. C'est légal, et
c'est gentil. Fortunatus près de Fortunata[1]. – Applau-
dissement de toute la table. Marius prit près de
75 Cosette la place de Jean Valjean ; et les choses s'arran-
gèrent de telle sorte que Cosette, d'abord triste de
l'absence de Jean Valjean, finit par en être contente.
Du moment où Marius était le remplaçant, Cosette
n'eût pas regretté Dieu. Elle mit son doux petit pied
80 chaussé de satin blanc sur le pied de Marius.

Le fauteuil occupé, M. Fauchelevent fut effacé ; et
rien ne manqua. Et, cinq minutes après, la table entière
riait d'un bout à l'autre avec toute la verve[2] de l'oubli.

[...]

3. L'inséparable

Qu'était devenu Jean Valjean ?

Immédiatement après avoir ri, sur la gentille
injonction[3] de Cosette, personne ne faisant attention à
lui, Jean Valjean s'était levé, et, inaperçu, il avait gagné
5 l'antichambre. C'était cette même salle où, huit mois
auparavant, il était entré noir de boue, de sang et de

---

1. « Fortuné près de Fortunée ».
2. Verve : fantaisie, vivacité.
3. Injonction : demande pressante.

poudre, rapportant le petit-fils à l'aïeul. La vieille
boiserie était enguirlandée de feuillages et de fleurs ; les
musiciens étaient assis sur le canapé où l'on avait déposé
10 Marius. Basque en habit noir, en culotte courte, en bas
blancs et en gants blancs, disposait des couronnes de
roses autour de chacun des plats qu'on allait servir. Jean
Valjean lui avait montré son bras en écharpe, l'avait
chargé d'expliquer son absence, et était sorti.

15 Les croisées de la salle à manger donnaient sur la
rue. Jean Valjean demeura quelques minutes debout et
immobile dans l'obscurité sous ces fenêtres radieuses.
Il écoutait. Le bruit confus du banquet venait jusqu'à
lui. Il entendait la parole haute et magistrale du grand-
20 père, les violons, le cliquetis des assiettes et des verres,
les éclats de rire, et dans toute cette rumeur gaie il distinguait la douce voix joyeuse de Cosette.

Il quitta la rue des Filles-du-Calvaire et s'en revint
rue de l'Homme-Armé.

25 [...]

Jean Valjean rentra chez lui. Il alluma sa chandelle et
monta. L'appartement était vide. Toussaint elle-même
n'y était plus. Le pas de Jean Valjean faisait dans les
chambres plus de bruit qu'à l'ordinaire. Toutes les
30 armoires étaient ouvertes. Il pénétra dans la chambre
de Cosette. Il n'y avait pas de draps au lit. L'oreiller de
coutil[1], sans taie et sans dentelles, était posé sur les
couvertures pliées au pied du matelas dont on voyait la
toile et où personne ne devait plus coucher. Tous les
35 petits objets féminins auxquels tenait Cosette avaient
été emportés ; il ne restait que les gros meubles et les
quatre murs. Le lit de Toussaint était également

---

1. **Coutil :** tissu épais, en fil ou en coton.

dégarni. Un seul lit était fait et semblait attendre quelqu'un, c'était celui de Jean Valjean.

40 Jean Valjean regarda les murailles, ferma quelques portes d'armoires, alla et vint d'une chambre à l'autre.

Puis il se retrouva dans sa chambre, et il posa sa chandelle sur une table.

Il avait dégagé son bras de l'écharpe, et il se servait 45 de sa main droite comme s'il n'en souffrait pas.

Il s'approcha de son lit, et ses yeux s'arrêtèrent, fut-ce par hasard ? fut-ce avec intention ? sur l'*inséparable*, dont Cosette avait été jalouse, sur la petite malle qui ne le quittait jamais. Le 4 juin, en arrivant rue de 50 l'Homme-Armé, il l'avait déposée sur un guéridon près de son chevet. Il alla à ce guéridon avec une sorte de vivacité, prit dans sa poche une clef, et ouvrit la valise.

Il en tira lentement les vêtements avec lesquels, dix ans auparavant, Cosette avait quitté Montfermeil ; 55 d'abord la petite robe noire, puis le fichu noir, puis les bons gros souliers d'enfant que Cosette aurait presque pu mettre encore, tant elle avait le pied petit, puis la brassière de futaine[1] bien épaisse, puis le jupon de tricot, puis le tablier à poche, puis les bas de laine. Ces 60 bas, où était encore gracieusement marquée la forme d'une petite jambe, n'étaient guère plus longs que la main de Jean Valjean. Tout cela était de couleur noire. C'était lui qui avait apporté ces vêtements pour elle à Montfermeil. À mesure qu'il les ôtait de la valise, il les 65 posait sur le lit. Il pensait. Il se rappelait. C'était en hiver, un mois de décembre très froid, elle grelottait à demi nue dans des guenilles, ses pauvres petits pieds tout rouges dans des sabots. Lui, Jean Valjean, il lui avait fait quitter ces haillons pour lui faire mettre cet

---

1. **Futaine :** étoffe de fil et de coton.

70 habillement de deuil. La mère avait dû être contente dans sa tombe de voir sa fille porter son deuil, et surtout de voir qu'elle était vêtue et qu'elle avait chaud. Il pensait à cette forêt de Montfermeil ; ils l'avaient traversée ensemble, Cosette et lui ; il pensait 75 au temps qu'il faisait, aux arbres sans feuilles, au bois sans oiseaux, au ciel sans soleil ; c'est égal, c'était charmant. Il rangea les petites nippes[1] sur le lit, le fichu près du jupon, les bas à côté des souliers, la brassière à côté de la robe, et il les regarda l'une après l'autre. Elle 80 n'était pas plus haute que cela, elle avait sa grande poupée dans ses bras, elle avait mis son louis d'or dans la poche de ce tablier, elle riait, ils marchaient tous les deux se tenant par la main, elle n'avait que lui au monde.

85 Alors sa vénérable tête blanche tomba sur le lit, ce vieux cœur stoïque[2] se brisa, sa face s'abîma[3] pour ainsi dire dans les vêtements de Cosette, et si quelqu'un eût passé dans l'escalier en ce moment, on eût entendu d'effrayants sanglots.

[Un nouveau cas de conscience se pose à Jean Valjean : a-t-il le droit de profiter, sous une fausse identité, du bonheur familial qu'on lui offre (V, VI, 4) ?]

---

1. **Nippes** : vêtements.
2. **Stoïque** : courageux, ferme, inébranlable.
3. **S'abîmer** : ici, s'enfoncer, plonger.

LIVRE SEPTIÈME :
LA DERNIÈRE GORGÉE DU CALICE

1. Le septième cercle et le huitième ciel

[Le lendemain matin, Jean Valjean va rendre visite à Marius, qui l'accueille très chaleureusement, et l'invite à déjeuner.]

– Monsieur, dit Jean Valjean, j'ai une chose à vous dire. Je suis un ancien forçat.

La limite des sons aigus perceptibles peut être tout aussi bien dépassée pour l'esprit que pour l'oreille. Ces mots : *Je suis un ancien forçat*, sortant de la bouche de M. Fauchelevent et entrant dans l'oreille de Marius, allaient au delà du possible. Marius n'entendit pas. Il lui sembla que quelque chose venait de lui être dit ; mais il ne sut quoi. Il resta béant[1].

Il s'aperçut alors que l'homme qui lui parlait était effrayant. Tout à son éblouissement, il n'avait pas jusqu'à ce moment remarqué cette pâleur terrible.

Jean Valjean dénoua la cravate noire qui lui soutenait le bras droit, défit le linge roulé autour de sa main, mit son pouce à nu et le montra à Marius.

– Je n'ai rien à la main, dit-il.

Marius regarda le pouce.

– Je n'y ai jamais rien eu, reprit Jean Valjean.

Il n'y avait en effet aucune trace de blessure.

Jean Valjean poursuivit :

– Il convenait que je fusse absent de votre mariage. Je me suis fait absent le plus que j'ai pu. J'ai supposé

---

1. **Béant** : qui regarde avec étonnement, la bouche et les yeux grand ouverts.

cette blessure pour ne point faire un faux, pour ne pas
introduire de nullité dans les actes du mariage, pour
25 être dispensé de signer.

Marius bégaya.

– Qu'est-ce que cela veut dire ?

– Cela veut dire, répondit Jean Valjean, que j'ai été
aux galères.

30 – Vous me rendez fou ! s'écria Marius épouvanté.

– Monsieur Pontmercy, dit Jean Valjean, j'ai été dix-
neuf ans aux galères. Pour vol. Puis j'ai été condamné
à perpétuité. Pour vol. Pour récidive. À l'heure qu'il
est, je suis en rupture de ban[1].

*[Marius est horrifié. Jean Valjean le rassure : il n'est
pas le père de Cosette.]*

35 – [...] Je ne suis rien à Cosette. Rassurez-vous.

Marius balbutia :

– Qui me prouve ?...

– Moi. Puisque je le dis.

Marius regarda cet homme. Il était lugubre et tran-
40 quille. Aucun mensonge ne pouvait sortir d'un tel
calme. Ce qui est glacé est sincère. On sentait le vrai
dans cette froideur de tombe.

– Je vous crois, dit Marius.

Jean Valjean inclina la tête comme pour prendre
45 acte, et continua :

– Que suis-je pour Cosette ? un passant. Il y a dix
ans, je ne savais pas qu'elle existât. Je l'aime, c'est vrai.
Une enfant qu'on a vue petite, étant soi-même déjà

---

1. Les forçats libérés qui échappaient à la surveillance policière en ne se
rendant pas dans la ville où ils devaient résider étaient dits *en rupture de
ban*. Jean Valjean, pour sa part, est un évadé du bagne depuis l'épisode du
vaisseau *L'Orion* (II, II, 3).

vieux, on l'aime. Quand on est vieux, on se sent grand-
50 père pour tous les petits enfants. Vous pouvez, ce me
semble, supposer que j'ai quelque chose qui ressemble
à un cœur. Elle était orpheline. Sans père ni mère. Elle
avait besoin de moi. Voilà pourquoi je me suis mis à
l'aimer. C'est si faible les enfants, que le premier venu,
55 même un homme comme moi, peut être leur pro-
tecteur. J'ai fait ce devoir-là vis-à-vis de Cosette. Je ne
crois pas qu'on puisse vraiment appeler si peu de chose
une bonne action ; mais si c'est une bonne action, eh
bien, mettez que je l'ai faite. Enregistrez cette circon-
60 stance atténuante. Aujourd'hui Cosette quitte ma vie ;
nos deux chemins se séparent. Désormais je ne puis
plus rien pour elle. Elle est madame Pontmercy. Sa
providence a changé[1]. Et Cosette gagne au change.
Tout est bien. Quant aux six cent mille francs, vous ne
65 m'en parlez pas, mais je vais au-devant de votre pensée, c'est un dépôt. Comment ce dépôt était-il entre
mes mains ? Qu'importe ? Je rends le dépôt. On n'a
rien de plus à me demander. Je complète la restitution
en disant mon vrai nom. Ceci encore me regarde. Je
70 tiens, moi, à ce que vous sachiez qui je suis.
Et Jean Valjean regarda Marius en face

*[Marius ne comprend pas : pourquoi M. Fauchelevent
a-t-il éprouvé le besoin de révéler son secret ? « C'est par
honnêteté », répond Jean Valjean.]*

– […] Je ne suis d'aucune famille, moi. Je ne suis
pas de la vôtre. Je ne suis pas de celle des hommes.
Les maisons où l'on est entre soi, j'y suis de trop. Il y

---

1. Après avoir été sous la protection de Jean Valjean, Cosette est maintenant
confiée à Marius.

75 a des familles, mais ce n'est pas pour moi. Je suis le
malheureux, je suis dehors. Ai-je eu un père et une
mère ? j'en doute presque. Le jour où j'ai marié cette
enfant, cela a été fini, je l'ai vue heureuse, et qu'elle
était avec l'homme qu'elle aime, et qu'il y avait là un
80 bon vieillard, un ménage de deux anges, toutes les
joies dans cette maison, et que c'était bien, je me suis
dit : Toi, n'entre pas. Je pouvais mentir, c'est vrai,
vous tromper tous, rester monsieur Fauchelevent.
Tant que cela a été pour elle, j'ai pu mentir ; mais
85 maintenant ce serait pour moi, je ne le dois pas. Il suffisait de me taire, c'est vrai, et tout continuait. Vous
me demandez ce qui me force à parler ? une drôle de
chose, ma conscience. Me taire, c'était pourtant bien
facile. J'ai passé la nuit à tâcher de me le persuader ;
90 vous me confessez, et ce que je viens vous dire est si
extraordinaire que vous en avez le droit ; eh bien, oui,
j'ai passé la nuit à me donner des raisons, je me suis
donné de très bonnes raisons, j'ai fait ce que j'ai pu,
allez. Mais il y a deux choses où je n'ai pas réussi ; ni à
95 casser le fil qui me tient par le cœur fixé, rivé et scellé
ici, ni à faire taire quelqu'un qui me parle bas quand je
suis seul. C'est pourquoi je suis venu vous avouer tout
ce matin. Tout, ou à peu près tout. Il y a de l'inutile à
dire qui ne concerne que moi ; je le garde pour moi.
100 L'essentiel, vous le savez. Donc j'ai pris mon mystère,
et je vous l'ai apporté. Et j'ai éventré mon secret sous
vos yeux.

*[Jean Valjean explique à Marius qu'il veut être en
paix avec sa conscience.]*

Jean Valjean fit encore une pause, avalant sa salive
avec effort comme si ses paroles avaient un arrière-
105 goût amer, et il reprit :

– Quand on a une telle horreur sur soi, on n'a pas le droit de la faire partager aux autres à leur insu, on n'a pas le droit de leur communiquer sa peste, on n'a pas le droit de les faire glisser dans son précipice sans qu'ils s'en aperçoivent, on n'a pas le droit de laisser traîner sa casaque[1] rouge sur eux, on n'a pas le droit d'encombrer sournoisement de sa misère le bonheur d'autrui. S'approcher de ceux qui sont sains et les toucher dans l'ombre avec son ulcère invisible, c'est hideux. Fauchelevent a eu beau me prêter son nom, je n'ai pas le droit de m'en servir ; il a pu me le donner, je n'ai pas pu le prendre. Un nom, c'est un moi. Voyez-vous, monsieur, j'ai un peu pensé, j'ai un peu lu, quoique je sois un paysan ; et vous voyez que je m'exprime convenablement. Je me rends compte des choses. Je me suis fait une éducation à moi. Eh bien oui, soustraire un nom et se mettre dessous, c'est déshonnête. Des lettres de l'alphabet, cela s'escroque comme une bourse ou comme une montre. Être une fausse signature en chair et en os, être une fausse clef vivante, entrer chez d'honnêtes gens en trichant leur serrure, ne plus jamais regarder, loucher toujours, être infâme au dedans de moi, non ! non ! non ! non ! Il vaut mieux souffrir, saigner, pleurer, s'arracher la peau de la chair avec les ongles, passer les nuits à se tordre dans les angoisses, se ronger le ventre et l'âme. Voilà pourquoi je viens vous raconter tout cela. De gaîté de cœur, comme vous dites.

Il respira péniblement, et jeta ce dernier mot :

– Pour vivre, autrefois, j'ai volé un pain ; aujourd'hui, pour vivre, je ne veux pas voler un nom.

---

1. Les forçats condamnés à perpétuité portaient la casaque et le bonnet rouges.

[La conversation est interrompue par l'arrivée joyeuse de Cosette. Les deux hommes font comme si de rien n'était. Marius demande à sa femme de les laisser seuls. Il autorise Jean Valjean à rendre visite à Cosette tous les soirs.

Marius, perplexe, ne parvient pas à s'expliquer la personnalité de Jean Valjean. Il reconnaît sa bonté envers Cosette, mais ses visites lui déplaisent. (V, VII, 2.)

Jean Valjean et Cosette se voient d'abord tous les soirs, dans une petite salle écartée, au rez-de-chaussée. Mais une gêne s'installe entre eux. Le vieil homme comprend peu à peu qu'il est indésirable, et arrête ses visites. (V, VIII.)]

LIVRE NEUVIÈME :
SUPRÊME OMBRE, SUPRÊME AURORE

[« Marius avait peu à peu soustrait Cosette à Jean Valjean. Cosette s'était laissé faire. » Abandonné par son enfant chérie, Jean Valjean dépérit. (V, IX, 1 et 2.)]

3. Une plume pèse
à qui soulevait la charrette Fauchelevent

Un soir Jean Valjean eut de la peine à se soulever sur le coude ; il se prit la main et ne trouva pas son pouls ; sa respiration était courte et s'arrêtait par instants ; il reconnut qu'il était plus faible qu'il ne l'avait encore
5 été. Alors, sans doute sous la pression de quelque préoccupation suprême, il fit un effort, se dressa sur son séant et s'habilla. Il mit son vieux vêtement d'ouvrier. Ne sortant plus, il y était revenu, et il le préférait. Il dut s'interrompre plusieurs fois en
10 s'habillant ; rien que pour passer les manches de la veste, la sueur lui coulait du front.

Depuis qu'il était seul, il avait mis son lit dans l'anti-chambre, afin d'habiter le moins possible cet appartement désert.

15 Il ouvrit la valise et en tira le trousseau de Cosette.

Il l'étala sur son lit.

Les chandeliers de l'évêque[1] étaient à leur place sur la cheminée. Il prit dans un tiroir deux bougies de cire et les mit dans les chandeliers. Puis, quoiqu'il fît 20 encore grand jour, c'était en été, il les alluma. On voit ainsi quelquefois des flambeaux allumés en plein jour dans les chambres où il y a des morts.

Chaque pas qu'il faisait en allant d'un meuble à l'autre l'exténuait, et il était obligé de s'asseoir. Ce 25 n'était point de la fatigue ordinaire qui dépense la force pour la renouveler ; c'était le reste des mouvements possibles ; c'était la vie épuisée qui s'égoutte dans des efforts accablants qu'on ne recommencera pas.

Une des chaises où il se laissa tomber était placée 30 devant le miroir, si fatal pour lui, si providentiel pour Marius, où il avait lu sur le buvard l'écriture renversée de Cosette. Il se vit dans ce miroir, et ne se reconnut pas. Il avait quatre-vingts ans ; avant le mariage de Marius, on lui eût à peine donné cinquante ans ; cette 35 année avait compté trente. Ce qu'il avait sur le front, ce n'était plus la ride de l'âge, c'était la marque mysté-rieuse de la mort. On sentait là le creusement de l'ongle impitoyable. Ses joues pendaient ; la peau de son visage avait cette couleur qui ferait croire qu'il y a 40 déjà de la terre dessus ; les deux coins de sa bouche s'abaissaient comme dans ce masque que les anciens sculptaient sur les tombeaux ; il regardait le vide avec

---

1. Jean Valjean a toujours gardé les chandeliers que Mgr Myriel lui avait donnés au début du roman.

un air de reproche ; on eût dit un de ces grands êtres tragiques qui ont à se plaindre de quelqu'un.

45 Il était dans cette situation, la dernière phase de l'accablement, où la douleur ne coule plus ; elle est pour ainsi dire coagulée ; il y a sur l'âme comme un caillot de désespoir.

La nuit était venue. Il traîna laborieusement une
50 table et le vieux fauteuil près de la cheminée, et posa sur la table une plume, de l'encre et du papier.

Cela fait, il eut un évanouissement. Quand il reprit connaissance, il avait soif. Ne pouvant soulever le pot à l'eau, il le pencha péniblement vers sa bouche, et but
55 une gorgée.

Puis il se tourna vers le lit, toujours assis, car il ne pouvait rester debout, il regarda la petite robe noire et tous ces chers objets.

Ces contemplations-là durent des heures qui sem-
60 blent des minutes. Tout à coup il eut un frisson, il sentit que le froid lui venait ; il s'accouda à la table que les flambeaux de l'évêque éclairaient, et prit la plume.

Comme la plume ni l'encre n'avaient servi depuis longtemps, le bec de la plume était recourbé, l'encre était
65 desséchée, il fallut qu'il se levât et qu'il mît quelques gouttes d'eau dans l'encre, ce qu'il ne put faire sans s'arrêter et s'asseoir deux ou trois fois, et il fut forcé d'écrire avec le dos de la plume. Il s'essuyait le front de temps en temps.

70 Sa main tremblait. Il écrivit lentement quelques lignes que voici :

« Cosette, je te bénis. Je vais t'expliquer. Ton mari a eu raison de me faire comprendre que je devais m'en aller ; cependant il y a un peu d'erreur dans ce qu'il a
75 cru, mais il a eu raison. Il est excellent. Aime-le toujours bien quand je serai mort. Monsieur Pontmercy, aimez toujours mon enfant bien-aimé. Cosette, on

trouvera ce papier-ci, voici ce que je veux te dire, tu vas voir les chiffres, si j'ai la force de me les rappeler,
80 écoute bien, cet argent est bien à toi. Voici toute la chose. Le jais[1] blanc vient de Norvège, le jais noir vient d'Angleterre, la verroterie noire vient d'Allemagne. Le jais est plus léger, plus précieux, plus cher. On peut faire en France des imitations comme en Allemagne. Il
85 faut une petite enclume de deux pouces carrés et une lampe à esprit de vin pour amollir la cire. La cire autrefois se faisait avec de la résine et du noir de fumée et coûtait quatre francs la livre. J'ai imaginé de la faire avec de la gomme-laque[2] et de la térébenthine[3]. Elle ne
90 coûte plus que trente sous, et elle est bien meilleure. Les boucles se font avec un verre violet qu'on colle au moyen de cette cire sur une petite membrure[4] en fer noir. Le verre doit être violet pour les bijoux de fer et noir pour les bijoux d'or. L'Espagne en achète beau-
95 coup. C'est le pays du jais… »

Ici il s'interrompit, la plume tomba de ses doigts, il lui vint un de ces sanglots désespérés qui montaient par moments des profondeurs de son être, le pauvre homme prit sa tête dans ses deux mains, et songea.
100 – Oh ! s'écria-t-il au dedans de lui-même (cris lamentables, entendus de Dieu seul), c'est fini. Je ne la verrai plus. C'est un sourire qui a passé sur moi. Je vais entrer dans la nuit sans même la revoir. Oh ! une minute, un instant, entendre sa voix, toucher sa robe,
105 la regarder, elle, l'ange ! et puis mourir ! Ce n'est rien de mourir, ce qui est affreux, c'est de mourir sans la voir. Elle me sourirait, elle me dirait un mot. Est-ce

---

1. **Jais :** pierre compacte et très noire (voir I, V, 2, p. 68).
2. **Gomme-laque :** beau vernis de Chine, noir ou rouge.
3. **Térébenthine :** sorte de résine liquide.
4. **Membrure :** armature.

que cela ferait du mal à quelqu'un ? Non, c'est fini,
jamais. Me voilà tout seul. Mon Dieu ! mon Dieu ! je
ne la verrai plus.

En ce moment on frappa a sa porte.

[Le même jour, Marius a reçu la visite d'un homme
louche, venu lui vendre un secret. C'est Thénardier, qui
croit apprendre au baron Pontmercy qu'il abrite un
assassin et un voleur. Mais Marius le sait : Jean Valjean
a, dit-il, volé M. Madeleine et tué l'inspecteur Javert.
Thénardier le détrompe, en lui montrant les coupures de
journaux qui attestent que Jean Valjean était M. Made-
leine, et que Javert s'est suicidé. Fort de ces révélations,
Thénardier poursuit. Il prétend que Jean Valjean est un
meurtrier : le 6 juin 1832, il l'a vu porter un cadavre
dans les égouts de Paris. Mais, en croyant perdre Jean
Valjean, Thénardier lui rend justice : Marius a enfin
retrouvé son sauveur. Il congédie vertement Thénardier,
et, en souvenir de Waterloo, lui donne suffisamment
d'argent pour qu'il parte en Amérique. Le lecteur
apprend qu'il y deviendra négrier.

Dès le départ du scélérat, Marius court chercher Cosette,
appelle un fiacre, et l'emmène rue de l'Homme-Armé. En
chemin, il lui explique toute l'histoire. (V, IX, 4)]

5. Nuit derrière laquelle il y a le jour

[Cosette se jette dans les bras de son « père », bouleversé
par la joie de la revoir. Les deux jeunes gens demandent
à Jean Valjean de venir vivre chez eux. Mais il est trop
tard. Le vieil homme sent que sa mort est proche.]

Cosette lui soutenait les épaules, et sanglotait, et
tâchait de lui parler sans pouvoir y parvenir. On distinguait, parmi les mots mêlés à cette salive lugubre qui

accompagne les larmes, des paroles comme celles-ci :

5 – Père ! ne nous quittez pas. Est-il possible que nous ne vous retrouvions que pour vous perdre ?

On pourrait dire que l'agonie serpente. Elle va, vient, s'avance vers le sépulcre, et se retourne vers la vie. Il y a du tâtonnement dans l'action de mourir.

10 Jean Valjean, après cette demi-syncope[1], se raffermit, secoua son front comme pour en faire tomber les ténèbres, et redevint presque pleinement lucide. Il prit un pan de la manche de Cosette et le baisa.

– Il revient ! docteur, il revient ! cria Marius.

15 – Vous êtes bons tous les deux, dit Jean Valjean. Je vais vous dire ce qui m'a fait de la peine. Ce qui m'a fait de la peine, monsieur Pontmercy, c'est que vous n'ayez pas voulu toucher à cet argent. Cet argent-là est bien à votre femme. Je vais vous expliquer, mes enfants, c'est

20 même pour cela que je suis content de vous voir. Le jais noir vient d'Angleterre, le jais blanc vient de Norvège. Tout ceci est dans le papier que voilà, que vous lirez. Pour les bracelets, j'ai inventé de remplacer les coulants[2] en tôle soudée par des coulants en tôle rapprochée.

25 C'est plus joli, meilleur, et moins cher. Vous comprenez tout l'argent qu'on peut gagner. La fortune de Cosette est donc bien à elle. Je vous donne ces détails-là pour que vous ayez l'esprit en repos.

La portière[3] était montée et regardait par la porte

30 entrebâillée. Le médecin la congédia, mais il ne put empêcher qu'avant de disparaître cette bonne femme zélée ne criât au mourant :

– Voulez-vous un prêtre ?

---

1. **Syncope :** évanouissement.
2. **Coulants :** anneaux utilisés en bijouterie.
3. **Portière :** concierge.

– J'en ai un, répondit Jean Valjean.

35   Et, du doigt, il sembla désigner un point au-dessus de sa tête où l'on eût dit qu'il voyait quelqu'un.

Il est probable que l'évêque en effet assistait à cette agonie.

[Le vieil homme fait venir ses « enfants » autour de lui, leur recommande d'être heureux, souhaite être enterré simplement et anonymement (« Pas de nom sur la pierre... »), et se rappelle tous les moments heureux qu'il a passés avec Cosette quand elle était petite. Il lui révèle alors le secret de sa naissance.]

– [...] Cosette, voici le moment venu de te dire le
40   nom de ta mère. Elle s'appelait Fantine. Retiens ce nom là : Fantine. Mets-toi à genoux toutes les fois que tu le prononceras. Elle a bien souffert. Et t'a bien aimée. Elle a eu en malheur tout ce que tu as en bonheur. Ce sont les partages de Dieu. Il est là-haut, il
45   nous voit tous, et il sait ce qu'il fait au milieu de ses grandes étoiles. Je vais donc m'en aller, mes enfants. Aimez-vous bien toujours. Il n'y a guère autre chose que cela dans le monde : s'aimer. Vous penserez quelquefois au pauvre vieux qui est mort ici. Ô ma
50   Cosette ! ce n'est pas ma faute, va, si je ne t'ai pas vue tous ces temps-ci, cela me fendait le cœur ; j'allais jusqu'au coin de la rue, je devais faire un drôle d'effet aux gens qui me voyaient passer, j'étais comme fou, une fois je suis sorti sans chapeau. Mes enfants, voici
55   que je ne vois plus très clair, j'avais encore des choses à dire, mais c'est égal. Pensez un peu à moi. Vous êtes des êtres bénis. Je ne sais pas ce que j'ai, je vois de la lumière. Approchez encore. Je meurs heureux. Donnez-moi vos chères têtes bien-aimées, que je mette mes
60   mains dessus.

Cosette et Marius tombèrent à genoux, éperdus, étouffés de larmes, chacun sur une des mains de Jean Valjean. Ces mains augustes ne remuaient plus.

65 Il était renversé en arrière, la lueur des deux chandeliers l'éclairait ; sa face blanche regardait le ciel, il laissait Cosette et Marius couvrir ses mains de baisers ; il était mort.

La nuit était sans étoiles et profondément obscure. Sans doute, dans l'ombre, quelque ange immense était 70 debout, les ailes déployées, attendant l'âme.

6. L'herbe cache et la pluie efface

Il y a, au cimetière du Père-Lachaise[1], aux environs de la fosse commune, loin du quartier élégant de cette ville des sépulcres[2], loin de tous ces tombeaux de fantaisie qui étalent en présence de l'éternité les hideuses modes 5 de la mort, dans un angle désert, le long d'un vieux mur, sous un grand if auquel grimpent les liserons, parmi les chiendents et les mousses, une pierre. Cette pierre n'est pas plus exempte que les autres des lèpres[3] du temps, de la moisissure, du lichen, et des fientes 10 d'oiseaux. L'eau la verdit, l'air la noircit. Elle n'est voisine d'aucun sentier, et l'on n'aime pas aller de ce côté-là, parce que l'herbe est haute et qu'on a tout de suite les pieds mouillés. Quand il y a un peu de soleil, les lézards y viennent. Il y a, tout autour, un frémissement 15 de folles avoines. Au printemps, les fauvettes chantent dans l'arbre.

---

1. Le **Père-Lachaise** est un grand cimetière situé dans l'est de Paris.
2. **Ville des sépulcres :** cimetière.
3. **Lèpres :** marques laissées par le temps qui « ronge » la pierre.

Cette pierre est toute nue. On n'a songé en la taillant qu'au nécessaire de la tombe, et l'on n'a pris d'autre soin que de faire cette pierre assez longue et 20 assez étroite pour couvrir un homme.

On n'y lit aucun nom.

Seulement, voilà de cela bien des années déjà, une main y a écrit au crayon ces quatre vers qui sont devenus peu à peu illisibles sous la pluie et la poussière, et 25 qui probablement sont aujourd'hui effacés :

Il dort. Quoique le sort fût pour lui bien étrange,
Il vivait. Il mourut quand il n'eut plus son ange ;
La chose simplement d'elle-même arriva,
Comme la nuit se fait lorsque le jour s'en va.

SOCIÉTÉ : la révolution manquée

1. Dans la quatrième partie, l'insurrection débutait dans l'allégresse et l'exaltation. Comment se termine-t-elle ? Comment expliquer son échec ?

2. Hugo eut une attitude modérée pendant les événements violents de juin 1848 : il fit partie des soixante commissaires envoyés par l'Assemblée constituante sur les barricades pour tenter de raisonner les insurgés. Quel rôle Jean Valjean joue-t-il sur la barricade ? Pourquoi refuse-t-il de tuer ? À partir de l'épisode de l'insurrection, peut-on se faire une idée des opinions politiques de l'auteur ?

THÈMES : l'égoïsme des gens heureux

3. Hugo lui-même, sous la monarchie de Juillet, est devenu un « notable ». Comment les rapports entre Marius et M. Gillenormand évoluent-ils dans cette partie ? Montrez que Marius, autrefois révolté contre son grand-père et contre la société, finit par s'installer dans un certain conformisme bourgeois.

4. Quelles questions Marius se pose-t-il après avoir découvert l'identité véritable de M. Fauchelevent ? Comprenez-vous qu'il l'éloigne peu à peu de Cosette ?

GENRES : un roman philosophique

5. Dans le mélodrame, le traître est un personnage entièrement mauvais, et il ne saurait en aucun cas appartenir à la police. Le personnage de Javert est très complexe, puisque c'est son attache-ment à la loi qui l'aveugle, jusqu'au retournement final. En quoi sa conversion est-elle inattendue ? Pourquoi est-il si bouleversé ? De quel principe supérieur a-t-il la révélation ?

6. Le roman forme ici une boucle : l'« histoire d'un homme » rejoint l'« histoire d'un saint » (voir p. 97). À quels indices perçoit-on la présence de l'évêque dans cette dernière partie ? Son sou-venir accompagne Jean Valjean jusqu'à la fin : quel rôle l'évêque aura-t-il joué dans le destin de l'ancien forçat ?

L'ART DU RÉCIT : un dénouement amer

7. Le dénouement n'est heureux que pour Cosette et Marius. Par ailleurs, le roman est assez pessimiste : le lecteur s'attendait-il à la mort de Gavroche ? Après la mort d'Éponine à la fin de la quatrième partie, dans quelle tonalité la dernière partie commence-t-elle ?

8. Les amis de Marius ont chacun une personnalité très différente. Par quels aspects de son caractère Enjolras est-il un être hors du commun ? En quoi sa mort fait-elle de lui un personnage sublime ?

9. Sait-on à qui appartient la mystérieuse main qui a écrit quatre vers au crayon sur la tombe de Jean Valjean ? Quelle interprétation symbolique pouvez-vous donner du fait qu'ils sont « probablement […] aujourd'hui effacés » ?

UNE INTRIGUE ÉCHEVELÉE

1. Le roman est construit sur l'entrelacement de plusieurs intrigues : certains personnages sont abandonnés à leur destin pendant plusieurs chapitres ou livres de l'histoire, pour reparaître bien plus tard, dans une situation différente. Donnez des exemples de cette construction narrative. Quels sont les effets de suspense ménagés par cette technique romanesque ?

2. De nombreux épisodes reposent sur des retrouvailles ou des coïncidences très improbables. Lesquels ? À l'inverse, le narrateur nourrit son récit de détails vrais qui créent de puissants effets de réel. Les invraisemblances de la fiction vous semblent-elles incompatibles avec l'expression d'une vérité ?

DES DESTINS CONTRASTÉS

3. Jean Valjean connaît tout au long du roman plusieurs cas de conscience, qui donnent lieu chaque fois à un violent combat intérieur, résolu finalement par une révélation lumineuse. Dans quels chapitres avons-nous rencontré cette structure ? Quel sens peut-on donner à la victoire de la lumière sur l'ombre ?

4. Le destin de Jean Valjean, orienté vers le rachat, peut se lire comme une « imitation » de la Passion du Christ. Quels sont les épisodes qui permettent de justifier cette comparaison ? Par les décisions qu'il prend, Jean Valjean parvient-il à donner un sens à sa souffrance ?

5. Le destin de Cosette est miraculeux : « petite chose » bâtarde et orpheline, enfant martyre, elle finit par réussir parfaitement son intégration sociale, grâce à Jean Valjean, qui la sauve de la misère et lui donne une éducation, et grâce à Marius, qui lui donne un nom. Devenue Mme la baronne Pontmercy, quelles valeurs nouvelles adopte-t-elle ? A-t-elle une personnalité propre ? Cosette est-elle plus attachante enfant, jeune fille, ou jeune femme ? Justifiez votre réponse.

6. D'un point de vue romanesque, quels destins vous semblent les plus exaltants : le bonheur des jeunes mariés, ou la mort des héros ? Pourquoi ?

INDIVIDU ET HISTOIRE

7. Si le thème des misères et du malheur est prépondérant dans le roman, c'est bien souvent l'amour qui est le moteur de l'action. Quels sont les personnages animés par ce sentiment ? Quels obstacles leur permet-il de surmonter ?

8. Après avoir assisté à la révolution de 1830, Hugo a choisi de raconter l'insurrection manquée de 1832. À l'époque où se déroule le roman, le peuple a le pouvoir de droit (depuis la Révolution française et la Déclaration des droits de l'homme), mais pas de fait ni sous la Restauration ni sous la monarchie de Juillet (temps de la fiction), à cause du suffrage censitaire, ni sous le Second Empire (temps de l'écriture), à cause de la dictature. Dans quelle mesure peut-on dire que le romancier donne ici aux misérables la parole dont la société les prive ?

9. Les principes moraux et sociaux de Mgr Myriel sont transmis à Jean Valjean. D'après *Les Misérables*, sur quelles valeurs peut-on espérer construire un monde meilleur ? Le destin des personnages (retrait de Jean Valjean, mort des jeunes révolutionnaires, mort d'Éponine et de Fantine, suicide de Javert, intégration sociale de Cosette et Marius) donne-t-il l'espoir que l'humanité est capable de progresser ?

L'UNIVERS
DE L'ŒUVRE

Dossier documentaire
et pédagogique

LE TEXTE
ET SES IMAGES

LE PEUPLE AU XIXᵉ SIÈCLE :
MISÈRE ET RÉVOLUTION (P. 2-3)

Le XIXᵉ siècle est souvent appelé « siècle des révolutions » : à celle de 1789 succèdent en effet les révolutions de 1830 et 1848, puis en 1871, l'insurrection de la Commune. Les romanciers se font l'écho des luttes politiques de leur époque. Mais la question politique est au fond sous-tendue par la « question sociale ».

1. Quelles correspondances peut-on établir entre les personnages du tableau de Delacroix, *La Liberté guidant le peuple* (ill. 1), et ceux du roman ?

2. Quelles sont les caractéristiques du personnage allégorique* représentant la Liberté (ill. 1) ?

3. Montrez comment la composition d'ensemble, les jeux de lumière et le mouvement des personnages traduisent dans ce tableau la violence et la force de l'histoire (ill. 1).

4. Dans la rue de Londres gravée par Gustave Doré (ill. 2), quels différents types de personnages peut-on repérer ? Comment la pauvreté est-elle représentée ?

REGARDS SUR JEAN VALJEAN (P. 4-5)

Tout au long du livre, Jean Valjean, l'homme sans nom, affronte le regard d'autrui, qui tour à tour le soupçonne et lui donne une individualité.

5. À quelle scène la photo n° 3 correspond-elle ? Que peut symboliser l'ombre de la visière de sa casquette sur le visage de Jean Valjean ? Quelle signification peut-on donner à cet échange de regards ?

6. Où se passe la scène représentée sur la photo n° 4 ? Quels rapports de force entre les personnages les regards et les mouvements de mains suggèrent-ils ?

7. À quelle scène la photo n° 5 correspond-elle ? Commentez la posture et les gestes des deux personnages. Quelle nouvelle relation leurs regards semblent-ils exprimer ?

8. Qui sont les personnages représentés sur la photo n° 6 ? Quel est apparemment le sujet central de ce cliché ? Vers quel autre personnage le regard de Javert détourne-t-il notre attention ? Que peut signifier ce regard du policier, à ce stade du récit ?

DES PERSONNAGES EMBLÉMATIQUES (P. 6-7)

L'une des particularités des *Misérables* est de comporter de nombreux personnages « secondaires » devenus aussi célèbres que le personnage principal, qui ont constitué de nouveaux « types » littéraires et culturels.

9. Qu'expriment la posture de l'enfant, le mouvement de son visage et de son corps (ill. 8) ? Quel effet supplémentaire le matériau choisi produit-il ?

10. Quels sont les accessoires et l'attitude caractéristiques du gamin de Paris (ill. 7) ?

11. Quel est l'effet produit par le cadrage en contre-plongée* sur le personnage de Gavroche (ill. 7) ?

MISERIA (P. 8)

Ce dessin avait été composé par Hugo pour le frontispice* des *Misérables*.

12. Quel personnage du roman ce dessin peut-il représenter ? Commentez l'expression du visage du personnage.

13. Que suggère ici la semi-nudité du personnage ? De quoi est-elle le symbole ?

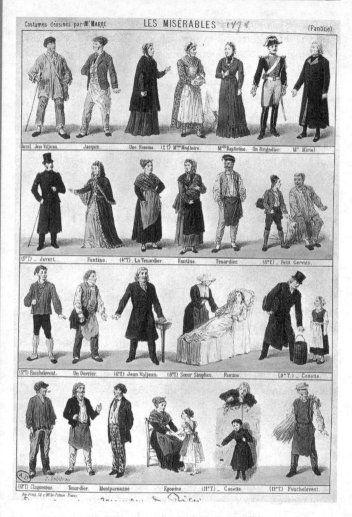

M. Marre, *Lithographie pour les costumes des* Misérables, 1878.
(Bibliothèque des arts décoratifs, Paris.)

LES ILLUSTRATIONS DE GUSTAVE BRION
(P. 28, 78, 112, 138, 164, 196)

Trois ans après la première parution des *Misérables*, une magnifique édition illustrée est publiée chez Hetzel et Lacroix. Les gravures de Gustave Brion sont restées célèbres.

14. Sur la gravure de la page 29, qui représente Jean Valjean, repérez les détails du vêtement et des accessoires qui correspondent à la description du texte, pages 28-30. Le décor est-il réaliste ? Quelle impression générale le personnage dégage-t-il ?

15. Dans le chapitre « Entrée en scène d'une poupée » (II, III, 4, p. 113), Cosette, partie chercher de l'eau, contemple une poupée dans une vitrine illuminée. Sur la gravure de la page 112, commentez la posture et la mine de l'enfant. Montrez comment les jeux de lumière et le cadre intérieur à l'image accentuent l'opposition entre le dedans et le dehors de la boutique.

16. Dans la gravure illustrant l'épisode de l'éléphant de la Bastille, page 196, commentez la posture de chaque enfant et les effets de lumière. Que suggère l'emboîtement des architectures (la charpente de l'éléphant et la tente) ?

Le combat pour la liberté d'expression au temps des *Misérables*

LA LIBERTÉ D'EXPRESSION :
UNE REVENDICATION CONSTANTE AU XIXe SIÈCLE

Après la Révolution française, la liberté d'expression est considérée comme un droit fondamental. L'une des causes directes de la Révolution de 1830 est d'ailleurs la restriction de la liberté de la presse et le raffermissement de la censure.

La censure est une institution qui peut soit interdire la parution d'un ouvrage dont on estime qu'il risque de choquer les bonnes mœurs ou de porter atteinte à l'ordre public et au pouvoir, soit en interdire la diffusion après son impression. Elle est particulièrement attentive au répertoire théâtral. En effet, parce qu'il s'adresse aussi à ceux qui ne savent pas lire, le théâtre touche un large public ; aussi est-il considéré comme potentiellement dangereux pour l'ordre social. La première pièce que Hugo propose à la Comédie-Française, en 1829, *Marion de Lorme*, est censurée, parce que le roi Louis XIII, ancêtre du souverain régnant Charles X, y est représenté sous un jour peu flatteur. Pour amadouer l'auteur, on lui propose le triplement de sa pension d'homme de lettres. Hugo refuse, et répond crânement : « Ma famille, noble dès l'an 1531, est une vieille servante de l'État. Mon père et mes deux oncles l'ont servi quarante ans de leur épée. [...] J'avais demandé que ma pièce fût jouée, je ne demande rien autre chose. »

L'année suivante, pour *Hernani*, Hugo situe l'intrigue en Espagne. Le censeur Briffaut est contraint de la laisser passer, même s'il réprouve le style de la pièce. Après la révolution de

1830, la censure est supprimée, jusqu'en 1835 : ce sont des années fastes pour le drame romantique. Il en ira de même après la révolution de 1848. Mais les gouvernements qui se succèdent au XIXᵉ siècle reviennent rapidement aux anciennes méthodes pour assurer leur pouvoir. Hugo en est victime en 1832 : *Le roi s'amuse*, pièce où il met en scène le roi François Iᵉʳ dans une situation désastreuse pour l'image du monarque, est interdite après la première représentation, pour cause d'outrage aux mœurs et trouble de l'ordre public. La censure étant officiellement abolie, Hugo intente un procès au Théâtre-Français, et prononce lui-même sa propre plaidoirie, aux accents prophétiques :

« Aujourd'hui on me fait prendre ma liberté de poète par un censeur, demain on me fera prendre ma liberté de citoyen par un gendarme ; aujourd'hui on me bannit du théâtre, demain on me bannira du pays ; aujourd'hui on me bâillonne, demain on me déportera ; aujourd'hui l'état de siège est dans la littérature, demain il sera dans la cité. De liberté, de garanties, de Charte, de droit public, plus un mot. Néant. Si le gouvernement, mieux conseillé par ses propres intérêts, ne s'arrête sur cette pente pendant qu'il en est temps encore, avant peu nous aurons tout le despotisme de 1807, moins la gloire. Nous aurons l'empire, sans l'empereur[1]. »

À partir de ce moment, Hugo militera âprement pour défendre la liberté du théâtre, tout comme de nombreux autres écrivains, qui luttent activement pour protéger leur liberté d'expression.

Le retour de l'Empire entraîne le renforcement de la censure, instrument de la dictature. Le régime de Napoléon III contrôle de près les imprimeurs et les théâtres, et la loi du 17 février 1852 autorise la suspension d'un journal après deux avertissements. Les pièces de Victor Hugo sont interdites de représentation. En province, ce sont les préfets qui sont chargés de la censure des ouvrages produits dans leurs départements. De peur de déplaire au pouvoir central, ils se montrent souvent plus zélés que les

---

1. Victor Hugo, « Discours prononcé le 19 décembre 1832 devant le tribunal de commerce », *Œuvres complètes*, t. I, *Théâtre*, Robert Laffont, « Bouquins », p. 845.

censeurs parisiens. À la censure politique s'ajoutent les **procès en justice**. Ainsi, en 1857, Baudelaire est poursuivi pour *Les Fleurs du mal* : son livre est condamné pour « immoralité » et expurgé de plusieurs poèmes. La même année, Flaubert ressort acquitté du retentissant procès de *Madame Bovary*.

HUGO BÂILLONNÉ : UN EXILÉ CÉLÈBRE

Plus fort encore que la censure, l'exil semble un moyen radical de museler les opposants politiques. Mais, paradoxalement, le **bannissement** va ouvrir un nouvel espace de parole à Hugo, entouré et encouragé par ses proches.

Hugo séjourne d'abord en Belgique, d'où il attaque Napoléon III et son régime dans un pamphlet, *Napoléon-le-Petit* (1852). Puis il se réfugie bientôt à Jersey, poursuivant sa critique de Napoléon III dans un recueil de poèmes, *Les Châtiments* (1853) ; en 1855, il déménage avec sa famille à Guernesey. En 1859, année où l'Empire devient « libéral », Napoléon III accorde l'amnistie aux bannis. Hugo la refuse, et publie cette déclaration :

« Personne n'attendra de moi que j'accorde, en ce qui me concerne, un moment d'attention à la chose appelée amnistie. Dans la situation où est la France, protestation absolue, inflexible, éternelle, voilà pour moi le devoir.

Fidèle à l'engagement que j'ai pris vis-à-vis de ma conscience, je partagerai jusqu'au bout l'exil de la liberté. Quand la liberté rentrera, je rentrerai. »

Par ce geste courageux, il s'interdit tout retour en France, mais s'assure une indépendance de parole et affirme son hostilité persistante au régime de Napoléon III.

Privé de tribune, Hugo déploie son activité critique dans l'écriture. Ainsi, son *Discours sur la misère*, si mal reçu à la Chambre en 1849, trouve un écho retentissant dans *Les Misérables*, et sera repris sous forme romancée dans *L'homme qui rit*. En outre, même si l'intrigue des *Misérables* se déroule principalement sous la Restauration et au début de la monarchie de Juillet, le lecteur de 1862 percevra néamoins, au-delà du texte écrit entre 1845 et 1848, le « texte-barricade » (Anne Ubersfeld) du proscrit et du prophète. Napoléon III a beau n'être pas directement visé, la dénonciation des injustices sociales et de la répression peut aussi évoquer la situation en France sous le Second Empire.

Un jeune éditeur bruxellois enthousiaste et hardi, Lacroix, entreprend de publier le roman, et entretient avec l'auteur une correspondance féconde. Après la publication triomphale des premiers volumes, qui émeuvent fortement l'opinion, Lacroix, alarmé par des bruits qui courent, s'inquiète, à la lecture des chapitres sur les barricades, de « l'éventualité » d'une interdiction, et recommande la « prudence ». Mais Hugo refuse les coupures, et répond à l'éditeur :

« Le dénouement sort de la barricade. Le tableau d'histoire agrandit l'horizon et fait partie essentielle du drame. Il est comme le cœur du sujet. Il fera le succès du livre en grande partie. Il faut donc prendre son parti de la situation que nous fait l'abominable régime actuel. C'est le despotisme. Il fera à sa fantaisie. Nous n'y pouvons rien que le faire repentir ensuite. Ce que vous devez dire et répandre dès à présent, c'est que si Bonaparte persécute *Les Misérables*, la littérature au-dedans de la France m'étant fermée, je reprendrai la littérature au-dehors et je recommencerai la guerre de *Napoléon-le-Petit* et des *Châtiments*. Ceci pour intimider la persécution et la faire reculer. »

Les Misérables ne sera pas interdit.

La misère, le peuple et l'Histoire
dans *Les Misérables*

L'écriture romanesque de Victor Hugo échappe à toute classi-
fication définitive. *Les Misérables*, roman d'aventures, roman policier, roman d'apprentissage, roman philosophique, roman
d'amour, est aussi un roman social où l'auteur témoigne d'une
réalité nouvelle. L'Avant-propos nomme les trois problèmes du
siècle : « la dégradation de l'homme par le prolétariat, la
déchéance de la femme par la faim, l'atrophie de l'enfant par la
nuit ». La question sociale préoccupe les contemporains de Hugo,
qui donne dans son roman la parole à ceux que la société ne peut
plus ignorer : les misérables.

« LA DÉGRADATION DE L'HOMME
PAR LE PROLÉTARIAT »

Les innovations techniques du XVIIIᵉ siècle s'intensifient au
siècle suivant, dans un processus qu'on appellera la « révolution
industrielle » et dont l'apogée se situe dans la seconde moitié du
XIXᵉ siècle. L'intrigue des *Misérables* se déroule à cette époque
charnière, où l'ancien artisanat laisse peu à peu la place à de nouvelles méthodes de travail techniquement plus évoluées, écono-
miquement plus rentables, mais socialement redoutables. La
mécanisation entraîne en effet l'apparition du chômage pour les
personnes non qualifiées, ayant pour seule ressource leur force
de travail. Le travail de l'ouvrier, pénible et parfois dangereux,
est mal rémunéré. Les logements sont très inconfortables. Les
familles s'entassent souvent dans une seule pièce, dans une pro-
miscuité fâcheuse. Hugo, qui a vu de ses yeux la misère noire
dans laquelle vivent les ouvriers entassés dans les caves de Lille,

dénonce la condition ouvrière dans plusieurs de ses œuvres, notamment dans le poème « Joyeuse Vie » des *Châtiments*, et le poème « Melancholia » des *Contemplations* (voir p. 310-311).

LES CONTRASTES DE LA SOCIÉTÉ PARISIENNE

Paris est alors une ville pleine de contrastes. On passe très vite des beaux quartiers, comme le faubourg Saint-Germain et ses hôtels particuliers[1], aux quartiers défavorisés où les bourgeois n'osent pas s'aventurer. Malgré les aménagements réalisés depuis l'Empire, la ville, dont l'urbanisme a peu évolué depuis le Moyen Âge, est vétuste et insalubre, car l'hygiène publique laisse à désirer et les égouts sont encore rares. Les travaux d'assainissement sont entrepris sous le Second Empire, à l'époque où Hugo rédige *Les Misérables*.

La population parisienne s'accroît régulièrement, enrichie de provinciaux et d'étrangers venus chercher du travail et de meilleurs salaires dans la capitale. Une nouvelle couche de jeunes provinciaux vit en marge des Parisiens de souche, habitant des garnis, vivant en concubinage, dans un relatif anonymat, loin des conventions morales imposées par la vie de province. Ils s'entassent dans les vieux quartiers de Paris : les Halles, l'Hôtel-de-Ville, la rue Saint-Denis, les faubourgs Saint-Jacques et Saint-Marceau[2]. Cette concentration dans de sordides habitations est dangereuse, car l'agitation politique peut facilement y dégénérer en émeute.

La pauvreté est inquiétante : en 1821, 80 % des personnes laissent moins de 75 euros à leur mort. Les trois quarts des Parisiens sont enterrés aux frais de la communauté ou jetés à la fosse commune. Les pauvres meurent plus jeunes que les gens aisés. La maladie, le veuvage, le chômage, non indemnisé, peuvent faire basculer soudain une famille dans la plus grande détresse matérielle. L'inégalité de la population devant la maladie et la mort est criante.

---

1. C'est dans ce quartier que se situe la rue Plumet du roman.
2. C'est dans ce quartier que se situe la masure Gorbeau.

BOURGEOIS ET PROLÉTAIRES

Les classes populaires comprennent des domestiques, des militaires, de petits artisans et de nombreux ouvriers salariés. Les travailleurs à domicile sont durement exploités. Certaines ouvrières ne gagnent qu'un franc par jour (environ trois euros). Les journées de travail sont de 12 heures, et parfois davantage.

La petite bourgeoisie est constituée essentiellement d'artisans et de petits boutiquiers. La moyenne bourgeoisie comprend des négociants, des médecins, des architectes, des fonctionnaires de grade moyen ou élevé. On trouve les grosses fortunes dans l'ancienne aristocratie et chez des bourgeois enrichis, propriétaires d'immeubles et de terres, ou chez les banquiers, comme Rothschild, Péreire, Delessert, sans oublier le très populaire Jacques Laffitte, homme d'affaires aventureux et libéral, archétype du *self made man*, chez qui M. Madeleine, dans *Les Misérables*, place sa fortune. De 1814 à 1848, les notables jouent un rôle politique considérable dans la vie de la nation, car leur richesse leur confère, grâce au système censitaire, le privilège d'élire les députés. Ces derniers appartiennent à la frange la plus riche de la population : en effet le cens exigible pour être éligible est encore plus élevé que le cens exigible pour être électeur !

La mobilité sociale est assez grande. Dans la première moitié du XIXᵉ siècle, des artisans, des boutiquiers ou des fils de paysans fortunés peuvent devenir industriels, comme M. Madeleine dans le roman. L'idéologie* libérale dominante, qui exalte les valeurs de la liberté d'entreprise, est difficilement compatible avec l'idée d'assistance publique.

La bourgeoisie du XIXᵉ siècle, dont les valeurs sont l'épargne, l'honnêteté, le sérieux, la sévérité des mœurs, la rigueur de l'éducation, a généralement bonne conscience : elle trouve normale l'inégalité des revenus et des conditions sociales. De nombreux bourgeois voient dans les classes laborieuses des classes dangereuses, et portent le même regard soupçonneux sur les ouvriers « barbares », les marginaux, les vagabonds, les pauvres et les criminels. Cependant, une partie compatissante de la bourgeoisie, choquée par la misère, cherche les moyens de la résorber : à partir de 1820, en France et en Angleterre, des **philanthropes**, aristocrates et bourgeois, s'efforcent de soulager les détresses les plus criantes. La société catholique de Saint-Vincent-de-Paul est formée en 1833 ; Lamennais s'intéresse à la question sociale et appelle l'Église à s'occuper des prolétaires. Des patrons avertis cherchent à construire des cités ouvrières salubres, mais ces initiatives restent isolées. Dans *Les Misérables*, le maire de Montreuil dote l'hôpital de dix lits supplémentaires, crée une salle d'asile, une caisse de secours pour les ouvriers vieux ou infirmes, et deux écoles, l'une pour les garçons, l'autre pour les filles ; il institue une pharmacie gratuite pour les indigents ; Jondrette s'adresse à des philanthropes pour leur demander assistance. Jean Valjean, devenu le bourgeois aisé Fauchelevent, vient lui rendre une visite de charité dans son galetas. Tout au long du roman, le héros s'enrichit, mais il utilise ses ressources à améliorer le sort de la collectivité. Digne et Montreuil-sur-Mer sont les deux utopies romanesques où Hugo expérimente des solutions, aussi limitées soient-elles, pour lutter contre la misère.

Le modèle de Montreuil-sur-Mer est nettement paternaliste. Il s'inspire des initiatives privées prises par de grands patrons philanthropes, comme les industriels du textile de Mulhouse, certaines grandes compagnies minières, métallurgiques ou ferroviaires (la Compagnie d'Anzin, Schneider, la Compagnie du Nord...), qui s'efforcent de créer des cités ouvrières salubres. Signalons aussi qu'il existait déjà quelques sociétés de secours mutuel, entérinées par les lois et décrets de 1850 et 1852. M. Madeleine double de sa poche le salaire des instituteurs, palliant les défauts du système public par sa générosité individuelle. Les initiatives de M. Madeleine, isolées, constituent un modèle de ce que devraient être une véritable assistance publique, une éducation nationale, une prise en charge par la collectivité, et non plus seulement par la charité, des questions sociales.

LA CONDITION FÉMININE

Le second problème soulevé par Hugo dans son Avant-propos est celui de la condition féminine. La dureté des conditions de travail des ouvrières et l'insuffisance des salaires peut facilement les mener à la prostitution, selon un mécanisme implacable qui interdit ensuite à ces « femmes perdues » toute possibilité de réintégration.

Ainsi, le narrateur rend la société responsable du destin de Fantine. Il décrit le processus fatal par lequel la jeune femme, abandonnée par Tholomyès, qui ne se sent aucun devoir envers elle, malgré la naissance de leur enfant, doit quitter Paris, se séparer de Cosette, garder le secret sur l'existence de son enfant, céder au chantage de Thénardier, subir la malveillance de ses collègues, la perte de son travail, la précarité de ses revenus, puis se résoudre à vendre ses cheveux, ses dents, son corps, et finalement succomber à la maladie.

Au-delà de la condition des femmes pauvres, c'est la condition féminine dans son ensemble qui est en jeu. Le Code civil fait de la femme une mineure, qui doit obéissance à son père, puis à son mari, et se trouve dépourvue de nombreux droits. La femme adultère est passible de prison (c'est le sort de la maîtresse de Hugo, Léonie Biard, en 1845 ; voir p. 17), et peut être poursuivie sur simple dénonciation, tandis que le mari adultère n'est inquiété que s'il entretient une maîtresse à domicile. Comme beaucoup de penseurs de son époque, Hugo s'offusque de ces injustices, et accorde son soutien aux mouvements féministes. Ainsi, en 1872, il témoigne de sa solidarité au rédacteur en chef du journal *L'Avenir des femmes* en ces termes :

« Il est douloureux de le dire : dans la civilisation actuelle, il y a une esclave. La loi a des euphémismes[1] ; ce que j'appelle une esclave, elle l'appelle une mineure ; cette mineure selon la loi, cette esclave selon la réalité, c'est la femme. L'homme a chargé inégalement les deux plateaux du Code [...]. Dans notre législation telle qu'elle est, la femme ne possède pas, elle n'est pas en

---

1. **Euphémisme :** expression atténuée d'une réalité.

justice, elle ne vote pas, elle ne compte pas, elle n'est pas. Il y a des citoyens, il n'y a pas de citoyennes. C'est là un état violent : il faut qu'il cesse. […] On en viendra, espérons-le, à comprendre qu'une société est mal faite quand l'enfant est laissé sans lumière, quand la femme est maintenue sans initiative, quand la servitude se déguise sous le nom de tutelle, quand la charge est d'autant plus lourde que l'épaule est plus faible ; et l'on reconnaîtra que, même au point de vue de notre égoïsme, il est difficile de composer le bonheur de l'homme avec la souffrance de la femme. »

La lutte des mouvements féministes sera encore longue : la revendication du suffrage véritablement universel est formulée en 1848, à la faveur de la révolution. Après la Première Guerre mondiale, de nombreux pays accordent le droit de vote aux femmes. Mais, en France, elles ne l'obtiendront qu'en 1945 !

« L'ATROPHIE DE L'ENFANT PAR LA NUIT »

Troisième problème, l'exploitation des enfants par les adultes. Le sort des enfants dans la nouvelle organisation du travail préoccupe les philanthropes et, en 1832, le docteur Louis Villermé est chargé par l'Académie des sciences morales de mener une enquête sur la condition ouvrière. Il découvre la misère des enfants exploités, qui commencent parfois à travailler dès six ans. Ils peuvent travailler jusqu'à quatorze heures par jour, pour un salaire dérisoire. Échappant à tout système scolaire, ils sont incultes et illettrés ; les jeunes filles dérivent vers la prostitution (c'est ce que suggère la scène des *Misérables* où Éponine est envoyée par son père pour séduire Marius, leur jeune voisin). Cosette donne un autre exemple de cette dégradation de l'enfant par la société : exploitée par les Thénardier, la petite fille devient laide, sournoise, menteuse ; sa souffrance physique et morale la fait ressembler à une petite vieille, vision atroce. Elle doit à l'intervention miraculeuse de Jean Valjean, qui lui donne une deuxième naissance, d'échapper à son destin servile. D'autres enfants, comme Gavroche ou Montparnasse, n'ont pas sa chance. Ils sont contraints par la misère à vivre d'expédients, ou à intégrer des réseaux de voleurs ou de criminels, tel le petit Olivier Twist du roman de Dickens (voir p. 311). Les causes sociales de la criminalité sont observables dès l'enfance.

Une partie de l'opinion s'indigne de cette nouvelle forme d'esclavage. Le rapport du docteur Villermé inspirera la loi de 1841 qui limite le travail des enfants dans les manufactures, et ramène la journée de travail à huit heures pour les plus petits, douze heures pour les jeunes de 12 à 16 ans. Hugo étudie de près cette loi pendant la première phase de rédaction des *Misérables*. Sous le Second Empire – à l'époque de la seconde phase de conception des *Misérables* –, d'autres améliorations sociales verront le jour, comme la constitution, encore limitée, d'un réseau d'assistance médicale gratuite. La durée du temps de travail des enfants sera encore réduite, et on élèvera encore l'âge minimum d'embauche dans les usines. Mais, comme en témoigne par exemple le cas des enfants Maheu dans *Germinal* de Zola (dont l'action se passe sous le Second Empire), le travail des enfants constitue un revenu non négligeable pour les familles ouvrières. C'est la création par Jules Ferry en 1882 de l'école obligatoire pour les enfants de 7 à 13 ans, qui mettra fin à cette exploitation.

LES ÉCRIVAINS ET LA « QUESTION SOCIALE »

Les problèmes posés par l'industrialisation et l'urbanisation éveillent chez les penseurs de graves préoccupations. À l'ancienne misère reconnue, celle des campagnes, s'ajoute donc maintenant une pauvreté plus effrayante, moins facile à circonscrire, celle des concentrations ouvrières urbaines : le prolétariat qui s'y entasse constitue une population misérable, sans culture propre, sans conscience de classe encore organisée, vivant à l'écart de la société institutionnalisée, dans ces « forêts [qui] ont leurs antres » où se cache une population redoutable de gens vivant en marge de la cité, hors-la-loi. Un nouveau point de vue sur la société est en train de naître : les révolutions récentes avaient situé la question sur le terrain politique, et les problèmes posés par la nouvelle criminalité urbaine avaient d'abord reçu une réponse de type policier et judiciaire, incarnée dans *Les Misérables* par Javert. Hugo lui-même affirme que le temps est venu de la « substitution des questions sociales aux questions politiques ». Dans son *Discours sur la misère* prononcé à la chambre des députés en 1849, il montre combien l'écart entre les droits de l'homme proclamés par la Révolution française, et la réalité des conditions de vie des prolétaires crée un écart douloureux et dangereux pour la cohésion et l'ordre social :

« L'homme du peuple aujourd'hui souffre avec le sentiment double et contradictoire de sa misère résultant du fait et de sa grandeur résultant du droit. (*Profonde sensation.*) »

Le scandale éclate quand Hugo proclame : « Je suis de ceux qui pensent et qui affirment qu'on peut détruire la misère. (*Réclamations. – Violentes dénégations à droite.*) » Ces propos peuvent en effet passer pour sacrilèges aux yeux de ceux qui considèrent que la misère fait partie de l'ordre divin des choses terrestres. Soutenu sur sa gauche, interrompu sur sa droite, Hugo force les députés à entendre ce que beaucoup refusent d'admettre :

« Il y a dans Paris, dans ces faubourgs de Paris que le vent de l'émeute soulevait naguère si aisément, il y a des rues, des maisons, des cloaques, où des familles, des familles entières, vivent pêle-mêle, hommes, femmes, jeunes filles, enfants, n'ayant pour lits, n'ayant pour couvertures, j'ai presque dit pour vêtements, que des monceaux infects de chiffons en fermentation. »

Les conditions de vie de la famille Thénardier dans la masure Gorbeau correspondent bien à cette description.

Après ce discours, Hugo poursuit son enquête en visitant les quartiers ouvriers de Lille en 1851 avec l'économiste Adolphe Blanqui. Il constate que la loi de 1841 sur le travail des enfants n'est pas véritablement respectée, et prépare un autre discours qu'il n'aura pas l'occasion de prononcer, à cause du coup d'État de décembre 1851, après lequel il est exilé. Mais on retrouvera de nombreux échos de ce discours dans son œuvre, notamment dans le poème des *Châtiments* « Joyeuse Vie », dont un vers est resté célèbre : « Caves de Lille, on meurt sous vos plafonds de pierre ! » ainsi que dans le discours de Gwynplaine à la Chambre des lords, dans *L'homme qui rit*. Le second discours sur la misère de Hugo, dont on a gardé la trace, se terminait par une mise en garde adressée aux hommes politiques :

« Ah ! songez-y, quand les temps sont proches, quand l'heure est venue, quand la mesure est comble, savez-vous ce qu'il y a de plus éloquent, ce qu'il y a de plus irrésistible, ce qu'il y a de plus terrible pour commencer les révolutions, ce n'est pas M. Thiers signant la protestation des journalistes de 1830, ce n'est pas M. Odilon Barrot agitant les banquets de 1847, ce n'est pas Chateaubriand, ce n'est pas Lamartine, ce n'est pas même Mirabeau, ce n'est pas même Danton, c'est un enfant qui crie à sa mère : j'ai faim ! »

La littérature romanesque se fait elle aussi militante, en apportant sa contribution à la description des problèmes sociaux. Dans *Olivier Twist*, Dickens décrit la misère ouvrière en Angleterre. En France, Eugène Sue décrit les bas-fonds de la société parisienne dans *Les Mystères de Paris*, George Sand réhabilite l'image de la classe ouvrière dans ses romans sociaux.

Les philanthropes remettent en cause le dogme libéral de la non-intervention de l'État dans les problèmes sociaux, en proposant l'organisation de caisses de secours pour venir en aide aux plus démunis. Mais il faudra attendre la seconde moitié du siècle pour que le prolétariat, prenant conscience de son importance économique et sociale, s'organise en associations ou en syndicats et fasse entendre sa voix.

LE BAGNE

À travers le personnage de Jean Valjean, ce sont aussi les aberrations du système pénal que Hugo veut dénoncer. Il avait visité le bagne de Toulon en 1834 et celui de Brest en 1839. Cette institution lui semble une punition d'un autre âge. Le thème est fréquent dans la littérature de l'époque, comme en témoignent le grand succès des *Mémoires* de Vidocq[1] et la fascination qu'exerce Vautrin (voir p. 317) sur les autres personnages du *Père Goriot*. Le bagne remplace, au milieu du XVIIIᵉ siècle, l'institution des galères. Les galériens travaillaient sur les bateaux du roi ; regroupés en longues chaînes, les cadènes, ils partaient deux fois l'an pour Lorient ou Toulon. Après la disparition des galères, devenues obsolètes avec l'apparition de techniques de navigation plus modernes, apparaissent, suite au décret du 27 septembre 1748, des lieux pénitentiaires où les condamnés aux travaux forcés purgent leur peine. Ils sont enchaînés deux à deux, au moins au début de leur peine, et surveillés par des « garde-chiourmes » (avant d'être policier, Javert était adjudant garde-chiourme au bagne de Toulon, où il a connu Jean Valjean). Ces bagnes sont créés dans des zones portuaires, à Toulon par exemple, car les bagnards participent à la construction ou à la réparation des navires. C'est ainsi que Jean Valjean se retrouve de corvée dans le vaisseau *L'Orion*, mouillé dans le port de Toulon, d'où il s'échappe en plongeant. Le bagne ne sera transféré en Guyane qu'au milieu du XIXᵉ siècle.

Jean Valjean, condamné en 1796, ne porte pas la marque au fer rouge (TF pour « travaux forcés ») qui permet d'identifier Vautrin, le personnage de Balzac *(Le Père Goriot)* ; cette marque, supprimée après 1791, est rétablie de 1810 à 1830. Le passeport jaune, frappé de la lettre F, est une autre marque d'infamie : les forçats libérés doivent se rendre au lieu de résidence qui leur est assigné, en présentant ce passeport à la mairie ou au commissariat de police de toutes les villes traversées. S'ils ne se rendent pas à leur résidence ou s'ils la quittent, ils sont en rupture de ban et donc recherchés. Jean Valjean est dans cette situation. Le lecteur perd sa trace après l'épisode du vol de la pièce à Petit-Gervais et comprend *a posteriori* qu'il ne s'est pas rendu à Pontarlier, où il était assigné. La confusion qui règne à Montreuil-sur-Mer le jour de son arrivée lui permet d'échapper à la vérification de son

---

1. **Vidocq** (1775-1857) : ancien bagnard, devenu chef de la police.

passeport. C'est ainsi qu'il peut se réinsérer sous le faux nom de M. Madeleine. Mais Jean Valjean est toujours recherché par la police, incarnée par Javert.

À l'époque où Hugo écrit *Les Misérables*, le sort des forçats commence à susciter l'intérêt de certains penseurs. Pour Hugo, le bagne est « cette chose difforme et noire », « cette affreuse mort vivante », « un brasier de damnation, un enfer ». Cette institution punitive est indigne, car elle ne laisse aucune chance véritable de réintégration dans la société : « On sort du bagne, mais non de la condamnation ». Le sort inhumain réservé aux bagnards fait d'eux des êtres dénaturés, ivres de vengeance contre la société. Dès lors, au lieu de corriger la délinquance, le bagne devient au contraire l'école du crime, d'où le forçat ressort plus dangereux encore qu'il n'y est entré, tel Jean Valjean sortant de Toulon avec « ce hideux trésor de pensées affreuses qu'il avait mis dix-neuf ans à ramasser sur le pavé du bagne ».

Comme il l'avait déjà fait dans *Le Dernier Jour d'un condamné* (1829), Hugo critique également la peine de mort dès l'ouverture des *Misérables*, en rapportant le sentiment d'horreur éprouvé par Mgr Myriel qui a accompagné un condamné à la guillotine. Pour Hugo, la question posée par la délinquance ne concerne pas que la police et la justice. Le problème de la criminalité est indissociable de la question sociale.

INSCRIPTION DU RÉCIT DANS L'HISTOIRE

Pour donner à sa fiction toute la force du témoignage, Hugo ancre son récit dans la réalité historique : l'auteur devient un personnage du roman, lorsqu'il relate sa visite sur la plaine de Waterloo, où il situe un épisode décisif pour l'intrigue, celui du sauvetage fortuit du père de Marius par Thénardier, détrousseur de cadavres. Il prend alors la parole en son nom propre, dans l'*incipit** du livre II : « L'an dernier [1861], par une belle matinée de mai, un passant, celui qui raconte cette histoire, arrivait de Nivelles et se dirigeait vers la Hulpe. Il allait. » La silhouette de l'auteur apparaît ainsi au lecteur, qui peut mesurer l'écart relatif entre le temps de l'écriture du roman et le temps de la fiction. La bataille de Waterloo (1815) fait ainsi l'objet d'une longue digression qui permet à Hugo d'envisager l'Histoire avec recul. L'insurrection de 1832 est longuement racontée : elle occupe une part importante de la quatrième partie.

Outre ces deux événements historiques, le narrateur multiplie les références à la réalité géographique, historique et sociale de son époque, au point que certaines pages sont de véritables documents. Mais ces références n'ont pas pour seule fonction la production d'effets de réel, destinés à accréditer la fiction. Elles ont aussi une signification symbolique : ainsi 1815 est l'année de Waterloo, mais aussi celle de la libération de Jean Valjean et de la naissance de Cosette. De même, la description des égouts est à la fois réaliste, donnant lieu à une longue réflexion de l'auteur sur les nouveaux principes de l'hygiène publique, et symbolique, puisqu'elle évoque dans le même temps le « chemin de croix » de Jean Valjean.

Le propos de l'auteur n'est pas pour autant de montrer l'épopée d'un peuple qui serait le héros positif du roman. Pour les misérables, l'avenir est plus qu'incertain. Au dénouement, les destins individuels l'emportent sur les destins collectifs : quelle que soit la sympathie qu'on éprouve pour les jeunes révolutionnaires, leur cause est perdue, et les motivations de Marius et de Jean Valjean pour aller sur la barricade sont avant tout personnelles. Si le peuple anonyme des *Misérables* n'a pas encore les moyens historiques de faire valoir ses droits, il trouve du moins dans le roman l'espace où proférer enfin une parole que la société a jusqu'ici refusé d'entendre.

Les métamorphoses du roman

UN ROMAN D'AVENTURES

Les Misérables est un roman-fleuve, dont la version intégrale occupe trois volumes dans les éditions de poche. Sa structure, très originale, déjoue toutes les attentes d'un roman traditionnel. Le récit est certes très architecturé, avec ses cinq parties, divisées en livres, eux-mêmes constitués de chapitres, trois cent soixante-cinq en tout, autant que de jours dans l'année ! Mais cette maîtrise de l'ensemble se combine avec une grande liberté de composition : ainsi, contrairement aux lois du genre, le héros n'intervient qu'au livre II, l'entrée de Jean Valjean dans Digne, initialement prévue pour constituer l'*incipit** du roman, ayant été décalée dans la version finale, où elle constitue une sorte de second début, à retardement. Puis le héros est oublié pendant cent pages. Les personnages secondaires, comme Fantine, Cosette, Gavroche, Marius, Thénardier, sont les héros principaux de certaines parties du roman, qui s'enchâssent dans la trame générale. L'écriture « démocratique » de Hugo passe aussi par cette égalité de traitement entre les personnages. Le roman est parcouru de centaines de figures, plus ou moins esquissées : certains personnages, sitôt évoqués, disparaissent définitivement du roman, comme la sœur et les neveux de Jean Valjean ou les jeunes amies de Fantine. Le lecteur ne saura pas ce que sont devenus ces misérables que le roman, comme la société, engloutit dans son ombre.

Les Misérables paraissent directement en volumes, mais sont inspirés par la technique du roman-feuilleton. Ce genre fort à la mode s'est développé depuis les années 1840, grâce à l'expansion de la presse. De nombreux romans de Balzac paraissent

ainsi dans les journaux avant d'être publiés en volumes individuels. Le plus grand succès du genre est *Les Mystères de Paris*
d'Eugène Sue, parus quotidiennement dans *Le Journal des
débats* en 1842-1843, qui suscitent un engouement extraordinaire auprès du public (certains lecteurs écrivent à l'auteur pour
lui demander d'infléchir le destin des personnages dans la direction qu'ils souhaitent). Cette forme de parution commande une
écriture en chapitres relativement courts, et la relance régulière
du suspense, pour maintenir l'intérêt du lecteur et l'inciter à
acheter la prochaine livraison du journal dans l'attente de la
suite. Selon une technique différente, mais comparable, le narrateur des *Misérables* entretient le suspense sur le destin du
bagnard, en ne révélant pas tout de suite l'identité de
M. Madeleine, ni celle de l'inconnu qui vient chercher Cosette
à Montfermeil. Dans le premier cas, Jean Valjean a disparu pendant deux livres, depuis le vol de la pièce à Petit-Gervais. Dans
le deuxième cas, le lecteur le croit mort après sa chute du vaisseau *L'Orion* ; sa disparition est alors certifiée par des coupures
de journaux. Le narrateur finit toujours, au moment de la révélation, par supposer que son lecteur complice a reconnu de lui-
même le héros, ce qui est le cas, bien sûr. Il arrive qu'il s'autorise
des retours en arrière, plus ou moins longs, qui permettent de
retracer l'itinéraire secret du fuyard.

Celui-ci est parfois difficile à reconstituer. Les grandes étapes
du parcours de Jean Valjean le mènent de Faverolles au bagne de
Toulon, puis à Digne. Se rendra-t-il à Pontarlier, où il est assigné
à sa sortie du bagne ? L'épisode du vol de la pièce à Petit-Gervais
semble l'en empêcher. On comprend *a posteriori* qu'il n'a pas
rejoint la ville où il devait se rendre (et être surveillé) : il est en
rupture de ban. On le retrouve à Montreuil-sur-Mer. Après le
procès d'Arras, où il dévoile sa véritable identité pour ne pas laisser condamner l'innocent Champmathieu à sa place, il retourne
au bagne, d'où il s'évade. Il réapparaît à Montfermeil, pour aller
chercher Cosette, qu'il ramène à Paris. Là, il doit bientôt fuir la
masure Gorbeau et se retrouve au couvent du Petit-Picpus, où il
reste plusieurs années, à l'abri derrière les murs de cette retraite

protectrice. Quand il en sort, il cherche à brouiller les pistes en changeant souvent de domicile. Dernier trajet symbolique : sa longue marche dans les égouts. La durée du récit de ces différents épisodes n'est pas homogène : ainsi, la narration de la nuit de Noël 1823 où il va chercher Cosette occupe un livre entier (II° partie, livre III), tandis que les cinq années passées au couvent du Petit-Picpus sont résumées en une phrase : « Plusieurs années s'écoulèrent ainsi ; Cosette grandissait. »

UNE FRESQUE SOCIALE : LES MISÈRES

« Tant qu'il y aura sur la terre ignorance et misère, des livres de la nature de celui-ci pourront ne pas être inutiles. » Dans son Avant-propos, l'auteur déclare son ambition de contribuer au progrès de l'humanité. Le roman, en décrivant par quel processus la misère pousse les pauvres gens à voler, à exploiter ou abandonner les enfants, les ouvrières à se prostituer, les jeunes à vagabonder, montre comment la société se retrouve menacée par ces bas-fonds qu'elle produit et exclut.

L'indignation de l'auteur perce souvent sous la narration, par exemple lorsque Cosette, sous les menaces de la Thénardier, se tord les mains, « ce qui est effrayant à dire dans un enfant de cet âge ». Mais il est difficile de dégager avec certitude la position de l'auteur sur certaines questions politiques et sociales : Jean Valjean a eu beau souffrir de l'exclusion, il n'est pourtant pas un révolutionnaire. M. Madeleine est un notable respectable, industriel et maire de sa ville. Il épargne pour que Cosette, devenue Mme la baronne Pontmercy, mène une existence aisée. Quant à Thénardier, il a beau être une crapule, il n'en tient pas moins des propos éclairants sur la bonne conscience bourgeoise.

Il ne s'agit pas d'un roman à thèse, dans la mesure où les solutions à la misère restent à inventer, et semblent difficiles à mettre en œuvre. Certes, le progrès paraît pouvoir venir du travail, de la charité, des bonnes mœurs et de l'éducation, qui sont les principes de M. Madeleine à Montreuil-sur-Mer. Mais cette expérience, limitée dans l'espace et le temps, puisque son succès s'évanouit avec le bienfaiteur, a dans le roman un caractère utopique. Dans ce roman social, Hugo est davantage prophète que partisan.

UN TÉMOIGNAGE HISTORIQUE

Dans *Les Misérables*, le romancier se fait le témoin de l'Histoire, dans une perspective qui rappelle celle d'écrivains ou d'historiens novateurs comme les frères Grimm ou Michelet. Comme le théâtre, le roman est à l'époque romantique l'une des formes de l'écriture de l'Histoire : délaissant l'essai, elle emprunte le biais de la fiction. Hugo raconte à la fois l'histoire « du dehors » celle des événements, et l'histoire « du dedans », celle des mœurs, car « nul n'est bon historien de la vie patente, visible, éclatante et publique des peuples s'il n'est en même temps, dans une certaine mesure, historien de leur vie profonde et cachée » (IVᵉ partie, livre VII, chap. 1). Victor Hugo se fait le chroniqueur de la Restauration et des premières années de la monarchie de Juillet, en racontant les grands événements politiques et militaires (comme Waterloo, ou l'insurrection de juin 1832), mais aussi la vie quotidienne des petites gens, à Paris et en province, et les débats d'idées qui divisent les diverses couches de la population. *Les Misérables* sont le premier roman de la littérature française dont le peuple est le héros (comme en témoigne son titre collectif). Il correspond de ce point de vue à la nouvelle conception romantique de l'Histoire, qui ne limite pas cette dernière aux grands événements, aux grandes batailles, aux couronnements et aux actions d'éclat des grands, mais l'envisage dans le temps plus long de l'activité des hommes, de leurs mœurs et de leurs conditions de vie.

L'HISTOIRE D'UNE ÂME

Dans sa *Préface philosophique*, Hugo annonçait un « livre religieux ». Si l'auteur s'est, en 1862, séparé de « toutes les Églises », son roman est malgré tout placé sous la figure tutélaire de Mgr Myriel, qui rachète au forçat son âme pour la donner à

Dieu, et dont le souvenir guidera Jean Valjean jusqu'à son dernier soupir. Les allusions à l'Évangile sont nombreuses : Jean Valjean se convertit au Bien, prend le nom de Madeleine, la pécheresse repentie, va chercher Cosette une nuit de Noël, porte Marius dans les égouts comme Jésus porte sa croix, et meurt apaisé, une fois ses fautes rachetées. Son trajet peut être comparé à la Passion du Christ.

Mais au-delà des références religieuses, ce sont les mémoires d'une âme qui nous sont ici donnés à lire, à travers la solitude radicale de Jean Valjean, « grande figure romantique du moi » (Nicole Savy). Cette histoire n'est pas différente de celle des hommes, car « faire le poème de la conscience humaine, ne fût-ce qu'à propos d'un seul homme, ne fût-ce qu'à propos du plus infime des hommes, ce serait fondre toutes les épopées dans une épopée supérieure et définitive » (I, VII, 3). Le moi des personnages romantiques s'ouvre ainsi à l'humanité entière, et notamment au moi du lecteur.

LE PLAISIR DES TITRES

La langue de Hugo est très imagée. L'alternance des styles est frappante et donne à l'écriture une grande richesse.

Hugo aime jouer avec les mots. C'est le cas par exemple dans les titres des livres et des chapitres, dont la forme syntaxique est très variable : il peut s'agir tout simplement du nom d'un personnage : « Petit-Gervais » (I, II, 13) ; d'un motif-épisode « La cadène » (IV, III, 8), « Le baril de poudre » (IV, 14, 4) ; d'indications spatio-temporelles : « Le champ de bataille la nuit » (II, I, 19) ou de l'annonce d'un épisode identifiable : « Le guet-apens » (III, VIII, 20). Mais il peut s'agir aussi de formules inattendues, qui permettent à l'auteur de jouer avec la complicité de son lecteur : maximes (« Confier, c'est parfois livrer » IV, IV) ; images symboliques (« Le septième cercle et le huitième ciel » V, VII, 1, « Une tempête sous un crâne » I, VII, 3) ; formules ironiques (« Le désœuvrement de M. Bamatabois » I, V, 12 ; « Désagrément de recevoir chez soi un pauvre qui est peut-être un riche » II, III, 8) ou souriantes (« La rose s'aperçoit qu'elle est une machine de guerre », IV, III, 5) ; commentaires sur la technique d'écriture : « Deux portraits complétés » (III, III, 2) ; entrées encyclopédiques : « Le sobriquet : mode de formation des noms de famille » (III, VI, 1) ; citations latines : « *Lux facta est* » (III, II, 6) ; programmes d'action : « Se préoccuper des fonds obscurs » (III, VIII, 19) ; commentaires sur l'action à la mode des romans picaresques : « Où le petit Gavroche tire parti de Napoléon le Grand » (IV, VI, 2). La lecture de la tables des matières est à elle seule tout un roman !

Les figures de style abondent dans ces titres : métaphore : « L'alouette » (I, IV, 3) ; antithèse : « Oreste à jeun et Pylade ivre » (V, I, 23) ; balancement : « Suprême ombre, suprême aurore » (V, IX) ; oxymore : « Les grandeurs du désespoir » (IV, XIV) ; « Buvard, bavard » (IV, XV, 1) joue sur une paronomase*. La formule de Rimbaud, pour qui *Les Misérables* sont « un véritable poème », s'applique déjà aux titres.

LA CRÉATION VERBALE

Hugo est inventif aussi dans la création des noms de personnages, qui comporte une dimension symbolique : on peut remarquer, dans le nom d'emprunt Fauchelevent et le surnom Leblanc, des mots comme *vent* ou *blanc* connotant l'absence d'identité du personnage ; Cosette et Fantine n'ont pas de nom de famille, la première est une « petite chose », la seconde, pourtant mère, une femme « enfantine ».

L'écrivain varie les registres de langue. Une partie du réalisme de l'œuvre tient à l'emploi de l'argot. Il s'agit à l'origine de la langue orale des voleurs, puis des misérables, forgée et utilisée par les initiés qui veulent échapper à la police en développant un vocabulaire parallèle, inaccessible aux bourgeois. C'est pourquoi elle est particulièrement riche dans le lexique de l'argent, de la justice, de l'architecture des maisons, dans celui des armes, de la police et de la justice, de la nourriture, du corps. Son emploi dans *Les Misérables* donne à l'écrivain le plaisir de la création lexicale, que l'on trouve dans la richesse du langage de

Gavroche (« Colle-toi ça dans le fusil », dit-il à son petit frère en lui tendant à manger), mais aussi de toute la famille Thénardier. Le niveau de langue trahit l'appartenance sociale : celle d'Éponine par exemple, qui note sur un papier : « Les cognes sont là[1] ». Hugo consacre un livre entier (IV, VII) à l'étude de cette langue originale, employée au Moyen Âge par François Villon, à son époque par Balzac et Eugène Sue, et analyse ce phénomène comme le signe de la maladie du peuple misérable.

La grande richesse stylistique des *Misérables* vient aussi de l'emploi des vocabulaires techniques (comme *radier, fontis, coulants*), qui contribuent au réalisme du récit et témoignent de l'immense curiosité linguistique de Hugo. Les images abondent également : les figures animales servent à peindre les caractères : Cosette est ainsi comparée à une alouette, Thénardier à un chacal, Javert à un faucon. L'abstrait est parfois désigné par des termes concrets (« des monstruosités cyniques »). Les antithèses (comme celle de l'ombre et de la lumière) structurent l'esthétique du roman : l'antithèse est en effet pour Hugo « cette loi de succession et de contraste qui est le fond même de la nature ». Elle ne peint pas un monde manichéen en noir et blanc. Elle permet, chez Hugo, de dire la complexité des choses, les contradictions internes des êtres : elle est donc l'un des moyens les plus appropriés pour traduire l'alliance du sublime et du grotesque.

La caractérisation des personnages, par la description, le dialogue et le monologue intérieur, est riche. L'alternance des points de vue narratifs (par exemple dans les épisodes de Petit-Gervais, ou de Cosette et la poupée) donne ainsi une grande souplesse au récit. Mais on notera un élément très particulier, invisible à la première lecture : dans le roman, le personnage principal reste aussi, jusqu'au bout, le plus mystérieux, non seulement par son caractère et son destin hors du commun, mais aussi par le sort particulier que lui réserve la narration. Jean

---

1. **Cognes** (argot) : gendarmes, policiers.

Valjean parle peu, très peu, et ses sentiments restent souvent secrets. Plusieurs scènes majeures sont décrites du point de vue des autres personnages : c'est le cas, notamment, dans la scène où il soulage Cosette du poids de son seau et la raccompagne à l'auberge. Il surgit d'on ne sait où (la dernière fois qu'il a été question de lui, c'était dans une coupure de presse qui annonçait sa mort par noyade), son nom n'est pas donné, et seuls les sentiments et les perceptions de Cosette sont évoqués. Cette technique permet au narrateur d'exacerber la curiosité du lecteur pour ce personnage, auquel chacun prête ses propres sentiments pour arriver à le comprendre. Ce mode de lecture entraîne donc non seulement la sympathie pour le personnage, mais aussi la compréhension intime de sa situation et des problèmes sociaux et psychologiques qu'il rencontre.

Les voix narratives sont variées. Hugo fait feu de tout bois pour élever *Les Misérables* à la dimension d'œuvre totale. D'autres genres littéraires viennent alimenter le roman, comme les discours politiques, les chansons, inventées par Hugo ou entendues dans la rue, les dialogues dramatiques. Les situations théâtrales sont nombreuses, ce qui explique la facilité avec laquelle on a pu, depuis un siècle et demi, adapter ce roman sur la scène, malgré sa taille impressionnante. Quant à la langue, elle fait appel à d'autres formes d'écriture parallèles : l'argot, les citations latines, les pages personnelles de carnet, les lettres, les coupures de journaux, les budgets, les rapports de police... Toutes techniques d'écriture novatrices, que l'on trouve fréquemment dans les romans contemporains. Le narrateur s'efface devant cette « prolifération des voix » (Annette Rosa), se faisant peu à peu aussi insaisissable, aussi anonyme que les misérables eux-mêmes.

LES THÈMES

LES « MISÉRABLES »

« Les infortunés et les infâmes se mêlent et se confondent dans un seul mot, mot fatal, les misérables. » Le mot *misérables* désigne à la fois les pauvres, les malheureux, et les malfaiteurs. Ces trois sens ne se recouvrent pas, mais Hugo montre comment la pauvreté et la détresse qui l'accompagne peuvent entraîner la chute dans la délinquance. L'auteur ne décrit pas en sociologue la misère des ouvriers. Il met plutôt en lumière la détresse des plus faibles, enfants, femmes, vieillards, et montre par quel mécanisme on finit par voir dans les « classes laborieuses » des « classes dangereuses ».

L'ENFANCE

Pour l'auteur, les enfants sont le symbole de l'innocence et leur souffrance, provoquée par la société ou par la méchanceté des hommes, est révoltante. La peinture des bas-fonds de Paris montre quel avenir la société réserve aux enfants livrés à eux-mêmes : Éponine, choyée par sa mère à Montfermeil, devient une gueuse mêlée aux sombres trafics de son père à Paris. Montparnasse, satisfait par l'état de voleur, ne voit pas l'intérêt de chercher du travail. Gavroche, abandonné par ses parents, invente un mode de vie autonome : il est le type du gamin de Paris, libre, spirituel, débrouillard, généreux envers plus misérable que lui. Contestataire, insouciant, inconscient du danger, il participe à l'insurrection, au cours de laquelle il meurt sous le feu des soldats. Cosette, bâtarde et pauvre, échappe à la déchéance qui guette les femmes grâce au dévouement de Jean Valjean, qui la sauve de la misère et lui donne une éducation. Son destin, qui est celui d'une héroïne de conte de fées, est beaucoup moins vraisemblable que celui des autres enfants du roman.

LES PRÉJUGÉS SOCIAUX

Les misérables sont rejetés par la société qui est en partie responsable de leur sort. Jean Valjean, le soir de son arrivée à Digne, est traqué par le regard des habitants avant d'être refoulé. Le forçat, dénoncé par son passeport jaune, n'a plus aucune chance de se réinsérer dans la société. Seul Mgr Myriel accepte de le recevoir sans tenir compte de son passé. La foule stupide et sans pitié se précipite pour voir passer la cadène avec une curiosité malsaine. Les habitants de Montreuil-sur-Mer nourrissent, sur l'identité de monsieur Madeleine, des soupçons qui disparaissent sitôt qu'il s'enrichit. Marius lui-même, à la fin du roman, ne peut s'empêcher de rejeter le « père » de Cosette en apprenant son identité.

Fantine, fille-mère abandonnée, sera victime des mêmes préjugés. Mme Victurnien obtient son renvoi de la fabrique sous prétexte que l'ouvrière a eu un enfant hors mariage. M. Bamatabois, bourgeois imbu de sa respectabilité, s'autorise à insulter et à maltraiter la « fille publique ». Lors de leur dispute, Javert arrête spontanément la prostituée, présumant le bourgeois innocent. C'est que le policier, « fils d'une tireuse de cartes dont le mari était aux galères », veut absolument échapper à son milieu d'origine et respecte aveuglément la loi et la normalité. À la fin du roman, Jean Valjean lui apparaît sublime, supérieur à la loi qui le condamne et, incapable d'assumer l'effondrement de ses certitudes, Javert se suicide.

IDENTITÉ ET MARGINALITÉ

La société officielle ne prend pas en compte les misérables, l'état civil semble les avoir oubliés. Entre eux, les liens de filiation se distendent : Cosette ne sait pas qui est sa mère, Gavroche et ses frères sont abandonnés par les Thénardier. Fantine, « petite enfant », n'a qu'un prénom, et sa fille Cosette est une « petite chose » sans nom, baptisée par la Thénardier « Mlle Chien-faute-de-nom », ou « cette autre ». Cosette adoptera le nom d'emprunt de son faux père, avant d'entrer de plein droit dans la société civile par son mariage avec Marius Pontmercy, dont elle prend légitimement le nom.

Jean Valjean est lui aussi un homme sans identité avouable. Le vide s'inscrit dans ses surnoms ou faux noms (Leblanc, Fauchelevent), et son patronyme officiel ne fait que répéter son prénom. Il doit au trouble de la nuit où il est arrivé à Montreuil-sur-Mer d'avoir pu se rebaptiser Madeleine. Il est en cela comparable à Thénardier, qui change d'identité à toute occasion, s'appelant Jondrette à Paris, signant ses lettres de demande de charité de noms d'artistes, comme Fabantou ou Genflot. Autant de noms, autant de masques. Jean Valjean feint d'avoir le bras en écharpe pour ne pas invalider le mariage de Cosette en signant d'un nom illégitime. Anonyme, il traverse ainsi toutes les couches de la société, passant du statut de bagnard à celui de petit industriel. Mais son nom, à jamais sali par le passeport jaune qu'il ne peut pas montrer, lui interdit d'usurper le bonheur familial que lui offrent Cosette et Marius, à qui il déclare : « Un nom, c'est un moi », et il disparaît sans laisser de traces, comme en témoigne l'état d'abandon de sa tombe, elle aussi anonyme.

L'ARGENT

L'un des principaux ressorts dramatiques de l'action des *Misérables* est la circulation de l'argent. Sa possession est déterminante dans l'accès à la respectabilité sociale. Jean Valjean vole un pain parce qu'il n'a plus de quoi assurer la subsistance de ses neveux. En arrivant à Digne, il n'a que sa masse, cent neuf francs quinze sous (environ 330 euros) gagnés en dix-neuf ans de bagne. Les couverts volés sont en argent, comme les chandeliers que lui donne Mgr Myriel. La réussite sociale de M. Madeleine se solde par un enrichissement jalousement protégé, argent placé d'abord chez le banquier Laffitte, puis soigneusement enterré dans un bois.

Même les enfants peuvent être achetés. Cosette est l'objet d'un odieux marchandage : Thénardier, qui a déjà détroussé des cadavres et poussé Fantine dans la tombe par son affreux chantage, vend l'enfant à Jean Valjean ; à Paris il monnaye ses deux plus jeunes fils. Lors du mariage, la dot de près de six cent mille francs que son « père » laisse à Cosette occupe une place déterminante, et Jean Valjean éprouve le besoin, avant de mourir, de certifier que cette somme a été honnêtement gagnée.

L'argent donné par Mgr Myriel a donc été utilisé à bon escient par Jean Valjean, qui a procuré du travail aux ouvriers de Montreuil-sur-Mer, exercé la charité philanthropique, et surtout sauvé Cosette de la misère. La circulation de l'argent concrétise ainsi l'achat de l'âme de Jean Valjean par Mgr Myriel au début du roman.

LE BIEN PUBLIC

Hugo espère, dans certaines pages, un avenir meilleur. Les solutions proposées dans le roman sont pourtant ponctuelles, et reposent avant tout sur l'initiative individuelle. À Digne, l'évêque tente d'améliorer le sort des nécessiteux en dotant l'hôpital, auquel il sacrifie son propre confort, et en restreignant ses dépenses au profit des pauvres. On retrouve des principes semblables chez M. Madeleine, qui lui aussi dote l'hôpital, fait construire deux écoles, double le salaire des instituteurs, crée une salle d'asile et une caisse de secours pour les vieux travailleurs, et tente d'instaurer des principes de moralité publique à Montreuil-sur-Mer. Devenu rentier, Jean Valjean continue son œuvre de charité, en secourant de pauvres gens comme Jondrette. Il donne aussi sa bourse au jeune voyou qui l'a agressé, après lui avoir fait une leçon de morale. Mais la charité des deux hommes est individuelle et leur œuvre disparaît avec eux.

LE RACHAT

Le roman commençait, dans la première version, par l'arrivée de Jean Valjean à Digne. Hugo a rajouté le premier livre de la première partie consacré à l'évêque, dont l'influence est décisive sur le destin de Jean Valjean. En effet, l'émondeur de Faverolles a basculé dans le Mal le jour où il a volé un pain, et le bagne a fait de lui un être dangereux et impie. Mais l'évêque lui par-donne le vol des couverts, lui donne en plus les chandeliers, et lui achète son âme pour la donner à Dieu.

La conversion de Jean Valjean au Bien doit passer par une première épreuve, qui agira comme une révélation. Le remords qu'il éprouve après avoir volé la pièce de Petit-Gervais constitue le premier combat spirituel de Jean Valjean. Viendront par la suite d'autres cas de conscience : la « tempête sous un crâne » avant le procès de Champmathieu, le trouble éprouvé à la lecture de la lettre de Marius, le désarroi qui suit le mariage de Cosette.

Les allusions à l'Évangile émaillent le roman. Le choix du nom de M. Madeleine rappelle immanquablement Marie-Madeleine, la pécheresse repentie. M. Madeleine n'oublie pas Mgr Myriel, dont il porte le deuil. Malgré ses bonnes intentions, qui se manifestent par sa philanthropie, il est poursuivi par un sentiment de culpabilité : Fantine a été chassée de sa fabrique. M. Madeleine va tenter de réparer le mal dont il se sent responsable, en prenant soin de la jeune femme déchue et en sauvant sa fille.

C'est par une nuit de Noël qu'il va chercher Cosette. Par le symbolisme de la nativité, cet épisode constitue une deuxième naissance pour la petite fille, et permet à Jean Valjean d'accéder à la paternité. Le pénible trajet dans les égouts est une sorte de chemin de croix où Jean Valjean porte Marius sur ses épaules, lourd fardeau qui causera son supplice, puisque Marius lui prendra Cosette, son bien le plus cher. Dès lors, la fin de sa vie prend la forme d'un renoncement : à l'amour de Cosette, qui ne lui appartient pas ; à sa fortune, qu'il lui offre comme dot ; à la reconnaissance de Marius, dont il est le sauveur inavoué. Au moment de mourir, ayant racheté ses fautes par ses souffrances, par sa Passion, Jean Valjean touche à la sainteté.

L'enfance malheureuse

CHARLES PERRAULT, *CENDRILLON*, 1697

Un motif de conte

« Il était une fois un Gentilhomme qui épousa en secondes noces une femme, la plus hautaine et la plus fière qu'on eût jamais vue. Elle avait deux filles de son humeur[1], et qui lui ressemblaient en toutes choses. Le Mari avait de son côté une jeune fille, mais d'une douceur et d'une bonté sans exemple ; elle tenait cela de sa Mere, qui était la meilleure personne du monde. Les noces ne furent pas plus tôt faites, que la Belle-mère fit éclater sa mauvaise humeur ; elle ne put souffrir les bonnes qualités de cette jeune enfant, qui rendaient ses filles encore plus haïssables. Elle la chargea des plus viles occupations de la Maison : c'était elle qui nettoyait la vaisselle et les montées[2], qui frottait la chambre de Madame, et celles de Mesdemoiselles ses filles ; elle couchait tout au haut de la maison, dans un grenier, sur une méchante[3] paillasse, pendant que ses sœurs étaient dans des chambres parquetées, où elles avaient des lits des plus à la mode, et des miroirs où elles se voyaient depuis les pieds jusqu'à la tête. La pauvre fille souffrait tout avec patience, et n'osait s'en plaindre à son père qui l'aurait grondée, parce que sa femme le gouvernait entièrement. Lorsqu'elle avait fait son ouvrage, elle s'allait mettre au coin de la cheminée, et s'asseoir dans les cendres[4], ce qui faisait qu'on l'appelait communément dans le logis Cucendron. La

---

1. **De son humeur :** du même caractère.
2. **Montées :** escaliers.
3. **Méchante :** vilaine, grossière.
4. **S'asseoir dans les cendres :** geste d'humiliation ou de pénitence.

cadette, qui n'était pas si malhonnête[1] que son aînée, l'appelait Cendrillon ; cependant Cendrillon, avec ses méchants habits, ne laissait pas[2] d'être cent fois plus belle que ses sœurs, quoique vêtues très magnifiquement. »

Charles PERRAULT, « Cendrillon »,
Histoires et Contes du temps passé.

QUESTIONS

1. Étudiez les relations entre les personnages du conte. Comparez la situation de Cosette chez les Thénardier (I, IV, 3) avec celle de Cendrillon.
2. Relevez les champs lexicaux* du Bien et du Mal. La belle-mère de Cendrillon et la Thénardier ont-elles les mêmes motivations ? Montrez que Hugo dépasse la portée psychologique et morale du conte, pour donner au thème de l'enfant martyrisé une dimension sociale.

HUGO, « MELANCHOLIA », 1856

Hugo : traitement poétique du thème

Les Contemplations *est un recueil de poésie lyrique qui ne traite pas seulement de sentiments intimes : la sensibilité du poète est un tout, où les questions privées et les questions publiques sont liées. Contrairement à ce que son titre pourrait laisser croire, le poème « Melancholia », ne traite pas de la mélancolie d'un sujet solitaire, mais de l'humeur noire (c'est l'étymologie du mot* mélancolie) qui est à la fois celle des miséreux exploités, de la société où ils vivent, et du poète qui en est le témoin.*

> « Où vont tous ces enfants dont pas un seul ne rit ?
> Ces doux êtres pensifs, que la fièvre maigrit ?
> 115 Ces filles de huit ans qu'on voit cheminer seules ?
> Ils s'en vont travailler quinze heures sous des meules ;
> Ils vont, de l'aube au soir, faire éternellement
> Dans la même prison le même mouvement,
> Accroupis sous les dents d'une machine sombre,

---

1. **Malhonnête :** impolie.
2. **Ne laissait pas d'être :** était néanmoins.

120 Monstre hideux qui mâche on ne sait quoi dans l'ombre,
Innocents dans un bagne, anges dans un enfer,
Ils travaillent. Tout est d'airain, tout est de fer.
Jamais on ne s'arrête et jamais on ne joue.
Aussi quelle pâleur ! la cendre est sur leur joue.
125 Il fait à peine jour, ils sont déjà bien las.
Ils ne comprennent rien à leur destin, hélas !
Ils semblent dire à Dieu : « Petits comme nous sommes,
Notre père, voyez ce que nous font les hommes ! »
Ô servitude infâme imposée à l'enfant !
130 Rachitisme ! travail dont le souffle étouffant
Défait ce qu'a fait Dieu ; qui tue, œuvre insensée,
La beauté sur les fronts, dans les cœurs la pensée,
Et qui ferait – c'est là son fruit le plus certain –
D'Apollon un bossu, de Voltaire un crétin !
135 Travail mauvais qui prend l'âge tendre en sa serre,
Qui produit la richesse en créant la misère,
Qui se sert d'un enfant ainsi que d'un outil !
Progrès dont on demande : « Où va-t-il ? que veut-il ? »
Qui brise la jeunesse en fleur ! qui donne, en somme,
140 Une âme à la machine et la retire à l'homme ! »

Victor HUGO, *Les Contemplations*, III, 2.

QUESTIONS

1. Étudiez la métaphore de la machine-monstre. Quelles sont les autres métaphores filées dans ce passage ?

2. Quelle est la position du poète face au progrès technique, d'après la fin du texte ?

DICKENS, *LES AVENTURES D'OLIVIER TWIST*, 1837-1839

La question sociale des orphelins

Quelques années avant Les Misérables, *le romancier anglais Charles Dickens s'intéresse lui aussi aux causes sociales de la criminalité. Le petit héros, Olivier Twist, né de père inconnu et*

d'une mère qui meurt en lui donnant le jour, est élevé par une
nourrice peu attentionnée, avant d'être placé dans un hospice
pour enfants nécessiteux, à la sortie duquel il sera enrôlé par une
bande de voleurs sans scrupules. La scène se passe à l'hospice.

« Les petits garçons ont généralement fort bon appétit. Olivier Twist et ses camarades supportèrent la torture d'une lente inanition trois mois durant : à la fin, ils devinrent si voraces, si enragés de faim, que l'un d'eux, qui était fort grand pour son âge et qui n'avait pas été habitué à ce genre de traitement (son père ayant tenu une petite rôtisserie), laissa entendre d'un air sombre à ses compagnons qu'à moins de recevoir une écuellée supplémentaire *per diem*[1], il craignait bien d'en arriver quelque soir à dévorer son voisin de lit, un chétif freluquet d'âge tendre. Il avait l'œil égaré et avide, et tous le crurent sans hésitation. On tint conseil et on tira au sort pour désigner celui qui le soir même, à la fin du dîner, irait trouver le surveillant pour lui demander un supplément ; le sort tomba sur Olivier Twist.

Vint le moment du dîner ; les enfants prirent place à table. Le surveillant, vêtu de sa tenue de cuisinier, se posta près de la chaudière ; ses assistantes indigentes se rangèrent derrière lui ; l'on servit le brouet[2] et l'on dit de longues grâces sur le bref ordinaire[3]. Le brouet disparut ; les garçons chuchotèrent entre eux et adressèrent des clins d'œil à Olivier, tandis que ses voisins immédiats le poussaient du coude. Tout enfant qu'il était, la faim et la détresse lui donnaient l'énergie farouche du désespoir. Il se leva de table, s'avança, écuelle et cuiller à la main, jusqu'au surveillant et dit, quelque peu effrayé de sa propre audace :

"S'il vous plaît, Monsieur, j'en voudrais encore."

Le surveillant était un gros homme, regorgeant de santé, mais il devint livide. Hébété de stupéfaction, il contempla quelques secondes le petit rebelle, puis s'agrippa à la chaudière en guise de soutien. Les assistantes étaient paralysées par la surprise, les enfants par la peur. »

---

1. *Per diem* (expression latine) : par jour.
2. **Brouet** : bouillon léger et peu nourrissant.
3. Les **grâces** sont une prière dite en remerciement avant le repas (**l'ordinaire**).

"Quoi ? fit enfin le surveillant, d'une voix faible.

– S'il vous plaît, répéta Olivier, j'en voudrais encore."

Le surveillant allongea un coup de sa louche sur la tête de l'enfant et enserra celui-ci dans ses bras en hurlant pour appeler le bedeau[1].

Le Conseil siégeait en conclave[2] solennel quand M. Bumble se précipita, tout excité, dans la pièce et dit à l'adresse du monsieur assis dans le grand fauteuil :

"Monsieur Limbkins, excusez-moi, Monsieur ! Olivier Twist en a redemandé !"

Il y eut un sursaut général. L'horreur se peignit sur tous les visages.

"Redemandé ! s'écria M. Limbkins. Remettez-vous, Bumble, et répondez-moi clairement. Dois-je comprendre qu'il a demandé un supplément, après avoir mangé le dîner alloué par le règlement ?

– Oui, Monsieur, répondit Bumble.

– Ce garçon finira au gibet, dit le monsieur au gilet blanc. Je suis certain qu'il finira au gibet."

Personne ne contredit cette prophétique opinion. Une discussion animée prit place. On ordonna qu'Olivier fût immédiatement enfermé et, le lendemain matin, un placard fut apposé à l'extérieur de la grille, offrant une récompense de cinq livres à quiconque voudrait débarrasser la paroisse de la personne d'Olivier Twist. En d'autres termes, on offrait cinq livres et Olivier Twist à tout homme ou toute femme désirant un apprenti en n'importe quel métier, commerce ou profession.

"Jamais de ma vie je n'ai été plus convaincu de quoi que ce soit que je ne le suis de ceci, dit le monsieur au gilet blanc tandis que le lendemain matin il frappait à la porte et lisait l'avis : ce garçon finira au gibet." »

Charles DICKENS, *Les Aventures d'Olivier Twist*,
traduit de l'anglais par Francis Ledoux,
© éditions Gallimard, 1958.

---

1. **Bedeau :** en Angleterre, employé laïque chargé de diverses fonctions subalternes.
2. **Conclave :** réunion des autorités (= le Conseil) dont dépend l'hospice.

1. Reconstituez et commentez le raisonnement sous-jacent à l'affirmation : « Ce garçon finira au gibet ».

2. Comparez le ton adopté par le narrateur des *Misérables* dans le portrait de Cosette exploitée par les Thénardier (« L'Alouette », p. 63) avec celui du narrateur des *Aventures d'Olivier Twist*.

JULES VALLÈS, *L'ENFANT*, 1879

Les privations

L'Enfant, *premier tome de la trilogie autobiographique de Jules Vallès, raconte sur un ton sarcastique les malheurs de son enfance. L'œuvre se donne une portée sociale plus générale, puisque l'auteur la dédie* « [à] tous ceux qui crevèrent d'ennui au collège ou qu'on fit pleurer dans la famille, qui, pendant leur enfance, furent tyrannisés par leurs maîtres ou rossés par leurs parents ».

« Les collègues de mon père, quelques parents d'élèves, viennent faire visite, on m'apporte des bouts d'étrennes.

"Remercie donc, Jacques ! Tu es là comme un imbécile."

Quand la visite est finie, j'ai plaisir à prendre le jouet ou la friandise, la boîte à diable ou le sac à pralines ; – je bats du tambour et je sonne de la trompette, je joue d'une musique qu'on se met entre les dents et qui les fait grincer, c'est à en devenir fou !

Mais ma mère ne veut pas que je devienne fou, elle me prend la trompette et le tambour. Je me rejette sur les bonbons et je les lèche. Mais ma mère ne veut pas que j'aie des manières de courtisan : "On commence par lécher le ventre des bonbons, on finit par lécher…" Elle s'arrête, et se tourne vers mon père pour voir s'il pense comme elle, et s'il sait de quoi elle veut parler ; – en effet, il se penche et montre qu'il comprend.

Je n'ai plus rien à faire siffler, tambouriner, grincer, et l'on m'a permis seulement de traîner un petit bout de langue sur les bonbons fins : et l'on m'a dit de la faire pointue encore ! Il y avait Eugénie et Louise Rayau qui étaient là, et qui riaient en rougissant un peu. Pourquoi donc ?

Plus de gros vernis bleu qui colle aux doigts et les embaume, plus le goût du bois blanc des trompettes !...

On m'arrache tout et l'on enferme les étrennes sous clef.

"Rien qu'aujourd'hui, maman, laisse-moi jouer avec, j'irai dans la cour, tu ne m'entendras pas ! rien qu'aujourd'hui, jusqu'à ce soir, et demain je serai bien sage !

– J'espère que tu seras bien sage demain ; si tu n'es pas sage, je te fouetterai. Donnez donc de jolies choses à ce saligot, pour qu'il les abîme."

Ces points vifs, ces taches de couleur joyeuse, ces bruits de jouet, ces trompettes d'un sou, ces bonbons à corset de dentelle, ces pralines comme des nez d'ivrognes, ces tons crus et ces goûts fins, ce soldat qui coule, ce sucre qui fond, ces gloutonneries de l'œil, ces gourmandises de la langue, ces odeurs de colle, ces parfums de vanille, ce libertinage du nez et cette audace du tympan, ce brin de folie, ce petit coup de fièvre, ah ! comme c'est bon, une fois l'an ! – Quel malheur que ma mère ne soit pas sourde !

Ce qui me fait mal, c'est que tous les autres sont si contents ! Par le coin de la fenêtre, je vois dans la maison voisine, chez les gens d'en face, des tambours crevés, des chevaux qui n'ont qu'une jambe, des polichinelles cassés ! Puis ils sucent, tous, leurs doigts ; on les a laissés casser leurs jouets et ils ont dévoré leurs bonbons.

Et quel boucan ils font !

Je me suis mis à pleurer.

C'est qu'il m'est égal de regarder des jouets, si je n'ai pas le droit de les prendre et d'en faire ce que je veux ; de les découdre et de les casser, de souffler dedans et de marcher dessus, si ça m'amuse...

Je ne les aime que s'ils sont à moi, et je ne les aime pas s'ils sont à ma mère. C'est parce qu'ils font du bruit et qu'ils agacent les oreilles qu'ils me plaisent ; si on les pose sur la table comme des têtes de mort, je n'en veux pas. Les bonbons, je m'en moque, si on m'en donne un par an comme une exception, quand j'aurai été sage. Je les aime quand j'en ai trop.

"Tu as un coup de marteau[1], mon garçon !" m'a dit ma mère un jour que je lui contais cela, et elle m'a cependant donné une praline.

"Tiens, mange-la avec du pain."

On nous parle en classe des philosophes qui font tenir une leçon dans un mot. Ma mère a de ces bonheurs-là, et elle sait me rappeler par une fantaisie, un rien, ce qui doit être la loi d'une vie bien conduite et d'un esprit bien réglé.

"Mange-la avec du pain !"

Cela veut dire : Jeune fou, tu allais la croquer bêtement, cette praline. Oublies-tu donc que tu es pauvre ! À quoi cela t'aurait-il profité ! Dis-moi ! Au lieu de cela, tu en fais un plat utile, une portion, tu la manges avec du pain.

J'aime mieux le pain tout seul. »

Jules VALLÈS, *L'Enfant*, chapitre 7.

---

1. **Tu as un coup de marteau :** tu es fou (familier).

QUESTIONS

1. Observez le rythme des phrases, le niveau de langue, le mode des discours rapportés : quelle est la tonalité générale du passage ?

2. Le personnage de la mère est complexe : quelle est sa philosophie de la vie ? Peut-on la comprendre ?

QUESTIONS D'ENSEMBLE

1. Quel lien peut-on établir entre le thème littéraire de l'enfance malheureuse, qui est initialement un motif de conte, et la question sociale de la misère au XIXe siècle ?

2. Quels sont les problèmes rattachés aujourd'hui, en France et dans le monde, au thème de l'enfance malheureuse ?

Le personnage du hors-la-loi dans la littérature du XIXe siècle

BALZAC, *LE PÈRE GORIOT*, 1835

Un autre ancien bagnard

Au début du Père Goriot, *le narrateur présente les locataires de la pension Vauquer. L'un d'eux, Vautrin, est un personnage mystérieux, dont on découvrira la véritable identité à la fin du roman : cet ancien forçat est un dangereux bandit.*

« Il était un de ces gens dont le peuple dit : Voilà un fameux gaillard ! Il avait les épaules larges, le buste bien développé, les muscles apparents, des mains épaisses, carrées et fortement marquées aux phalanges par des bouquets de poils touffus et d'un roux ardent. Sa figure, rayée par des rides prématurées, offrait des signes de dureté que démentaient ses manières souples et liantes. Sa voix de basse-taille[1], en harmonie avec sa grosse gaieté, ne déplaisait point. Il était obligeant[2] et rieur. Si quelque serrure allait mal, il l'avait bientôt démontée, rafistolée, huilée, limée, remontée, en disant : « Ça me connaît. » Il connaissait tout d'ailleurs, les vaisseaux, la mer, la France, l'étranger, les affaires, les hommes, les événements, les lois, les hôtels et les prisons. Si quelqu'un se plaignait par trop, il lui offrait aussitôt ses services. Il avait prêté plusieurs fois de l'argent à madame Vauquer et à quelques pensionnaires ; mais ses obligés[3] seraient morts plutôt que de ne pas le lui rendre, tant, malgré son air bonhomme, il imprimait de crainte par un certain regard profond et plein de résolution. À la manière dont il lançait un jet de salive, il annonçait un sang-froid imperturbable qui ne devait pas le faire reculer devant un crime

---

1. **Voix de basse-taille :** voix grave (terme de musique).
2. **Obligeant :** aimable, serviable.
3. **Ses obligés :** les personnes qui lui sont redevables du service qu'il leur a rendu.

pour sortir d'une position équivoque[1]. Comme un juge sévère, son œil semblait aller au fond de toutes les questions, de toutes les consciences, de tous les sentiments. [...] Il savait ou devinait les affaires de ceux qui l'entouraient, tandis que nul ne pouvait pénétrer ni ses pensées ni ses occupations. Quoiqu'il eût jeté son apparente bonhomie, sa constante complaisance et sa gaieté comme une barrière entre les autres et lui, souvent il laissait percer l'épouvantable profondeur de son caractère. Souvent une boutade[2] digne de Juvénal[3], et par laquelle il semblait se complaire à bafouer les lois, à fouetter la haute société, à la convaincre d'inconséquence avec elle-même, devait faire supposer qu'il gardait rancune à l'état social, et qu'il y avait au fond de sa vie un mystère soigneusement enfoui. »

Honoré de BALZAC, *Le Père Goriot*.

QUESTIONS

1. Balzac décrit très précisément son personnage et le montre en action. Quels détails permettent de déduire la personnalité de Vautrin de son portrait physique et de son comportement ?

2. Quels sont les points communs apparents entre Vautrin et Jean Valjean ? Quelles sont leurs différences ?

3. Comparez la manière dont Balzac (dans ce texte) et Hugo (I, II, 1) entretiennent le mystère sur l'identité et le passé de leurs personnages respectifs, dès leur première apparition.

HUGO, « LA CONSCIENCE », 1859

Le mythe de Caïn, ou la culpabilité originelle

Le motif du repentir du criminel est fréquent dans Les Petites Épopées, *première série de* La Légende des siècles, *volume poétique contemporain de la rédaction définitive des* Misérables.

---

1. **Équivoque :** embarrassante.
2. **Boutade :** trait d'esprit.
3. **Juvénal :** poète latin du IIe s. apr. J.-C., qui critiqua dans ses *Satires* les vices de son époque.

Les premiers poèmes sont des réécritures de l'Ancien Testament. Le personnage de Caïn, premier fils d'Adam et Ève, qui a assassiné son frère Abel, incarne la présence originelle du Mal dans le cœur de l'homme, mais aussi l'existence de sa conscience morale. On rapprochera l'image de l'œil de la pièce de monnaie dont la simple vue accuse Jean Valjean, « comme si cette chose qui luisait là dans l'obscurité eût été un œil ouvert fixé sur lui » (voir p. 59, l. 125-126).

« Lorsque avec ses enfants vêtus de peaux de bêtes,
Échevelé, livide au milieu des tempêtes,
Caïn se fut enfui de devant Jéhovah,
Comme le soir tombait, l'homme sombre arriva
Au bas d'une montagne en une grande plaine ;
Sa femme fatiguée et ses fils hors d'haleine
Lui dirent : "Couchons-nous sur la terre, et dormons."
Caïn, ne dormant pas, songeait au pied des monts.
Ayant levé la tête, au fond des cieux funèbres,
Il vit un œil, tout grand ouvert dans les ténèbres,
Et qui le regardait dans l'ombre fixement.
"Je suis trop près", dit-il avec un tremblement.
Il réveilla ses fils dormant, sa femme lasse,
Et se remit à fuir sinistre dans l'espace.
Il marcha trente jours, il marcha trente nuits.
Il allait, muet, pâle et frémissant aux bruits,
Furtif, sans regarder derrière lui, sans trêve,
Sans repos, sans sommeil ; il atteignit la grève
Des mers dans le pays qui fut depuis Assur.
"Arrêtons-nous, dit-il, car cet asile est sûr.
Restons-y. Nous avons du monde atteint les bornes."
Et, comme il s'asseyait, il vit dans les cieux mornes
L'œil à la même place au fond de l'horizon.
Alors il tressaillit en proie au noir frisson.
"Cachez-moi !" cria-t-il ; et, le doigt sur la bouche,
Tous ses fils regardaient trembler l'aïeul farouche.
Caïn dit à Jabel, père de ceux qui vont
Sous des tentes de poil dans le désert profond :

"Étends de ce côté la toile de la tente."
Et l'on développa la muraille flottante ;
Et, quand on l'eut fixée avec des poids de plomb,
"Vous ne voyez plus rien ?" dit Tsilla, l'enfant blond,
La fille de ses fils, douce comme l'aurore ;
Et Caïn répondit : "Je vois cet œil encore !"
Jubal, père de ceux qui passent dans les bourgs
Souffrant dans des clairons et frappant des tambours,
Cria : "Je saurai bien construire une barrière."
Il fit un mur de bronze et mit Caïn derrière.
Et Caïn dit : "Cet œil me regarde toujours !"
Hénoch dit : "Il faut faire une enceinte de tours
Si terrible, que rien ne puisse approcher d'elle.
Bâtissons une ville avec sa citadelle,
Bâtissons une ville, et nous la fermerons."
Alors Tubalcaïn, père des forgerons,
Construisit une ville énorme et surhumaine.
Pendant qu'il travaillait, ses frères, dans la plaine,
Chassaient les fils d'Énos et les enfants de Seth ;
Et l'on crevait les yeux à quiconque passait ;
Et, le soir, on lançait des flèches aux étoiles.
Le granit remplaça la tente aux murs de toiles,
On lia chaque bloc avec des nœuds de fer,
Et la ville semblait une ville d'enfer ;
L'ombre des tours faisait la nuit dans les campagnes ;
Ils donnèrent aux murs l'épaisseur des montagnes ;
Sur la porte on grava : "Défense à Dieu d'entrer."
Quand ils eurent fini de clore et de murer,
On mit l'aïeul au centre en une tour de pierre ;
Et lui restait lugubre et hagard. "Ô mon père !
L'œil a-t-il disparu ?" dit en tremblant Tsilla.
Et Caïn répondit : "Non, il est toujours là."
Alors il dit : "Je veux habiter sous la terre
Comme dans son sépulcre un homme solitaire ;
Rien ne me verra plus, je ne verrai plus rien."
On fit donc une fosse, et Caïn dit : "C'est bien !"

Puis il descendit seul sous cette voûte sombre ;
Quand il se fut assis sur sa chaise dans l'ombre
Et qu'on eut sur son front fermé le souterrain,
L'œil était dans la tombe et regardait Caïn. »

Victor HUGO, La Légende des siècles.

QUESTIONS

1. Dégagez la structure du texte en repérant les étapes-clefs et leurs éléments récurrents : lieux, actions de Caïn et des siens, retour de l'œil, réaction, nouveau départ. Remarquez comment le mot *œil* se déplace dans le vers. Quel est l'effet produit ?

2. Commentez la chute du poème.

3. Dans les deux textes, explicitez la métaphore de l'œil, image d'un Dieu transcendant (extérieur, dominant, et omniscient), mais aussi d'une conscience intime.

DOSTOÏEVSKI, *CRIME ET CHÂTIMENT*, 1866

Le retour de la conscience dans le rêve

Le héros du roman, Raskolnikov, étudiant pauvre et orgueilleux, croit que les lois morales ne s'appliquent pas aux « hommes extraordinaires » dont il estime faire partie. Aussi pense-t-il prouver sa supériorité en tuant. Il se repentira, poussé par une force intérieure qui l'incitera à se dénoncer et à rechercher son châtiment. Après avoir assassiné une vieille usurière pour lui dérober son argent, le souvenir de son crime lui revient en rêve.

« Il était là et attendait. Il attendit longtemps et, plus la lune était calme, plus son cœur battait fort, plus il lui faisait mal. Et toujours ce silence. Soudain se fit entendre un craquement sec, instantané, comme si on avait cassé une baguette ; puis tout retomba dans le silence. Une mouche réveillée soudain, dans son vol frappa la vitre et bourdonna plaintivement. À ce moment même, dans le coin entre la petite armoire et la fenêtre, il distingua un manteau qui paraissait pendu au mur. "Pourquoi ce manteau ici ? pensa-t-il, il n'y était pas, avant…" Il s'approcha tout doucement et devina que derrière ce manteau quelqu'un devait être caché. Prudemment, il écarta de la main le manteau et vit qu'il y avait là une chaise, et sur la chaise était assise une mauvaise petite vieille, toute recroquevillée et baissant la tête, de sorte qu'il ne pouvait distinguer son visage ; mais c'était elle. Il resta là devant elle : "Elle a peur !" pensa-t-il. Tout doucement il dégagea de son nœud la hache et frappa la vieille sur la nuque, une fois, une seconde fois. Mais, chose singulière, elle n'a même pas bougé sous les coups, comme si elle était de bois. Il eut peur, se baissa davantage et se mit à la dévisager ; mais elle baissa la tête encore plus bas. Il se baissa alors jusqu'au plancher, et la regarda de bas en haut ; il la regarda et crut mourir : la mauvaise petite vieille était assise et riait – elle se tordait dans un rire silencieux, à peine perceptible, en faisant tous ses efforts pour qu'il ne l'entendît pas. Il lui sembla soudain que la porte de la chambre à coucher venait de s'entr'ouvrir, et que là-bas aussi on riait et on chuchotait. La rage s'empara de lui : de toutes ses forces il se mit à frapper la vieille sur la tête, mais à chaque coup de hache les rires et les chuchotements retentissaient de plus en plus fort, tandis que la mauvaise petite vieille elle-même se dodelinait de rire. Il voulut s'enfuir, mais toute l'entrée était déjà pleine de gens, la porte donnant sur le palier était largement ouverte, et ce palier, l'escalier, en allant vers le bas, n'étaient que gens, tête contre tête, tous regardaient, mais tous faisant le mort et attendant en silence… Son cœur était serré comme dans un étau, ses jambes refusaient d'avancer, clouées sur placc… Il voulut crier et… il s'éveilla.

Il respira péniblement. Chose singulière, son rêve semblait encore se prolonger : sa porte était grande ouverte, et sur le seuil se tenait un homme absolument inconnu de lui… qui le regardait fixement. »

Fedor DOSTOÏEVSKI, *Crime et Châtiment*, III, 6,
traduit du russe par Pierre Pascal,
© éditions Flammarion, « GF », 1984.

1. Repérez la structure du rêve : ses étapes successives, ses motifs principaux. Quels sont les procédés stylistiques qui mettent en valeur l'atmosphère de rêve ?

2. À quels signes perçoit-on l'affleurement de la conscience morale du héros dans le rêve ?

ALEXANDRE DUMAS, *ANTONY*, 1831

Le jeune premier criminel au théâtre

Antony est le plus grand succès public du drame romantique. Ce personnage de jeune premier ténébreux, que sa bâtardise a empêché d'épouser la femme qu'il aime, et qu'il finira par tuer pour sauver son honneur perdu, incarnait, selon son auteur, les contradictions mêmes de la société de la monarchie de Juillet, libérale et puritaine. La tirade qui suit se situe au début de la pièce. Antony n'a pas encore commis l'assassinat d'Adèle, qui interviendra au dénouement, mais le récit qu'il fait de son passé à sa bien-aimée, qu'il vient de retrouver mariée après des années, donne des indices permettant de comprendre le processus par lequel l'exclusion sociale peut engendrer le crime.

« ANTONY. Et pourquoi les [les lois de la société] accepterais-je, moi ?... Pas un de ceux qui les ont faites ne peut se vanter de m'avoir épargné une peine ou rendu un service ; non, grâce au ciel, je n'ai reçu d'eux qu'injustice, et ne leur dois que haine... Je me détesterais du jour où un homme me forcerait à l'aimer... Ceux à qui j'ai confié mon secret ont renversé sur mon front la faute de ma mère... Pauvre mère !... Ils ont dit : « Malheur à toi qui n'as pas de parents !... » Ceux à qui je l'ai caché ont calomnié ma vie... Ils ont dit : « Honte à toi qui ne peux pas avouer à la face de la société d'où te vient ta fortune !... » Ces deux mots, honte et malheur, se sont attachés à moi comme deux mauvais génies... J'ai voulu forcer les préjugés à céder devant l'éducation... Arts, langues, science, j'ai tout étudié, tout appris... Insensé que j'étais d'élargir mon cœur pour que le désespoir pût y tenir ! Dons naturels ou sciences acquises, tout s'effaça devant la tache de ma nais-

---

sance : les carrières ouvertes aux hommes les plus médiocres se fermèrent devant moi ; il fallait dire mon nom, et je n'avais pas de
nom. Oh ! que ne suis-je né pauvre et resté ignorant ! perdu dans
le peuple, je n'y aurais pas été poursuivi par les préjugés ; plus ils se
rapprochent de la terre, plus ils diminuent, jusqu'à ce que, trois
pieds au-dessous, ils disparaissent tout à fait.

ADÈLE. Oui, oui, je comprends... Oh ! plaignez-vous ! plaignez-
vous !... car ce n'est qu'avec moi que vous pouvez vous plaindre !

ANTONY. Je vous vis, je vous aimai ; le rêve de l'amour succéda à
celui de l'ambition et de la science ; je me cramponnai à la vie, je
me jetai dans l'avenir, pressé que j'étais d'oublier le passé... Je fus
heureux... quelques jours... les seuls de ma vie !... Merci, ange !
car c'est à vous que je dois cet éclair de bonheur, que je n'eusse
pas connu sans vous... C'est alors que le colonel d'Hervey...
Malédiction !... Oh ! si vous saviez combien le malheur rend
méchant ! combien de fois, en pensant à cet homme, je me suis
endormi la main sur mon poignard !... et j'ai rêvé de Grève et
d'échafaud !

ADÈLE. Antony !... vous me faites frémir...

ANTONY. Je partis, je reviens ; il y a trois ans entre ces deux
mots... Ces trois ans se sont passés je ne sais où ni comment ; je
ne serais pas même sûr de les avoir vécus, si je n'avais le souvenir
d'une douleur vague et continue... Je ne craignais plus les injures
ni les injustices des hommes ; ... je ne sentais plus qu'au cœur, et
il était tout entier à vous... Je me disais : « Je la reverrai... Il est
impossible qu'elle m'ait oublié... je lui avouerai mon secret... et
peut-être qu'alors elle me méprisera, me haïra. »

ADÈLE. Antony, oh ! comment l'avez-vous pu penser ?

ANTONY. Et moi, à mon tour, moi, je la haïrai aussi comme les
autres ; ... ou bien, lorsqu'elle saura ce que j'ai souffert, ce que
je souffre, ... peut-être elle me permettra de rester près d'elle...
de vivre dans la même ville qu'elle !

ADÈLE. Impossible.

ANTONY. Oh ! il me faut pourtant haine ou amour, Adèle ! je veux
l'un ou l'autre... J'ai cru un instant que je pourrais repartir ;

insensé !… je vous le dirais, qu'il ne faudrait pas le croire ; Adèle, je vous aime, entendez-vous ?… Si vous vouliez un amour ordinaire, il fallait vous faire aimer par un homme heureux !… Devoirs et vertu !… vains mots !… Un meurtre peut vous rendre veuve… Je puis le prendre sur moi, ce meurtre ; que mon sang coule sous ma main ou sous celle du bourreau, peu m'importe !… il ne rejaillira sur personne et ne tachera que le pavé… Ah ! vous avez cru que vous pouviez m'aimer, me le dire, me montrer le ciel… et puis tout briser avec quelques paroles dites par un prêtre… Partez, fuyez, restez, vous êtes à moi, Adèle !… à moi, entendez-vous ? je vous veux, je vous aurai… Il y a un crime entre vous et moi ?… Soit, je le commettrai… Adèle, Adèle ! je le jure par ce Dieu que je blasphème ! par ma mère, que je ne connais pas !…

ADÈLE. Calmez-vous, malheureux !… vous me menacez !… vous menacez une femme… »

Alexandre DUMAS, Antony.

QUESTIONS

1. Étudiez, dans le dialogue, les signes de la gestuelle et de l'intonation des acteurs romantiques.

2. Montrez comment Antony fait dériver sa personnalité de sa condition sociale.

3. Quels sont les indices du dénouement présents dans cette scène ?

QUESTIONS D'ENSEMBLE

1. Les textes ici réunis mettent une même catégorie de personnages dans des genres différents (roman, théâtre, poésie). Quels sont les enjeux propres à chaque type de texte ?

2. La société du XIXe siècle est hantée par la question du Mal : le criminel est-il le produit inévitable du déchet organique de la société, ou est-il poussé au mal par le fonctionnement même de cette dernière ? Dans quels termes cette question se pose-t-elle de nos jours ?

3. Le cinéma contemporain propose lui aussi divers types de hors-la-loi, depuis l'incarnation du mal absolu, jusqu'au bandit-justicier, en passant par le malheureux poussé au crime par la misère. Analysez ces différents types en prenant les exemples de votre choix.

LECTURES
DES *MISÉRABLES*

Tout en reconnaissant son génie, Lamartine a souvent été agacé par le style de Hugo, qu'il juge excessif. Il a trouvé le roman *Notre-Dame de Paris* immoral par manque de religion. Tout en reconnaissant le talent prodigieux de l'auteur des *Misérables*, il reproche au livre d'être dangereux, par l'espoir déraisonnable qu'il est susceptible de donner aux malheureux.

« Le livre est dangereux, parce que le danger suprême en fait de sociabilité, l'excès séduisant l'idéal, le pervertit. Il passionne l'homme peu intelligent pour l'impossible : la plus terrible et la plus meurtrière des passions à donner aux masses, c'est la passion de l'impossible ! Presque tout est impossible dans les aspirations des *Misérables*, et la première de ces impossibilités, c'est l'extinction de toutes nos misères.

Ne trompez pas l'homme, vous le rendriez fou ; et quand, de la folie sacrée de votre idéal, vous le laisseriez retomber sur l'aridité et la nudité de ses misères, vous le rendriez fou furieux. […]

La société, tout imparfaite qu'elle est, parce qu'elle est l'expression d'un être imparfait, est le grand fait accompli des siècles. Il faut le reconnaître ou s'appeler Titan ; tout remettre en question, comme les utopistes ; se constituer en état de révolte radicale contre la forme de l'humanité tout entière, c'est-à-dire en état de démence et de frénésie contre la FORCE DES CHOSES, cette souveraineté absolue de Dieu.

Que la société, sans cesse pénétrée de l'esprit divin, qui est un esprit de paix et non de guerre, s'interroge sans cesse elle-même pour savoir ce qu'elle peut introduire d'améliorations pratiques dans ses formes et dans ses lois sans faire écrouler l'édifice, qu'elle s'appelle tour à tour oligarchie, aristocratie, monarchie, démocratie, république, selon que la force des choses, la tradition, l'innovation lui indique dans quelle région de la hiérarchie humaine se trouve le plus de droit, de force conservatrice, d'autorité nécessaire, de lumière législative, de responsabilité et de passion du bien général. C'est l'acte même de la vie sociale ; c'est la pulsation du pouls, c'est le battement du cœur de l'humanité ; ce sont quelquefois les changements d'attitude, debout ou assis, des peuples en révolution ; c'est la FORCE DES CHOSES en législation.

Mais qu'on fasse espérer aux peuples, fanatisés d'espérances, le renversement à leur profit des inégalités organiques créées par la FORCE DES CHOSES, et maintenues par la nature elle-même sous peine de mort ; qu'on leur persuade que les deux bases fondamentales de toute société non barbare, la propriété et la famille, ces deux constitutions de Dieu et non de l'homme, peuvent être déplacées par le radicalisme sans que tout s'écroule à la fois sur la tête des radicaux comme des conservateurs, c'est là le rêve, c'est là la démence, c'est là le sacrilège, c'est le drapeau rouge ou le drapeau noir de la philosophie sociale ! Tout ce qu'il y a de raison, de bon sens, de lumière dans l'intelligence humaine, doit se rallier et protester contre ces doctrines qui seraient le suicide de l'humanité. [...]

Malgré ses protestations sincères et courageuses contre toute coercition violente à ses fins, la seule magie de son éloquence, les seuls mirages de ses promesses, la seule séduction de ses songes dorés, font de son livre un livre malsain de fait. Il est trop beau pour être innocent. Il ne sait pas dire à la société humaine d'assez rudes vérités ; il lui masque la face impassible de la FORCE DES CHOSES ; il la soulève contre le fait accompli ; il la flatte plus qu'il ne l'éclaire ; il donne tort partout à la société contre la misère, contre la nécessité, contre le crime ; il lui reproche ses impuissances.

Les utopistes sont souvent plus à craindre que les scélérats eux-mêmes, parce qu'on ne s'en défie pas et qu'on aime ses flatteurs. Platon, Fénelon, Morus, ont peut-être fait verser autant de sang que Catilina. Que Victor Hugo prenne garde à ce côté de son génie ! et qu'avant d'énoncer sa théorie du progrès sans limites, il étudie profondément la FORCE DES CHOSES, la loi de la nature, incommutable comme la nature elle-même.

Nous sommes tous des *misérables*, et nous ne serons jamais des dieux !

Mais, pour tempérer nos misères et pour désarmer l'utopie, le ciel nous a laissé un divin intermédiaire, l'assistance mutuelle, cette charité de tous pour tous.

Que la société l'introduise en plus forte dose dans ses lois, à chaque misère sociale qui se révèle.

La charité légale est le traité de paix entre nous. [...]

En résumé, *Les Misérables* sont un sublime talent, une honnête intention, et un livre très dangereux de deux manières :

Non seulement parce qu'il fait trop craindre aux heureux, mais parce qu'il fait trop espérer aux malheureux. »

Alphonse de LAMARTINE
(extraits des Entretiens 83 à 87 du *Cours familier de littérature*, parus de novembre 1862 à mars 1863).

Baudelaire fait paraître dans *Le Boulevard* un article admiratif sur *Les Misérables*. En même temps, il confie à sa mère, dans sa correspondance privée, qu'il trouve ce livre « inepte et immonde ». On peut penser qu'il est sincère dans les deux cas, Hugo ayant toujours excité chez Baudelaire des sentiments contradictoires : admiration pour son génie visionnaire et son écriture souveraine, distance à l'égard de son humanisme progressiste. Réciproquement, Hugo n'adhère pas à la doctrine de « l'art pour l'art », et l'a écrit à Baudelaire en 1859.

« Valjean, c'est la brute naïve, innocente ; c'est le prolétaire ignorant, coupable d'une faute que nous absoudrions tous sans aucun doute (le vol d'un pain), mais qui, punie légalement, le jette dans l'école du Mal, c'est-à-dire au Bagne. Là, son esprit se forme et s'affine dans les lourdes méditations de l'esclavage. Finalement il en sort, subtil, redoutable et dangereux. Il a payé l'hospitalité de l'évêque par un vol nouveau ; mais celui-ci le sauve par un beau mensonge, convaincu que le Pardon et la Charité sont les seules lumières qui puissent dissiper toutes les ténèbres. En effet, l'illumination de cette conscience se fait, mais pas assez vite pour que la bête routinière, qui est encore dans l'homme, ne l'entraîne dans une nouvelle rechute. Valjean (maintenant M. Madeleine) est devenu honnête, riche et puissant. Il a enrichi, civilisé presque, une commune, pauvre avant lui, dont il est maire. Il s'est fait un admirable manteau de respectabilité ; il est couvert et cuirassé de bonnes œuvres.

Mais un jour sinistre arrive où il apprend qu'un faux Valjean, un sosie inepte, abject, va être condamné à sa place. Que faire ? Est-il bien certain que la loi intérieure, la Conscience, lui ordonne de démolir lui-même, en se dénonçant, tout ce pénible et glorieux échafaudage de sa vie nouvelle ? « La lumière que tout homme en naissant apporte en ce monde » est-elle suffisante pour éclairer ces ténèbres complexes ? M. Madeleine sort vainqueur, mais après quelles épouvantables luttes ! de cette mer d'angoisses, et redevient Valjean par amour du Vrai et du Juste. Le chapitre où est retracée, minutieusement, lentement, analytiquement, avec ses hésitations, ses restrictions, ses paradoxes, ses fausses consolations, ses tricheries désespérées, cette dispute de l'homme contre lui-même (*Tempête sous un crâne*), contient des pages qui peuvent enorgueillir à jamais non seulement la littérature français, mais même la littérature de l'Humanité pensante. Il est glorieux pour l'Homme Rationnel (*sic*) que ces pages aient été écrites ! Il faudrait chercher beaucoup, et longtemps, et très longtemps, pour trouver dans un autre livre des pages égales à celles-ci, où est exposée, d'une manière si tragique, toute l'épouvantable Casuistique inscrite, dès le Commencement, dans le cœur de l'Homme Universel (*sic*).

Il y a dans cette galerie de douleurs et de drames funestes une figure horrible, répugnante, c'est le gendarme, le garde-chiourme, la justice stricte, inexorable, la justice qui ne sait pas commenter, la loi non interprétée, l'intelligence sauvage (peut-on appeler cela une intelligence ?) qui n'a jamais compris les circonstances atténuantes, en un mot la Lettre sans l'Esprit, c'est l'abominable Javert. J'ai entendu quelques personnes, sensées d'ailleurs, qui, à propos de ce Javert, disaient : « Après tout, c'est un honnête homme ! » Pour moi, je le confesse, au risque de passer pour un coupable (« ceux qui tremblent se sentent coupables », disait ce fou de Robespierre), Javert m'apparaît comme un monstre incorrigible, affamé de justice comme la bête féroce l'est de chair sanglante, bref, comme l'Ennemi absolu.

Il n'est pas nécessaire, je présume, de raconter et d'expliquer toutes les beautés tendres, navrantes, que Victor Hugo a répandues sur le personnage de Fantine, la grisette déchue, la femme moderne, placée entre la fatalité du travail improductif et la fatalité de la prostitution légale. Nous savons de vieille date s'il est habile à exprimer le cri de la passion dans l'abîme, les gémissements et les pleurs furieux de la lionne-mère privée de ses petits ! Ici, par une liaison toute naturelle, nous sommes amenés à reconnaître une fois de plus avec quelle sûreté et aussi quelle légèreté de main ce peintre robuste, ce créateur de colosses, colore les joues de l'enfance, en allume les yeux, en décrit le geste pétulant et naïf. On dirait Michel-Ange se complaisant à rivaliser avec Lawrence ou Velasquez.

[...]

Les Misérables sont donc un livre de charité, un étourdissant rappel à l'ordre d'une société trop amoureuse d'elle-même et trop peu soucieuse de l'immortelle loi de fraternité ; un plaidoyer pour les *misérables* (ceux qui *souffrent* de la misère et que la misère *déshonore*), proféré par la bouche la plus éloquente de ce temps. Malgré tout ce qu'il peut y avoir de tricherie volontaire ou d'inconsciente partialité dans la manière dont, aux yeux de la stricte philosophie, les termes du problème sont posés, nous pensons, exactement comme l'auteur, que *des livres de cette nature ne sont jamais inutiles.*

Victor Hugo est pour l'Homme, et cependant il n'est pas contre Dieu. Il a confiance en Dieu, et pourtant il n'est pas contre l'Homme.

Il repousse le délire de l'Athéisme en révolte, et cependant il n'approuve pas les gloutonneries sanguinaires des Molochs et des Teutatès.

Il croit que l'homme est né bon, et cependant, même devant ses désastres permanents, il n'accuse pas la férocité et la malice de Dieu.

Je crois que pour ceux mêmes qui trouvent dans la doctrine orthodoxe, dans la pure théorie Catholique, une explication, sinon complète, du moins plus compréhensive de tous les mystères inquiétants de la vie, le nouveau livre de Victor Hugo doit être le *Bienvenu* (comme l'évêque dont il raconte la victorieuse charité) ; le livre à applaudir, le livre à remercier. N'est-il pas utile que de

temps à autre le poète, le philosophe, prennent un peu le Bonheur égoïste aux cheveux, et lui disent, en lui secouant le mufle dans le sang et l'ordure : « Vois ton œuvre et bois ton œuvre » ?
Hélas ! du Péché Originel, même après tant de progrès depuis si longtemps promis, il restera toujours bien assez de traces pour en constater l'immémoriale réalité ! »

Charles BAUDELAIRE, *Le Boulevard*, 20 avril 1862.

Flaubert éprouve pour Hugo une admiration certaine, mais celui-ci ne fait pas partie de ses modèles. Sa correspondance témoigne de la grande déception qui est la sienne à la lecture des *Misérables*, où il ne voit que démagogie et populisme.

« [...] *Les Misérables*. [...] Il n'est pas permis d'en dire du mal. On a l'air d'un mouchard. La position de l'auteur est inexpugnable, inattaquable. – Moi qui ai passé ma vie à l'adorer, je suis présentement *indigné* ! Il faut bien que j'éclate, cependant.
Je ne trouve dans ce livre ni vérité, ni grandeur. Quant au style, il me semble intentionnellement incorrect et bas. C'est une façon de flatter le populaire. [...] Où y a-t-il des prostituées comme Fantine, des forçats comme Valjean et des hommes politiques comme les stupides cocos de l'A, B, C ? Pas une fois on ne les voit *souffrir*, dans le fond de leur âme. Ce sont des mannequins, des bonshommes en sucre, à commencer par Mgr Bienvenu. Par rage socialiste, Hugo a calomnié l'Église comme il a calomnié la misère. Où est l'évêque qui demande la bénédiction d'un conventionnel ? Où est la fabrique où l'on met à la porte une fille pour avoir eu un enfant, etc. ? Et les digressions ! Y en a-t-il ! Le passage des engrais a dû ravir Pelletan. Ce livre est fait pour la crapule catholico-socialiste, pour toute la vermine philosophico-évangélique. [...] C'était un bien beau sujet pourtant. Mais quel calme il aurait fallu et quelle envergure scientifique ! Il est vrai que le père Hugo méprise la science. Et il le prouve. [...]
La postérité ne lui pardonnera pas, à celui-là, d'avoir voulu être un penseur, malgré sa nature. – [...] Il n'est pas plus penseur

que Racine ou La Fontaine qu'il estime médiocrement. C'est-à-dire qu'il résume comme eux le courant, l'ensemble des idées banales de son époque – et avec une telle persistance qu'il en oublie son œuvre, et son art. Voilà mon opinion […]. Je la garde pour moi, bien entendu. Tout ce qui touche une plume doit avoir trop de reconnaissance à Hugo pour se permettre une critique. Mais je trouve, intérieurement, que les dieux vieillissent. Quel insouci de la beauté ! Que l'on me cite une de ces pages (comme il en avait […]).
J'attends votre réponse et votre colère. »

Gustave FLAUBERT, lettre à Edma Roger des Genettes.

Rimbaud a seize ans quand son professeur Georges Izambard lui fait lire *Les Misérables* (au grand scandale de la mère du jeune homme). Dans sa lettre à Paul Demeny du 15 mai 1871, dite *Seconde Lettre du Voyant,* il fait un sort spécial à la production de Hugo :

« Hugo, trop cabochard, a bien du Vu dans les derniers volumes : *Les Misérables* sont un vrai poème. »

Exaspéré par le culte du grand homme, Barbey d'Aurevilly s'acharne pendant toute sa carrière contre l'œuvre de Victor Hugo. Tout en reconnaissant son génie, il conspue son style excessif, emphatique, et considère qu'avec *Les Misérables,* il se montre démagogue et prostitue son talent, tout en menaçant les institutions par ses idéaux démocratiques.

« Eh bien, hâtons-nous de le dire d'abord : le livre n'est point raté, et ce n'est pas une platitude, comme on pouvait le croire et comme nous l'avons cru nous-même après avoir lu les intelligentes citations des journaux ! […] Je ne sais pas si M. Victor Hugo tient à l'honneur d'être dangereux, mais je sais qu'il est à un point qui épouvanterait un honnête homme, pour peu qu'il eût ce qui manque parfois à la force : le regard d'assez de portée pour voir jusqu'où atteint la main. […]
Le dessein du livre est de faire sauter toutes les institutions sociales, les unes après les autres, avec une chose plus forte

que la poudre à canon, qui fait sauter les montagnes, – avec des larmes et de la pitié. Il s'est dit, avec assez de raison, que, dans l'humanité, ce qui fait la foule, le nombre et les publics, ce sont les femmes et les jeunes gens, ces femmes momentanées, qui bien souvent restent femmes toute leur vie par impossibilité de mûrir et indigence de cerveau, et c'est sur tous les cœurs, peu surmontés de tête, qu'il a essayé d'opérer. C'est pour tous ces cœurs, impétueusement ou tendrement sensibles, qu'il a combiné les effets d'un livre arrangé de manière à donner toujours raison à l'être que la société punit contre la société qui le punit. Conception, je l'ai dit, méprisable, mais rendue formidable par l'exécution. [...]

M. Hugo interrompt son récit, l'arrête, le coupe de réflexions, de *contemplations*, qui durent parfois tout un chapitre, – puis il le reprend, ne le rattache pas, ne le recolle pas, mais l'égaille, le débraille et l'éraille. Il fait ce qu'il veut. Il est chez lui, non pas sous son dais d'autrefois, les jours de présentation et de baise-mains romantiques, mais pantoufles aux chenêts, les mains dans les poches, avec le sans-gêne d'un homme mené plus qu'il ne le croit par la mystérieuse logique des choses, et qui, ayant répudié l'art pour la politique, – et même pour le sans-culottisme politique, – devait un jour ou l'autre, arriver au sans-culottisme littéraire. Il y est arrivé. Il y est neuf encore, mais il s'y fera. Il s'y acclimatera. Il s'y complétera. Il s'y consommera. À cette heure, son sans-culottisme littéraire n'a pas l'irréductible pureté vers laquelle il tend. Il a encore des taches, – des taches de talent, – çà et là, mais elles disparaîtront bientôt, ces taches lumineuses. Il atteindra littérairement, un jour qui n'est pas éloigné, allez ! à la pureté de ce sans-culottisme politique, immaculé et accompli, celui-là, que je trouve dans *Les Misérables*, dans ce livre où ces régicides confessent des évêques et où Louis XVII est comparé au frère de M. Cartouche. [...]

Et j'ai tout dit. J'ai dit l'idée première du livre, les caractères, l'action, le récit. J'ai montré la vulgarité de tout cela, la vulgarité qui certainement en fera la fortune, car le mélodrame est plus fort que la distinction même de l'esprit qui le juge. Tout est portière pour y pleurer. Ce bilan de la platitude terminé, il reste à faire le compte du talent qui s'y mêle, ce qui ne sera pas long, puisque, excepté dans *Les Contemplations*, jamais Hugo n'a mis moins de talent que dans ces *Misérables*. Il y en a pourtant, ne vous y trompez pas ! et je veux le noter. Ainsi, dans l'ordre de la pensée, il y a deux fois dans *Les Misérables*, le spectacle très beau de la conscience de ce Valjean, observée avec une impartialité singulière pour un esprit comme celui de M. Hugo, très emporté, toujours, au-delà des justesses de l'analyse et de ses subtilités. La première fois, c'est quand Valjean passe du crime au repentir et fait son dernier vol, comme pour protester contre sa conscience qui revient, – sa dernière tentative contre elle, trait superbe de nature humaine ! La seconde fois, c'est quand il délibère s'il ira se dénoncer comme étant Valjean le forçat, dans ce chapitre qui n'avait pas besoin de ce titre gongorique : *Une tempête sous un crâne*, pour être beau. Mais, au-dessus de tout, selon moi, il y a l'inspecteur de police Javert, composé si bien qu'on dirait qu'il est vrai, l'inspecteur de police nuancé avec un art nouveau dans M. Hugo et dominant toutes les autres figures du livre, qui ne sont au fond que des charges : l'évêque, le forçat, la fille-mère. Complexe réalité, profondément étudiée, mais qui soufflette tout le système de M. Hugo et la conception de son livre, en montrant combien la société est auguste dans ses répressions et dans ses disciplines, puisqu'elle communique tant de grandeur à l'abjection même d'un mouchard. Force irrésistible d'une idée vraie, le mouchard a, malgré sa vileté, sous la plume anti-sociale de M. Hugo dans *Les Misérables*, une grandeur que n'a pas Valjean, malgré ses hauts mérites de forçat ! Voilà, dans l'ordre de la pensée, les trois beautés indéniables que j'ai rencontrées dans ce livre. Dans l'ordre du style, elles seront moins éclatantes, mais plus nombreuses, et je veux aussi les compter. Les bons comptes font les bons amis.

Chez M. Victor Hugo, le talent est surtout de style, c'est l'expression, c'est l'invention dans le verbe, c'est enfin toute cette matérialité enflammée de mots et d'images qu'on peut ne pas aimer, mais dont on ressent la puissance. Eh bien, c'est par là qu'il est encore aujourd'hui. Victor Hugo, et que, par là, il échappe au triste destin de n'être plus que l'imitateur d'Eugène Sue. [...] Seul, le style, et non partout, le style, à quelques places, en ces deux volumes, éclate à travers le système et rappelle aux esprits littéraires l'ancien Victor Hugo. Ainsi je suis très sûr, et j'ai compté : mettez *dix* charmantes lignes sur mademoiselle Baptistine, la sœur de l'évêque Bienvenu ; – *trois* pages très *enlevées* sur la religion du sénateur ; – *deux* pages intitulées *L'Onde et l'Ombre* ; – *une* page et *demie* sur la sœur Simplice ; – le délicieux paradoxe, cité par M. Janin, sur le bonheur d'être aveugle, et vous avez tout, car c'est tout ! L'addition, comme vous le voyez, n'est pas difficile, et je suis vraiment désolé de n'avoir pas trouvé davantage [...]. M. Hugo, je n'en doute pas, entraînera de son côté tous les esprits ardents et faibles, toutes les âmes de portière, plus nombreuses qu'on ne croit [...] ; enfin tous les enthousiastes pleurards qui larmoieront d'admiration sur le Bienvenu et qui ne savent pas que là, parmi nous, sur le terrain de la réalité, il y avait, quand M. Hugo écrivait ses *Misérables*, un vrai prêtre (le curé d'Ars), plus sublime que le sien, justement parce qu'il *était plus prêtre*, et que, pour cette raison, il n'aurait pas voulu copier. Oui, M. Hugo aura tout ce monde-là pour lui, et peut-être (je le regretterais davantage) les gouvernements, qui le laissent en paix attaquer la société et ses institutions salvatrices avec ces larmes qu'il ne songe à faire couler que pour mieux la noyer dedans. Mais ce n'est pas une raison, tout cela, pour que la critique littéraire, qui doit être toujours de la critique morale, ne dise pas son mot, et il sera net. *Les Misérables* ne sont pas un beau livre, et, de plus, c'est une mauvaise action. »

Jules BARBEY D'AUREVILLY, *Le Pays*, 19 avril 1862.

LIRE, VOIR, ENTENDRE

BIBLIOGRAPHIE

Texte intégral des *Misérables*

Victor HUGO, *Les Misérables*, édition d'Yves Gohin, Gallimard, « Folio », 1973, rééd. 1999.

Victor HUGO, *Les Misérables*, édition de Guy Rosa, commentaires de Nicole Savy, Librairie générale française, « Les Classiques de poche », 1998.

Victor HUGO, *Les Misérables*, édition de Annette et Guy Rosa, Robert Laffont, « Bouquins », 1985 (rééd. 2002).

Sur Victor Hugo

Catherine BALAUDÉ, *Hugo*, Nathan, « Balises », 1991. Une présentation aisément accessible.

Patrick BESNIER, *L'ABCdaire Victor Hugo*, Flammarion, 2002.

Yves GOHIN, Victor Hugo, PUF, coll. « Que sais-je ? » 1987. Un ouvrage de référence.

Jean-Marc HOVASSE, *Victor Hugo*, Fayard, 2001. La biographie la plus complète et la mieux informée, écrite avec hauteur de vue et humour.

Arnaud LASTER, *Pleins feux sur Victor Hugo*, Comédie-Française, 1981. Une mine de renseignements sur la vie et l'œuvre de Hugo, aisée à consulter.

Franck LAURENT, édition commentée d'une anthologie des *Écrits politiques* de Hugo, Le Livre de poche, 2001. On y trouve notamment les plus célèbres discours de Hugo à la Chambre.

Évelyne POIREL (dir.), *Lorsque l'enfant paraît...* Victor Hugo et l'enfance, catalogue de l'exposition de Villequier, avril-juillet 2002, Somogy/musée Victor Hugo de Villequier, 2002.

Marie-Laure PRÉVOST (dir.), *Victor Hugo, l'homme océan : le cahier*, Bibliothèque nationale de France, « Cahiers pédagogiques des expositions », 2002.

Annette ROSA, *Victor Hugo, l'éclat d'un siècle*, Messidor/La Farandole, 1985. Une biographie inspirée, vivante, accessible sur Internet sur le site du groupe Hugo : http ://groupugo.div.jussieu.fr

Sur *Les Misérables*

Pierre BRUNEL (textes réunis par), *Victor Hugo, Les Misérables*, Mont-de-Marsan, Éditions Interuniversitaires, 1994.

Gabrielle CHAMARAT (textes réunis par), *Les Misérables, nommer l'innommable*, Paradigme, 1994.

José-Luis DIAZ (textes réunis par), Victor Hugo, *Les Misérables. La preuve par les abîmes*, SEDES, « Romantisme. Colloques », 1995.

Louis CHEVALIER, *Classes laborieuses, classes dangereuses*, 1958. Réédité en 1978, Hachette, « Pluriel ».

Claude GÉLY, *Les Misérables de Hugo*, Hachette, « Poche critique », 1975. Nouvelle édition aux Éditions interuniversitaires, 1995.

René JOURNET et Guy ROBERT, *Le Mythe du peuple dans Les Misérables*, Éditions sociales, 1964.

Pierre LAFORGUE, *Gavroche*, SEDES, 1994.

Myriam ROMAN et Marie-Christine BELLOSTA, *Les Misérables, roman pensif*, Belin, « Lettres Sup », 1995.

Guy ROSA (textes réunis par), *Misérables*, Klincksieck, « Parcours critique », 1995.

Anne UBERSFELD et Guy ROSA (textes réunis par), *Lire Les Misérables*, José Corti, 1985.

FILMOGRAPHIE

Adaptations

Bille AUGUST, *Les Misérables*, avec Michael Collins, 1998.

Raymond BERNARD, *Les Misérables*, avec Harry Baur, 1933.

Albert CAPPELLANI, *Les Misérables*, avec Henry Krauss, 1912.

Josée DAYAN, *Les Misérables*, avec Gérard Depardieu, 2000.

Henri FESCOURT, *Les Misérables*, avec Gabriel Gabrio, 1925.

Robert HOSSEIN, *Les Misérables*, avec Lino Ventura, 1982.

Jean-Paul LE CHANOIS, *Les Misérables*, avec Jean Gabin, 1957.

Claude LELOUCH, *Les Misérables du vingtième siècle*, avec Jean-Paul Belmondo, 1995.

LES TERMES DE CRITIQUE

Allégorie : représentation d'une idée par un personnage (ex. : Delacroix, *La Liberté guidant le peuple* ; voir ill. 1 p. 2).

Allitération : répétition expressive d'une même consonne.

Anaphore : répétition expressive d'un même terme en tête de propositions successives.

Antithèse : opposition dans une même phrase de deux idées ou images contrastées.

Apologie : fervent éloge d'une personne ou d'une chose.

Assonance : répétition expressive d'une même voyelle.

Champ lexical : ensemble de termes apparentés par une ou plusieurs notions communes (ex. : *effroi, tremblant, redouter* font partie du champ lexical de la peur).

Comparaison : rapprochement explicite entre deux termes, fondé sur un rapport de ressemblance.

Connotation : sens particulier d'un mot évoqué dans un certain contexte (ex. : selon les contextes, le rouge peut connoter la colère, l'amour, ou la révolution).

Contre-plongée : angle de vue cinématographique où la caméra est placée en contrebas de son sujet, qui est donc vu par en dessous.

Discours rapporté : paroles d'un personnage retranscrites par le narrateur au style direct, indirect, ou indirect libre.

Dramatique : qui se rapporte à l'action, au déroulement de l'intrigue.

Ellipse : omission par le narrateur d'une circonstance du récit, que le lecteur doit rétablir lui-même.

Épique, épopée : une épopée est le récit des exploits d'un héros ou d'un peuple. Le style épique magnifie le récit de l'histoire.

Fantastique (adj.) : qui relève de l'imaginaire ou du surnaturel. Le *fantastique* (subst.) consiste à introduire des éléments inquiétants ou surnaturels dans un contexte réaliste.

Feuilleton : roman qui paraît par épisodes réguliers dans un journal ou une revue, et dont le ressort dramatique principal repose sur le suspense ménagé à la fin de chaque séquence.

Frontispice : illustration accompagnant le titre d'un ouvrage.

Idéologie : ensemble d'idées et de valeurs propres à une époque, à une société ou à une classe sociale.

Incipit : début (première phrase, ou premier paragraphe) d'un roman, ou d'un chapitre.

Jeune premier, jeune première : personnage positif de jeune homme ou de jeune fille, traditionnellement traité comme le héros ou l'héroïne d'un roman ou d'une pièce.

Métaphore : figure de style consistant à désigner un être ou un objet par une comparaison implicite.

Métonymie : figure de style consistant à remplacer un mot par un autre mot qui entretient avec le premier une relation logique (ex. : *boire un verre* : métonymie au contenant pour le contenu ; *lire un Zola* : métonymie de l'auteur pour l'œuvre).

Narrateur : celui qui, dans un roman prend en charge la narration, c'est-à-dire le récit de l'histoire ; à distinguer de l'auteur du livre.

Oxymore : association syntaxique de deux termes incompatibles par le sens (ex. : « une souffrance heureuse », I, V, 6).

Paradoxe : énoncé qui contredit apparemment le sens commun, mais dont on peut déceler la logique sous-jacente.

Paronomase : figure de style consistant à associer deux mots de sens différents, mais très proches par la sonorité (ex. : *fleurs / pleurs*).

Périphrase : figure de style qui consiste à désigner un objet ou un personnage par une définition qui le caractérise (ex. : *le vainqueur d'Austerlitz*, pour *Napoléon*).

Personnification : figure de style attribuant à une chose ou à un animal une caractéristique humaine.

Point de vue narratif : perspective adoptée par le narrateur dans le récit. Le point de vue est *extérieur* lorsque le narrateur décrit les personnages et l'action comme un observateur neutre ; il est *intérieur* lorsque le narrateur adopte la perspective d'un personnage ; il est *omniscient* lorsque le narrateur connaît toutes les motivations des personnages et toutes les circonstances de l'action.

Question rhétorique : interrogation dont la réponse est prédéterminée par le contexte de la question.

Rythme : mouvement, cadence de la phrase.

Suspense : effet d'attente créant une tension dans la narration.

Synecdoque : désignation d'un tout par l'une de ses parties (ex. : *une voile* pour *un bateau*).

POUR MIEUX EXPLOITER
LES QUESTIONNAIRES

Ce tableau fournit la liste des rubriques utilisées dans les questionnaires, avec les renvois aux pages correspondantes, de façon à permettre des **études d'ensemble** sur tel ou tel de ces aspects (par exemple dans le cadre de la lecture suivie).

RUBRIQUES	PAGES
L'ART DU RÉCIT	98, 136, 170, 270
CARACTÈRES	48, 215, 243
GENRES	48, 118, 133, 169, 270
MISE EN SCÈNE	222
PERSONNAGES	60, 67, 89, 105, 136, 151, 162, 169, 175, 184, 198, 222, 251
QUI PARLE ? QUI VOIT ?	31, 67, 89, 118, 133, 151, 251
REGISTRES ET TONALITÉS	67, 105, 137, 162, 198, 215, 222
SOCIÉTÉ	48, 67, 89, 97, 151, 169, 184, 215, 270
STRATÉGIES	60, 80, 162
STRUCTURE	31, 80, 105, 175, 237, 243
THÈMES	31, 60, 80, 97, 118, 133, 136, 162, 170, 175, 184, 198, 215, 222, 237, 243, 251, 270

TABLE DES MATIÈRES

L'UNIVERS DE L'ŒUVRE

ANNEXES

COUVERTURE : Léon-Adolphe Willette (1857-1926), *Gavroche à la barricade* (détail), 1862. (Maison Victor Hugo, Paris.)

CRÉDITS PHOTO :
Couverture : Ph. © Jeanbor/Archives Larbor – p. 2 : Ph. © H. Josse/Archives Larbor/T – p. 3 : Ph. Coll Archives Larbor – p. 4 bas : Ph. Roger Corbeau © Ministère de la Culture, France/T – p. 4 ht : Ph. Roger Corbeau © Ministère de la Culture, France/T – p. 5 ht : Ph. © Enguerand/DR/T – p. 5 bas : Ph. Roger Corbeau © Ministère de la Culture, France/T – p. 6 : Ph. Coll Archives Larbor – p. 7 : Ph. © Photothèque des Musées de la Ville de Paris/Daniel Lifermann – p. 8 : Ph. © Photothèque des musées de la ville de Paris/T – p. 13 : Ph. L. de Selva © Archives Larbor – p. 20 : Ph. © H. Josse/T – p. 28 : Ph. Coll Archives Larbor/T – p. 78 : Ph. Coll Archives Larbor/T – p. 108 : Ph. © Pathé/T – p. 112 : Ph. © Bulloz/RMN/T – p. 138 : Ph. Coll Archives Larbor/T – p. 164 : Ph. Coll Archives Larbor/T – p. 196 : Ph. J. L Charmet © Archives Larbor/T – p. 278 : Bibliothèque des Arts décoratifs, Paris. Ph. © Archives Larbor/T.

Direction éditoriale : Pascale Magni – *Coordination et édition* : Franck Henry – *Révision des textes* : Luce Camus – *Iconographie* : Christine Varin – *Maquette intérieure* : Josiane Sayaphoum – *Fabrication* : Jean-Philippe Dore – *Compogravure* : PPC.

© Bordas, Paris, 2003 – ISBN : 978-2-04-730359-7

Imprimé en France par France Quercy – N° de projet : 10155207 – Dépôt légal : octobre 2008
Dépôt légal 1re éd. : juillet 2003